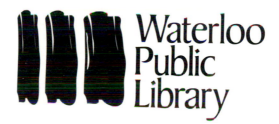

How It Works®

Science and Technology

Third Edition

Volume 20

Index

Marshall Cavendish

New York • London • Toronto • Sydney

Marshall Cavendish
99 White Plains Road
Tarrytown, NY 10591

Website: www.marshallcavendish.com

Third edition updated by Brown Reference Group plc.

Library of Congress Cataloging-in-Publication Data
How it works: science and technology.—3rd ed.
p. cm.
Includes index.
ISBN 0-7614-7314-9 (set)   ISBN 0-7614-7346-7 (Vol. 20)
1. Technology—Encyclopedias. 2. Science—Encyclopedias.
[1. Technology—Encyclopedias. 2. Science—Encyclopedias.]
T9 .H738 2003
603—dc21   2001028771

Consultant: Donald R. Franceschetti, Ph.D., University of Memphis

Brown Reference Group
Editor: Wendy Horobin
Associate Editors: Paul Thompson, Martin Clowes, Lis Stedman, Dawn Titmus
Managing Editor: Tim Cooke
Design: Alison Gardner
Picture Research: Becky Cox
Illustrations: Mark Walker, Darren Awuah
Index: Kay Ollerenshaw

Marshall Cavendish
Project Editor: Peter Mavrikis
Production Manager: Alan Tsai
Editorial Director: Paul Bernabeo

Printed in Malaysia
Bound in the United States of America
08 07 06 05 04   6 5 4 3 2

Contents

Volume 20

Bibliography

Biology and Medicine

Ackefors, H., Huner, J. V., and Konikoff, M. *Introduction to the General Principles of Aquaculture*. New York: Food Products Press, 1994.

Ahrens, F. A. *Pharmacology*. Baltimore, Maryland: Williams & Wilkins, 1996.

Alberts, et al. *Molecular Biology of the Cell*. 4th edition. New York: Garland, 2002.

Aldridge, A. *The Thread of Life: The Story of Genes and Genetic Engineering*. New York: Cambridge University Press, 1996.

Animal Breeding and Infertility. Edited by M. Meredith. Boston: Blackwell Scientific Publications, 1995.

Ash, M. *Wheeler's Dental Anatomy, Physiology, and Occlusion*. 7th edition. Philadelphia: W. B. Saunders, 1997.

Bender, A. E. *Bender's Dictionary of Nutrition and Food Technology*. 7th edition. Boston: Butterworth-Heinemann, 1999.

Benson, R., and Pernoll, M. *Benson and Pernoll's Handbook of Obstetrics and Gynecology*. 10th edition. New York: McGraw-Hill, 2001.

Bushberg J. *The Essential Physics of Medical Imaging*. Baltimore: Williams & Wilkins, 1994.

Byatt, A., Fothergill, A., and Holmes, M. *Blue Planet*. New York: DK Publishing, 2002.

Clark, W. R. *At War Within: The Double-Edged Sword of Immunity*. New York: Oxford University Press, 1995.

Encyclopedia of Agricultural Science. Edited by C. Arntzen and E. Ritter. San Diego: Academic Press, 1994.

Encyclopedia of Family Health. Tarrytown, New York: Marshall Cavendish Corporation, 1998.

Fact Book of U.S. Agriculture. United States Department of Agriculture: Washington, D.C., 1997.

Fix, G. *An Analysis of Brewing Techniques*. Boulder, Colorado: Brewers Publications, 1997.

Fukuyama, Francis. *Our Posthuman Future: Consequences of the Biotechnology Revolution*. New York: Farrar Straus & Giroux, 2002.

Hall, D. C. *Economics of Pesticides, Sustainable Food Production, and Organic Food Markets*. Greenwich, CT: JAI Press, 2002.

Hanan, J. J. *Greenhouses: Advanced Technology for Protected Horticulture*. Boca Raton, Florida: C.R.C. Press, 1998.

The History of Agriculture and the Environment. Edited by D. Bowers. Washington D.C.: Agricultural History Society, 1993.

Hoopes, K., and Thwaits, R. *Principles of Veterinary Science*. Baltimore: Williams and Wilkins, 1997.

Hurt, D. *American Agriculture: A Brief History*. Ames, Iowa: Iowa State University Press, 1994.

Jay, J. *Modern Food Microbiology*. 5th edition. New York: Aspen Publishers Inc., 1998.

Jones, B. J. *Hydroponics: A Practical Guide for the Soilless Grower*. Boca Raton, Florida: St. Lucie, 1997.

Koch, F. K. *Mariculture: Farming the Fruits of the Sea*. New York: Franklin Watts, 1992.

Kolata, G. *Clone: The Road to Dolly, and the Path Ahead*. New York: William Morrow & Company, 1997.

Kuby, J. et al. *Kuby Immunology*. New York: W. H. Freeman & Co., 2000.

Livestock for a Small Earth. Edited by J. Aaker. Washington, D.C.: Seven Locks Press, 1994.

Lufkin, Robert B. *Pocket Atlas of Head and Neck MRI Anatomy*. Philadelphia: Lippincott Williams & Wilkins Publishers, 2000.

Manci, W. *Farming and the Environment*. Milwaukee: Gareth Stevens Publishers, 1993.

McCullough, J. *Blood Transfusion: A Practical Guide*. New York: McGraw-Hill, 1997.

Newton, J. *Profitable Organic Farming*. Cambridge, Massachusetts: Blackwell Scientific Publishers, 1995.

Plaster, E. *Soil Science and Management*. 3rd edition. New York: Delmar Publishers, 1997.

Rosenthal, M. *The Fertility Sourcebook*. Los Angeles: Lowell House, 1995.

Sterelny, K. *Dawkins vs Gould*. Blue Ridge Summit, Pennsylvania: Totem Books, 2001.

Taintor, J. F., and Taintor, M. J. *The Complete Guide to Better Dental Care*. New York: Facts on File, Inc., 1997.

Youngson, R. *The Surgery Book: An Illustrated Guide to 73 of the Most Common Operations*. New York: St. Martin's Press, 1993.

Chemistry and Materials Science

Amato, I. *Stuff: The Material the World Is Made Of*. New York: Basic Books, 1997.

Ball, P. *Designing the Molecular World*. Princeton, New Jersey: Princeton University Press, 1994.

Ball, P. *Made to Measure: New Materials for the 21st Century*. Princeton: Princeton University Press, 1997.

Barsoum, M. W. *Fundamentals of Ceramics*. New York: McGraw-Hill, 1997.

Birley, A., and Haworth, B. *Physics of Plastics: Processing, Properties, and Materials Engineering*. New York: Hanser, 1992.

Brydson, J. *Plastics Materials*. Boston: Butterworth-Heinemann, 1995.

Carter, G. *Materials Science and Engineering*. Materials Park, Ohio: ASM International, 1991.

Chemistry and Technology of the Cosmetics and Toiletries Industry. Edited by D. Williams and W. Schmitt. New York: Blackie Academic & Professional, 1996.

Epp, D. *The Chemistry of Food Dyes*. Middletown, Ohio: Terrific Science Press, 1995.

Fahey, J. *A Century of Western Mining*. Seattle: University of Washington Press, 1990.

Fenichell, S. *Plastic: The Making of a Synthetic Century*. New York: HarperBusiness, 1996.

Herakovich, C. *The Mechanics of Fibrous Composites*. New York: John Wiley & Sons, 1998.

Herbst, W. *Industrial Organic Pigments: Production, Properties, and Applications*. New York: VCH, 1993.

Hewlett, P. C. *Lea's Chemistry of Cement and Concrete*. 4th edition. New York: John Wiley & Sons, 1997.

Jones, D. *Principles and Prevention of Corrosion*. Englewood Cliffs, New Jersey: Prentice-Hall, 1996.

Laser Interaction with Atoms, Solids, and Plasmas. Edited by M. Richard. New York: Plenum Press, 1994.

McMurray, J. *Chemistry*. Englewood Cliffs, New Jersey: Prentice-Hall, 1995.

Miller, R. *Lubricants and their Application*. New York: McGraw-Hill, 1993.

Neely, J. *Practical Metallurgy and the Materials of Industry*. New York: Prentice-Hall, 1994.

Ouellette, R. J. *Organic Chemistry: A Brief Introduction*. Second Edition. Upper Saddle River, New Jersey: Prentice-Hall, 1998.

Principles of Paint Formulation. Edited by R. Woodridge. New York: Chapman & Hall, 1991.

Schuler, M. L., and Kargi, F. *Bioprocess Engineering: Basic Concepts*. New York: Prentice-Hall, 1991.

Selinger, B. *Chemistry in the Marketplace*. 5th edition. New York: Harcourt, Brace, Jovanovich, 1997.

Senter, B. *Color Transfer*. New York: Watson-Guptill, 1990.

Shape Memory Materials. Edited by K. Otsuka and C. M. Wayman. New York: Cambridge University Press, 1999.

Soaps and Detergents. Edited by L. Spitz. Philadelphia: American Society of Oil Chemists, 1996.

Stiles, A., and Koch, T. A. *Catalyst Manufacture*. New York: M. Dekker, 1995.

Wittcoff, H. A., and Reuben, B. G. *Industrial Organic Chemicals*. New York: John Wiley & Sons, 1996.

Zollinger, H. *Color Chemistry*. 3rd revised edition. New York: John Wiley & Sons, 2001.

Computers, Communications, and Information Technologies

Advances in Wireless Communications. Edited by J. Holtzmann and M. Zorzo. Boston: Kluwer Academic Publishers, 1998.

Alkin, G. *Sound Recording and Reproduction*. Woburn, Massachusetts: Focal Press, 1996.

Artificial Intelligence. Edited by M. Boden. San Diego: Academic Press, 1996

Baert, L. *Digital Audio and Compact Disc Recording Systems*. Woburn, Massachusetts: Focal Press, 1996.

Bellamy, J. *Digital Telephony*. New York: John Wiley & Sons, 2000.

Black, U. *Emerging Communications Technologies*. Upper Saddle River, New Jersey: Prentice-Hall, 1997.

Cawsey, A. *The Essence of Artificial Intelligence*. Englewood Cliffs, New Jersey: Prentice Hall, 1998.

Dodd, A. *The Essential Guide to Telecommunications*. Upper Saddle River, New Jersey: Prentice-Hall, 1998.

Gralla, P. *How the Internet Works*. Emeryville, California: Ziff-Davis Press, 1996.

Grotta, D. *The Illustrated Digital Imaging Dictionary*. New York: McGraw-Hill, 1998.

Hagen, J. B. *Radio-frequency Electronics: Circuits and Applications*. New York: Cambridge University Press, 1996.

Nellist, J. *Understanding Telecommunications and Lightwave Systems: An Entry-level Guide*. New York: IEEE Press, Institute of Electrical and Electronics Engineers, 1996.

Pelton, J. *Wireless and Satellite Communications*. Upper Saddle River, New Jersey: Prentice-Hall, 1995.

Picton, P., Rzevski, G. *Mechatronics: Designing Intelligent Machines*. Boston: Butterworth-Heinemann, 1995.

Prosise, J. *How Computer Graphics Work*. Emeryville, California: Ziff-Davis, 1994.

Rheingold, H. *The Virtual Community*. Cambridge, Massachusetts: MIT Press, 2000.

Vaz, M. C., and Duignan, P. R. *Industrial Light and Magic: Into the Digital Realm*. New York: Ballantine Books, 1996.

Vince, J. *Essential Virtual Reality Fast*. New York: Springer Verlag, 1998.

Yoder, A. R. *Home Audio*. New York: McGraw-Hill, 1998.

Construction and Civil Engineering

Advances in Acoustics Technology. Edited by J. Hernandez. Chichester, New York: John Wiley & Sons, 1995.

Bennet, D., Steinkamp, J., and Foster, N. *Skyscrapers: Form and Function*. New York: Simon & Schuster, 1995.

Bloch, H. *A Practical Guide to Steam Turbine Technology*. New York: McGraw-Hill, 1996.

Bridger, R. *Introduction to Ergonomics*. New York: McGraw-Hill, 1995.

Brown, C. *Spacecraft Mission Design*. 2nd edition. Reston, Virginia: American Institute of Aeronautics and Astronautics, 1998.

Brown, D. J. *Bridges: 3000 Years of Defying Nature*. New York: Macmillan, 1993.

Chadwick, A. *Hydraulics in Civil and Environmental Engineering*. New York: Routledge, Chapman & Hall, 1998.

Crowley, T. *Beam Engines*. Princes Risborough, England: Shire Publications, 1999.

Encyclopedia of Acoustics. Edited by M. Crocker. New York: John Wiley & Sons, 1997.

Fetherstone, D. *The Chunnel: The Amazing Story of the Undersea Crossing of the English Channel*. New York: Times Books, 1997.

Frisk, G. *Ocean and Seabed Acoustics: A Theory of Wave Propagation*. Englewood Cliffs, New Jersey: Prentice-Hall, 1994.

Janovsky, L. *Elevator Mechanical Design*. 2nd edition. New York: Ellis Horwood, 1993.

Kavanagh, B. *Surveying: Principles and Applications*. Englewood Cliffs, New Jersey: Prentice-Hall, 1996.

Kennedy, J. L. *Oil and Gas Pipeline Fundamentals*. 2nd edition. Tulsa, Oklahoma: PennWell Books, 1993.

Korn, P. *The Woodworker's Guide to Hand Tools*. Newtown, Connecticut: The Taunton Press, 1997.

Marine Engineering. Revised edition. Edited by R. Harrington. Jersey City: Society of Naval Architects and Marine Engineers, 1992.

Massel, S. *Ocean Surface Waves: Their Physics and Prediction*. River Edge, New Jersey: World Scientific, 1996.

Matthews, F., and Rawlings, R. *Composite Materials: Engineering and Science*. New York: Chapman & Hall, 1994.

Orlemann, E. *Giant Earth Moving Equipment*. Osceola, Wisconsin: Motorbooks International, 1995.

Pierce, M., and Jobson, R. *Bridge Builders*. New York: John Wiley & Sons, 2002.

Powell, R. *Rethinking the Skyscraper*. New York: Whitney Library of Design, 1999.

Shapiro, H. I., Shapiro, J. P., and Shapiro, L. K. *Cranes and Derricks*. New York: McGraw-Hill Professional Publishing, 1999.

Tsinker, G. *Marine Structures Engineering: Specialized Applications*. New York: Chapman & Hall, 1995.

Vanderwarker, P. *The Big Dig: Reshaping an American City*. New York: Little, Brown and Co., 2001.

Earth, Space, and Environmental Science

Abbott, P. *Natural Disasters*. Dubuque, Iowa: William C. Brown Publishers, 1996.

Aquaculture and Water Resource Management. Edited by D. Baird. Malden: Blackwell Science, 1996.

Barbee, J. *A Journey Through Time: Exploring the Universe with the Hubble Space Telescope*. New York: Penguin Studio, 1995.

Biological Wastewater Treatment. Edited by L. Grady, G. Daigger, and H. Lim. 2nd edition. New York: Marcel Dekker, 1998.

Botkin, D., and Keller, E. *Environmental Science: Earth as a Living Planet*. New York: John Wiley & Sons, 1995.

Bryant, A. *Tsunami: The Underrated Hazard*. New York: Cambridge University Press, 2001.

Chiras, D., Owen, O., and Reganold, J. *Natural Resource Conservation*. Englewood Cliffs, New Jersey: Prentice-Hall, 1998.

Clearcut: The Tragedy of Industrial Forestry. Edited by B. Devall. San Francisco: Sierra Club Books, 1995.

Davies, J. and Mazurek, J. *Pollution Control in the United States*. Washington, D.C.: Resources for the Future, 1998.

Dutton, A. *Handbook on Quarrying*. Adelaide, Australia: Department of Mines and Energy, 1993.

Environmental Forest Science. Edited by K. Sassa. Boston: Kluwer Academic Publishers, 1998.

Fagan, B. *In the Beginning: An Introduction to Archaeology*. New York: HarperCollins College Publishers, 1994.

Gleick, P. *Environmental Consequences of Hydroelectric Development: The Role of Facility Size and Type*. New York: Pergamon Press, 1992.

Global Energy Strategies: Living with Restricted Greenhouse Gas Emissions. Edited by J. White. New York: Plenum Press, 1993.

Hawking, S. *The Universe in a Nutshell*. New York: Bantam Books, 2001.

Jobin, W. R. *Sustainable Management for Dams and Waters*. Boca Raton: Lewis Publishers, 1998.

Opie, J. *Ogallala: Water for a Dry Land*. Lincoln, Nebraska: University of Nebraska Press, 1993.

Ramage, J. *Energy: A Guidebook*. New York: Oxford University Press, 1997.

Stein, S. *Introduction to Seismology: Earthquakes and Earth Structure*. Boston: Blackwell Scientific Publishers, 1994.

Theodore, M., and Theodore, L. *Major Environmental Issues Facing the 21st Century*. Upper Saddle River, New Jersey: Prentice-Hall, 1996.

Voit, M. *Hubble Space Telescope: New Views of the Universe*. New York: Harry N. Abrams, 2000.

Walker, L. *The North American Forests: Geography, Ecology, and Silviculture*. Boca Raton, Florida: C.R.C. Press, 1998.

Water Management. Edited by M. Goosen, W. Shayya. Lancaster: Technomic Publishing Co., 1999.

Electrical Engineering

Adamczyk, P., et al. *Electricity and Magnetism*. Tulsa, Oklahoma: Usborne, 1994.

Bridgman, R. *Electronics*. New York: Dorling Kindersley/HarperCollins, 1993.

Clifford, M. *Electric/Electronic Motor Data Handbook*. Englewood Cliffs, New Jersey: Prentice-Hall, 1990.

Fisher, D., and Fisher, M. *Tube: The Invention of Television*. Washington, D.C.: Counterpoint, 1996.

Fuel Cell Systems. Edited by L. J. Blowen and M. N. Mugerwa. New York: Plenum Press, 1993.

Gerrish, H. *Electricity*. South Holland, Illinois: Goodheart-Wilcox Company, 1994.

Gray, J. *Advanced Robotics and Intelligent Machines*. London: Institution of Electrical Engineers, 1996.

Horn, D. T. *Basic Electronics Theory*. Blue Ridge Summit, Pennsylvania: TAB Books, 1994.

Komp, R. *Practical Photovoltaics*. Ann Arbor, Michigan: Aatec Publications, 1995.

Litman, T. *Efficient Electric Motor Systems Handbook*. Lilburn, Georgia: Fairmont Press, 1995.

Smith, R. J., et al. *Circuits, Devices and Systems*. 5th edition. New York: John Wiley & Sons, 1991.

Tapping into the Sun: Today's Applications of Photovoltaic Technology. Washington, D.C.: U.S. Department of Energy, 1995.

Velvey, V. F. C. *The Benchtop Electronics Reference Manual*. New York: TAB Books, 1994.

Weaver, R., and Dale, D. *Machines in the Home (Discoveries and Inventions)*. New York: Oxford University Press, 1994.

Fundamentals of Science

Anderson, J. *Fundamentals of Aerodynamics*. New York: McGraw-Hill, 1991.

Ardley, N. *The Science Book of Color*. Fort Worth: Harcourt, Brace, Jovanovich, 1991.

Atkins, P. *The Second Law: Energy, Chaos and Form*. New York: W. H. Freeman, 1994.

Barnett, J. *Time's Pendulum: The Quest to Capture Time—From Sundials to Atomic Clocks*. New York: Plenum Trade, 1998.

Brosseau, C. *Fundamentals of Polarized Light: A Statistical Optics Approach*. New York: John Wiley & Sons, 1998.

Coyne, G. S. *The Laboratory Companion: A Practical Guide to Materials, Equipment, and Technique*. New York: John Wiley & Sons, 1995.

Crummett, W., and Western, A. *University Physics: Models and Applications*. Dubuque, Iowa: William C. Brown/McGraw-Hill, 1994.

De Pinna, S. *Forces and Motion*. Austin, Texas: Raintree Steck-Vaughn, 1998.

Dilson, J. *The Abacus*. New York: St. Martin's Press, 1994.

Feynman, R. *The Character of Physical Law*. New York: Modern Library, 1994.

Gerrish, H. *Electricity*. South Holland, Illinois: Goodheart-Wilcox Company, 1994.

Griffith, W. *The Physics of Everyday Phenomena*. Dubuque, Iowa: Brown Publishers, 1992.

Hobson, A. *Physics: Concepts and Connections*. Englewood Cliffs, New Jersey: Prentice-Hall, 1995.

Lamb, H. *Hydrodynamics*. New York: Cambridge University Press, 1993.

Livingston, J. D. *Driving Force: The Natural Magic of Magnets*. Cambridge, Massachusetts: Harvard University Press, 1996.

Macaulay, D. *The New Way Things Work*. New York: Dorling Kindersley, 1997.

McEvoy, J. P. *Introducing Quantum Theory*. Blue Ridge Summit, Pennsylvania: Totem Books, 2001.

Pain, H. *The Physics of Vibrations and Waves*. Chichester, New York: John Wiley & Sons, 1999.

Peitgen, H.-O., et al. *Chaos and Fractals: New Frontiers of Science*. New York: Springer Verlag, 1992.

Rankin, W. *Introducing Newton and Classical Physics*. Blue Ridge Summit, Pennsylvania: Totem Books, 2000.

Rubin, S. *Toilets, Toasters, and Telephones: The How and Why of Everyday Objects*. San Diego: Browndeer Press, 1998.

Vecchione, G. *Magnet Science*. New York: Sterling Publishing Co., 1995.

Instrumentation and Analytical Technology

Bently, J. *Principles of Measurement Systems*. 3rd edition. New York: John Wiley & Sons, 1995.

Contemporary Chemical Analysis. Edited by J. Rubinson and K. Rubinson. Upper Saddle River, New Jersey: Prentice-Hall, 1998.

DeFelice, T. *An Introduction to Meteorological Instrumentation and Measurement*. Paramus, New Jersey: Prentice-Hall, 1998.

Gaussorgues, G. *Infrared Thermography*. New York: Chapman & Hall, 1994.

Kocis, S., and Figura, Z. *Ultrasonic Measurements and Technologies*. London: Chapman & Hall, 1996.

Norden, K. *Electronic Weighing: Fundamentals and Applications*. Boston: Butterworth-Heinemann, 1993.

Principles of Electronic Instrumentation. Edited by D. James and B. Holden. Philadelphia: W. B. Saunders, 1997.

Light, Optics, and Photography

Aaland, M. *Digital Photography*. New York: Random House, 1992.

The Age of Videography: Twenty Years That Changed the Way We See Ourselves. Edited by B. McKernan. New York: Miller Freeman, 1996.

Blair, P. *Cartoon Animation*. Laguna Hills, California: Walter Foster, 1994.

Brown, B. *Motion Picture and Video Lighting*. Boston: Focal Press, 1996.

Cheo, P. *Fiber Optics and Opto-electronics*. Englewood Cliffs, New Jersey: Prentice-Hall, 1990.

Crisp, C. *Introduction to Fiber Optics*. Boston, Massachusetts: Newnes, 1996.

Electro-Optical Displays. Edited by M. Karin. New York: Marcel Dekker, 1992.

Farace, J. *Digital Imaging: Tips, Tools, and Techniques for Photographers*. Woburn, Massachusetts: Focal Press, 1994.

The Focal Encyclopedia of Photography. Edited by L. Stroebel and R. Zakia. Woburn, Massachusetts: Focal Press, 1993.

Goff, D. R. *Fiber Optic Reference Guide: A Practical Guide to the Technology*. Woburn, Massachusetts: Focal Press, 1999.

Freeman, M. *The Complete Guide to Digital Photography*. New York: Silver Pixel Press, 2001.

Hecht, J. *Understanding Fiber Optics*. Carmel, Indiana: Howard W. Sams & Co., 1990.

Holland, G. *Inventors and Inventions: Photography*. Tarrytown, New York: Marshall Cavendish, 1996.

Malkiewicz, K. *Cinematography*. New York: Simon & Schuster, 1992.

Sklar, R. *Movies Made America*. New York: Random House, 1994.

Walker, B. H. *Optical Engineering Fundamentals*. New York: McGraw-Hill, 1995.

Manufacturing and Industry

Ball P. *Made to Measure: New Materials for the 21st Century*. Princeton, New Jersey: Princeton University Press, 1997.

Barlow, C. *The World Rubber Industry*. New York: Routledge, 1994.

Beck, D. *Gas-Turbine Regenerators*. New York: Chapman & Hall, 1996.

Conway, G. *Garment and Textile Dictionary*. Albany: Delmar Publishers, 1997.

DeAlmeida, A. *Autonomous Robotic Systems*. London: Springer-Verlag, 1998.

Dickerson, K. *Textiles and Apparel in the Global Economy*. Upper Saddle River, New Jersey: Merrill, 1999.

DuBois and Pribble's Plastics Mold Engineering Handbook. Edited by Eric L. Buckleitner. New York: Chapman & Hall, 1995.

Fatikow, S. *Microsystem Technology and Microbiotics*. New York: Springer-Verlag, 1997.

Gary, J. *Petroleum Refining: Technology and Economics*. New York: Marcel Dekker, 1993.

Gingery, D. *Working Sheet Metals*. Springfield, Missouri: D. J. Gingery, 1993.

Middleton, A. *Rugs and Carpets: Techniques, Traditions and Designs*. London: Mitchell Beazley, 1996.

The Mining Industry. Edited by D. Banks. Philadelphia: Hanley & Belfus, 1993.

Neely, J. *Practical Metallurgy and the Materials of Industry*. New York: Prentice-Hall, 1994.

Polymers: Fibers and Textiles: A Compendium. Edited by J. Kroschwitz. New York: John Wiley & Sons, 1990.

Rickwood, D., Ford, T., and Steensgard, J. *Centrifugation: Essential Data*. New York: John Wiley & Sons, 1994.

Rock Mechanics for Underground Mining. Edited by B. Brady and E. Brown. 2nd edition. New York: Chapman & Hall, 1993.

Walsh, R. A. *Machining and Metalworking Handbook*. New York: McGraw-Hill, 1998.

Waters, T. *The Fundamentals of Manufacturing for Engineers*. Bristol, Pennsylvania: UCL Press, 1996.

Mechanical Engineering

Avery, W., and Wu, C. *Renewable Energy from the Ocean*. Oxford: Oxford University Press, 1994.

Baines, A. C. *The Concise Oxford Dictionary of Musical Instruments*. New York: Oxford University Press, 1992.

Bodansky, D. *Nuclear Energy: Principles, Practices, and Prospects*. Woodbury, New York: American Institute of Physics, 1996.

Brown, W. *Alternative Sources of Energy*. New York: Chelsea House Publishers, 1994.

Clean Energy from Waste and Coal. Edited by M. R. Khan. Washington, D.C.: American Chemical Society, 1993.

Ewert, R. *Gears and Gear Manufacture: The Fundamentals*. New York: Chapman & Hall, 1997.

Fowler, K. *The Fusion Quest*. Baltimore: Johns Hopkins University Press, 1997.

Gieras, G. *Linear Induction Drives*. New York: Oxford University Press, 1994.

Gipe, P. *Wind Energy Comes of Age*. New York: John Wiley & Sons, 1995.

The Illustrated Encyclopedia of Musical Instruments. Edited by Robert Dearling. New York: Schirmer Books, 1996.

Indirect Solar, Geothermal, and Nuclear Energy. Edited by T. N. Veziroglu. New York: Nova Science Publishers, 1991.

Jiandong, T., et al. *Mini Hydropower*. New York: John Wiley & Sons, 1997.

Nanotechnology. Edited by Gregory Timp. New York: Springer Verlag, 1999.

Organ, A. J. *The Regenerator and the Stirling Engine*. Bury St. Edmunds, United Kingdom: Mechanical Engineering Publications, 1997.

Parsa, Z. *Future High Energy Colliders*. Woodbury, New York: American Institute of Physics, 1997.

Ross, D. *Power from the Waves*. Oxford: Oxford University Press, 1995.

Walker, J. *UNESCO Energy Engineering Series: Wind Energy Technology*. New York: UNESCO, 1997.

Wohletz, K. *Volcanology and Geothermal Energy*. Berkeley: University of California Press, 1992.

Military Technology

Alexander, J. *Future War: Nonlethal Weapons in Modern Warfare*. New York: St. Martin's Press, 1999.

Baker, A. *The Naval Institute Guide to Combat Fleets of the World 2002/2003*. Annapolis, Maryland: Naval Institute Press, 2002.

Blakelock, J. H. *Automatic Control of Aircraft and Missiles*. New York: John Wiley & Sons, 1991.

Builder, C., and Nichiporuk, C. *Information Technologies and the Future of Land Warfare*. Santa Monica, California: Rand, 1995.

Bull, S. *20th-Century Arms and Armor*. New York: Facts On File, 1996.

Chant, C. *The New Encyclopedia of Handguns and Small Arms*. New York: Prion/Multimedia Books, 1995.

Cole, H. *Understanding Radar*. Boston: Blackwell Scientific Publications, 1992.

Davis, J. K. *Aircraft Carriers and the Role of Naval Power in the 21st Century*. Cambridge, Massachusetts: Institute for Foreign Policy Analysis, 1993.

Ford, R. *The Grim Reaper: The Machine-Gun and Machine-Gunners*. London, England: Sidgwick & Jackson, 1996.

Gelbert, M. *Tanks: Main Battle Tanks and Light Tanks*. London: Brassey's, 1996.

Gudmundsson, B. I. *On Artillery*. Westport, Connecticut: Praeger, 1993.

Jane's Ammunition Handbook 2000/2001. Alexandria, Virginia: Jane's Information Group, 2000.

McMahon, K., and Warner, J. *Pursuit of the Shield: The U.S. Quest for Limited Ballistic Missile Defense*. Lanham, Maryland: University Press of America, 1997.

Norris, J., and Fowler, W. *NBC: Nuclear, Biological and Chemical Warfare on the Modern Battlefield*. Herndon, Virginia: Brassey's, 1998.

Performance of Protective Clothing. Edited by J. S. Johnson and S. Z. Mansdorf. Washington, D.C.: American Society for Testing, 1997.

Polmar, N. *The Naval Institute Guide to the Ships and Aircraft of the U.S. Fleet*. Annapolis, Maryland: The United States Naval Institute, 2001.

Price, R. M. *The Chemical Weapons Taboo*. New York: Cornell University Press, 1997.

Rhodes, R. *The Making of the Atomic Bomb*. London: Simon & Schuster, 1986.

Tchudi, S. *Lock and Key: The Secrets of Locking Things Up, In, and Out*. New York: Maxwell Macmilan International, 1993.

The First Information War: The Story of Communications, Computers, and Intelligence Systems in the Persian Gulf War. Edited by E. Campen. Fairfax, Virginia: AFCEA International Press, 1992.

Van der Vat, D. *Stealth at Sea: The History of the Submarine*. London: Wiedenfeld & Nicolson, 1994.

Transportation and Leisure

Advanced Technology for Road Transport. Edited by I. Catling. Boston: Artech House, 1994.

Baker, D. *Spaceflight and Rocketry: A Chronology*. New York: Facts on File, 1996.

Batchelor, R. *Henry Ford, Mass Production,*

Modernism, and Design. Manchester, U.K.: Manchester University Press, 1994.

Birch, T. *Automotive Suspension and Steering Systems*. Fort Worth: Saunders College Publishing, 1993.

Birch, T. W. *Automotive Braking Systems*. Philadelphia: W. B. Saunders, 1994.

Brooks, M. *Subway City: Riding the Trains*. New Brunswick, New Jersey: Rutgers University Press, 1997.

Brown, C. *Spacecraft Mission Design*. Reston, Virginia: American Institute of Aeronautics and Astronautics, 1998.

Campbell, J. *Automatic Transmissions and Transaxles*. Englewood Cliffs, New Jersey: Prentice-Hall, 1995.

Cannon, J. S. *Harnessing Hydrogen: The Key to Sustainable Transportation*. New York: Inform, 1995.

Carlton, J. *Marine Propellers and Propulsion*. Boston: Butterworth-Heinemann, 1994.

Chilton's Guide to Small Engine Repair. Radnor, Pennsylvania: Chilton Book Company, 1994.

Compton, S. W., and Rhein, M. J. *The Ultimate Book of Lighthouses*. San Diego: Thunder Bay Press, 2000.

Comstock, H. *The Iron Horse: An Illustrated History of Steam Locomotives*. 2nd edition. Sykesville: Greenberg Publishing, 1992.

Coughlan, J. *Green Cars: Earth-Friendly Electric Cars*. Mankato: Capstone Press, 1994.

Coyle, S. *The Art and Science of Flying Helicopters*. Ames, Iowa: Iowa State University Press, 1996.

DeLuchi, M. A. *Hydrogen Fuel-cell Vehicles*. Davis, California: Institute of Transportation Studies, University of California, 1992.

Doganis, R. *The Airport Business*. London; New York: Routledge, 1992.

Dole, C. *Flight Theory for Pilots*. Casper, Wyoming: IAP Inc., 1993.

Dwiggins, B. *Automotive Electricity and Electronics: Concepts and Applications*. Englewood Cliffs, New Jersey: Prentice-Hall, 1996.

Electric Vehicles: Driving Towards Commercialization. Edited by R. Sims. Warrendale, Pennsylvania: Society of Automotive Engineers, 1997.

Fishbein, S. B. *Flight Management Subsystems*. Westport, Connecticut: Praeger, 1995.

Fuel Spray Technology. Warrendale, Pennsylvania: Society of Automotive Engineers, 1994.

Ganesan, V. *Internal Combustion Engines*. New York: McGraw-Hill, 1996.

Garratt, C. *Hamlyn History of Trains*. New York: Hamlyn, 2000.

Green, M., and Petersen J. *Amphibious Vehicles (Land and Sea)*. Minneapolis, Minnesota: Capstone Press, 1997.

Gurzadian, G. *Theory of Interplanetary Flight*. Amsterdam: Gordon and Breach, 1996.

Halderman, J. *Automotive Chassis Systems: Brakes, Steering, Suspension, and Alignment*. Englewood Cliffs, New Jersey: Prentice-Hall, 1996.

Harris, K. *World Electric Locomotives*. London: Jane's Publishing Company, 1981.

Hovercraft Technology, Economics, and Application. Edited by J. Amyot. Amsterdam, New York: Elsevier, 1990.

Isakowitz, S. J., and AIAA Space Transportation Systems Technical Committee. *International Reference Guide to Space Launch Systems*. Washington, D.C.: American Institute of Aeronautics and Astronautics, 1991.

Keiper, D. *Hydrofoil Voyages: Williwaw, From Dream to Reality*. Cape Girardeau, Missouri: Hinsdale Press, 1996.

Kemp, P. *Oxford Companion to Ships and the Sea*. New York: Oxford University Press, 1994.

Kerrebrock, J. *Aircraft Engines and Gas Turbines*. Cambridge, Massachusetts: MIT Press, 1992.

Kozloski, L. *U.S. Space Gear: Outfitting the Astronaut*. Washington, D.C.: Smithsonian Institution Press, 1994.

Larsson, L., and Eliasson, R. *Principles of Yacht Design*. Camden, Maine: International Maritime Publishing, 1994.

McCartney, B. *Inland Navigation: Locks, Dams, and Channels*. Reston, Virginia: American Society of Civil Engineers, 1998.

Mechanical Power Transmission Components. Edited by D. South and J. Mancuso. New York: Marcel Dekker, 1994.

Mott, L. *The Development of the Rudder: A Technological Tale*. London, England: Chatham, 1996.

Newton, K., Steeds, W., and Garrett, T. *The Motor Vehicle*. Boston: Butterworth-Heinemann, 1996.

Noble, D. L. *Lighthouses and Keepers: The U.S. Lighthouse Service and Its Legacy*. Annapolis, Maryland: U.S. Naval Institute Press, 1997.

Outlaw, B. *FAA Parachute Basics*. Washington, D.C.: Federal Aviation Administration, Regulatory Support Division, 1998.

Pike, D. *An Introduction to Powerboat Cruising*. New York: Hearst Marine Books, 1989.

Pulkrabek, W. *Engineering Fundamentals of the Internal Combustion Engine*. Englewood Cliffs, New Jersey: Prentice-Hall, 1997.

Raimond, V. D. *Transportation*. Edinburgh, Texas: New Santander, 1996.

Rawson, K., and Tupper, E. *Basic Ship Theory*. 5th edition. Woburn, Massachusetts: Butterworth-Heinemann, 2001.

Safety Belts, Airbags, and Child Restraints: Research to Address Emerging Policy Questions. Washington, D.C.: Transportation Research Board, National Research Council, 1998.

Scott, P. *The Shoulders of Giants: A History of Human Flight to 1919*. Reading, Massachusetts: Addison-Wesley, 1995.

Shaw, R. E. *Canals for a Nation: The Canal Era in the United States, 1790–1860*. Lexington, Kentucky: Kentucky University Press, 1993.

Steering and Suspension Technology. Warrendale, Pennsylvania: Society of Automotive Engineers, 1997.

Stockel, M. W., and Stockel, M. T. *Auto Mechanics Fundamentals*. South Holland, Illinois: Goodheart-Willcox, 1990.

Stover, J. F. *The Routledge Historical Atlas of the American Railroads*. New York: Routledge, 1999.

Suvorov, V. *The First Manned Spaceflight: Russia's Quest for Space*. Commack, New York: Nova Science Publishing, 1997.

Turner, J. E. *Air Traffic Controller*. New York: Prentice-Hall, 1994.

Visual Navigation: From Biological Systems to Unmanned Ground Vehicles. Edited by Y. Aloimonos. Mahwah, New Jersey: Lawrence Erlbaum Associates, 1997.

Wells, A. T. *Commuter Airlines*. Malabar, Florida: Krieger, 1996.

Wildenburg, T. *Gray Steel and Black Oil: Fast Tankers and Replenishment at Sea in the U.S. Navy*. Annapolis, Maryland: U.S. Naval Institute Press, 1996.

Williams, J. *From Sails to Satellites: The Origins and Development of Navigational Science*. New York: Oxford University Press, 1994.

Wilson, H. *The Encyclopedia of the Motorcycle*. New York: Dorling Kindersley, 1995.

Web sites

Abacus
http://www.ee.ryerson.ca:8080/~elf/abacus

Alternative Fuels Data Center
http://www.afdc.doe.gov

Animation World Network
http://www.awn.com

Artificial Intelligence
http://www.aaai.org

The Association for Automatic Identification and Data Capture Technologies
http://www.aimglobal.org

Automobile News: Car and Driver
http://www.caranddriver.com

Bioenergy Information Network
http://bioenergy.ornl.gov/links.html

Bridges
http://www.pbs.org/ktca/newtons/12/bridges.html

Carpet Making: The Carpet and Rug Institute
http://www.carpet-rug.com

CERN (European Organization for Nuclear Research)
http://press.web.cern.ch/Public

Chandra X-Ray Observatory Center
http://chandra.harvard.edu

Channel Tunnel: Eurotunnel
http://www.eurotunnel.com

Chemistry: Frequently Asked Questions
http://antoine.frostburg.edu/chem/senese/101/index.shtml

Chemistry: Periodic Table
http://www.webelements.com

Civil Engineering: The American Society of Civil Engineers
http://www.asce.org

Coal Mining, History of
http://www.history.ohiostate.edu/projects/Lessons_US/Gilded_Age/Coal_Mining

Coal: The Kentucky Coal Council
http://www.coaleducation.org

Color
http://acept.la.asu.edu/PiN/mod/light/colorspectrum/pattLight3.html

Computer History Museum
http://www.computerhistory.org/index.page

Computers: Glossary of Computing Terms
http://www.geek.com/glossary/glossary_search.htm

Consumer Electronics Association
http://www.cemacity.org

Contemporary College Physics Simulation Library
http://webphysics.ph.msstate.edu/jc/library

Conversion Tables: Convert it!
http://microimg.com/science

Deep Sea and Diving: Jacques-Yves Cousteau
http://www.france.diplomatie.fr/label_france/ENGLISH/SCIENCES/cousteau/cousteau.html

Defense Meteorological Satellite Program
http://www.ngdc.noaa.gov/dmsp/dmsp.html

Eden Project
http://www.edenproject.com

Electric Vehicle Association of the Americas
http://www.evaa.org

Electronics: The Institute of Electrical and Electronics Engineers
http://www.ieee.org

Energy, Alternative: Solar, Wave, and Wind Power
http://www.alt-energy.com/index.cgi

Environmental: Automobiles and Carbon Monoxide
http://www.epa.gov/OMSWWW/03-co.htm

Environmental Protection: Envirofacts Warehouse
http://www.epa.gov/enviro/html/ef_overview.html

European Space Agency
http://sci.esa.int

Fastening and Joining: The American Welding Society
http://www.aws.org

Federation of American Scientists
http://www.fas.org

Fermi National Accelerator Laboratory
http://www.fnal.gov

Fibers: The Natural Fibers Research and Information Center
http://www.utexas.edu/depts/bbr/natfiber

Fishing Industry: Food and Agriculture Organization
http://www.fao.org/fi/default.asp

Gas Laws
http://www.chemistry.ohio-state.edu/betha/nealGasLaw

Gas, Natural: The Natural Gas Supply Association
http://www.naturalgas.org/

General: How Stuff Works
http://www.howstuffworks.com

Genetics
http://www.dnaftb.org/dnaftb

Helicopters: Helicopter Association International
http://www.rotor.com

History of Robotics
http://web.mit.edu/sts001/www/Team10/team10page1.html

HubbleSite
http://hubble.stsci.edu

Human Genome
http://www.nature.com/genomics

Hydroelectricity: General
http://www.usbr.gov/power/edu/edu.htm

Imagine the Universe
http://imagine.gsfc.nasa.gov/index.html

Index of African American Inventors
http://www.princeton.edu/~mcbrown/display/inventor_list.html

Internal Combustion Engine: Rudolf Diesel
http://www.invent.org/hall_of_fame/42.html

Internet, History of
http://www.isoc.org/internet/history

Internet: World Wide Web
http://press.web.cern.ch/Public/ACHIEVEMENTS/WEB/Welcome.html

Sources for Further Study

Inventors
http://inventors.about.com/library/bl/bl12.htm

Invent Now (National Inventors Hall of Fame)
http://www.invent.org/index.asp?bhcp=1

Iron and Steel: The International Iron and Steel Institute
http://www.worldsteel.org

ITER (Nuclear Fusion Research)
http://www.iter.org/ITERPublic/ITER/physics_text.html

Light and Optics
http://acept.la.asu.edu/PiN/mod/light/pattLightOptics.html

Machine Tools: An Introduction
http://electron.mit.edu/~gsteele/mirrors/www.nmis.org/EducationTraining/machineshop/outline.html

Magnetism: The National High Magnetic Field Laboratory
http://www.magnet.fsu.edu

Masonry: The International Masonry Institute
http://www.imiweb.org

Mass Transit: Innovative Technologies
http://faculty.washington.edu/jbs/itrans

Materials Science
http://www.nmsi.ac.uk/on-line/challenge

Meteorology: Office of Meteorology Home Page
http://www.nws.noaa.gov/om/index.html

Meteorology: The Weather Channel
http://www.weather.com/?from=globalnav

MIT Artificial Intelligence Laboratory
http://www.ai.mit.edu

Monorail: The Monorail Society
http://www.monorails.org

Motorcycles: The American Motorcyclist Association
http://www.ama-cycle.org

NASA
http://www.nasa.gov

The National Academies
http://nationalacademies.org

National Oceanic and Atmospheric Administration
http://www.noaa.gov

National Renewable Energy Laboratory
http://www.nrel.gov

Nature Magazine
http://www.nature.com/nature

Nobel Foundation
http://www.nobel.se/index.html

Nuclear Fusion: The Princeton Plasma Center
http://www.pppl.gov/oview/pages/fusion_energy.html

Nuclear Issues: Bulletin of the Atomic Scientists
http://www.bullatomsci.org

Nuclear Safety: The International Nuclear Safety Center
http://www.insc.anl.gov

Nuclear Weapons: Los Alamos National Laboratory
http://www.lanl.gov/worldview

Paint: What Is Paint?
http://www.sinopia.com/paint.html

Petroleum: Offshore Drilling Technology
http://otrc.tamu.edu

Planetarium: International Planetarium Society
http://www.ips-planetarium.org

Pollution: Lead in the Environment
http://www.tmc.tulane.edu/ECME/leadhome

Princeton Plasma Physics Laboratory
http://www.pppl.gov

Printing Industry: Graphion's Online Type Museum
http://www.slip.net/~graphion/museum.html

Printing: Color Printing in the 19th Century
http://www.lib.udel.edu/ud/spec/exhibits/color

Printing: Offset Lithography
http://nmaa-ryder.si.edu/posters/process.html

Radar: NASA Observatorium
http://observe.ivv.nasa.gov/nasa/education/reference/radar/gif.html

Railroads: Trains across America
http://ipl.sils.umich.edu/exhibit/trains

Road Systems and Traffic Control: U.S. Traffic Signs
http://members.aol.com/rcmoeur/signman.html

Robotics: An Introduction
http://www.thetech.org/exhibits_events/online/robots/intro

Rocketry: Marshall Space Flight Center
http://history.msfc.nasa.gov/rocketry

Roslin Institute Online: Web Links on Cloning and Nuclear Transfer
http://www.ri.bbsrc.ac.uk/library/research/cloning/cloneweb.html

Science Is Fun
http://scifun.chem.wisc.edu/scifun.html

Science Museum
http://www.sciencemuseum.org.uk

Scientific American
http://www.sciam.com

SI Units: Bureau International de Poids et Mésures
http://www.bipm.fr

Smithsonian National Air and Space Museum
http://www.nasm.si.edu

Soap and Detergent Association
http://www.sdahq.org

Solar Energy
http://www.eren.doe.gov/RE/solar.html

Space Probes: Planetary and Earth observation missions
http://nssdc.gsfc.nasa.gov

Space Stations: The International Space Station
http://spaceflight.nasa.gov/station/index.html

Space Photography
http://www.nix.nasa.gov

Space Technology
http://www.space-technology.com/index.html

Spectroscopy: The Basics of NMR
http://www.cis.rit.edu/htbooks/nmr

Steam Engine Library
http://www.history.rochester.edu/steam

Technology Review Magazine
http://www.techreview.com

TechWeb Technology Encyclopedia
http://content.techweb.com/encyclopedia/defineterm.cgi

Telecommunications: ISDN
http://www.ralphb.net/ISDN

Telephone, History of
http://inventors.about.com/library/inventors/bltelephone.htm

Telescope: Mauna Kea Observatory
http://www.ifa.hawaii.edu/mko

Telescope: Parkes Observatory
http://www.parkes.atnf.csiro.au

Textiles: The Internet Center for Canadian Fashion and Design
http://www.ntgi.net/ICCF&D/textile.htm

Time Standard (NIST)
http://nist.time.gov

Time: General Information
http://physics.nist.gov/GenInt/Time/time.html

Time: The Quartz Watch
http://www.si.edu/lemelson/Quartz/coolwatches/index.html

Tunnels: The American Underground-Construction Association
http://www.auca.org

United States Department of Agriculture
http://www.usda.gov

United States Environmental Protection Agency
http://www.epa.gov

United States Geological Survey
http://www.usgs.gov

University of British Columbia Liquid-Mirror Home Page
http://www.astro.ubc.ca/LMT/index.html

Visual Effects Headquarters
http://www.vfxhq.com

Waste Disposal: Recycling
http://www.recycle.net/recycle/index.html

Watch Escapements in Motion
http://home.talkcity.com/Terminus/mvhw/escapement.html

What is Engineering? (Whiting School of Engineering, Johns Hopkins University)
http://www.jhu.edu/virtlab

Women in Engineering: Famous Female Engineers and Opportunities
http://www.nae.edu/nae/cwe/cwe.nsf/Homepage

Women in Physics
http://www.physics.ucla.edu/~cwp

Woodworking: Popular Woodworking
http://www.popularwoodworking.com

Zoology
http://www.si.edu/resource/faq/nmnh/zoology.htm

Other Useful Resources

Magazines

Magazines and journals often have the most current and interesting information about topics in technology and the applied sciences. Here follows a list of titles you may find useful. If these magazines are not available from your local library, you can contact the publisher directly or via the Internet to obtain a subscription or single copies.

American Scientist – Sigma Xi
99 Alexander Drive
P.O. Box 13975
Research Triangle Park
NC 27709-3975
(919) 549 0097
http://www.amsci.org

Astronomy
P.O. Box 1612
Waukesha, WI 53186-4055

(800) 446 5489
http://www.kalmbach.com/astro/astronomy.html

Discover
Walt Disney Magazine Publishing Group, Inc.
114 5th Avenue
New York, NY 10011
(800) 829 9132
http://www.discover.com

New Scientist
151 Wardour Street
London W1F 8WE, UK
Boston office:
(617) 558 4939
http://www.newscientist.com

Popular Mechanics
810 Seventh Avenue
New York, NY 10019
(212) 586 5562
http://www.popularmechanics.com

Popular Science Magazine
2 Park Avenue, 9th Floor
New York, NY 10016
(212) 481 8062
http://www.popsci.com

Science News
1719 N Street NW
Washington, D.C. 20036
(202) 785 2255
http://www.sciencenews.org

Science Now
American Association for the Advancement of Science
1200 New York Avenue NW,
Washington, D.C. 20005
(202) 326 6400
http://sciencenow.sciencemag.org

Scientific American
415 Madison Avenue
New York, NY 10017-1179
(212) 754 0550
http://www.sciam.com

The Scientist
3535 Market Street
Suite 200
Philadelphia, PA 19104
(215) 386 9601
http://www.the-scientist.com/homepage.htm

Museums

As well as places of interest to visit, many museums are also research institutions that have scientists on staff who will answer your questions about topics that fall within their field. If you have a question you have not been able to answer on your own, you might try calling your local science museum. Following are the addresses, telephone numbers, and websites of some of the more well known of these institutions.

THE EAST COAST

Marine Biological Laboratory
7 MBL Street
Woods Hole, MA 02543
(508) 548 3705
http://www.mbl.edu

Museum of Science
Science Park
Boston, MA 02114
(617) 723 2500
http://www.mos.org/home.html

New York Hall of Science
47-01 111th Street
Queens, NY 11368
(718) 699 0005
http://www.nyhallsci.org/index.html

THE SOUTHEAST

Kennedy Space Center
Kennedy Space Center Visitor Complex
Mail Code: DNPS
Kennedy Space Center, FL 32899
http://www.KennedySpaceCenter.com

National Air and Space Museum
Smithsonian Institution
7th and Independence Avenue, SW
Washington, D.C. 20560
(202) 357 2700
http://www.si.edu/activity/planvis/museums/i-nasm.htm

The Science Place
Main Building
1318 2nd Avenue
Dallas, TX 75210
http://www.scienceplace.org/index.html

THE MIDWEST

Museum of Science and Industry
57th Street and Lake Shore Drive
Chicago, IL 60637
(773) 684 9844
http://www.msichicago.org

National Inventors Hall of Fame Inventure Place
221 South Broadway Street
Akron, OH
(330) 762 4463
http://www.invent.org

Science Museum of Minnesota
120 W Kellogg Boulevard
St. Paul, MN 55102
(651) 221 9444
http://www.sci.mus.mn.us

United States Air Force Museum
1100 Spaatz Street
Wright-Patterson AFB
OH 45433
(937) 255 3286
http://www.wpafb.af.mil/museum/index.htm

THE WEST

Arizona Science Center
600 E. Washington
Phoenix, AZ 85004
(602) 716 2000
http://www.azscience.org

International Space Hall of Fame
The New Mexico Museum of Space History, Alamogordo, NM 88311-5430
(505) 437 2840
http://www.zianet.com/space/index.html

National Atomic Museum
Building 20358
Wyoming Blvd. SE
Kirtland AFB East
Albuquerque, NM 87117
(505) 284 3242
http://www.atomicmuseum.com

THE PACIFIC COAST

The Exploratorium
3601 Lyon Street
San Francisco, CA 94123
(415) 561 0360
http://www.exploratorium.edu

Lawrence Hall of Science
University of California at Berkeley
Berkeley, CA 94720-5200
(510) 642 7723
http://www.lhs.berkeley.edu

The Tech Museum of Innovation
201 South Market Street
San Jose, CA 95113
(408) 294 TECH
http://www.thetech.org

Pacific Science Center
200 Second Avenue North
Seattle, Washington 98109
(206) 443 2001
http://www.pacsci.org

AUSTRALIA

Australian Museum
6 College Street
Sydney, NSW 2010
(612) 9320 6000
http://www.austmus.gov.au

Powerhouse Museum
500 Harris Street
Ultimo, Sydney
NSW 2007
(612) 9217 0111
http://www.phm.gov.au/home3.htm

CANADA

The Ontario Science Center
770 Don Mills Road
Don Mills
Toronto, Ontario M3C 1T3
(416) 696 1000
http://www.ontariosciencecentre.ca

Science World
1455 Quebec Street
Vancouver, B.C.
V6A 3Z7
http://www.scienceworld.bc.ca

UNITED KINGDOM

Science Museum
Exhibition Road
London SW7 2DD
(0870) 870 4771
http://www.sciencemuseum.org.uk

The Glasgow Science Center
50 Pacific Quay
Glasgow G51 1EA
(0141) 420 5000
http://www.gsc.org.uk

Glossary

aberration Optical defect of mirror or lens caused by its shape or material and preventing the formation of a true image.

abrasive Hard, sharp, or rough material used to rub or grind a surface.

absolute zero Lowest temperature theoretically attainable, 0 K, or –459.67°F (–273.15°C).

absorptiometer Device for measuring the concentration of a solution by the amount of light the solution absorbs.

absorption Taking in of a substance, such as a gas dissolving in a liquid.

acceleration Rate of change of velocity over a given time; measured, for example, in meters per second per second.

accumulator Rechargable cell for storing electricity. Also known as a secondary cell or battery.

acetate Salt or ester of acetic acid, commonly cellulose acetate. Also used in making fibers and sheet material.

acetic acid (CH_2COOH) Pungent smelling organic acid found in vinegar. Also used in plastics manufacture.

acetylene (C_2H_2) Hydrocarbon gas used for welding and production of organic compounds.

achromatic lens Lens free from chromatic aberration (colored fringes to the image) and made from elements of two kinds of glass bonded together.

acid anhydride Nonmetallic oxide that combines with water to form an acid.

acid salt Compound formed from an acid where some of the hydrogen has been replaced by a metal.

adiabatic Process that takes place without heat entering or leaving the system.

adsorption Adhesion of the molecules of a gas, liquid, or dissolved substance to the surface of another substance.

airfoil Shape creating lift by the differential air pressure caused by the airflow over it.

airscrew Propeller that operates in air.

air thermometer Temperature-measuring device in which change in gas volume at constant pressure, or pressure at constant volume, is used.

alcohol Organic compound derived from hydrocarbons by replacing one or more hydrogen atoms by hydroxyl (OH) groups. Also used for ethyl alcohol (C_2H_5OH).

aldehyde Organic compound related to alcohols and carboxylic acids, e.g., formaldehyde (H·CHO), used as preservative and in plastics manufacture.

algae Group of simple plants, of which the largest is seaweed.

algebra Branch of mathematics using general symbols to deal with the properties of and relations between quantities.

alginates Chemicals derived from algae, used in food processing and elsewhere.

algorithm Systematic mathematical procedure used to solve a problem in a finite number of steps.

allotropy Phenomenon in which an element may exist in various forms (allotropes) with identical chemical properties, but different physical ones owing to different arrangements of atoms; e.g., graphite and diamond are both allotropes of carbon.

alpha particle Particle consisting of two protons and two neutrons (a helium nucleus), emitted during the decay of various radioactive elements.

alternating current (AC) Electric current with rapid and regular reversals of its direction of flow.

alternator Generator producing alternating current of constant frequency.

alumina (Al_2O_3) Aluminum oxide, found as corundum, emery, and bauxite.

alums Generally hydrated crystal double sulfate salts. The name is commonly used for aluminum potassium sulfate ($K_2SO_4 \cdot Al_2(SO_4)_3 \cdot 24H_2O$), which forms large colorless crystals and occurs naturally.

amines Organic compounds derived from ammonia by replacing one or more hydrogen atoms with a hydrocarbon alkyl or amyl group. Replacement of one hydrogen atom gives a primary amine, of two a secondary, and the replacement of all three gives a tertiary amine.

amino acids Group of organic compounds that are the constituents of proteins and peptides. They contain both an amino group and a carboxyl group. Essential amino acids are needed in the diet for conversion into proteins.

ammeter Device for measuring electric current in amperes.

ammonia (NH_3) Colorless, pungent-smelling gas readily soluble in water to form ammonium hydroxide (NH_4OH); used as refrigerant and to make explosives, fertilizers, etc.

ampere (A) Basic unit of electric current.

amphoteric Exhibiting both acidic and basic properties, e.g., zinc oxide and aluminum oxide.

amplitude modulation (AM) Method of imposing a signal on a carrier wave by varying the amplitude of the carrier.

anabolism Chemical changes in living organisms in which complex molecules are synthesized from simpler ones.

anaerobic Able to live and grow where there is no air or oxygen.

analog Having the same behavior as the system under investigation, with the input being continuously variable. In an analog computer, the variables are generally represented by voltages or currents.

angle of attack Angle between an air-frame or airfoil and its direction of movement.

ångstrom (Å) Unit of length measurement, used for measuring wavelength of light; 10^{-10}m (one ten-thousand-millionth of a meter); now succeeded by the nanometer, which is ten times larger.

angular velocity Angle through which a rotating object turns in a given time.

anhydrous Containing no combined water.

anode Positively charged electrode to which negative ions move in electrolysis or in a vacuum tube.

anodizing Electrolytic treatment of metals to give them a protective surface coating of oxide.

antibiotic Destructive of, or preventing growth of, bacteria in the body; substance, generally derived from mold or a synthetic version of such a substance, which does this.

antibodies Proteins produced by animal and human plasma cells to combine with foreign organic material and render it harmless. Production of the appropriate antibodies can provide immunity against infective organisms.

antigenic shift Process by which infective agents (such as viruses and bacteria) change their characteristics so as to evade the body's immune defenses.

antiknock Substance added to gasoline to prevent pre-ignition in an internal combustion engine.

antinode Point of maximum displacement in a stationary wave.

antiparticles Elementary particles with equal mass but opposite charge to conventional particles. The antiparticle of the electron is the positron.

aphelion Point of a celestial body's orbit at its greatest distance from the Sun.

apogee Point of a satellite orbit at the greatest distance from Earth.

aquifer Water-bearing body of permeable rock.

arc (electric) Luminous, high-temperature discharge produced by electric current flowing through a gap between two electrodes.

Archimedes' screw Water-raising device consisting of a rotating screw in an inclined cylinder.

armature Moving part of an electromagnetic circuit, such as the rotating coils of an electric motor or generator.

aromatic Literally, smelly; term applied to organic compounds derived from benzene.

asphalt Semisolid composed mostly of bitumen, found near some oil deposits.

astigmatism Defect of lens (especially in the eye) caused by the curvature varying in two perpendicular planes so that a single point is focused as two images, causing distortion.

astrocompass Compass used to determine direction by taking sightings of the stars.

astronomical clock Clock measuring sidereal time, i.e., with reference to the stars, rather than solar or "ordinary" time, with reference to the Sun.

atmospheric pressure Pressure caused by the weight of the atmosphere and varying with weather changes; for scientific purposes, standard atmospheric pressure is 100 kN/m^2 (1 bar—now an obsolete unit—or about 760 mm of mercury in a barometer).

atom Smallest whole unit of an element which cannot be divided by chemical means; composed of subatomic particles, which can be separated by electrical means.

atomic clock Clock regulated by vibration of atoms of an element, e.g., cesium; this vibration is very regular, providing great accuracy.

atomic number Number of protons in nucleus of an atom, giving a convenient method of listing elements in order of increasing atomic weight.

atomic weight Weight of an atom relative to that of an atom of carbon-12, which has an atomic weight of 12.

audio frequency Frequency of signal within range of human hearing (about 20–20,000 Hz).

Aurora Borealis (Northern Lights) Display of colored light, mainly red and green, seen in sky above North and South Poles (at latter, should strictly be called Aurora Australis); caused by

streams of charged particles from the Sun, particularly during times of high sunspot activity.

autoclave Pressure vessel, similar to a pressure cooker, in which fluids can be heated to above their atmospheric boiling point. Used for sterilization in industry and medicine.

autotransformer Transformer with single coil serving as both primary and secondary, from which different voltages can be obtained by connection to the coil at different points.

auxin Substance producing growth in a plant.

Avogadro's Number Number of molecules in a gram-molecule (1 gram x the molecular weight) of a substance; this is a constant, 6.025×10^{23}.

axis Imaginary line about which a rotating object is considered to turn.

azo Name of a chemical group formed of two nitrogen atoms with a double bond—N=N—. Also of a large range of synthetic dyes, mainly red and yellow, containing the group.

bacteria Single-celled organisms responsible for various beneficial processes, including some kinds of fermentation, as well as causing many diseases.

balance wheel Time-regulating device in a watch or clock, which is oscillated back and forth against the force of a spring.

ballistic missile Long-range missile that is propelled and guided by preset mechanisms along a ballistic trajectory to the target.

band pass filter Electronic device allowing passage of signals within a certain frequency range, and blocking others.

bank (aircraft) Tilt to one side, often when turning.

bar Unit of pressure, now replaced by kilonewtons per square meter (kN/m^2).

barograph Recording barometer.

barometer Device for measuring atmospheric pressure, either by means of a column of mercury (hence the common expression of pressure in mm Hg—millimeters of mercury) or an aneroid (literally liquidless) barometer, in which a metal box partly exhausted of air expands and contracts with pressure changes.

baryon Class of subatomic particle of relatively high weight, e.g., proton, neutron.

base (chemistry) Compound that reacts with an acid to produce a salt and water; most bases are metal oxides, and all alkalis are bases.

base (electronics) Region that lies between the emitter and collector of a transistor.

base (genetics) Repeating organic nucleotide forming part of the DNA (deoxyribonucleic acid) structure. Genetic information is coded by the base sequence.

base (mathematics) A number chosen as the framework for a system of numeration, e.g., 10 for the decimal system and 2 for the binary.

base metals Metals that corrode on exposure to the air, as opposed to noble metals.

binding energy Energy that has to be applied to a nucleus to split it into its constituent neutrons and protons.

basicity Number of replaceable hydrogen atoms in a molecule of an acid; thus nitric acid (HNO_3) is monobasic and sulfuric acid (H_2SO_4) dibasic.

basic salt Salt formed by partial neutralization of a base, but still containing a definite proportion of molecules of the original base.

bathymetry Measurement of depth of the sea.

bathyscaphe Deep-sea exploration device consisting of a bathysphere attached to a flotation and propulsion system.

bathysphere A pressure-resistant steel sphere with windows, used for deep-sea exploration, either lowered from a surface ship or part of a bathyscaphe.

bauxite ($Al_2O_3 \cdot xH_2O$) Natural hydrated aluminum oxide, the most important ore of aluminum.

benchmark Permanent surveyor's mark indicating elevation, often cut into rock.

benzene (C_6H_6) Compound found in coal tar; the simplest of the aromatic series of hydrocarbons; widely used as a solvent and in the manufacture of many other substances.

Bessemer process Method of making steel from cast iron: molten iron is poured into a large converter vessel and air blown through from below to oxidize its carbon content and thus remove it; now supplanted by the basic oxygen process.

beta particle Fast-moving electron or positron emitted from the nucleus of a radioactive isotope during the process of beta decay.

beta ray Stream of fast-moving beta particles.

bias Nonsignal input fed to an electronic device to establish the required operating conditions.

bicarbonate Acid salt of carbonic acid (H_2CO_3) with half the hydrogen replaced by a metal, e.g., sodium bicarbonate ($NaHCO_3$).

bimetallic strip Two flat strips of different metals bonded together. A change in temperature causes the two metals to expand by different amounts, so that the strip bends. The device is used in thermostats and thermometers.

biodegradable Capable of being easily decomposed by naturally occurring microorganisms.

bioluminescence Production of light by living organisms, such as glow worms.

biomass Weight of living matter present in a specific area.

bit Binary digit, which may be either 0 or 1; thus a unit of information in a computer.

blackbody Theoretically perfect absorber of heat or light radiation, etc.

bleaching Removal of color by chemical means.

boiling point Temperature (for a specific pressure) at which a liquid changes state to turn into a gas.

bolometer Device for measuring very low levels of heat radiation.

bond Link between one atom and another in a molecule, caused by the sharing or transfer of electrons. Bonds may be covalent, where an electron pair is shared between one atom and another; ionic, the simplest type of bonding, where an electron is transferred from one atom to another; or dative, where one atom gives an electron pair to another; and some atoms, e.g., carbon, can form double and triple bonds as well as single ones.

brake horsepower Useful power of an engine measured by testing against a dynamometer brake.

brass Alloy of copper and zinc, possibly with other metals such as nickel or tin.

breeder reactor Nuclear reactor that produces more fissionable material than it uses.

brine Solution of common salt.

British Thermal Unit Heat required to raise the temperature of 1 lb. of water through 1 degree Fahrenheit.

broadband amplifier Amplifier capable of giving uniform amplification of signals over a wide frequency range.

bromide Any salt of hydrobromic acid (HBr), e.g., silver bromide (AgBr), used in photographic paper; hence *bromide* as a term for a photographic print.

bronze Alloy of copper, tin, and possibly some other metals. The term is also used for some other alloys such as aluminum bronze.

Brownian movement Movement of microscopic particles suspended in a gas or liquid, caused by surrounding molecules of the suspension medium colliding with the suspended particles.

browser A program used to open and view Web pages on the Internet.

buffer solution A solution with a definite pH that does not change on dilution or with the addition of small amounts of an acid or an alkali.

buoyancy Upward thrust on an immersed object, equal to the weight of fluid displaced by the object.

burette Glass measuring tube with scale marked on its side and a tap at the bottom, used in chemical analysis.

byte Group of bits (binary digits), generally 8 but may be 16 or 32.

calcium carbonate ($CaCO_3$) Compound occurring in many rocks, e.g., chalk, limestone, marble, as well as shells and bones.

calcium chloride ($CaCl_2$) Compound in form of strongly hygroscopic (water-attracting) white powder; used as drying agent.

calcium hydroxide ($Ca(OH)_2$) Slaked lime, formed by action of water on quicklime (calcium oxide); used in agriculture to reduce acidity of soil.

calcium oxide (CaO) Quicklime, a compound made by heating limestone (calcium carbonate).

calculus Branch of mathematics dealing with variable quantities and their rates of change.

calorie Unit of heat: the amounts required to raise the temperature of 1 gram of water through 1°C. Dieticians use kilocalories, conventionally written as Calories, which are a thousand times as large.

calorific value Amount of heat produced by complete burning of given amount of a fuel or food.

calorimeter Device for measuring thermal constants, such as latent heat.

cam Device that gives a specific motion to a follower riding on the cam edge, or in a cam groove.

camera obscura Room or enclosure with a lens arrangement to project an image of the outside world onto a wall or table.

candela SI unit of luminous intensity replacing the original candlepower, which was defined by the light produced from a standard candle. The candela has approximately the same magnitude but is more exactly defined.

cantilever Member, or beam, fixed at one end and unsupported at the other.

capacitance Unit of ability to hold an electric charge; measured in farads. Capacitance = charge ÷ potential.

capillary action Term for various phenomena occurring on the boundary of a liquid, such as its attraction into a tube with a very narrow bore (a capillary tube).

carat (karat) Either a unit of weight for precious stones (0.2 g) or a measure of the fineness (purity) of gold, expressed as the number of parts of gold per 24; e.g., 24 k is pure gold.

carbide Compound of carbon and a metal; e.g., calcium carbide (CaC_2), which is often referred to simply as carbide and is used to produce acetylene gas (C_2H_2) for lamps, etc.

carbonate Salt of carbonic acid (H_2CO_3); e.g., calcium carbonate ($CaCO_3$).

carbon dioxide (CO_2) Colorless gas present in the atmosphere and produced, for example, by combustion of carbon.

carbonic acid Weak acid formed by carbon dioxide dissolving in water.

carbon monoxide (CO) Colorless, poisonous gas produced by incomplete combustion.

carbon tetrachloride (CCl_4) Colorless liquid, an efficient solvent once used for dry cleaning but now (because it is poisonous) largely abandoned; it is still used in fire extinguishers.

carbonyl Compound of metal and carbon monoxide, e.g., nickel carbonyl ($Ni(CO)_4$).

Carborundum Silicon carbide (SiC), a synthetically manufactured abrasive.

carboxylic acids Group of organic acids containing the carboxyl group (COOH), e.g., formic acid (HCOOH).

Carnot cycle Cycle of operations in a perfect heat engine. The four stages are adiabatic compression, isothermal expansion, adiabatic expansion, and isothermal compression, which return the system to its original temperature, pressure, and volume.

carrier wave Radio wave of constant amplitude and frequency on which a signal is imposed by amplitude, frequency, or pulse code modulation.

Cartesian coordinates System used to locate a point with respect to a set of axes (usually perpendicular). Each coordinate is the distance from one axis, measured perpendicular to the other axes.

cartography The art or practice of making charts or maps.

cast iron Iron–carbon alloy containing 2 to 4 percent carbon and small amounts of other elements. Characteristically hard and brittle, though ductile forms are produced for engineering applications.

catheter Thin tube inserted for example into blood vessel.

cathode Negatively charged electrode to which positive ions move in electrolysis. Source of electrons in a vacuum tube.

caustic Corrosive to living material; a substance, such as caustic soda (sodium hydroxide, NaOH) or caustic potash (potassium hydroxide, KOH) that has this effect.

cavitation Formation of low-pressure gas or vapor bubbles in a moving liquid due to low local pressures caused by the flow conditions, for example, on a propeller blade or pump impeller where it can reduce efficiency and lead to damage.

CD-ROM Compact-disc read-only memory. A type of compact disc on which digital information

is engraved. It can be read, but not altered, by a scanning laser device.

cell, electrical Device for producing electric current by chemical action.

cellulose Carbohydrate that is the main structural tissue of plants; used in manufacture of paper, rayon, plastics, etc., for which it is obtained from wood pulp, cotton, and other plant material.

cellulose acetate Material obtained by treating cellulose with acetic anhydride; used in manufacture of plastics and rayon.

cellulose nitrate Material formed by treating cellulose with nitric and sulfuric acid, used in manufacture of plastics, paint, and explosives.

Celsius scale Scale of temperature measurement (also called Centigrade and, besides Fahrenheit scale, the most widely used) in which the freezing point of water is 0 and its boiling point 100.

center of gravity Fixed point through which the gravitational force (weight) acts, whatever the position of the body.

centrifugal force Outward pull caused by inertia of object being made to move in a circle.

centripetal force Inward force needed to make an object move in a circle.

chain reaction Self-sustaining atomic or chemical reaction.

charge Quantity of (static) electricity on a body; to add charge to a body.

chemiluminescence Cold light produced by chemical reaction, e.g., bioluminescence, but the same effect can now be achieved artificially.

chemisorption Form of adsorption in which absorbed substance is held by stronger-than-usual forces, similar to those operating in chemical bonds.

chlorate Salt of chloric acid, for example, the salt sodium chlorate ($NaClO_3$).

chloride Salt of hydrochloric acid (HCl); e.g., sodium chloride (common salt, NaCl).

chlorophyll Green pigment found in plants that uses solar energy to form carbohydrates by the process of photosynthesis.

cholesterol Fatlike substance produced by body cells (mainly in the liver) and carried in the blood.

chord (mathematics) Straight line joining two points on circumference of circle.

chromatic aberration Formation of colored fringes by nonachromatic lenses due to variation of the refractive index of the lens material with the wavelength of the light.

chromosomes Threadlike structures found in cell nuclei and carrying the genetic information.

chronometer Very accurate clock or watch meeting recognized standards; used in navigation, etc.

circuit Complete path through which electric current flows away from and back to its source; also used with reference to magnetism.

clutch Device for engaging and disengaging drive on a shaft.

coaxial cable Cable for carrying high frequency currents. One conductor is in the form of a tube that completely encloses the other but is insulated from it.

coefficient Numerical constant relating to a property. In algebraic expressions, the factor by which a variable is multiplied.

coherent (physics) Of radiation: with all waves in

step with each other, as in a laser beam, but not in ordinary light.

coke Solid residue from the gasification of coal. Contains about 80 percent carbon.

colloid System of particles dispersed in a medium (usually liquid) but not in solution.

color Property of visible light depending on its wavelength, or mixture of wavelengths.

combustion Combination of a substance with oxygen to yield heat and light.

commutator Current-reversing device used in dynamos and some electric motors to change alternating current to direct current. Consists of a rotating ring formed from mutually insulated metal segments connected to the windings and making contact with a fixed brush.

complementary colors Any pair of colors which, when additively mixed, produce white light.

complex number Number consisting of real and imaginary parts and expressed in the form $A + iB$ where i is the square root of minus one.

compound (chemistry) A substance made from two or more elements chemically combined in fixed proportions by weight.

condensation (meteorology) Change of state from vapor to liquid.

condenser (chemistry, etc.) Device for assisting vapor to condense into liquid, generally by a process of cooling.

condenser (optics) Lens used in microscope to concentrate illumination on specimen.

conduction Of heat and electricity: passage through an object, which is known as a conductor. Substances easily allowing this are said to be good conductors or highly conductive.

conductivity (electric) Reciprocal of the resistivity of a conductor. Measured in siemens (or reciprocal ohms—mhos) per meter.

conductivity (thermal) Rate of transfer of heat by conduction. Measured in terms of the heat flow per unit area under a unit temperature gradient.

constant (mathematics) In an algebraic equation or expression, a quantity that does not vary.

contact (electricity) Piece of conductive material touching and transferring current to another.

contact process Sulfuric acid production process.

continuum Something absolutely continuous. (Term used, e.g., of space–time.)

convection Heat transfer in liquids and gases by currents, i.e., bodily movements of molecules.

conventional current Direction in which electric current was thought to flow (from positive to negative) before the discovery of the electron; the terminology is still in use.

converging (optics) Lens that focuses a beam of light to a point.

copper sulfate ($CuSO_4 \cdot 5H_2O$) Blue, crystalline compound used as fungicide.

corrosion Chemical reaction on the surface of a solid (usually a metal) with air, moisture, or chemicals in the environment and resulting in damage to the surface.

cosmic rays Radiation, mainly consisting of charged particles, such as protons, falling on Earth from outer space.

cosmogeny, cosmogony Any system of theories concerning the origin of the Universe.

cosmology Any system of theories concerning the nature of the Universe.

coulomb SI unit of electricity; the amount transferred by one ampere in one second.

cracking Pyrolysis: decomposition of a chemical substance by controlled heating. (Term used especially of oil refining.)

creep Gradual change in shape of a metal under constant stress.

critical mass Mass of fissionable material required to allow a chain reaction to be self-sustaining.

critical temperature Temperature above which a gas cannot be liquefied by pressure alone.

critical velocity Velocity at which the flow of a liquid becomes turbulent.

cryostat Vessel for maintaining very low temperatures, especially below 0°C.

crystal oscillator Device in which a fixed frequency is determined by the piezoelectric oscillations of a crystal (often quartz).

cupric, cuprous Terms describing compounds of copper. In cupric compounds the copper is bivalent, in cuprous compounds it is univalent.

curie Unit used for measuring radioactive disintegration rates. Equal to 3.7×10^{10} disintegrations per second.

curing Originally, chemical treatment of meat, etc., to preserve it; but the term has now been extended to various hardening treatments for resins and other synthetic materials.

current, electric Movement of electric charge through a conductor; measured in amperes (A).

cybernetics Theory of communication and control mechanisms in living beings and machines.

cycle Series of changes in, or operations performed by, a system, which brings it back to its original state. The frequency of cycles is measured in hertz (Hz)—cycles per second.

cytoplasm The protoplasm and cytosol of a living cell excluding the nucleus.

daguerreotype Early type of photograph in the form of direct positive on metal plate.

damping Decrease of oscillation with time due to applied forces.

decomposition (chemistry) Breaking up of a compound into simpler parts.

decompression Slow reduction of pressure surrounding a surfacing diver to avoid the formation of gas bubbles in body tissue, which cause decompression sickness.

dehydration Removal of water.

delta In the form of a triangle; e.g., delta wing.

denier Unit used for fiber measurement and given by the mass divided by the length. One denier corresponds to a fiber with a weight of 1 gram for 9,000 meters length.

depletion layer (electronics) Region of a semiconductor where the density of mobile charge carriers is insufficient to overcome the fixed charge density of the donors and acceptors.

depletion (nuclear) Term applied to the reduction in the proportion of fissile isotopes in a nuclear fuel as the fission reaction proceeds.

derived unit Unit of measurement other than the fundamental unit of mass, length, and time, but derived from them; e.g., meters per second.

desiccant A substance used to withdraw moisture from other materials.

destructive distillation Heating a substance to produce chemical changes in it and to drive off and collect volatile substances; e.g., obtaining coal gas from coal.

developer Chemical that brings out the latent image on an exposed photographic film by decomposing the particles of silver halide into dark colored metallic silver.

dew point Temperature at which moisture in the atmosphere becomes saturated and starts to condense into dew or water droplets.

dialysis Separation of colloids from dispersion by passage through a semipermeable membrane; e.g., in an artificial kidney machine.

diamagnetism Possession of small negative magnetic susceptibility; a property of all substances, which may be masked by stronger properties such as ferromagnetism.

diaphragm Thin flexible sheet of material used as a separating member. Used in a microphone to pick up sound waves, which cause it to vibrate.

diatomic Having two atoms in a molecule, as in the case of oxygen (O), which is therefore conventionally written as O_2.

diatonic Term used of ordinary major or minor musical scale to distinguish it from chromatic or other types of scale or mode.

diazo Of an organic compound: having the general formula RN=NR′ (R, R′ are radicals). Many diazo compounds are dyes. See also azo.

dichroism In certain anisotropic materials, the property of having different absorption coefficients for light polarized in different directions.

die A forming device; types exist for cutting threads, drawing wire, stamping sheet metal, and as molds in diecasting.

dielectric Not conducting electricity. A material in which an electric field displaces a charge but no charge flows.

diesel Internal combustion engine in which fuel is ignited by the heat generated as air is compressed in the engine cylinder.

differential Gear system arranged so that the speed of one (input) shaft is proportional to the sum or difference of the other (output) shafts. Used in automobile transmission to allow the driven wheels to run at different speeds when cornering.

diffraction grating An optical device for dispersing electromagnetic waves (light or X rays) into their constituent wavelengths; in the case of light, this will produce a spectrum. One design consists of a transparent or reflective plate ruled with fine parallel lines.

diffusion (in gases and liquids) The spreading and scattering of matter under the influence of a concentration gradient.

diffusion (in solids) The actual transportation of mass, in the form of discrete atoms, through the lattice of a crystalline solid.

digital In discrete units (see analog); represented in numerical form.

diorama Realistic display of scene made up of models and pictures.

dip The angle between direction of Earth's magnetic field and horizontal; a freely suspended compass needle will dip to this angle.

dipole Two equal point electric charges or magnetic poles of opposite sign separated by a small distance.

direct current (DC) Electric current flowing always in the same direction.

discharge Flow of current through a gas or air owing to ionization.

discrete Separate or distinct.

disinfectant Capable of destroying harmful bacteria; a substance that does this.

dislocation Irregularity in crystal structure.

dispersed phase Material in a colloidal state.

dispersion medium Medium in a colloidal dispersion in which the disperse phase is scattered.

dissociation Reversible breakup of a molecule into simpler parts, as opposed to decomposition.

distillate Liquid condensed from vapor produced by distillation.

distortion Undesirable change in the shape of waveform of a signal.

distributor Device used to supply the ignition spark to the spark plug of an internal combustion engine at the correct time.

diurnal Daily; something carried out every 24 hours. Opposite of nocturnal.

diverging Lens that causes a beam of light to spread out. Concave.

DNA (deoxyribonucleic acid) Long threadlike molecule in a cell that carries the hereditary (genetic) information.

domain Small region in ferromagnetic material in which magnetic forces are acting together in a certain direction.

doping Addition of controlled amounts of impurities into a semiconducting substance to modify its properties.

drawing Reducing diameter of a wire by pulling it through a small hole in a die.

dry cell Electric cell or battery in which the electrolyte is in the form of paste rather than a liquid.

ductility Property of materials, usually metals, which can be drawn out or elongated without breaking.

dynamics Study of motion of objects and forces acting on them, as opposed to statics.

dynamo Generator that produces direct current electric power.

e "Natural number" (in connection with natural logarithms): 2.718282 to six decimal places.

echo sounding Technique used for finding the depth of water, such as the sea, by using sound waves reflected from the bottom.

ecliptic Sun's apparent annual path in the sky relative to the fixed stars.

eddy currents Induced electric currents set up in metals; in armatures of generators and cores of transformers these are undesirable and waste power.

efficiency For a machine, the ratio of output energy to input energy. For processes, the proportion of output product to the inputs.

efflorescence Property of some crystalline salts, which give up water of crystallization to the air, thus becoming dry and powdery.

elastic limit Greatest extent to which a material can be distorted and still recover its original shape and size.

elastic modulus Ratio of stress to strain in a given material; i.e., extent to which it will distort when subjected to a certain force.

electric charge Excess or deficiency of electrons in a material compared to its uncharged, neutral state. An excess causes a negative charge and a deficiency a positive charge. Such a state is a static charge; if the charge flows, it is said to be a current.

electric field Region where forces are exerted on any charged particle present.

electrochemistry Interaction of electric and chemical energy.

electrode Conductor by which an electric current enters or leaves a liquid (such as an electrolyte in electrolysis), a vacuum (such as in a vacuum tube), or a gas (such as in a discharge tube). *See also* anode *and* cathode.

electrodeposition Depositing a layer of material, often a metal, by means of electrolysis.

electroencephalograph Device for picking up and recording electric impulses in the brain.

electroluminescence Luminescence of certain materials caused by electricity, apart from simple phenomena such as the glow of a white-hot filament in a bulb.

electrolyte Substance that carries an electric current by the movement of ions, as in electrolysis.

electromagnetic induction Production of magnetic effect by electric current.

electromotive force (emf) Voltage.

electron Subatomic particle orbiting the nucleus of an atom and whose movement is responsible for electric phenomena.

electronic circuit Network of conductors with active and passive electronic components and having at least one closed path for the control of electron motion.

electron lens Magnetic or electric field used to focus beam of electrons in, e.g., cathode-ray tube.

electron microscope Microscope using an electron beam to scan objects too small to see with the longer wavelengths of visible light.

electron volt (eV) Unit of energy used in nuclear physics, representing increase in energy of 1 volt by 1 electron; since this is a very small amount, figures are generally in larger units such as mega electron volts (MeV, millions of electron volts).

electroplating Depositing a layer by means of electrolysis, with the object to be plated being the cathode of the cell.

electroscope Simple device for detecting presence of electric charge.

elevator (airplane) Tail-control surface of aircraft regulating pitch. On delta-winged aircraft, this is combined with the aileron and called an elevon.

emulsion One liquid suspended in another in the form of tiny droplets; the two liquids are known as phases. Also used to describe the emulsion coating on a photographic film.

endothermic Of a reaction: absorbing heat.

entropy Measure of the degree of disorder in a system and so of the availability of energy to do useful work. Total entropy of a system always increases with a change; it cannot decrease.

epoxy Containing oxygen bound to two other atoms, often carbon, to give a ring structure. Often applied to a range of synthetic resins that are used as adhesives.

equator Great circle lying in a plane perpendicular to Earth's axis and equidistant from the poles. The magnetic equator is the line of zero magnetic dip and generally lies close to the geographic equator.

equinox The moment at which the Sun crosses the celestial equator, at which time day and night are the same length.

escape velocity Velocity a space vehicle must have to escape from a planet's gravitational field. For Earth this is approximately 25,000 mph (11,200 m/s). Also called parabolic velocity.

ester Compound that corresponds in organic chemistry to a salt in general chemistry; i.e., it is formed when the hydrogen of an acid is replaced by an organic radical or group. Many flavoring essences, oils, and fats are or contain esters.

ether (chemistry) $(C_2H_5OC_2H_5)$ Liquid derived from alcohol used as anesthetic and solvent.

Euclidean geometry The main subject matter of the 13-volume work called *The Elements*, written about 300 B.C.E. by the Greek mathematician Euclid. Regarded as a milestone in the history of scientific thought.

evaporation Conversion of liquid into vapor below its boiling point.

exothermic Of a reaction: giving out heat.

explosive Substance that undergoes a rapid chemical change with the production of large amounts of gas when heated or struck.

exponent (mathematics) Small number written above base indicating power to which it is raised; e.g., 10^2 (= 100), 10^{-2} (= 0.01).

exponential function The exponential of a function x is equal to the natural number e to the power of a constant times x. $f(x) = e^{ax}$.

exposure Taking of a picture with a camera; but the term is more specifically used to mean the setting at which the picture was taken.

extrusion Forcing metal, plastics, and other materials through a die to form a shaped section.

factor (mathematics) Number exactly divisible into another number; thus the factors of 6 are 1, 2, and 3.

Fahrenheit scale Temperature scale in which water freezes at 32° and boils at 212°.

fanjet Jet engine incorporating a large ducted fan, which blows air around the outside of the engine to mix with the jet exhaust and give an increased thrust.

farad (F) Unit of capacitance; a capacity of one farad requires one coulomb to raise its potential one volt. Since the unit is large, the microfarad (one-thousandth of a farad) is used for most practical applications.

fatigue Deterioration of metals caused by repeated stresses above a critical level, which produces changes in the crystalline structure.

fats Mixtures of various glycerides of fatty acids; may be either animal or vegetable in origin. The difference between fats and (non-mineral) oils is simply one of melting point.

fatty acids Organic monobasic acids with the general formula R·COOH, where R is hydrogen or a group of carbon and hydrogen atoms.

ferric, ferrous Terms used to describe iron compounds. In ferric compounds, the iron is trivalent; in ferrous compounds, it is divalent.

ferrimagnetism Magnetic property of some materials, often ceramic, due to the partial orientation of the atomic moments of some atoms or the unequal strength of the individual atomic moments. Generally not as powerful as ferromagnetism.

ferromagnetism Permanent magnetism of, e.g., iron and nickel.

fibrillation Uncontrolled movements of the heart.

field lens Lens in a compound optical instrument that is placed farthest from the eyepiece.

field winding Winding that carries the current used to set up a magnetic field in an electric machine.

filament Thin wire or other material. Often heated by passage of an electric current so it emits light or electrons.

filter (electronics) Circuit allowing easy passage of certain frequencies and blocking others.

filter (chemistry) Any sievelike device for separating solids from a liquid.

filter (optics) Sheet of transparent material used to restrict the passage of certain wavelengths of light, or to polarize it.

fissile Isotopes that can undergo nuclear fission.

fixer Chemical used in photographic processing that dissolves and removes unexposed silver halide.

flashpoint Lowest temperature at which a substance gives off sufficient flammable vapor to ignite when a small flame is applied.

flocculation Coagulation of a finely dispersed solid material in a liquid to form larger particles that can be separated from the liquid by sedimentation or filtration.

flotation process Extraction technique, often used for ores, in which solids are separated by causing one to float in surface froth and one to sink in the flotation medium.

fluid Liquid or gas.

fluidics Control systems operated by fluid flow in narrow channels. The method is analogous to the flow of electric currents in circuits.

fluorescence Absorption of light and reemission at new wavelength.

flux (chemical) Substance added to assist fusion.

flux (physics) Of a vector quantity (i.e., a quantity having a stated direction) and its action through an area: the product of the area and the component of the vector at right angles to the area.

flywheel Heavy rotating wheel acting as a store of rotating energy. Often used to smooth out energy fluctuations, as in an internal combustion engine.

focus, principal Point at which parallel rays of light converge after refraction by convex lens or reflection by concave mirror; or, for concave lens or convex mirror, point from which diverging rays appear to have come.

food chain Natural system in which some animals feed on plants, other animals feed on these animals, and so on.

foot–pound–second system (FPS system) System of units in which the foot is the unit of

distance, the pound the unit of mass, and the second the unit of time.

force External agency capable of altering the state of rest or motion in a body; measured in newtons.

formalin Solution of formaldehyde (*see* aldehyde) in water.

fossil fuel Coal, oil, and natural gas, all formed over long periods from decayed organic matter.

four-stroke cycle Sequence of operations in an internal combustion engine in which the piston moves up and down twice for each power stroke. The four strokes are compression, expansion, exhaust, and induction.

fractional distillation (fractionation) Simultaneous distillation of several liquids with closely similar boiling points by vaporizing them, passing the vapors up a fractionating column, and drawing them off at various points as they condense in order on the way up.

Frasch process Method of extraction of underground sulfur deposits by melting them with steam and pumping them out.

Fraunhofer lines Dark lines in the spectrum of the Sun caused by the absorption of some of the wavelengths of the light by elements present in the outer layers of the Sun.

freezing Change of state from liquid to solid; all pure substances have characteristic freezing points, constant under the same conditions of pressure.

frequency Number of repetitions of a cycle in a given time; measured in hertz (cycles per second).

frequency modulation Method of imposing radio signals on a carrier wave by varying the frequency of the carrier.

Fresnel lens Thin lens formed by repeatedly stepping back one of the curved faces.

frictional electricity Triboelectricity, or static electricity.

fuel cell Cell that produces electric power directly from chemical energy, with the power output being continuous as long as fuel is supplied.

fuel injection System used in internal combustion engines in which metered amounts of fuel are directly injected into the air intake or the cylinder, instead of being mixed with the air in a carburetor.

fundamental Of wave motion: lowest frequency that a vibrating object can produce. This is accompanied by higher overtones at whole multiples of that frequency.

fusion Melting, also the mingling of melted substances.

g Acceleration due to gravity. This varies slightly at different points on Earth's surface and is normally taken as 32.2 ft. per sec. per sec. (9.81 cm/s^2).

gallon Unit of volume used for liquid measurement. The U.S. gallon is 231 cu. in. and the British gallon slightly larger at approximately 277 cu. in.

galvanizing Coating iron and steel with protective layer of zinc.

galvanometer Instrument for measuring small electric currents.

gamma radiation Electromagnetic radiation with the shortest wavelength—less than 0.1 nanometer.

gas State of matter in which molecules move freely in space and spread out to fill any container.

gasket Sealing element, such as layer of rubber, between two stationary members.

gate Switching element in logic circuit.

gel Semisolid form of colloidal dispersion in which the dispersed phase has formed mesh structure.

gene Basic unit of biological inheritance.

genetic Concerned with processes of biological inheritance and specifically with the genes.

geodesy Surveying taking into account curvature of Earth. (Adjective: geodetic)

geology Study of Earth's crust.

geomorphology Study of the shape of the features of Earth's surface and how they are related to its structure.

gimbal Pivoted mounting that allows free movement in two planes.

gland (biology) A cell, group of cells, or organ that produces substances useful to an organism or secretes excretory products.

gland (mechanical) Device used to prevent leakage where a shaft emerges from a pressurized vessel.

glidepath Path followed by landing aircraft.

gluons Hypothetical subatomic particles with zero mass that are responsible for strong interactions between quarks.

glyceride Ester of glycerol with an organic acid.

glycerol (glycerine, $CH_2OH \cdot CHOH \cdot CH_2OH$) Sweet-tasting, sticky fluid made from oils and fats; used in cosmetics, resins, and explosives.

gradient Rate at which a quantity, such as elevation, varies with distance.

gram Unit of mass. The basic SI unit of mass is the kilogram, which is equal to 1,000 grams.

gram molecular volume Volume occupied by one gram of a gas; for a perfect gas at standard temperature and pressure this is 22.4 liters. From this its molecular weight can be calculated.

gram molecule Molecular weight of a compound (e.g., 18 for water) expressed as a weight in grams (e.g., 18 g). This quantity is also known as a mole.

gravimeter Sensitive weighing device used to detect local gravity variations by their action on a standard mass.

graviton Hypothetical particle or quantum of gravitational energy.

gravure Printing process in which ink is distributed by hollow cells in plate.

ground effect Increase in aerodynamic lift caused by proximity of ground.

gunpowder Explosive mixture of potassium nitrate, powdered charcoal, and sulfur.

gypsum Calcium sulfate ($CaSO_4 \cdot 2H_2O$ in its naturally hydrated form); used for plaster.

Haber process Industrial preparation of ammonia from atmospheric nitrogen.

hadron Class of subatomic particles including baryons and mesons.

half life Time taken for the activity of a radioactive element to decay to half its original level (for half the atoms to decay).

hard water Water containing various metal salts, causing failure to lather with ordinary soap and formation of scale deposits in pipes, etc.

harmonic Of wave motion: wave superimposed on fundamental wave, with frequency that is a whole multiple of that of the fundamental. In music, a harmonic is often called an overtone.

heat Kinetic energy of molecules of a substance.

heat, latent Total heat absorbed or liberated during a change of phase, for example from solid to liquid or liquid to vapor.

hematite Naturally occurring red iron oxide (Fe_2O_3), a commercially important iron ore.

hemoglobin Red pigment in blood that carries oxygen around the body.

henry SI unit of inductance such that a rate of change of current of one ampere per second induces an electromotive force of one volt.

hertz (Hz) Unit of frequency: an oscillation of 1 cycle per second.

heterodyne Beat effect produced by superimposing two waves of different frequency.

high explosive Explosive that can be detonated by a sudden shock (normally from a primer) to give a very rapid release of energy.

high tension High voltage.

horsepower Power unit, widely used by the automobile industry: equal to a rate of work of 550 foot-pounds per second. One horsepower equals 745 watts.

HTML Hypertext markup language. Computer language that is used to produce pages for multimedia products such as CD-ROMs, and for posting pages on the World Wide Web.

humidity Weight of water vapor present in a given volume of air; either absolute (actual) or relative (ratio to weight of water that would saturate air at that temperature).

hunting In a governor: oscillation.

hybrid computer Computer that can handle both analog and digital signals.

hydrated Of a compound: containing chemically combined water (water of crystallization).

hydraulic mechanisms Mechanisms based on hydraulically powered operating elements.

hydride Compound of element with hydrogen.

hydrocarbon Strictly, a compound containing only hydrogen and carbon.

hydrochloric acid Strong acid consisting of solution of hydrogen chloride gas (HCl) in water; much used in industry and for etching.

hydrofluoric acid Strong acid consisting of a solution of hydrogen fluoride (HF) gas in water. Will attack glass and is used for glass etching.

hydrogenation Process used in food industry to convert liquid oils to hard fats by adding hydrogen atoms to their molecules.

hydrogen peroxide (H_2O_2) Liquid, soluble in water and which decomposes into water and free oxygen; used as bleach, disinfectant, and oxidant for rocket fuel.

hydrology Study of natural water resources.

hydrolysis Alteration or decomposition of a chemical substance by water, which is itself decomposed.

hydrometer Device for measuring liquid density or specific gravity. Commonly, a float marked with a scale, the level at which it floats indicating the fluid level.

hydrophilic Water-absorbing or attracting.

hydroplane Control surface regulating dive and climb in a submarine. Small fast boat that rides—or planes—on the water surface.

hydroxyl ion (OH^-) Negatively charged ion present in solutions of bases, corresponding to the hydrogen ion (H^+) in an acid and reacting with it to form water (H_2O).

hygroscopic Of a compound: absorbing moisture from the air, but not so much as to become liquid.

hypermetropia Farsightedness.

hypersonic Traveling over 5 times faster than sound (Mach 5; see Mach number).

hypersonic (acoustics) Sound frequencies above 500 MHz.

hysteresis Delay in recovering from stress (in elastic materials) or from magnetization.

ice point Exact temperature of freezing point of water at normal atmospheric pressure; the standard for 0°C.

ignition point Of a substance: temperature to which it must be heated before it will burn.

illumination Amount of light falling on unit area of surface per second; measured in lumens.

immiscible Incapable of being mixed.

impedance Of an electric circuit: unwillingness to pass an alternating current.

impeller (fluid) Rotating member of a pump or turbine, which applies propulsive forces to the working medium.

impeller Rotor used to provide a rapidly moving stream of particles, as in shot blasting.

implosion Violent collapse of an evacuated vessel under the external pressure.

incandescence State of being hot enough to emit light, e.g., an electric light filament.

incendiary Of a bomb, etc.: intended to cause fire.

incident ray Light ray falling on reflecting or refracting surface; its angle to the normal (perpendicular) is termed the angle of incidence.

inclinometer Device for measuring angle of slope.

indicator Chemical compound that changes color to show, for example, the pH of a solution. More generally, a warning device.

inductance Creation of an electromotive force by a change in the current flowing through a circuit. This force resists the current flow and is measured in henrys.

induction coil Device using induction in magnetically linked coils to create high voltages when supplied with lower ones.

infrared radiation Electromagnetic radiation with wavelength slightly longer than that of visible light (700 mm to 1 mm); given off by hot objects, and having a heating effect.

inorganic Branch of chemistry that does not deal with carbon (organic) compounds.

insulator Substance that does not conduct, e.g., electricity or heat.

integer Whole number, e.g., 1, 2, 3.

interference (mechanical) Assembly of components with a negative clearance so the natural elasticity provides a gripping force.

interference (wave) Effect of combining wave motions, which may reinforce each other (constructive interference) or cancel one another out (destructive interference).

interferometer Instrument in which optical light, microwaves, or sound waves are allowed to produce interference fringes. Used to make accurate measurements of wavelength and distance, the testing of optical components, and similar applications.

interferometry Use of an interferometer for measurement purposes.

interferon Protein produced by cells in response to organisms such as viruses and acting on unaffected cells to prevent attack by the virus.

invar Nickel–iron alloy that hardly expands when heated; used in accurate measuring instruments.

inverse ratio Relationship in which increase in one factor produces decrease in another.

inverter Device for turning direct current into alternating current.

investment casting Casting method in which a mold is made from a wax original that is melted, drained away, and replaced with metal.

iodide Salt of hydroiodic acid, HI, e.g., silver iodide (AgI; used in photographic film).

ionized Atom or molecule that has lost or gained an electron to become electrically charged.

ionosphere Ionized region of Earth's atmosphere, which reflects radio waves.

ISDN Integrated Services Digital Networks. System that sends digital signals directly through telephone lines without using a modem.

isomer Any of two or more chemical compounds having the same constituent elements in the same proportion by weight but differing in physical and chemical properties because of differences in the structure of their molecules.

isotherm Line on weather map connecting points of equal temperature.

isotope One of several forms of an atom of an element differing in the number of neutrons in the nucleus and hence in the atomic mass.

ISP Internet service provider. Organization that mediates between individual users of the Internet and the high-capacity Internet routes that carry information over long distances.

jacquard Mechanism on loom, controlling weaving pattern by means of punched cards.

jamming Masking of radio signal by broadcasting another at same frequency.

jetstream Stream of high-speed winds in Earth's upper atmosphere.

jig Framework ensuring accurate alignment between tools and parts to be worked on.

joule (J) SI unit of work, energy, and heat; work done by current of 1 ampere flowing through resistance of 1 ohm for 1 second.

junction transistor Transistor with the base electrode and two or more electrodes (collector and emitter) connected to a junction between two different types of semiconductor.

kaon Subatomic particle: a meson.

Kelvin scale Scale of absolute temperature (once called absolute scale) starting at absolute zero (–273.15°C) and using Celsius-size degrees, so that 273 K is 0°C.

ketone Organic compound containing a carbonyl (CO) group with a pair of bonding carbon atoms; for example, acetone ($CH_3 \cdot O \cdot CH_3$).

Kevlar Trade name for an aromatic aramid fiber with exceptional strength.

kilogram SI unit of weight and mass, defined by a physical prototype. Equal to 2.205 lbs.

kiloton Unit used for indicating the power of atomic explosives and bombs. An explosive power equal to 1,000 tons of TNT.

kinematics Another name for dynamics.

kinetic energy Energy a body possesses because of its motion. For a mass m moving at a velocity v, the kinetic energy is $mv^2/2$.

klystron Electron tube in which an electron beam is velocity-modulated to amplify or produce high-frequency (microwave) electromagnetic radiation. Used in radar systems.

knock In an internal combustion engine, a noise caused by pre-ignition.

knot Speed of 1 nautical mile per hour.

laminar flow Fluid flow that smoothly follows a surface without turbulence occurring.

latent Not apparent but nevertheless available.

latent heat Total heat absorbed or liberated during a change of phase, for example, from solid to liquid or liquid to vapor.

lattice, crystal Regular pattern of atoms in a crystalline solid.

laughing gas Nitrous oxide (N_2O), an anesthetic.

lava Rock surfacing from interior of Earth in molten state.

leaching Washing out a soluble component by passing a solvent through the material.

Leclanché cell Electric cell using zinc negative and carbon positive electrodes, ammonium chloride electrolyte, and manganese dioxide depolarizer; dry form of this cell is the ordinary "dry battery."

lepton Class of subatomic particles of low weight, such as the electron. Also includes the muon and neutrino. Sub-group of fermions.

letterpress Printing method in which raised areas of the type or illustration blocks carry the ink and transfer it to the paper.

light-emitting diode (LED) Semiconductor device that gives off light when a current is passed through it. Arrays of these are used for displays.

light meter Device used to time exposure of photographs; intensity of light falling on photoelectric cell varies flow of current to milliammeter with scale giving exposure times and apertures.

light year Astronomical distance equal to the distance light travels in one year; 5.88×10^{12} miles (9.46×10^{12} km).

linear motor Electric motor in straightline form, without rotating parts.

liquefaction Turning a gas into a liquid, which may be done by cooling or compression, or both.

liter Metric unit of volume. Defined as 100 cubic centimeters and equal to the volume of 1 kg of water at a temperature of 4°C.

litmus Dye used as indicator; turns red in acid, blue in alkaline solution.

load Weight or force supported by a structure. Electric power drawn by equipment.

local-area network (LAN) Connection between computers occupying a relatively small area, e.g., an office or a building (see wide-area network).

locus Of a point: line that can be drawn through adjacent positions of the point, thus tracing out its path in space.

lodestone Natural magnet composed of magnetite (Fe_3O_4), an iron ore.

logarithm Alternative expression of number as a power, to a given base. Common logarithms are to base 10; natural or Napierian logarithms to base 2.718282 (a number known as e).

logarithmic scale Scale in which increase of one unit denotes tenfold increase in quantity.

logic circuit Electric, electronic, or fluidic circuit operating according to principles of logic; these range in complexity, e.g., from relay-operated lift-control system to part of computer.

longitudinal wave Wave in which vibrations are along its direction of travel.

lubrication Reduction of friction between two surfaces by separating them with film of a fluid.

Mach number Speed compared to speed of sound (Mach 1), which is 761 mph (1,225 km/h) at sea level and 15°C, but falls with increasing altitude and decreasing temperature to 691 mph (1,112.5 km/h) at 36,000 ft. (11,000 m).

magnetic compass Direction finding device that uses a permanent magnet, which aligns itself with Earth's magnetic field.

magnetic field Field of force that is said to exist at any point if a small coil of wire carrying a current experiences a force when placed at that point; may be caused both by a permanent magnet and by a conductor carrying current.

magnetic pole Apparent concentration of magnetism at either end of a magnet; the two ends are called north and south; unlike poles attract, like poles repel.

magnetic storm Disturbance of Earth's magnetic field associated with sunspot activity and Aurora Borealis; affects magnetic compasses and radio.

magneto Combined generator and ignition coil sometimes used for the ignition system of an internal combustion engine.

magnetomotive force (mmf) Potential causing magnetic flux to flow.

majority carrier Type of carrier (hole or electron) that makes up more than half the carriers in a semiconductor.

manganese dioxide (MnO_2) Manganese ore, occurring naturally as pyrolusite, also used in Leclanché cells, as oxidizing agent and catalyst, and in glass manufacture.

mass Amount of matter an object contains, determining its inertia; unlike weight, mass does not vary with the force of gravity.

matrix (mathematics) Rectangular or square formation of real or imaginary numbers.

matte (metallurgy) Mixture of sulfides of iron and copper obtained at intermediate stage in copper smelting.

mechanics Study of behavior of matter under action of a force; includes dynamics and statics.

melting point Temperature at which a solid turns into a liquid; this is constant, provided pressure remains the same.

meniscus Convex or concave shape of edge of liquid where it touches the edge of its container, depending on its surface tension; water and most other liquids (though not mercury) exhibit a concave meniscus.

meson Class of subatomic particle intermediate in mass between leptons and baryons; types distinguished by Greek letters: kappa-meson (kaon for short), pi-meson (pion) etc. The mu-meson (muon), however, has been reclassified as a lepton.

metallurgy Science and technology of metals. In particular, their extraction, alloying, and heat treatment.

meter SI unit of length. Defined as the length of the path travelled by light in a vacuum during a time interval of 1/299,792,458 of a second.

meter–kilogram–second system (MKS system) System of units using these as basic units; this is the name of the immediate predecessor of the current SI system, but SI also uses the same basic units.

metric system Original name of the 19th-century system that introduced the meter, etc.; still loosely used to mean the present SI system.

mica Group of minerals that can be readily split into pieces and sheets. They are excellent insulators and resistant to high temperatures.

microchip Semiconductor substrate carrying an integrated circuit.

micron One-millionth of a meter.

microprocessor Silicon chip containing computer arithmetic, logic, and interface functions.

mild steel Steel of low carbon content (0.12–0.25 percent), so that it is comparatively soft.

milliammeter Loosely used term for a small, sensitive ammeter (i.e., measuring milliamperes).

mineral Any substance occurring naturally in the earth, whether inorganic (e.g., metal ore) or organic (e.g., coal, oil, etc.).

mineralogy Study of minerals.

minute One-sixtieth of a degree, as well as of an hour.

miscible Capable of being mixed.

mode Characteristic frequency of oscillation; functional state; (in music) early form of scale.

moderator Substance used in nuclear reactor to slow down neutrons; e.g., graphite, heavy water.

modulation Imposition of signal on carrier wave.

modulus Constant factor or multiplier for conversion of units from one system to another.

moiré Interference pattern produced by intersecting grids.

molar Of a solution: containing one gram molecule per liter.

mole Same as gram molecule.

molecule Smallest part of an element or compound capable of existing on its own and retaining the properties of the original substance.

moment (mechanics) Turning effect of a force, stated in terms of the magnitude of the force and its distance from the axis of rotation.

moment of inertia For a body, the moment of inertia about an axis is the sum of the products of the mass of each element and the square of its distance from the axis.

momentum Mass times velocity.

monochromatic Of light: of one wavelength.

monoclonal antibody Very specific antibody that acts on only one antigen.

monocoque Type of construction in which the stresses are carried by the skin of the structure. Widely used for automobiles.

monoculture Agricultural system based on the continuous growing of a single crop.

monolithic In one block. Term used to describe a block of stone, a structure made from a continuous mass of material, and for integrated circuits.

monomer Compound consisting of single molecules, as opposed to polymer.

mordant Substance used to fix a dye to the fibers of a fabric.

mule Early yarn-spinning device, so called because it was a hybrid of two existing mechanisms.

multiplex Use of a single communications channel to carry more than one signal at the same time.

muon Negatively charged subatomic particle; though name is short for "mu-meson," it is now classed not as a meson but a lepton.

mutation Sudden change in the chromosomes of an organism, leading to different characteristics.

nadir The point on the celestial sphere that is vertically downward from the observer; opposite of zenith.

napalm Incendiary mixture consisting of oil or gasoline converted to a gel form by the addition of aluminum soap.

natural gas Mixture of hydrocarbons, mostly methane (CH_4); usually found in association with petroleum deposits.

nautical mile Distance equivalent to one angular minute of latitude measured along the Equator: 1.852 km (an Imperial land mile is 1,609 km).

negative (photography) Exposed, processed film with tones and (if any) colors reversed.

negative charge Charge caused by the presence of electrons, not their absence. See conventional current.

neutral (chemistry) Neither acid nor alkaline, having a pH of 7.

neutralization Reaction between acid and base producing salt and water only (i.e., with no acid or alkali residue, so that the result is neutral).

neutrino Subatomic particle with no charge, little or no rest mass, and one-half unit of spin. Very hard to detect but known to exist.

neutron Subatomic particle (classified as a baryon) with no charge, found in the nuclei of all atoms except hydrogen.

newton SI unit of force: that which, acting for 1 second on a mass of 1 kilogram, produces an acceleration of 1 meter per sec. per sec.

Newton's rings Concentric colored rings produced by an interference effect in refracted light; visible in film of oil on water.

nitrate Salt of nitric acid (HNO_3), e.g., potassium nitrate (saltpeter or niter, KNO_3).

nitric acid (HNO_3) Colorless, highly corrosive acid; powerful oxidizing agent; widely used in chemical industry, e.g., to make dyes, explosives, plastics, and photographic materials.

nitrogen cycle Natural circulation of nitrogen compounds through living organisms, to which nitrogen is essential. Plants take nitrogen from the soil, while quantities are kept "topped up" by nitro-

gen-fixing bacteria, which can extract it directly from the air, and the electric action of lightning.

noble metals Metals such as silver, gold, and platinum, which do not corrode in air or water, as opposed to base metals.

node One of the points of least vibration in a stationary wave, e.g., the end of a vibrating string.

noise (electronics) Unwanted random addition to signal.

nondestructive testing Testing of products in quality control by means such as X rays and ultrasonic techniques, which measure it in some way but do not consume or damage it.

normal (chemistry) Of a solution: containing the gram equivalent weight of a compound dissolved in a liter of water.

normal (mathematics, optics, etc.) Of a line: at right angles to a surface.

n-type Doped semiconductor in which the number of electrons is greater than the number of holes.

nuclear magnetic resonance Form of spectroscopy based on exciting the atomic nuclei with a radio frequency field. Used to determine the structure of complex molecules and in body scanners.

nuclear reaction Reaction changing nature of atomic nucleus, e.g., fission, fusion, and isotope formation, as opposed to a chemical reaction, which leaves the nucleus unaffected.

nucleus (cell) Central body enclosed by a membrane and containing the chromosomes.

nucleus (physics) Central mass of atom, comprising nearly all its mass; consists of protons and neutrons (except for hydrogen, which consists of 1 proton only) and carries an overall positive charge.

nylon Long chain synthetic polymeric amide molecules. Used for fibers, sheet, and solid materials.

octane number Antiknock rating of gasoline measured by comparing it to a mixture of iso-octane and heptane. The octane number is equal to the percentage of iso-octane.

octant Sector of one-eighth of area of circle; hence a navigational instrument of that shape.

octave Interval between one frequency and double or half that frequency; in a musical scale, this is eight notes (counting inclusively).

odometer Device for recording distance by counting revolutions of wheel.

offset Printing technique in which image is transferred indirectly to paper via a roller.

ohm Unit of electric resistance (symbol Ω); that of a conductor through which a current of 1 ampere passes when a potential difference of 1 volt is maintained across its ends.

opaque Not allowing transmission. (Term used of X rays, etc., as well as for ordinary light.)

optic Lens, mirror, or prism in optical device.

optical activity (or optical rotation) Property of some substances and solutions of rotating plane of polarized light passed through them. Rotation is to the left or right of levorotatory or dextrorotatory substances respectively, and some substances have two forms, or isomers, which are mirror images of each other (stereoisomers) and one of which does each; e.g., the sugars glucose (called dextrose) and fructose (called levulose).

optical fibers Flexible transparent fiber devices, used for either image or data transmission, in which light propagates by total internal reflection.

ore Any naturally occurring rock which contains a commercially significant, extractable quantity of a desired substance, generally a metal.

organism Animals, plants, fungi, and micro-organisms.

orthochromatic Of film: an early type of black-and-white film that was insensitive to red, so that this came out black (*see* panchromatic).

oscillation Regular vibration.

oxidation Chemical reaction in which substance gains oxygen or loses hydrogen.

oxide Compound of oxygen and one other element.

oxyacetylene Term for welding and cutting torches burning mixture of oxygen and acetylene.

ozone (O_3) Poisonous form of oxygen with triatomic (three-atom) molecules, formed from atmospheric oxygen by electric discharges.

panchromatic Of film: modern type of black-and-white film giving good response to all colors. See orthochromatic.

pantograph Parallelogram-shaped arrangement of pivoted arms used as a contact-carrying assembly on overhead wire electric traction systems, e.g., street cars and electric trains. Also used for mechanical enlargement or reduction of outlines.

parabola Curved path traced by a point that moves so that its distance from a fixed point (the focus) is equal to its distance from a fixed straight line (the directrix). Path followed by a projectile, and the profile used for a parabolic reflector, which focuses a parallel beam of light to a point.

paraffin Name of hydrocarbon series starting with gases (in order of increasing molecular weight: methane, ethane, propane, butane), continuing through liquids and ending with solids (paraffin wax). Paraffin oil (kerosene) is a mixture of liquids.

parallax Difference in apparent position of objects when seen from different points.

parallel (electricity) Term used of conductors set side by side in a circuit so that if one is interrupted, current can still flow through the other.

parallelogram of forces Means of finding resultant of two forces acting at an angle to each other: if each force is drawn as a line leading from a point in the direction in which it acts, and with its length proportional to the size of the force, and these two lines are made two sides of a parallelogram, then the diagonal of that parallelogram running from the point will show the direction of the resultant, and its length the size.

parallelogram of velocities Technique similar to parallelogram of forces for finding resultant of two velocities.

paramagnetism Possession of a small amount of magnetic permeability due to unbalanced electron spins or orbital motion.

parameter Variable kept constant to allow study of other variables.

paravane Device towed behind a ship, often to one side and maintaining a constant depth. Used for cutting the mooring wires of naval mines.

parsec Astronomical unit of distance equal to a parallax of one second of arc. Equal to 3.26 light years.

pasteurization Moderate heating, e.g., of milk to kill bacteria and thus prolong keeping time.

pathogen Organism causing disease.

peat Partly decomposed plant matter; first stage in formation of coal.

pentode Vacuum tube with five electrodes.

penumbra Region of half shadow around dark central shadow (umbra), cast when object is illuminated by a large source of light. An observer in the penumbra sees part of the source of light, as in a partial eclipse of the Sun.

percussion cap Detonating device that sets off explosion when struck.

perigee Point of orbit of an object, such as a satellite, at its smallest distance from Earth.

perihelion Point of orbit of a heavenly body at smallest distance from Sun.

period Time taken to complete one cycle of a repeated action, e.g., a wave motion or the swing of a pendulum.

permanganate Salt of permanganic acid ($HMnO_4$); but term is commonly used to mean potassium permanganate ($KMnO_4$) rather than any other permanganate.

permeability (general) Property of a substance that allows the passage of another substance through itself.

permeability (magnetism) Ease with which magnetic flux is developed in a material by a magnetomotive force.

permittivity (electronics) Specific inductive capacity of a dielectric (insulating) substance when used as the dielectric in a capacitor, compared to that of a vacuum.

peroxide Oxide that yields hydrogen peroxide (H_2O_2) with an acid; any oxide that contains more oxygen than the usual form of that oxide; term loosely used to mean hydrogen peroxide.

persistence of vision Characteristic of the eye, which perceives a quick succession of "still" images of an object in different positions as a moving object; this makes cinematography possible.

petroleum Crude oil: mixture of hydrocarbons formed over long periods from the remains of marine organisms.

pewter Alloy of tin, lead, and a little antimony.

phase (chemistry) Separate part of a heterogenous system. For example, ice and water form a two-phase system.

phase (physics) Stage of wave motion: two points are in phase if their displacements are of the same magnitude and varying in the same manner.

phenol Carbolic acid (C_6H_5OH), a disinfectant derived from coal tar and used in the manufacture of plastics and dyes, also the name of a whole group of related aromatic compounds, of which this is one.

phosphate Salt of phosphoric acid (H_3PO_4); e.g., calcium phosphate ($Ca_3(PO_4)_2$).

phosphorescence Type of luminescence that differs from fluorescence in that the material continues to glow after it has absorbed light.

phosphors Substances that exhibit fluorescence or phosphorescence.

photocathode Photosensitive cell that emits electrons when exposed to light.

photochemical Of a reaction: accelerated by exposure to light.

photoconductor Photosensitive material whose conductivity increases when exposed to light.

photodiode Semiconductor diode in which the current flow varies according to the intensity of the incident light.

photoengraving (photogravure) Printing technique in which a gravure plate is made by coating it with photographic emulsion, exposing it to the image, and developing it so that the image areas are washed off; these exposed areas are then etched with acid.

photometer Instrument for comparing light intensities.

photon Quantum of radiant energy, e.g., light; its properties are best explained by sometimes treating it as a subatomic particle, and sometimes as a wave.

photosensitive Of a material: altered by exposure to light; e.g., photographic film.

pH value Measure of acidity or alkalinity in terms of hydrogen or hydroxyl ion concentration; the pH scale runs from 0 (extremely acid) through 7 (neutral) to 14 (extremely alkaline).

pi (π) The ratio of the circumference of a circle to diameter; not an exact amount: it has been calculated to a million places of decimals. To 20 decimal places pi is 3.14159265358979323846.

pinion (engineering) Small gear wheel.

pion Subatomic particle: a meson.

pipette Device used in chemical analysis for drawing up a measured volume of liquid and transferring it to another vessel: a thin glass tube with a bulge in the middle.

pitch (chemistry) General term for various dark, tarry substances obtained from wood, coal tar, asphalt, etc.

pitch (physics) Measure of frequency, either of a musical note or of the spacing of a screw thread; by extension from this, the blade angle of a propeller (i.e., considering its spiral motion through a medium such as air or water as that of a screw).

pitchblende Uranium ore, mostly as uranium oxide (U_3O_8); also contains a little radium, and is the principal source of this.

pixel Smallest unit of an electronic picture image.

Planck's constant Universal constant connecting the frequency of radiation with its quantum of energy: 6.624×10^{-20} joules seconds.

plasma Region in a gas discharge containing roughly equal numbers of positively and negatively charged particles. In thermonuclear reactions, the plasma is very hot with a high level of ionization.

plasticizer Substance added to plastic, clay, or cement to make it more flexible.

pneumatics Study of gases under pressure.

polyethylene A plastic made by the polymerization of ethylene (C_4H_4); a tough, waxy, electrically highly insulative thermoplastic.

polygon Geometrical figure with several sides.

polyhedron Solid figure that consists of faces that are polygons.

positive (photography) Of a picture: with colors "the right way around," as in a finished print.

positron Subatomic particle with same mass as an electron but positively charged; the antiparticle of the electron.

potash Potassium carbonate (K_2CO_3).

potassium nitrate (KNO_3) Also called niter and saltpeter. Used as an ingredient of gunpowder and in food preservation.

potential Ability to act in some way, e.g., do work.

potential (electric) Work that has to be done to move a unit electric charge from one point to another against an electric field.

potential difference Difference in voltage between two points in a conductor.

pound Unit of mass; defined as 0.4535924277 kilogram.

power (mathematics) Property of number multiplied by itself; e.g., $4 \times 4 \times 4$ is said to be "four to the power of three," and is written 4^3.

precession Motion characteristic of a gyroscope; when this is rotating about one axis and given a push at right angles to this axis, it moves along the third axis at right angles to the other two.

precipitate Insoluble substance that comes out of a solution in a chemical reaction.

preignition Premature ignition of fuel–air mixture in a gasoline engine, before the spark plug has time to set it off; this produces a sound called "knock."

presbyopia Eye defect associated with aging, in which the eyes lose their power of focusing on near objects, so that reading glasses are needed.

pressing (engineering) Forming of sheet metal parts by stamping in a press.

pressure Force acting on unit area of surface.

pressure vessel Vessel that can withstand high internal pressures. Often used for carrying out chemical reactions.

primary color Red, blue, and green are known as the primary colors of additive color mixing, i.e., mixing of colored light, because any other color can be produced by mixing them. In mixing of pigments, known as subtractive color mixing because pigments filter out colors they do not reflect, the primaries are red, blue, and yellow, none of which can be obtained by mixing pigments of other colors.

prime mover Any engine converting natural energy into power, e.g., a fuel-burning engine but not an electric motor.

prime number Number other than 1 with no factors, i.e., not divisible by any whole number other than itself and 1.

principal focus Point where parallel rays of light converge after refraction by a convex lens or concave mirror; or point from which they appear to diverge from a concave lens or convex mirror.

program A logical sequence of operations to be performed by a digital computer in solving a problem or in processing data. Also coded instructions and data for such a sequence.

projectile Any body thrown or fired; the study of projectiles is termed ballistics.

propellant Fuel, including oxidant, used in a rocket. Also a liquefied or compressed gas used in an aerosol can.

proportional Equality between ratios.

prosthesis Artificial substitute for part of body.

protocol (computing) An agreed upon set of rules to which communicating computers in a network must conform.

proton Subatomic particle found in varying numbers in nuclei of all atoms; positively charged.

protoplasm Complex colloidal substance containing proteins found in cells of all living organisms.

proximity fuse Fuse used to detonate a warhead when the target is within a preset range. May use radar or photoelectric sensors.

p-type Doped semiconductor in which the number of holes is greater than the number of electrons.

pulsar Collapsed neutron star that emits rapid pulses of electromagnetic radiation, probably because it is revolving.

pulse code modulation (PCM) Method of imposing signal on radio carrier wave by first reducing it to binary code.

pulse jet Crude form of jet engine with vanes that open and shut, so that it fires in short bursts.

pumice Light rock formed of lava filled with gas bubbles; used as aggregate in lightweight concrete.

pumped storage Energy storage method to meet demand for peak-hour electricity: water is pumped up to a high lake during times of low demand, then, when necessary, allowed to flow back, driving the pumps as turbines to generate electricity.

pyrites Sulfide of certain metals, characterized by shining appearance; e.g., iron pyrites (FeS_2), copper pyrites ("fools gold," $CuFeS_2$).

pyrometer Device for measuring temperature of a furnace; there are many types using thermoelectric effects, measuring the intensity of the light emitted, and using ceramic cones that melt at a known temperature.

pyrotechnic Connected with fireworks or flares.

quadrant Quarter circle; hence a navigational instrument of that shape.

qualitative Dealing with kind or type; e.g., qualitative analysis, examination of a compound or mixture to find what materials are present, but not to measure their proportions.

quantitative Dealing with amount; e.g., quantitative analysis, examination of a compound or mixture to find the proportions of its constituents.

quantum Individual, smallest possible unit of energy; quanta of electromagnetic radiation are called photons. (The word is also used to describe other things that occur in small "packets" or units.)

quantum mechanics Mathematical theory developed from quantum theory and used to explain the motion of atomic particles.

quark Hypothetical subatomic particle from which other particles are built up.

quartz Natural crystalline silica (silicon dioxide, SiO_2); sometimes clear (rock crystal) but generally colored or made opaque by impurities; used in powder form as an abrasive, and in crystal form for quartz oscillators in clocks, etc.

quartz halogen Type of light bulb with a tungsten filament and a quartz envelope filled with halogen vapor. It can operate at high filament temperatures and has an intense light output.

quartz oscillator Quartz crystal made to vibrate at its natural frequency by passing an alternating current through it; this frequency is extremely regular and makes an excellent regulator for timekeeping.

quasar Quasistellar astronomical object with large red shift. Generally has a small optical diameter but a large radio diameter.

quick freezing Freezing of food as quickly as possible by dividing it into small pieces and using powerful refrigerating equipment: this reduces damage to the texture caused by formation of large ice crystals.

rack Straight, toothed bar meshing with gear wheel; used in steering systems and to provide traction in mountain railways.

rad Former unit of radiation dosage, generally used for absorption by the body. Replaced by the SI unit the Gray (GY), which is equal to 1 joule/kg.

radial engine Aircraft piston engine with cylinders on circle around crankshaft.

radial ply Of a tire; with cords running radially, and a reinforcing band under the tread.

radian SI unit of angle: angle subtended at center of circle by arc equal in length to the radius. One radian is equal to 57.296 degrees.

radiation Emission of waves or particles. See also electromagnetic radiation.

radiation detector Device for detecting radioactivity, such as a particle detector, or a film badge: a small piece of photographic film, screened from light, worn by a worker. Any radiation will mark the emulsion, so that, developed at the end of each day, the badge indicates the total dose over the time; such a device is called a dosimeter.

radical (chemistry) Groups of atoms that act as a unit in a reaction, retaining their identity, but which are unable to exist on their own. An example is the ammonium radical (NH_4^+).

radioactive decay Spontaneous disintegration of radioactive substances into other substances, with the emission of radioactive particles.

radiocompass Navigational device that picks up radio signals from fixed "beacon" transmitters and uses the direction from which they have come to determine heading and position of aircraft or ship.

radiography Use of X rays to make photographs (strictly speaking, radiographs).

radioimmunoassay A method using the reaction of antigen with specific antibody, permitting measurements of the concentration of virtually any substance of biological interest.

radioisotope Radioactive isotope of any element, the unbalanced number of neutrons in its atomic nuclei making it unstable; may be natural or artificially produced; used as source of radiation for medical or industrial purposes, or examined in radioisotope dating techniques.

radiosonde Weather balloon carrying recording instruments that send readings to the meteorologist by radio.

ram, hydraulic Piston and cylinder arrangement for converting hydraulic pressure into mechanical force. Also a water-raising device worked by the energy of flowing water.

ramjet Jet engine in which the air for combustion is compressed by the forward movement of the engine. This design works only at high airspeeds.

rangefinder Distance-measuring device used for cameras and gunnery. Optical versions work by the parallax effect, with images from two separate viewfinders being adjusted until they are superimposed, the degree of adjustment giving a measure of the distance.

rare earth elements The group of 17 elements with atomic numbers 21, 39, and 57–71. Although widely distributed in nature, they generally occur in low concentrations. They are found in high concentrations as mixtures in a number of minerals.

ratchet Device allowing free movement in one direction but acting against movement in the other direction, often by a system of interlocking teeth.

ratio Relationship between two or more quantities, sizes, or amounts of the same kind.

rayon Textile fiber artificially made from cellulose (as opposed, e.g., to cotton, which is natural cellulose); there are two types, viscose and acetate.

reactance Of an alternating current circuit; quantity that, together with resistance, makes up the impedance of the circuit.

reaction (physics) Equal and opposite force resisting any action, as stated in Newton's Third Law of Motion; e.g., centrifugal and centripetal force.

reactor Container in which a nuclear or chemical reaction takes place; the term is used in the latter sense for some industrial processes.

reciprocal Of a number: 1 divided by that number; e.g., the reciprocal of 4 is ¼.

reciprocating Of motion: back and forth; e.g., a piston in an engine.

recoil Reaction force causing gun to move backward when bullet leaves it in a forward direction.

rectifier Device for converting alternating current to direct current, e.g., using a diode.

red shift Increase in wavelength of light (so that it becomes redder) of stars moving away from the Earth at high velocities; due to Doppler effect.

reduction Chemical reaction in which substance gains hydrogen or loses oxygen.

refining Increasing purity, e.g., of metal after initial extraction from ore, which is known as smelting.

refining (oil) Conversion of crude petroleum into finished products such as gasoline, lubricating oils, and chemical feedstocks.

refraction Diversion of path of light when it passes from one medium to another.

refractive index Measure of the extent to which a medium refracts light. Given as the ratio of the sine of the angle of incidence to the sine of the angle of refraction.

refractory Material that can withstand very high temperatures. Used in the construction of furnaces and high-temperature equipment.

refrigerant Substance used for heat transfer in the refrigeration cycle; e.g., ammonia and fluorocarbons.

regenerative braking Braking system used on some electric vehicles in which the wheels are used to drive the motor as a generator, so that some energy is recovered and used to recharge the battery.

relative molecular mass The mass of a molecule of an element or compound relative to ¹⁄₁₂ of the mass of a molecule of carbon-12.

relay Device in which a small current is used to switch a larger current in another circuit. In electromagnetic relays, the first current is passed through a coil to produce a magnetic field that closes the contacts for the second current.

reluctance (magnetic) Impedance to flow of magnetic flux. The ratio of the magnetomotive force in a circuit to the magnetic flux.

rennin Enzyme used to coagulate milk in cheese making.

resin Noncrystalline or viscous liquid, which may be a natural gum, etc., or a synthetic material.

resist Coating used to prevent adherence of ink in lithography, or of dye in batik, to nonimage areas.

resistance thermometer Thermometer working by measurement of resistance, which varies with temperature, in a platinum wire.

resistivity Specific resistance of a substance, measured as the resistance between opposite faces of a cube of given size.

resolution Degree of resolving power, e.g., of camera to distinguish between two tiny objects very close together, or of spectroscope to distinguish between two nearly identical wavelengths.

resonator Any device designed to have a natural frequency of vibration or oscillation and be excited into resonating at that frequency; e.g., a klystron.

respiration Process by which living organisms take in oxygen for the processes of metabolism and give off carbon dioxide.

rest mass Mass of a body when at rest relative to the observer; this concept is necessary because the theory of relativity shows that the mass of a body varies with its velocity.

resultant Single force having the same effect as, or resulting from, two or more forces acting together.

retardation Rate of decrease of velocity; opposite of acceleration.

retort Vessel used for distillation (or, occasionally, an autoclave).

reverberatory furnace Furnace in which heat is reflected off the roof onto the material to be melted, thus keeping fuel from mixing with it.

reversible reaction Chemical reaction that can be made to proceed in either direction by varying the conditions in which it takes place; it will not go to completion unless one of the products is removed.

rheostat Variable electric resistor.

ring compound Chemical compound in molecule of which some atoms are arranged in form of a ring; e.g., benzene and all its related compounds.

RMS (root mean square) Square root of the mean of the individual squares. Mathematical method of finding average value of quantity alternating in a sine waveform, such as ordinary alternating current electricity. For the United States, AC reaching a peak voltage of ±156 has an RMS voltage of 110 V. In countries with a peak voltage of ±339 V, the RMS voltage is 240 V.

RNA (ribonucleic acid) Substance in living cell that picks up and transfers hereditary information coded in DNA.

robot Term used to describe machine that automatically performs work that would normally be done by a human, e.g., in an industrial process.

rolled gold "Sandwich" of two thin sheets of gold with thicker layer of cheap metal between, rolled out thin and used to make inexpensive jewelry.

röntgen Unit of measurement for X rays and gamma rays. The amount of radiation that will produce ions with a charge of 2.58 x 10^{-4} coulombs per kilogram of dry air.

rotary converter Device for converting DC to DC of another voltage, or to AC, using a motor driven by the input current to drive a generator.

rotary drives Devices used to transmit the output of a mechanical power source using a rotating shaft. Special couplings (universal joints are used to allow for misalignment between driving and driven shafts.

rotary engine Term originally used to describe early aircraft engine in which entire cylinder block rotated around stationary crankshaft; later used for Wankel engine and other engines in which main parts rotate instead of reciprocate.

rotary valve Valve used in some engines; a disc or drum with a hole in it revolves to cover and uncover a port.

rust Hydrated form of iron oxide ($Fe_2O_3 \cdot H_2O$) formed on iron through action of moist air.

sal ammoniac Ammonium chloride (NH_4Cl); used in Leclanché cells.

salinometer Hydrometer used to find specific gravity of seawater and other saline solutions.

saltpeter Potassium nitrate (KNO_3): also called niter; used in food preservation and as ingredient of gunpowder.

saturated vapor pressure Pressure exerted by a saturated vapor.

saturation Maximum level of vapor in a gas or solute in a solvent.

sawtooth wave Waveform in which each pulse builds up gradually to a maximum, then falls instantaneously; used as a time base.

scalar quantity Quantity having magnitude but not direction; e.g., mass, but not velocity.

scan Covering an area with a moving detector; e.g., traversing an image in strips to record its features in a television camera.

scattering of light Random reflection and diffraction of light passing through a medium; light of short wavelength is scattered to a greater extent than of long, so that atmospheric scattering of sunlight makes the sky blue.

schlieren photography Technique for examining flow variations in fluids by taking photographs of the associated changes in refractive index.

scintillation counter Particle detector using a block of material that emits light when crossed by a high-energy particle, with a photomultiplier to detect and amplify the emitted light.

second Unit of time. Angular measurement of $\frac{1}{60}$ degree.

secondary emission Emission of electrons from solid material struck by electrons or ions.

sector Portion of circle cut off by two radii; e.g., slice of round cake.

sedimentary Of rocks: laid down as sediment. This sediment is formed from other rocks, the hard parts of organisms, and salts deposited from solution, e.g., limestones formed under the sea from the compacted shells of dead sea creatures, as distinct from rocks of volcanic origin.

seine Type of fishing net extended in form of enormous bag and gradually drawn in.

semiconductor device Electronic device making use of the properties of semiconductor material.

semipermeable Of a membrane: allowing the passage of some liquids (and gases) but not others; this property is important in osmosis and dialysis.

series (electronics) Conductors or components connected in a line so the current passes through them in turn.

series (mathematical) Sum of a sequence of mathematical expressions that have a regular form or relationship.

shear Stress applied to a body in the plane of one of its faces.

shock wave Wave of very high compression sent through, e.g., air by explosion or supersonic aircraft.

short circuit Connection accidentally or deliberately made across a circuit, having a lower resistance than the circuit so that most of the current flows along it.

SI (System Internationale d'Unités) International system of units of measure, consisting of the following six units plus their multiples and submultiples: length—meter (m); mass—kilogram (kg); time—second (s); electric current—ampere (A); thermodynamic temperature—kelvin (K); and luminous intensity—candela (cd).

sideband (radio) Band of frequencies just above or below carrier frequency.

sidereal day Time taken by Earth to rotate once relative to the stars, rather than the Sun; a little shorter than a solar day (ordinary day).

sidereal year Time taken by the Sun to (apparently) perform a complete revolution with reference to the stars.

siemens Unit of conductance, the SI name for the mho; the ratio of the current flowing through a conductor, measured in amperes, to the voltage difference between the ends of the conductor.

silica Silicon dioxide (SiO_2). Occurs naturally as quartz, flint, and sand. Used in the manufacture of glass and for the production of silicon.

silica gel Highly porous granular form of hydrated silica that absorbs water from the atmosphere and is used as a drying agent.

silicate Defined as a salt of silicic acid (H_2SiO_3), but more important, a type of compound commonly found in rocks, many of which are silicates of aluminum, calcium, magnesium, etc.

silver nitrate ($AgNO_3$) White, soluble crystalline salt, used in marking ink, chemical analysis, and as a caustic substance in medicine.

simple harmonic motion Oscillation along a line about a central point so that acceleration toward this point is always proportional to distance from it; e.g., motion of a pendulum.

slag Nonmetallic residue of smelting process, generally floating on the surface of the metal; some slags are useful, e.g., basic slag as a soil treatment, and others as aggregate in concrete.

slipstream Flow of air behind a moving object, or of moving air behind a stationary object.

smelting Extracting metal from its ore, normally by chemical reduction, though aluminum is smelted by electrolysis.

smoothing (electronics) Term used for flattening and evening out of choppy waveform of DC coming from a rectifier by means of circuits incorporating inductors, etc.

soap General term for various mixtures of sodium and potassium salts obtained by saponification; one such salt is sodium stearate ($C_{17}H_{35} \cdot COONa$).

soda Baking soda, sodium bicarbonate ($NaHCO_3$); caustic soda, sodium hydroxide ($NaOH$); washing soda, sodium carbonate ($Na_2CO_3 \cdot 10H_2O$ in hydrate crystal form). Soda water is basically plain water with dissolved carbon dioxide (CO_2), though it contains a little sodium bicarbonate for flavoring.

solar cell Device for converting energy of sunlight directly into electricity.

solder Alloy with low melting point used for joining metals. Soft solders, as used for electric connections, etc., are lead–tin alloys; hard solders for brazing are copper–zinc; and there are special silver and gold solders.

solid state (electronics) Of a circuit: employing semiconductor rather than thermionic components.

solstice Time of year at which Sun is at maximum angular distance from Equator; summer solstice (from point of view of Northern Hemisphere), when Sun is farthest north, is about June 21; winter solstice about December 21.

solvent Substance that dissolves another.

sonic boom Loud sound resulting from shock wave propagated by aircraft traveling at the speed of sound.

space–time Concept of the three dimensions of space and dimension of time being welded together into a four-dimensional continuum.

spark chamber Particle detector in which passage of a particle causes ionization in a gas between two highly charged wires or plates, so that a spark jumps between them; this can be photographed. Normally, spark chambers consist of a whole row of separate detectors.

spark plug Device used for the propagation of the ignition spark in the cylinder of an internal combustion engine.

specific gravity Measure of density of substance (i.e., its weight per unit volume) compared with that of water at 39°F (the temperature at which water is densest; if cooled further, it expands prior to freezing). Also called relative density.

specific heat Heat required to raise unit mass of a substance through a temperature of one degree.

specific impulse Ratio of thrust produced by a rocket to the rate of fuel consumption.

spectrum Result of resolving any wave phenomenon, e.g., light, into its constituent wavelengths or frequencies; in the case of light, this produces the familiar rainbow colors, blue having the shortest wavelength and red the longest. Various kinds of light spectrum exist: emission spectra are produced by bodies emitting light, and if continuous the result is white light. When this light passes through a semitransparent medium, certain frequencies are absorbed, leaving gaps in the spectrum; this is an absorption spectra. Some substances emit only certain wavelengths, producing a line spectrum, e.g., of the yellow light produced by sodium. The spectra are characteristic of the substances causing them, thus allowing spectra to be used in analysis.

spherical aberration Distortion of image formed by lens or mirror caused by light from the edges coming to a focus in a different position to that from the center.

spin Form of energy that subatomic particle may possess in addition to other forms (e.g., charge), and due to it spinning on its axis in a particular direction; this energy is connected with magnet-

ism, and is also an important concept in the studies of particle physics and wave mechanics.

spot welding Welding process in which two sheets of metal or plastic are joined by a series of point welds.

square wave Waveform having a very rapid rise to a maximum, remaining there for a moment, then falling away equally rapidly.

stabilizer (chemistry) Substance that has the opposite effect to that of an ordinary catalyst, slowing down a chemical reaction; stabilizers are used by the food industry to retard spoilage.

stainless steel Class of steels containing up to 25 percent chromium, and other metals such as nickel. None rust, but all corrode a little, 18–8 (chromium and nickel percentages) steel being the least affected.

static electricity Electricity in the form of a stationary charge, rather than a current.

statics Branch of mechanics dealing with nonmoving bodies.

stationary wave Wave, e.g., in a guitar string, where the position of nodes and antinodes remains constant, as opposed to a traveling wave, such as one of sound.

steam Water in the gaseous state, above boiling point; this is invisible—visible "steam" is in fact condensed droplets of water vapor.

steam point Exact boiling point of water at standard atmospheric pressure; the standard for 212°F (100°C).

steel Iron alloy containing 0.1 to 1.5 percent carbon and, generally, small amounts of other alloying elements.

steradian SI unit of solid angle: that solid angle that encloses a surface on the sphere equal to the square of the radius.

stereochemistry Branch of chemistry dealing with the arrangement in space of the atoms within a molecule.

stereoisomer One of a pair of isomers of a substance, each of which is a mirror image, in terms of atomic arrangement, of the other.

stereophonic Of a sound system: with two channels, giving the illusion of breadth and depth.

sterilize Application of heat to kill bacteria.

still (chemical industry, etc.) Apparatus for distilling liquids.

storage battery Rechargeable cell for storing electricity.

strain Ratio of change in dimension to original dimension in a body subjected to stress.

stratosphere Layer of atmosphere between troposphere (the base layer) and ionosphere; not much weather at this altitude apart from "jetstream" winds; used by airliners.

streamline Of flow: smooth, laminar, as opposed to turbulent.

stress Force per unit area applied to a body.

strong force Interaction between subatomic particles occurring at very short range and acting to hold the atomic nucleus together.

subatomic Of particles: smaller than, or forming part of, an atom.

sublimate Undergo sublimation; or a solid obtained by direct condensation from vapor, without passing through the liquid state.

subsonic Traveling below the speed of sound.

sugar General term for soluble carbohydrates, particularly sucrose ($C_{12}H_{22}O_{11}$) but also glucose and fructose (both $C_6H_{12}O_6$, stereoisomers) and lactose and maltose (both isomers of sucrose).

sulfuric acid (H_2SO_4) Strongly corrosive acid; a colorless, oily liquid; used as electrolyte in lead acid storage batteries; much of the sulfur used in industry is in this form.

sunspots Large, dark patches on surface of Sun, often occurring in groups and appearing to cross the Sun's surface as it rotates; appear in greatest number every 11 years, and are connected with terrestrial phenomena such as the Aurora Borealis.

supercooling Cooling of liquid below its freezing point without normal solidification; with some substances, supercooling is possible, but introducing a particle of the solid substance will cause it to crystallize, solidify, and heat up to its normal freezing point; in other cases this does not happen e.g., glass, which has no crystalline structure, may be considered as a form of supercooled liquid.

superheating Heating of substance above the temperature needed for a change of state without the change occurring.

supersaturated solution Solution holding more solute than in a saturated solution at the same temperature.

supersonic Traveling at a speed greater than that of sound; *see* Mach number and hypersonic.

surface action Range of effects exhibited, e.g., by detergents, altering the wetting and spreading properties of water; substances having effects of this kind are called surfactants.

surface tension State of tension on open surface of a liquid, as if held in by an elastic membrane, and allowing it to form drops and bubbles; caused by attractive forces between molecules.

susceptibility (magnetism) The capacity of a substance for being magnetized, expressed in the ratio of the extent of magnetization to the strength of the magnetizing force.

suspension Dispersion of very small solid particles in a liquid; e.g., muddy water.

synchromesh Device in manual transmission to make gear changing smoother: gear wheels are in constant mesh and engaged and disengaged as needed by means of cone clutches.

synthetic Built up by artificial means from simpler materials; thus synthetic fibers include nylon, a complex polymer built up from simple organic compounds, but not rayon, which is a modified form of the complex compound cellulose.

tachometer Instrument measuring angular speed of rotation of a machine, e.g., an engine, usually in revolutions per minute.

tanning Converting raw animal skin into leather by treating it with chemicals, many of which contain tannic acid and tannins, esterlike compounds extracted from vegetables.

tar General name for various dark, viscous organic materials; e.g., asphalt, bitumen, coal tar.

telemetry Method of recording events (usually measurements) at a distance, often using radio links. For example, the transmission of satellite measurements to an Earth station.

telephoto lens Lens used on camera to take enlarged pictures of distant objects.

tempering Form of heat treatment involving heating the material to a specific temperature and controlled quenching (cooling).

terminal velocity Maximum velocity attainable by body subjected to a constant force (e.g., falling because of gravity) in a viscous medium (such as air).

tesla SI unit of magnetic flux density. Equal to one weber per square meter.

theodolite Surveyor's instrument for measuring angles: consists of a telescope pivoted against a scale of degrees.

theorem Statement proved by logical reasoning.

therm Practical unit of quantity of heat, used, e.g., for fuel suppliers; originally 100,000 British thermal units, but now 100,000 kilojoules, a little smaller (= 0.948 "old" therms).

thermistor Semiconductor device whose resistance alters with temperature, so that it can be used in thermometers or thermostats.

thermocouple Two strips of different metals joined end to end, the other ends completing a circuit through, e.g., a galvanometer. Heating the junction causes a small current to flow, so the device can be used as a thermometer.

thermoelectricity Electricity generated directly by heat, as in a thermocouple.

thermoluminescence Radioisotope dating technique used for ceramics: decay of isotopes present in, e.g., quartz causes accumulation at a certain rate of electrons "trapped" in its crystal structure, but these can be driven off by heating; the quantity of electrons accumulated, measurable by the glow they produce on reheating, reveals the time since the ceramic object was originally fired.

thermonuclear Nuclear fusion reaction in which the interacting particles have very high kinetic energies. Used to describe the hydrogen bomb, which requires a very high temperature (obtained from a fission bomb) to initiate the fusion process.

thermopile "Battery" of thermocouple junctions connected in series; such a device can produce a small but usable electric current.

thermostat Temperature-regulating switch or valve used, e.g., in heating systems; a temperature-sensing device such as a bimetallic strip turns the power off when it reaches a certain temperature, then on again when it cools.

thixotropy Property found naturally in quicksand, and imparted to some paints and adhesives, increasing in viscosity if left undisturbed, but becoming less viscous immediately if shaken or stirred.

three-phase current Form in which alternating current is generated and distributed to industrial users, though not to household users.

threshold Term used to describe value or level at which an event begins.

throttle Choking device used to regulate the flow of a fluid; hence variation of the power of an internal combustion engine by reducing or increasing the air flow into the engine.

thrust Propulsive force, as of a rocket.

titration Method of measuring strength of a chemical solution by adding a known volume of a solution with which it reacts, at a known strength,

to a known volume of the solution under test. The amount that has to be added to neutralize the test solution (this is ascertained with a chemical indicator) allows its strength to be figured out.

toluene ($C_6H_5 \cdot CH_3$) Hydrocarbon of the benzene series: a colorless, flammable liquid extracted from coal tar; used to make dyes, drugs, artificial sweeteners, and explosives (TNT).

tomography X-ray technique giving picture of cross section of patient.

ton Unit of weight equal to 2,000 lbs. in the United States. Also known as the short ton.

tone Term used to mean both a sound of a certain frequency and the combination of frequencies of a particular sound.

tonne 1,000 kg, metric tonne = 2,204.62 lbs.

topography General arrangement of the features of a surface (usually the land), including height and slope details.

torque convertor Device for changing the torque/speed relationship between input and output shafts. Often uses hydrodynamic mechanisms.

torquemeter Type of dynamometer for measuring torque produced by an engine.

torr Unit of pressure used in vacuum measurements and equal to 1 mm of mercury.

torsion Strain produced by torque; the extent to which something is twisted.

torsion balance Force-measuring device in which the force is made to push a bar that twists a wire to a certain extent, the deflection of the bar indicating the force.

total internal reflection Reflection of light off the inside of the surface of a transparent medium because its angle of incidence exceeds the critical angle, and it cannot therefore be refracted out.

toxicology Study of poisons.

tracer (ammunition) Round placed at intervals in a belt, e.g., of machine gun ammunition; when fired, the bullet leaves a glowing trail so that direction of fire can be checked.

tracer (radioactive) Radioisotope of an element substituted for the ordinary form so that its progress through a system (pipeline, plant, animal, etc.) can be monitored with a radiation detector.

transfer printing Method used for transferring printed designs onto material that cannot be printed on by ordinary means, e.g., chinaware: the design, possibly in several colors, is printed onto a flexible sheet from which it can be detached and pressed onto the article.

transmission (mechanical) Means by which power is transferred, for example, from an automobile engine to the road wheels.

transmutation Changing of one element into another by nuclear fission or fusion.

transonic Of speed: in the region of the speed of sound, or just over it (see Mach number).

transparent Permitting passage of light in a sufficient orderly way to give a clear image.

transuranic elements Periodic table classification of radioactive elements, starting just below uranium and continuing beyond it to the heaviest elements yet discovered.

transverse wave Wave in which vibrations take place across the direction in which it is traveling; e.g., electromagnetic waves, but not sound.

traveling wave Wave that moves bodily, as opposed to stationary wave.

triangle of forces Representation of three forces acting on a point by three sides of a triangle, their angles showing the direction of the forces and their lengths proportional to the size of each force; if the three lines form a closed triangle, the forces will be in equilibrium.

triangle of velocities Representation of velocities by similar method to that of triangle of forces; if the triangle is closed, the body will be at rest.

triangulation Surveying method in which country is divided into triangles and positions and distances found by trigonometry.

triboelectricity Static electricity caused by friction; e.g., rubbing a piece of glass.

tribology Study of friction and lubrication.

trigonometry Branch of mathematics in which unknown distance and angle measurements can be discovered by treating them as sides and angles of a right-angled triangle; if three facts (e.g., two sides and an angle) about the triangle are known, the rest can be found out by the use of trigonometric ratios, of which tables have been drawn up. These ratios are expressed as, e.g., the sine of an angle (abbreviated to sin), which is the ratio of two sides when the angle is a certain size. If a vertical line AB is drawn perpendicular to a base line OB and a third line drawn from A to O to close it into a triangle, the ratios are: sine of angle AOB (sin AOB; referring to the angle at O made by sides AO and OB) is AB/AO (side AB divided by side AO); cosine (cos) AOB is OB/AO; tangent (tan) AOB is AB/OB; cosecant (cosec) AOB is AO/AB; secant (sec) AOB is AO/OB; cotangent (cot) AOB is OB/AB.

trinitrotoluene ($C_6H_2 \cdot CH_3(NO_2)_3$) The explosive TNT; an ingredient of other high explosive mixtures, such as dynamite.

triple point Unique set of values of temperature pressure and volume at which vapor, liquid, and solid phases of a particular substance are in equilibrium and can exist together.

tropics Two lines of latitude 23° 28′ north (Tropic of Cancer) and south (Tropic of Capricorn) of the Equator, at which the Sun is directly overhead at the summer (northern) and winter (southern) solstices respectively; the regions between these are tropical regions.

troposphere Lowest layer of the atmosphere, reaching from sea level to height of 7–16 km; this is the layer in which most weather phenomena occur.

tungsten halogen Term for high output light bulb used, e.g., for car headlights, and having a tungsten filament set in a quartz tube containing halogen elements such as iodine (vaporized).

tuning fork Fork-shaped resonating device for producing a note of a particular pitch.

turbocharger Supercharger driven by a turbine powered by engine exhaust gases and used to force extra air into the engine.

turbojet Jet engine in which the turbine is used only to drive the compressor. The propulsive force comes from reaction of the hot exhaust gases.

turboshaft Type of jet engine (or strictly speaking gas turbine) turning a shaft to operate, e.g., the rotors of a helicopter.

turbulent flow Fluid flow in which the local velocity and direction of flow undergo rapid variations.

two-stroke cycle Sequence of operations in internal combustion engine in which piston moves up and down once for each explosion of fuel mixture.

Tyndall effect Scattering of light by particles in the light path, so giving a visible beam.

type metal Alloy of lead, antimony, and tin that expands on solidifying to fill the mold completely and give a well-defined casting.

UHF Ultra-high frequency: radio waveband used for TV broadcasting and some short-range radio transmission.

ultimate stress Load at fracture divided by the original cross section at the point of fracture.

ultrasonic Sound too high for human hearing. Typically above 20,000 Hz.

ultraviolet Electromagnetic radiation with wavelength shorter than that of visible light but longer than X rays, ranging from 400 nm to 5 nm; ultraviolet radiation in sunlight, though mostly absorbed by the atmosphere, causes sunburn and affects photographic film (UV filters are often used on cameras to avoid this).

umbra Region of complete shadow at center of penumbra (half shadow) caused when object is illuminated by large source of light; during a total eclipse of the Sun, for example, an observer on Earth is in the umbra.

uncertainty principle Impossibility of determining accurately both the position and momentum of a subatomic particle simultaneously; a problem in the science of wave mechanics.

unity (mathematics) One.

urea ($CO(NH_2)_2$) Organic compound: a white, crystalline solid; occurs in urine; was the first organic compound to be synthesized; used to make urea formaldehyde resins and plastics.

vaccination Use of vaccines to provide immunity to diseases.

vacuum distillation Distillation at lower than normal temperature by use of partial vacuum to lower boiling point.

vacuum gauge Instrument for measuring pressure reduction in evacuated container; generally a Bourdon gauge.

valency Combining power of an atom with other atoms; the combination occurs in fixed numerical ratios, though one element may have several valencies; valency is stated in terms of the number of hydrogen atoms the element would combine with. The numerical ratios in bond formation are explicable in terms of electron transfer: *see* bond.

van de Graaff generator Device for generating very high voltages; used as a particle accelerator.

van der Waals' force Force of attraction that exists between atoms and molecules of all substances; not very strong and easily overcome by other forces.

vapor Substance in gaseous state, but below its critical temperature, so that it may be liquefied simply by increasing the pressure.

vapor density Measure of density of a gas or vapor, usually relative to oxygen or hydrogen.

vapor diffusion pump High-vacuum pump in which jets of vapor are used to carry away gas molecules.

variable (mathematics) Any changing quantity in a calculation, as opposed to a constant.

variable geometry Aircraft term describing swing-wing arrangements where wings stretch out straight for takeoff and landing, and move back for high-speed flight.

vector Quantity that requires a direction to be stated to define it completely, e.g., velocity.

velocity Speed in a particular direction. Measured as the distance covered per unit time.

velocity ratio In a machine: the distance moved by applied effort, divided by the distance moved by the load.

verdigris Green deposit on copper: a mixture of various basic copper acetates.

vernier Device used to obtain accurate readings on a scale. Normally, a sliding scale adjacent to the main scale with subdivisions ‰ of those on the main scale so as to allow fractional readings.

VHF Very high frequency: radio waveband used for local transmissions and (in some countries) for television.

vibration, plane of Alternative term for plane of polarization of light (*see* polarization).

vinyl Name of an organic radical (CH_2=CH) found in, e.g., vinyl chloride (CH_2=CHCl) that is polymerized to make polyvinyl chloride (PVC) plastic, often loosely called "vinyl" itself.

virus Small disease-causing agent midway between a large molecule and a living organism.

virtual particle Particle considered as existing for a very short period during the interaction of two other particles.

viscometer Device for comparison of viscosities of different fluids by speed at which they flow through a tube, or objects sink through them.

viticulture Growing grapes for wine.

vitrification Formation into a glassy material.

vitriol, oil of Old name for sulfuric acid (H_2SO_4).

volatile Of liquids: with a high vapor pressure, and thus readily vaporizing.

volt (V) Unit of electromotive force or potential difference. One volt gives one joule of energy to each coulomb of electricity supplied.

voltage Electric potential causing current to flow; measured in volts. The voltage of a current is equal to the power in watts divided by the current size in amperes.

voltage divider Also called potential divider: both are alternative terms for a potentiometer.

voltaic cell Earliest type of electric cell invented (by Volta): one copper and one zinc plate dipped in dilute sulfuric acid.

voltaic pile Battery of voltaic cells.

voltameter Device for measuring quantity of electricity by amount of metal it deposits in an electrolytic cell.

voltmeter Device for measuring voltage.

volumetric analysis Chemical analysis to determine proportion by volume of constituents of a compound or mixture.

volute Spiral shape (like a snail shell), e.g., of centrifugal pump housing.

V/STOL, VTOL Aircraft term: vertical or short takeoff and landing, vertical takeoff and landing.

vulcanite Hard insulating material made from rubber and sulfur by vulcanization; now largely replaced by plastics.

vulcanization Treatment of rubber with sulfur to make it hard and durable.

Wankel engine Internal combustion engine that uses shaped rotor instead of reciprocating pistons.

water gas Gas consisting of carbon monoxide (CO) and hydrogen, made by passing steam over red-hot coke; an excellent fuel gas, but the reaction is endothermic (loses heat), so has to be kept going by passing air over the coke to make inferior producer gas.

water jet Propulsion method suitable for boats in shallow water, or wherever propellers are liable to damage. Water is drawn in at the bows and pumped out at the stern through a swiveling nozzle.

watt (W) SI unit of power; joules per second.

wattage Power: the wattage of electricity is equal to the voltage multiplied by the amperage.

wattmeter Device for measuring power of an electric current; it has two coils, which measure the voltage and amperage and combine the result.

waveband Range of radio wavelengths, arbitrarily selected according to broadcasting requirements.

wavelength Distance on a wave between any successive points of equal phase.

wave mechanics Study of the behavior of subatomic particles treating them as waves. A development of quantum mechanics.

wave number Measurement used instead of wavelength for infrared radiation: reciprocal of wavelength in centimeters.

weak force Force in atomic nucleus of radioactive elements controlling rate of decay.

weber Unit of magnetic flux. The flux that produces an emf of 1 volt in a single-turn circuit as it decays to zero over a period of 1 second.

weight Force of attraction of Earth (usually) on a given mass.

weighting Technique used in noise measurement, where measurements of sound energy are deliberately biased to allow for the different effect of different pitches on a human listener.

Wheatstone bridge Experimental apparatus for finding value of an unknown resistor by comparing it with those whose resistance is known.

wide-angle lens Camera lens of short focal length, giving a wide field of view; in its most extreme form it is called a fisheye lens.

wide-area network Computer network covering a wide area, e.g., the Internet.

work Movement of the point of application of a force through a distance; expended energy; measured in joules.

World Wide Web Part of the Internet that features interactive graphical displays called websites that are accessed by computer.

wort Alcoholic liquor at intermediate stage of brewing or similar process.

wrought iron Iron with a very low carbon content, but containing a small amount of slag, so that it has a fibrous structure. Malleable, ductile, tough and relatively corrosion-resistant.

xerography Photocopying technique using static electricity to attract toner (dry, powdered ink) to image areas on a drum.

xeroradiography X-ray examination technique producing pictures by xerography.

X plates Electrically charged plates in oscilloscope tube deflecting electron beam horizontally.

X-ray collimator Tube containing row of slotted plates used for producing a straight beam of X rays, which cannot be focused by a conventional lens.

X-ray crystallography Method of finding atomic structure of a crystal by passing X rays through it onto photographic film; the atoms diffract the X rays into a characteristic pattern (Laue pattern) depending on their arrangement.

X-ray fluoroscopy X-ray examination technique producing immediate image on fluorescent screen, without using photographic film. (Term also, confusingly, used for analysis by X-ray spectrometer.)

X rays Electromagnetic radiation with wavelengths in the region of 0.01 to 5 nanometers; intermediate between gamma rays and ultraviolet. X-ray examination techniques are much used in medicine and industry, on account of the rays' ability to pass through objects opaque to light. When they are used to produce an image on photographic film, the technique is called radiography.

X-ray tube Vacuum tube used for the production of X rays by causing rapidly moving electrons to collide with a target.

xylene ($C_6H_4(CH_3)_2$) Liquid resembling toluene, and, similarly, extracted from coal tar; used as solvent, etc.

Yagi antenna Directional antenna with one or two dipoles, a reflector behind the dipole and a series of reflectors in front of the dipole.

yaw Of an aircraft: turn without banking.

yeast Single-celled plant organism used in various fermentation processes, including bread, beer, and winemaking and direct production of animal feed from waste materials.

yield point Point at which increase of tension (beyond the elastic limit) results in a sudden increase of elongation.

Y plates Electrically charged plates in oscilloscope tube deflecting electron beam vertically.

Zamboni pile Early type of high-voltage battery.

zenith Highest point; opposite of nadir.

zeppelin Old term for airship, after Count Zeppelin, the airship pioneer.

Zernicke microscope (phase contrast microscope) Uses interference effects produced by zone plate to make translucent specimens easier to see.

zodiac Path in the sky across which the Sun, Moon, and planets move; extends about 9 degrees above and below the ecliptic.

zone plate Plate marked with concentric rings that produce interference effects on light or other radiation, depending on their spacing; can be used as a crude focusing device, even for X rays, which go straight through a lens.

zoom lens Camera lens with continuously adjustable focal length.

Weights and Measures

Use this table to convert the English system (or the imperial system), the system of units common in the United States (e.g., inches, miles, quarts), to the metric system (e.g., meters, kilometers, liters) or to convert the metric system to the English system. You can convert one measurement into another by multiplying. For example, to convert centimeters into inches, multiply the number of centimeters by 0.3937. To convert inches into centimeters, multiply the number of inches by 2.54.

To convert	into	multiply by
Acres	Square feet	43,560
	Square yards	4840
	Square miles	0.00156
	Square meters	4046.856
	Hectares	0.40468
Celsius	Fahrenheit	First multiply by 1.8 then add 32
Centimeters	Inches	0.3937
	Feet	0.0328
Cubic cm	Cubic inches	0.06102
Cubic feet	Cubic inches	1728
	Cubic yards	0.037037
	Gallons	7.48
	Cubic meters	0.028317
	Liters	28.32
Cubic inches	Fluid ounces	0.554113
	Cups	0.069264
	Quarts	0.017316
	Gallons	0.004329
	Liters	0.016387
	Milliliters	16.387064
Cubic meters	Cubic feet	35.3145
	Cubic yards	1.30795
Cubic yards	Cubic feet	27
	Cubic meters	0.76456
Cups, fluid	Quarts	0.25
	Pints	0.5
	Fluid ounces	8
	Milliliters	237
	Tablespoons	16
	Teaspoons	48
Fahrenheit	Celsius	First subtract 32 then divide by 1.8
Feet	Centimeters	30.48
	Meters	0.3048
	Kilometers	0.0003
	Inches	12
	Yards	0.3333
	Miles	0.00019
Gallons	Quarts	4
	Pints	8
	Cups	16
	Fluid ounces	128
	Liters	3.785
	Milliliters	3785
	Cubic inches	231
	Cubic feet	0.1337
	Cubic yards	0.00495
	Cubic meters	0.00379
	British gallons	0.8327
Grams	Ounces	0.03527
	Pounds	0.0022
Hectares	Square meters	10,000
	Acres	2.471
Horsepower	Foot-pounds per minute	33,000
	British thermal units (Btu) per minute	42.42
	British thermal units (Btu) per hour	2546
	Kilowatts	0.7457
	Metric horsepower	1.014

To convert	into	multiply by
Inches	Feet	0.08333
	Yards	0.02778
	Centimeters	2.54
	Meters	0.0254
Kilograms	Grams	1000
	Ounces	35.274
	Pounds	2.2046
	Short tons	0.0011
	Long tons	0.00098
	Metric tons (tonnes)	0.001
Kilometers	Meters	1000
	Miles	0.62137
	Yards	1093.6
	Feet	3280.8
Kilowatts	British thermal units (Btu) per minute	56.9
	Horsepower	1.341
	Metric horsepower	1.397
Kilowatt-hours	British thermal units (Btu)	3413
Knots	Statute miles per hour	1.1508
Leagues	Miles	3
Liters	Milliliters	1000
	Fluid ounces	33.814
	Quarts	1.05669
	British gallons	0.21998
	Cubic inches	61.02374
	Cubic feet	0.13531
Meters	Inches	39.37
	Feet	3.28083
	Yards	1.09361
	Miles	0.000621
	Kilometers	0.001
	Centimeters	100
	Millimeters	1000
Miles	Inches	63,360
	Feet	5280
	Yards	1760
	Meters	1609.34
	Kilometers	1.60934
	Nautical miles	0.8684
Miles, nautical U.S. and international	Statute miles	1.1508
	Feet	6076.115
	Meters	1852
Miles per minute	Feet per second	88
	Knots	52.104
Milliliters	Fluid ounces	0.0338
	Cubic inches	0.061
	Liters	0.001
Millimeters	Centimeters	0.1
	Meters	0.001
	Inches	0.03937
Ounces, avoirdupois	Pounds	0.0625
	Grams	28.34952
	Kilograms	0.0283495
Ounces, fluid	Pints	0.0625
	Quarts	0.03125
	Cubic inches	1.80469
	Cubic feet	0.00104
	Milliliters	29.57353
	Liters	0.02957

To convert	into	multiply by
Pints	Quarts	0.5
	Fluid ounces	16
	Cubic inches	28.8745
	Cubic feet	0.01671
	Milliliters	473.17647
	Liters	0.473176
Pounds	Ounces	16
	Grams	453.59237
	Kilograms	0.45359
	Tons	0.0005
	Tons, long	0.000446
	Metric tons (tonnes)	0.0004536
Quarts	Fluid ounces	32
	Pints	2
	Gallons	0.25
	Cubic inches	57.749
	Cubic feet	0.033421
	Liters	0.946358
	Milliliters	946.358
Square feet	Square inches	144
	Square meters	0.093
	Square yards	0.111
Square inches	Square centimeters	6.452
	Square feet	0.0069
Square kilometers	Hectares	100
	Square meters	1,000,000
	Square miles	0.3861
Square meters	Square feet	10.758
	Square yards	1.196
Square miles	Acres	640
	Square kilometers	2.59
Square yards	Square feet	9
	Square inches	1296
	Square meters	0.836
Tablespoons	Fluid ounces	0.5
	Teaspoons	3
	Milliliters	14.7868
Teaspoons	Fluid ounces	0.16667
	Tablespoons	0.3333
	Milliliters	4.9289
Tons, long	Pounds	2240
	Kilograms	1016.047
	Short tons	1.12
	Metric tons (tonnes)	1.016
Tons, short	Pounds	2000
	Kilograms	907.185
	Long tons	0.89286
	Metric tonnes	0.907
Tons, metric (tonnes)	Pounds	2204.62
	Kilograms	1000
	Long tons	0.984206
	Short tons	1.10231
Watts	British thermal units (Btu) per hour	3.415
	Horsepower	0.00134
Yards	Inches	36
	Feet	3
	Miles	0.0005681
	Centimeters	91.44
	Meters	0.9144

Periodic Table

Actinium — Ac
Aluminum — Al
Americium — Am
Antimony — Sb
Argon — Ar
Arsenic — As
Astatine — At
Barium — Ba
Berkelium — Bk
Beryllium — Be
Bismuth — Bi
Bohrium — Bh
Boron — B
Bromine — Br
Cadmium — Cd
Calcium — Ca
Californium — Cf
Carbon — C
Cerium — Ce
Cesium — Cs
Chlorine — Cl
Chromium — Cr
Cobalt — Co
Copper — Cu
Curium — Cm
Dubnium — Db
Dysprosium — Dy
Einsteinium — Es
Erbium — Er
Europium — Eu
Fermium — Fm

Key:
- 23 — Atomic number
- V — Symbol
- 50.942 — Atomic mass
- Metals
- Metalloids
- Nonmetals

Groups

Period	1	2	3	4	5	6	7	8	9	10	11	12	13	14	15	16	17	18
1	1 H 1.0079																	2 He 4.0026
2	3 Li 6.941	4 Be 9.0122											5 B 10.811	6 C 12.011	7 N 14.007	8 O 15.999	9 F 18.998	10 Ne 20.180
3	11 Na 22.990	12 Mg 24.305											13 Al 26.982	14 Si 28.086	15 P 30.974	16 S 32.066	17 Cl 35.453	18 Ar 39.948
4	19 K 39.098	20 Ca 40.078	21 Sc 44.956	22 Ti 47.867	23 V 50.942	24 Cr 51.996	25 Mn 54.938	26 Fe 55.845	27 Co 58.933	28 Ni 58.693	29 Cu 63.546	30 Zn 65.39	31 Ga 69.723	32 Ge 72.61	33 As 74.922	34 Se 78.96	35 Br 79.904	36 Kr 83.80
5	37 Rb 85.468	38 Sr 87.62	39 Y 88.906	40 Zr 91.224	41 Nb 92.906	42 Mo 95.94	43 Tc [97.907]	44 Ru 101.07	45 Rh 102.91	46 Pd 106.42	47 Ag 107.87	48 Cd 112.41	49 In 114.82	50 Sn 118.71	51 Sb 121.76	52 Te 127.60	53 I 126.90	54 Xe 131.29
6	55 Cs 132.91	56 Ba 137.33	57-70 *	71 Lu 174.97	72 Hf 178.49	73 Ta 180.95	74 W 183.84	75 Re 186.21	76 Os 190.23	77 Ir 192.22	78 Pt 195.08	79 Au 196.97	80 Hg 200.59	81 Tl 204.38	82 Pb 207.2	83 Bi 208.98	84 Po [208.98]	85 At [209.99]	86 Rn [222.02]
7	87 Fr [223.02]	88 Ra [226.03]	89-102 †	103 Lr [262.11]	104 Rf [263.11]	105 Db [262.11]	106 Sg [266.12]	107 Bh [264.12]	108 Hs [269.13]	109 Mt [268.14]	110 Uun [271.15]	111 Uuu [272.15]	112 Uub [277]		114 Uuq [285]		116 Uuh [289]		118 Uuo [293]

*	57 La 138.91	58 Ce 140.12	59 Pr 140.91	60 Nd 144.24	61 Pm [144.91]	62 Sm 150.36	63 Eu 151.96	64 Gd 157.25	65 Tb 158.93	66 Dy 162.50	67 Ho 164.93	68 Er 167.26	69 Tm 168.93	70 Yb 173.04
†	89 Ac 227.03	90 Th 232.04	91 Pa 231.04	92 U 238.03	93 Np [237.05]	94 Pu [244.06]	95 Am [243.06]	96 Cm [247.07]	97 Bk [247.07]	98 Cf [251.08]	99 Es [252.08]	100 Fm [257.10]	101 Md [258.10]	102 No [259.10]

Fluorine — F
Francium — Fr
Gadolinium — Gd
Gallium — Ga
Germanium — Ge
Gold — Au
Hafnium — Hf
Hassium — Hs
Helium — He
Holmium — Ho
Hydrogen — H
Indium — In

Iodine — I
Iridium — Ir
Iron — Fe
Krypton — Kr
Lanthanum — La
Lawrencium — Lr
Lead — Pb
Lithium — Li
Lutetium — Lu
Magnesium — Mg
Manganese — Mn
Meitnerium — Mt

Mendelevium — Md
Mercury — Hg
Molybdenum — Mo
Neodymium — Nd
Neon — Ne
Neptunium — Np
Nickel — Ni
Niobium — Nb
Nitrogen — N
Nobelium — No
Osmium — Os
Oxygen — O

Palladium — Pd
Phosphorus — P
Platinum — Pt
Plutonium — Pu
Polonium — Po
Potassium — K
Praseodymium — Pr
Promethium — Pm
Protactinium — Pa
Radium — Ra
Radon — Rn
Rhenium — Re

Rhodium — Rh
Rubidium — Rb
Ruthenium — Ru
Rutherfordium — Rf
Samarium — Sm
Scandium — Sc
Seaborgium — Sg
Selenium — Se
Silicon — Si
Silver — Ag
Sodium — Na
Strontium — Sr

Sulfur — S
Tantalum — Ta
Technetium — Tc
Tellurium — Te
Terbium — Tb
Thallium — Tl
Thorium — Th
Thulium — Tm
Titanium — Ti
Tin — Sn
Tungsten — W
Ununbium — Uub

Ununhexium — Uuh
Ununnilium — Uun
Ununoctium — Uuo
Ununquadium — Uuq
Unununium — Uuu
Uranium — U
Vanadium — V
Xenon — Xe
Ytterbium — Yb
Yttrium — Y
Zinc — Zn
Zirconium — Zr

SI Prefixes

Multiple	Prefix	Symbol	Example
1,000,000,000,000,000,000 (10^{18})	exa-	E	Eg (exagram)
1,000,000,000,000,000 (10^{15})	peta-	P	PJ (petajoule)
1,000,000,000,000 (10^{12})	tera-	T	TV (teravolt)
1,000,000,000 (10^{9})	giga-	G	GW (gigawatt)
1,000,000 (10^{6})	mega-	M	MHz (megahertz)
1,000 (10^{3})	kilo-	k	kg (kilogram)
100 (10^{2})	hecto-	h	hm (hectometer)
10	deca-	da-	daN (decanewton)
1/10 (10^{-1})	deci-	d	dC (decicoulomb)
1/100 (10^{-2})	centi-	c	cm (centimeter)
1/1,000 (10^{-3})	milli-	m	mA (milliampere)
1/1,000,000 (10^{-6})	micro-	µ	µF (microfarad)
1/1,000,000,000 (10^{-9})	nano-	n	nm (nanometer)
1/1,000,000,000,000 (10^{-12})	pico-	p	ps (picosecond)
1/1,000,000,000,000,000 (10^{-15})	femto-	f	frad (femtoradian)
1/1,000,000,000,000,000,000 (10^{-18})	atto-	a	aT (attotesla)

Science Time Line

2,500,000 B.C.E.
Earliest known stone tools.

41,000 B.C.E.
Earliest mine: iron ore (used as pigments) in Swaziland.

4000–3500 B.C.E.
Copper alloy and smelting of gold and silver known by the Egyptians and Sumerians. Bamboo rafts used in China. Canals constructed in Iraq. Earliest known security lock.

3500–3000 B.C.E.
Potter's wheel, wheeled vehicles, and linen in use. Egyptians use boats with sails. First known written language (Sumerian). Earliest known dam is constructed in Jordan. Construction of Stonehenge is begun.

3000–2500 B.C.E.
Weaving loom used in Europe. Egypt adopts a 365-day calendar. First iron objects forged. Great Pyramid of Giza built (ca. 2600 B.C.E). Chinese cultivate silkworms and weave silk.

2500–2000 B.C.E
Egyptians using papyrus. First form of plow used in Egypt. Bow and arrow used in warfare.

2000–1500 B.C.E.
Mercury used in Egypt. Contraceptives in use in Egypt. Earliest known metal water pipes in Egypt. Crete adopts a decimal counting system. The chariot becomes an effective battle vehicle.

1500–1000 B.C.E.
Iron Age in Syria and Palestine. First Chinese dictionary. Phoenicians import tin from England.

1000–900 B.C.E.
Natural fabric dyes used in Mediterranean area. Underground water system built in Jerusalem.

900–800 B.C.E.
Iron and steel production in Indo-Caucasian culture. Earliest known printed book.

800–700 B.C.E.
Hand cranks used by Etruscans. Spoked wheels and horseshoes in use in Europe.

700–600 B.C.E.
Assyrians devise water clocks. Phoenicians introduce the first war galleys. Earliest astronomical observatory in Korea. Lydia (ancient land of western Asia minor) mints first coinage.

600–500 B.C.E.
Ore smelting and casting, water level, lock and key, and turning lathe credited to Theodorus of Samos. Persian Empire establishes postal service. Darius the Great (Persia) lays pontoon bridges across the Bosphorus and Danube.

500–400 B.C.E.
Cataract operations performed by Indian surgeon Susrata (ca. 500 B.C.E.). Democritus of Abdera proposes an atomic theory of the Universe.

400–300 B.C.E.
Siege catapults first in use. In *Organon*, Aristotle explains logical reasoning. Lathe in use in Egypt.

300–250 B.C.E.
The first lighthouse, the Pharos of Alexandria, is built. Greek prisoners of war introduce medicine to Romans.

250–200 B.C.E.
Parchment introduced at Pergamum. Eratosthenes of Alexandria makes close estimate of Earth's circumference. Chinese weights and measures standardized. Great Wall of China built. Ctesibus of Alexandria invents the force pump.

200–150 B.C.E.
Hipparchus of Nicaea invents trigonometry. Riding stirrups appear in India.

150–100 B.C.E.
Crates of Mallus makes a globe representing Earth. Mathematician Heron founds first college of technology at Alexandria (ca. 105 B.C.E.).

100–50 B.C.E.
Pompey the Great's trainer, Atticus of Naples, invents the medicine ball. Water mills in use in the Roman empire.

50–2 B.C.E.
Julian calendar introduces leap year.

1–100 C.E.
First reference to diamonds (ca. 16). Cranes first used in Greco–Roman world. Pliny reports the use of glass mirrors in the Roman world.

100–200
Chang Hêng (China) makes a seismometer. Galen uses plant juices as medicine (ca. 190). First wheelbarrow developed in China (ca. 200).

250–300
Compass probably first used in China. Cog wheel, lever, pulley, screw, and wedge described by Pappus of Alexandria.

300–350
Grand Canal of China begun with 120-mile (193 km) stretch: eventually finished between 1280 and 1300 to a length of 1,100 miles (1,700 km).

500–600
First paddle-wheel boats with animal drive. Book printing in China.

620
Porcelain produced in China.

650–750
Earliest known windmills in Persia (644). First printed newspaper appears in Beijing (748).

750–850
Pictorial book printing in Japan (765). Persian scientist and mathematician Muhammed Ibn-Musaal-Kwarazmi writes book on equations and invents the term *algebra* (810).

900–950
Paper manufacturing in Cairo. Persian doctor Abu-Bakr Muhammed Ibn-Zakariya al-Razi describes plague, consumption, smallpox, and rabies.

950–1000
Persian astronomer Abd-al-Rahman Al Sufi provides the first documented observation of a star system outside our galaxy (963). Arabic numerals brought to Europe (975). Chinese perfect gunpowder (1000).

1000–1200
Water-driven mechanical clock constructed in Beijing (1090). Chinese use explosives in warfare (1151). Trebuchet super-heavy siege stonethrower comes into use (1200).

1250–1300
Goose quill used for writing (1250). Earliest record of human dissection (1275).

1300–1350
First reference to eyeglasses (1303). Cannon used at Siege of Metz (1324). Invention of the sawmill (1328). First scientific weather forecast, by William Merlee of Oxford, England (1337).

1400–1450
Dutch fishermen first to use drift nets (1416). Coiled springs replace weights in clocks (1430).

1450–1500
Johannes Gutenberg (Germany) invents printing with movable metal type (1452). Leonardo da Vinci (Italy) draws a parachute (1480) and observes capillary action (1490). Earliest surviving terrestrial globe made in Nuremberg by geographer Martin Behaim (Germany) (1492).

1500–1550
Leonardo da Vinci (Italy) designs horizontal water wheel (water turbine) (1510). Spinning wheel in general use in Europe. Nicholas Copernicus (Poland) proposes that Earth and other planets move around the Sun (1530). Gerardus Mercator (Flanders, now Belgium) discovers Earth's magnetic poles (1546).

1550–1600
Georgius Agricola (Germany) publishes a scientific text on mining and metallurgy, *De Re Metallica* (1556). Gerardus Mercator (Flanders, now Belgium) designs a flat world map that represents

the spherical shape of Earth (the Mercator projection, 1569). Galileo (Italy) invents the thermometer (1593). Sir John Harington (England) invents a flush toilet (1596).

1601–1620

Johannes Kepler (Germany) devises the three laws of planetary motion. Hans Lippershey (Germany) invents the telescope (1608).

1621–1630

Willebrord Snell (Holland) discovers the law of light refraction (Snell's law, 1621). William Harvey (England) publishes his discovery of the circulation of the blood (1628).

1641–1650

Evangelista Torricelli (Italy) invents the barometer (1643). Athanasius Kircher (Germany) publishes a book showing the design for a projection lantern (magic lantern) (1646). Blaise Pascal (France) devises the basic laws of hydraulic systems (Pascal's principle, 1647).

1651–1660

Christiaan Huygens (Holland) invents the pendulum clock (1656). Robert Hooke (England) invents the balance spring for watches (1658) and discovers the law of elasticity (1660).

1661–1670

Sir Isaac Newton (England) devises the first calculus system (1660s). Robert Boyle (Ireland) coins the word *element* for a simple pure substance (1661) and discovers that the volume and pressure of a gas are inversely proportional (Boyle's law, 1662). Robert Hooke (England) discovers plant cells (1665). Francesco Grimaldi (Italy) publishes a paper on the diffraction of light (1665).

1671–1680

Anton van Leeuwenhoek (Holland) discovers microorganisms (1670s). Sir Isaac Newton (England) invents the reflecting telescope (1671). Christiaan Huygens (Holland) discovers the polarization of light and proposes the wave theory of light (1678).

1681–1700

Sir Isaac Newton (England) proposes three laws of motion and a law of gravitation (1687). Plate glass is made for the first time (1688). Denis Papin (France) designs a steam piston engine (1690). Thomas Savery (England) invents the first practical steam engine (1698).

1701–1710

Charles Townshend (England) devises the four-field crop rotation system (the Norfolk system, 1700s). Sir Isaac Newton (England) demonstrates that white light is made up of different colors (1704). Thomas Newcomen (England) designs the first steam engine with a separate boiler (1705).

1711–1730

Gabriel Daniel Fahrenheit (Germany) invents the first accurate mercury thermometer (1714). James Puckle (England) invents the first machine gun (1718). Gabriel Daniel Fahrenheit (Germany) devises the Fahrenheit temperature scale (1724).

1731–1740

John Kay (England) invents the flying shuttle for textile manufacture (1733). John Harrison (England) invents the first marine chronometer for determining longitude (1735). Daniel Bernoulli (Holland) discovers the principle of fluid flow (Bernoulli's principle, 1738).

1741–1750

Anders Celsius (Sweden) devises the original Celsius, or centigrade, temperature scale (1742). Ewald Jurgen von Kleist (Germany) invents the electric capacitor (1745).

1751–1770

Benjamin Franklin (United States) invents the lightning conductor (1753). Henry Cavendish (England) discovers that hydrogen is less dense than air. (1766). Nicolas Gugnot (France) constructs the first steam carriage for use on roads (1769). James Watt (Britain) patents his design for a more efficient steam engine (1769).

1771–1780

Joseph Priestley (Britain) identifies oxygen. David Bushnell (United States) builds the first submarine (1776). Antoine Lavoisier (France) discovers that combustion occurs as a result of reactions with oxygen in air (1777). Abraham Darby III (Britain) constructs the first cast-iron bridge (1779).

1783

Joseph and Jacques Montgolfier (France) invent the first passenger-carrying hot-air balloon. Jacques-Alexandre-César Charles (France) invents the hydrogen balloon.

1784

Joseph Bramah (Britain) designs an unpickable lock. Henry Shrapnel (Britain) invents a shell with an inner core of lead shot designed to explode over the enemy, the shrapnel shell. Pierre Aimé Argand (Switzerland) invents the first efficient oil lamp, the Argand burner. Henry Cavendish (England) determines the composition of water.

1787

John Fitch (United States) builds the first successful steam-powered boat. Jacques-Alexandre-César Charles (France) discovers that under constant pressure the volume of a gas is directly proportional to its temperature (Charles's law).

1788

James Watt (Britain) invents a centrifugal governor for steam engines.

1789

Antoine Lavoisier (France) devises the first list of chemical elements. First steam-driven cotton factory, at Manchester, England. Antoine Jussieu (France) introduces modern plant classification in his book *Genera plantarum*. Oliver Evans (United States) patents a design for a high-pressure steam engine (1790).

1791–1795

William Murdock (Scotland) devises a method of making, purifying, and storing coal gas (1790s). Eli Whitney (United States) invents the cotton gin and the milling machine (1793). Joseph Bramah (Britain) invents the hydraulic press (1795).

1796–1800

J. T. Lowitz (Russia) prepares pure ethyl alcohol. Edward Jenner (Britain) develops the first successful vaccine (for smallpox). Alois Senefelder (Germany) invents lithography (1798). Alessandro Volta (Italy) invents the first electrical battery, the voltaic pile (1800).

1801–1810

Thomas Young (Britain) revives the wave theory of light and devises the trichromatic (three-color) theory of vision. Richard Trevithick (Britain) designs and constructs the first steam-driven railroad locomotive (1804). Joseph-Marie Jacquard (France) invents a loom that uses a system of punched cards to control the weaving pattern (1805).

1811–1820

Friedrich Mohs (Germany) devises the scale of mineral hardness (the Mohs's scale, 1812). Sir Humphry Davy (Britain) invents a safety lamp for miners. Robert Stirling (Britain) invents the gas engine (the Stirling engine, 1816). Hans Christian Oersted (Denmark) demonstrates that an electric current produces a magnetic effect (1819). René Théophile Hyacinthe Laënnec (France) invents the stethoscope (1819).

1821–1825

Charles Babbage (Britain) makes early attempts to construct mechanical computers (1820s). Sir Michael Faraday (Britain) produces an early electric motor (1821). Thomas Johann Seebeck (Estonia) discovers the thermoelectric effect (the Seebeck effect, 1822). André-Marie Ampère (France) establishes the laws of electrodynamics (1822). George Stephenson (Britain) builds the first public passenger steam railroad locomotive (1825). Hans Christian Oersted (Denmark) uses electrolysis to isolate aluminum from its ore (1825).

1826–1830

Joseph Nicéphore Niepce (France) produces the earliest surviving photograph (1826). Georg Simon Ohm (Germany) discovers that the electrical current in a resistor is directly proportional to the voltage and inversely proportional to the resistance (Ohm's law, 1827). Joseph Henry (United States) discovers electromagnetic induction (1830) independently of Faraday.

1831–1835

Sir Michael Faraday (Britain) discovers electromagnetic induction independently of Henry (1831) and produces the basic laws of electrolysis (Faraday's laws of electrolysis, 1833). Samuel Colt

(United States) invents the modern revolver (1830s). Thomas Davenport (United States) invents the electric streetcar (1834). Samuel Finley Breeze Morse (United States) invents the electric telegraph (1835).

1836–1840

Sir Francis Pettit Smith (Britain) and John Ericsson (Sweden) invent independently the screw propeller (1836). Louis Jacques Mandé Daguerre (France) invents the first useful photographic process (the daguerreotype process, 1837). William Henry Fox Talbot (Britain) invents negative–positive photography (1839). Charles Goodyear (United States) invents the vulcanization process for strengthening rubber.

1841–1845

Christian Johann Doppler (Austria) discovers the frequency change of a wave due to the relative motion between its source and the observer, the Doppler effect. Ada Lovelace (Britain) predicts the use of computers for nonmathematical functions and invents possibly the first computer program (1845).

1846–1850

William Thomas Morton (United States) pioneers the use of ether as an anesthetic (1846). William Thomson (Lord Kelvin) (Britain) devises the absolute temperature scale; the Kelvin scale (1848). Armand-Hippolyte-Louis Fizeau (France) makes the first accurate measurement of the speed of light (1849). Sir George Cayley (Britain) designs and constructs the first passenger-carrying glider (1849). Rudolf Clausius (Germany) formulates the Second Law of Thermodynamics and kinetic theory of gases (1850).

1851–1855

William Kelly (United States) invents a process of making steel, independently of Sir Henry Bessemer (1850s). Elisha Graves Otis (United States) invents an automatic safety device for elevators (1853). Alexander Parkes (Britain) discovers cellulose nitrate; parkensine (1855).

1856–1860

Sir Henry Bessemer (Britain) invents a process of making steel, the Bessemer process (1856), independently of William Kelly. Jean-Joseph Étienne Lenoir (Belgium) invents the first practical internal combustion engine (1860). Louis Pasteur (France) establishes that microorganisms are responsible for fermentation.

1861

Ernest Solvay (Belgium) invents a process for producing sodium carbonate; the Solvay process.

1862

Alphonse Eugène Beau de Rochas (France) patents the four-stroke internal combustion engine. Alfred Bernhard Nobel (Sweden) invents the mercury fulminate detonator for nitroglycerine. Julius Sachs (Germany) demonstrates that starch is produced by photosynthesis.

1863

Pierre Émile Martin (France) invents the open-hearth process for the production of steel (the Siemens-Martin process).

1864

James Clerk Maxwell (Britain) formulates the fundamental equations of electromagnetism. Louis Pasteur (France) demonstrates that microorganisms in foods such as wine and milk are destroyed by heating (pasteurization).

1865

Baron Joseph Lister (Britain) introduces the use of antiseptic techniques in surgery. Atlantic telegraph cable is completed. Thaddeus Lowe (United States) invents the ice machine.

1866

Alfred Bernhard Nobel (Sweden) invents dynamite. Georges Leclanché (France) invents the forerunner of the dry-cell battery (the Leclanché cell). Robert Whitehead (Britain) invents underwater torpedo.

1870–1875

Andrew Smith Hallidie (Britain) invents the cable car (1870s). Alfred Bernhard Nobel (Sweden) invents blasting gelatin, gelignite (1875).

1876

Alexander Graham Bell (Britain) invents the telephone. Thomas Alva Edison (United States) establishes the first industrial research laboratory. Samuel Plimsoll (Britain) invents the load-line on ships (the Plimsoll mark).

1877

Thomas Alva Edison (United States) invents the phonograph. In the United States, the first public telephones are installed and used.

1878

Sir Joseph Wilson Swan (Britain) invents a carbon-filament lightbulb, independently of Edison. Carl Gustaf Patrik de Laval (Sweden) invents the first modern centrifuge.

1879

Thomas Alva Edison (United States) invents a carbon-filament lightbulb, independently of Swan. Lars Nilson (Sweden) discovers element scandium.

1880

Pierre Curie (France) discovers the piezoelectric effect. Louis Pasteur (France) discovers a chicken cholera vaccine. Charles Laveran (France) discovers parasite *Plasmodium*, which causes malaria.

1882

Robert Koch (Germany) discovers the microorganisms that cause tuberculosis. Thomas Alva Edison (United States) builds the first hydroelectric plant, at Appleton, Wisconsin.

1883

Robert Koch (Germany) discovers the microorganisms that cause cholera. Thomas Alva Edison (United States) discovers thermionic emission (the Edison Effect). Nikola Tesla (Serbia/United States) constructs the first induction motor.

1884

Sir Charles Algernon Parsons (Britain) invents the modern steam turbine. Svante August Arrhenius (Sweden) discovers electrolytic dissociation.

1885

Carl Benz (Germany) designs and builds the first practical automobile for use by the public. Louis Pasteur (France) devises rabies vaccine. Gottlieb Daimler (Germany) builds the first motorcycle. Hiram Stevens Maxim (United States) demonstrates his fully automatic belt-fed machine gun.

1886

Paul Louis Toussaint Héroult (France) and Charles M. Hall (United States) independently invent an electrolytic process (the Hall-Héroult process) for extracting aluminum from bauxite.

1887

William Holabird and Martin Roche (United States) design the first steel-frame skyscraper. Heinrich Rudolph Hertz (Germany) transmits and receives radio waves for the first time.

1888

John Boyd Dunlop (Britain) invents the pneumatic tire. George Eastman (United States) perfects the Kodak box camera.

1889

Gottlieb Daimler (Germany) designs and builds one of the earliest gasoline-powered motor cars. Alexandre Gustave Eiffel (France) constructs the Eiffel Tower.

1890

Rubber gloves used for the first time in surgery, at Johns Hopkins Hospital, Baltimore.

1891

Edward Goodrich Acheson (United States) develops a method for synthesizing Carborundum (silicon carbide). First automatic telephone exchange. Rudolf Christian Karl Diesel (Germany) patents a design for a compression-ignition engine (the diesel engine).

1892

Nikola Tesla (Serbia/United States) invents the Tesla coil and predicts the advent of the radio.

1895

Wilhelm Konrad Röntgen (Germany) discovers X rays. Guglielmo Marconi (Italy) invents radio telegraphy with experiments near Bologna. Louis and Auguste Lumière (France) invent the cinématographe, the first successful film projector.

1896

Antoine Henri Becquerel (France) discovers radioactivity. George Washington Carver (United States) begins the process of revolutionizing farm-

ing in the southern states by developing commercial uses for agricultural crops such as peanuts. Ernest Rutherford (New Zealand) discovers the emission of alpha and beta particles during radioactive decay. Guglielmo Marconi (Italy) invents a successful system of radio telegraphy. Scipione Riva-Rocci (Italy) invents the sphygmomanometer.

1897

Sir Joseph John Thomson (Britain) discovers the electron. Ferdinand Braun (Germany) develops the cathode-ray tube.

1898

Marie Curie (Poland/France) and Pierre Curie (France) discover the radioactive elements radium and polonium.

1900

Max Karl Ernst Ludwig Planck (Germany) devises quantum theory. Ernest Rutherford (New Zealand) discovers the emission of gamma rays during radioactive decay.

1901

Karl Landsteiner (Austria) discovers human blood groups.

1902

Willis Haviland Carrier (United States) invents air conditioning.

1903

Wilbur and Orville Wright (United States) design, construct, and fly the first powered airplane, the Wright *Flyer*.

1904

Sir John Ambrose Fleming (Britain) invents the diode. The first ultraviolet lamps are made. First telegraphic transmission of photographs, by Arthur Korn (Germany).

1905

Albert Einstein (Germany) publishes a paper explaining the photoelectric effect and formulates the special theory of relativity.

1906

Lee De Forest (United States) invents the triode valve amplifier. Reginald Aubrey Fessenden (United States) broadcasts first voice-and-music radio program. Charles Franklin Kettering (United States) invents the electric cash register.

1907

Bertram Borden Boltwood (United States) discovers ionium, a radioactive isotope of thorium, and revolutionizes geology by introducing radioactive decay as a method of dating rocks and establishing the age of Earth.

1908

Fritz Haber (Germany) discovers how to manufacture ammonia from nitrogen and hydrogen (the Haber process). Hans Geiger (Germany) invents a device for detecting radiation (the Geiger counter).

1909

Paul Ehrlich (Germany) discovers salvarsan, a cure for syphilis. Louis Blériot (France) crosses English Channel by airplane. Leo H. Baekeland (Belgium) invents the first synthetic plastic (Bakelite).

1910

Georges Claude (France) invents neon lighting. Carl Bosch (Germany) develops the synthesis of ammonia on an industrial scale (the Haber-Bosch process).

1911

Heike Kamerlingh Onnes (Holland) discovers superconductivity. Ernest Rutherford (New Zealand) discovers the atomic nucleus.

1913

Neils Bohr (Denmark) propounds the orbiting electron theory of atomic structure. Irving Langmuir (United States) invents a gas-filled, tungsten-filament lightbulb.

1916

Albert Einstein (Germany) devises the general theory of relativity. Blood for transfusion is refrigerated. F. W. Mott (Britain) suggests theory of shell shock.

1917

Allied Anti-Submarine Detection Investigation Committee produces prototype asdic, or sonar.

1920

Ernest Rutherford (New Zealand) discovers the proton and predicts the existence of the neutron.

1921

Sir Frederick Grant Banting (Canada) and Charles Herbert Best (United States) discover the hormone insulin and administer it to diabetic patients.

1924

Hans Berger (Germany) records brain waves for the first time. Clarence Birdseye (United States) invents a food-freezing process for use in retailing. John Logie Baird (Britain) invents mechanical television.

1925

George L. McCarthy patents a practical microfilm machine, the Checkograph.

1926

Robert Hutchings Goddard (United States) invents the first successful liquid-fuel rocket. Erwin Schrödinger (Austria) introduces wave mechanics.

1927

Werner Heisenberg (Germany) introduces the uncertainty principle of quantum physics.

1928

Sir Alexander Fleming (Britain) discovers the antibiotic penicillin. Hans Geiger (Germany) and Walther Müller (Germany) construct an improved Geiger counter (the Geiger-Müller tube).

1929

Hans Berger (Germany) invents the electro-encephalograph (EEG). Edwin Hubble (United States) establishes that the Universe is in a state of expansion.

1930

Ernest O. Lawrence (United States) invents the cyclotron particle accelerator. Clyde W. Tombaugh (United States) discovers the planet Pluto. Sir Frank Whittle (Britain) invents the turbojet engine.

1931

Ernst Ruska (Germany) invents the electron microscope. Julius A. Nieuwland (United States) devises a process for producing synthetic rubber (neoprene). Harold C. Urey (United States) discovers heavy hydrogen (deuterium).

1932

Sir James Chadwick (Britain) discovers the neutron. Sir John Douglas Cockcroft (Britain) and Ernest Thomas Sinton Walton (Ireland) invent the electrostatic accelerator. Francis Bacon (Britain) develops the first practical fuel cell.

1934

Ernest Rutherford (New Zealand) creates tritium in the first nuclear fusion reaction. Enrico Fermi (Italy) produces radioisotopes via neutron bombardment.

1935

Sir Robert Alexander Watson-Watt (Britain) invents and develops radar. Wallace Hume Carothers (United States) invents nylon.

1936

German dirigible *Hindenburg* makes first transatlantic flight. Inge Lehmann (Denmark) postulates existence of Earth's solid inner core by seismology.

1937

Alan Mathison Turing (Britain) develops the concept of a universal computing machine (the Turing Machine), forerunner of the digital computer.

1938

Chester F. Carlson (United States) invents xerography. Lazlo Biro (Hungary) invents the first practical ballpoint pen.

1939

Otto Hahn (Germany), Lise Meitner (Austria), and Fritz Strassmann (Germany) discover nuclear fission. German Heinkel HE178 is the world's first jet aircraft to fly.

1941

Konrad Zuse (Germany) invents the first general-purpose calculator. Rex Whinfield (Britain) and James Dickson (Britain) invent polyester.

1942

Enrico Fermi (Italy) produces the first self-sustaining nuclear fission chain reaction at the University of Chicago. Igor Ivanovich Sikorsky

(Ukraine/United States) invents the first practical helicopter, the VS-316A.

1943

Willem Johan Kolff (Netherlands) develops the first kidney dialysis machine. Jacques-Yves Cousteau (France) invents the aqualung with Émile Gagnan.

1945

J. Robert Oppenheimer and colleagues (United States) invent the atomic bomb.

1947

Dennis Gabor (Hungary/Britain) invents holography. Walter Houser Brattain (United States), John Bardeen (United States), and William Bradford Shockley (United States) invent the transistor. Willard Frank Libby (United States) develops the process of radiocarbon dating.

1948

Claude Elwood Shannon (United States) devises a theory of communication technology (information theory). Peter Goldmark (United States) invents the long-playing record.

1950

Alan Mathison Turing (Britain) devises a test of a computer's capacity for "thought" (the Turing test).

1951

Eric Roberts Laithwaite (Britain) develops the first maglev train. Electric power produced from atomic energy at Arcon, Idaho.

1952

William Bradford Shockley (United States) proposes the field-effect transistor (FET). Donald A. Glaser (United States) invents the bubble chamber.

1953

John H. Gibbon Jr. (United States) invents the heart-lung machine. Charles Hard Townes (United States) invents the maser around the same time that it is also invented by the team of Nikolay Gennadiyevich Basov (Russia) and Alexsandr Mikhailovich Prokhorov (Russia). Francis Crick (Britain) and James Watson (United States) discover the helical structure of DNA.

1954

Hyman George Rickover (Russia/United States) heads the team that develops the first nuclear submarine, the *Nautilus*.

1956

Felix Wankel (Germany) invents the rotary engine. Clyde Cowan (United States) and Frederick Reines (United States) discover the neutrino, an elementary particle. The video recorder is invented.

1957

John Bardeen (United States), Leon Niels Cooper (United States), and John Robert Schrieffer (United States) develop the BCS (Bardeen, Cooper, Schrieffer) theory of superconductivity. *Sputnik I*, the first orbiting satellite, is launched.

1958

The first modem is invented. Jack St. Clair Kilby (United States) invents the integrated circuit, independently of Robert Noyce.

1959

Robert Noyce (United States) invents the integrated circuit, independently of Jack St. Clair Kilby. Richard Feynman (United States) develops the theory of quantum electrodynamics (QED). Sir Christopher Cockerell (Britain) builds the first practical hovercraft.

1961

Edward Norton Lorenz (United States) discovers that chaos theory applies in weather systems. Theodore Maiman (United States) develops the laser. Yuri Gagarin (USSR) is first man in space and spends 89 minutes orbiting Earth in *Vostok 1*. Alan Shephard makes first U.S. suborbital rocket flight; John Glenn orbits Earth in 1962.

1963

Edward Norton Lorenz (United States) describes the "butterfly effect." The compact cassette tape recorder is introduced by Phillips.

1964

Murray Gell-Mann (United States) and George Zweig (United States) propose independently a theory of subatomic particles. Gell-Mann names these particles "quarks."

1965

Insulin is synthesized. Soviet cosmonaut Alexei A. Leonov makes first space walk. *Mariner 4* space probe flies by Mars.

1967

Christiaan Neethling Barnard (South Africa) performs the first human heart transplant. Jocelyn Bell (Britain) and Antony Hewish (Britain) discover pulsars, collapsed neutron stars.

1969

U.S. astronauts make the first crewed Moon landing. George Smith (United States) and William Boyle (United States) invent the charge-coupled device at Bell Laboratories. An early form of the Internet, ARPANET, is established.

1971

Intel produces the first microprocessor, the 4004.

1974

The Internet's transmission control protocol (TCP) and Internet protocol (IP) are devised.

1976

First Concorde supersonic airliner passenger flight. The lander module of the space probe *Viking 1* lands successfully on Mars.

1977

The genetic code of the human growth hormone is determined. Raymond Damadian (United States) invents magnetic resonance imaging (MRI).

1978

The first global positioning satellite, *GPS Block I*, is launched. Birth of the first "test tube" baby.

1979

Seymour Cray (United States) invents the supercomputer. Cellular phone invented.

1981

John F. Burke (United States) and Ionnis V. Yannas (United States) develop artificial skin to treat burns. Heinrich Rohrer (Switzerland) and Gerd Binnig (Switzerland) invent the scanning tunneling microscope. The first flight of the space shuttle takes place.

1982

Introduction of the audio compact disc (CD).

1983

Kary Mullis (United States) invents the polymerase chain reaction (PCR) for amplifying minute amounts of DNA. Luc Montagnier (France) identifies the human immunodeficiency virus (HIV), the virus responsible for AIDS.

1984

First successful cloning of a mammal, a sheep, with cells taken from an early post-fertilization stage of development, a process known as "twinning."

1985

Alec Jeffreys (Britain) devises genetic fingerprinting. The computer program Windows is released by Microsoft.

1986

Alex Müller (Switzerland) and Georg Bednorz (Germany) create a ceramic compound that superconducts at 30 K. Introduction of the antidepressive drug Prozac.

1989

Development of the World Wide Web begun by Tim Berners-Lee (Britain) and colleagues at CERN, Switzerland.

1990

Hubble Space Telescope is launched.

1992

The first web browser is introduced.

1993

The Pentium processor is introduced.

1995

Top quark is discovered at Fermilab.

1996

Ian Wilmut (Britain) heads the team that produces the first successful clone from an adult mammal, Dolly the sheep. The digital versatile disc (DVD) is introduced.

2001

Rough draft of the human genome is completed.

GEOLOGICAL TIMESCALE

EON	ERA	PERIODS	EPOCHS	BEGINNING OF INTERVAL (millions of years)	LIFE FORMS
Phanerozoic	Cenozoic	Quaternary	Holocene	0.01	
			Pleistocene	1.8	First humans
		Tertiary	Pliocene	5	
			Miocene	23	First hominids
			Oligocene	38	
			Eocene	54	First grasses
			Paleocene	65	First large mammals and primitive primates
	Mesozoic	Cretaceous	Upper	98	Epoch ends with extinction of dinosaurs
			Lower	146	First flowering plants
		Jurassic		208	First birds and mammals
		Triassic		245	First dinosaurs
	Paleozoic	Permian		286	
		Carboniferous			
		Pennsylvanian		325	First reptiles
		Mississippian		360	First winged insects
		Devonian		410	First vascular plants and amphibians
		Silurian		440	First land plants and insects
		Ordovician		505	First corals
		Cambrian		544	Trilobites and earliest fish
Proterozoic	Precambrian			2,500	First soft-bodied invertebrates and colonial algae
Archeozoic				4,500	First life forms appear: earliest algae and primitive bacteria

Picture Credits

Volume 1

Title Page: **Alias Wave Front:** Columbia Pictures
3M (UK) Plc.: 18t; **Aerospace Plc.:** 72; **Airship Industries:** 91t; **Albright & Wilson Ltd.:** 23; **Alias Wave Front:** Columbia Pictures 136, 139; **Allsport:** Terry Duffy 39t; **Apis:** 50; **Aviation Authority:** 95; **BACO:** 108; **David Baker:** 43; **Ed Baxter:** 106; **Bell Aerospace:** 80b; **BNF Metals:** 102; **Babcock Power Ltd.:** 107; **Bob Godfrey Films:** Grange Calverly 137; **Paul Brierley:** 29b, 105, 129; **British Aerospace Plc.:** 66, 117b; **British Aircraft Corporation:** 38; **British Hovercraft Corp.:** 80m, 81l, 111b; **British Oxygen Co. Ltd.:** 131; **British Telecom International:** 142t; **Cable & Wireless Plc.:** 127, 141, 142b; **Cameron Iron Works:** 18b; **Case IH:** Bozell & Jacobs 49; **Central Office of Information:** 123t; **Ciba-Geigy:** 29t, 30m, 30t; **Colorific!:** John Olson/ Life 1969, Time Inc. 44; **Corbis:** Macduff Everton 28, Robert Holmes 59, Kit Materson 93, Stephanie Maze 62, Reuters 83, Ted Spiegel 25, John Wilkinson 61; **Daily Telegraph Colour Library:** Space Frontiers Ltd. 39m, 85b; **John Elard:** 26, 6; **English Abrasives:** 111t; **Fenamec Ltd.:** 90; **Ford Motor Company:** 46; **Genetics Co. Ltd.:** 53b; **International Aeradio:** 89t; **Jim Marshall (UK) Ltd.:** 126b, 126t; **Johnson Matthey Plc.:** 104; **David Kelly:** 101; **Lockheed:** 84; **Loctite (UK) Ltd.:** 32t; **Maglev-Railway Institute Systems Department:** 8t; **Michael Holford Library:** 15b; **MOD:** Sgt. R. Hudson 144; **Monsanto:** 53t; **NASA:** 85t, David Baker 65, 70, Dryden Research Center 73, Jet Propulsion Laboratory 4l, 33, Human Space Flight Center 5; **National College of Agricultural Engineering:** 51; **National Farmers Union:** 56, 57; **Neilson Hardell Ltd.:** 138; **NOAA:** Mohammed Al Momany, Aqaba, Jordan 14r; **Novosti Press Agency:** 81r; **Pearson Television Stills Library:** 140; **Photri:** 78; **Picturepoint:** 7; **PO Peter Holgate:** 122; **Rio Tinto Zinc:** 109, 110; **Robert Harding Associates:** 135, John Ross 76; **Rolls Royce Ltd.:** 15t, 89b; **Royal Ordance Factory:** 117t; **Dr. Royle:** Long Ashton Research Station 54t; **Science Museum:** Hoffman 77; **Science Photo Library:** Bob Edwards 134, Mauro Fermariello 112, Jim Gipe/AGSTOCK 45, 60, Peter Menzel 52, NASA 41; **Silsoe Research Inst.:** 55; **SNCF French Railways Ltd.:** 36, 37t; **Stevens Guitars:** 14l; **Sylvia Cordaiy Photo Library:** 58, Humphrey Evans 88; **The Distillers Company:** 97; **The Partially Sighted Society:** 19; **Toby Churchill Ltd.:** 21, 22; **TRH Pictures:** DOD 69, McDonnell Douglas 42; **Unicorn Industries:** 17; **University of Southampton:** 54b; **U.S. Navy:** 80t, 123b, 143; **Vaisala, Finland:** 130; **Visum:** George Fischer 113; **Wild Heerbrugg:** 34b, 34t; **ZEFA:** 87, 99, 100, 114.

Volume 2

Title Page: **NASA**
Airviews Ltd.: 159l, 159r; **Alan Hutchison Library:** 258, Felix Greene 241m; **Allsport:** 241t, Tony Duffy 162t; **Alltek Hospital Supplies Ltd.:** 282t; **Ann Ronan Picture Library:** 240; **Barden Co.:** 233b; **Barnaby's Picture Library:** 212t; **Berger Chemicals:** 149; **Bibliotheque Nationale:** 274r; **Blatchford:** 253t; **Boeing Aerospace:** 212b; **Paul Brierley:** 226, BP Research 233t; **Brinks Incorporated:** 168; **Bristol Composite Materials Engineering Ltd.:** 276b; **Celltech Ltd.:** James Holmes 266; **Central Office of Information:** 166, 275r, 276t; **CERN:** 150t, 151b, 183; **Chase Manhattan Bank:** 192b; **Colorific!:** 256, Alexander Tsiaras/Life Magazine 278b; **Corbis:** AFP 198, Dave Bartruff 237; Richard A. Cooke III 153, Richard T. Nowitz 245, Neal Preston 189, Rafael Roa 244, Joseph Sohm 229b; **Courage Central:** 235t; Courtesy of University of Glasgow: Galaxy Picture Library 180b; **Daily Telegraph Colour Library:** Space Frontiers Ltd. 229t; **Charles Day:** 282b; **Douglas Dickins:** 274t; **Dornier:** 174; **Dyson:** 172; **Ecoscene:** Joel Cress 259; **English Heritage Photo Library:** 156t; **European Colour Library:** Carlo Berilacqua 210; **Fiat Auto (UK) Ltd.:** Trevor Lawrence 228t; **Ford:** 201; **Forestry Commision:** 160t; **Galaxy Picture Library:** Robin Scagell 180bl; **Gallenkamp:** 214t; **General Motors Overseas Corp.:** 199; **Grass Valley:** 187; **Grundy:** Mike St. Maur Sheil 205; **Sonia Halliday:** 214b; **Nelson Hargreaves:** 202; **Image Bank:** Jeff Smith 20; **Imperial College London:** Dr. J. M. Squire 261t, 262t, 262b; **Intermed/J. E. Hanger & Co.:** 253c, 253b; **Janus Foundation:** 260; **J. E. Hanger & Co. Ltd.:** 255; **John Hillelson Agency:** John Guichard-Sygma 213, Howard Sochurek 279; **JVC (UK) Ltd.:** 188t; **Kobal Collection:** 273l, 273m, 273r; **Lightweight Body Armour Ltd.:** 163; **Lloyds Bank Plc.:** 192t; **Lucas Industries Ltd.:** 228b; **Andy Luckhurst:** 234tl; **William Macquitty:** 241b, 277b; **Mansell Collection:** 225; **MARS:** Fairchild Industries: 284b; **Mary Rose Trust:** 160b; **Tessa Musgrove:** 216t; **NASA:** 175, 176, 179, 181, 248, 269, CFA/J. McClintock & M. Garcia 268, Galaxy Picture Library 173; **NCR Ltd.:** 191; **NHPA:** Laurie Campbell 152b; **Tim O'Leary:** 156b; **Oxford University:** 261b, Research Lab. for Archaeology 157tr; **Pharmaceutical Proteins:** 264; **Photo Courtesy of Andrew Karplus and John Clardy:** Gregory Van Duyne/Cornell University 263t, 263b; **Photri:** 283, 285; **Picturepoint:** 275l, 277t; **Planet Earth Pictures:** Keith Scholey 152t; **PO Peter Holgate:** 217; **Reinhard Henning:** 260; **Renault:** 206, 208t, 208b; **Royal Aeronautical Society:** 211; **Royal Greenwich Observatory:** 178; **RSAF:** Richard Gliddon 196; **Salter Industrial Measurement Ltd.:** 215; **Science Museum:** Chris Barker 224; **Science Photo Library:** Martin Dohrn 270, John Durham 252b, Adam Hart-Davis 171, Laguna Design 182; **Seaport:** 154; **Soldier Magazine:** 284t; **Sony (UK) Ltd.:** 188b; **Spectrum Colour Library:** 234b; **Jon Stewart:** 242, 243t; **Tass:** 167; **Time Inc.:** 243b; **Tom Tracey:** 170; **TRH Pictures:** 161, 286; **TSI Communications:** 169t, 169b; **United Breweries Ltd.:** 236b; **United Kingdom Energy Authority:** 190; **University of Bradford:** 157tl; **University of Cambridge:** Erika Hagelberg 158; **University of Pennslyvania:** Dr. R. L. Brinster 265; **University of Sussex:** Dr. Andrew Smith 251, 252t; **U.S. Army Photo:** 216b; **Vision International:** 282c; **John Watney:** 278t, 280b; **Werner Foreman:** 162b; **Whitechapel Bell Foundry:** David Hoffman: 238; **John Wyand:** 234t, 234bl, 235b, 236f; **Jerry Young:** 218, 220tl, 220tr; **ZEFA:** 274l.

Volume 3

Title Page: **Corbis:** David H. Wells
AKG London: 331, Marion Kalter 318; **Alfa Laval:** 422; **Ann Ronan Picture Library:** 429; **Barnotts (London) Ltd.:** Chris Barker 302t, 302c, 302b; **Bachelors:** 382; **Ed Baxter:** 366; **BICC Plc.:** 346; **Biophotos Associates:** 412; **John Bouchier:** 368; **Breeding Institute Cambridge:** 390; **Paul Brierley:** 287, 393b; **British Ropes Ltd.:** 352; **British Steel Corporation:** 402, 403, 404; **Bruce Coleman:** Jane Burton 305t, Manfred Kage 311b; **C &CA:** 420; **Cable & Wireless Plc.:** 348, Michael Newton 345, 349; **Canon (UK) Ltd.:** 367; **Casio:** 361b; **Central Electricity Generating Board:** 344; **CERN:** 333; **Colorific!:** 379, Joe McNally © 1981 Time Inc.; **Corbis:** AFP 293, 353, 372, 415, 432, David Cumming 330, Nick Hawkes 398, Earl Kowall 385, Kevin R. Morris 343, Joel W. Rogers 363, Joseph Sohm 355, David H. Wells 377; **Courtaulds Ltd.:** 394t; **CPU (UK) Ltd.:** 423b; **Daily Telegraph Colour Library:** Patrick Ward 322; **Andrew de Lory:** 301t, 301b; **Rhein-Main Donau:** 373t, 373b; **Dr. K. P. Games:** 323; **Leslie Garland Picture Library:** Vincent Lowe 376; **Guinness Ltd.:** 384t, 384b; **Thun Habegger:** 357; **ICI:** 405; **Imperial Tobacco Ltd.:** 304t; **Institute of Geological Sciences:** 391t; **Paul Kemp:** 388; **Kings College, London:** Dr. Tony Brain 378; **Life Magazine:** Alexander Tsiaras 358; **Leo Mason:** 306; **Johnson Matthey Plc.:** 407; **Metal Box Company:** Michael Newton 381t, 381c, 381b; **Monroe Calculators:** 359t, 361t; **Mullard Ltd.:** 409; **NCR Ltd.:** 399, 401; **Michael Newton:** 386; **Nokia (UK) Ltd.:** 400b, 416; **Novosti Press Agency:** 333, **Oxford Scientific Films:** J. A. L. Cooke 368; **Photos Horticultural:** 304b; **Photri:** 417, 423t; **Picturepoint:** 336, 426b; **Pirelli General Cable Works Ltd.:** 350; **Port of New Orleans:** 375; **Professor Pearse:** 389; **Renold Plc.:** 428; **Royal Armouries, HM Tower of London:** 308; **Royal Doulton:** 424, 425t, 425b; **Colin Salmon:** 393t; **Scala:** 332; **Science Museum:** 339; **Science Photo Library:** Tim Beddow 378, Biophoto Associates 413t, Dr. Jeremy Burgess 303, Maximillian Stock 406, Dr. John Mazziotta/ETAL Neurology 311t, Tom McHugh 337, Alfred Pasieka 430t, Gregory Sams 431, Prof. S. Tolansky 391b, John Walsh 413b; **Sinclair Radionics Ltd.:** 359b; **Site Academy Editions:** 335; **Grant Smith:** 337; **Staatsbibliothek Berlin:** 320; **Steel Casting Research & Trade Association:** 426t; **Sweda Cash Registers:** 400t; **Homer Sykes:** 364; **Travel Ink:** Tony Page 325; **TRH Pictures:** E. Nevill 294; **V-Dia:** 298; **Volvo Truck & Bus Company:** 342; **Washington University, School of Medicine:** 414t, 414b; **John Watney:** 356; **ZEFA:** 321, 327, 328, 329, 374.

Volume 4

Title Page: **Science Photo Library:** Sam Ogden
Alcan Industries Ltd.: 565t; **AM&S Europe:** 496; **Apple Macintosh:** 531; **Aspect Picture Library:** 489b; **Barnaby's Picture Library:** 499; **BASF:** 473, 546T; **BNR Europe Ltd.:** 551b; **Ron Boardman:** 548b; **Paul Brierley:** Aerostyle Ltd. 519b, Southampton University 546b, 569b; **British Petroleum:** 459; **British Steel Corporation:** 549; **Broomwade Ltd.:** 519t; **California Institute of Technology:** 461b; **Canon:** 544, 545; **ChocoSuisse:** 500t; **Warwick Clarke:** 443; **Colorific!:** 502b, Mr. Laff & VA Norton/IBM/Discover ©1982 Time Inc. 535; **Cooper Bridgeman Library:** 481b; **Corbis:** 452, James L. Amos 449, 450, Yves Forestier 531; **Courtaulds Ltd.:** 489t; **Daily Telegraph Colour Library:** 438; **De Beers:** 563; **English China Clay:** 466; **Exeter University:** Dr. J. Littlechild 458; **Exxon Corp.:** 497; **FBC Ltd., Cambridge:** 469; **Ferranti:** 437; **Fiat Auto (UK) Ltd.:** 570; **Frank Spooner Pictures:** 478b; **French Railways:** 476; **Gaggia Espanola SA, Barcelona, Spain:** 504t; **Gerber Technology:** 490; **Sonia Halliday:** 568; **Richard Harrington:** 502t; **Hershey Corporation, Pennsylvania:** 500b; **Hewlett Packard Ltd.:** 543; **Hulton Getty:** 524b; **IBM:** 534b, 534t; **Image Bank:** Melford, INC, MIC 542; **Inco (Europe) Ltd.:** 507c; **Institute of Geological Sciences:** 472; **Keystone Press Agency:** 488t; **Koll Morgan (UK) Ltd.:** 512b; **Manufacturers Federation:** 564b; **Met. Office:** 525; **Michael Holford Library:** 482, 484, 488b; **Microsoft:** 523; **MOD:** 439; **NASA:** Hubble 572, 573, 574t, 574b, Jet Propulsion Laboratory 480; **National Coal Board:** 493b, 493t, 494b; **National Portrait Gallery, London:** 498; **Nestle:** 503b; **Net Gear:** 539; **Omniclock Ltd.:** David G. Jones 486; **Oxford Magnets:** 553b; **Polaroid:** 512c; **Psion Computers Plc.:** 530; **QA Photos:** 475; **Ready-Mixed Concrete Ltd.:** 547; **Rio Tinto Zinc:** 566b, 566t, 567; **Rothmans International:** 565b; **Royal Doulton:** 467b, 467t, 468; **Royal Mint:** 508bl, 508br, 508tl, 508tr; **Salmer:** 507b; **Sanyo Energy:** 552; **Science Photo Library:** Biosym Technologies Inc. 462, Deep Light Productions 445, Dick Luria, 453, NASA GSF 479, Sam Ogden 529, The Royal Inst. 464, Arthur Winfree 463, Jerome Yeats 527; **Shell:** 471, 569t; **Sipa-Press:** 520; **Somerset Levels Project:** 478t; **Sony (UK) Ltd.:** 513, 514b, 517, 528; **Spaceport:** 541; **Starbucks:** 504b; **Statoil:** 548t; **Roy Szweda:** 460; **Telegraph Colour Library:** L. Lefkowitz 524t, Paul Von Stroheim 557; **The City University, London:** 560t, 561t, 562b, 562t; **Travel Ink:** 526, Derek Allan 474, Kevin Nicol 537; **University of Cambridge:** Dr. C. J. Adkins 551t, 553t; **University of Dundee:** Dr. R. Gibson 550; **University of Sussex:** Dr. Harry Kroto 455; **University of Wisconsin, Madison:** 461t; **ZEFA:** 447, 481t, 494t, 495, 503t.

Volume 5

Title Page: **Corbis:** Roger Ressmeyer
Alan Hutchison: 600; **Allsport:** Tony Duffy 714b; **Barnaby's Picture Library:** 608, 658; **BASF:** 691; **Bavaria Verlag:** 605; **BBC Hulton Picture Library:** 675; **Theo Bergstrom:** 686; **Blohm &**

Voss: 669; **Paul Brierley:** 654b, 657, Instron 713, 715; **British Museum:** 584; **British Petroleum:** 683; **Bruce Coleman Ltd.:** Colin Molyneux 607; **Colorific!:** 663, 705, NASA 707; **Coloursport:** 694b; **Corbis:** Michelle Garrett 631, Philip Gould 615, Ed Kashi 611, 684, Kevin R. Morris 614, Roger Ressmeyer 612, 616, 696, Reuters New Media Inc. 646, Scott T. Smith 700, Michael S. Yamashita 708; **Courtaulds Ltd.:** 693; **De Beers:** 637, 639; **De Beers Industrial Diamonds Divisions:** 638b; **Dixence SA:** 604; **Eastman Dental Hospital:** 620; **Elf France:** 617; **Empics:** Steve Mitchell 685; **Robert Estell:** 602; **Frank Spooner Pictures:** 636; **General Electric:** 720b; **Glaxo Kendal:** 603t; **Herema:** 671; **Imperial College:** Dr. Windle 598t; 679; **David Kelly:** 664t; **Keystone Press Agency:** 690b; **Klargester:** 674; **La Spirotechnique (UK) Ltd.:** 666; **Laing:** 585; **Leslie Garland Picture Library:** 609; **Maglev-Railway Institute Systems Department:** 717; **Marshall Fowler:** 701; **Martin-Baker:** 711; **Michael Holford Library:** 603b, 641; **Mieke Co. Ltd.:** 660; **Ministry of Energy:** Harza Engineering Company 606; **Colin Molyneux:** 586; **NASA:** Aldus Books 706; **Neil & Spencer:** 687; **Oceaneering International:** 667; **Orenstein & Koppel:** 676, 704; **Oxford Instruments Ltd.:** 589, 591; **Philips Laservision:** 650; **Photo Library International:** 656; **Photri:** 678; **Picturepoint:** 589b, 644, 699; **Popperfoto:** Eriko Sugita/Reuters 649; **Racal-Datacom Ltd.:** 595; **Robert Bosch Ltd.:** 659b, 659t; **Sci-Tex:** 628, 629; **Science Photo Library:** 597b, 597t, James Bell 710, Dr. J. Durst 709, Pascal Goetgheluck 583, Hank Morgan 626, Alfred Pasieka 599, Volker Steger 593, Volker Steger/Peter Arnold Inc. 622; **Peter Scoones:** 665; **Shell:** 681, 682, 719; **Ship and Ocean Foundation, Japan:** 719; **Siemens:** 621; **Sony:** 652; **Southern Water:** 673; **Spectrum:** 690t; **Tony Stone:** David H. Endersbee 670; **Sunday Times:** 596; **Switched Reluctance Driver:** 718b, 718t; **Thorn Electrical Industries Ltd.:** 654t; **Thorn Lighting:** 655; **United Kingdom Atomic Energy Authority:** 623, 625; **Volvo:** 720t; **John Watney:** 643, 664b; **Dr. G. A. Webster:** 714t; **Weir Westgarth Ltd.:** 625; **Simon Wheeler:** 581b, 581t; **ZEFA:** 668b.

Volume 6

Title Page: **Corbis:** Joseph Sohm
Allied Breweries: 842t; **Dr. P. Andrews:** 824; **Ardea:** 825b; **ASEA:** 731; **Atlanta:** 811; **Mark Balakjian:** Mike St. Maur Shiel 804; **BASF:** 859; **Beecham Pharmaceuticals:** 841; **Bell Asbestos Engineering Ltd.:** 847b; **BICC Plc.:** 730; **Ron Boardman:** 734; **Paul Brierley:** 766t, STL/ITT 728; **KJA Brookes:** 769t; **Peter Burt:** 760, 761; **Cable & Wireless:** 744; **Camera Press:** 739; **Central Electricity Generating Board:** 798; **Central School of Art & Design:** 805t; **CERN:** 768, 770b; **Colorific!:** 849, 856, John Drysdale 861b, J. H. Pickerell 862; **Corbis:** Richard T. Nowitz 790, Roger Ressmeyer 729, 791, Joseph Sohm 793, Paul Thompson/Ecoscene 808; **Courtaulds Ltd.:** 851, 852; **Crown Copyright:** ERDE 829; **Daily Telegraph Colour Library:** John de Visser 839; **Dista Products:** 840; **Edward Curran Ltd.:** 779; **Enviroco Ltd.:** 846; **European Colour Library:** Carlo Berilacqua 767t; **Extell**

Group: Dave King 759, 762b, 762t; **Frank Spooner Pictures:** 806, 807; **GE Medical Systems:** 756t; **Guinness Breweries:** 842b; **Healey of Leicester Ltd.:** 735; **Humboldt University:** Museum für Naturkunde 823; **Icelandic Photo & Press Service:** 786; **Image Bank:** Anthony Johnson 836; **International Wool Secretariat:** 850t; **John Hillelson Agency:** 743t; **Frank Lane:** Hugo Binz 725; **William Macquitty:** 850b; **Michael Holford Library:** 749, Victoria & Albert Museum 780t; **Ken Moreman:** 758; **Motorola Inc.:** 755; **NASA:** MIT 763; **Michael Newton:** 857b, 857t; **Otis:** 774; **PBI:** 845; **Bury Peerless:** 833; **Philips:** 754b, 754t; **Photographic Library of Australia:** 794; **Photri:** 741t, 766b, 775, 819, 848, 861t; **Picturepoint:** 741b, 742, 747, 756b, 820; **Porsche:** 802; **Port Authority of New York & New Jersey:** 860; **Public Health Laboratory Service:** 812; **Rayrolle Parson Ltd.:** 726; **Rex Features:** 796, Lehtikuva Oy 864; **Robert Harding Picture Library:** SH&DH Cavanaugh 837t; **Royal Aeronautical Society:** 767b; **Science Photo Library:** 743b, 788, 853, Adam Hart-Davis 727, James King-Holmes 783, Jerry Mason 815, Maximilian Stock Ltd. 738, Will & Deni McIntyre 781, L. Medard/Eurelios 772, David Parker/Seagate Microelectronics Ltd. 752, David Parker 773, Science Pictures Ltd. 777, Paul Shambroom 750, Andy Walker/Midland Fertility Services 778; **SIC/PTT:** 855; **Siemens:** 757; **Skyscan Photo Library:** Peter Smith 816; **Smith Industries:** 813; **Spectrum:** 817b, 826t; **Spillers:** 776; **Survival Anglia Ltd.:** Alan Root 825t; **Susan Griggs Agency:** Adam Woolfitt 858; **The City University:** 831; **The Moving Picture Co.:** 814; **Travel Ink:** Abbie Enock 818; **Tropix:** M & V Birlev 809; **Turner & Newall:** 847t; **V-DIA:** 826b; **Yardley:** 837b; **ZEFA:** 780b, 817t, Gerolf Kalt 844.

Volume 7

Title Page: **Corbis:** Ed Kashi
Actualit: 929; **Architectural Association:** 983; **Aspect Picture Library:** 882; **Axminster Carpets:** John Goldblatt 894b; **Barnaby's Picture Library:** 928; **BH Morris & Co. (Radio) Ltd.:** 903; **Biophoto Associates:** 980; **Birdseye:** 906t, 912; **Paul Brierley:** 899, UKAEA 947, Corning Glass 1001, 1002b; **Bruce Coleman Ltd.:** Inigo Everson 875, 921, 958, 959, 1000b; **Allen Bushboake:** 914; **Cellmark Diagnostics:** 919; **Central Electricity Generating Board:** 971; **Ciba-Geigy:** 881; **Compass Graphic:** 930; **Corbis:** Morton Beebe 979, Nicole Duplaix 870b, Robert Estall 904, Ed Kashi 917, Stephanie Maze 962, Reuters New Media Inc. 978, Roger Ressmeyer 900, 943, 946, Bob Rowan 909, Paul A. Souders 949; **Daily Telegraph Colour Library:** Harry Gruyaert 874; **Dartington Glass:** Michael Newton 1000t; **Du Pont:** 880; **Ray Duns:** 953b; **ESRI (UK):** 985; **ESSO:** 969; **Explorer:** V. Pascal 869; **Farm Gas Ltd:** Steve Cross 957; **Ferodo Ltd.:** 933; **Forbo-Nairn Ltd.:** 892, 894t; **Frank Spooner Pictures:** 997; **GEC Switchgear Ltd.:** 944b; **Golden Wonder Ltd.:** 911; **Hart Associates:** 878; **Denis Hughes-Gilbey:** 905; **IDG Netherlands:** 890; **Donald Innes:** 873; **Institute of Geological Sciences:** 988t; **Jet Joint Undertaking:** 948; **Leonard Kamsler:** 915, 916; **Kent Industrial Measurements Ltd.:** 897; **Dave**

King: 944t; **Lancaster Carpets Ltd.:** 895; **Tim Langley:** 951b, 951m; **Lawrence Livermore National Laboratory:** 936; **Lucas:** Mike St. Maur Shiel 937t, 937b; **Marshall Cavendish Library:** 924; **Mike Turner Associates:** 870t; **Tony Morrison:** 923; **NASA:** Jet Propulsion Laboratory 993, 995; **National Coal Board:** 901; **NEI Thompson Ltd.:** 934; **Ommi Micro Technology Ltd.:** 952; **Overseas Containers:** 931; **Oyo (UK) Ltd.:** 994t, 994b; **PA Photos:** John Giles 891; **Picturepoint:** 970; **Planet Earth Pictures:** Ken Lucas 925; **Reading University:** V. Rae 982; **Rediffusion Simulation Ltd.:** 886, 887; **Rex Features:** 953t; **Rio Tinto Zinc:** 942; **Science Photo Library:** Volker Steger 906b, BSIP Laurent 973, Peter Menzel 976, Phillipe Plailly 977, NASA 986, Adam Jones 987, Simon Fraser 996, Dr. David Miller 998, David Parker 1006; **Skyscan Photo Library:** 888; **Snark:** Edouard Rousseau 913; **Susan Griggs Agency:** Adam Woolfitt 1005; **Sylvia Cordaiy Photo Library:** Graham Horner 999; **The Gas Council:** 963t, 963b; **The Port of Manchester:** 932; **TRH Pictures:** Rolls Royce 964, EADS 965, MAN Technologie 1008; **United Kingdom Atomic Energy Authority:** 877; **John Ward:** 879; **WaterAid:** Jim Holmes 981; **T. Wray:** 871; **Jerry Young:** 961; **ZEFA:** 893, 907, 908, 988b.

Volume 8

Title Page: **NASA**

Alan Hutchison Library: 1087; **Ann Ronan Picture Library:** 1140; **Autair:** 1067t; **BASF:** 1034; **Robin Bath:** 1022; **Theo Bergstrom:** 1083t; **Blue Room Loudspeakers Ltd.:** 1074t, 1074b; **Board of Trinity College, Dublin:** 1149; **Paul Brierley:** 1108, Borax 1139, Cambridge Consultants Ltd. 1080, Claredon Laboratories 1053, Hawker Siddeley 1101; **Simon Butcher:** 1060t; **Central Electricity Generating Board:** Stuart Clark 1017; **Colorific!:** 1049; **Coloursport:** 1142; **Colt:** 1061; **Corbis:** Shelley Gazin 1071, Richard Glover 1076, Roger Ressmeyer 1147, Vanni Archive 1056, Ed Young 1150, Jim Zukerman 1094; **Courtaulds Ltd.:** 1090; **Davin Optical Ltd.:** 1130b, 1131; **Empics:** Phil O'Brien 1143; **Massey Ferguson:** 1104; **Ferranti:** 1144; **General Dental Institute:** 1036; **Richard & Sally Greenhill:** 1135b; **Grove Cranes:** 1102; **Gunshots:** 1026; **Claus Hansmann:** 1013t; **Hart Associates:** 1023; **Image Bank:** Ben Weaver 1121; **Infinity Features:** 1047; **Keystone Picture Agency:** 1044; **Kings College, London:** Dr. Tony Brain 1137t; **Kodak Ltd.:** 1078; **Leicester Museum:** Mike St. Maur Sheil 1093b; **Lucas:** 1125; **Marchwood Engineering Laboratories:** 1082; **MARS:** 1067t; **Microsoft Corporation:** Box Shot reprinted with permission from Microsoft Corporation 1148; **Ken Moreman:** 1051t; **MRC/Common Cold Unit:** 1134; **NASA:** 1020, Goddard Space Flight Center 1098, Hubble Heritage Team 1021, Kennedy Space Centre 9, 1118, Planetary Photojournal 1097; **Michael Newton:** 1105; **Nohab Tampella:** 1115; **Oxford Scientific Films:** 1120, Stephen Dalton 1077; **Parker Pen Company Ltd.:** 1151; **Photri:** 1013b, 1035; **Pilkington:** 1016; **Pobjoy Mint:** 1015; **Pretty Polly:** 1091, 1092; **Ransomes:** 1018; **Raytheon Infrared:** 1129b, 1129t; **Research Consultants:** 1152; **Rex Features:** 1033; **Robert**

Bosch Ltd.: 1043; **RSAF:** Richard Gildon 1130t; **Sanyo:** 1073; **Schwarzkopf:** 1032; **Science Photo Library:** 1109, CC Studio 1041, Mary Clarke 1085, CNRO 1137b, Nigel Dennis 1084, Mauro Fermariello 1070, Dr. Alexander Lawton 1135t, NASA 1113b, Novosti Press Agency 1112, David Parker 1122, Tek Image 1046, Biology Media 1132; **Nigel Snowdon:** 1124; **Sony:** 1072, 1075; **Sperry:** 1028; **Sperry Gyroscope:** 1146; **Mike St. Maur Sheil:** 1030; **Sunday Times:** Ian Yeomans 1052; **Travel Ink:** Jeremy Philips 1088, David Toase 1065; **Travelnol Laboratories:** 1051b; **TRH Pictures:** McDonnell Douglas 1039, Pilkington 1128; **United Kingdom Atomic Energy Authority:** 1048; **Dr. Harry Wagnall:** 1093b, 1093t; **Westminster Children's Hospital:** 1133; **Woods of Colchester Ltd.:** 1060b; **York:** 1063; **Jerry Young:** 1038; **ZEFA:** 1100, 1111, 1116.

Volume 9

Title Page: **Corbis:** Kevin Wilson

AI Ceramic Products Limited: 1200; **Air Products:** 1246; **Alan Hutchison Library:** 1272; **AM&S Europe Ltd.:** 1220t, 1221; **Amsterdam Musee de la Bible:** 1267t; **Anders Einsiedel:** 1205; **Architectural Association:** 1185; **ASEA:** 1189; **Dr. A. Attridge:** 1226, 1227; **Blue Room Loudspeakers Ltd.:** 1284; **Boskalis Westminster/Delta-Phot:** 1208; **Paul Brierley:** 1219t, 1259; **British Petroleum Co. Ltd.:** 1291; **British Telecom:** 1209; **British Wool Marketing Board:** 1281b; **Brown Reference Group:** 1179; **Bruce Coleman Ltd.:** 1234b; **BS&W Whiteley Ltd.:** 1163; **Cable & Wireless Plc.:** 1279; **Colorific!:** F Goro/Life © 1965 Time Inc. 1214; **Corbis:** Bettmann 1167, Pablo Corral 1196, Mark E. Gibson 1160, Peter Harholdt 1204, Craig Lovell 1232, Roger Ressmeyer 1257, Bob Rowan 1191, Bill Varie 1182, Kevin Wilton 1289; **Daily Telegraph Colour Library:** 1288; **Sergio Dorantes:** 1270; **EasyJet:** 1177; **Ecoscene:** Alex Bartel 1162, Graham Neden 1242; **Elizabeth Photo Library:** 1210; **ESSO:** 1290; **Robert Estall:** 1266; **Eye Indentify Inc.:** 1269; **Fairchild Industries:** 1277; **Ferranti:** 1213t; **Ford Motor Company:** 1187; **Gainsmead:** Graham Finlayson 1197b; **Google:** 1180, 1181; **Mike Hardy:** 1234t; **Holmes Halls Tanneries:** Jon Wyand 1222b, 1222t, 1223; **IBM:** 1194; **JVC (UK) Ltd.:** 1275; **Lead Development Association:** 1220b; **Maglev-Railway Technical Research Institute Systems Department:** 1252, 1255; **Mary Evans Picture Library:** 1281t; **Mazda Cars (UK) Ltd.:** 1172; **John Melville:** 1175t; **MM Rathore:** 1238b; **Mt. Isa Mines Ltd.:** 1219b; **Angela Murphy:** 1243; **NASA:** 1201, Jet Propulsion Laboratory 1235; **National Maritime Museum Picture Library:** 1215; **National Meteorological Library:** HMSO 1216b; **National Semiconductor Corporation:** 1166; **Michael Newton:** 1267b; **Denis O'Regan:** 1197t; **Photo Library International:** 1175b; **Photographic Library of Australia:** 1280, 1293; **Photri:** 1294, 1295b; **Picturepoint:** 1265, 1283, 1287; **Chance Pilkington:** 1225, 1229; **PIRA:** 1264b, 1264t; **Professor Laithwaite:** 1256; **Rentokil Initial Plc.:** 1217; **Rijksvoorlichting Dienst:** B. Hofmeester 1206; **Robert Harding Associates:** 1295t; **Rover Group:** 1169, 1171, 1176; **Royal**

Ordance Factories: 1292; **Science Photo Library:** 1212, Dr. Jeremy Burgess 1161, Stanley Cohen 1233, Deep Light Productions 1260, Maximilian Stock Ltd. 1262, Peter Menzel 1250, David Parker 1238t, George Post 1240, Volker Steger 1236, Amy Eve Trustham 1244; **Spectrum Colour Library:** 1216t; **St. George's Hospital, Tooting:** Jon Watney 1218b, 1218t; **Telegraph Colour Library:** 1193t; **Texas Instruments:** 1164b, 1164t; **Thames Water Authority:** 1199; **Travel Ink:** Frances Balham 1274; **Abbie Enock:** 1273; **TRH Pictures:** Peugeot 1286; **Trinity House Lighthouse Service:** 1249; **United Kingdom Atomic Energy Authority:** 1237; **John Walsh:** 1168; **John Watney:** 1248; **Victor Watts:** 1224b, 1224t; **Werner Forman Archive:** 1190; **George Wright:** 1228.

Volume 10

Title Page: **Corbis:** Roger Ressmeyer
Edward Allington: 1346; **ASEA:** 1387; **Jack Avery:** 1414; **R. Barrett:** 1352, 1353; **BASF:** 1311, 1312t, 1312b; **James Blake:** 1384; **BMW (GB) Ltd.:** 1364b; **Paul Brierley:** 1313, 1372, Avdel Ltd 1379, BNFMRA 1309, GPO Southampton 1323, Solitron Corporation 1382; **British Ceramic Research:** 1340; **Bruce Coleman Ltd.:** 1302; **Bundesminster für Post- und Fermeldewesen:** 1321b, 1324t, 1324b; **Cincinnati Milacron:** 1310; **Corbis:** Jonathan Blair 1332, Dean Conger 1306, Eye Ubiquitous 1308, Amos Nachoum 1320, Charles O'Rear 1429, Neil Rabinowitz 1335, Roger Ressmeyer 1327, David Spears 1359; **Davey-Loewy:** 1388; **Delco Electronics:** 1418; **Ecoscene:** Anthony Cooper 1345; **Elizabeth Photo Library:** 1392; **Empics:** Tony Marshall 1373, Lloyd Rogers 1334; **Fairey Survey:** 1331t; **Ford Motor Company:** 1380; **General Post Office:** 1321t; **Tony Hammond:** 1386t; **Hart Assoc.:** 1421; **Hewlett Packard:** 1427b, 1428; **Hunting Surveys:** 1331b; **Hurco Europe Ltd.:** 1366t; **IBM:** Kurt Peterson 1420; **Johnson Matthey Plc:** 1377; **David Kelly:** 1406; **Goring Kerr:** 1385, 1386b; **Lumonics:** 1363t; **Michael Holford Library:** 1403; **More & Wright:** 1422; **Ken Moreman:** 1326; **NASA:** Hubble Space Telescope 4r, 1362; **NASA/ESA:** Solar and Heliospheric Observatory 10t, 1361; **Nikon:** 1433; **Nippon Electric Co.:** 1341; **NOAA:** National Weather Service 1398; **Photo Courtesy of the Welding Institute, Cambridge, UK:** 1366b; **Planet Earth Pictures:** Robert Hessler 1333; **PRA Communications:** 1365; **Queen Mary's Hospital, Roehampton:** 1436, 1440t, 1440b; **G. A. Robinson:** 1396; **Science Photo Library:** 1430, CNRI 1370, 1409, A. B. Dowsett 1367, Eve of Science 1419, 1431, Bruce Frisch 1351, James Holmes 1342, Hank Morgan 1368, 1400, NASA 1401, Alfred Pasieka 1371, Sandia National Laboratories 1416, Lee Simon/Stammers 1412, Sinclair Stammers 1338, Geoff Tomkinson 1411t, D. Vo Trung/Eurelios 1415, John Wilson 1411b; **Siemens:** 1426; **Sony (UK) Ltd:** 1423; **Spectrum Colour Library:** 1394; **St. Mary's College, Twickenham:** Dept. of Movement Studies 1303; **The Nippon Foundation:** 1319; **The Ord-Hume Picture Library:** 1408; **Thomas Moriarty Association:** 1364t; **Bob Thomas:** 1336; **Thyssen Industrie AG Henschel:** 1363b; **Tinto Zinc:** 1378; **TRH Pictures:** Lockhead

Advanced Development Co 1350; **Tropix:** P. Frances 1369; **Unimation Inc.:** 1339; **United Kingdom Atomic Energy Authority:** 1344; **Carol Unkenholz:** 1399; **Vision International:** CNRI 1305; **Washington Metropolitan Area Transit Authority:** 1348; **Henry Wiggins:** 1390; **Xerox Corporation:** 1413.

Volume 11

Title Page: **Corbis**
Air Products: 1528, 1529b; **Art Directors Photo Library:** M. Barnett 1571, 1573b; **Australian Atomic Energy Authority:** 1548; **Avid Technology:** 1498, 1500; **B&K:** 1530; **BOC Ltd.:** 1525; **Bruce Coleman Ltd.:** Gene Cox 1506t, 1506b; **Brucker Spectrospin Ltd.:** 1541; **Camera Press:** BSS 1533t; **Casio Inc. 2000:** 1491; **Pat Caulfield:** 1463; **Central Office of Information:** UKAEA 1552; **Charles F. Thackery Ltd.:** 1582; **Columbia University:** 1556; **Commissiarat à l'Energie Atomique:** 1550; **Corbis:** 1532, Toby Gipstein 1501, Philip Gould 1575, Richard T. Nowitz 1502, David and Peter Turnley 1534, Michael S. Yamashita 1503; **Crown Copyright:** 1581; **Daily Telegraph Colour Library:** Space Frontiers 1520b; **Sergio Dorantes:** 1529t; **Esko Keski-Wa:** 1516, 1517t, 1517b, 1518; **David Farrell:** 1497, 1499t, 1499b; **Ferranti:** 1512; **G. Lubb Parsons:** 1464; **General Dynamics Corp.:** 1467; **Habeggar Thun:** 1482b; **Image Bank:** Butch Martin Inc. 1472; **Inco Alloy Products Ltd:** 1522b, 1524, Doncaster Blaenavon Ltd. 1522t, Rolls Royce 1523; **Irvine Mat:** 1495; **Israel Military Industries:** 1533b; **Julia Lamm:** 1578; **LKB:** 1446; **Maj. Gen. F. W. E. Fursdon:** 1454t, 1454b; **Mannesmann Demag:** 1461; **Marconi International Marine:** 1510; **Michael Holford Library:** 1513, MMM 1511; **Mobil North Sea Ltd.:** 1574; **MOD:** 1453; **NASA:** 1558t, Hubble Space Telescope 10b, 1560, Ocean Color Data Resources 1568b; **NCB:** 1458; **NOAA:** 1566b, 1566t, 1569, National Geophysical Data Center 1565; **Novosti Press Agency:** 1460; **ORLAU:** R. Jones & A. Hunt/Orthopaedic Hospital 1470; **Oxford Research Instruments:** 1540; **PA Photos:** Michael Stephens 1469; **Pictor International:** 1583; **Picturepoint:** 1451; **Geoff Renner:** 1573t; **Rex Features:** 1557, 1558b, Sipa Press 1484; **Rio Tinto Zinc:** 1462; **G. R. Roberts:** 1452; **Ronald Grant Archive:** 1493; **Royal Observatory, Edinburgh:** 1561; **Science Photo Library:** 1480m, 1480b, Dr. Jeremy Burgess 1564t, Simon Fraser 1570, Jerry Mason 1478, Maximilian Stock Ltd. 1539b, Peter Menzel 1480t, Hank Morgan 1479, Royal Observatory, Edinburgh 1562, Saturn Stills 1563, Sinclair Stammers 1477, Alexander Tsiaras 1535, 1564b, Hugh Turvey 1490, U.S. Department of Energy 1537; **Seaport:** 1567; **Sharp:** 1447; **Shell:** 1579, 1580; **Spectrum Colour Library:** 1482t; **Susan Griggs Agency:** Adam Woolfitt 1584; **Sylvia Cordaiy Photo Library:** Chris Parker 1481; **The New York Times Company:** 1519; **Tony Stone Associates:**1504; **Travel Ink:** Trevor Creighton 1473, Kevin Nicol 1515; **TRH Pictures:** 1551; **United Kingdom Atomic Energy Authority:** , 1544, 1545, American EP Co./Donald C. Cook 1542; **U.S. Navy:** 1465; **Vessa Ltd.:** 1471; **Weston Simfire:** 1486; **Woods Hole Oceanographic Institution:** 1568t.

Volume 12

Title Page: **Corbis:** Bohemian Nomad Picture Makers
Heather Angel: 1676b, 1677; **Ardea:** P. Morris 1632t; **Aspro:** Andrew de Lory 1624t; **BASF:** 1693t; **Ron Boardman:** 1610; **Chris Bonnington:** 1618; **Paul Brierley:** 1606,1682, 1723, Matrix Ltd. 1595; **Bruce Coleman Ltd.:** 1633, Jane Burton 1678, 1719, Lyn Stone 1699; **Bryant & May:** 1700; **BSC:** 1617b; **CERN:** 1652, 1654b; **Chessell Ltd.:** 1666; **Colorific!:** John Moss 1591t; **Corbis:** 1651, Paul Almasy 1667, 1725, Bohemian Nomad Picture Makers 1708, Eye Ubiquitous 1605, Kevin Fleming 1654t, Owen Franken 1690, Mitchell Gerber 1697, Craig Lovell 1698, Roger Ressmeyer 1726, 1727, 1728, Phil Schermeister 1597, 1681, Paul A. Souders 1634, Yogi Inc. 1674; **Crown Paints & Wallcoverings Group:** 1627, 1630; **Decca:** John Goldblatt 1694t, 1694b, 1695; **Douglas Dickins:** 1639b; **Dickinson Robinson Group:** 1624b; **Dolley & Palmer:** 1622; **Sergio Dorantes:** 1703l, 1703r; **Fenamec Ltd.:** 1680t, 1680b; **Fermi National Accelerator Laboratory:** 1649; **Heidelberg:** 1594, HD-Scanners 202 1592; **Hoechst:** 1625; **Ilford:** 1709; **Institute of Dermatology:** Prof. I. A. Magnus 1724t; **Institute of Oceanography:** Dr. P. J. Herring 1724b; **Intel Corp.:** 1686, 1688; **Keymed:** 1612l, 1612r; **Keystone Press Agency:** 1628, 1629; **Kodak Ltd.:** 1713b; **Lily Industries Ltd.:** 1656t; **Sally McFall:** 1670; **Michael Holford Library:** Royal Observatory Greenwich 1665; **MM Rathore:** 1718; **Munro & Foster:** 1611; **NASA:** 1707, Hubble Space Telescope 1599; **Norlin Music (UK) Ltd.:** 1601; **Denis O'Regan:** 1604; **Ordnance Survey:** 1706; **Outboard Marine Corporation:** 1615t; **Baker Perkins:** 1623; **Photo Me:** 1714; **Photri:** 1616; **Pictor International:** 1676t; **Popperfoto:** 1640; **Pye Unicam:** 1693b; **Rainbow:** Dan McCoy 1590; **Reed Paper & Board (UK) Ltd.:** 1638; **Rockwell International:** 1620; **Kim Sayer:** 1705; **Scan Optics:** 1593; **Science Museum:** 1671; **Science Photo Library:** 1658, Dr. Brad Amos 1715, James Bell 1716, E. H. Cook 1659, Martin Dohm 1644b, Eye of Science 1655, Guy Gillet 1589, Eric Grave 1721, Adam Hart-Davis 1646, Maximilian Stock Ltd. 1626, Andrew McClenaghan 1692, Philippe Plailly 1631, Stammers Sinclair 1644t, 1645, Geoff Tompkinson 1685, Alexander Tsiaras 1613t; **Spectrum:** 1602; **Sylvia Cordaiy Photo Library:** Dizzy De Silva 1713t, Chris Taylor 1596; **Thorn EMI Electron Tubes Ltd.:** 1717; **Patrick Toseland:** 1657; **Toshiba:** 1701; **Tom Tracy:** 1687; **United Kingdom Atomic Energy Authority:** 1648; **John Watney:** 1591b, 1724m; **Wersi Ltd.:** 1603; **Jack Wynter:** 1615b; **ZEFA:** 1608, 1639t, 1641, 1642, 1691.

Volume 13

Title Page: **Corbis:** Lawrence Manning
Adel Roostein (London): Ray Leaning 1772; **Aerospace Plc.:** 1826; **Alan Hutchison Library:** 1791; **Edward Allington:** 1871; **Heather Angel:** 1799b; **Ann Ronan Picture Library:** 1825b, 1834; **Apex Photo Agency Ltd.:** 1768; **Associated Press:** Topham 1734t, 1734m, 1734b; **Atlas Copco:** 1840b; **ATO Chemical Products (UK) Ltd.:** 1776b; **Auriema Ltd.:** 1808; **Babcock Power Ltd.:** 1827, 1828, 1829; **BASF:** 1775t, 1775b,

1776t, 1812; **Timothy Beddow:** 1851; **BICC Plc.:** 1837; **Black Star:** 1800b; **Alastair Black:** 1840t; **Bozell & Jacobs:** 1744; **Paul Brierley:** 1794b, 1853, 1865t, 1865b; **British Alcan Tubes Ltd.:** 1752; **British Industrial Plastics Ltd.:** 1769; **British Steel Corporation:** 1749, 1751; **Broomwade Ltd.:** 1789b; **Bruce Coleman:** Bill Wood 1792; **Malcolm Bryan:** 1861; **Central Electricity Generating Board:** 1830, 1831; **Circuits Consultants Ltd.:** Pan Publicity 1845; **Corbis:** Bettmann 1801, Bohemian Nomad Picture Makers 1860, Anna Clopet 1807, Marc Granger 1833, Farrell Grehan 1819, Lawrence Manning 1854, Kate Holmes-Tweedy 1790; **Courtesy of The Powder Coating Institute:** 1823; **Crosfield Electronics Ltd.:** 1852; **Daily Telegraph Colour Library:** 1737; **Douglas Dickins:** 1820t; **Du Pont:** 1771, 1805, 1813, 1814, 1815; **Ecoscene:** Kjell Sandved 1753, Alan Towse 1788; **Englehard Industries:** 1783; **ESSO:** 1754; **Ferranti:** 1838; **John Goldblatt:** 1740t, 1740m, 1740b; **Richard Greenhill:** 1816; **Tessa Hammond:** 1866; **Heidelberg Graphic Equipment:** 1847, 1848t, 1848b; **Hepworth Iron:** 1750; **Johnson Matthey Plc.:** 1782, Rustenburg Platinum Mines Ltd. 1781; **David Kelly:** 1849l, 1849r; **Dave King:** 1855t; **Kodak Ltd.:** 1855b; **Magnum:** Eric Lessing 1738; **Mansell Collection:** 1868; **Tor Mavestrand:** 1804; **Michael Holford Library:** 1825t; **Arcangelo Moles/Mauro Matteini:** 1743l, 1743r, 1743b; **Andrew Morland:** 1842; **MRC Brain Metabolism Unit, Edinburgh:** 1862t; **NASA:** AnimAlu Production/Jet Propulsion Laboratory 1758l, 1758r, 1759l, 1759r, 1760, Galaxy Picture Library 1761, Planetary Photojournal 1757, 1803; **National Geographic Society:** Winfield Parks 1870t; **Newmarket Transistor:** 1844, 1846b; **Olympia Business Machines Ltd.:** 1846t; **PA Photos:** EPA European Press Agency 1741; **Roger Phillips:** 1841b; **Picturepoint:** 1820b; **Pirelli:** 1836; **Queen Victoria Hospital, East Grinstead, Sussex:** 1766; **Rex Features-Sipa Press:** 1777; **Robert Harding Associates:** 1832; **GR Roberts:** 1802b; **John Rose & John Dyble:** 1789t; **Science Photo Library:** Pascal Goetgheluck 1770, 1797, Lawrence Livermore National Laboratory 1762, Astrid Michler & Hanns-Frieder 1794t, David Parker 1733, 1763b, Philippe Plailly 1864, Saturn Stills 1818, Paul Shambroom 1763t, A. Sternberg 1809; **Skinkis:** Aviation Photographs International 1859; **Spectrum Colour Library:** 1765l, 1765m, 1765r, 1870b; **St. Bartholomew's Hospital:** 1843b; **Sunday Times:** 1843t; **Thames Water Authority:** 1799t; **The Electron Machine Corporation:** 1793; **The New York Times Company:** 1850; **Travel Ink:** Neil Egerton 1839, Abbie Enock 1817; **Tussaud's London Planetarium:** Tussaud's Group 1755; **GKN Vandervell:** 1862b; **W Vinten Ltd.:** 1747; **John Ward:** 1786; **Dave Waterman:** 1742t ,1742b; **Westminster Medical School:** 1767t, 1767b; **WL Gore & Associates (UK) Ltd.:** 1863; **Martin Woodford:** 1800t; **ZEFA:** 1802t.

Volume 14

Title Page: **PA Photos:** EPA
3M (UK) Ltd.: 1944; **Air Products Ltd.:** 1945t; **Albright & Wilson Ltd.:** 2014; **Edward Allington:** 1985; **Argonne National Laboratory:**

1905; **ASEA:** 1987; **Atlas Copco:** 1977t; **Babcock Power Ltd.:** 1998; **BASF:** 1961; **BBC Hulton Picture Library:** 1950; **Bildarchiv Preussischer Kulterbesitz:** 1992; **Biophotos Associates:** 1945b; **Alastair Black:** 2008; **BOH Chemicals Ltd.:** 2015; **Paul Brierley:** 1960, 1984b; **British Airways:** 1962; **British Railway Board:** 1926; **British Standards Institute:** 1877, 1879; **British Transport Films:** 1878; **Bruce Coleman Ltd.:** 2012, Eric Crichton 1957; **Cable & Wireless Plc.:** 1927; **Cementation Costain:** 1974, 1977b; **Corbis:** Sheldan Collins 1963, Eye Ubiquitous 1901, Neal Preston 1935, Roger Ressmeyer 1911, Douglas Slone 1978, Joseph Sohm/ChromoSohm Inc. 1893t, 1943, Paul A Souders 1923, Vince Streano 2004; **Gerry Cranham:** 1967; **Desoutter Ltd.:** 1889; **Douglas Dickins:** 1998t; **Ecoscene:** Peter Currell 1933; **Fiat Auto (UK) Ltd.:** Trevor Lawrence 1918t; **GEC Elliot Traffic Automation:** 1984t; **GLC Department of Public Health Engineering:** 1939, 1941; **Goodyear Ohio:** 2001; **Grumman:** 1893b; **Hadley Hobbies Ltd., London:** 1915; **Heather Angel:** 1959; **Hencoup Enterprises:** 1983; **Holland & Holland:** 1969, 1970; **ISR/PG Harvery:** 1999; **Kleeper:** Bruno Herdt 2006b, 2006t, 2007; **LAT Photographic:** 1888; **Lockheed:** 1948; **Lucas Industries:** 1918b; **Malaysian Rubber Research & Development Board:** 1997, 1998b; **Marconi Radar:** 1897; **Marconi Communications Systems Limited:** 1937; **MARS: Crown Copyright (MOD):** 1956; **Midland Oil Refineries:** 1942; **MOD:** 1991; **NASA:** 1994, 1995, Canadian Space Agency 1955b, Jet Propulsion Laboratory 1910, Kennedy Space Center 1990, Planetary Photojournal 12, 1900; **National Peace Council:** Hiroshima/Nagasaki 1908; **New York State Thruway Authority:** 1981; **Norden Systems:** 1898; **Oxford Scientific Films:** Peter Parks 1958b, 1958t; **PA Photos:** EPA European Press Agency 1986; **Philips Electronics:** Ray Duns 1913, 1936; **Plessey:** 1895; **Science Photo Library:** CNRI 1917, Fermilab 1881, Victor Habbick/Visions 1989, James King Holmes 1916, Chris Madeley 1899, Dr. K. Milne/David Parker 1912, National Institute of Standards and Technology (NIST) 1880, Space Telescope Institute/NASA 1954, U.S. Department of Energy 1907; **Scott Polar Institute:** 1904; **SNCF:** French Railways Ltd. 1928; **Nigel Snowdon:** 1887; **Steel Corporation:** Manfred Kage 1919; **Sylvia Cordaiy Photo Library:** Geoffrey Taunton 1929; **Topham Picture Library:** 1971; **Transport & Road Research Laboratory:** 1982l, 1982r; **Travel Ink:** Derek Allan 1973, Tony Page 1964; **Union Carbide (UK) Ltd.:** 1947; **United Kingdom Atomic Energy Authority:** 1955t; **Varian-TEM Ltd.:** 1922; **Vautier/de Nanxe:** 1932; **Vision International:** CNRI 1920; **Walker Wingsail Systems Ltd.:** 2009; **John Watney:** 2011; **Wilkinson Sword Group:** 1936t; **Andy Wilsheer:** 1890, 1891; **ZEFA:** 1921, 1938, 2016.

Volume 15

Title Page: **NASA:** Johnson Space Center **Architectural Association:** 2094, 2095; **ASEA:** 2054b; **Asprey Plc:** 2080; **Austin Rover:** 2066; **Autonumis Ltd.:** 2109; **BBC:** 2073t; **Paul Brierley:** 2140b; **British Geological Survey:**

2047; **British Transport Films:** 2069; **Brooklands Museum:** 2023; **Brother UK Ltd.:** 13t, 2058, 2059, 2060; **Bruce Coleman Ltd.:** Nicholas Devore 2110, Michael Freeman 2103; **Canadair:** 2035, 2036; **Chubb:** 2042; **Corbis:** 2068b, Jonathan Blair 2021, Christopher Cormack 2136, Judy Griesedieck 2061t, Wolfgang Kaehler 2068t, Larry Lee 2092b, Buddy Mays 2067, Roger Ressmeyer 2131, James A. Sugar 2046, 2054t, Adam Woolfit 2084, Ed Young 2052; **Daily Telegraph Colour Library:** Michael Hardy 2040; **J. Kim Van Diver:** 2031t; **EMI:** 2044t; **European Space Agency:** 2025; **Fisions Ltd.:** 2111; **Frank Spooner Pictures:** 2048t; **Freedom Ship:** 2072; **Sally & Richard Greenhill:** 2089; **P. F. Hancock:** 2086; **John Heseltine:** 2081; **Kelvin Hughes:** 2063; **Image Bank:** Elyse Lewin Studio Inc 2099; **Institute of Geological Sciences:** 2048b, 2076b, 2076t; **Institute of Sound & Vibration Research:** 2141; **Johnson Matthey Plc:** 2079, 2130; **Rob Kesseler:** 2091, 2092t; **Dave King:** 2147; **Lloyds Bank Plc.:** 2045; **Marconi:** 2127t; **Mary Rose Trust:** 2022t, 2022b; **Giuseppe Mazza:** 2105; **Ian Mckinnel:** 2082; **Meat & Livestock Commision:** 2096, 2097, 2098; **Michael Holford Library:** National Maritime Museum 2062; **MOD:** 2128; **NASA:** 2056, 2120b, Dryden Flight Research Center 2114, Goddard Space Flight Center 2028, Hubble Space Telescope 2154t, Human Space Flight Center 2024, 2153, 2154b, 2155, Jet Propulsion Laboratory 2118, 2157b, 2157t, 2160, Johnson Space Center 2027, Johnson Space Center/Space Science Branch 2151, Kennedy Space Center 2152, Mars Odyssey 2156, MIX 2026, 2159, Planetary Photojournal 2120t, 2121, 2122, 2123b, 2123t, Transition Region and Coronal Explorer 2119; **NASA/ESA:** Solar and Heliospheric Observatory 2158r, 2158l; **Naval Research Laboratory:** 2133l, 2133r; **Neve:** 2139; **Novosti Press Agency:** 2073b; **PA Photos:** European Press Agency 2126, 2142, 2149; **Peter Abbot & Co.:** 2032; **Pfaff (Britain) Ltd.:** 2061b; **Photographic Library of Australia:** 2116; **Popperfoto Ltd.:** 2127b; **Reid Marine:** 2050; **Royal National Lifeboat Institute:** A Ferry 2039l, Peter Hadfield 2039rb, David Trotter 2039rt; **Science Photo Library:** Pascal Goetgheluck 2078, C. S Langlois/ Publiphoto 2138, 2146, Peter Menzel/Dinamation 2137, NASA 2150, P. Plailly/Eurelios 2135, H. Raguet/Eurelios 2087, Dr. G. Settles 2031b; **Silicon Fabrications:** 2077; **Smiths Industries:** 2055; **Solar Energy Research Institute:** 2117; **Sunday Times:** 2044b; **The Ronald Grant Archive:** 2148b; **Transport & Road Research Laboratory:** 2113; **Travel Ink:** Clive Geoffrey 2090; **U.S. Coastguard:** 2038b, 2038t, 2051; **Vauxhall Motors Ltd.:** 2064, 2065; **Patrick Ward:** 2101, 2102; **John Watney:** 2140t; **Yardley of London Ltd.:** 2107.

Volume 16

Title Page: **Gotland**
Allsport: 2225b, Vandystadt 2225t; **Ann Ronan Picture Library:** 2193, 2234; **Beken of Cowes:** 2208b; **Boulevard Distillers & Importers Inc.:** 2215, 2218; **Paul Brierley:** Oxford University Clarendon Laboratory 2267; **British Aerospace Dynamics Group:** 2251t, 2251b; **British Sugar Corporation:** 2295, 2297t, 2297b; **British**

Sulphur Corporation: 2299; **Bruce Coleman Ltd.:** 2286t; **Brucker Spectrospin Limited:** 2195; **Corbis:** 2250, Rick Doyle 2188, Eye Ubiquitous 2187, 2276, Lynn Goldsmith 2233, Catherine Karnow 2185, Roger Ressmeyer 2285t, Joel W. Rogers 2242, The Military Picture Library 2252, Tim Thompson 2246, Manuel Zambrana 2189; **Courtaulds Ltd.:** 2212; **CXJB Underwater Engineers Ltd.:** 2244; **Daily Telegraph Colour Library:** John Perkins 2208t, 2223b; **Dawe Instruments Ltd.:** 2286b; **Anthony Dawson:** 2209t; **De Beers:** 2271; **Distillers Co. Ltd.:** 2217; **Dunlop Sports Ltd.:** 2220, 2223t; **EMI:** 2203; **Empics:** Ian Crawford 2260; **ESSO:** 2300; **Fotogram:** 2202; **Freedman Panter:** 2235; **Genesis Space Photo Library:** 2176; **Goddard & Gibbs Studios Ltd.:** 2238l, 2238r; **Gotland:** 2266; **Sonia Halliday:** 2236; **Hart Associates:** 2228; **David Hoffman:** 2199, 2282; **Dave Hoskins:** 2273; **Image Bank:** Barros & Barros 2279, Guido Alberto Rossi 2224; **Institute of Geological Sciences:** 2270, 2272, 2298; **Keystone Press Agency:** 2301t; **Klepper:** 2219; **Lawrence Lee:** 2237; **Leeds University:** Mike Lindsay 2226; **London Art Tech:** 2303b; **Michael Holford Library:** 2243, 2301b; **Missile Defense Agency:** 2179, 2180, 2182, 2183; **Alison Moody:** 2239, 2240; **Andrew Moorland:** 2303t; **NASA:** 2166, 2169, 2172, 2173, 2255, Human Space Flight Center 2170, 2174t, 2174b, 2175, 2178, Johnson Space Center 2165, John J. Olson 2171, Planetary Photojournal 2264; **Michael Newton:** 2194; **NOAA:** OAR/National Undersea Research Program (NURP); JAMSTEC 2292, 2294; **PA Photos:** EPA 2204; **Phonic Ear International Photo Library:** 2227; **Rex Features:** 2192; **RI Harding Ltd.:** Simon de Courcy Wheeler 2263; **Rieter:** 2214; **Robert Bosch Ltd.:** 2285b; **Roberts & Saunders (Brighton) Luthiers:** James Blake 2284; **Royal Navy:** 2290; **Royal Scottish Musuem:** Syntax Films 2259; **Science Photo Library:** Hank Morgan 2200; **Seaphot:** 2293; **Slazenger Ltd.:** 2221; **Smiths Industries:** 2209b; **Nigel Snowdon:** 13b, 2205; **Spectrum Colour Library:** 2257t, 2257b, 2302; **Spring Steel Productions:** 2230; **Stevens Guitars:** 2283; **Stirling Power Station:** 2269; **Sylvia Cordaiy Photo Library:** John Howard 2256; **Tate & Lyle Plc.:** 2296; **TM Lucas Film Ltd.:** 2190; **Toronto Transit Commission:** 2278; **TRH Pictures:** Northrop Grumman Corporation 2254; **U.S. Air Force:** 2184; **U.S. Department of Defense:** 2289; **Vision Express:** 2191; **Vosper Thornycroft Limited (UK):** 2232; **John Watney:** 2211, 2265; **Jerry Young:** 2222.

Volume 17

Title Page: **NASA**
Aerospace & Defence Review: Smiths Industries 2423; **AGA Infrared Systems:** 2422; **AMF:** 2445; **Anglo-American Telescope Board:** 2379; **Anglo-Australian Observatory:** David Malin 2316; **Ann Ronan Picture Library:** 2361; **Architectural Association:** 2397; **ASEA:** 2433b; **AT & T Bell Laboratories:** 2312; **Barnaby's Picture Library:** 2356; **Belinda:** 2404; **Theo Bergstrom:** 2410b; **BKS Surveys Ltd.:** 2337t; **Paul Brierley:** BNFMRA 2323; **British Steel Corporation:** 2322t, 2322b; **British Telecom:** 2348, 2349t, 2349b; **British Telecommunications**

Subject Indexes

Biology and Medicine

A

abscesses, dental (gumboils) 5:619
abscisic acid 3:305
accessibility aids 1:19–22
Acetobacter 7:911
acetylcholine 3:413, 414; 11:1506
  organophosphates and 12:1700
  in plants 3:305
  receptors 3:*414*
acetylcholinesterase 4:437
acetyl coenzyme A (acetyl CoA) 10:1374, 1375
acetylsalicylic acid *see* aspirin
acids and alkalis, acids, poisoning from 13:1791
acromegaly 6:782
actin 1:865
actinomycetes 10:1409
addiction, drug 12:1685
adenine 7:973–4; 11:1477, 1478
adenosine diphosphate (ADP) 10:1373, 1374, 1376; 12:1700
adenosine monophosphate (AMP) 10:1373, 1376
adenosine triphosphate (ATP) 9:1234; 10:1373, 1374, 1375, 1376; 12:1700
adipose tissue 6:836
ADP *see* adenosine diphosphate
adrenal glands 6:781; 8:1086
adrenaline *see* epinephrine
aging, study of *see* gerontology
agonists 2:252
AIDS (acquired immunodeficiency syndrome) 6:811–12; 8:1137; 10:*1368*, 1369–70
  anti-HIV therapy 12:1688
  virus *see* HIV
Air Rescue Service 1:113
albinism 7:*979*, 980
albumin 2:*264*
  technetium-labeled 14:1918
alburnum 9:1294
aldosterone 6:781; 8:1085, 1086
algae 12:*1719*
algal blooms 19:2663
  blue-green 6:823; 10:1412
  used in pollution control 13:1803
  used in sewage treatment 8:1108; 13:1803; 19:2645
alkaloids 12:1686–7; 13:*1790*
allergies 8:1135
  asthma and 10:1305
  to food additives 7:907
altitude sickness 10:1305
alveoli 10:1303, *1304*
  and cancer 12:*1655*
Alzheimer's disease 3:414; 7:*996*, 997; 13:*1865*
amalgams, dental 5:619; 10:1371; 15:2080
ambulances 1:112–13
  aircraft 1:113; 8:1067, *1070*
amino acids 1:114; 2:251; 4:458; 7:974; 13:1864, 1866
  essential 11:1557; 13:1866
ammonites 7:*989*; 12:*1633*
amniocentesis 11:1564
amnioscopes 6:785
amoebas
  binary fission 14:1957
  detection of chemicals 15:2105

digestion by 5:645
AMP *see* adenosine monophosphate
Ampalax 7:997
amphetamines 12:1681, 1682
amphibians (animals)
  evolution 6:824
  reproduction 14:1957, 1958–9
amylase 5:642, 643
amyotrophic lateral sclerosis (ALS) 19:*2615*
anabolism 6:810; 10:1376
analgesics 12:1681, 1683
anastomoses 10:1437, 1438, *1440*
anemia 11:1558
  sickle-cell 7:980
anencephaly 12:1660
  anesthetics 1:131–2; 10:1368; 11:1582, *1583*; 12:1681; 17:2328–9
  for dentistry 5:618
  epidural 1:132
  inhalation 1:131–2; 12:1620, 1621
  liquid 1:131
  local 1:132; 5:618; 17:2328
  pressure measurement 13:1843
  see also surgery
angina pectoris 8:1052
angiograms, nuclear 14:1919
angioplasty, balloon 8:1052
animals
  cells 3:411–12
  cloned 1:52; 2:264; 7:*978*
  cold-blooded and warm-blooded 6:836–7
  experimental (for pathology) 12:1656
  eyes 6:832
  feedstuffs for 6:810; 7:914; 13:1866
  genetically-engineered 1:52–3; 2:263–4
    transgenic 2:*264, 265, 266*
  intensively-reared livestock 1:56–7
  smell used by 15:2105
  study of (zoology) 19:2733–6
  tracking 19:*2734, 2736*
  see also veterinary science and medicine
anisometropia 4:560
ankylosing spondylitis 10:1369
anorexics (diet pills) 12:1682
antagonists 2:252
anthrax
  as a biological weapon 4:437, 438, 441
  vaccines 18:2555
antibiotics 12:1681, 1687
  discovery 10:1368
  penicillin 6:*841*
  testing 10:*1411*
antibodies (immunoglobulins) 2:264; 8:1133–5, *1137*
  and cancer 3:380
  monoclonal 2:265, *266*
    manufacture 8:1137
    for radiotherapy 14:1922
  resistance to 10:1411
antidepressants 12:1681; 13:1868
antidiuretic hormone (ADH) 6:781; 8:1085
antigenic drift and shift 18:2556–7
antigens 8:1133
  manufacture 7:978

antihistamines 12:1682, 1689
antihypertensives 12:1682
anti-inflammatory drugs 12:1682
antioxidants 16:2225
antisepsis 17:2328
alpha-1 antitrypsin 2:266
ants
  pheromones 12:1690
  slaves 12:1644
anxiety 10:1369
anxiolytic antidepressants 12:1681
aphids, alfalfa 12:1678
Apligraf 18:2500
appendix 5:644
aqueous humor 6:830, 831; 9:1240
Archaebacteria 10:1412
Archaeopteryx 6:*823*, 825; 12:1635
Argentinosaurus 12:1635
Aricept 7:997
Armillaria 12:1645
arms
  artificial 2:254–5
  reattachment 13:1765–6
arsenic, poisoning 12:1659
arteries
  blocked using radiology 14:*1918*
  cerebral, blocked 10:*1438*
  coronary 8:1046
    and heart disease 8:1046–7, 1052
  nanorobots in 10:*1419*
arthritis 10:1369; 19:*2721*
arthroscopy 10:1437, 1439–40
artificial insemination, in cows 1:52
asbestos 15:2077
  diseases related to 6:847; 10:1305
asbestosis 6:847
Ascaridia galli 12:1645
ascorbic acid *see* vitamins, C
asepsis 10:1367–8; 17:*2327*, 2329
asparagine 1:*114*
asparginase 13:1866
Aspergillus oryzae 19:*2726*
aspiration, fluid 2:280
aspirin 8:1047; 12:1686
  mode of action 12:1683
  in plants 3:305
  various effects 12:1681
asthma 10:1305
  drugs for 2:252
astigmatism 6:832; 9:*1241*; 12:1597, 1598
astrobiology (exobiology) 9:1235
atherosclerosis 6:837; 8:1046; 11:1559
  coronary artery 8:1046–7, 1052
  treatment, using phototherapy 12:1723–4
ATP *see* adenosine triphosphate
atrioventricular node 8:1046
atropine 12:1686–7; 13:1792
audiometers 8:104
auditory tubes (Eustachian tubes) 8:1042
autism 18:2556
autoclaves 2:190; 3:382; 13:1841
autoimmunity 8:1135; 10:1369
autopsies (postmortems) 12:1658
auxins, and weed control 19:2679
aye-ayes 19:2736
azathioprine 18:2499
AZT (azidodeoxythymidine; zidovudine) 12:1688

B

babies
  congenital defects, heart 8:1046, 1051; 12:1660
  crib deaths 12:1661
  crying 16:2200
  premature 12:1661
  Rhesus 2:272
  skeleton 3:297
  sleep 15:*2099*
  "test tube" 7:980; 11:1564
backcrosses 1:53
bacteria 10:1409
  at temperature extremes 9:1232
  corrosion-inducing 4:571
  effect on iron 7:982
  and food spoilage 7:904–5
  and genetic engineering 7:977
  gold-depositing 10:1412
  and human health 10:1410–11
  immune response to 8:1136
  mesophilic 7:904
  and the origins of life 10:1412
  photosynthetic, fossils 7:988
  proteolytic 7:905
  psychrophilic 7:904
  spores 7:904
    affecting canning and bottling 3:381
  "superbugs" 4:440-1 10:1411
  symbiotic 10:1333
  thermophilic 7:904
  used by man 10:1411–12
    as animal feedstuff 10:1412
    as biological weapons 4:438
    methane production 2:259–60; 10:1411
    waste management 10:1411; 13:1802–3
bacteriophages 10:1410, *1412*
  and genetic engineering 7:977
balance 8:1043
barbiturates 12:1682
  poisoning 13:1791
Barnard, Christiaan 18:2501
Basic Metabolic Rate (BMR) 8:1085
bathing aids, for the disabled 11:1472
bats 18:*2532*
Bayliss, Sir William 8:1084
beetle banks 1:55
beetles
  Colorado 3:303; 12:1676
  ladybug 12:1677, 1678
  and past climates 4:477, *478*
behavior therapy 13:1868
bends, the 2:155; 5:667; 11:1528; 16:2292; 18:2537
  and saturation diving 18:2537–8
benthic species 10:1332
beta carotene 11:1558–9
bile 5:643
bile duct, obstruction 14:*1918*
binary fission 14:1957
biochemistry 2:251–2
biodiversity 2:262, 266
  in forests 7:922
biodynamics 1:58
bioengineering (biomedical engineering; bionics) 2:253–7
  heart pacemakers 2:257; 8:1048
  prosthetic eyes 12:*1613*
bioinorganic chemistry 4:452

biological control 1:58, 61; 12:*1677*, 1678
  in aquaculture 2:153
  using parasites 12:1645
  using pheromones 12:1691
biology
  astrobiology (exobiology) 9:1235
  botany 3:**303–5**
  cell 2:251; 3:**411–14**
  marine *see* marine biology
  microbiology 10:**1409–12**
  molecular 11:**1477–80**
  zoology 19:**2733–6**
  see also biotechnology
bioluminescence 10:1301, 1302
biomes, in the Eden Project 7:984
biomineralization 10:1412
biophysics 2:**261–2**
biopsies 2:280; 3:378; 12:1657
bioremediation 10:1411; 13:**1802–3**
biosynthesis *see* anabolism
biotechnology 2:**263–6**
  and agriculture 1:52; 2:265–6
    cloned animals 1:52; 2:264; 7:*978*
  DNA probes 2:265
  engineered bacteria 1:55; 2:263, *264*
  for food additives 7:914
  and medicine 2:263, *264*
    "anti-sense" drugs 2:265
    bioengineered vaccines 2:264–5, 266
    monoclonal antibodies 2:265
  to make new proteins 2:266
  transgenic animals 2:*264*, 265, 266
  see also genetic engineering
biotin 19:2613
biowarfare *see* chemical and biological warfare
bipolar disorder 4:452
birds
  brood parasitism 12:1644
  droppings (guano) 12:*1698*, 1700
  migratory 11:1514; 19:2734
  reproduction 14:1959
  salt glands 8:1087
  song 16:2200
bladder, operations on 18:2550
blastocysts 6:777, 778
bleaches, ingested 13:1791
blind spot 9:1240
blinking 6:830
blood 2:**271–3**
  artificial 2:**272–3**
  calcium levels 6:782
  carbon dioxide level 10:1305
  cells
    counts 12:1656–7
    freeze etching 5:*592*
    red 3:*413*
  circulation discovered 13:1733
  clots 8:1047
  flow detected 2:280; 10:1438; 18:2531
  glucose, testing for 12:1657
  groups 2:271; 17:2328
    typing 2:271–2, *273*
  plasma 12:1657
  of porphyria victims 12:*1724*
  substitutes 13:*1733*
  testing 12:1656–7
  transfusions 2:272, *273*; 17:2328
blood pressure
  measuring
    automated monitors 6:757–8
    sphygmomanometers 10:1326; 16:**2211**
  regulation 3:413–14
blood pumps, external 4:*520*
bloodsucking animals 5:645
blood vessels

joined using microsurgery 10:1437, 1438, *1440*
  see also arteries; veins
blubber 6:836
blue-baby syndrome 8:1046
bodies, and cryogenics 5:*592*
body scanners 2:**278–82**
  BEAM 2:*280*; 3:312
  CAT (CT) scans 2:278–9, *280*; 14:*1919*; 19:2723
  MRI 2:282; 3:312; 4:448; 5:718; 11:1540, *1541*; 12:1657; 14:*1966*
  positron emission tomography (PET) 2:151, 281; 3:312
  radionuclide (scintigraphy) 2:281; 14:*1917*
  thermographic 2:281, *282*; 6:743; 17:*2422*
  ultrasound *see* ultrasonics
  xerography 2:281
bone
  grafts 13:*1766*; 18:2504
  necrosis 5:667
  scans 14:1917–18
bone marrow 3:298–9
  transplants 3:380; 18:*2499*, *2502*, 2503–4
bones, and fracture treatment 3:**297–300**
  see also joints (body parts)
botany 3:**303–5**
  paleobotany 12:1634
  see also plants
bovine somatotropin (BST) 1:57
bovine spongiform encephalopathy (BSE) 18:2587
Boyle's apparatus 1:131–2
brachiation 9:*1234*
brain 3:**309–12**
  Alzheimer's disease 13:*1865*
  death, defined 18:2498
  drug entry into 12:1683–5
  olfactory lobe 15:*2103*, *2104*
  scans 6:756
    BEAM 2:*280*; 3:312
    CAT (CT) 2:278–9, *280*; 3:*311*
    EEG 3:312; 6:756, *758*; 15:2099–2100
    MRI 3:312; 7:*996*
    PET 2:281; 3:312
    ultrasound 18:2532
    X-ray fluoroscopy 19:*2724*
  and sleep 15:2099, *2100*
  and speech and language 3:310; 16:2201
  surgery 10:*1438*, 1440; 17:*2328*, *2329*, 2330
Brain Electric Activity Mapping (BEAM) 2:*280*; 3:312
breasts, cosmetic surgery 13:1764–5; 15:*2078*
breathing 10:**1303–5**
breeding
  plant 1:*52*, 53–4; 8:1089
  selective breeding of livestock 1:56
Brenner, Sydney, 7:975
bronchi 10:1303
bronchioles 10:1303
bronchitis, chronic 10:1305
bronchoscopes 6:785; 17:2331
brucellosis, as a biological weapon 4:438
BSE (bovine spongiform encephalopathy) 18:2587
budding 14:1957
  yeasts 19:*2726*, 2727
buffers, chemical, in living cells 1:114
bulimia nervosa 12:1658
burns 2:281
butterflies, monarch 19:2733
Byssochlamys spp. 7:905

C

cadmium, poisoning 13:1801
caecum 5:644
Caenorhabditis elegans 11:1480
calciferol 19:2613
calcitonin 8:1086
calcium, in the blood 6:782
Calvin cycle 12:**1720–1**
cancer
  breast 2:*282*; 7:997; 12:1687
  and calcium levels in the blood 6:*782*
  causes 2:252; 3:377, 378; 11:1479
  cervical 17:*2331*
  childhood 12:1661
  detection
    using scintigraphy 14:*1917*
    using thermography 2:281, *282*
  diagnosis 3:378
  formation 3:377
  head and neck 13:1767
  holographic visualization 8:1083
  immunity 3:378; 8:1137
  lung 3:*378*; 6:847; 10:1305; 11:1529; 12:*1655*
  skin 6:806; 15:2089
  throat 12:1613
  treatment 3:**377–80**
    antibody-directed drug therapy 3:380
    anti-sense drugs 2:265
    bone marrow transplants 3:380
    chemotherapy 3:*377*, 379, 380; 12:1685, 1687
    gene therapy 3:380
    hormone therapy 3:379–80
    internal phototherapy 12:*1723*, 1724
    photodynamic therapy (PDT) 3:380
    platinum drugs 13:1783
    radiotherapy 3:*378*, 379, 380; 14:1920–2; 19:2723
    surgery 3:378–9, 380; 17:2331
    use of growth factors 2:273
    using lasers 17:*2331*
    vaccines 2:265; 3:380
  see also leukemia
Candida utilis 19:2727
captive breeding 18:2588; 19:2736
carbohydrates 3:**388–90**; 11:1557
  metabolism 8:1085–6
carbolic acid 10:1367
carbon cycle 9:1233
carbon dioxide
  and anesthesia 1:132
  blood levels 10:1305
carbon monoxide, poisoning 13:1792; 18:2488
cardiology, nuclear 14:1919
cardiopulmonary bypass 8:1049
  see also heart-lung machines
cardiovascular drugs 12:1682
caries, dental 5:618–19
carnivores 5:644
carpels 14:1958
casein 5:600
casting, air-pressure, for artificial limbs 2:253
catabolism 6:810; 10:**1373–5**
catalysts, biological *see* enzymes
cataplexy 15:2102
cataracts 6:806, 832; 12:1589
catheterization, cardiac 8:1052
cats, veterinary medicine and 18:2583–5, 2588
CAT scanners *see* Computed Axial Tomography
cattle
  beef and veal production 1:57
  dairy *see* cows

growth hormones 18:2588
  slaughtering 15:2096, 2098
cell biology 2:251; 3:**411–14**
CellCept 18:2499
cell membrane 3:411
cellulose 3:**389–90**
  digestion 5:644
cement, dental 5:619
central nervous system (CNS), drugs acting on 12:**1683–5**
centromere (kentochore) 7:*980*
cephalosporin 12:1687
cerebellum 3:310
cerebral palsy, mobility aids for 11:**1470–1**
cerebrospinal fluid 3:310
cervix, cancer 17:*2331*
chaperonins 2:252
charcoal, activated 13:1791
chemical and biological warfare 4:**437–41**
chemicals, carcinogenic 3:378
chemotherapy 3:*377*, 379, 380; 12:1685, 1687
chiasma 3:309
chickens 1:56–7
  parasites of 12:1645
  slaughtering 15:2098
chimpanzees 19:2733, *2734*
chiropractic 10:1370
chlorine, as a chemical weapon 4:437, 438; 8:1036
chloroform, poisoning 13:1791
chlorophyll 3:412; 12:1719–20, 1722
chloroplasts 3:412, *413*; 12:1719, *1721*, 1722
cholecystokinin 5:643
cholera 6:811; 19:2648
  chicken 18:2554–5
  vaccine 18:2556, 2557
cholesterol 6:837; 8:1046, 1052; 11:*1558*, 1559
cholinesterase, inhibitors 7:997
Chomsky, Noam 16:2201
chordae tendinae 8:1045
chorionic villus sampling 11:*1563*, 1564
choroid 6:830
Christmas disease 7:980
chromosomes 3:411, 412–13; 6:823; 7:979, *980*
  sex (X and Y) 3:412–13
  and genetic disorders 7:980
  in situ hybridization 7:980
  see also DNA; genes; genetics
chronic fatigue syndrome 13:1868
chyme 5:643
cigarette smoke, lung damage 10:1305
ciliary body 6:830
ciliary muscles 9:1240
cirrhosis 18:2532
citric acid cycle *see* Krebs cycle
classification, plant and animal 12:**1632–3**
clean-room technology, for surgery 11:**1582–3**
cleft lip and palate 13:1766–7
cloning, animals 1:52; 2:264; 7:*978*
Clostridium
  acetobutylicum 6:842
  botulinum 7:905, 911
clozapine 13:1868
cocaine 5:618; 12:1687
cochlea 15:2132
cochlear implants 8:1044; 12:1612
codeine 12:1687; 16:2226
codons 7:975; 11:1478
coelacanths 12:*1632*
cognitive therapy 13:1868
coliform count 19:2662
collagen 3:298; 19:2614

collimators, multileaf **14**:1922
colon **5**:644
  and endoscopy **6**:*784*, 785
colonoscopes **6**:785
color blindness **4**:510; **12**:1598
colostomy **3**:379
communication
  animal **19**:2733
    by smell **15**:2104–5
Computed Axial Tomography (CAT; CT) scans **2**:278–9, *280*; **14**:*1919*; **19**:2723
computer voice-stress analyzers (CVSAs) **13**:1808
condoms **13**:1818
condors, Californian **18**:2587–8; **19**:*2733*, 2735–6
congenital defects **12**:1660
  heart **8**:1046, 1051; **12**:1660
conservation, animal **19**:2734–6
contact lenses **4**:**560–3**
contraceptives **13**:1818
  from cotton **5**:*581*
  oral **12**:1682; **13**:1818
control question tests (CQTs) **13**:1808
convulsants, poisoning **13**:1791
Cope, Edward Drinker **12**:1633
corals, digestion by **5**:645
corn
  breeding **1**:*52*, 53
    emasculation **3**:303
    genetically-engineered **3**:303
cornea **6**:830; **9**:1240
  and laser surgery **12**:1590
coronary arteries, dilating **17**:2330
coronary-artery bypass graft (CABG) surgery **8**:1052
coronary sinus **8**:1045
corpses, and forensic science **7**:919–20; **8**:1083
corpus callosum **3**:309
corticosterone **8**:1085
cortisol **6**:781; **8**:1086
cortisone **2**:186; **12**:1682
Corynebacterium glutamicam **7**:914
cosmetic surgery **13**:1764–5
cowpox **8**:*1134*
cows
  artificial insemination of **1**:*52*; **18**:*2585*
  and biotechnology **2**:*266*
  hormones and **1**:52, 57
  improving herds **1**:52
  veterinary work and **18**:*2585–6*, 2588
  see also milk
cranes, whooping **19**:2736
craniofacial surgery **13**:1767
Creutzfeldt-Jakob disease (CJD), new-variant **18**:2587
Crick, Francis **7**:973, 975
cross breeding **1**:52
crowns, dental **5**:*619*
cryosurgery **5**:591; **17**:2330
CS gas **4**:437
ctenophores **10**:*1301*
CT scanners (CAT scanners) *see* Computed Axial Tomography
cuckoos **12**:1644
curare **12**:1687; **13**:*1791*
Cuvier, Georges **12**:1633
cyanide
  detection in blood **12**:*1657*
  poisoning **13**:1792
cyanocobalamin **19**:2613
cyclic-AMP **2**:251; **8**:1087
cyclopropane **12**:1681
cyclosporin **18**:2499, 2503
cysteine **13**:1864
cystic fibrosis **7**:980; **12**:1660
cytochromes **13**:1865

cytokinins **3**:305
cytological specimens, for cancer investigations **3**:378
cytoplasm **3**:411, 413
cytosine **7**:973–4; **11**:1477, 1478

D

daphnia **12**:*1716*
Darwin, Charles **6**:822, 823, *825*; **12**:1633
DDT **1**:61; **12**:1676, 1678
deafness
  and bionic ears **2**:*257*
  cochlear implants for **8**:1044; **12**:1612
  hearing aids for **8**:1043–4
  spectacles to aid deaf people **9**:1243
death
  definition of **9**:1232
  time of **7**:919–20; **12**:1658–9
decompression sickness *see* bends, the
decongestants **12**:1682
defibrillators **6**:757; **8**:1047
Demikar, Vladimir **18**:2500
dementia, senile **14**:1919
Demikar, Vladimir **18**:2500
dendrites **3**:309
dentine **18**:2466
dentistry **5**:**618–22**; **13**:*1782*
  amalgams **5**:619; **10**:1371; **15**:2080
  drills **2**:233; **5**:621–2
  holographic dental records **8**:1083
  sealants **1**:32
  see also teeth; toothpaste
dermabrasion **13**:1767
dermatitis (eczema) **15**:2089
dermis **15**:2087, *2088*
Desulfivibrio **7**:982
dextrin **6**:842
diabetes **3**:414; **6**:782; **8**:1085–6; **10**:1375
  blood tests **12**:1657
  and exercise **16**:2225
  immune system and **8**:1136
  insulin injections **18**:*2557*
  recent developments in research **13**:1733–4
  and sight **12**:*1590*
dialysis machines **5**:**633–6**; **12**:1609; **18**:2549–50
dialyzers **5**:634–5
diastole **8**:1045
diathermy, surgical **6**:758; **17**:2329
diatoms, in the blood **7**:919
diazepam (Valium) **12**:1682; **13**:1791
diet *see* nutrition and food science
"diet pills" **12**:1682
diets
  and health **6**:837; **7**:996; **8**:1047
digestive system **5**:**642–5**
digits, replacement **10**:1439
dihydroxyacetonephosphate **10**:1374
dinosaurs **6**:825; **12**:1635
  extinction **7**:989; **10**:1395; **11**:1568
  fossils **12**:*1631*, *1634*, 1635
dioxin **4**:438
1,3-diphosphoglycerate **10**:1374
disabled, the, aids for *see* accessibility aids; mobility aids
disaccharides **3**:389
diseases
  bacteria and **10**:1410–11
  from animals (zoonoses) **18**:2586–7
  inherited **12**:1660–1
  notifiable **6**:811
  skin **15**:2089
  study of *see* epidemiology; pathology
diuretics **12**:1682

dizziness **8**:1043
DNA (deoxyribonucleic acid) **1**:114; **3**:412; **6**:823; **7**:973, 979; **9**:*1233*
  automated synthesizers **11**:*1478*
  fingerprinting (genetic fingerprinting) **7**:920, 978; **16**:2249; **19**:2736
  and genetic engineering **7**:977–8
  microarrays **11**:1480
  probes **12**:1657
  and protein synthesis **7**:974–5; **11**:1477–8; **12**:1657
  recombinant **7**:977; **18**:2556
  redundant and "junk" **11**:1478
  replication **7**:975
  sequencing **7**:975–6; **11**:*1480*
  structure **2**:261; **7**:973–4; **11**:1477
  to test for genes ("DNA probes") **2**:265
  see also chromosomes; genes
DNA polymerase **7**:*974*, 978; **11**:1478
docosahexaenoic acid (DHA) **11**:1559
dogs
  microchipped **18**:2588
  veterinary medicine and **18**:2583–5, 2588
Dolly the sheep **2**:264
dolphins **19**:2733
dopa, L- **12**:1684
dopamine **12**:1684
Down's syndrome, testing for **11**:1564
doxorubicin **12**:1687
dreaming **15**:2100–1
Drosophila **6**:778
drought **13**:*1819*
drowning, and forensic pathology **7**:919
drugs, medical *see* pharmaceuticals; pharmacology
DSM (*Diagnostic and Statistical Manual of Mental Disorders*) **13**:1867
DTaP vaccine **18**:2556
duodenum **5**:643
duramen **9**:1294
dwarfism **6**:781; **8**:1086
dyes, and medicine **1**:135

E

ear, nose, and throat (ENT) *see* otolaryngology
ears **8**:1041–3; **15**:2131, 2132
  bionic **2**:*257*
eating disorders, bulimia nervosa **12**:1658
Ebola virus **4**:440–1
E. coli see Escherichia coli
*Eco*RI (restriction enzyme) **11**:1478
ectoderm **6**:777
ectoparasites **12**:1644
eczema (dermatitis) **15**:2089
EEGs (electroencephalograms) **3**:312; **6**:756, *758*
  and sleep **15**:2099–2100
eicosapentaenoic acid (EPA) **11**:1559
EKGs *see* electrocardiographs
elbows, prosthetic **2**:255
electrocardiographs (EKGs) **6**:756–7; **8**:*1046*; **12**:1666
electroconvulsive therapy (ECT) **13**:1868
electrophoresis, gel **11**:*1480*
elephants **19**:*2733*, *2734*, 2735
ELISA (enzyme-linked immunosorbent assay) **6**:*811*; **18**:2584
embolisms, pulmonary **14**:1918
embryology **6**:777–8

embryos **6**:777
  gene testing in **7**:980
emphysema, drugs for **2**:*264*, 266
enantiomers, drug **12**:1689
encephalins **3**:311
Encephalitis lethargica (sleeping sickness) **12**:1684
encephalograms **3**:312
endocrinology **6**:**781–2**
endoderm **6**:777
endometrium, removal **11**:1563–4
endonucleases, restriction **7**:975; **11**:1479
endoparasites **12**:1644
endoplasmic reticulum **3**:411
endoprostheses **2**:255–6
endorphins **3**:311
endoscopes **6**:**783–5**, 856; **17**:2330–1, 2332; **18**:*2550*
  in veterinary medicine **18**:*2584*
endothelium-derived relaxing factor (EDRF) **3**:414
energy, for living organisms **10**:1373
ENT (ear, nose, and throat) *see* otolaryngology
Enterococcus faecium **10**:1411
enterogastrone **5**:643
enterokinase **5**:643
entomology, forensic **7**:919–20
enzyme-linked immunosorbent assay (ELISA) **6**:*811*; **18**:2584
enzymes **1**:114; **6**:810
  are catalysts **3**:*406*, 407; **6**:810; **13**:1865
  denatured **6**:810
  in detergents **5**:632
  digestive **5**:642–3
  and food spoilage **7**:905
  from transgenic animals **2**:*264*, 266
  and ligands **2**:*252*
  pacemaker **10**:1376
  restriction **7**:975, 976; **11**:1478
  structure **2**:*251*, 252
  used in brewing **1**:98; **3**:*406*
  in yeast **6**:841–2
epidemics **6**:811; **13**:1816
epidemiology **6**:**811–12**
epidermis **15**:2087, *2088*
epiglottis **10**:1303
epilepsy, and strobe lamps **16**:2286
epinephrine (adrenaline) **6**:781; **8**:1085
  receptors **8**:1087
erepsin **5**:643
Erlich, Paul **10**:1368
erythropoietin (EPO) **2**:273, **10**:2549
  abuse, detecting **5**:684; **16**:2226
Escherichia coli (*E. coli*) **10**:1409
  and genetic engineering **2**:263; **7**:977, 978; **10**:1409
  for blood substitutes **13**:*1733*
  infection by viruses **10**:1410, *1412*; **11**:1480
  and water quality **19**:2662
esophagus **5**:642
estradiol **8**:1086
estriol **8**:1086
estrogen(s) **8**:1086; **12**:1687
  the menopause and **7**:997
  in plants **3**:305
estrone **8**:1086
estrus **14**:1959
ether, anesthesia using **10**:1368; **17**:2327–8
eukaryotes **6**:823; **9**:1235; **10**:1412
Euphorbia spp., fuel produced from **7**:*963*
Eustachian tubes **8**:1042
evolution **6**:**822–5**; **12**:*1633*, 1634–5
  language **16**:2200
  smell and **15**:2106
exercise **7**:997; **16**:2225–6

exobiology (astrobiology) **9**:1235
expectorants **12**:1682
extinction **12**:1635
  dinosaurs **7**:989; **10**:1395; **11**:1568
eyes **6**:830–2
  and color vision **4**:510
  compound **6**:832
  contact lenses **4**:**560**–3
  defects **6**:832
  diseases and disorders **12**:1589–90, 1598
  in animals **18**:2584
  refractive state **12**:1596–8
  surgery **12**:*1589*, 1590; **17**:2329
    plastic surgery **13**:*1764*
    using lasers **9**:1213, 1214; **12**:1590; **17**:*2330*

F

Factor VIII **7**:978
FAD **10**:1373
FADH₂ **10**:1373, 1374, 1375
fallopian tubes **6**:777
families, and the aging population **13**:1819
farsightedness *see* hyperopia
fatigue, driver **18**:2508
fat(s) **4**:457; **6**:**836**–7; **11**:1557
  saturated and unsaturated **6**:836, 837; **11**:1557
  storage in the body **6**:836
fatty acids **6**:836; **11**:1557
Faverin (fluvoxamine) **13**:1868
feet, prosthetic **2**:254
fertilization, in-vitro ("test tube baby" method) **7**:980; **11**:1564
fertilizers
  organic **1**:61
  manures **6**:843–4
fetuses **6**:777
  and fetal stethoscopes **16**:2265
  screening **11**:*1563*, 1564; **18**:2531
fever **6**:810
Fibonacci series **11**:*1555*
fibrillation, ventricular **8**:1047
fibroblasts **3**:*300*
fibroplasia, retrolental **19**:2613
fillings, dental **5**:*618*, 619; **10**:1371
fingerprinting, DNA (genetic fingerprinting) **7**:920, 978; **16**:2249; **19**:2736
fingers, fused **13**:*1766*
fireflies **10**:1301
fish
  evolution **6**:824
  parasitic **12**:1645
  puffer fish poison **13**:1792
  reproduction **14**:1958
  taxidermy **17**:2354
fish oils **11**:1559
FIV (feline immunodeficiency virus) **18**:2588
Fleming, Alexander **10**:1368
flies
  and forensic entomology **7**:919
  fruit **6**:778
  photomicrograph of **12**:*1715*
fluoride, and teeth **5**:620; **8**:1034, *1036*; **18**:2466; **19**:2666
fluoroscopy **8**:1052; **19**:2723
  television **19**:2723–4
fluoxetine *see* Prozac
flurbiprofen **12**:1682
fluvoxamine **13**:1868
folic acid **19**:2613
follicle-stimulating hormone (FSH) **6**:782; **8**:1086
food
  additives **7**:914
  carbohydrates **3**:*388*, 389, *390*

energy from **12**:1617
genetically-modified **1**:53; **3**:303, 304; **7**:978; **12**:1676
  organic **1**:*58*, 61
  slimming foods **3**:390
  spoilage **7**:904–5
  sterilization **5**:601; **7**:912; **18**:2533
  synthetic
    artificial meats **7**:913–14
    from single-cell proteins **7**:914; **13**:*1866*
Food and Drug Administration (FDA) **12**:1689
food poisoning **7**:904
  Clostridium botulinum **7**:905
food science *see* nutrition and food science
foot and mouth disease **2**:261; **18**:2587
forensic science, forensic pathology **7**:919–20; **12**:1658–9
fossils **6**:822, *823*, 825; **7**:987–8; **12**:1631–5
  ammonites **7**:*989*; **12**:*1633*
  coelacanth **12**:*1632*
  microfossils **12**:1634
  "fossy jaw" **12**:*1700*
fovea **6**:831; **9**:1240
fractures, bone, treatment **3**:299–300
Franklin, Rosalind **7**:973
free radicals **11**:1559; **16**:2225
Freud, Sigmund **13**:1867
frogs
  calls **19**:2733
  curare from **13**:*1791*
  reproduction **14**:*1957*, 1958–9
fructose **3**:389
fructose-1,6-diphosphate **10**:1374
fructose-6-phosphate **10**:1374
fruits
  dehydration **12**:1610
  dietary **11**:1558
  premature ripening **1**:55
fungi **10**:1409–10
  infections in animals **18**:2585
  parasitic **12**:1644–5
  reproduction **14**:*1958*
  use in pest control **12**:1645
  see also yeast

G

gadolinium texaphyrin **12**:1724
galactose **3**:389
Galapagos Islands **6**:825
gallbladder, removal **17**:2331
galls **12**:1646, 1659
gallstones **6**:784
  removal **6**:785
galvanic skin response (GSR) **13**:1807
gamma rays
  dangers of **6**:745
  gamma-camera scans of the body **14**:1917, 1919
gastric lavage **13**:1791
gastroscopes **6**:785; **17**:2331
genes **3**:412; **6**:823; **7**:973, 979–80; **11**:1477
  and aging **7**:996
  banks **8**:*1120*; **11**:1478–9
  in development **6**:778
  dominant and recessive **6**:823; **7**:980
  housekeeping **11**:1479
  intermediate **7**:980
  isolation **11**:1478
  jumping (transposons) **3**:*303*
  libraries **11**:1478
  mutated *see* mutations
  polygenic **7**:980

selector (homeotic genes) **6**:778
  see also chromosomes; DNA; genetics
gene therapy **3**:380; **7**:978
genetic engineering **1**:52; **7**:**973**–8; **11**:1478
  of animals **1**:52–3; **2**:263–4; **7**:978
  and biological weapons **4**:440
  for blood substitutes **13**:*1733*
  gene therapy **3**:380; **7**:978
  and horticulture **8**:1089
  for insulin **7**:978; **13**:1733–4; **19**:2727
  of plants and crops (food) **1**:53; **3**:303, 304; **7**:978; **12**:1676
    herbicide-tolerant crops **19**:2681
  to produce biosteel **2**:163
  and transplants **13**:1734
  see also biotechnology; DNA
genetic fingerprinting *see* fingerprinting, DNA
genetics **7**:**979**–80
  definition of life **9**:1233
  genetic disorders **7**:980
  high-tech plant breeding **1**:53–4
  mapping the genome **1**:53–4; **7**:980; **11**:1479–80
  see also chromosomes; DNA; genes
genome **7**:976; **11**:1478
  mapping **1**:53–4; **7**:980; **11**:1479–80
    Human Genome Project **7**:976, **11**:1479–80
genus **12**:1632
germ theory **10**:1367
gerontology **7**:**996**–7
gibberellic acid **3**:305
gigantism **6**:781; **8**:1086
Gigantosaurus **12**:1635
gingivitis **5**:619–20
Ginko biloba **7**:997
glands
  endocrine **6**:781–2; **8**:1084
  see also hormones
glaucoma **17**:2332
glowworms **10**:1301, *1302*
glucagon **10**:1375; **13**:1792
  receptors **1087**
glucocorticoids **8**:1086
glucose **3**:389
glucose-6-phosphate **10**:1374
glucose tolerance tests **12**:1657
glue, surgical **1**:31
glutamate **3**:414
glyceraldehyde-3-phosphate **10**:1374
glycogen **3**:389, 390; **8**:1085
  and the slaughter of animals **15**:2096
glycolysis **10**:1374, 1376
GM-CSF **2**:263, 265, 273
  and gene therapy **3**:380
gnotobiotic environments **8**:*1133*
goiter **8**:1036, *1087*
Golgi apparatus **3**:411; **8**:1084
gonads **6**:781
G proteins **2**:252
graft versus host disease (GVHD) **18**:*2499*, 2503
granulocytes **3**:*413*
groundwater, pollution from nitrates **1**:54
growth factors **2**:273
growth hormone(s)
  and aging **7**:997
  for farm animals **1**:52, 57; **18**:2588
  human (HGH) **2**:263; **6**:781, 782; **7**:997; **8**:1086; **16**:2226
  rat **2**:265
guanine **7**:973–4; **11**:1477, 1478
gum disease **5**:619–20
gynecology and obstetrics **11**:1563–4

H

Haemophilus influenzae **8**:1137
hagfish **12**:1645
hair **15**:2087
  beard **14**:1935
  lanugo **14**:1935
  structure **1**:10
halothane **1**:131
hands
  artificial **2**:254–5
  rheumatoid arthritis **19**:*2721*
  transplants **10**:1439; **18**:2504
  virtual **17**:2332
Harvey, William **10**:1367; **13**:1733
Haversian canals **3**:298, *299*
hayfever **8**:1135
hearing **8**:**1041**–4, 1072; **9**:1284; **11**:1530; **15**:2142
  damage **11**:*1530*
  the ears and **8**:1041–3; **15**:2131, 2132
hearing aids **8**:1043–4
heart **8**:**1045**–7
  artificial **2**:256–7; **8**:*1047*
  disorders **8**:1046–7
    cardiovascular drugs **12**:1682
    congenital defects **8**:1046, 1051; **12**:1660
    monitoring
      electrocardiographs (EKGs) **6**:756–7; **8**:*1046*; **12**:1666
      ultrasound scans **2**:*282*
  muscle **11**:1504, 1505–6
  pacemaker *see* heart pacemaker
  radiological scans **14**:1919
  surgery on *see* heart surgery
  transplants *see* transplants, heart
  see also stethoscopes
heart attack (myocardial infarction) **6**:837; **8**:1047, 1052; **10**:1305; **11**:1559
heart block **8**:1047
heart disease, coronary **8**:1046–7; **10**:1305; **11**:1559
heart failure, congestive **8**:1047
heart-lung machines **8**:1049, 1050, *1051*, *1052*; **18**:*2501*
heart pacemaker **8**:**1048**
  external **8**:1048
  implantable **2**:257; **8**:1048
  natural **2**:257; **11**:1506
heart surgery **8**:**1049**–52
  see also heart pacemaker
Helicobacter pylori **10**:*1367*, 1411
hematoporphyrin derivative (HPD) **12**:*1613*
hemodialysis *see* dialysis machines
hemoglobin **1**:134; **9**:1188; **13**:1865; **18**:2488
  synthetic **13**:*1733*
hemolysis, and heart-lung machines **8**:1050
hemophilia **7**:978, 980
hemorrhage, gastrointestinal **6**:785
heparin **8**:1050
hepatitis **18**:2532
  hepatitis B **10**:1369; **12**:*1659*
    vaccine **2**:266; **18**:2555, 2556
herbivores **5**:644
heredity *see* genetics
hermaphrodites, hydras **14**:1958
hibernation **10**:1376
high pressure nervous syndrome **5**:667
hip joints
  artificial **2**:254, *255*, 256; **10**:1352; **14**:1917–18
  dysplasia, in dogs **18**:2584
Hippocrates **10**:1367
histopathology **12**:*1655*
HIV (human immunodeficiency

virus) 10:1369–70
  and anti-HIV therapy 12:1688
  tracking 6:811–12
  vaccine 18:2555
  see also AIDS
HLA (human leukocyte antigen)
    system 18:2498
Hodgkin's disease 3:379
honeybees 10:1317
hooks, split (hand substitutes) 2:255
hormone replacement therapy
    (HRT) 3:298; 6:782; 7:997
hormones 2:251; 3:413; 6:781–2;
    8:1084–7
  and aging 7:997
  for cancer treatment 3:379–80
  growth see growth hormone(s)
  as medicines 12:1687
  plant 3:305
  sex 8:1086–7
  see also endocrinology
horses
  taxidermy 17:2354
  veterinary work and 18:2584, 2587
hospitals, waste disposal 19:2641
HRT (hormone replacement
    therapy) 3:298; 6:782; 7:997
Human Genome Project (HGP)
    7:976, 980; 11:1479–80
humans
  cloning 2:266
  evolution 6:825; 12:1633
    language 16:2200
    origins 12:1635
    pheromones 12:1691
hummingbirds, migration 19:2733
Huntington's chorea 3:414; 7:980
hybridization, and agriculture 1:52
hybridomas 2:265; 8:1137
hydras 14:1957, 1958
hydrocephalus 12:1660
hydrochloric acid, in the stomach
    5:642
hydrolases 6:810
hydroxyl ions 12:1692
hyperfractionation 14:1921
hyperglycemia 12:1657
hypermetropia see hyperopia
hyperopia (hypermetropia; farsight-
    edness) 6:832; 12:1597; 16:2191
hyperparasitism 12:1644
hypertension, pulmonary 18:2502
hyperthyroidism 8:1085
hyphae, fungal 12:1644–5
hypnotherapy 10:1370
hypnotics 12:1682
  poisoning 13:1791
hyposomnia 15:2101–2
hypothalamus 3:310
hypothermia, for heart surgery
    8:1049–51
hypothyroidism 8:1085
hysteria 13:1868

I

ibuprofen 4:458; 12:1682
ichthyosaurs 6:825
ileum 5:642, 643
immunity
  adaptive 8:1132, 1133
  autoimmunity 8:1135
  natural 8:1132–3
immunization 8:1135
  active and passive 8:1137
  see also vaccines
immunodeficiency
  AIDS 8:1137
  feline 18:2588
  SCIDs 8:1133
  see also AIDS

immunoglobulins see antibodies
immunology 8:1132–7
  and cancer 3:378; 8:1137
  see also vaccines
immunostimulation 8:1137
immunosuppression 8:1137; 18:2499
implant materials, Nitinol 1:107
indigestion 5:645
indole-acetic acid 3:305
infertility, in animals 18:2584
influenza 8:1135
  monitoring 6:811
  vaccines 18:2556–7
inhalers 1:40
inhibin 6:782
inositol triphosphate 2:252
insects 19:2736
  hormones 8:1087
  reproduction 14:1958
insemination, artificial 1:52
insomnia 15:2101–2
insulin 2:263; 5:643; 8:1085–6;
    10:1375
  from genetic engineering 7:978;
    13:1733–4; 19:2727
  injections 18:2557
  receptors 8:1087
intensive care units 11:1584
intercostal muscles 10:1303
interferon 2:263; 3:380; 7:977;
    8:1133, 1137
  computer graphics model 5:599
interleukin-2 3:380
intestines
  large 5:644–5
  small 5:642, 643–4
intrauterine devices (IUDs) 13:1818
invertase 5:643; 6:841
invertebrates, paleontology
    12:1634–5
invert syrup 3:389
in-vitro culturing 2:266
in-vitro fertilization ("test tube baby"
    method) 7:980; 11:1564
ion channels 3:413
ionizers 9:1184
iris 6:830; 9:1240
isoflurane 1:132
isomerases 6:810

J

Jacobson's organ 15:2105
jaundice 6:784
  neonatal 12:1724
jejunum 5:643
jellyfish 12:1724
Jenner, Edward 8:1132; 18:2554
joints (body parts)
  artificial 2:254, 255–6; 10:1352;
    17:2332; 18:2504
  examined by endoscopes see
    arthroscopy
  movement 3:297–8
  shoulder 9:1234

K

keratin 15:2087
keratinocytes 15:2087, 2089
keratoconus 4:560
kidneys
  artificial (dialyzers) 5:634–5
  failure 5:633; 18:2549
  functions 5:633, 634
  radiological tests 14:1918–19
  removal 17:2332
  stones 18:2532, 2549, 2550
  structure 5:634
  transplants 6:782; 18:2498, 2499

see also dialysis machines
kinases 2:251
Koch, Robert 10:1367, 1409
Krebs cycle (citric acid cycle; TCA
    cycle) 10:1374, 1375, 1376

L

laboratories, hospital, electronic
    apparatus 6:758
lactic acid, in muscles 6:840
Lactobacillus bulgaricus 5:603; 7:904
lactoferrin 1:131; 2:266
lactose 3:389; 5:600, 602
ladybugs 12:1677, 1678
Laënnec, René 16:2265
Lamarck, Jean Baptiste de 6:822;
    12:1633, 1634
lambda (virus) 11:1480
lampreys 12:1645
Landsteiner, Karl 17:2328
Langerhans, islets of 10:1375;
    13:1734
language see speech and language
laparoscopy 6:785; 17:2331–2;
    18:2549
larynx 10:1303
  endoscopic surgery 12:1612, 1613
  papillomata 12:1613
lasers and masers
  lasers
    used for cancer treatment
      12:1613
    used for dentistry 5:622
    used for surgery 6:785, 856;
      9:1214; 11:1564; 12:1590,
      1613; 13:1767; 17:2330, 2332
L-dopa 12:1684
lead, and health 9:1221
leaves, structure 12:1719, 1721
Leclerc, Georges-Louis 12:1633
Leeuwenhoek, Antonie van 10:1367,
    1434; 13:1733
left ventricular assist devices (LVADs)
    2:256–7
legs
  artificial 2:253–4
  bone transplants 18:2504
leishmaniasis 8:1136
Lemaire-Boucher movement 1:59
lenses
  eye 6:830, 832; 9:1240
  uncorrected 9:1241
leprosy, treatment 18:2555
leukemia 2:273; 3:379; 12:1661
  treatment 12:1687; 13:1866;
    14:1920
lie detection 13:1807–8
life 9:1232–5
  conditions artificially created
    9:1235
  definitions 9:1232–3
  development on Earth 1:62–3;
    5:700; 6:823; 9:1234–5;
    10:1412; 12:1633–4
  extraterrestrial? 4:446; 9:1235;
    15:2121
life expectancy 13:1819
ligases 6:810
ligatures 17:2329
light and optics, light, light, treat-
    ment of medical conditions
    using 12:1723–4
lilies, voodoo 3:304, 305
limbs
  artificial 2:253–5
  reattachment 10:1439; 13:1765–6
  transplanting 10:1439; 18:2504
Linnaeus, Carl 12:1632
lions, mountain 19:2736
lipases 5:643; 6:836

liposuction 13:1767
lips, cleft lip and palate 13:1766–7
Lister, Sir Joseph 10:1367; 17:2328
lithium carbonate 4:452
lithotripsy 18:2549, 2550
lithotripters 17:2330
liver
  transplants 18:2498
    from animals 13:1734
lividity 12:1659
locusts, desert 19:2736
LSD (lysergic acid diethylamide)
    4:437
luciferase 10:1302
luciferin 10:1302
lungs 10:1303–5
  cancer 3:378; 6:847; 10:1305;
    11:1529; 12:1655
  radiological tests 14:1918
  transplants 18:2499
lupus vulgaris, treatment 12:1723
luteinizing hormone (LH) 8:1086
lutetium texaphyrin 12:1723–4
lyases 6:810
Lyell, Sir Charles 6:822
lymph nodes 3:377, 378
lymphocytes 8:1132, 1133, 1134–5,
    1136, 1137
  and graft versus host disease
    18:2503
lysergic acid diethylamide (LSD)
    4:437
lysine 3:303
lysosomes 3:411
lysozyme 8:1132, 1136

M

macronutrients 11:1557
macrophages 8:1132
macula 6:831; 12:1589
magnetic resonance imaging (MRI)
    2:282; 3:312; 4:448; 5:718;
    11:1540, 1541; 12:1657;
    14:1966
magnetite, in humans 16:2275
malaria 18:2555
  spread 12:1644, 1646
malnutrition 10:1370; 11:1558
maltase 1:98; 5:643; 6:810, 842
Malthus, Thomas 6:822
maltose 3:389; 6:842
mammals
  evolution 6:825
  pheromones 12:1691
  reproduction 14:1959
manures 6:843–4
  excess nitrates from 1:54
  green 6:844
marine biology 10:1332–3; 11:1567,
    1569; 18:2540
  and sonar 15:2126, 2128
Marsh, Othniel Charles 12:1633
marsupials 14:1958
mastitis, in cows 18:2586
medicine 10:1367–70
  "alternative" 10:1370
  electronics in 6:756–8
  forensic 7:919
  sports 16:2225–6
  see also veterinary science and
    medicine
medicines see pharmaceuticals (med-
    ical drugs); pharmacology
meditation, and raising body temper-
    ature 10:1376
meiosis 3:412
melanin 15:2088
  in hair 8:1033
melanocytes 15:2088, 2089
melanoma 6:806

membranes, semipermeable **12**:1609
memory (personal) **3**:310
menaquinone **19**:2613
Mendel, Gregor **6**:823; **7**:979
Ménière's disease **8**:1043
menopause **7**:997
menstrual disorders, sports and **16**:2226
mercury (metal)
  toxicity **10**:1372; **12**:1659; **13**:1801; **16**:2197
  uses, in dental fillings **5**:620; **10**:1371
mescaline **4**:437
mesoderm **6**:777
mesophyll, palisade and spongy **12**:1719, *1721*
mesothelioma **6**:847; **10**:1305
metabolic rate, and body size **2**:262
metabolism **6**:810; **10**:1373–6
  anabolism **6**:810; **10**:1376
  catabolism **6**:810; **10**:1373–5
metaphyses **3**:298
Methylophilus methylotrophus **6**:810; **7**:914
mice
  pest control of **12**:1677
  pheromones **12**:1691
microarrays, DNA **11**:1480
microbiology **10**:1409–12
  see *also* bacteria; fungi; micro-organisms; protozoa; viruses
microlenses **17**:2330
micronutrients **11**:1557–8
  see *also* minerals; vitamins
microorganisms
  affecting canning and bottling **3**:381, 382, 385
  and fermentation **6**:840
  influencing corrosion **4**:571
micropaleontology **12**:1634
microscopes, binocular, for operations **12**:*1589*, 1590
microsurgery **10**:1436–40; **13**:1765–6
  on the eye **12**:1590
  limb reattachment **10**:1439; **13**:1765–6
  skin grafts **10**:1438–9
  see *also* plastic surgery
microwaves, danger to health **11**:1450
Miescher, Friedrich **7**:973
migration **19**:2733–4
  birds' **11**:1514; **19**:2734
milk
  as a food **5**:600
  from genetically-modified animals **7**:977
Minamata disease **13**:1801
mineralocorticoids **8**:1086
minerals, dietary **11**:1557, 1558
mistletoe **12**:1644
mites
  harvest **18**:2585
  red spider **12**:1677
mitochondria **3**:411, *413*, *414*; **10**:1375
mitosis **3**:*412*, 413
MMR vaccine **18**:2556
mobility aids **11**:1469–72
modeling, molecular **12**:1688–9
molds (fungi), and food spoilage **7**:905
molecular biology **11**:1477–80
  molecular biophysics **2**:261
  see *also* DNA; genetic engineering; genetics
Moniliella acetobutans **7**:907
monkeys, vervet **19**:2733
monoamine-oxidase inhibitors (MAOIs) **12**:1681–2; **13**:1868

monoamines **3**:311
monosaccharides **3**:388–9
monosodium glutamate, allergy to **7**:907
morphine **12**:1685, 1687
morphogens **6**:778
mosquitoes **10**:1367; **12**:*1644*, 1646
  weapons against **12**:1678
moths
  codling **19**:2736
  control of prickly pear using **19**:2679
  peppered **6**:823; **13**:*1799*
  pheromones **12**:1690–1; **19**:2736
motor neurone disease **13**:1734
mouth **5**:642
MRI see magnetic resonance imaging
MRSA (methicillin-resistant *Staphylococcus aureus* **10**:1411
multichannel physiological recorders (MCPRs) **6**:758
multiple sclerosis, mobility aids for **11**:1471
muscle relaxants **12**:1682
muscles **11**:1504–6
  cells **3**:411; **11**:1505–6
  movement at the molecular level **2**:262
muscular dystrophy
  Duchenne's **7**:980
  mobility aids for **11**:1470–1
mustard gas **3**:379
  as a chemical weapon **4**:437, 438
mutations **6**:778, 823; **9**:1233; **11**:1479
  deletion, detected **11**:1479
  induced in plants **1**:54
  somatic **8**:1134, 1135
Mycoderma aceti **6**:842
myeloid cells **8**:1133
myocardial infarction see heart attack
myocarditis **8**:1047
myofibrils **11**:1505
myopia (nearsightedness) **6**:832; **9**:1213; **12**:1596–7
  laser surgery and **12**:1590
myosin **13**:1865

N

NADH **10**:1373, 1374, 1375
nailing, intramedullary **3**:300
narcolepsy **15**:2102
narcotics, poisoning **13**:1791
natural selection **6**:822
nearsightedness see myopia
nematodes, parasitic **12**:*1644*, 1645
nerve cells see neurons
nerve gases **4**:437, 438–9
neural tube defects **12**:1660
neuritis, optic **12**:1590
neurochemistry **3**:311
neurology **3**:312
neurons (nerve cells) **3**:411
  in the brain **3**:309, 311
   diaphorase neurons **3**:414
neurotransmitters **3**:311, 413–14; **11**:1506
  and parkinsonism **12**:1684
niacin **19**:2613
nictitating membrane **6**:832
nightmares **15**:2102
nightshade, deadly **13**:*1790*
Nitinol, and shape memory **1**:106–7
nitric oxide, biological roles **3**:413–14
nitric oxide synthase **3**:414
nitrogen
  atmospheric, fixed by bacteria **6**:843; **11**:*1526*
  cycle **11**:*1526*

nitrogen narcosis **2**:155; **18**:2538
nonsteroidal anti-inflammatory drugs (NSAIDs) **12**:1682
norepinephrine (noradrenaline) **3**:414; **6**:781
  in plants **3**:305
nose
  cancer **12**:1613
  plastic surgery **13**:1764, *1765*
  and smell **15**:2103, 2105–6
  see *also* sinuses, nasal
Novocain **1**:132
novocaine **12**:1681
NSAIDs (nonsteroidal anti-inflammatory drugs) **12**:1682
nucleic acid **7**:973
  hybridization **12**:1657
nucleoside analogs **12**:1688
nucleotides **7**:973
  as probes **10**:1333
nucleus, cell **3**:411, *413*
nutrient film technique (NFT) **8**:1120–1
nutrition and food science **11**:1557–9
  milk **5**:600
  and sports medicine **16**:2225–6
  see *also* vitamins

O

oak trees, galls **12**:1646
obesity **6**:837
obstetrics and gynecology **11**:1563–4
octreotide **6**:782
oculists (ophthalmologists) **12**:1589, 1596
odontology, forensic **7**:919
olfactory lobe **15**:2103
olfactory system **15**:2103, 2105–6
oligonucleotides **11**:1479
omnivores **5**:644–5
oncogenes, ras **2**:252
oncology, radiation see radiology
On the Origin of Species (Darwin) **6**:823; **12**:1633
operating rooms **6**:758; **11**:1581–4; **17**:*2327, 2329, 2332*
  patient surveillance units **6**:757
  see *also* anesthetics; surgery
ophthalmology **12**:1589–90
  ophthalmologists (oculists) **12**:1589, 1596
ophthalmoscopes **12**:*1591*, 1598
opium **13**:1791
opticians
  dispensing **12**:1596
  ophthalmic **12**:1596
optic nerve, damage to **12**:1589–90
optoisolators **6**:757
optometrists **12**:1589
organophosphates **12**:1677
  toxicity **12**:1700
organs, artificial creation of **6**:778
orthodontics **5**:618, 622
osmosis **12**:1609–10
  and kidney dialysis **5**:633
osseointegration **5**:620
osteoarthritis **10**:1369
osteocytes **3**:*300*
osteopathy **10**:1370; **12**:1611
osteoporosis **3**:298; **7**:997
otolaryngology **12**:1612–13
outpatient departments, electronic equipment **6**:758
overwearing syndrome **4**:561
owls, eyes **6**:*830*
oxazolidinones **10**:1411
oxidoreductases **6**:810
oxyhemoglobin **9**:1188
oxytocin **6**:781–2

P

pacemakers, cardiac see heart pacemaker
paleobotany **12**:1634
paleontology **12**:1631–5
  invertebrate **12**:1634–5
  see *also* evolution; fossils
palynology **12**:1634
pancreas **5**:643; **6**:781
  artificial **13**:1734
  cancer **6**:784
  endoscopy **6**:784
  transplants **6**:782
   cells **13**:1734
pantothenic acid **19**:2613
papillomata, laryngeal **12**:1613
paramecia **14**:*1958*
paramedics **1**:112
parasitology and parasites **12**:1644–6
parathormone see parathyroid hormone
parathyroid gland **6**:781
parathyroid hormone (parathormone) **6**:781, 782; **8**:1085
parathyroid hormone-related protein **6**:782
Paré, Ambroise **13**:1764; **17**:2327
Parkinson's disease **12**:1684
  treatment **3**:414; **5**:592
parthenogenesis **14**:1957
pasteurization, milk **5**:600, 601, *603*; **7**:906–7, 911
Pasteur, Louis **6**:840; **7**:906; **10**:1367, 1409; **17**:2328; **18**:2554–5
  and fermentation **19**:2725
pathology **12**:1655–9
  clinical **12**:1655, 1656–7
  comparative **12**:1655–6
  forensic **7**:919–20; **12**:1655, 1658–9
  plant **12**:1659
patient-monitoring systems **6**:757, 758
Pauling, Linus **19**:2614
PCR (polymerase chain reaction) **11**:1479
pediatrics **12**:1660–1
pellagra **19**:*2614*
penicillin **6**:841; **8**:1108; **10**:1409
Penicillium spp. **12**:*1682*
  for cheesemaking **5**:602
  for penicillin production **6**:*841*
pentoses **3**:389
peridontal disease **5**:619–20
perimysium **11**:1504
periosteum **3**:298
peristalsis **5**:642, 643
pest control **12**:1676–8
  biological see biological control
  in forests **7**:925
  pest avoidance **1**:61
  pesticides **6**:*844*; **12**:1676–8
   applying **12**:*1676*, 1677
   microencapsulated **10**:1414
   organic **1**:58, *59*
   organochlorine **12**:1676–7
   organophosphorus **12**:1677
   resistance to **12**:1678
   synthetic **1**:54–5, 61
PET see positron-emission tomography
phage vectors **7**:977
phagocytosis **8**:*1132*, 1133
pharmaceuticals (medical drugs) **12**:1681–5
  administration **12**:1683
  anticancer see chemotherapy
  for asthma **2**:252
  combinations **12**:1685
  cytotoxic **18**:2499
  dependency **12**:1685

design, using computer graphics 4:*534*; 12:1689
development of 3:414
dosage 12:1682–3
drug distribution 12:1683–5
encapsulated 10:1413, 1414
from biotechnology 2:263
"anti-sense" drugs 2:265
from transgenic plants and animals 2:*264*, 266
immunosuppressive 18:2499
inhalers for 1:40
mode of action 12:1683, 1687–8
molecular modeling 12:1688–9
pain relief 12:1683
receptors 12:1687–8
resistance 12:1685
side effects 12:1685, 1689
targeting 12:1689
testing of new 12:*1685*, 1689
trials 6:*811*
types 12:1681–2
sulphonamide 1:135
see also anesthetics; antibiotics
see also pharmacology; vaccines
pharmacology 12:**1686–9**
see also pharmaceuticals
pharynx 10:1303
pheromones 12:**1690–1**; 15:2105; 19:2736
traps 12:1678, 1691
phobias 10:1369
phosgene (carbonyl chloride), as a chemical weapon 4:437, 438
phosphoenolpyruvate (PEP) 10:1374
phosphofructokinase 10:1376
3-phosphoglycerate 12:1720
phosphoinositide system 2:252
photochemotherapy 12:1724
photodynamic therapy (PDT) 3:380
photosynthesis 1:62; 3:389, 412; 5:645; 10:1373; 12:**1719–22**
photosystems I and II 12:1722
phototherapy (photodynamic therapy) 12:**1723–4**
physic nuts 2:260
physiology 13:**1733–4**
definition of death 9:1232
phytoplankton 10:1332
pigeon's milk 8:1087
pigs
cloned 7:*978*
intensively-reared 1:*56, 57*
organically-reared 1:*61*
organs, for transplants 18:2504
slaughtering 15:2090–7, 2098
transgenic 18:2504
and truffles 12:*1690*
veterinary work and 18:2586
pill, contraceptive 13:1734, 1818
pinning, bone fractures 3:300
pituitary gland 6:781–2; 8:1085, *1086*
cell culture, and insulin production 13:1733–4
placebos 12:1689
placenta, hormones 6:782
plague 6:811
plankton 10:1332, 1333
plants
and the atmosphere 1:62, 63
carnivorous 5:645
cells 3:412, *413*
communication between 3:304–5
evolution 7:988
fat-reducing 6:837
genetically-engineered *see* genetic engineering
grown in water (hydroponics) 8:1120–2; 9:1194
high-tech breeding 1:53–4
in-vitro culturing 2:266
leguminous 11:*1526*

natural fibers from 6:849–50
and nickel 11:1524
parasitic 12:1644
photosynthesis 1:62; 3:389, 412; 5:645; 10:1373; 12:**1719–22**
reproduction 14:1958
sense of touch 3:303–4, *305*
size and metabolic rate 2:262
transgenic 19:2681
plaque
arterial 8:1046–7, 1052
dental 5:619
plasmids 1:53; 2:263, *264*; 7:977
plasmolysis 12:1609
plaster casts 3:300
plastic surgery 13:**1764–7**
on gums 5:620
limb reattachment 13:1765–6
see also microsurgery; skin, grafts
pneumographs 13:1807
pneumonia, vaccine 18:2557
poison gas 4:437
poisons 13:**1790–2**; 16:2197
and forensic science 7:918–19; 13:1792
polio, vaccines 18:2555, 2556
pollen 10:*1431*; 14:1958
pollution
effects on the lungs 10:1305
and free radicals 11:1559
polymerase chain reaction (PCR) 11:1479
polypeptides 13:1864–5
polyps, colon 6:*784*, 785
polysaccharides 3:389–90
population 13:**1816–19**
control *see* contraceptives
porphyria 12:*1724*
porphyrins 12:1723
positron-emission tomography (PET) 2:151, 281; 3:312
postmortems (autopsies) 12:1658
post-traumatic stress disorder (PTSD) 13:1867
potatoes, genetically-engineered 3:303, 304
poultry, slaughtering 15:2098
pregnancy 11:**1563–4**; 14:*1958*
ectopic 6:785
medical drugs taken during 12:1685
nutrition during 8:1047
preterm delivery 12:1661
rubella during 12:1589
tests during 8:*1135*; 11:*1563*, 1564
tests for 2:263
see also in-vitro fertilization; obstetrics and gynecology
prehension 2:255
presbyopia 6:832; 16:2191
prickly pear, control of 19:2679
primates, evolution 6:825
proctoscopes 17:2331
progesterone 12:1687
prohormones 8:1084
prokaryotes 6:823; 9:1235
prolactin 8:1087
prostaglandins 12:1683
in plants 3:305
prostate gland, operations on 18:2550
prostheses 2:253–7; 13:1764, 1767
eye 12:*1613*; 13:1767
see also bioengineering
proteins 2:261; 13:**1864–6**
chiral 4:458
complete and incomplete 11:1557
dietary 11:1557; 13:*1866*
fibrous 13:1865
functions 13:1865
see also enzymes
globular 13:1865

manufacture
single-cell protein (SCP) foods 6:810; 7:914; 13:*1866*
using genetic engineering 7:978
structure 2:261; 13:1864–5
from computer graphics 13:*1864*, 1866
synthesis 7:974–5; 11:1477–8; 12:1657
uses 13:1865–6
see also amino acids
protozoa, immune response to 8:1136
Prozac (fluoxetine) 12:1682; 13:1868
Pseudomonas spp. 9:1168; 10:1411
psoralen compounds 12:1723; 18:*2533*
psoriasis 12:*1724*; 15:2089; 18:*2533*
psychiatry 13:**1867–8**
psychoacoustics 1:26–7
psychoanalysis 13:1867
psychochemicals 4:437
psychology, sports 16:2226
ptyalin 5:642
pulse meters 16:2224
pupils, eye 6:830, *831*; 9:1227
Purkinje fibers 11:1506
pyrethrum 12:*1676*
pyridoxine 19:2613

Q

Q fever, as a biological weapon 4:438
quinine 12:1686
quinuclidinyl benzilate (BZ) 4:437

R

rabies, vaccines 18:2555, 2556
radar, safety 14:1898
radiation
effects on the body
cause of cancer 3:378
dangers from cell phones 3:416
from radiotherapy 14:1921
in space 16:*2175*
radioactive in-situ hybridization 11:*1480*
radiography 19:*2722–3*
see also X-ray imaging
radiology 14:**1917–19**
see also body scanners; X-ray imaging, of the body
radionuclide scanning *see* scintigraphy
radiotherapy 3:*378*, 379, 380; 14:**1920–2**; 19:2723
conformational therapy 14:1922
radon, a health hazard 11:1529
Rafflesia arnoldi 12:1644
rats, pest control of 12:1677, 1678
RDAs (recommended dietary allowances) 11:1558
receptors, cell 3:413
recommended dietary allowances (RDAs) 11:1558
rectum 5:644
red drop 12:1722
refraction, refractive state of the eye 12:1596–8
rehydration therapy, oral 10:1370
renal failure 5:633
renin 18:2549
rennet 5:602
rennin 5:643
renograms 14:1918–19
repetitive strain injury (RSI) 11:1491
replication 9:1233
reproduction 14:**1957–9**
reptiles, evolution 6:824, 825

respiration
aerobic 6:840
anaerobic 6:840
see also lungs
restriction fragment length polymorphisms (RFLPs) 1:53–4; 11:1479
retina 4:510; 6:830–1; 12:1589
and color blindness 12:1598
detached 12:1589
repaired using lasers 12:1590
retinitis pigmentosa 12:1589
retinol 19:2613
retinoscopy 12:1597–8
retinulae 6:832
reverse transcriptase 11:1478
RFLPs (restriction fragment length polymorphisms) 1:53–4; 11:1479
Rhesus (Rh) factor 2:271–2
rhinoplasty 13:*1765*
rhodopsin 6:831
riboflavin (vitamin B2) 5:600; 6:837; 19:2613
ribosomes 3:411–12; 11:1477, 1478
ribulose 1,5-biphosphate 12:1720
rice, lysine in 3:303
ricin 4:438; 13:1792
rickets 11:1558
rifampicin 6:812
rigor mortis 7:919; 12:1658–9
ringworm 18:2585
RNA (ribonucleic acid) 7:973
messenger (mRNA) 7:974, 975; 11:1477; 12:1657
transfer (tRNA) 11:1478
Robodoc 17:2332
robotics
nanorobots, in blood vessels 10:*1419*
for surgery 10:1440; 17:2331–2; 19:*2616*
Rodale, J. I. 1:59
rods and cones 6:831; 9:1240
rubella 12:1589
rumen 5:644
ruminants 5:644

S

Sabin, Albert Bruce 18:2555
Saccharomyces
bailii 7:907
cerevisiae 7:963; 10:1409–10; 19:2725
sake 19:2726
SAD (seasonal affective disorder) 12:1724
Sagan, Carl 9:1234
salbutamol 2:252
salicylic acid 12:1686
and plants 3:305
saliva 5:642
Salk, Jonas Edward 18:2555
Salmonella 7:906
salt *see* sodium chloride
salt glands 8:1087
salvarsan (arsphenamine) 1:135; 10:1368
sapwood 9:1294
sarcolemma 11:1504–5
Sarin 4:437, 439, *441*
Sarracenia plants 15:*2105*
saxitoxin 4:438
scanners, body *see* body scanners
scarring 15:2089
schistosomiasis 12:1646
schizophrenia 13:1868
Schizosaccharomyces pombe 10:1410; 11:1479

scintigraphy (radionuclide scanning) 2:281; 14:1917
sclera 6:830
scrapie 18:2587
scurvy 11:1558; 19:2614
seabirds, salt glands 8:1087
seals, elephant 10:1332
seasickness 8:1043
seasonal affective disorder (SAD) 12:1724
sebaceous glands 15:2088
sebum 15:2088
secretin 5:643
sedatives 12:1682
selective serotonin reuptake inhibitors (SSRIs) 12:1681–2; 13:1868
semen, bull, frozen 14:1947
semicircular canals 8:1042, 1043
senility, blood flow and 14:1919
sequence homology 11:1478
serology
    forensic 7:919
    veterinary 18:2584
serotonin, in plants 3:305
Severe Combined Immune Deficiency (SCID) 8:1133
sex-change operations 13:1765
sharks, teeth 5:645
sheep
    cloned 2:264
    Judas 15:2096
    milk from transgenic ewes 2:264, 266
    slaughtering 15:2096–7
    veterinary work and 18:2586
shock lung 13:1791
shunts, arterio-venous (A-V) 5:635, 636
sickle-cell disease 2:273
SIDS (sudden infant death syndrome) 12:1661
Silent Spring, The (Carson) 1:61
silkworms 6:849
    bioengineered 2:266
sinoatrial node 8:1046; 11:1506
sinuses, nasal
    blocked 12:1612–13
    cancer 12:1613
    endoscopic surgery 12:1613
    sinusitis 12:1612
size ratios, in nature 2:262
skeletons 3:297
    and archaeology 2:158
    identifying people from 7:920
skiaskopy (retinoscopy) 12:1597–8
skin 15:2087–9
    animal 9:1222
    artificial 15:2087, 2088–9
    color 15:2089
    diseases 15:2089
        in animals 18:2585
        cancer 6:806; 15:2089
    galvanograph records 13:1807
    grafts 10:1438–9; 13:1765, 1766; 15:2087; 18:2500
    resurfacing 13:1767
    structure 15:2087, 2088
skull
    boring holes into 17:2327
    X-ray image 19:2724
sleep 15:2099–2102
    deprivation 15:2101
    disorders 15:2101–2
sleeping sickness (African trypanosomiasis) 1:135
sleepwalking 15:2102
sleeping sickness (Encephalitis lethargica) 12:1684
smallpox 10:1368–9
    as a biological weapon 4:437
    inoculation (variolation) 18:2554

vaccines 2:264; 8:1132, 1134; 18:2554
smell and taste 15:2103–6
    smell 3:310; 15:2103–6
    taste 15:2103–4, 2106
Smith, William 6:822; 12:1633
smoking
    and free radicals 11:1559
    and lung damage 10:1305
snakes
    feeding 5:645
    and infrared radiation 6:742
    venom 13:1792
sodium chloride (salt), and health 7:907; 8:1035
soil
    effect of lightning on 6:725
    erosion, reduction 1:61; 6:816–18
    improvement, in forests 7:924
    tillage 1:55
Soil Association, The 1:59
somatoform disorder 13:1867–8
somatostasin 6:782
somatotrophin 18:2588
sound, hearing 8:1041–4
soybeans 6:837; 13:1865
    artificial meats from 7:913–14
    herbicide-tolerant 19:2681
species 12:1632
speech and language 16:2200–3; 19:2615
    and the brain 3:310; 16:2201
sphygmomanometers 10:1326; 16:2211
spina bifida
    mobility aids for 11:1470–1
    testing for 11:1564
    vitamin supplements and 19:2614
Spirulina maxima 7:914
splints 3:299
spondylitis, ankylosing 10:1369
sports medicine 16:2225–6
SSRIs (selective serotonin reuptake inhibitors) 12:1681–2; 13:1868
stains, laboratory 1:135
stamens 14:1958
Staphylococcus aureus, methicillin resistant (MRSA) 10:1411
staples, for joining tissues 17:2330
starch 3:389, 390
Starling, Ernest 8:1084
Steiner, Rudolf 1:58
stem cells 7:997; 8:1132
    embryonic 3:414; 6:778
stents 8:1052; 14:1918
stereoradiography 16:2264
stereoscopy
    medical applications 16:2264
    optical 16:2264
sterilization
    autoclaves 2:190
    food 5:601; 7:912; 18:2533
    of hospital laundry 9:1218
    using gamma rays 6:745
sterilization (surgical) 13:1818
sternomastoid muscles 10:1303
steroids 6:781
    drug testing for 16:2226
    in plants 3:305
sterols, plant 6:837
stethoscopes 16:2265
Still, Andrew Taylor 12:1611
stomach 5:642–3, 644
stomach pumps 13:1791
stomatitis, angular 5:600
strabismus (squint) 6:832
Streptococcus 12:1682
    thermophilus 5:603; 7:904
streptokinase 8:1047
Streptomyces spp. 10:1409; 12:1687
strokes, vascular 3:414; 10:1438
stromatolites 5:700; 7:988

sucrose 3:389, 390
sudden infant death syndrome (SIDS) 12:1661
sugar 3:389
    in food 7:907
sugar beet 16:2295, 2296
sugarcane 16:2295, 2296
suicide 10:1369
sulfa drugs 11:1368
"superbugs" 4:440–1; 10:1411
surgery 17:2327–32
    alternatives to 17:2330
        see also body scanners
    aseptic 10:1367; 17:2327, 2329
    cold-probe 5:592
    cryosurgery 5:591; 17:2330
    diagnostic 12:1657–8
    endoscopes used in 6:785; 12:1613; 17:2330–1, 2332
    eye 12:1589, 1590
        using lasers 9:1213, 1214; 12:1590; 17:2330
    heart (cardiovascular) 8:1049–52
    history 17:2327–8
    "keyhole" 18:2549
    laser 6:785, 856; 9:1214
    plastic, glues used in 1:32
    preparation for 11:1581–2; 17:2328–9
    and robotics 10:1440; 17:2331–2; 19:2616
    stereotactic 17:2330
    telesurgery 17:2332
    veterinary 18:2584–5
    virtual 17:2332
        see also anesthetics; microsurgery; operating rooms
surveillance, sentinel 6:812
Sutherland, Thomas 13:1867
sutures 17:2329
SV40 (simian virus 40) 7:977
sweat glands 15:2105
symbiosis, parasitism 12:1644
synapses 3:309, 311
    neuromuscular 3:414; 11:1506
syncytial cells 11:1506
syndactyly 13:1766
synovial fluid 3:297
syphilis, treatment 1:135
systole 8:1045

T

tabun 4:437
tamoxifen 12:1687
tartar, dental 5:619–20
tartrazine 7:907
taste 15:2103–4
    taste buds 15:2106
taxidermy 17:2353–4
Tay-Sachs disease 7:980
TCA cycle see Krebs cycle
tear gases 4:437; 11:1532, 1534; 14:1972
tear glands 6:830
teeth 5:642; 18:2466
    of animals 5:645
    decay 5:618–19, 622
    false 5:620, 622
    fluoride and 5:620; 8:1034, 1036; 18:2466; 19:2666
    identifying people from 7:920
    replacement 5:620
    structure 5:618
        see also dentistry; toothpaste
telesurgery 17:2332
teletherapy, cobalt 14:1921
temperature
    body
        raised during meditation 10:1376

regulation 15:2087–8
tendons 11:1504
teratogenesis 12:1685
termites, pheromones 12:1690
testosterone(s) 8:1087
    in plants 3:305
"test tube baby" procedure 7:980; 11:1564
tetrodotoxin 13:1792
thalamus 3:309
thalidomide 12:1685
thermograms and thermography, of the body 2:281, 282; 6:743; 17:2422
thermolysin 13:1864
Thermophilus aquaticus 7:978
thiamine 19:2613
throat
    cancer 12:1613
    endoscopic surgery 12:1612, 1613
thrombin 8:1047
thrombosis, coronary 8:1046–7
thumbs, replacement 10:1439
thylakoids 12:1722
thymine 7:973–4; 11:1477, 1478
thymus 8:1134
thyroid gland 6:781; 8:1085, 1087
thyroxine 6:781; 8:1085
tillage, soil 1:55
tinnitus 8:1041
tissue plasminogen activator 2:263
tissues, artificial creation of 6:778
tissue typing 18:2498
toads, poisonous 13:1792
tobacco 3:304
    disease-resistant 1:55
tocophenol 19:2613
tongue 15:2106
toothpaste 1:17; 18:2466
tortoises, giant 9:1232
total body irradiation (TBI) 14:1920
total crop management 1:55
toxicology, forensic 7:918–19; 13:1792
Toxocara vitalorum 12:1645
trachea 10:1303
traction 3:300
tranquilizers 12:1682
transcription factors 6:778
transferases 6:810
transfusions, blood 2:272, 273; 17:2328
transpiration 19:2665
transplants 18:2498–504
    animal organs (xenotransplants) 13:1734; 18:2504
    bioprosthetic valves 18:2500
    bone marrow 3:380; 18:2499, 2502, 2503–4
    hand 10:1439; 18:2504
    heart 12:1660; 18:2498–9, 2500–2
        extra-heart operations 18:2502
        heart–lung 12:1660; 18:2499, 2502
        valves 18:2499, 2500
        see also heart, artificial
    kidney 6:782; 18:2498
    limb 10:1439; 18:2504
    liver 13:1734; 18:2498
    microsurgery techniques 10:1438–9
    pancreas 6:782
    rejection 8:1137
        drug control of 18:2499
        graft versus host disease (GVHD) 18:2499, 2503
    skin grafts 10:1438–9; 13:1765, 1766; 15:2087; 18:2500
    spare-part surgery 18:2499–2500, 2503
        growing organs for 6:778; 18:2500

tooth 5:622
see also joints (body parts), artificial
transposons (jumping genes) 3:303
tree of life 6:822
trees
    hardwood and softwood 9:1293–4
    rubber 14:1997
trepanning 17:2327
tricarboxylic acid cycle (TCA) cycle
    see Krebs cycle
trichloroacetic acid (TCA) 13:1767
trichloroethylene 1:131
Trichoderma 12:1645
tricyclic antidepressants 12:1681;
    13:1868
trilobites 6:824; 12:1634–5
trophosomes 11:1567
truffles 12:1690
trypanosomiasis 8:1136
trypsinogen 5:643
tuberculosis (TB) 6:811, 812;
    10:1305, 1370
    in cattle 18:2587
tube worms 10:1333
tubocurarine 12:1687
tularemia, as a biological weapon
    4:438
tumors
    holographic visualization 8:1083
    malignant and benign 3:377
    see also cancer
typhoid
    as a biological weapon 4:437
    vaccine 18:2557

U

ulcers, stomach 10:1367, 1411
ultrasonics
    uses
        body scans 2:279–80, 282;
            12:1657; 18:2531
        brain exploration 18:2532
        dentistry 5:622
        scans during pregnancy 11:1564;
            18:2531, 2586
        therapy 18:2532, 2550
ultraviolet lamps, for healing 18:2534
umbilical cord 6:777
ureters 18:2549

urethra 18:2549
Urey, Harold 9:1234
urine, tests 12:1657; 18:2457
urograms 18:2549
urology 18:2549–50
    see also dialysis machines; kidneys

V

vaccines 8:1137; 10:1369, 1370;
    18:2554–7
    against biological weapons 4:440
    genetically-engineered 2:264–5,
        266; 7:978
    see also immunization
vacuoles, cell 3:412
V agents 4:437
Valium (diazepam) 12:1682; 13:1791
valves, heart 8:1045, 1046; 18:2568
    surgery 8:1049, 1051
vasectomy 13:1818
vasodilation 10:1376
vasopressin 8:1086
vegetables, dietary 11:1558
veins, pulmonary 8:1045
vena cava, inferior and superior
    8:1045
ventilators, automatic 1:132
ventriculoscopes 6:785
Venus's flytrap 5:645
vertebrae, slipped disks, detection
    19:2723–4
vertebrates
    evolution 6:824
    smell used by 15:2105
veterinary science and medicine
    18:2583–8
villi 5:642, 643, 644
viruses (microorganisms) 10:1410
    bacteriophages 10:1410
    and bioengineered vaccines 2:264
    as biological weapons 4:438
    and cancer 3:378
    foot-and-mouth-disease (FMDV)
        2:261
    hepatitis B 12:1659
    immune response to 8:1136
    reproduction 14:1957
    see also HIV (human immunodefi-
        ciency virus)

vision 6:830–1; 9:1240
    persistence of 12:1607
    quantifying 6:832
    stereoscopic 6:831; 16:2263
    visual acuity 12:1596
visual purple 6:831
vitamins 11:1557–8; 19:2612–14
    A 19:2612, 2613, 2614
    antioxidant 11:1558–9
    B complex 19:2612, 2613, 2614,
        2727
    B2 5:600; 6:837; 19:2613
    C 11:1558–9; 19:2612, 2613, 2614
    D 19:2612, 2613
    deficiency 11:1558; 19:2612, 2613,
        2614
    E 7:997; 11:1558–9; 19:2613
    as food additives 7:914
    from fats 6:837
    K 19:2613
    supplements 19:2614
vitiligo 12:1723
vitreous humor 6:830; 9:1240
vocal cords, growths 12:1613
voice see speech and language
voice-stress analysis 13:1808
vomeronasal organ (VNO) 12:1691

W

walking frames 11:1472
Wallace, Alfred 6:822
wasps
    for biological control 1:61
    gall 12:1646
water, consumption 11:1557
water boatmen 10:1359
water fleas (daphnia) 12:1716
water hyacinths 5:608; 13:1803
Watson, James 7:973
wax, ear 8:1041
weed control 19:2678–81
weevils, control using parasites
    12:1645
whales 19:2733, 2734–5
    whaling and 19:2685–8
wheat, genetically-engineered 3:303
whiplash injuries 2:209
withdrawal symptoms, to drugs
    12:1685

wood, dust, a health hazard 19:2711
worms
    immune response to 8:1136
    muscles 11:1504
    nematode 1:61
        life span 7:996
    on the seabed 11:1567

X

xenotransplants 13:1734; 18:2504
xerography, body scans using 2:281
xerophthalmia 11:1558
X-ray imaging
    of the body 12:1657; 14:1917;
        19:2721, 2722–3, 2724
    of animals 18:2584
    dental 5:619
    fractures 3:300
    see also Computed Axial
        Tomography; radiotherapy
xylocaine 12:1687

Y

yeast 6:840; 10:1409–10; 19:2725–7
    enzymes in 6:841–2
    and food spoilage 7:905
    food yeast 19:2726–7
    and protein production 6:810;
        7:914; 13:1866; 19:2726–7
    industrial uses 19:2727
    used in baking, brewing, and fer-
        mentation 2:236, 237; 3:406;
        19:2725–6
yellow fever 6:811
    as a biological weapon 4:438
    mosquitoes carrying 12:1644

Z

zidovudine (AZT) 12:1688
Zimmer frames 11:1472
zoology 19:2733–6
    see also entomology
zoonoses 18:2586–7
zooplankton 10:1332
zymase 1:98; 6:841

Chemistry and Materials Science

A

abrasives 1:17–18; 17:2322
    aluminum oxide 1:17, 18, 111
    diamond 1:18; 5:638
    made by crystal synthesis 17:2347
    used in grinding machines
        10:1309–10
ABS (acrylonitrile-butadiene-
    styrene) rubber 13:1772;
    14:2001
acetates, fibers see cellulose acetate;
    cellulose triacetate
acetic acid, and sodium acetate
    12:1693
acetic anhydride 6:852
acetone see propanone
acetylene see ethyne
acids and alkalis 1:23–5
    acids
        Lewis acids 1:23
        organic 1:23
        protonic 1:23
    alkalis 1:23

see also pH
acrylamide (propenamide) 13:1771
acrylic acid (propenoic acid) 12:1629
acrylic fibers 6:853
acrylic resins 1:30–1; 12:1629
acrylics 13:1771
acrylonitrile (propenonitrile) 7:880;
    14:1999
    polymers of 6:853; 13:1771
actinides 6:765; 12:1673; 18:2485,
    2487
actinium 18:2485
activation energy 9:1202
adhesives and sealants 1:28–32
    adhesives 1:28–32
        anaerobic 1:32
        thermoplastic and thermosetting
            1:30
        wood 19:2718
    sealants 1:28, 32
adrenaline see epinephrine
air 1:62–4
    composition 1:62
    origins 1:62–3

uses for gases 1:64
aircraft
    materials 1:43, 44
alchemy 4:449; 5:661
alcohol 1:97–8
    for beverages see beer and brewing;
        spirits; winemaking
    as a biofuel 2:258–9; 6:794
    distillation 1:97, 98; 5:661;
        16:2215–18
    industrial 6:842
    production 1:98
    surface tension 17:2321
aldehydes 4:456
aldrin 12:1676
alembics 5:661
alicyclic compounds 4:455
aliphatic compounds 8:1105
alkali metals 1:99–101; 12:1673
alkaline earth metals 12:1673
alkanes (paraffins) 4:454, 456;
    8:1105, 1106
alkenes (olefins) 4:454–5, 456;
    8:1105, 1107

catalytic hydrogenation 15:2129,
    2130
    fibers derived from 6:853
alkoxide ions 4:456
alkylation 11:1576, 1579
alkylbenzine sulfonate (NSD) 5:631,
    632
alkyl phenol polyethylene oxide
    5:631
alkynes 4:454, 455, 456; 8:1105, 1107
alloys 1:102–7; 10:1387
    amorphous (metallic glasses) 1:107
    dental amalgams 5:619; 10:1371;
        15:2080
    fusible 1:106
    heat treatment of steel 1:104;
        10:1387
    intermetallic compounds 1:104;
        10:1351
    multiphase 1:103
    powder metallurgy 1:104–6
    precipitation hardening 1:104
    shape-memory 5:622; 10:1351–2,
        1363

alloys (cont.)
  Nitinol 1:106–7; 10:1351–2, 1363
  solid solutions 1:103
  superconductivity 17:2312
  uses 1:105–7
    aircraft construction 1:44, 106; 10:1363
    bioengineering 2:256
    coins 4:507
    superplastic forming 10:1363
  see also names of individual alloys
alumina see aluminum oxide
aluminum 1:108–11
  alloys 1:106, 108, 109–10; 3:332
  compounds, uses 1:109–10
  corrosion resistance 4:570
  discovery 4:449
  extraction 1:109, 110; 6:738; 10:1378
  foil 1:109
  manufacture 1:110–11; 10:1388
  occurrence 1:109
  powdered 1:108–9
  properties 1:108
  recycling 14:1940–1
  uses 1:108–10
    bicycle frames 2:243
    boat building 2:277
    in buildings 3:336
    cans 3:385
    in paints 12:1628
    in power cables 3:344
  welding 1:111; 11:1529
aluminum bronze 3:332
aluminum chloride 12:1616
  anhydrous 4:449
  hydrated (aluminum chlorohy-drate) 1:110
aluminum hydroxide 1:109; 19:2664
aluminum oxide (alumina) 1:109, 110
  aluminum manufactured from 1:110–11
  forming gemstones 5:599
  melting point 3:424
  uses 3:426
    abrasives 1:17, 18, 111
    in ammonia synthesis plants 3:407
    in batteries 2:229
aluminum silicate 15:2077
aluminum sulfate 1:109
alums 1:109
amalgams 1:106; 10:1372
  dental 5:619; 10:1371; 15:2080
amber 6:725
americium 6:765
amides 4:457; 11:1527
amine oxides 6:851
amines 11:1527
amino acids 1:114; 2:251; 4:458; 7:974; 13:1864, 1866
aminobenzene see aniline
aminophenols 8:1108
ammonia
  manufacture 1:25, 115; 3:405, 407; 4:451; 11:1525–6
  uses 11:1526–7
    for maser action 9:1211–12
    refrigeration 14:1946
ammoniac see ammonium chloride
ammonium chloride (ammoniac) 11:1527
ammonium dihydrogen phosphate (ADP) 13:1744–5
ammonium diuranate 11:1537
ammonium hydrogen sulfate, elec-trolysis 12:1621
ammonium ions 14:2015
ammonium nitrate
  explosive 6:827, 829
  fertilizer 4:450; 6:829, 843, 844

ammonium nitrate fuel-oil mixture (ANFO) 6:828
ammonium perchlorate 14:1994
ammonium phosphate, production 14:2014
ammonium salts 14:2014–15
ammonium sulfate, fertilizer 6:844
ammonium thioglycolate 8:1032
amosite 6:846
amphiboles 6:846
anatase 5:599
ANFO (ammonium nitrate fuel-oil mixture) 6:828
angle grinders 1:17
aniline (phenylamine; aminobenzene) 1:133; 4:453, 457, 498; 8:1107
  steam distillation 5:663
aniline and azo dyes see dyes
anisotropy 9:1257–8
anodizing 17:2323
anthracene 4:498
anthracite (hard coal) 4:494
anthraquinones 5:691
antifouling techniques 2:149
antifreeze 1:73, 97; 6:802
antimony, alloys with lead 9:1221
aquamarines 16:2272
aqua regia 1:25; 13:1782
aragonite 16:2240
aramids 6:852; 13:1805, 1806; 17:2405
  inflammability 7:880
  see also Kevlar
argentite 15:2079
argon 11:1528, 1529
  separation from air 5:590
armor
  body 2:161–3
  tank 2:167
aromatic compounds 4:455; 8:1106, 1107–8
  aromatic rings as functional groups 4:456
  from petroleum 4:453
arsenic, in groundwater 7:981
asbestos 6:846–7; 7:953
asparagine 1:114
aspartame 7:914
Aspergillus niger 19:2727
asphalt
  as a fuel 6:797
  liquid, transportation 7:929
astatine 8:1036
atomic mass, relative 6:763, 764
austenite 10:1387
Avogadro's Law 7:961
azeotropes 5:663

B

Baekeland, Leo 13:1770
Bakelite 8:1108; 9:1162; 13:1770, 1773; 17:2370
barite 16:2299
barium oxide 12:1618
barium peroxide 12:1618
barium sulfate 19:2723
barium titanate 3:426; 13:1745
Barrer, Richard 19:2728, 2729
bauxite 1:109, 110; 10:1378
Bayer, Adolf von 13:1770
beer and brewing 1:98; 2:234–7; 3:406; 6:841
benzene 4:455, 498; 8:1105–6
  bonds in 4:444; 8:1105–6
  from oil refining 11:1578–9
  industrial uses 8:1107; 11:1578–9
  ring structure 8:1106, 1108
benzine 5:687
benzol 4:498
benzoyl peroxide 1:100; 13:1771,

1810
berkelium 6:765
beryllium, atomic structure 2:182
Berzelius, J. J. 15:2076
beta decay 6:765, 771; 14:1907
biochemistry 2:251–2
bioconversion 2:258
biodiesel 2:259; 6:794; 7:963
bioethanol 2:259
biofuels 2:258–60; 6:794
biogas 2:259–60; 3:343
bioinorganic chemistry 4:452
biosteel 2:163
biscuit ware 3:426
bismuth, removal from lead 9:1220–1
bisphenol 13:1772
bitumen 1:30; 5:663; 6:817
  from oil refining 11:1575, 1579
blacktop (tarmacadam) 1:30; 14:1973, 1975
Boltzmann distribution 4:463; 12:1728; 17:2416
bond polarization 4:459
bonds, chemical see chemical bonding and valency
bone ash (calcium phosphate) 3:425
bone meal 6:844
boranes 4:451
borax (sodium borate) 1:100; 12:1709
borazon 11:1527
boron carbide 1:18
boron hydrides 4:451
boron nitride 2:163; 11:1527; 17:2347
borosilicate glass 11:1549–50
Boyle, Robert 4:449; 6:763; 7:960; 12:1671
Brand, Hennig 12:1698
brass 1:106, 107; 3:316–17; 19:2731
  manufacture 1:102; 3:316
  working 3:316–17
Bravais lattices 5:598
brewing see beer and brewing
brimstone 16:2298
brocade 17:2405, 2406–7
bromine 8:1036
  compounds, flame-retarding 7:881
  extraction from seawater 8:1036; 11:1569
  uses 8:1036
bromochlorodifluoromethane (BCF) 8:1034
bromoethane 4:459
bronze 1:106; 3:331–2
  bells cast in 2:238
Brownian motion 9:1203
buckminsterfullerenes (buckyballs) 4:451; 10:1360
buckyballs see buckminsterfullerenes
buffers, chemical
  buffer solutions 12:1693
  in living cells 1:114
Buna rubbers 13:1771; 14:1999
Bunsen burners 3:339; 7:878
but-1-ene 13:1770; 15:2129
but-2-ene 4:455; 8:1105
butadiene 4:460; 8:1106; 13:1771; 14:1999–2001
butane 4:454; 5:625; 7:955, 959
  from oil refining 11:1577
  liquefied 8:1106
butanone 11:1579
butyl alcohol 6:842

C

cabochons 16:2270, 2272
cadmium, poisoning 13:1801
caesium, in atomic clocks 4:485, 488
calcining 19:2729

calcite 16:2239, 2240
calcium 18:2486
calcium carbide, action of water on 8:1107
calcium carbonate
  in toothpaste 18:2466
  see also limestone
calcium chloride, electrolysis 6:738
calcium hydroxide (slaked lime; lime)
  production 1:25
  uses 1:25; 3:417; 19:2656
calcium magnesium silicate 15:2077
calcium oxide (quicklime; lime), pro-duction 9:1200
calcium phosphate 3:298
californium 6:765
  isotopes 14:1907
caprolactam 13:1804, 1811
capsaicin 11:1532
carbamates, pesticides 12:1677
carbohydrates 3:388–90
carbolic oil 4:498
carbon 3:391–3
  activated 3:322; 4:476
  allotropes 3:392; 10:1360
  bonds 3:393; 4:454
  inorganic compounds 4:449
  isotopes 2:157; 3:393; 6:763; 9:1276; 14:1906
    and carbon dating 2:157; 3:393; 9:1276; 14:1908, 1916
  nanotubes 10:1420
  organic compounds see chemistry, organic
  phase diagrams of 10:1362
carbon black 10:1311; 12:1628, 1696
carbon dating 2:157; 3:393; 9:1276; 14:1908, 1916
carbon dioxide
  atmospheric, from ice-core sam-ples 13:1800
  cycle 1:64
  in fire extinguishers 6:863
  a greenhouse gas 4:477, 479; 6:807; 7:998
  lasers using 9:1213
  liquid 18:2569
    as an explosive 6:829
    as a cleaning solvent 5:689
    solid 5:664; 18:2570
carbon disulfide 4:464
carbon fiber 3:394–5; 17:2405
  manufacture 3:394–5
carbonic acid, in the water supply 13:1786
carbon monoxide, molecules 4:462
carbon tetrachloride 8:1106
carbonyl chloride see phosgene
carborundum see silicon carbide
carboxylic acids 1:25; 4:457
  production 1:25
carnauba wax 5:716
Carothers, Wallace 13:1804
casein 9:1224
cassiterite 17:2447
Castner cells 1:100
catalysts 3:402–7; 4:452, 464
  chiral 4:458
  and fluidized beds 7:901
  transition-metal 3:405; 4:452; 18:2488
catechol 8:1108
cathodic protection 4:571; 13:1754; 19:2732
caustic potash see potassium hydroxide
caustic soda see sodium hydroxide
cellophane 3:390; 12:1626; 13:1769
Celluloid 3:390; 13:1768
cellulose 3:389–90; 6:852
  adhesive 1:29–30; 3:390
  and cellophane manufacture

12:1626; **13**:1769
combustion **7**:881
paper made from **12**:1636–7
plastics derived from **13**:1768–9
regenerated, for textiles **6**:851;
13:1769
cellulose acetate **3**:390; **5**:634; **6**:852;
12:1609–10; **13**:1769; **16**:2191
cellulose nitrate **3**:390; **13**:1768–9;
16:2191
cellulose triacetate **6**:852
cellulose triethanoate **13**:1769
cellulose xanthate **6**:851
cement
asbestos **6**:846–7
pipes **13**:1750
cold-setting acrylic (dental
cement) **2**:256
hydraulic **1**:31
macro-defect-free (MDF) **3**:421
manufacture **3**:417–21
reinforced **3**:421; **4**:546
glass-reinforced (GRC) **7**:1003
ceramics **3**:424–7; **10**:1340
piezoelectric **3**:426; **13**:1745
smart **10**:1352–3
superconducting **5**:718;
17:2312–13
uses
in bulletproof jackets **2**:163
as insulators **3**:346; **9**:1162
ceramides **8**:1033
cerium **18**:2485
cesium **1**:99, 101
and atomic clocks **17**:2443
isotopes **14**:1921
CFCs see chlorofluorocarbons
chabazite **19**:2728
chain mail **2**:161, 162
chalcopyrite **16**:2299
chamber process **1**:23–4; **4**:452
charcoal
activated **7**:953; **15**:2130
fuel **2**:258; **3**:391
Chardonnet, Hilaire de **6**:851
chemical and biological warfare
4:437–41
chemical bonding and valency
4:442–4; **6**:787
coordinate bonds **4**:444
covalent bonds **4**:442, 443; **5**:597
hydrogen bonds **4**:444; **5**:597;
19:2654–5
ionic bonds **4**:442–3; **5**:597
metallic bonding **4**:442, 444; **5**:597
polar bonds **4**:444
van der Waals forces **5**:598;
15:2129
chemical reactions
exothermic and endothermic **4**:464
kinetics **4**:464; **9**:1202
oxidation and reduction
12:1616–17
chemical vapor deposition (CVD)
5:639; **10**:1418
chemisorption **15**:2129–30
chemistry
analytical **4**:445–8
drug and alcohol testing
5:684–6; **16**:2226
inorganic **4**:449–52
organic **4**:453–8
see also hydrocarbons
organometallic **4**:459–60
physical **4**:461–4
chiffon **17**:2407
Chile saltpeter see sodium nitrate
china clay (kaolin) **1**:109; **3**:424;
4:466
chipboard **19**:2709
manufacture **19**:2709–10
chirality (optical activity) **4**:457

chiral synthesis **4**:458
chlorine **8**:1034–5
compounds **8**:1035–6
manufacture **4**:452; **8**:1035
uses **8**:1035
as a chemical weapon **4**:437,
438; **8**:1036
in the water supply **4**:476
chloroacetophenone **8**:1036; **11**:1532
chlorobutadiene (chloroprene)
14:2001
chloroethene (vinyl chloride) **7**:880,
892–3; **8**:1035, 1107
copolymer **12**:1696
chlorofluorocarbons (CFCs) **1**:40;
4:480; **6**:806, 807; **8**:1034;
13:1798
as refrigerants **8**:1062
chloroform **8**:1036; **10**:1368
chloromethane **4**:459
chlorine isotopes in **10**:1344
chloroprene (chlorobutadiene)
14:2001
chloroxylenol **8**:1108
cholesteryl benzoate **9**:1257
chromic oxide **4**:472
chromium **4**:472–3; **18**:2486
extraction **4**:472
powder **1**:105
uses **4**:472, 473
chrysoberyl **16**:2270
chrysoidine **5**:691
chrysotile (white asbestos) **6**:846
cinnabar **10**:1371; **16**:2299
citric acid **19**:2727
clathrate compounds **11**:1529
clay **15**:2077
and brick manufacture **3**:323–4
heavy **3**:424
cling film **12**:1626
clothing, bulletproof **2**:163; **13**:1806
CN gas (Mace) **11**:1532; **14**:1972
coacervation **10**:1413, 1414
coal **2**:258; **3**:391
destructive distillation of **5**:664
"seacoal" **4**:497
types **4**:494
coal tar **4**:453, 498
aniline dyes from **1**:133–4
cobalt, isotopes **7**:911; **14**:1921
cobalt (II) chloride **14**:2015
coconut fiber **6**:850
coir **6**:850
coke **4**:494
coking, on catalysts **3**:406
collodion **12**:1708
collodion cotton **3**:390
combustion **12**:1617, 1620
flame-retarding agents **7**:880–1;
13:1771
slow **7**:879
composites **10**:1353
for aircraft **1**:43, 44
carbon fibers used in **3**:395
for prostheses **2**:255
smart **10**:1353
compounds, intermetallic **1**:104;
10:1351
compression **5**:714
condensers (distillation), Liebig
5:662
conditioners, hair **8**:1033
contact process **1**:23, 24; **4**:452
cooperite (platinum sulfide) **13**:1781
coordination **18**:2488
copal **13**:1741, 1742–3
copolymers **13**:1812
self-polishing (SPCs) **2**:149
synthetic rubber **14**:1999–2001
vinyl acetate **12**:1696; **13**:1771
copper **4**:566–8
alloys **1**:102; **4**:568; **15**:2080

blister **4**:567
electrical properties **4**:568
electrolytic **4**:568
etched copper printed circuit
boards **13**:1845–6
extraction **4**:566–7
oxygen-free **4**:568
patina **4**:571
pipes, scale **13**:1787
powder **1**:105
refined **4**:567–8
refining **4**:567; **6**:738
tough-pitch **4**:568
see also brass; bronze
copper arsenate, chromated (CCA)
9:1295
copper ferrocyanide **12**:1609
copper (I) oxide (cuprous oxide)
2:149
copper (II) oxide (cupric oxide) **2**:149
copper phosphide **3**:332
copper phthalocyanine **12**:1628
copper sulfate (blue vitriol) **4**:566
copper sulfide **4**:566
copper uranite **18**:2546
cordite **3**:390
cork
floor tiles **7**:893
production **7**:925
corrosion **12**:1617
prevention **4**:569–71
in cars **2**:199
in pipelines **13**:1754
corundum **1**:18, 109; **16**:2270
cotton **5**:581–2; **6**:848, 849; **17**:2404,
2405
flame-resistant **7**:881; **13**:1862
Courtelle **6**:853
cracking **4**:453; **11**:1575–6, 1578
catalytic **4**:459; **11**:1576
hydrocracking **8**:1119; **11**:1576,
1578
thermal **11**:1578
creosote oil **4**:498
crepe **17**:2407
crepon **17**:2407
cresols **8**:1108
cretonne **17**:2407
crocidolite (blue asbestos) **6**:846
Crookes, Sir William **12**:1671
cross-linkers **12**:1628–9
crude oil see petroleum
cryolite **6**:738
crystals and crystallography **4**:550;
5:597–9
birefringence of crystals **9**:1239;
13:1794
bonds **5**:597–8
cleavage planes **5**:598
covalent crystals **5**:597
crystal formation **5**:599
crystals in industry **5**:599
impurities **5**:599
ionic crystals **4**:443; **5**:597
liquid crystals **4**:551; **9**:1257–9;
10:1352, 1362
metallic crystals **5**:597
periodic structures **5**:598
synthetic crystals **17**:2346–7
unit cells **5**:598; **10**:1359; **13**:1744
X-ray crystallography, X-ray diffraction **2**:261, 262; **4**:462, 551;
5:598–9, 641; **12**:1689; **19**:2724
see also gemstones
CS gas **4**:437; **11**:1532
cupronickels **4**:568; **11**:1523
Curie point **13**:1745
curium **6**:765
cyanates **11**:1527
cyanides **11**:1527
cyanoacrylates **1**:31–2
cyclamates **7**:914

cyclic-AMP **2**:251
cycloalkenes **4**:455
cycloalkynes **4**:455
cyclohexane **4**:455; **8**:1107; **11**:1579
Cyclonite see RDX
cyclononyne **4**:455
cyclopropane **4**:455; **8**:1106; **12**:1681
cyclopropene **4**:455
Czochralski method **15**:2077;
17:2347

D

2,4-D **19**:2679
Dacron **3**:350; **6**:853; **13**:1772
Dalapon **19**:2679
Dalton, John **2**:182; **4**:461; **6**:763;
12:1671
damask **17**:2407
dammar **13**:1741, 1742–3
Davy, Sir Humphry **1**:100; **4**:449;
8:1034
DDT **1**:61; **12**:1678
dehydration, osmotic **12**:1610
dendrimers **13**:1812
denim **17**:2407
density **10**:1359
desalination (desalting) **5**:623–5, 662
reverse osmosis for **5**:625;
12:1610; **19**:2666
using solar energy **5**:624; **15**:2116
descaling **2**:223
Despeissis, Louis-Henri **6**:851
detergents
manufacture **5**:631–2
in toothpaste **18**:2466
zeolites and **19**:2730
deuterium **7**:947; **8**:1118; **19**:2655
in hydrogen bombs **11**:1553
deuterium hydrogen oxide **19**:2655
deuterium oxide (heavy water)
11:1553; **19**:2655–6
in nuclear reactors **11**:1545
deuterons **7**:946
dextrin **3**:390; **6**:842
Dextron **19**:2611
1,4-diaminobenzene (p-phenylenedi-
amine) **12**:1710
1,6-diaminohexane **13**:1806
diamonds **5**:637, 640; **10**:1360;
12:1679
covalent crystals **3**:393; **4**:443;
5:597
identity patterns **9**:1243
properties **3**:391, 392; **5**:639
melting point **3**:393
synthetic (industrial) **1**:18; **3**:392;
5:599, 637, 639; **17**:2346
Diaplex **10**:1352
diastase **6**:842
dicalcium orthophosphate **12**:1699
dicalcium phosphate **12**:1699
dicalcium silicate **3**:419
dichlorodimethylsilane **15**:2078
1,1-dichloroethene **7**:880
dichloromethane **8**:1106
dieldrin **12**:1676
diethylamine **4**:456
diethyl ether see ethoxyethane
diffusion **5**:633
difluorodichloromethane **8**:1036
dihexylamine nitrate **4**:571
dihydroxyl-5,6-indole **8**:1033
diisooctyl phthalate (DOP) **13**:1771
dilatency **19**:2609–10
dimethylbenzene see xylene
2,3-dimethylbuta-1,3-diene, polymerization **14**:1999
2,2-dimethylbutane **4**:454
dimethylether (DME) fuel **3**:343
dioxins **4**:438

dioxins (*cont.*)
  decomposition of **5**:720
  elimination from soil **7**:901
disaccharides **3**:389
distillation and sublimation **5:661–4**
  distillation **4**:445; **5**:661
    alcohol **1**:*97, 98*; **5**:661;
      16:2215–18
    azeotropic **5**:663
    continuous **16**:2215
    destructive **5**:664
    fractional **5**:662–3; **11**:1576
    molecular **5**:664
    of petroleum (crude oil) **5**:661;
      11:1576, 1577–9
    reduced pressure (vacuum)
      5:*661*, 663; **18**:2560
    steam **5**:663
    of water **5**:623–5; **15**:2116
  sublimation **5**:664; **18**:2570
    dye **6**:834
dolomite, uses **7**:901
Downs cells **1**:100
dry ice **18**:2570
dubnium **6**:765
Duralumin **1**:106, 109
dyes **4**:*498*
  aniline and azo **1**:*133–5*; **5**:690–1
  disperse **5**:691–2; **6**:852
  dyeing process **5:690–3**
  fading in sunlight **4**:464
  fastness **5**:693
  and medicine **1**:135
  natural **5**:690
  reactive **5**:691
  structures **1**:134
  sulfur **5**:691
  synthetic **5**:690–1
  triarylmethane **1**:134–5
  uses
    carpets **7**:894
    fabric printing **6**:834
    optical filters **6**:858
    synthetic fibers **5**:692; **6**:852
  vat **5**:691
dynamite **6**:827
  manufacture **6**:828
dysprosium **18**:2486

E

earthenware **3**:425; **4**:465
Ehrlich, Paul **1**:135
einsteinium **6**:765
elasticity **5**:713–14; **10**:1361
  elastic collisions **9**:1202–3
  and springs **16**:2229
elastic limit **5**:713; **16**:2229
elastic modulus *see* Young's modulus
elastic region **5**:713
elastomeric fibers **6**:853
elastomers **15**:2078
electrochemical series (electromotive
  series) **17**:2324
electrochemistry **4**:464; **6**:727
  see also electrolysis
electrolysis **6:737–8**; **9**:1184
  Castner-Kellner cells **6**:738
  of sodium chloride **1**:25; **4**:450,
    452; **6**:737; **8**:1118; **9**:1184
  uses
    aniodic stripping/cathodic
      polishing **2**:160
    in electrochemical machining
      6:735, 736
    in gold refining **8**:1015
    metal plating *see* electroplating
    to conserve metals **2**:160
    to extract alkali metals **1**:99
    to extract aluminum **1**:110–11;
      6:738

to extract metals **6**:738
    to extract zinc **19**:2731
electrons, transfer, in oxidation and
  reduction **12**:1616
electroplating **6**:738; **17**:2323–4
  with chromium **4**:473
  with nickel **4**:473; **11**:1523
  preparation before **1**:17
  and waste disposal **19**:*2641*
electropolishing **17**:2325
electrorheological fluids **10**:1353
electrum **4**:507
elements, chemical **6:763–6**
  abundance **10**:1377
  atomic number **14**:1905–6
  classifications **6**:764
  elements 110 to 112, synthesis
    6:766
  elements beyond 112 **6**:766
  mass number **14**:1906
  origins of **6**:*763*, 764
  synthetic **6**:764–6
  theories and discoveries of **4**:449;
    6:763
  transition *see* transition elements
  see also isotopes; periodic table
Elinvar **1**:106; **11**:1524
Eloner's reaction **8**:1015
emeralds **4**:472
  synthetic **17**:2346
emery **1**:18, 109
Emulsan **19**:2611
enamels
  stoving **12**:1629–30
  vitreous (porcelain enamel)
    6:779–80
enantiomers **4**:457, 458
  drug **12**:1689
epinephrine (adrenaline) **8**:1108
epitaxy **17**:2347
EPNS (electroplated nickel silver)
  11:1523; **15**:2080
Epsom salts *see* magnesium sulfate,
  hydrated
erbium **18**:2486
esters **4**:457
  as biofuels **2**:259
Estron **6**:852
ETFE (ethyltetrafluoroethylene)
  7:984
ethane **1**:*97, 98*; **4**:454; **8**:1105, 1106
ethanediol *see* ethylene glycol
ethanoate ions **4**:457; **14**:2015
ethanoic acid (acetic acid) **1**:23; **4**:457
  manufacture **1**:25
ethanol (ethyl alcohol) **1**:*97, 98*;
  4:456
  as a biofuel **2**:259
  in gasoline **6**:842
  for petroleum-like hydrocarbons
    4:458
  production **1**:98; **5**:663; **8**:1107
    from biomass **7**:962–3
ethene *see* ethylene
ethene dichloride **8**:1107
ethenyl ethanoate *see* vinyl acetate
ether
  anesthesia using **17**:2327–8
  evaporation **5**:592
ethers, crown **4**:458
ethoxyethane (diethyl ether) **4**:456
ethyl alcohol *see* ethanol
ethylamine **4**:456
ethyl chloride **8**:1106
ethylene (ethene) **4**:454, 456; **8**:1105,
  1107
  hydration of **1**:98
  polymerization **13**:1810; **18**:2488
ethylene bromide **8**:1036
ethylene glycol (ethanediol) **1**:73, *97,
  98*; **6**:802; **8**:1107
ethylene oxide **8**:1107

2-ethylhexanol **13**:1771
ethyl-magnesium bromide **4**:459
ethyltetrafluoroethylene (ETFE)
  7:984
ethyne (acetylene) **4**:455; **8**:1105,
  1107
  oxyacetylene welding **12**:1620
ethynyl radicals **10**:1419
evaporation **5**:661
explosives **6:826–9**

F

fabrics *see* textiles
fat(s) **4**:457; **6:836–7**
  and detergents **5**:631–2
  saturated and unsaturated **6**:836,
    837
  see also oils
fatty acids **6**:836
Fehlings solution **16**:2295
feldspar **1**:109
felt **17**:2404
FEP (fluorinated ethyene-propylene)
  13:1815
fermentation **1**:98; **6:840–2**; **19**:2725
  acetic **6**:842
  for baking **6**:841
  for biofuels **2**:258–9
  brewing and **2**:234, 236–7; **3**:*406*;
    6:841
  for protein production **7**:914;
    13:*1866*
  for winemaking **6**:840–1; **19**:2700,
    2701–2, *2703*
fermium **6**:765
ferric chloride **9**:1188
ferric oxide *see* iron (III) oxide
ferrocene **4**:*459*, 460
ferrosilicon powder **5**:638
fertilizers **6:843–5**
  ammonium nitrate **4**:*450*; **6**:829,
    843, *844*
  phosphorus **6**:844–5; **12**:*1698*,
    1699, 1700
  and water pollution **6**:845; **12**:1700
fiberboard **19**:2711
fiberglass, for insulation **9**:1160–1
fibers
  mineral **6:846–7**
  natural **6:848–50**; **17**:2404
    see also cotton; silk; wool
  nonwoven fabrics **17**:2404
  synthetic **4**:490; **5**:691–2; **6:851–3**;
    17:2404–5
    cellulose-derived **6**:851–2;
      13:1768–9
    dyes for **5**:692; **6**:852
    flammability **7**:880
fibroin **6**:849
film formers **12**:1627
fireworks and flares, fireworks **1**:*100*
fission, nuclear **2**:248; **6**:796;
  7:876–7; **11**:1543–6; **12**:*1727*;
  13:1832
flame retarding agents **7:880–1**;
  13:1771
flannel **17**:2407
flash point **5**:687; **9**:1291
flax **6**:848, 849, 850; **17**:2405, 2406,
  2408
flocculation **19**:2656
floor coverings **7:892–5**
flow, plastic *see* plastic deformation
fluorescein **10**:1302
fluoride, and teeth **5**:620; **8**:1034,
  1036; **18**:2466
fluorine **4**:442; **8**:1034
fluorocarbons **19**:2660
fluothane **8**:1034
flurane anesthetics **1**:131

fluxes **10**:1382
foam
  firefighting **6**:862, 863
  plastic **13**:1772, 1776
  "sticky" **11**:*1532*
fog sprays **11**:1532
foil, aluminum **1**:109
formic acid *see* methanoic acid
fractionating columns **5**:662–3;
  11:*1575*, 1576
francium **1**:99, 101
Frasch, Herman **16**:2299
freons **8**:1036, 1062; **14**:1947
fructose **3**:389
fuchsin, basic (dye) **1**:134, 135
fullerenes **4**:451, *455*
  buckminsterfullerenes (buckyballs)
    4:451; **10**:1360
functional groups **4**:456–7
fusain (mineral charcoal; mother-of-
  coal) **4**:497
fusion, latent energy of **4**:463

G

gadolinium **11**:1549; **18**:2486
galactose **3**:389
galena **9**:1219; **16**:2299
gallic acid **12**:1708
gallium arsenide **9**:1213; **15**:2116
gallium indium phosphide **15**:2116
galvanizing **4**:571; **17**:*2322*, 2323,
  2325–6; **19**:*2732*
garnets **1**:18; **7**:982; **16**:2271
gases **10**:1359, 1362
  atmospheric **1**:62
  dew point **8**:*1123*
  elasticity **5**:713
  energy distribution of molecules
    9:1203
  gas laws **7:960–1**
  ideal **7**:960; **10**:1362
  kinetic theory of **7**:960–1; **9**:1203
  liquefaction **1**:63–4; **5**:590
  and pressure **7**:960–1; **13**:1840
  vapor density **5**:617
gas oil **11**:1579
gasoline **8**:1106
  biofuel replacements **2**:258, 259;
    6:794
  containing alcohol **6**:842; **7**:962
  containing lead **9**:1221
  containing toluene (heavy gaso-
    line) **5**:617
  from oil refining **11**:1576, 1580
  and the greenhouse effect **6**:794
  lead-free **8**:1036; **11**:*1578*
  octane numbers **8**:1106; **11**:*1578*
  straight-run **11**:1577
  synthetic **7:962–3**
  tetraethyl lead additive **4**:459;
    13:1802
gelatin
  blasting **6**:827
  for optical filters **6**:857, 858
gels, polyelectrolyte **10**:1353
gemstones **5**:598
  coloration **4**:472
  cutting **16**:2270–2
  diamonds **5**:*637*, 638
  polished **1**:18
  synthetic **17**:2346, *2347*; **18**:*2487*
geochemistry **7:981–2**
germanium **6**:752; **15**:2052
gilding metal **3**:317
glass **3**:425–6; **4**:493; **7:999–1001**;
  10:1360
  cutting **16**:2237
  didymium **6**:858
  etching **6**:805
  and forensic science **7**:917

heat-resistant 7:1001
incising patterns on 1:17; 5:*638*
laminated safety 1:30; 2:209
light-sensitive 7:1001
optical and ophthalmic 7:1001
    for optical filters 6:858
patterned 7:1001
photochromatic 16:2192
powdered 6:779
production 4:493; 7:999–1001
safety 7:1001
stained 6:858; 7:*999*; 16:**2236–8**
wired 7:1001
see also enamels, vitreous; glass
    fibers
glass fibers 7:**1002–3**
    covering the Millennium Dome
        3:*337*
    GRPs see plastics, glass-reinforced
    manufacture 7:1002–3
    Teflon-coated glass fiber fabric
        17:2399, *2400*, 2401
    see also fiberglass
glass-reinforced plastic (GRPs) see
    plastics, glass-reinforced
glass-reinforced polyester (GRP)
    3:337
Glauber, Johann Rudolf 11:1525
glucose 3:389
glue 1:29
    marine 1:30
    superglue 1:30
    surgical 1:31
    see also adhesives
glufinosate (Liberty) 19:2681
glycerine see glycerol
glycerol (glycerine) 1:97, 98; 4:457;
        6:836, 837
glyceryl monothioglycolate 8:1032
glycogen 3:389, 390
glycyrrhizin 4:*558*
glyphosate (Roundup) 19:2681
gold 8:**1013–16**
    alloys 8:1016
    deposited by bacteria 10:1412
    extraction 8:1013–15
    isotopes 14:1921
    jewelry 8:1016
    rolled 16:2191
    uses 8:*1013*, 1016
Gore-Tex 13:1861, *1863*
Graham, Thomas 12:1609
graphite 3:392, *393*, 395; 9:1289;
        10:1360–1; 12:1679
    diamonds created from 17:2346
gravimetric analysis 4:446
Grignard reagents 4:459
grit blasting 1:17; 17:2322
groundwater
    analysis 7:*982*
    arsenic in 7:*981*
gum arabic 1:30
gums, plant, adhesive 1:29–30
guncotton 3:390; 6:827
gunmetals 3:331
gunpowder 4:449; 6:826, 829
    black 1:101, 120
gutta percha 3:347
gypsum 3:417; 16:2240, 2299

H

Haber (or Haber-Bosch) process
    1:25, 115; 4:451; 11:1525–6
    catalysts 3:*405*, 407
hafnium 18:2485
hair, treatment 8:**1032–3**
half-life 11:1547
halite 14:2016
haloalkanes 4:456, 459
halogens 8:**1034–6**

halon 1301 (bromotrifluoromethane)
    6:863
halon bromochlorodifluoromethane
    (BCF) 6:862
halothane 1:131
hapticity 4:460
hardness, Moh's scale of 1:17
hassium 6:766
heat capacity 4:463; 12:1728
heavy water see deuterium oxide
helium 11:1528–9
    atomic structure 2:*182*
    in balloons and airships 1:91, 92;
        2:219
    isotopes 11:1528–9
    liquid 5:591–2; 11:1529
    nucleus, binding energy 2:248
    produced by the Big Bang 4:573–4
    superfluidity 4:553; 5:592; 7:934;
        10:1362; 11:1528–9
    and underwater diving 5:667;
        11:1528; 18:2538
helium burning 6:764
hematite 9:1186
hemp 3:350
herbicides 19:2679–80
    microencapsulated 10:1414
heulandite 19:2728
hex-1-ene 11:1770
hex-3-ene, cis and trans 4:*454*
hex-3-yne 4:*454*
hexacyanoferrate ions 18:2488
hexane 4:*454*, 459; 11:1579
    isomerization 11:1578
Hexogen see RDX
Hoffmann, August 1:133–4
hollow bar 13:1752
holmium 18:2486
Hooke's law 5:713; 16:2229
hopcalite 7:953
humidification
    in air-conditioning systems 8:1061
    and desalination 5:624
hydrazine 11:1527
hydrazoic acid 11:1527
hydrocarbons 8:**1105–8**
    branched, detection by mass spec-
        trometry 10:1344
    saturated and unsaturated 8:1105
hydrochloric acid 1:23, 25
    uses 1:25
hydrochlorofluorocarbons 14:1947
hydrodesulfurization 3:406
hydrofluoric acid 6:805
hydrofluorocarbons 14:1947
hydrogen 8:**1118–19**
    bonds
        with electronegative atoms
            (hydrogen bonds) 4:444; 5:597;
            19:2654–5
        in molecular hydrogen 4:443
    ions, and pH measurement
        12:1692
    isotopes 7:946; 8:1118; 13:1763
    liquid 1:64; 6:795; 9:1287
    monoatomic 10:1317
    uses 8:1119
        ammonia manufacture 1:115;
            3:*405*
        in balloons and airships 1:91, 92;
            2:219
        in bubble chambers 3:334
        cooling dynamos 8:1119
        cutting and welding 1:119
        hydrocracking 8:1119; 11:1578
        hydrofining 8:1119; 11:1580
        in nuclear fusion 7:946, 947
        vehicle fuel 8:1119; 9:1287–8
hydrogenation 3:406; 13:1782;
    15:2107
hydrogen bromide 7:881; 8:1119

hydrogen burning 6:764
hydrogen chloride 8:1035, 1119;
    9:1163
hydrogen cyanide 8:1119
hydrogen fluoride 8:1034, 1119
hydrogen iodide 8:1119
hydrogen peroxide 8:1119; 12:1621
    manufacture 12:1621
hydrogen sulfide 7:956; 16:2299,
    2300
hydrolysis 7:962–3
hydroquinone 12:1713

I

ibuprofen 4:458
ice 10:*1360*, 1361; 19:*2665*
    forms of 19:2655
Icynene 9:1161
incineration, of chemical weapons
    4:440
Indura 13:1860
ink 8:**1151–2**
    for banknotes 5:583, 584
    electronic 10:*1413*, 1414
    for gravure processes 8:1152
intermetallic compounds 1:104;
    10:*1351*
Invar 1:106; 11:1524
inversion (hydrolysis of sucrose)
    16:2295
inversion (molecular motion) 9:1212
invertase 5:643; 6:841
invert syrup 3:389
iodine 8:1036
    isotopes 8:1036; 14:1907, 1908,
        1921
    preparation 8:*1035*
    sublimation 5:*664*
iodoform 8:1036
ion exchange
    chromatography 4:471
    for desalination 5:625
    for lens surfaces 9:*1225*
    to soften water 19:2656
ionic materials
    solids 4:443, 555–6; 9:1163
    solutions 4:556
iridium 10:1395; 13:1781, 1782
    isotopes 14:1921
iron see iron and steel
iron (II) chloride (ferrous chloride)
    12:1616
iron (III) chloride (ferric chloride)
    9:1188
iron disulfide (iron pyrite) 8:1024
iron (III) oxide (ferric oxide) 9:1188;
    12:1628
    hydrated (rust) 4:570; 9:1188;
        12:1617, 1621; 17:2325–6
    inks 5:584
    on magnetic tapes 10:1311
    and thermic lances 17:2412
iron and steel 9:**1185–90**
    corrosion 4:569, 570; 12:1621
        prevention 4:571
    iron
        burning in oxygen 12:1617
        cast (pig iron) 1:106; 7:942;
            9:*1185*, 1187–8; 17:2448
        compounds 9:1188
        effect of bacteria on 7:982
        manufacture 3:391, *392*
        ores 9:1185–6; 11:1458
        physical properties 9:1185
        powder 1:105
        recycling 14:1940
        wrought 9:1187
    steel 1:106; 9:1188
        abrasion of 1:*18*
        austenitic 13:1830

bicycle frames 2:243
for boat building 2:277
bridges 3:329, 330
in buildings 3:335–6
in bulletproof jackets 2:163
cans 3:382, 383
carbon content 9:1189
casting 3:*403*; 9:1190
chromium 4:473
heat treatment of 1:104;
    10:1387
history 9:1188–9
plastic-coated 17:*2322*
production 9:1188–90; 12:*1617*,
    1619
recycling 14:1940
refining 9:*1189*, 1190
for reinforced concrete 3:329,
    420; 4:547
stainless 4:473, 570; 11:1523–4
tin-free (TFS) 3:383
tin-plated 3:382, 383; 4:571
tool 4:507–8
with an aluminum bronze
    cladding 6:*829*
islands of stability 6:766
isobutylene (methylpropene)
    14:2001
isocyanates 11:1527
isocyanides 11:1527
isomerism
    alcohols 1:98
    geometric 4:455
    polarimeters and 13:1793
isooctane 8:1106
isopentane 13:1776
isoprene, polymers 14:1997, 2001
isopropanol 1:*98*
isotopes 6:763–4
    carbon see carbon, isotopes
    and mass spectrometry 10:1344
    radioactive 11:1547
    scanning using 2:281; 3:378
    to label organic compounds 2:251
    uranium see uranium, isotopes

J

jackets, flak 2:163
jean 17:2407
jersey 8:1091
joints (mechanical), adhesive 1:28–9
jute 6:849, 850

K

kaolin see china clay
kapok 6:849
Kauri-Butanol scale 5:687
Kekulé, Friederich A. 8:1108
kenaf 6:848
kerogen 11:1572
kerosene 5:687; 8:1106; 11:1575,
    1579
ketones 4:456
Kevlar 1:44; 2:220; 6:852; 7:880;
    13:1805, 1806; 17:2405
    uses 13:*1805*, 1806
        on boat hulls 13:*1771*, *1804*
        clothing and textiles 2:163;
            3:295; 13:1806, 1860
        in sailboards 14:2006
kieselguhr 6:827
kinases 2:251
kinetics 9:**1201–3**
    chemical reaction 4:464; 9:1202
    kinetic theory of gases 7:960–1;
        9:1203
krypton 11:1529
krypton difluoride 11:1529

L

lacquers and varnishes 9:1204–5
  lacquers 9:1204, 1205
  varnishes 9:1204, *1205*
    manufacture 9:1205
    on paintings 13:1741, 1742–3
    solvents 13:1823
    uses 3:385; 9:1205
lactic acid
  chirality 4:457
  and fermentation 6:842
  in milk 7:905
  in muscles 6:840
lactose 3:389; 5:602
lanthanides (rare earth elements)
  12:1673; 18:2487, 2488
lanthanum 18:2485, 2487
lasers and masers, lasers, and chemical bonds 4:*461*
latex 14:1997, 1998
laughing gas (nitrous oxide) 1:131;
  11:1527
Lavoisier, Antoine 4:449; 6:763, 788;
  12:1618; 15:2076
lawrencium 6:765
lead 9:1219–21
  alloys 9:1221
  compounds 9:1221
  and health 9:1221
  occurrence and extraction 9:1219
  properties 9:1221
  red 9:1221; 12:1628
  refining 9:1219–21
  uses 9:1221
    roofing 9:*1220*
  white 12:1628
lead azide 6:827; 9:1221; 11:1527
leaded-tin bronzes 3:332
lead sulfide 9:1219, *1220*
lead tetraethyl *see* tetraethyl lead
lead–tin–antimony alloys 1:104
lead zirconate titanate (PZT) 3:426;
  10:1352, 1364; 13:*1745*
leather 13:1860
Leblanc process 4:450
lecithin 4:500
ligands 2:251, *252*
lignite 4:494
limestone
  cave decorations 16:2239
  uses 7:901
limonite 9:1186
Lindane 12:1676
linen 17:2404, 2408
  flame-resistant 7:881
linoleum (lino) 7:892, *894*
linseed oil 9:1204
  and linoleum 7:892
  in paints 12:1628
liquefaction
  of gases 1:63
    air 1:64; 5:590
liquefied petrolem gas 2:200
liquid crystals 4:551; 9:*1257–9*;
  10:1352, 1362
liquid petroleum gas (LPG) 7:955,
  959; 8:1106
  from oil refining 11:1577
liquid propane gas, a vehicle fuel
  7:959
liquids 10:1359, 1361
  boiling point 18:2569–70
  elasticity 5:713
  electrical conduction 6:728
  pressure applied to 8:1109
  specific gravity 5:616–17
Listerine 8:1108
litharge 9:1221
lithium 1:99–100
  lithium-6 11:1553, 1554
  in stars 13:1761

lithium-7 2:*182*
lithium aluminum hydride 8:1119
lithium carbonate 1:99; 4:452
lithium chloride 8:1123
lithium deuteride 11:1554
lithium hydride 1:99; 8:1119
lithium stearate 1:99
lithium tantalate, piezoelectric 5:599
lithopone 12:1628
litmus 12:1692
London dispersion forces 4:444
low-energy electron diffraction
  (LEED) 15:2129
lutetium 18:2487
Lycra 6:853

M

magic numbers 6:766
magma 12:1680
magnesia *see* magnesium oxide
magnesium
  burning in air 12:1617
  extraction 6:738; 10:1378
  and flash photography 3:365
  reaction with chlorine 12:1616
magnesium oxide (magnesia) 3:424,
  426
magnesium sulfate, hydrated (Epsom
  salts) 5:*598*
magnetorheological fluids 10:1353
majolica ware 3:425
malathion 12:1700
maltase 1:98; 5:643; 6:810, 842
maltose 3:389; 6:842
manganate (VII) salts 4:443
manganese, oxidation numbers
  12:1616
manganese carbonyl 18:2488
manganese dioxide 3:324
martensite 10:1351, 1388
mastic 13:1742–3
materials science 10:**1350–3**
  see also petrology
matter
  dark 4:575–6; 8:*1021*
  law of conservation of 4:449; 6:788
  properties of 10:1359–62
  wavelike properties 14:1882;
    19:2674
  see also gases; liquids; solids; super-
    fluids
mauveine (dye) 1:133, 134; 4:453;
  5:690
MDF (medium density fiberboard)
  19:2711
mechanochemistry 10:1420
medium density fiberboard (MDF)
  19:2711
meitnerium 6:766
melamine-formaldehyde polymers
  13:1773
membranes, semipermeable 12:1609
mendelevium 6:765
Mendeleyev, Dmitri 4:449; 12:1671;
  18:2485
mercuric chloride 2:226; 13:1801
mercuric sulfate 10:1372; 13:1801
mercuric sulfide 10:1371
mercury (metal) 10:**1371–2**
  alloys *see* amalgams
  extraction 10:1371
  occurence 10:1371
  superconducting 17:2309, 2314
  surface tension 10:*1371*; 17:2321
  uses 10:1371–2; 13:1801
    in barometers 2:222–3; 10:*1372*
    in batteries 2:227; 10:1372
    in dental fillings 5:620; 10:1371
    in discharge lamps 5:658;
      10:*1372*; 14:1980; 18:2533–4

    in liquid-mercury telescopes
      11:1464; 17:2380
mercury fulminate (mercury II iso-
  cyanate) 6:827; 8:1024
metallic glasses (amorphous alloys)
  1:107
metallocene 4:460
metals 10:**1377–8**
  alkali *see* alkali metals; alkaline
    earth
  bonds 4:442, 444
  conserving 2:160
  crystal structure 1:102, *103*
  electrical conduction 4:550, 556;
    17:2417–18
  heavy 13:1801
  joints 1:29
  melting point, casting and 3:404
  rare earth *see* lanthanides
  recycling 14:1940–1
  tests for, qualitative and quantita-
    tive 4:446
  transition *see* transition elements
  see also alloys
methacrylate esters 13:1771
methacrylic acid (2-methylpropenoic
  acid) 12:1629; 13:1771
methane 4:454; 8:1105, 1106
  a biogas 2:259–60
  bonding in 4:*442*, 455
  in fuel cells 7:936
  for hydrogen production 8:1118
  induced dipoles 9:1163
  as landfill gas 14:*1939*
  liquefied, transportation 7:929
  and the ozone layer 13:1798
  reaction with oxygen 6:787; 7:878
methanoic acid (formic acid) 1:25
methanol (methyl alcohol; wood
alcohol) 1:97; 16:2215
  in fuel cells 7:936
  for petroleum-like hydrocarbons
    4:458
  production 1:98
methanolysis 13:1776
methyl alcohol *see* methanol
methylamine 4:444
methylchloride 15:2078
2-methylhexane 10:1344
methyllithium 4:459
methyl orange 12:1692
methylpotassium 4:459
methylpropane 4:454
methylpropene (isobutylene)
  14:2001
2-methylpropenoic acid (methacrylic
  acid) 12:1629
methyl salicylate (oil of wintergreen)
  1:98
micafill *see* vermiculite
micas 15:2077
  muscovite 15:*2075*, 2077
  in paints 12:1628
microfiltration 12:1610
mineral charcoal (fusain) 4:497
mineral oils, for lubrication 9:1289,
  1290–1
mineral wools 9:1161
misch metal 18:2487
Moh's scale of hardness 1:17
molasses 16:2297
  blackstrap 16:2296, 2297
molecular sieving 19:2729–30
molecules
  computer graphics 4:*534*
  custom-built, using nanotech-
    nology 10:1419
  and quantum physics 12:1728
  rotational and vibrational energy
    9:1209
  structure established 4:462
molybdenum disulfide 9:1289

monazite 18:2487
monocalcium orthophosphate
  12:1699
monocalcium phosphate 12:1699
monomethylhydrazine 15:2029
monosaccharides 3:388–9
monosodium glutamate 7:907
  production 7:914
mordanting 5:690–1
mortar 3:417
mother-of-coal (fusain) 4:497
muriatic acid 2:160
muscovite 15:*2075*, 2077
muslin 17:2407
  Dacca 5:582
mustard gas, as a chemical weapon
  4:437, 438; 7:953; 8:1036

N

nanofiltration 12:1610
naphtha 11:1575, 1577–9
naphthalene 4:455, 498
  and BBICs 9:1168
natrolite 19:2728
neodymium 5:622; 9:1212
neon 4:442; 11:1529
neoprene 13:1771–2, 1862; 14:2001
neptunium 6:764–5
Nichrome 14:1963
nickel 11:**1522–4**
  alloys 4:568; 10:*1390*; 11:1522,
    1523–4
    cupronickels 4:568; 11:1523
    Elinvar 1:106; 11:1524
    Invar 1:106; 11:1524
    nickel silver (German silver)
      3:317; 4:568; 11:1523
    Nimonic (superalloys) 1:106;
      4:473; 11:*1523*, 1524
    in steels and cast irons
      11:1523–4
    see also Nitinol
  catalysts 18:2488
  corrosion 4:569
  occurrence and extraction
    11:1522–3
  plating 6:738
  powder 1:105
nickel carbonyl 11:1523; 12:1616;
  18:2488
nickel oxide 4:569; 11:1523
nickel sulfide 11:1523
Nimonic alloys (superalloys) 1:106;
  4:473; 11:*1523*, 1524
niobium 3:404
  alloys 3:346; 17:2312
niobium tin 3:346; 17:2312
niobium titanium 17:2312, 2314
Nitinol, and shape memory 1:106–7;
  10:1351–2, 1363
nitrating phenol 6:828
nitric acid 1:24
  bonds in 4:*444*
  preparation 1:24–5; 4:451;
    11:1525; 13:*1783*
  uses 1:25
nitric oxide, biological roles
  3:413–14
nitrobenzene 1:133
nitrocellulose 3:390; 6:827; 13:1768
nitrogen 11:**1525–7**
  atmospheric 1:62
    fixed by bacteria 6:843; 11:*1526*
  bonds in 4:442
  compounds 11:1525–6
  cycle 11:*1526*
  isotopes 11:1525
  liquid 1:*62*; 5:591; 11:1525, *1527*
    transport 14:1927
  production 11:1525

uses 1:64; 11:1525
nitrogen mustard 3:379
nitrogen tetroxide 15:2029
nitroglycerine 3:390; 6:827
nitromethanol 14:*1891*, 1892
nitrous oxide 11:*1527*
  anesthetic (laughing gas) 1:131;
    11:1527
  bonds in 4:444
nobelium 6:765
noble-gas configurations 4:442;
  9:1183
noble gases 4:442; 11:*1528–9*;
  12:1672
  see also helium; krypton; neon;
    radon; xenon
Nomex 7:*880*; 13:1806, 1860
nuclear stability 6:*765*, 766
nucleic acid 7:973
nylons 6:852; 13:*1769*, 1804–5, 1811,
  1812; 17:2404
  manufacture 6:852; 17:*2405*
  uses
    bulletproof jackets 2:163
    parachute material 12:1643
    ropes 3:350–1
    tires 18:2456

O

oct-1-ene 13:1770
octane numbers, gasoline 8:1106;
  11:*1578*
oil length 9:1204
"oil rig" (mnemonic) 12:1616
oils
  in paints 12:1628
  recycling 14:1942
  see also fat(s)
oil of wintergreen (methyl salicylate)
  1:98
olefins see alkenes
oleum 1:24
Optyl 16:2191
organophosphates 12:1677
  toxicity 12:1700
Orlon 6:853
orthophosphoric acid 12:1699
osmium 13:1781, 1782
osmosis 12:1609–10
  reverse 12:1609–10
    for desalination 5:625; 12:1610;
      19:*266*
oxidation and reduction 12:1616–17
oxidation numbers 12:1616
oxidation state 4:443
oxides 12:1620–1
oxygen 12:1618–21
  atmospheric 1:62–3; 12:1620,
    1719
    in ancient times 6:823, 824;
      7:988
  discovery 12:1618
  liquid 5:591; 14:1927
  manufacture 12:1618
    separation from air 5:590;
      12:1618–19
  oxides 12:1620–1
  synthesis in stars 6:*763*
  uses 1:64; 12:1619–20
  see also ozone
ozone 12:1621
  used in water treatment 19:2664–6

P

paints 12:1627–30
  acrylic 12:1629
  alkyd 12:1628–9
  antifouling 2:149

emulsion (latex) 12:1629
  luminescent 10:1302
  manufacture 12:1630
  metallic 12:1628
  oil 12:1628
  pearlescent 12:1628
  pigments 12:1627–8, 1630
  solvents 13:1823
    reduction 12:1630
  stoving enamels 12:1629–30
palladium 13:1781, 1783; 15:2130;
  18:2485
paper, litmus 12:*1692*
papyrus 12:1636
paraffins see alkanes
paraquat 7:918; 19:2679
pararosaniline chloride 1:134–5
Parkesine 13:1768
patina, of copper 4:571
pearlite 10:1387
pectin 7:911, 912
Peg-Board 19:2711
penetration number 9:1291
peninsula of stability 6:766
pentaerythritol tetranitrate (PETN)
  1:116; 6:827, 828
pentane 4:454; 9:1161; 17:2424
pentoses 3:389
pepper sprays 11:1532–3; 14:1972
peptide bonds 13:1864
perchloroethylene (perc) 5:687–9;
  8:1036
perfluorocarbons 2:273
periodic structures 5:598
periodic table 4:449; 6:764;
  12:*1671–3*
  oxidizing and reducing agents
    12:1616
  see also elements, chemical
Perkin, William 1:134; 4:*498*; 5:*690*
perlite 8:1122
Perspex 4:560; 13:1770
PET see polyethylene terephthalate
petrochemicals see hydrocarbons
petroleum (crude oil) 3:391
  alternatives from fermentation
    4:458; 6:842
  chemicals from 4:453; 5:663;
    11:1577–80
  compositions 11:1577
  oil spills 10:1411
  sulfur content 11:1577, 1580;
    16:*2300*
  synthetic, for cleaning textiles
    5:689
petrology 12:1679–80
pewter 9:1221; 17:2448
  conservation 2:160
Pfeffer, Willhelm 12:1609
pH
  measurement 12:1692–3
  pH meters 12:1692–3
  titration and 4:446
phase diagrams 10:*1360*, 1362;
  12:1680
phases, of matter 10:1362
PHB (polyhydroxybutyrate) 3:303
phenacetin 8:1108
phenol 4:457, 498; 8:1107, 1108
phenolase 7:905
phenolics, as adhesives 1:30
phenolphthalein 12:1692
phenols, polyhydric 8:1108
phenylamine see aniline
phenylethene see styrene
phenylmercuric acetate 10:1372
phosgene (carbonyl chloride)
  13:1772
  as a chemical weapon 4:437, 438;
    7:953; 8:1036
phosphine 12:1700
phosphor bronze 3:332; 16:2230

phosphoric acid 1:23
phosphors 5:599; 10:1302
  manufacture 18:2487
phosphorus 12:**1698–1700**
  allotropes 3:392; 12:1698
  compounds 12:1699–1700
  fertilizers 6:844–5; 12:*1698*, 1699,
    1700
  manufacture 12:1698–9
  sources 12:*1698*, 1700
  uses 12:1699
phosphorus pentachloride
  12:1699–1700
phosphorus sesquisulfide 12:*1700*
phosphorus trichloride 8:1034;
  12:1699–1700
photochemistry 4:464; 9:1202
phthalic acid 12:1628
picric acid (trinitrophenol) 6:827,
  828; 8:1108; 11:1527
picture restoration 13:1741–3
piezoelectric material 5:599;
  10:1364; 13:1744–5
  ceramics 3:426; 13:1745
  quartz 5:599; 12:1606; 13:1744,
    1745
    in clocks and watches 4:487;
      17:2442, 2445–6; 19:2650
  as smart ceramics 10:1352–3
  as transducers 13:1745, 1843;
    18:2474, 2529–30
  use in ink-jet printers 4:545
pigments
  in butter 5:602
  in paint 12:1627–8, 1630
pitchblende 18:2487
pitch (material) 4:498; 10:1359
pitting 4:569
plaster, gypsum 3:417
plastic flow see plastic deformation
plastics 13:**1768–72**
  cellulosic 13:1768–9
  epoxies 13:1772
  from plants 3:303
  glass-reinforced (GRPs) 7:1003
    in boat building 2:274, 276–7
    in bows 3:307, 308
    for mannequins 13:*1772*
    for pipes 5:675; 13:1750, 1751
    in trucks 18:2507
  plating 17:2324
  polyalkenes 13:1770–1
    see also polyethylene; polypropy-
      lene
  polyamide see polyamides
  polycarbonates 9:1229, 13:*1768*,
    1772
  polyester see polyesters
  polyurethane see polyurethanes
  processing 13:1773–6
  PTFE see polytetrafluoroethylene
  recycling 10:1366; 12:1625;
    13:1776; 14:1941
  reinforced, with asbestos 6:847
  synthetic 13:1769–70
    see also polychloroethene; poly-
      styrene
  synthetic rubber see rubber,
    synthetic
  thermosets 13:1750
  uses
    batteries 2:229
    bearings 2:233
    bicycle frames 2:243
    in buildings 3:337
    contact lenses 4:560
    food and drink containers 3:382,
      385; 12:1625
    pipes 13:1750–1, 1787
    see also fibers, synthetic
    see also thermoplastics
platforming 11:1576

plating
  electroless 17:2324
  see also electroplating
platinum 10:*1377*; 13:1781
  as a catalyst 3:406; 13:1782;
    15:*2129*
  in resistance thermometers
    17:2424
platinum diarsenide (sperrylite)
  13:1781
platinum metals 13:1781–3; 18:2485
platinum sulfide (cooperite) 13:1781
Plexiglas 4:560; 13:1770; 16:2191,
  2192
plutonium 14:1906–7
  in heart pacemakers 8:1048
  isotopes 7:877; 11:1544, 1547
  and nuclear fission 11:1538, 1539,
    1546; 13:1831
    nuclear weapons 11:1552–3
  recovery 6:766
plutonium dioxide 11:1539
plutonium nitrate 11:1539
plutonium nitride 11:1538
plywood 19:2709
  manufacture 19:2710–11
    adhesives used in 1:30; 19:2709
  uses
    boatbuilding 2:275–6
    for buildings 3:336
poisons 13:1790–2
polishing 17:2325
pollucite 1:101
polonium 11:1276
polyacrylonitrile (PAN; Acrilan)
  3:394, 395; 6:853; 13:1771
  gels 10:1353
polyalkenes (polyolefins) 6:853;
  13:1770
  see also polyethylene; polypropy-
    lene
polyamides 13:1772, **1804–6**, 1811
  aromatic see aramids
  Nomex 7:*880*; 13:1806, 1860
  polyimides 13:1804, 1806
  uses, car washes 3:398
  see also Kevlar; nylons
polybutadiene 4:460
polycarbonates 13:*1768*, 1772
  for lenses 9:1229
polychlorinated biphenyls 7:901
polychloroethene (polyvinyl chloride; PVC) 7:880, 893; 8:1035;
  13:1769–70, 1771; 17:2448
  baton rounds 11:1533
  and cling film 12:1626
  plasticized 12:1696; 13:1770, 1771
polydimethylsiloxane (PDMS)
  15:2078
polyelectrolyte gels 10:1353
polyesters 6:853; 13:1772
  dyeing 5:692, 693
  glass-reinforced (GRP) 3:337
  as membranes on tensile structures
    17:2398
  for powder coatings 13:1823–4
  production 6:853; 13:1811
  recycling 13:1776
  for rope making 3:350–1
polyethene see polyethylene
polyethylene (polyethene; polythene)
  6:853; 13:1770, 1773
  chlorinated (CPE) 14:1941
  formation 13:1810
  low- and high-density 13:1770–1
  strengthening 6:745
  uses 2:*255*; 13:1770–1
    car washes 3:398
    cling film 12:1626
    food packaging 7:908; 12:1676;
      13:1770–1
polyethylene glycol 2:159, 160

polyethylene terephthalate (PET)
  6:853; **12**:*1622*; **13**:1772;
  14:1941
polyhydroxybutyrate (PHB) **3**:303
polyhydroxyethyl-methacrylate
  4:561
polyimides **13**:1804, 1806
polyisobutene **14**:1994
polyisocyanurate **9**:1161
polyisoprene **13**:1771
polymers and polymerization
  13:**1809–12**
  polymerization
    processes **13**:1809–12
    reactions **13**:1809
  polymers
    architecture **13**:1812
    for batteries **2**:229
    coatings *see* powder coatings
    cyanoacrylate **1**:32
    for fiber-optic cables **6**:856
    "living" **4**:460
    shape-memory **10**:1352;
      12:1624
    smart **10**:1352
  see also copolymers; plastics;
    polyamides
polymethylmethacrylate **4**:560;
  13:1770
polyolefins *see* polyalkenes
polyols **1**:98
polypropene *see* polypropylene
polypropylene (polypropene)
  13:1770, *1809*
  biaxially oriented **12**:1626
  uses **3**:384; **4**:*546*; **6**:853; **13**:*1769*
polysaccharides **3**:389–90
polysiloxanes *see* silicones
polystyrene **8**:1108; **9**:1161; **13**:1770,
  1772, *1775*
  expanded (Styrofoam) **13**:1776
  plating **17**:2324
polytetrafluoroethylene (PTFE;
  polytetrafluoroethene; Teflon)
  8:1034; **13**:*1769*, 1771, **1813–15**
  manufacture **13**:1813–14
  uses **2**:233; **3**:*337*; **9**:1289; **13**:1771,
    1814–15
    on razor blades **14**:1936
    on saws **18**:2463
    Teflon-coated glass fiber fabric
      17:2399, *2400*, 2401
    tubing **13**:1752
polythene *see* polyethylene
polyurethane rubbers **14**:2001
polyurethanes (PUs) **13**:1772
  foams **13**:1772, 1776; **15**:2023,
    2051
  uses
    for artificial feet **2**:254
    for baton rounds **11**:1533
    for filling wall cavities **9**:1161
    for marine salvage **15**:2023
polyvinyl acetate (PVA) **4**:*546*
  adhesives based on **1**:30; **19**:2718
polyvinyl chloride *see* polychloroethene
polyvinylidene chloride **13**:1744
potassium **1**:99, 101
  electron orbitals **2**:185
  fertilizers **6**:845
potassium aluminum sulfate **14**:2015
potassium bromide **1**:101; **12**:1708,
  1711
potassium carbonate **1**:100, 101
potassium chloride **1**:101; **6**:845
potassium dichromate **2**:226;
  12:1711
potassium hexacyanoferrate **12**:1711;
  14:2015
potassium hydroxide (caustic potash)
  1:23, 101

  in batteries **2**:227
  in fuel cells **7**:936
  preparation **1**:25
  and soap manufacture **15**:2107
potassium iodide **1**:101
potassium nitrate (saltpeter) **8**:1024;
  11:1525
potassium perchlorate **7**:869
potassium sodium tartrate (Rochelle
  salt) **13**:1744–5
potassium sulfate **6**:845
powder coatings **13**:**1823–4**
powder metallurgy **1**:104–6, *107*;
  3:404
pozzolana **3**:417; **4**:546
praseodymium **18**:2485, 2488
precipitates, and qualitative analysis
  4:446
precipitation hardening **1**:104
Priestley, Joseph **12**:1618; **15**:2109
Proban **7**:880; **13**:*1862*
propanal **4**:456
propane **3**:334; **4**:454; **7**:955, 959;
  8:1105
  from oil refining **11**:1577
  liquefied **8**:1106
propanol **1**:*98*
propanone (acetone) **4**:456
propenamide (acrylamide) **13**:1771
propene (propylene) **4**:454; **8**:1105
  polymers **13**:1812
  see also polypropylene
propenoic acid (acrylic acid) **12**:1629,
  13:1771
propenonitrile *see* acrylonitrile
propyne **4**:455; **8**:1105
proteins **2**:261; **13**:**1864–6**
  chiral **4**:458
  structure **2**:261; **13**:*1864–5*
    from computer graphics
      13:*1864*, 1866
  see also amino acids
PTFE *see* polytetrafluoroethylene
pulverised fuel ash (PFA) **13**:1831
pumice **1**:17, 18
PVC (polyvinyl chloride) *see* polychloroethene
pyrethrum **12**:1677
pyridine **4**:455
pyrite **16**:2299
pyrolysis **13**:1776

Q

quartz **7**:981; **15**:*2075*; **16**:*2270*
  in clocks and watches **4**:486–8;
    17:2442, 2445–6; **19**:*2649*, 2650
  piezoelectric **5**:599; **12**:1606;
    13:1744, 1745
quicklime *see* calcium oxide
quinine **1**:134

R

radar-absorbent materials (RAMs)
  10:*1350*
radiocarbon dating **2**:157; **3**:393;
  9:1276; **14**:1908, 1916
radioisotopes, of nitrogen **11**:1525
radioisotopic dating **14**:**1916**
  carbon dating **2**:157; **3**:393;
    9:1276; **14**:1908, 1916
  of rocks **7**:995; **14**:1916
radon **5**:708; **11**:1529
  isotopes **11**:1529
Ramsay, Sir William **11**:1528, 1529
rare earths *see* lanthanides
rayon **13**:1860
RDX (Hexogen; Cyclonite) **1**:116;
  6:828

red gum **7**:869
redox reactions **12**:1616, 1617
reduction *see* oxidation and reduction
refinery gas **8**:1118
reforming **4**:453; **11**:1576, 1579
Regnault, Henri **13**:1769
Resazurin test **5**:601
resins
  acrylate **10**:*1419*
  acrylic **1**:30–1; **12**:1629
  alkyd **9**:1204; **12**:1628–9
  epoxy **1**:30; **13**:1772
  ion-exchange **15**:2130
  melamine-formaldehyde (MF)
    12:1629
  natural
    for adhesives **1**:30
    for varnishes **9**:1204; **13**:1742–3
  phenolic **13**:1775
  polyester **1**:31; **13**:1823
  synthetic **1**:30; **12**:1629; **13**:1743
  thermosetting **13**:1773, 1775
  urea-formaldehyde (UF) **12**:1629
  vinyl **1**:30
resonance (in chemical bonding)
  4:444
restoration, picture **13**:**1741–3**
retrosynthesis **4**:458
rhodamine 6G **1**:1213
rhodium **13**:1781, 1782, 1783
rigidity modulus (torsion modulus)
  5:714
RNA (ribonucleic acid) **7**:973
Rochelle salt **13**:1744–5
rocks
  artificial **12**:1679–80
  chemical composition **7**:981–2
  magnetism **7**:992
    in the past (paleomagnetism)
      7:990, *991*, 992–3; **13**:1777
  types **7**:981–2, *987*; **12**:1679
  see also geochemistry; petrology
rock wool **9**:1161
rosins **10**:1382
rubber
  bearings **2**:233
  elasticity **5**:714
  high-hysteresis **17**:2339
  natural **14**:**1997–8**
    for adhesives **1**:30
    synthetic **14**:2001
    vulcanized **14**:1997; **18**:2454
  scrap recovery schemes **5**:591
  synthetic **1**:31; **13**:1771–2;
    14:**1999–2001**
    ABS **13**:1772
    flooring **7**:893
    tires **18**:2454
rubidium **1**:99, 101
  in atomic clocks **4**:485
rubies **1**:109; **4**:472; **5**:599; **16**:2270,
  2271, 2272
  for jewel bearings **2**:233
  for lasers and masers **5**:599;
    9:1211, 1212
  synthetic **17**:2346
Runge, Friedlieb **1**:133
rust **4**:569, 570; **9**:1188; **12**:1617,
  1621; **17**:2325–6
ruthenium **13**:1781, 1782
rutherfordium **6**:765
rutile **5**:599; **12**:1627

S

saccharin **7**:914
sacrificial protection **4**:571
SAE values **9**:1291
salbutamol **2**:252
salt *see* sodium chloride
saltpeter *see* potassium nitrate

salts, chemical **14**:**2014–15**
salvarsan (arsphenamine) **1**:135;
  10:1368
sand, an abrasive **1**:18
sandblasting **1**:17; **17**:2322, *2325*
sandpaper **1**:17, 18
saponification **1**:25; **15**:2107
sapphires **1**:109; **5**:599; **16**:2271,
  2272
  for jewel bearings **2**:233
  synthetic **17**:2346
saran **13**:1771
Sarin **4**:437, 439, *441*; **12**:1700
SBR (styrene-butadiene rubber)
  14:2001
scandium **18**:2485, 2487
Scheele, Carl Wilhelm **8**:1034;
  11:1525; **12**:1618, 1698
Schrödinger, Erwin **2**:150, 183, 184;
  4:461; **14**:1883
Schrödinger equation **2**:183–5;
  4:462; **6**:726
scums **19**:2656, 2666
Seaborg, Glen **12**:1673
seaborgium **6**:765, 766
sealants **1**:28, 32
seersucker **17**:2407
selenium **7**:982; **19**:2727
self-polishing copolymer (SPC)
  2:149
semipermeable membranes **5**:633,
  634
Semon, Waldo **13**:1770
serge **17**:2407
shampoos **8**:1033
shantung **17**:2407
shape-memory effect (SME)
  1:106–7; **10**:1351
  polymers **10**:1352
  see also alloys, shape-memory
shape selectivity **3**:406
shear modulus **5**:714
Sheffield plate **15**:2080
shellac **12**:1696
sherardizing **17**:2323
shot blasting **17**:2322
sialons **3**:427
siderite **9**:1186
silica (silicon dioxide) **15**:2076
  abrasive **1**:17, 18
  dust **7**:954
  gel **15**:2130
  see also quartz
silicates **15**:2077
silicon **4**:449; **15**:**2076–7**
  cantilevers **10**:1418
  compounds **15**:2077
  and photolithography **10**:1417–18
  production **15**:2076
    manufacture of crystals **5**:599;
      15:2076–7
  as a semiconductor **4**:552; **5**:599;
    6:752; **15**:2076
silicon carbide (carborundum) **1**:18;
  3:426; **17**:2347
silicones (polysiloxanes) **1**:32;
  15:2077, **2078**
  sealants **1**:32
  silicone rubbers **14**:2001; **15**:*2077*
  and water-repellent textiles
    19:2660
silicon nitride **3**:426, 427
silicon-tellurium-arsenic-germanium
  (STAG) **4**:552
silk **6**:849, *850*; **17**:2404, 2408
  artificial **3**:390; **6**:851
silver **15**:**2079–80**; **18**:2485
  EPNS (electroplated nickel silver)
    11:1523; **15**:2080
  extraction **9**:1220; **15**:2079–80
  solid **15**:2080
  sterling **15**:2080

silver bromide 8:1036; 12:1652, 1709; 15:2080
silver chloride 12:1709; 15:2080
silver iodide 8:1096; 12:1708, 1709
silver nitrate 12:1708; 15:2080
silver sulfide 15:2079, 2080
sisal 3:350; 6:849, 850
slag wool 9:1161
slaking 1:25
smart materials 10:1350–3, 1363–4
smelting 12:1617, 1620
soaps 4:457; 5:631
   lithium 1:99
soda see sodium carbonate
soda ash see sodium carbonate
sodamide 1:101
sodium 1:99, 100; 4:442
   production 1:100
   reaction with water 1:101
   uses 1:100–1
sodium acid pyrophosphate 12:1699
sodium alkyl suphates 1:101
sodium aluminate 1:109
sodium azide 11:1525
sodium borate (borax) 1:100; 12:1709
sodium carbonate (soda; soda ash) 1:100; 12:1709
sodium cellulose xanthate 12:1626
sodium chlorate 19:2679
sodium chloride (salt) 1:100
   bonds 4:442–3; 5:597, 598
   and corrosion 4:570, 571
   electrical conduction 4:555–6
   electrodialysis, for desalination 5:625
   electrolysis 1:25; 4:450, 452; 6:737; 8:1118; 9:1184
   and erosion 6:819
   as a food additive 7:907
   formation 9:1183
   production 14:2016
      from evaporation 11:1569; 14:2016
      mining 11:1462; 14:2016
   unit cells 10:1359
sodium cyanide, preparation 1:100–1
sodium diuranate 11:1537
sodium fluoride 18:2466
sodium hydroxide (caustic soda) 1:23; 12:1709
   preparation 1:25; 6:738
   and soap manufacture 15:2107
sodium hypochlorite 1:25
sodium laureth sulfate 8:1033
sodium monofluorophosphate 10:2466
sodium nitrate (Chile saltpeter) 1:24–5, 100; 6:826; 11:1525
   use in curing 7:905
sodium nitrite, uses 7:905
sodium perborate 5:632
sodium peroxide 1:100
sodium salicylate 7:869
sodium silicate (water glass) 1:30
sodium stannate 17:2448
sodium sulfite 12:1709
sodium thiosulfate 12:1708
sodium tripolyphosphate 5:631; 12:1699
softboard 19:2711
solders 1:31, 106; 10:1381–2; 17:2448
solids 10:1359–60
   allotropes 10:1360
   elasticity 5:713; 10:1361
   electrical properties 10:1360–1
   ionic 4:443, 555–6; 9:1163
   magnetic properties 10:1361
   saturated vapor pressure 18:2570
   thermal properties 10:1361
solid solutions 1:103
Solvay process 4:450

solvent extraction 4:446
solvent(s), water as a 19:2655
sorbants, use in fluidized beds 7:901
soybean oil, in paints 12:1628
spermaceti 19:2685
sperrylite (platinum diarsenide) 13:1781
sphalerite 9:1219; 19:2731
spider silk, and body armor 2:163
spinels 16:2271
spirits 1:97; 5:661, 663; 6:841; 16:2215–18
   poteen 5:664
   rectified 5:663
spodumene 1:99
stannic chloride 17:2448
stannous chloride 17:2448
stannous fluoride 18:2466
stannous sulfate 17:2448
starch 3:389, 390
starches, adhesive 1:29–30
steam 10:1360
steel see iron and steel
stilbite 19:2728
stills 5:663
   molecular 5:664
strain 5:713
stress (on materials) 5:713, 714
   analysis
      holographic interferometry 8:1083
      photoelastic 9:1237; 13:1796
strontium-90 17:2418
styrene (phenylethene) 8:1107; 12:1629; 13:1770, 1771, 1772; 14:1999–2001
Styrofoam 13:1776
sublimation see distillation and sublimation
submarines 16:2287–91
sucrose 3:389, 390
sugar 3:389
   bonds in 5:597
sulfanilamide 8:1108
sulfate ions 9:1183
sulfonyurea 19:2681
sulfur 13:1794; 16:2298–300
   allotropes 16:2298
   amorphous 16:2299
   compounds 16:2300
   in crude oil (petroleum) 11:1577, 1580; 16:2300
   flowers of 16:2299
   from seawater 11:1569
   occurrence and extraction 16:2299
   oxidation numbers 12:1616
   plastic 16:2298–9
sulfur dioxide 11:1527
sulfur hexafluoride 9:1162
sulfuric acid 1:23
   industrial manufacture 1:23–4; 4:452
   uses 1:24
      in batteries 2:225–6
superalloys see Nimonic alloys
supercooling 7:999
superfluids 4:550, 553; 5:592; 7:934; 10:1362; 11:1528–9
superglue 1:30
superphosphate, fertilizers 6:844–5
superplastic forming 10:1363
surface treatments 17:2322–6
   coatings 17:2323
      surface-alloy 1:107
      see also galvanizing
   polishing 17:2325
   using water jets 17:2322–3
   see also abrasives; electroplating
surfactants 5:631, 632
Swan, Sir Joseph 6:851
synmetals 2:229
synthetic crystals 17:2346–7

synthetic diamonds see diamonds, synthetic

T

tabun 4:437; 12:1700
taffeta 17:2407
tallows 10:1382
tannin 8:1151
tantalum 3:404
tarmacadam see blacktop
tartaric acid 4:447
tartrazine 7:907
TBTO (tributyltin oxide) 2:149
TCA (trichloroanisole) 19:2703
TCP 8:1108
tear gases 4:437; 8:1036; 11:1532, 1534; 14:1972
technetium, isotopes 14:1907
Teflon see polytetrafluoroethylene
Tencel 6:851; 13:1769
terbium 18:2486
terephthalic acid 8:1107
terracotta 4:467
Terylene 8:1108
tetrachloromethane 4:462
tetraethyl lead 1:97, 101; 4:459; 8:1036, 1106; 9:1221; 13:1802
tetrafluoroethene (tetrafluoroethylene) 13:1813, 1814
textiles 17:2404–8
   for the clothing industry 4:490
   fabrics 17:2406–8
      conservation 2:160
      fire-resistant 7:880, 881
      nonwoven 17:2408
      optical brighteners for 5:632, 693; 10:1302
      water-repellant finishes 19:2659–60
      woven 17:2405–6
   finishing processes 17:2408
   high-strength materials 17:2405
      see also carbon fiber; Kevlar
   see also fibers, natural; fibers, synthetic
thermodynamics 4:463–4
thermoplastics
   pipes 13:1750
   powder coatings 13:1823–4
   processing of 13:1773, 1774–5
   recycling 14:1941
thermosets 13:1775
   for pipes 13:1750
   for powder coatings 13:1824
Thinsulate 13:1861, 1863
thiokol 14:2001
thiophene 4:455
thiourea 12:1712
thixotropy 19:2609
Thomson, J. J. 2:182; 3:408; 6:726, 767
thorium 18:2487
   as a nuclear fuel 11:1539
thorium oxide 18:2487
tin 17:2447–8
   alloys 17:2448
      see also bronze; pewter; solders
   compounds 17:2448
   cry of 17:2448
   occurrence and production 17:2447
   tin-plated steel 3:382, 383; 4:571
   uses, in canning 3:382, 383; 17:2448
   white 17:2448
tin chloride 15:2080; 17:2448
tinplate 17:2448
tissue, glass 7:1002–3
titanium 18:2486
   alloys 10:1351; 18:2485

titanium-nickel 5:622; 10:1351
   uses 2:243, 256; 16:2191
titanium chloride 12:1627; 18:2488
titanium dioxide
   forms 5:599
   in paints 12:1627, 1628, 1630
   synthetic 5:599
titanium oxide 6:779
titration 4:446–7
TNT see trinitrotoluene
toluene 4:498; 5:617; 8:1107, 1108
   from oil refining 11:1578–9
toluene diisocyanate (TDI) 8:1107; 13:1772
toothpaste 1:17; 18:2466
tornadoes 8:1094, 1097–9
torsion modulus (rigidity modulus) 5:714
transactinides 6:765
transesterification 2:259
transition elements 12:1673; 18:2485–8
   as catalysts 3:405; 4:452; 18:2488
   compounds 4:443; 18:2488
   see also platinum metals
transmutation
   artificial 11:1525
   of nuclear waste 11:1550
transuranium (transuranic) elements 6:764–5; 18:2487
trass 3:417
Travers, Morris W. 11:1529
Trevira 6:853
tributyl phosphate (TBP) 11:1539
tributyltin oxide (TBTO) 2:149
tricalcium aluminate 3:419
tricalcium silicate 3:419, 420
Tricel 6:852; 13:1769
trichloroethylene 5:687; 8:1036
trichloromethane 13:1769
trichlorosilane 15:2076
triethylamine 4:456
trihalomethanes 4:476
trimethyl gallium 4:460
trinitrophenol (picric acid) 6:827, 828; 8:1108; 11:1527
trinitrotoluene (TNT) 1:116; 6:828; 8:1107, 1108; 11:1527
tritium 1:99; 7:947; 8:1118
   in hydrogen bombs 11:1553
tritons 7:946
tungsten 18:2486
   for lightbulbs 9:1244, 1245, 1246; 13:1782–3; 14:1960; 18:2485
   thoriated 18:2565
tungsten carbide, uses 5:680
turpentine 5:661
twill 17:2406

U

ultrafiltration 5:633; 12:1610
unit cells 5:598; 10:1359; 13:1744
Universal Indicator 12:1692
uranium 14:1906–7; 18:2487, 2546–8
   isotopes 6:764; 7:877; 8:1034; 11:1539, 1544, 1551–2; 14:1907; 18:2547
   decay series 14:1908, 1916
   separation (enrichment) 3:423; 11:1537–8, 1544; 18:2548
   nuclear fission 2:248; 7:876, 877; 11:1544, 1551–2; 14:1907; 18:2548
   occurrence and extraction 11:1457, 1462, 1537; 18:2546–7
   radioactivity 7:970; 14:1907; 18:2546
   reprocessing of spent fuel 11:1538–9, 1549

uranium (*cont.*)
  uses
    in aircraft **1**:69
    in nuclear reactors **6**:796;
      11:1537–9; **13**:1831; **18**:2548
    in nuclear weapons **11**:1551–2
uranium carbide **3**:426
uranium dioxide **11**:1538
uranium hexafluoride **6**:764; **8**:1034;
  11:1537–8, 1539; **18**:2546, 2548
uranium nitrate **11**:1539
uranium nitride **11**:1538
uranium oxides **18**:2546, 2547
uranium tetrafluoride **11**:1538;
  18:2546
uranyl carbonate **11**:1537
uranyl fluoride **11**:1538
uranyl ions **18**:2546
uranyl nitrate **18**:*2546*, 2547
uranyl sulfate **11**:1537
urea **4**:453
  fertilizers **6**:845
urea formaldehyde (UF) **19**:2709

V

V agents **4**:437
valency **4**:442
vanadium pentoxide **1**:24; **4**:452;
  18:2488
van der Waals forces **5**:598; **15**:2129
vaporization, latent heat of **4**:463
vapors **10**:1362
varnishes *see* lacquers and varnishes
veneers **18**:*2578–9*; **19**:2710–11
vermiculite (micafill) **8**:1122; **9**:*1161*
vinyl acetate **7**:892–3; **13**:1771
  copolymers **12**:1696; **13**:1771
vinyl chloride *see* chloroethene
vinyl floorings **7**:892–3

vinylidene chloride **7**:880; **13**:1771
  copolymers **13**:1771
viscose **3**:390; **6**:851; **7**:881; **13**:1769
viscosity **14**:1961; **19**:2609–11
  coefficient of **19**:2609, 2610, 2611
  SAE values **9**:1291
vitallium **2**:256
VOCs (volatile organic compounds,
  or components) **13**:1823;
  19:2641
vulcanization **14**:1997, 2001; **18**:2454

W

warfarin **12**:1677, 1678
water **19**:2654–6
  bonds in **4**:444; **19**:2654–5
  carbonated **15**:2109
  cycle **19**:2665
  drinking **19**:2656, 2662–3
  from brackish or seawater *see*
    desalination
  hard **13**:1786–7; **19**:2656, 2666
  heavy *see* deuterium oxide
  phases **10**:1361
    phase diagrams **10**:*1360*
  physical properties **12**:1621;
    19:2654, 2655
  pure water polymer **12**:1620–1
  shortages **6**:809
  softening **12**:1699; **13**:1787;
    19:2656, 2666, 2730
  solvent power **19**:2655
  surface tension **10**:*1359*, 1361–2
  triple point **17**:2395
  see also ice
water glass (sodium silicate) **1**:30
water-repellant finishes **19**:2659–60
wax
  corrosion-prevention by **4**:*570*

from oil refining **11**:1579
  sealing **1**:30
  uses
    food packaging **7**:908
    in water-repellent fabrics
      19:2660
white lead **12**:1628
winemaking **1**:98; **6**:840–1;
  19:*2700–3*
Wöhler, Friedrich **4**:453
Wollaston, W. H. **13**:1781
wood
  fuel **2**:258
  laminated **19**:2711
  paper made from **12**:1637, 1638
  veneers **18**:*2578–9*; **19**:2710–11
wood alcohol *see* methanol
wood composites **19**:2709–11
Wood's metal **1**:106; **9**:1221
wool **6**:848–9, 850; **17**:2404, 2408
  glass **7**:1002, 1003

X

xanthan gum **19**:2611
xenon **5**:*655*; **11**:1529
xenon oxide **11**:1529
xenon oxyfluoride **11**:1529
xenon tetrafluoride **11**:1529
xylene (dimethylbenzene) **4**:498;
  8:1108
  from oil refining **11**:1578–9
  isomerization of **3**:406
xylenes **8**:1107

Y

yarn, glass **7**:1003
yellow cake **11**:1537

Young's modulus (elastic modulus)
  5:713; **15**:2131; **16**:2229
yttrium **18**:2485, 2487
yttrium–aluminum garnet (YAG)
  9:1212; **18**:*2487*

Z

zein **12**:1677–8
zeolites **3**:406; **4**:471; **7**:953; **15**:2130;
  19:*2728–30*
  as catalysts **3**:406; **19**:2730
  computer graphical representation
    4:*464*; **19**:*2730*
  synthesis **19**:2729
zephyr **17**:2407–8
Ziegler–Natta polymerization catalysts **4**:460; **13**:1770, 1810;
  14:2001
zinc **19**:2731–2
  alloys **19**:2731, 2732
  see also brass
  galvanizing with **4**:571; **17**:*2322*,
    2323, 2325–6; **19**:*2732*
  production **19**:2731–2
  rolled **19**:2732
zinc blende (sphalerite) **9**:1219;
  19:2731
zinc oxide **10**:1352; **17**:2326;
  18:*2529*; **19**:2732
zinc phosphate **5**:619
zinc sulfide **19**:2731, 2732
zircon **7**:988
zirconia **3**:426
zirconium boride **3**:426
zirconium dioxide **7**:936
zirconium oxide **12**:1609
zircons **16**:2271
zone refining **17**:2347
zymase **1**:98; **6**:841

Computers, Communications, and Information Technologies

A

accelerated graphics port (AGP)
  4:534–5
accumulators (storage registers)
  10:1428
Adobe Pagemaker **11**:1518
Adobe PhotoShop **12**:1594
ADSLs (asymmetric digital subscriber lines) **11**:1476, 1517;
  17:2358
advanced intelligent tape (AIT)
  10:1312
Advanced Research Projects Agency
  (ARPA) **11**:1501
aerials *see* antennas
air-traffic control (ATC) **1**:93–6;
  11:1513
  radar **1**:88, 94–5; **3**:410;
    14:1895–6, *1897*
  virtual reality and **19**:*2608*
algebra, Boolean **9**:1277, 1279
ALUs (arithmetic and logic units)
  4:528; **10**:1428
AM *see* amplitude modulation
amplification, measured **9**:*1275*
amplifiers, turbulence (fluidic
  devices) **7**:899
amplitude modulation (AM) **11**:1473;
  14:1902–3
  quadrature, in modems **11**:1475
analog and digital systems **1**:127–9
  analog audio **4**:513–14; **8**:1071,
    1076; **15**:2144–5

analog-to-digital converters
  (ADCs) **1**:127, 128–9; **2**:189
  in cell phones **3**:416
  computers **1**:127
  digital audio **8**:1076; **15**:2145
  digital computer animation **1**:138
  digital encryption **5**:594; **6**:762
  digital imaging (image intensifiers)
    8:1131
  digitally-encoded sound **1**:26;
    6:755
    on compact discs **4**:514–15
  digital mapping **10**:1330–1
  digital radio **6**:755; **14**:1904
  digital television *see* television
    broadcasting, digital TV
  digital-to-analog converters
    (DACs) **1**:127
  digital video (DV) **19**:2602
  displays
    analog **1**:127
    digital *see* digital displays
  signals **1**:128
analog-to-digital converters (ADCs)
  1:127, 128–9; **2**:189
androids **14**:1989
animation **1**:136–40; **4**:536;
  16:2189–90
antennas **1**:141–2
  automobile **6**:740
  cell phone **3**:415, 416
  dish **1**:*141*, 142
  microwave **1**:*141*, 142; **6**:741–2,
    744

monopole and dipole **1**:142
  radio **1**:141–2; **6**:741; **14**:1904
  receiving **1**:141–2
  satellite-tracking **15**:2057
  television **1**:142; **19**:*2671*
  transmitting **1**:141, *142*
  radar **14**:*1897*
application service providers (ASPs)
  9:1182
ARISE satellite **14**:*1910*, 1911
arithmetic and logic units (ALUs)
  4:528; **10**:1428
arms, robotic **14**:1986, 1987, *1988*;
  15:*2056*; **16**:2169
ARPANET **9**:1178
artificial intelligence **2**:169–72
  and computer games **11**:1503
  and personal computers **4**:531
  and reading devices **1**:20
  see also robotics
artificial reality (projected reality)
  19:2604
ASCII **2**:247; **4**:529
asdic **15**:2126, *2127*
ASPs (application service providers)
  9:1182
assembly language **4**:530
asymmetric digital subscriber lines
  (ADSLs) **11**:1476, 1517;
  17:2358
atmospheric windows **6**:743
atomic weight **2**:182
audio and video recording **1**:129;
  2:186–9; **4**:513–14; **15**:2143–4

compact discs (CDs) **4**:514–15
magnetic tape **2**:186–7; **10**:1311,
  1312; **15**:2144–5
  see also digital audio tapes
  for movie production **11**:1498–9
  multitrack **10**:1312
  records **12**:1694–5, 1697
  video cassettes **2**:187–8; **10**:1312;
    19:2600–2
  compared with DVDs **5**:652
  see also phonography; sound effects
    and sampling; sound mixing;
    sound reproduction; video cam-
    eras; video recorders
augmented reality (AR; mixed reality)
  19:2608
automatic teller machines (ATMs)
  2:191–2
avatars **11**:1503

B

Babbage, Charles **2**:*171*; **4**:523
backup storage **5**:609
backward chaining **2**:171
Baird, John Logie **17**:2383, 2392;
  19:2597
bar codes **3**:401; **8**:1082, *1083*;
  12:1624
  for letters **10**:1322
  scanners *see* optical scanners,
    bar code
  for stock control **10**:1341

Bardeen, John **18**:2481
batteries, in calculators **3**:360–1
Baudot, Jean-Maurice-Emile **3**:354; **11**:1474
baud rate **3**:354; **4**:541; **11**:1474
BBICs *see* biointegrated circuits
Bell, Alexander Graham **12**:1694; **17**:2368–9
Bell Telephone Laboratories **18**:2480–1
Berners-Lee, Timothy **8**:1147; **9**:1178; **11**:1502
binary system **1**:128; **2**:245–7
  and computers **2**:246; **4**:524, 529
  and digital audio recording **4**:514–15
  and digital audio tapes **2**:189
biointegrated circuits (biolumines-cent bioreporter integrated circuits; BBICs) **9**:1168
BIOS (basic input-output system) **9**:1167
bitmaps **4**:533; **12**:1594, 1595
bits (computer)
  named **8**:1148
  parity (check bits) **4**:541–2; **5**:612; **8**:1148
"black box" flight recorders *see* FDRs
blind, the, aids for *see* accessibility aids
block diagrams **9**:1278
books
  ISBNs **8**:1149
  library classification system **8**:1149
  talking **1**:19
Boole, George **9**:1277
Braille **1**:19
Brattain, Walter **18**:2481
broadband ISDN **11**:1476
buses (data paths) **10**:1428
bytes **5**:610

C

cable networks **3**:353–5
  see also telecommunications
cables
  between computers **4**:539
  coaxial **4**:539
  polymer, for fiber optics **6**:856
  submarine (undersea) **3**:347–9; **18**:2471
  telephone **3**:347; **17**:2356, 2357, 2371; **18**:2471
caching **9**:1167
calorimetry **4**:462–3
camcorders **18**:2592
  tapes **2**:187
cards
  for automatic teller machines **2**:191
  CD business cards **4**:515
  credit and debit **3**:401
  identity **3**:341
  memory (PC cards) **5**:615
  plug-in **4**:539
  punched, for data input **5**:609
Carnivore **6**:762
carrier frequency **14**:1901; **15**:2144
  processing **10**:1331
cash dispensers *see* automatic teller machines
cash registers **3**:399–401
cassettes
  audio **2**:186; **10**:1312
  video **2**:187–8; **10**:1312
cathode-ray tubes (CRTs) **3**:408–10; **12**:1647–8
  for computer monitors **3**:409; **4**:532
  in oscilloscopes **3**:409; **12**:1607

in radar displays **14**:1897–8
in television receivers **3**:409; **12**:1647–8; **17**:2392, *2393*
CAVE (cave automatic virtual environment) **11**:1503
cave rooms **19**:2604
CCDs *see* charge-coupled devices
CCTV (closed-circuit television) **3**:340; **14**:1977; **15**:2042, 2044
CD-ROMs *see* compact discs
CDs *see* compact discs
cellular telephones (cell phones) **3**:415–16; **17**:2358–9
  answering service **17**:2367
  Internet access via **4**:540; **8**:1147
  traffic monitoring using **14**:1985
central processing units (CPUs) **10**:1416–17
  and caching **9**:1167
  in calculators **3**:360
  in computers **4**:527, 528, 529, 530; **10**:1428–9
  in mobile phones **3**:416
  see also microprocessors
Chappe, Ignace and Claude **17**:2360, *2361*
charge-coupled devices (CCDs) **3**:432
checks, sorting by MICR **12**:1595
chess, played on computers **2**:*169*, 171
ciphers **5**:594
CISC **10**:1428
clocks, talking **17**:2348–9
clock speeds **10**:1429
CNC (computer numerical control) **10**:1340; **18**:*2464, 2465*
colorimetry **4**:447, *510–12*
color mapping **4**:533–4
color-register encoding **4**:534
COMPAC network **3**:348
compact discs (CDs)
  audio **1**:129; **4**:*513–17*; **5**:650
    amplifiers **1**:126; **4**:*514*
    CD jukeboxes **9**:1197
    CD players **4**:*517*; **5**:650
  CD-ROMs **5**:614, 650; **6**:*754*
    drives **4**:527
    multimedia **11**:1502
    rewritable **5**:614
  manufacture **5**:*614*, 651
  trucks **18**:2507
  see also digital versatile discs (DVDs)
compression techniques **15**:2145
  computer **4**:533, 534
  and DVDs **5**:651
computer-aided design (CAD) **4**:532; **6**:814–15; **10**:*1364*, 1365
  and aerodynamic shapes **1**:37
  and chip circuitry **6**:*750*
  and clothing manufacture **4**:489
  and electrodischarge machining **6**:736
  see also computer graphics; ergonomics
computer-aided manufacture (CAM) **4**:532; **10**:1365
computer-assisted retrieval (CAR) systems **10**:1415
Computer Generated Images (CGIs) **7**:887; **16**:2190
computer graphics **1**:138, 139; **4**:*532–6*
  of chemicals **4**:*464*; **5**:*599*
  of protein structure **13**:*1864*, 1866
  of voiceprints **16**:*2200*
  of zeolites **4**:*464*; **19**:*2730*
  see also computer-aided design
computer models, of reservoir systems **7**:890
computer output microfilmers

(COMs) **10**:1415
computer printers **4**:528, **543–5**
  dot-matrix **19**:2720
  ink-jet **1**:40; **4**:544–5; **19**:2720
    bubble-jet **4**:544
  laser **4**:528, 543; **19**:2720
  line **4**:545
    barrel printers **4**:545
    train and chain printers **4**:545
  plotters **4**:528
  printing photographs **3**:372
computers **4**:523–31
  analog and digital **1**:127; **4**:523
  and animated movies **1**:137–8, 139, 140
  at airports **1**:*88*
  in aviation **1**:44
  and the binary system **2**:246; **4**:524, 529
  chess-playing **2**:*169*, 171
  components **4**:*527*, 528
    CPU *see* central processing units
    drives *see* data storage
    power supply unit (PSU) **4**:529
    see also integrated circuits
  customized **10**:1341
  development of **2**:*171*; **4**:523–4
  and digital cameras **3**:370
  electronics **6**:754–5
  in engineering **10**:1365
  fluidic digital **7**:899
  future of computing **4**:531
  graphical user interfaces (GUIs) **4**:*531*; **8**:1147; **11**:1490, 1501
  graphics cards (video cards; adapters) **4**:527
  and the hexadecimal system **2**:246–7
  languages **4**:530; **10**:1428
    high-level **2**:*246*; **4**:530
  laptop **4**:526; **19**:2720
  logic functions **9**:1277–9
  machine code **10**:1428
  mainframe **4**:526
  memory **5**:609; **9**:1167
    optical **9**:*1213*
    random access *see* RAM
    read-only (ROM) **5**:609
  minicomputers **4**:525, 526
  monitors (VDUs; visual display units) **3**:409; **4**:527; **5**:599
    color **4**:532, 533
    liquid crystal display (LCD) **4**:532; **9**:1259
    monochrome **4**:533
  multimedia **4**:525, 534–5
  and music **17**:2345
  networks **4**:*526*, 537–42; **8**:1150
    infrared **19**:2707
    local-area (LANs) **4**:526, 537, 538–9, 541
    power-line **19**:2707
    wide-area (WANs) **4**:537, 539–40, 542
  notebook **11**:*1491*
  operating systems **4**:525, 530
  output devices **4**:527–8
  palmtop **4**:526
  personal organizers **4**:*530*
  personal (PCs) **4**:*523*, 525, 526–7
    desktop **4**:526
    future developments **4**:531
    input devices **4**:527
    output devices **4**:527–8
    parity-bit checking **4**:542
  printers *see* computer printers
  programming and software **4**:523, 529–30; **8**:1148
    image-manipulation software **5**:629
    photographic editing software **4**:534

spreadsheets **8**:1150
see also databases; word processors
scanners *see* optical scanners
security **4**:530–1
  and data interception **6**:761–2
serial- and parallel processing **2**:*172*
stereoscopic images **16**:2264
see also artificial intelligence; data storage; mice and pointing devices; modems and ISDN
contact image sensor (CIS) system **12**:1592
cryptology **5**:593–6
CVRs (Cockpit Voice Recorders) **7**:884, 885

D

databases **8**:1148–50
Data Encryption Standard (DES) **5**:594; **6**:762
data gloves **11**:1503, **19**: 2603–6
data rate **5**:612
data storage **5**:609–15
  on digital cameras **3**:370–2
  floppy disks **5**:609, 612
  hard disk drives **5**:609, 610–12; **9**:1167
  magneto-optical discs **5**:*613*, 614–15
  memory cards (PC cards) **5**:615
  microfilm **10**:1415
  optical systems
    CD-ROMs *see* compact discs
    DVDs *see* digital versatile discs
    WORM drives **5**:614
  tape drives **5**:612–13
    digital audio tapes (DATs) **1**:129; **2**:189; **5**:612, *615*
  using scanning tunneling microscopes (STMs) **4**:552
  Zip drives and disks **4**:527; **5**:612
DATs *see* digital audio tapes
day-color-light signals **14**:1924
deaf, the, aids for **1**:22
Deep Space Network **15**:2156–7
degradation, chemical, of toxic agents **4**:440
demodulation **11**:1473
design *see* computer-aided design; ergonomics
desktop publishing (DTP) **5**:626–30; **19**:2720
Dewey Decimal Classification **8**:1149
Difference Engine **2**:*171*; **4**:523
digital audio broadcasting (DAB) **14**:1904
digital audio tapes (DATs) **1**:129; **2**:189; **5**:612, *615*
digital displays **1**:127; **5**:646–8
digital linear tape (DLT) **10**:1312
digital mapping **10**:1330–1
digital subscriber lines (DSLs) **4**:540; **17**:2358
  asymmetric (ADSLs) **11**:1476, 1517; **17**:2358
digital systems *see* analog and digital systems
digital-to-analog converters (DACs) **1**:127
digital versatile discs (DVDs) **1**:129; **3**:354; **5**:614, **649–52**; **8**:1148; **11**:1500
  multimedia **11**:1502
  recording on **5**:652
digital video discs *see* digital versatile discs
digital video (DV) **19**:2602
digitizers *see* graphics tablets

diodes 5:653–4; 14:1937
  avalanche 19:2621
  light-emitting (LEDs) 15:2054
    in calculators 3:361; 5:654
    in cameras 3:367
    and fiber optics 3:355
    in matrix displays 5:646, 647
    in optoisolators 6:757
    in planar displays 5:648
    in watches 19:2650
  semiconductor 5:653–4; 6:752;
    15:2053–4; 18:2481–2
  vacuum-tube (valves) 5:653;
    6:750–1; 18:2480, 2563–4
  zener 19:2619–21
dipoles (antennas) 1:142
  half-wave 6:740
disabled, the, aids for see accessibility
  aids
discrete multitone (DMT) 17:2358
distributed processing 4:538
dithering 4:533–4
DNC (direct numerical control)
  10:1340
Dolby systems 15:2147–8
  Dolby Digital 5:652; 15:2148
domain names 9:1180
domains (magnets), on hard disks
  5:610
doping 9:1164, 1166; 10:1427;
  15:2053
DRAM (dynamic random access
  memory) 6:753; 9:1167
drives, computer 4:527, 528;
  5:610–15
DSLs see digital subscriber lines
DTS (Digital Theater Sytems)
  process 15:2148
dual-in-line (DIL) package 3:359–60
DVDs see digital versatile discs
Dynabook 11:1501

E

Echelon 6:762
ECMs (electronic countermeasures)
  16:2250–3
E-Com 10:1325
Edison, Thomas
  and sound recording 2:186; 4:513;
    12:1694
  and the telegraph 3:353
EEPROMs (electrically erasable-
  programmable read only
  memories) 9:1167
electrochemical deposition 10:1418
electronic countermeasures (ECMs)
  16:2250–3
electronic funds transfer at point of
  sale (EFTPOS) 3:401
electronic news gathering (ENG)
  17:2389; 18:2592
electronic point-of-sale (EPOS)
  terminals 3:401
electrophotography 12:1701
e-mail 4:537; 9:1179; 10:1325;
  17:2363
  addresses 9:1180
  attachments 9:1182
  interception systems 6:762
  newsletters via 11:1519
  viruses 4:531
encoding, electronic 5:596
Enhanced Thematic Mapper Plus
  (ETM+) 17:2337
ENIAC computers 4:524
Enigma machine 5:593, 595–6
Enquire (computer program) 9:1178
EPROMs (erasable-programmable
  read only memories) 9:1167
erbium-doped fiber amplifiers

(EDFAs) 6:856
ergonomics 6:813–15
  see also computer-aided design
Ethernet 4:539, 541
expert systems 2:170–1

F

facsimile transmission (faxes)
  10:1325; 17:2357, 2363
faxes 10:1325; 17:2357, 2363
FDDI (fiber-optic digital device
  interface) 4:539
FDRs (Flight Data Recorders)
  7:884–5
feature analysis 19:2616
feature extraction 12:1595
Federal Communications
  Commission (FCC) 18:2496,
  2497
fiber-optic digital device interface
  (FDDI) 4:539
fiber optics 6:854–6
  optical fibers 6:855
    and holography 8:1082
    low-attenuation 6:856
    types 6:855, 856
    as waveguides 19:2671
  uses 6:856
    in cable networks 3:354–5;
      4:539, 542; 6:856; 17:2356–7,
      2371
    in submarine (undersea) cables
      3:349; 17:2357
files (data) 5:612
films, animated see animation
FLAG (fiber optic link around the
  globe) 3:355
flash cards 5:615
flight recorders 1:67; 7:884–5
flight simulators 7:886–7; 11:1501;
  19:2603–4
floppy disks 5:609, 612
fluorescent multilayer discs (FMDs)
  5:652
fly-by-wire (FBW) systems 1:44, 66;
  2:213
flying-spot scanners 17:2384
FM see frequency modulation
fonts 5:627
Frequency Division Multiple Access
  (FDMA) 3:416
frequency hopping 5:596; 6:762
frequency modulation (FM) 11:1473
  and electronic organs 12:1603–4
  and mobility aids 1:21
  and television receivers 17:2393
  and video recorders 19:2599–600
frequency shift keying 11:1474
fuzzy logic 2:171; 3:431; 9:1277;
  19:2635–6

G

games, computer 4:536; 11:1503
geographical information systems
  7:985, 986
"ghosts" (false frequencies) 15:2145
GIF (graphics image format) 4:534;
  12:1594
global system for mobile communications (GSM) 3:416
goggles, virtual-reality 4:532
gramophones 12:1694
graphical user interfaces (GUIs)
  4:531; 8:1147; 11:1490, 1501
graphics, computer see computer
  graphics
graphics cards (video cards; adapters)
  4:527

graphics image format (GIF) 4:534;
  12:1594
graphics tablets (digitizers) 4:535;
  11:1492
graphophones 12:1694
gray-scale imaging 4:533

H

Hamming, Richard 8:1148
Hamming code 8:1148
handoff 3:415
handshaking 4:541
handwriting, and optical character
  recognition 12:1595
Hawking, Stephen, and voice synthesis 19:2615, 2617
head-coupled displays (HCDs)
  19:2605
head-mounted displays (HMDs)
  19:2604–5, 2606
  and augmented reality 19:2608
head-up displays (HUDs) 1:68;
  8:1039–40, 1082
  in cars 6:813; 8:1040, 1129
hearing aids 1:22; 12:1612
Hertz, Heinrich 14:1893
heuristics 2:171, 172
hexadecimal system 2:246–7
Hollerith, Herman 4:523
HTML (hypertext markup language)
  9:1179; 11:1502
http (hypertext transfer protocol)
  9:1177
hubs, computer-network 4:539
hypertext markup language (HTML)
  9:1179; 11:1502
hypertext transfer protocol (http)
  9:1177

I

IBM System 360 computers 4:525
iconoscope cameras 17:2383, 2384
identity cards 3:341
illustrator programs 5:629
image-manipulation software 5:629
images
  three-dimensional
    and computer graphics 1:139;
      4:536
    viewed on computer screens
      9:1257
in-flight interceptor communications
  system (IFICS) 16:2184
information technology 8:1147–50
information theory 8:1148
Infrared Astronomical Satellite
  (IRAS) 2:176–7
integrated circuits (silicon chips;
  microchips) 2:169–70; 6:750,
  754–5; 9:1164–8
  in calculators 3:359–60
  in cell phones 3:416
  complexity
    large scale integration (LSI)
      2:169; 3:359; 4:525; 6:755
    medium-scale integration (MSI)
      4:525; 6:755
    ultra-large-scale integration
      (ULSI) 4:525; 6:755
    very-large-scale integration
      (VLSI) 2:169; 3:416; 4:525;
      6:755; 10:1426
  in computers 4:524, 525; 9:1165,
    1277
  latch circuits 9:1277, 1279
  copper 4:524
  manufacture 6:751, 752; 9:1166,
    1264; 10:1427, 1428; 13:1763

testing 6:752; 9:1166–8;
  14:1879
  metal oxide–silicon (MOS) 3:361
  in sewing machines 15:2060
  switches 4:552
  to monitor animals 18:2588
  in watches 19:2650
  see also microprocessors
Intel, landmark processors 10:1429
Intelpost 10:1325
Intelsat VI (satellite) 15:2027;
  16:2165; 17:2359
interblock gaps 5:613
interfacing 5:646
Internet 4:537, 539–40; 9:1177–82
  in 3-D 11:1503
  addresses 9:1180
  animation on 1:140
  browers 9:1180–1
  future 9:1182
  history of 9:1178–9
  Internet microwaves 11:1450
  newspaper production and
    11:1516–17, 1519
  and riot control 14:1971
  search engines 2:170–1; 9:1180,
    1181, 1279
  via cable networks 3:354
  and viruses 4:531
  webcams and 18:2592
  see also e-mail; World Wide Web
Internet service providers (ISPs)
  4:526; 9:1178–9, 1180; 10:1325
  and e-mail interception 6:762
  modems and 11:1474
  protocols 11:1475
interpolation 12:1593
inverter gates 6:754
iris, recognition 2:192; 9:1269
ISBNs 8:1149
ISDN see modems and ISDN
ISPs see Internet service providers
item coding 3:401

J

Jacquard, Joseph Marie 4:523
jamming techniques 16:2250–3
Joint Photographic Experts Group
  (JPEG) 4:534; 12:1594
journalism, electronic 17:2389
joysticks, computer 4:535; 11:1492
JPEG (Joint Photographic Experts
  Group) 4:534; 12:1594

K

keyboards, computer 4:527, 535
keypads, itemized 3:400–1
Kismet (robot) 4:529
Kodak Image Management System
  (KIMS) 10:1415

L

Landsat satellites 1:35; 6:743;
  10:1330; 17:2337
LANs (local-area networks) 4:526,
  537, 538–9, 541
laptops (laptop computers) 4:526;
  19:2720
large-scale integration (LSI) see
  integrated circuits
Laryngophones 1:22
Laserdisc (video disc) 5:649, 650
  manufacture 5:651
lasers and masers
  lasers
    and compact discs (CDs)

4:515–16
and digital verstile discs (DVDs) **5**:650
and fiber optics **4**:542; **9**:1214; **17**:2371
and magneto-optical discs **5**:613, 614–15
rubies used in **5**:599; **9**:1211, 1212
LEDs *see* diodes, light-emitting
libraries **8**:1149, *1150*
robotics in **5**:612
light pens **4**:535; **11**:1492
linear predictive coding (LPC) **19**:2616
liquid crystal displays (LCDs) **5**:*647*, 648; **9**:1258–9
uses **9**:1259
in calculators **3**:361
in projectors **13**:1855
for screens and monitors **4**:532; **9**:1259
in watches **5**:646; **19**:*2649*, 2650
liquid crystals **4**:551; **9**:**1257–9**; **10**:1352
see also liquid crystal displays
local-area networks (LANs) **4**:526, 537, 538–9, 541
logic **9**:**1277–9**
fuzzy *see* fuzzy logic
in microprocessors **9**:1277; **10**:1427–8
logic gates **6**:754
loop-disconnect (LD) dialing **17**:2371
loran (long-range-navigation system) **11**:1511–12
for aircraft **1**:67
for fishing vessels **7**:872–3
LP (long-playing) records **12**:1696
LSI *see* integrated circuits

M

machine code **10**:1428
MACs (media access controllers) **11**:*1475*
magnetic-ink-character-recognition (MICR) **12**:1595
magnetic tapes and films **2**:186–7; **10**:**1311–12**
for computers **5**:612–13
digital **1**:129
DATs *see* digital audio tapes
materials **10**:1311
video tape **10**:*1312*
magneto-optical discs **5**:*613*, 614–15
magnetophones **10**:1311
Mandala machines **19**:2604
Marconi, Guglielmo **1**:142; **11**:1511; **17**:2392; **18**:2493
matrix displays **5**:646
using light-emitting diodes (LEDs) **5**:646, 647
full-color video displays (RGB displays) **5**:647
matrixing **15**:2148
media access controllers (MACs) **11**:*1475*
medium-scale integration (MSI) *see* integrated circuits
Memex **11**:1501
memory **9**:1167
modules **9**:1167
see also computers, memory
memory cards (PC cards) **5**:615
MERLIN (multi-element radio link interferometer network) **14**:1910
mice and pointing devices **4**:535; **11**:**1490–2**
mice **4**:527, 535; **11**:1490–1

microarrays, DNA **11**:1480
microchips *see* integrated circuits
microcomputers *see* computers, personal
microfilm **10**:**1415**
microphones **10**:**1423–5**; **11**:1531
as computer input devices **4**:527
microprocessors **6**:755; **10**:**1426–9**; **15**:2054
on automobiles **2**:202, 204
on farm machinery **1**:51
for "intelligent prostheses" **2**:254
logic operations **9**:1277; **10**:1427–8
and optoelectronics **6**:755
see also central processing units; integrated circuits
Microsoft
Internet Explorer **9**:1180, 1181
MS-DOS **4**:525
Windows **4**:525, 539
microwaves **6**:741–2
antennas **1**:*141*, *142*; **6**:741–2, *744*
communications **6**:746; **17**:2359
generation **6**:741, 745, 751
uses, in computer networks **4**:542
waveguides and **19**:2668–71
see also radar
MIDI (Musical Instrument Digital Interface) **12**:1604; **17**:2345
minicomputers **4**:525, 526
mixed reality (augmented reality; AR) **19**:2608
mixing desks **15**:2138–9
video **17**:*2390*
MMX processors **10**:1428
mobile phones *see* cellular telephones
models
computer *see* computer models
virtual **19**:*2607*, 2608
modems and ISDN **11**:**1473–6**
ISDN **4**:540; **11**:1476, 1517; **17**:2357–8
broadband **11**:1476
and newspaper production **11**:1519
modems **1**:129; **4**:540; **8**:1148; **11**:*1473–5*, 1476; **17**:2357
cable **11**:*1475*, 1476; **17**:2358
protocols **11**:1475–6
see also ADSLs
monopoles **1**:142
Monte Carlo modeling **2**:172
Morse, Samuel **3**:353; **17**:2361
Morse system **5**:593; **17**:2357, 2361
and paper-tape **17**:2361–2
MOSFETs **9**:1165; **10**:1426
mouse, computer *see* mice and pointing devices
MP3 players **15**:*2142*
MPEG (Moving Picture Experts Group) **18**:2497
MPEG-2 process **5**:651
MTSOs (mobile telephone switching offices) **17**:2359
multifrequency tone (MFT) dialing **17**:2371
multimedia **11**:**1501–3**
see also flight simulators; virtual reality
multiplexing **4**:535, 542; **17**:2356
time-division (TDM) **1**:129; **17**:2356, 2365
museums, virtual **11**:1503

N

natural-language processing **2**:172
see also voice recognition and synthesis
Netscape **9**:1180

networks, computer *see* computers, networks
news gathering, electronic (ENG) **17**:2389
Nexrad **10**:1398
Nixie tubes **5**:647
notebook computers **11**:*1491*
NTSC system **17**:2394
Nyquist's theorem **15**:2145

O

oNLine System (NLS) **11**:1501
operating systems, computer **4**:525, 530
Optacons **1**:20
optical character recognition (OCR) systems **1**:20; **4**:527; **5**:626; **12**:*1593*, 1594–5
mail-sorting **10**:1323, 1324
in newspaper production **11**:1518
optical mark recognition (OMR) machines **12**:1595
optical scanners **4**:527, 535; **5**:*626*; **12**:*1592–5*
bar-code **3**:401; **8**:1082, *1083*, *1150*; **10**:1341
are 1-bit scanners **12**:1593
on microwave ovens **11**:1450
color **12**:1593
drum **12**:1592–3
flatbed **5**:628; **12**:1592, 1593
image resolution **12**:1593–4
magnetic-ink-character-recognition (MICR) **12**:1595
OCR *see* optical character recognition (OCR) systems
optical mark recognition (OMR) machines **12**:1595
sensors **12**:1592–3
storing images **12**:1594
optometry **12**:**1596–8**
Optophones **1**:19–20
orthicons **17**:2383, 2384
image **17**:2384
OTP (one-time programmable) cards **5**:615

P

packet switching **4**:541
PAL (phase alternating line) system **17**:2394
pan and scan **5**:*652*
parallel processing **4**:526
parity checking **4**:541–2; **5**:612
passwords, computer **4**:530–1
PBXs (private branch exchanges) **17**:2372
PCMCIA modems **11**:1475
PCs *see* computers, personal
Pentium processors **10**:1429
personal organizers **4**:*530*
phase-shift keying (PSK) **11**:1475
phonoautographs **12**:1694
Phonodisc **19**:2597
phonography (records and vinyl discs) **4**:513–14; **8**:1076; **12**:**1694–7**; **15**:2144
photocopiers **12**:**1701–3**
photographic editing software **4**:534
photoresist **5**:651
phototypesetting **9**:1261
pipelining, and microprocessor performance **10**:1429
pixels **3**:432; **4**:532, 533
and video cameras **18**:2590–1
planar displays **5**:648
plan position indicators (PPIs) **1**:94; **14**:1898

plotters **4**:528
point-of-sale terminals, electronic (EPOS) **3**:401
point-to-point protocol (PPP) **11**:1475–6
polarization (radio transmission) **6**:741
portraits, computer **7**:920
power supply units (PSUs) **4**:529
printed circuits **13**:**1844–6**
printers, computer *see* computer printers
printing, and desktop publishing **5**:630
process-control modules **9**:*1168*
program counters **10**:1428
programmable logic controllers (PLCs) **10**:1365
programming, computer *see* computers, programming and software
projected reality (artificial reality) **19**:2604
PROMs (programmable read only memories) **9**:1167
protocols **4**:537
modem **11**:1475–6
proximity caching **11**:1503
PSK (phase-shift keying) **11**:1475
PSUs (power supply units) **4**:529
public-key cryptosystems (PKCs) **6**:762
publishing, desktop *see* desktop publishing
pulse-code modulation (PCM) **1**:128–9
and electronic organs **12**:1603

Q

Quark Xpress **11**:1518
quartz, in computer motherboards **4**:529

R

radar **6**:*742*; **14**:**1893–8**
air traffic control **1**:88, 94–5; **3**:410; **14**:*1895–6*, *1897*
displays **14**:1897–8
plan position indicators (PPIs) **1**:94; **14**:1898
Doppler **1**:68; **5**:672; **8**:1097–8; **14**:1897
search and surveillance **14**:*1896*, 1897
for space navigation **11**:1514
to monitor the weather **10**:1397, 1398; **14**:1898
and traffic monitoring **14**:1985
pulsed **14**:1894, *1896*
range and wavelength **14**:1895–6
and remote-sensing satellite pictures **7**:986
secondary surveillance (SSR) **1**:94–5; **14**:1897
synthetic aperture (SAR) **12**:1707; **17**:2337
to calculate altitude **1**:68
tracking **14**:1896
of space debris **15**:2150
transmitters **14**:1895
radio **6**:740–1; **14**:**1901–4**
AM (amplitude modulation) **11**:1473; **14**:1902–3; **18**:*2496*
and diodes **18**:2564
antennas **1**:141–2; **6**:741; **14**:1904
broadcasting **18**:2493–4, 2495–6
and cell phones **3**:415–16; **17**:2358–9
communication **17**:2358

radio (*cont.*)
  see also cellular telephones
  digital **6**:755; **14**:1904
  distortion **14**:1903
  and feedback theory **6**:839
  FM (frequency modulation) **11**:1473; **14**:1903
  IF (intermediate frequency) **14**:1903
  long-wave **1**:142; **6**:739; **18**:2494
  medium-wave **1**:142; **18**:2494
  modulation **14**:1901
  noise **14**:1903
  radio bugs **6**:*759, 760, 761, 762*
  short-wave **18**:2494
  speed of radio waves **14**:1894
  stereo broadcasting **15**:2144
  telemetry **17**:2365
  telescopes **11**:1562; **14**:1909
    amplifiers **14**:1911
    antennas **14**:1909–10
    output devices **14**:1911
    Very Large Arrays (VLAS) **14**:*1909*, 1910–11
  transistor **18**:2494
  transmitters **6**:740
    to track animals **19**:2734
  tuning circuits **12**:1606; **14**:1966
  UHF **1**:142
  VHF **1**:142; **6**:739; **14**:*1901*; **18**:2494
    and air-traffic control **1**:94, *95*
  VLF **6**:740
  see also radar
Radio Corporation of America (RCA) **12**:1694
RAM (random-access memory) **4**:528, 529; **5**:609; **9**:1167; **10**:1429
  dynamic (DRAM) **9**:1167
  static (SRAM) **5**:615; **9**:1167
RAMAC 350 computers **5**:609
RAM-ROM packs **12**:1604
random-access memory *see* RAM
raytracing **4**:536
reading aids **1**:19–20
read-only memory *see* ROM
recognition systems **3**:341; **9**:1269; **15**:2043–4
  iris or retina **2**:192; **9**:1269
  voice *see* voice recognition and synthesis
record players **9**:1284; **12**:1697; **13**:1739
  adjusting the turntable speed **16**:2286
records (discs) *see* phonography
recrystallization **4**:445
rectification **18**:2480
  half- and full-wave **14**:1937
reduced-instruction-set computer (RISC) processors **4**:526; **10**:1428
remotely operated vehicles (ROVs) **14**:1987
  submersibles **15**:2023; **16**:2294
repeaters, submarine-cable **3**:347–9
RGB displays **5**:647
RISC (reduced-instruction-set computer) processors **4**:526; **10**:1428
robotics **2**:*172*; **10**:1366; **14**:*1986–9*
  and agricultural machinery **1**:51
  androids **14**:1989
  arms **14**:1986, 1987, *1988*; **15**:*2056*
    on space stations **15**:*2056*; **16**:2169, 2173, *2174*
  for bomb and mine disposal **3**:294, 295, *296*; **14**:1956; **18**:2471
  continuous-path (CP) robots **14**:1987
  early robots **14**:1886
  fractal shape-changing **9**:1255

industrial robots **14**:1986–7
  for mass production **10**:*1339*, 1340, *1365*; **15**:*2066*
  in libraries **5**:*612*
  linear motors used in **9**:1255
  for milking cows **11**:1452
  nanorobots **10**:1420; **14**:*1989*
    in blood vessels **10**:*1419*
  point-to-point (PTP) robots **14**:1987–8
  for remote handling, of nuclear fuel **14**:*1905*
  robots with facial expressions **4**:*529*
  second generation robots **14**:1987–8
  senses **14**:1988–9
  submersible robots **16**:2294
  for surgery **10**:1440; **17**:2331–2; **19**:*2616*
  vacuum cleaners **18**:2562
  and voice recognition **14**:1989; **19**:*2616, 2617*
  see also artificial intelligence
ROM (read-only memory) **9**:1167
  ROM cards **5**:615
ROSAT (satellite) **2**:174
routers **4**:541
ROVs *see* remotely operated vehicles
rule of thumb method **2**:171
run-time engines **11**:1502

S

satellites, artificial **15**:*2024–9*
  communications **4**:540, *541*, 542; **15**:*2025*, 2029; **17**:2359
  electricity from **15**:2117
  and global positioning systems **2**:204; **7**:1006–7
  remote sensing **7**:986, *995*; **15**:2029
    photography **1**:*33*, 35; **2**:156; **6**:*743*
    radar **7**:986
    surveying for oil deposits **11**:1571
  to track animals **19**:2735
SCADA (system control and data acquisition) systems **10**:1340, 1348; **19**:2667
scanners, optical *see* optical scanners
SEACOM network **3**:348
search engines **2**:170–1; **9**:*1180*, 1181, 1279
Seasat (satellite) **8**:*1097*; **11**:1569
semaphore signals **17**:2360, *2361*
  railway **14**:1924
semiconductors **4**:552, 555, 556; **6**:728; **10**:1361; **15**:*2052–4*
  intrinsic and extrinsic **15**:2053
  lasers **9**:1213, 1214; **15**:2054
  p-n junction (depletion layer) **5**:654; **6**:752; **15**:2053, 2116–17; **18**:2481
  p-type and n-type **5**:*653*, 654; **6**:752; **15**:2053; **18**:2481–2
  silicon as **4**:552; **5**:599; **6**:752; **15**:2076
  uses **15**:2053–4
    in calculators **3**:359
    in CCDs **15**:*2054*
    in electronic devices **6**:752
    in pressure transducers **15**:2054
    in rectifier applications **14**:1938; **15**:2053
    in thyristors **17**:2432
  see also integrated circuits; microprocessors
Serial Line Internet Protocol (SLIP) **11**:1475–6

servers (in computer networks) **4**:526, 537, 538
service providers, Internet **4**:540
Shannon, Claude **8**:1148
shift registers **1**:129
Shockley, William **18**:2481
silicon chips *see* integrated circuits
simulators
  cab **19**:2603–4
  see also flight simulators
SLIP (Serial Line Internet Protocol) **11**:1475–6
software *see* computers, programming and software
software, computer *see* computers, programming and software
Solar Maximum Mission (Solar Max) satellite **2**:173; **15**:2029; **16**:2169
solvent extraction **4**:446
Sony's Dynamic Digital Sound (SDDS) **15**:2148–9
sound effects and sampling **15**:2136–7
sound mixing **8**:*1071*; **13**:1822; **15**:2138–9
sound reproduction **15**:2142–5
  on DVDs **5**:652
  quadraphonic **15**:2145
  see also audio and video recording; stereophonic reproduction
soundtracks **15**:2146–9
  music scores **11**:1499, 1500; **15**:2149
Spacenet 1 (satellite) **15**:*2025*
spam **4**:531
special effects **16**:2185–90
  see also animation
speech disabilities, aids for **1**:22
spellcheckers **5**:626
Spider system **5**:596
spreadsheets **8**:1150
SRAM (static random access memory) **5**:615; **9**:1167
stealth technologies **16**:2250–5
  electronic countermeasures **18**:2550–3
stereophonic reproduction **15**:2142–3
  stereophonic recording **1**:27; **15**:2143
    onto records **12**:1697; **15**:2144
stereo systems **6**:755; **8**:1072
styluses, record **12**:*1696*, 1697
"subcode data" **4**:516
supercomputers **4**:*525*, 526
super video graphics arrays (SVGAs) **4**:532
switches (intelligent hubs) **4**:539
system control and data acquisition *see* SCADA

T

tagged image file format (TIFF) files **12**:1594
talking clocks **17**:2348–9
TAT 1 cable **3**:348–9
TAT-2 cable **3**:349
TAT-8 cable **17**:2357
TCP/IP (transmission control protocol/Internet protocol) **9**:1178, 1179–80
TDM (time-division multiplexing) **1**:129; **17**:2356, 2365
telecommunications **17**:2356–9
  cable networks **3**:353–5; **17**:2356
    data transmission **17**:2357
    fiber optics **3**:354–5; **4**:539, 542; **6**:856; **17**:2356–7, 2371
    submarine cables **3**:347–9; **18**:2471

    and data interception **6**:761–2
  high-speed data transfer **17**:2357–8
  operations centers **1**:*127*
  radio (earthbound) **17**:2358–9
    cell phones *see* cellular telephones
    signals **1**:129; **17**:2359
    see also radio
  satellite links **4**:540, *541*, 542; **15**:*2025, 2027, 2029*; **17**:2359
  using holography **8**:1082
  using microwaves **6**:746; **17**:2359
  see also modems and ISDN
teleconferencing **4**:525
  virtual reality (teleimmersion) **19**:2606
telegraph **17**:2357, **2360–3**
  cables **3**:347
  facsimile transmission **10**:1325; **17**:2363
  history **3**:353–4; **17**:2360–2
  telex network **17**:2357, 2362–3
  see also e-mail
teleimmersion **19**:2606
telemetry **17**:2364–5
  electric **17**:2364–5
  multiplex **17**:2365
  pulse-rate **17**:2365
  radio **17**:2365
  space probe antennas **15**:2156
  uses **2**:257; **17**:2365
telephone answering machines **17**:2366–7
telephone systems **17**:2368–72
  cables **3**:347; **17**:2356, *2357*, 2371; **18**:2471
  cell phones *see* cellular telephones
  cordless telephones **17**:2370
  digital techniques **6**:755
  and electronic surveillance **6**:759, 760
  exchanges **17**:2371–2
    answering services **17**:2367
    signaling **17**:2370–1
  handsets **17**:2369–70
    and amplification **1**:22; **17**:2369
  invention **17**:2368–9
  IP (Internet protocol) telephony **17**:2370
  local distribution **17**:2371
  long-distance calls **17**:2372
  "smart" telephones **17**:*2369*
  and speaking clocks **17**:2348–9
  third generation **3**:416
  using fiber optics **6**:856
  vending-machine payment via **18**:2577
  see also modems and ISDN
telepresence **19**:2604
teleprompters **17**:2373–5
telesurgery **17**:2332
teletype **11**:1516; **17**:2362
television broadcasting **6**:*741*; **18**:2494–6; **19**:*2671*
  cable television (community antenna television; CATV) **3**:354; **17**:2356; **18**:*2494*, 2496–7
  digital TV (DTV; high-definition TV – HDTV) **6**:754, 755; **11**:1498; **17**:2385, *2392*; **18**:2497
  and editing **17**:2390–1; **18**:2495
  satellite **1**:*141*, 142; **3**:354; **18**:2497
television receivers **5**:599; **17**:2392–4
  antennas **1**:142
  black-and-white **3**:409
  cable **3**:354; **17**:2356; **18**:2496–7
  cathode-ray tubes **3**:409; **12**:1647–8; **17**:2392, *2393*
  closed-circuit (CCTV) **3**:340;

14:1977; 15:2042, 2044
color 3:409; 4:511; 17:2385, 2393–4
digital (DTV; high-definition TV - HDTV) 6:754, 755; 11:1498; 17:2385, 2392; 18:2497
diodes 5:654
flat-screen 3:410
NTSC system 17:2394
PAL system 17:2394
picture reception 17:2392–3
plasma-technology 17:2394
signal decoding 17:2393
and sound 17:2393
watches as 19:2650
widescreen 6:754
telex 17:2357, 2362–3
template matching 19:2615
terminal guidance systems (TGSs) 2:288
Terra (satellite), images from 7:995
text editors 19:2719
text-to-speech communication aids 1:22
Thematic Mapper 6:743
Enhanced Thematic Mapper Plus (ETM+) 17:2337
ticker tape 5:609
TIFF (tagged image file format) files 12:1594
Time Division Multiple Access (TDMA) 3:416; 17:2359
time-division multiplexing (TDM) 1:129; 17:2356, 2365
TIROS-N (satellite) 4:479
TOPEX/Poseidon (satellite) 11:1569
TOPS (total operations processing systems) 14:1926
touch screens 11:1492
trackballs 4:535; 11:1492
trackpads 4:535; 11:1492
trackpoint sticks 11:1492
transducers and sensors, transducers, electret 5:715, 716
transmission, broadcasting 18:2493–7

transmitting antennas 1:141, 142
transmit-receive (TR) cells 14:1894, 1896
traveling-wave tubes 6:741
TR (transmit-receive) cells 14:1894, 1896
truth tables 9:1278
turntables, record-player 12:1697
typefaces 5:627
typewriters 18:2521–3; 19:2719
typography 5:627

U

ultra-large-scale integration (ULSI) see integrated circuits
uncommitted logic arrays (ULAs) 10:1427–8
Unimate robotic arms 14:1986
UNIVAC machines 4:524
universal serial bus (USB) sockets 11:1474
URLs (uniform resource locators) 9:1180, 1181
USB (universal serial bus) sockets 11:1474

V

vacuum tubes, in computers 2:169; 4:524; 6:754
VDUs (visual display units) see computers, monitors
Very Large Arrays (VLAS) 14:1909, 1910–11
very-large-scale integration (VLSI) see integrated circuits
Very Long Baseline Array 14:1910–11
very long baseline interferometry (VLBI) 14:1910–11
video cameras 18:2589–92
charge-coupled devices 3:432; 18:2590, 2591–2

sound recording 15:2149
video conferencing 3:353; 17:2370
videomicrographics 10:1415
video-on-demand 3:354
videophones 3:415
videoplace system 19:2604
video recorders 2:186, 188; 10:1311, 1312; 19:2597–2602
video cassettes 2:187–8; 10:1312; 19:2600–2
see also audio and video recording
video signals 17:2393
video tape 10:1312
vidicons 17:2384
vinyl discs see phonography
ViOS (visual Internet operating system) browser 11:1503
virtual reality (VR) 11:1503; 19:2603–8
goggles 4:532
for surgery 17:2332
weather processes 4:534
see also flight simulators
viruses (computer) 4:530, 531
vision, aids for impaired vision see accessibility aids
visual display units (VDUs) see computers, monitors
visually coupled displays 19:2604
vitalism 4:453
VLSI see integrated circuits
voice-controlled wheelchairs 11:1470
voice mail 17:2367
voice recognition and synthesis 2:169, 172; 19:2615–17
at automatic-teller machines 2:192
recognition 2:172; 9:1269; 16:2202–3; 19:2615–17
for desktop publishing 5:626
and forensic science 7:916
and robotics 14:1989; 19:2616, 2617
synthesis 1:22; 2:172; 16:2200, 2202, 2203; 19:2617
see also natural-language processing

W

WANs (wide area networks) 4:537, 539–40, 542
WAP (wireless access protocol) phones 8:1147
Watson-Watt, Sir Robert 14:1893
WCDMA see wide band code-division multiple access
webcams 18:2592
Wheatstone, Charles 3:353; 17:2360
wide area networks (WANs) 4:537, 539–40, 542
wide band code-division multiple access (WCDMA) 3:416; 4:540
widescreen recording 5:652
WIDE visual display system 7:886
Windows (operating system) 4:525, 539
wireframes 1:139; 4:536
word processors 19:2719–20
word-processing programs 5:626; 8:1150; 11:1491
see also desktop publishing; typewriters
workstations 4:526
World Wide Web 8:1147; 9:1177, 1178, 1179; 11:1502–3
multimedia applications 11:1503
see also search engines
WORM (write once read many) drives 5:614

X

xerography 12:1701–3
Xerox Alto 11:1501
X rays, for etching silicon chips 9:1168

Z

Zip drives and disks 4:527; 5:612
Zworykin, Vladimir 17:2383

Construction and Civil Engineering

A

acoustics, architectural 1:26, 27
aggregate 4:546
for lightweight concrete 4:549
air hammers 13:1746
airports, tensile structures at 17:2400, 2401, 2402
Akashi Kaikyo Bridge 4:474
Alamillo Bridge 4:474–5
alignments 16:2273
aluminum, uses, in buildings 3:336
angledozers 5:705
Annapolis Royal barrage 17:2438
arches, and dam construction 5:607
architecture
capsule 3:338
see also building techniques; vault construction
Aswan High Dam 5:608; 6:819; 9:1191
auditoriums, design 1:26, 27
Autobahnen 14:1973

B

ballotini 12:1630; 14:1977
barrages, tidal 17:2437–8

Big Muskie (earthmoving machine) 5:702
biobricks 3:324
blacktop (tarmacadam) 1:30; 14:1973, 1975
and paving machines 14:1976
blowout preventers (BOPs) 5:682
bricks 3:336
insulating 9:1161
manufacture 3:323–4
recording Earth's magnetism 10:1317
bridges 3:325–30; 4:474
adhesives used in 1:29
amphibious bridging rigs 1:123
design 16:2243
erection 3:330; 4:549; 14:1977
materials 3:329–30
plastic 4:476
natural frequency 14:1964–5
support columns, protection 14:1981
types
arch 3:327–8
Bailey 3:328
bascule 3:325
beam 3:325; 17:2402
box girder 3:325, 329
cable-stayed 3:326, 327, 329;

4:474–5, 476
cantilever and suspended-span 3:325
lifting 3:327
suspension 3:325–7; 4:474
Brunel, Marc Isambard 18:2512
Buckminster Fuller, Richard 7:983; 17:2402
buildings
heat loss detected 17:2422
insulation see insulation, thermal
intelligent 3:338
building techniques 3:335–8
in earthquake zones 5:707–8
tensile structures 3:338; 17:2397–402
vault construction 18:2571–4
see also cranes; geodesic structures; skyscrapers
bulldozers 5:705; 18:2471
tracks 18:2470

C

cablenets 17:2397–8, 2400
cables
for bridges 3:326, 327, 329
power, installation 3:346

submarine (undersea), manufacture 3:348, 350
in tensile structures 17:2397–8, 2399, 2400
caissons 1:85; 15:2091
canals 3:373–6
locks 9:1266
tunnels 18:2512
cat's eyes 14:1982
cement 3:335; 4:546
macro-defect-free (MDF) 3:421
reinforced 3:421; 4:546
see also concrete
ceramics, structural 3:336
Channel Tunnel 4:475; 7:1008
rail link through 4:476
Charles River Bridge 4:476
Chek Lap Kok Airport 4:474; 5:677
Chicago Tribune Tower 15:2092
chlorine, in the water supply 4:476
Chrysler Building 15:2092
civil engineering 4:474–6
see also bridges; dams; geodesic structures; railroad systems; roads, construction; tunneling; water supply
clay, in soil 15:2110, 2111–12
Columbia Basin Project 5:605
compacters 5:703

concert halls *see* auditoriums
concrete 3:417; 4:**546–9**
  blocks and walls, splitting 17:2412
  bonding sections together 1:*29*
  corrosion 4:571
  lightweight 4:549
    aerated 4:*547*, 549
  polymer-impregnated (PIC) 4:549
  precast 4:547–8
  prestressed 3:329–30, 335;
    4:548–9; 13:1750
  reinforced 3:329–30, 335, 420;
    4:547; 13:1750
  sealants over 1:*32*
  uses
    boat building 2:277
    for bridges 3:329–30; 17:*2402*
    for buildings 3:335, 338
    pipes 13:1750
    roads 14:1975–6
  see also cement
concrete masonry units (CMUs)
  9:1161
construction
  earthmoving machinery and 5:701
  see also building techniques
Corinth Canal 3:*374*
cranes 5:**585–8**
  bridge 5:585–6
  for containers 5:*586*, 588, 670;
    7:931, *932*
  crawler 5:*585*
  floating 5:588, 669, *671*; 15:2022
  gantry 5:585, 586, 670
  goliath 5:586, 588
  jib (derrick cranes) 5:586–7
    Stülcken derricks 5:*669*
  straddle carriers 7:*931*
  telescoping boom 5:587
  tower 5:*585*, *587*, 588
  on wharfs and docks 5:588, *668*,
    669, 671
crash barriers, road 14:1979–81
cuttings, and road construction
  14:1974

D

dams 5:**604–8**
  and beach erosion 6:819
  circular 17:*2438*
  coffer 5:608
  earth-fill 5:605–6
  and flooding 7:888–9, 891; 9:1191
  homogenous 5:605
  hydropower 5:605; 8:1112
  and irrigation 9:1191, 1192
  multiple-arch 5:607
  rock-fill 5:606
  solid-masonry arch 5:607
  solid-masonry gravity 5:606–7
  spillways in 7:888–9
  steel and timber 5:608
  see also barrages, tidal
Delta Project 7:*890*, 891; 9:1206
Denver International Airport
  17:2402
derricks
  crane *see* cranes, jib
  oil rig 5:680
deserts, reclamation 9:1207
diggers 5:703
ditches 5:674, 675
dolmen 16:2273
domes, geodesic 1:*108*; 3:*336*;
  7:983–4; 16:2245; 17:*2400*
dozers, tracks 18:*2469*, 2471
draglines 5:703
drainage 5:**673–5**
dredgers (dredges) 5:**676–7**
drilling, directional 3:346

drilling rigs, oil 4:*548*; 5:**680–3**;
  11:*1570*
drills, use in tunneling 18:2513
drop hammers 13:1746
ducted installations, of power cables
  3:346

E

earthmoving machinery 5:**701–5**;
  14:1974
earthquakes, and dams 5:608
Eddystone light 9:1248
Eden Project 7:984; 13:*1768*
embankments, and road construction
  14:1974
Empire State Building 3:337;
  15:2092, 2094
  elevators 15:2095
excavators
  hydraulics 5:704; 8:*1100*
  steam-powered 5:701
  see also earthmoving machinery

F

Flatiron Building 15:*2092*, 2094
flood control 7:**888–91**
  peak flow reduction 7:888
  reservoirs 7:888–90
  rivers 7:888, 890–1
  tidal flooding 7:891
flooding
  behind dams 5:608
  chemical, fire, or steam, for oil
    recovery 5:683
Florida Festival, tensile structures
  17:*2398*, *2399*, 2400
fog, monitors on roads 14:1977
footings, spread 15:2091
Forth Railway Bridge 3:328
Fort Peek Dam 5:606
foundations, on clay soils 15:2112
frameworks, structural 16:2244–5
Franklin Park Zoo, Massachusetts
  17:2400
Frei, Otto 17:2399, 2400
French drains 5:675
furnaces, construction 7:940–1

G

gabbards 5:588
gabions 9:1206–7
gantries, crane 5:585, 586
geodesic structures 7:**983–4**
  domes 1:*108*; 3:*336*; 7:983–4;
    16:2245; 17:*2400*
George Washington Bridge 3:326
geotextiles 17:2408
glass-reinforced polyester (GRP)
  3:337
Golden Gate Bridge 3:329
grabs, clamshell 5:704
graders (scrapers) 5:703; 14:1974
Grand Canal (China) 3:376
Grand Coulee Dam 5:605
Great Belt *see* Store Baelt
Great Pyramid of Cheops 13:*1870*,
  1871–2
groins 18:2571
grout, epoxy adhesive 1:*29*

H

harbors, lighthouses 9:1247
highways, major 14:1979
Home Insurance Company Building

  (Chicago) 15:2090–1
Hong Kong
  Chek Lap Kok Airport 4:474;
    5:677
  harbor, tunnel under 18:*2513*,
    2516
Hoover Dam 5:608; 18:2520
Humber Bridge 3:329; 4:474

I

Icynene 9:1161
IJssel Lake (IJsselmeer) 9:1208
Industrial Revolution
  building techniques 3:335
  dams 5:604–5
  earthmoving operations 5:701
insulation
  thermal 9:**1160–1**
    glass fibers for 7:1002; 9:1160–1
    vacuums and 17:2425; 18:2560
iron and steel
  steel
    bridges 3:329, 330
    in buildings 3:335–6, 337;
      15:2091, 2095

J

jackhammers 9:1195; 13:*1840*
Jeddah International Airport, Hajj
  Terminal 17:*2400*, 2401
Jenney, William Le Baron 15:2090–1
John Hancock Center 15:*2094*

K

Kariba Dam 19:*2667*
kelly 5:680
keystones 18:2574

L

land, drainage 5:673–4; 19:2695
landfill, reclamation 9:1207–8
land reclamation 9:**1206–8**; 19:2695
lasers and masers
  lasers
    and earthmoving machines
      5:705
    used in surveying 9:1214
    used in tunneling 18:2516
laterite 15:2112
lighthouses and lightships 9:**1247–9**;
  11:*1514*
lightning conductors 9:1250–1
Llyn Brianne Dam 5:*607*
loaders
  back-end 5:704–5
  front-end 5:704
locks (in waterways), canal, construction 9:1266

M

MacAdam, John 14:1973
manholes 5:675
median strips 14:1979
megaliths 16:2273, 2274–5
menhirs 16:2273
Metropolitan Life Building 15:2092
micafill *see* vermiculite
microtunneling machines 18:2516
Mies van der Rohe, Ludwig 15:2093
Millennium Bridge, London
  14:*1964*, 1965
Millennium Dome, London 3:*337*,

  338; 17:2401–2
mineral wools 9:1161
moles (machines) 18:2516
moling 3:346
mud mills 5:676

N

Netherlands
  flood control 7:*890*, 891
  land reclamation 9:1206, 1208;
    19:2695
Nile River
  Aswan High Dam 5:608; 6:819;
    9:1191
  flooding 7:891; 9:1191, 1206
no-fines concrete 4:549

O

Ohio Bridge 3:329
oil rigs *see* drilling rigs
Olympic Games, Munich, tensile
  structures 17:2402
oxygen-fuel lances 17:2412

P

paving machines 14:1976
Petronas Twin Towers 15:*2090*
pile drivers 13:**1746**
piles
  and building techniques 3:338
  sheet and bearing 13:1746
pipes, underground, for drainage
  5:674, 675
plastics, uses, in buildings 3:337
platforms, oil-drilling 5:*680*, *681*,
  682–3; 11:*1574*
plows
  mole 5:674
  underwater cable-laying 3:349
plywood, uses, for buildings 3:336
pneumatic tools
  jackhammers 9:1195; 13:*1840*
  see also pile drivers
polders 9:1206, 1208
polyesters
  glass-reinforced (GRP) 3:337
  as membranes on tensile structures
    17:2398
polyurethanes (PUs), for filling wall
  cavities 9:1161
pozzolana 3:417; 4:546
prefabricated building components
  3:338
pulleys 13:*1869*, 1872
pyramids 13:**1870–2**
  Mayan 11:*1560*; 16:2275

Q

quarrying 14:**1885–6**

R

railroad systems 4:475–6; 10:1364–5;
  14:**1923–8**
  tunnels 18:2512
Rance barrage 17:2437, *2438*
Raskin, John Jakob 15:2092
reservoirs 8:1112
  and flood control 7:888–90
  and pumped-storage schemes
    6:798; 8:1112, *1115*; 13:1827;
    18:2520
  siltation 5:608

for water supply 19:2661–2, 2663
reverberation time (RT), of auditoriums 1:27
road breakers 13:1789
roads
  arrester beds alongside 14:1981
  construction 5:701; 14:1973–7,
    1981
    adhesives used in 1:30
    earthmoving machinery 5:703
  crash barriers 14:1979–81
  drainage 5:675; 14:1975, 1981
  markings 14:1976–7, 1982
  signs 14:1982–4
road systems and traffic control
  14:1978–85
Rockefeller Center 15:2094
rock wool 9:1161
roofing, lead 9:1220
rumble strips 14:1982

S

Salt Springs Dam 5:606
sands, in soil 15:2110, 2111
Schnirch, Bedrich 17:2402
scrapers (graders) 5:703; 14:1974
Sears Tower 15:2093–4
  elevators 15:2095
septic tanks 5:674; 19:2648
Severn tidal project 17:2438
sewers 5:673, 674–5
  concrete 4:549
  remote-controlled cameras in
    19:2648
sheet piles 9:1207
shovels, steam-powered 5:701, 703
Sidney Meyer Music Bowl,
  Melbourne 17:2400, 2402

silt, in soil 15:2110
siltation, of reservoirs 5:608
Skylon sculpture 17:2402
skyscrapers 15:2090–5
  construction 15:2093
    cranes used in 5:588
    substructure 15:2091–2
slag wool 9:1161
slip-form machines 14:1976
soil
  compacters 5:703
  drainage 5:673–4
  earthmoving affecting 5:701
  engineering 15:2110–12
  lateritic 15:2112
  profiles 15:2112
  research 15:2110–13
  see also earthmoving machinery
soundproofing 15:2140–1
spillways 5:604
  in dams 7:888–9
steel see iron and steel
Stonehenge 11:1560; 16:2273–4
stone monuments 16:2273–5
stop signals, road 14:1983
Store Baelt (Great Belt) 3:329; 4:474
stormwater overflows 5:675
struts 16:2244, 2245
superelevation, of highways 14:1979
Swiss Grande Dixence Dam 5:604
Sydney Harbor Bridge 3:329

T

Tacoma Narrows Bridge 3:327;
  14:1965
tarmacadam see blacktop
Telford, Thomas 3:374; 14:1973
tellurometers 10:1328; 14:1898

tensile structures 3:338;
  17:2397–402
testing, nondestructive, using sound
  waves 1:27
Thames, River, tunnels under
  18:2512–13
Thames Barrier 5:605; 7:888, 889,
  891
Three Gorges Dam 5:608; 8:1115
thrusts 18:2573
tidal fences 17:2438
tiercerons 18:2573
ties 16:2244, 2245
timber, for buildings 3:336
Tower Bridge 3:325
tractors, crawler 5:703
trass 3:417
trenches 5:701
  cables laid in 3:346
  for pipes 5:674, 675, 703
Trésaguet, Pierre-Marie-Jérome
  14:1973
Tsing Ma Bridge 4:474
tunneling 4:475; 18:2512–16
  air locks used in 1:85
  cut-and-cover method 10:1347;
    18:2512
  machines 18:2512, 2514, 2515,
    2516
  in mines 11:1461
  New Austrian Tunneling Method
    4:475
tunnels, lighting 14:1980
tunnel shields 18:2512–13

U

United Nations Headquarters (New
  York City) 15:2094

V

vault construction 18:2571–4
vermiculite (micafill) 9:1161
Verrazano Narrows Bridge 3:327

W

water, and urban drainage 5:674–5
water supply 4:476; 13:1786–7;
  19:2661–7
  wells 19:2683–4
wells
  oil exploration 11:1571–3
  oil recovery 11:1573
  set ablaze 6:806
  water 19:2683–4
winches and windlasses 19:2689
  band brakes for winched loads
    3:313
wind bracing 15:2092, 2094
windlasses see winches and windlasses
wind power, and land reclamation
  9:1206, 1208; 19:2695
wood composites, building with
  19:2711
Woolworth Building 3:337; 15:2092
World Trade Center 15:2092–3,
  2095

Z

Zuider Zee 9:1208

Earth, Space, and Environmental Sciences

A

ABE (Autonomous Benthic Explorer)
  16:2294
accretion 2:270; 13:1759
  accretion disks 2:268; 10:1362
acid rain 1:25; 13:1798; 16:2300
active galactic nuclei (AGNs) 2:174
Advanced Camera for Surveys (ACS)
  15:2155; 17:2382
airstreams 10:1400
Amazon Basin, deforestation 15:2113
Antarctic 11:1566
  maps 10:1330
  ozone layer over 4:480; 6:806
  pollution monitoring in 13:1800
  sub-ice lake 7:998; 9:1235
anticyclones 10:1399; 14:1932
antimatter, antiparticles, and black
  holes 2:270
aphelion 12:1599
Apollo missions
  fuel cells 7:936
  photography 15:2152
  space suits 16:2177
archaeoastronomy 16:2274–5
Arctic, pollution monitoring in
  13:1800
Ariane launch vessels 1:43
Armstrong, Neil 15:2152, 2154
asteroids 5:698; 13:1761; 15:2123
  and extinction of the dinosaurs
    7:989
  and source of water on Earth
    13:1761

astroarchaeology 16:2274–5
astronauts
  dietary needs 11:1558, 1559
  and g-forces 3:423
  suits see space suits
  weightlessness 8:1020
astronomy 2:173–7
  eclipses 5:709–10
  observatories 11:1560–2
  radio 14:1909–12
  X-ray 19:2724
    and black holes 2:268, 270;
      19:2724
    and the Chandra telescope
      17:2381
    and stars 2:174; 19:2724
  see also astrophysics; telescopes
astrophysics 2:178–81
  astronomical spectroscopy 2:178;
    16:2197
  see also astronomy
Atlantic Ocean, relief map 7:991
Atlantis (space shuttle) 1:85; 2:173;
  16:2169, 2174
atmosphere 5:699–700
  corrosion in 4:571
  creation 5:700
  depressions 10:1399
    and tides 7:891
  ions in 9:1184
  levels 1:62, 63
  oxygen see oxygen, atmospheric
  pollution see pollution, atmos-
    pheric
  and solar radiation 10:1396

vapor pressure 18:2570
  water in 10:1396; 18:2570;
    19:2655, 2665
auroras 14:1899, 1900
Australia, Great Artesian Basin
  9:1194; 19:2684

B

biosphere 5:700
black holes 2:174, 180, 267–70;
  8:1021–2; 17:2315
  annihilation radiation from 6:745
  and radio astronomy 14:1912
    the ARISE satellite 14:1910
  and time 17:2443
black smokers 13:1780
blazars 2:267

C

Callisto (moon) 15:2121
Canopus (star) 15:2157
Cape Canaveral, vehicle assembly
  building 8:1062; 14:1996
carbon, "sinks" 6:807–8
carbon dioxide, a greenhouse gas
  4:477, 479; 6:807; 7:998
cartography see maps, mapmaking
  techniques
Cassini (space probe) 15:2122, 2160
caves, stalactites and stalagmites
  16:2239–40

Cepheid variables 4:573
Cerise (satellite) 15:2151
Challenger (space shuttle) 15:2029;
  16:2168
  and space debris 12:1600
Chandra X-ray Observatory 2:174
Charon (moon) 15:2122
charts, weather 10:1398–1400
Chicxulub crater 7:989
Chiron (asteroid) 15:2123
chlorofluorocarbons (CFCs) 1:40;
  4:480; 6:806, 807; 8:1034;
  13:1798
chondrites 10:1392
  carbonaceous 3:393
chondrules 10:1392
chromosphere 11:1528
clear-cutting, forests 7:921–2
climatology 4:477–80
  Earth's climatic divisions 14:1932
  El Niño 4:478–9; 15:2029
  global warming 4:479–80;
    6:807–8; 7:922; 13:1800
  past climates 4:477–8; 7:998;
    11:1568
  see also meteorology; ozone layer
clouds 19:2665
  classification 10:1400–1
  formation 10:1401; 14:1931–2;
    18:2570
  ionization 17:2429–30
  nacreous 9:1240
  noctilucent 9:1240
  seeding 8:1096; 18:2570
  thunder (cumulonimbus) 9:1250;

clouds, thunder (*cont.*)
10:*1399*, 1401; 17:*2428*, 2429
coasts
continental coastlines 7:990
erosion of 6:818–19
length of British coastline 3:431
COBE (Cosmic Background
Explorer) 4:*573*
Columbia (space shuttle) 1:43;
16:*2166*, 2167; 17:*2364*
crystal growth experiment 19:*2729*
comets 15:2123
Halley's 10:*1393*
orbits 12:1599
Shoemaker-Levy 9 2:176; 15:2121
Compton Observatory 2:173–4
conic sections, and planetary orbits
12:1599
continental drift 4:478; 7:990;
13:1777
see also plate tectonics
continental shelves 11:1566
convection currents, and plate
tectonics 5:699
Coriolis effect, and hurricanes
8:1094
Coriolis force 5:699–700; 8:1143;
10:1399; 17:2440
coronagraphs 5:*709*
Crab nebula 17:2316, 2317
currents, ocean 5:700; 11:1568–9
cyclones (depressions) 14:1932
cyclones (storms) *see* hurricanes
Cygnus Loop (supernova) 17:*2315*
Cygnus X-1 2:269; 19:*2724*

D

DART (Deep Ocean Assessment and
Reporting of Tsunamis) 18:2511
days 5:696, 697; 17:*2441*
Deep Sea Drilling Project 11:1568;
13:1777
Deep Space 1 (space probe) 14:*1994*,
1995; 15:2123
deserts, formation 9:*1207*
dew, for irrigation 9:1193–4; 18:2570
Discovery (space shuttle) 9:*1201*;
15:*2024*
Doppler effect (Doppler shift)
and astrophysics 2:178
and tornado detection 8:1097–8
drizzle 19:*2665*
dust storms 6:819

E

Earth 5:696–700; 13:1757
age 5:698; 6:824; 13:1757–8
climatic divisions 14:1932
development of life on 1:62–3;
5:700; 6:823; 9:1234–5;
10:1412; 12:1633–4
"free oscillations" 5:708
interior tides (Earth tides) 17:2440
layers, detection 15:2048
light pollution 13:*1803*
magnetic field
humans and 16:2275
and the solar wind 14:*1900*
orbit 15:2114
origin 5:698; 6:764
precession 5:696
radiation belts 14:**1899–900**
rotation 8:1143
gyrocompasses and 8:1028–9
pendulums and 12:1665
source of water on 13:1761
structure 5:697; 15:2048
core 5:697; 15:2048, 2049

tilt 5:696
see also atmosphere; geology; plate
tectonics
earthquakes 5:**706–8**; 7:*993*; 15:2049
detection using fiber optics 6:856
plate tectonics and 5:706, 707;
13:*1777*, 1780
scales of intensity
Mercalli scale 15:2049
Richter scale 9:1276; 15:2049
and the soil 15:2113
and tsunamis 18:2509, 2510
see also seismology
Earth Summit (1992) 6:807–8
eclipses 5:*709–10*
electromagnetic radiation, from
space 2:173–7
elementary particles, leaked by black
holes 2:270
El Niño 4:478–9; 15:2029
El Niño-Southern Oscillation
(ENSO) 4:478, 479
Endeavour (space shuttle) 14:*1955*;
16:*2165*, 2168, 2169; 17:*2359*
Enterprise (space shuttle) 16:2166–7
environmental science 6:**806–9**
ozone depletion 4:480; 5:687;
6:806–7; 13:*1798*, 1947
see also geography; global warming; pollution
epicenters, earthquake 5:*706*, 707
Eros (asteroid) 15:2123
erosion 6:**816–19**
tectonic 13:1778
ERS-1 (satellite) 15:2151
Europa (moon) 15:2120, 2160
European Center for Medium-Range
Weather Forecasting 10:*1400*,
1401
eutrophication 12:1700
event horizon 2:267, 269, 270
Explorer 1 (satellite) 14:1899
Extreme Ultraviolet Explorer
(EUVE) 2:175

F

Far Ultraviolet Spectroscopic
Explorer (FUSE) 2:*174*, 175–6;
17:*2382*
faults, geological 5:707
radar interferometry 7:*993*
transform faults 13:1780
fires
forest 6:809, 863; 7:924–5
fighting 6:861; 7:925
and pollution 6:*808*
oil well 6:806
Floyd, Hurricane 8:*1098*
fog 10:1401; 18:2570
Fujita tornado scale 8:1099
fumaroles 9:1235
Fundy, Bay of 17:2438, 2440
FUSE (Far Ultraviolet Spectroscopic
Explorer) 2:*174*, 175–6; 17:*2382*

G

galaxies
accretion disks 10:*1362*
active 14:1912
black holes in 2:*268*, 269, 270;
17:*2443*
Cartwheel 2:*179*
Centaurus A 2:*269*
distance estimated 2:178
and gravitational lensing 4:*572*
M87 10:*1362*; 17:*2443*
NGC 628 17:*2378*
our *see* Milky Way

polar-ring 8:*1021*
and radio astronomy 14:*1912*
receding 4:573
Seyfert 2:174, 267
"starburst" 2:177
"ultra-faint" 2:174
Galileo (spacecraft) 15:2120, 2121,
2123
gamma rays
from space 2:173–4; 6:745
black holes 2:268
Ganymede (moon) 9:*1235*; 15:2121
Gaspra (asteroid) 15:2123
Gemini 5 (spacecraft) 7:*936*
Gemini, Project 15:2152
geography 7:**985–6**
see also environmental science
geologic traps 11:1572
geology 7:**987–90**
economic 7:989–90
geologic timescale 6:824–5; 7:988
radioisotopic dating 7:995;
14:*1916*
see also plate tectonics
geophysics 7:**991–5**
gravimeters 7:992; 11:1571
oil and gas exploration 7:993–4
see also paleomagnetism; plate
tectonics; seismology
geostationary Earth orbits (GEOs)
space debris 15:2150, *2151*
see also satellites, artificial, orbits
geysers 5:700
Giotto (spacecraft) 15:2123
glaciology 7:*998*
Global Climate Observing System
(GCOS) 4:479
Global Surveyor (spacecraft) *see* Mars
Global Surveyor
global warming 4:479–80; 6:807–8;
7:922; 13:*1800*
Gondwanaland 7:990
gravity, and black holes 2:269, 270;
17:2443
Great Artesian Basin 9:1194; 19:2684
greenhouse gases 4:*477*, 479; 6:794,
807; 7:998
Grigg-Skjellerup (comet) 15:2123
Gulf Stream 11:*1568*

H

Hawking radiation 2:270
helioseismology 15:2046
Herschel, William 6:742; 11:1560
Himalayas 5:699
Hubble Space Telescope (HST)
pictures by 2:*175*; 4:*572*; 17:*2382*
space shuttle missions to
16:2168–9; 17:*2381*
hurricanes and tornadoes 8:**1094–9**
hurricanes 8:1094–6, *1098*;
15:*2028*
and tsunamis 18:2510
tornadoes 8:1094, *1095*, 1097–9
Huygens (space probe) 15:2122
Huygens, Christiaan 4:*482*, 483, 486;
12:1664; 19:2651
hydrothermal vents 10:1333;
11:1567; 13:1780
hypernovas 17:2317

I

Iapetus (moon) 3:393
ice, glacial, investigations 7:998
ice ages 4:478; 6:809
icebergs
fresh water from 19:2667
radio tagging 14:*1904*

ice cores 6:809; 13:*1800*
integrated thermal meteoroid garments (ITMGs) 16:2177
interferometry, space telescopes and
17:2382
intergalactic medium (IGM) 2:175
International Space Station (ISS)
1:43; 14:*1955*, 1956; 15:*2056*,
2153
construction 16:2169, 2173
detected for damage 15:2155
science programs 16:2174–5
and telemetry 17:*2364*
International Ultraviolet Explorer
(IUE) 2:174
Io (moon) 11:*1520*; 15:2121
ionosphere 1:62; 9:*1183*
isobars 10:1399

J

Jupiter 13:1757, 1758, 1760;
15:2118, 2121
auroras 14:*1900*; 15:2121
moons 9:*1235*; 11:*1520*; 14:*1900*;
15:2121–2
eclipses 5:710

K

Kepler, Johannes 8:1020; 15:2157;
16:2301
and planetary orbits 12:1599
third law 11:1521
Kepler's star 17:2317
Kobe, earthquake 5:*708*
K-T boundary 7:989
Kuiper Belt 2:176; 13:1761
Kyoto Protocol 6:807, 808

L

land reclamation 9:**1206–8**; 19:*2695*
landslides 5:707; 6:816
La Niña 4:479; 15:2029
Large Magellanic Cloud 2:180;
17:*2316*
LEASATs (satellites) 15:2029
lithosphere 5:697; 13:1777, 1778–9
longitude 4:*488*
Luna space probes 15:2157

M

M87 (galaxy) 10:*1362*; 17:*2443*
Maas River, damming of 7:891
Magellan (spacecraft) 15:2119–20,
2121; 17:2337
magnetism
Earth's 10:1316–17; 13:1777
of rocks in the past (paleomagnetism) 7:990, 991, 992–3; 10:1317;
13:1777
magnetopause 14:*1900*
magnetosphere 14:1899, 1900
mantle, Earth's 5:697
maps
geochemical 7:982
geological 7:989–90
mapmaking techniques
10:**1327–31**
photogrammetry 10:1329;
12:*1706–7*; 17:2334
see also surveying
ocean floor 7:991; 11:*1565*;
15:2127, 2128; 18:2531
weather 10:*1398*
see also charts

Marianas Trench **1**:69; **10**:1333; **11**:1566
  pressure at **11**:1568
MARIE *see* Mars Radiation Environment Experiment
Mariner space probes **15**:2156, 2159
  Mariner 9 **15**:2159
  Mariner 10, orbit **12**:*1600*
Mars **13**:1757; **15**:2118, 2120–1
  "face" **12**:*1707*
  future bases on? **16**:*2171*
  life on? **4**:*446*; **9**:1235; **15**:2121
  mapping **12**:1707; **17**:2337
  rovers on **15**:2158
Mars Global Surveyor (MGS) **12**:*1707*; **15**:2120
Mars Odyssey (space probe) **15**:*2156, 2157*, 2158, 2160; **17**:2337
Mars Radiation Environment Experiment (MARIE) **15**:2158, 2160
Mercator, Gerardus **10**:1327
Mercury (planet) **13**:1757; **15**:2118, 2119
  traveling to **12**:*1600*
Mercury, Project **15**:2152; **16**:2176–7
meridian, prime **9**:1215
Messenger (space probe) **15**:2119
Meteor Crater (Arizona) **10**:*1392*, 1394
meteoroids **10**:1392
meteorology **10**:**1396–1401**
  thermometers for **17**:2424
  upper atmosphere studies **10**:1401
  weather
    fronts **10**:*1397, 1398,* 1400
    mapping and forecasting **6**:746; **10**:1397–1400, 1401; **14**:1898; **15**:*2028*
    modeling **3**:430
    observations **10**:1396–7
    records **4**:477
    virtual reality **4**:*534*
    see also clouds
  see also climatology; hurricanes and tornadoes; rain and rainfall; thunderstorms
meteors and meteorites **10**:**1392–5**; **11**:1568
  carbon-rich **3**:393
  craters **10**:*1392, 1393,* 1394, 1395
  dating **5**:698
  from Mars **9**:1235; **15**:2121
microbursts **10**:1397
micrometeorites **10**:1392
Mid-Atlantic Ridge **10**:*1333*; **11**:*1565*
Milankovitch cycles **4**:478
Milky Way **2**:270; **5**:696
  annihilation radiation from **6**:745
Mir (space station) **1**:43; **15**:*2150*, 2151; **16**:2172
Montreal Protocol **6**:807
Moon
  Earth's gravitational pull on **11**:1521
  eclipse **5**:709–10
  lasers bounced off **9**:1214; **14**:1944
  photography on **15**:*2152*, 2154
  Surveyor craft landing on **15**:2157
  and tides on Earth **5**:696–7; **8**:*1022*; **11**:1521; **17**:2436–7, 2439, *2440*
  and tsunamis **18**:*2511*
Moons, tidal effects on **11**:*1520*
mountains, formation **5**:699; **11**:1565

N

Navstars **7**:1006; **11**:1514; **15**:2026
Near-Shoemaker (space probe)

  15:2123
nebulas
  Crab **2**:137; **17**:2317
  Eagle **2**:176
  Eskimo **2**:*175*, 176
  Horsehead **17**:*2382*
  Hourglass **2**:*248*
  Orion **2**:177
Negev Desert, for irrigation **9**:1193–4
Neptune **13**:1757, 1758, 1761; **15**:2118, 2122
  discovery (eighth planet) **5**:694
  rings around **5**:710
Next Generation Space Telescope (NGST) **2**:177; **17**:2382
Niagara Falls, hydroelectric projects **8**:*1113*
NOAA (National Oceanic and Atmospheric Administration) **10**:1398
  satellites **8**:*1096*
nodules, metal-bearing, seafloor **11**:1462
North Sea
  natural gas from **7**:956
  seismic surveying **7**:*992*

O

observatories **11**:**1560–2**
Ocean Drilling Program **11**:1568
ocean floor
  geological samples **7**:989
  hydrothermal vents **10**:1333; **11**:1567; **13**:1780
  life on **11**:1567
  maps **7**:*991*; **11**:*1565*; **15**:2127, 2128; **18**:2531
  mining **11**:1462
  ocean ridges **7**:995; **10**:1317, 1333; **11**:*1565*
  spreading **7**:995; **11**:1565; **13**:1777
  temperature **17**:*2396*
oceanography **11**:**1565–9**
  satellites and **11**:1569; **15**:2029
  see also ocean floor; oceans; sea levels; undersea habitats
oceans
  currents **5**:700; **11**:1568–9
  density **11**:1566
  energy from the temperature gradient of **6**:793, 795; **8**:1054
  pressure beneath **11**:1568
  resources **11**:*1569*
  salinity **11**:1566
  temperature **11**:1566
Ocean Thermal Energy Conversion (OTEC) **6**:795; **8**:1054
oil spills **10**:1411
orbits
  spacecraft **12**:1599–1600
    and monitoring space debris **15**:2150–1
  see also satellites, artificial, orbits
Origins program **17**:2382
Orionids **10**:*1393*
Orion nebula **13**:1760
OTEC (Ocean Thermal Energy Conversion) **6**:795; **8**:1054
oxygen
  atmospheric **1**:62–3; **12**:1620, 1719
  in ancient times **6**:823, 824; **7**:988
ozone layer **1**:62; **4**:479; **6**:806, 824; **7**:988; **12**:1621
  depletion **4**:480; **6**:806–7; **13**:1798
  dry-cleaning solvents and **5**:687
  refrigerants and **14**:1947
  research planes **10**:*1401*

P

Palapa B-2 (satellite) **15**:2029; **16**:2169
paleomagnetism **7**:990, *991, 992–3*; **10**:1317; **13**:1777
Pandora (moon) **12**:*1599*
Pangaea **5**:699
Pathfinder (space probe) **15**:2158
perihelion **12**:1599
petrology **12**:1679–80
Pioneer space probes **12**:1707; **15**:2156
  Pioneer 10 **14**:1913
planetarium projectors **13**:1755–6
planetars **13**:1760
planetary science **13**:**1757–61**
  planets
    age **13**:1757–8
    chaotic bombardment of **13**:1759
    and eclipses **5**:710
    extrasolar **13**:1759–60; **14**:1912
    formation **13**:1758–9
    free-floating **13**:1760
    gaseous (gas giants; outer planets) **13**:1757, 1758, 1760–1; **15**:2118
    habitable **13**:1761
    migration **13**:1761
    orbits **12**:1599; **13**:1761
    and planetarium projectors **13**:1755–6
    relief mapping **12**:1707
    terrestrial (inner planets) **13**:1757, 1759; **15**:2118
    see also Solar System; space probes
planetesimals **13**:1758, 1759
plate tectonics **5**:698–9; **7**:990, 995; **11**:1565, 1568; **13**:**1777–80**
  and earthquakes **5**:706, 707; **13**:*1777*, 1780
  see also continental drift
Pluto **15**:2118, 2122–3
  moon **15**:2122–3
  orbit **13**:1761
pollution
  acid rain **1**:*25*; **13**:1798; **16**:2300
  atmospheric **13**:1797–8
    and corrosion **4**:571
    emission control **13**:1800–2
    from forest fires **6**:*808*
    from oil-well burning **6**:806
  light **13**:1802, *1803*
  monitoring and control **13**:**1797–1803**
    from automobiles **2**:205; **13**:1802
    natural remedies **10**:1411; **13**:1802–3
    using BBICs **9**:1168
    using LIDAR **13**:*1797*
  noise **13**:1802
  soil **15**:2113
  transport-related **5**:720
  visual **5**:647
  water **13**:1798, *1799*, 1802
    from crude oil **6**:806
    from fertilizers **6**:845; **12**:1700
    from tankers **17**:2352
    in the water supply **4**:476
precession **5**:696
projections, mapmaking **10**:1327
projectors, planetarium **13**:1755–6
protoplanetary disks (proplyds) **13**:1759–60
PSR 1257+12 (pulsar) **14**:1912
pulsars **17**:2316–17
  and radio astronomy **14**:1912
  X-ray **17**:*2316*; **19**:2724

Q

quantum theory, quantum mechanics, and black holes **2**:270
quasars **2**:174, 267, *270*; **14**:1904

R

radar, to map planets **12**:1707
radiation belts **14**:**1899–90**
radioactivity, from igneous rocks **7**:995
radio astronomy **14**:**1909–12**
radioisotopic dating, of rocks **7**:995; **14**:1916
rain and rainfall **14**:**1931–2**; **19**:2665
  acid rain **1**:*25*; **13**:1798; **16**:2300
  generation **10**:*1397*, 1398; **14**:1931–2
  weather fronts and **10**:*1397*
  see also clouds; thunderstorms
Ranger space probes **15**:2157, 2159
red giants **17**:2315, *2316*
remote handling, by space shuttles **14**:*1955*, 1956; **15**:*2056*; **16**:2168, 2169
rivers
  erosion by **6**:818
  flood control **7**:888, 890–1
rocks
  artificial **12**:1679–80
  chemical composition **7**:981–2
  magnetism **7**:992
    in the past (paleomagnetism) **7**:990, *991, 992–3*; **13**:1777
  sedimentary, oil exploration and **11**:1571
  types **7**:981–2, *987*; **12**:1679
  see also geology; petrology
Roemer, Olaus **5**:710; **9**:1240
ROSAT (satellite) **2**:174
rovers, on planets **15**:2158

S

Sahara Desert, water beneath **19**:2667
St. Helens, Mount, eruption **7**:925; **17**:*2415*
St. Michel, Mont **17**:*2439*
saltdomes, sulfur in **16**:2300
salt marshes **6**:819
Salyut (space station) **1**:43; **16**:2170
San Andreas fault **5**:706, 707, 708
San Francisco, earthquakes **5**:706
satellites, artificial **1**:42–3; **15**:**2024–9**
  astronomical **2**:173, 174, 176–7
    ARISE **14**:*1910*, 1911
    COBE **4**:*573*
    IRAS **2**:176–7
    X-ray **19**:2724
    see also telescopes, space
  attitude control **15**:2028–9
  construction **15**:2026–8
  and earthmoving machines **5**:705
  first **1**:42
  launch techniques **15**:2026
  and mapping **10**:1330
  mechanics **15**:2024–5
  military, as targets for space weapons **16**:2180–2
  oceanographic **11**:1569; **15**:2029
  orbits **12**:1599–1600; **15**:2025–6; **16**:2180–1
    geostationary (parking orbits) **8**:1096; **10**:*1397*; **12**:*1600*; **15**:2025, 2150; **17**:2359
  as space mines **16**:2181
  and telemetry **17**:2365

satellites, artificial (*cont.*)
  thermal cameras 17:*2422*
  weather and climate 4:*479*; 7:986;
    8:1095–6, *1098, 1099*; 10:*1397,
    1398*; **15**:*2028*, 2029
  working environment 15:2026
  working life 15:2029
Saturn 13:1757, 1758, 1761;
  15:2118, 2122
  moons 12:*1599*; 13:*1760*; **15**:2122,
    2160
  rings 12:*1599*; 13:*1760*
scatter, tropospheric 19:*2668*
Schwarzschild, Karl 2:270
seafloor *see* ocean floor
sea levels
  and global warming 4:480; 6:807
  varying 11:1566; 13:*1780*
  measured 11:1569
Seasat (satellite) 8:*1097*; 11:1569
seasons 5:696
sediment, ocean, cores 4:478
seismology 7:991; **15:2046–9**
  four-dimensional 7:994–5
  for oil and gas exploration 7:*992,
    993–4*; 11:1570–1; 15:*2048*,
    2135
  seismic sections 7:993–4
  seismographs 15:2046–7
  three-dimensional reflection 7:994
  and tsunamis 18:2510
  see also earthquakes
Shoemaker-Levy 9 (comet) 2:176;
  15:2121
singularities 2:267
sinks, carbon 6:807–8
sky, appears blue 15:2114
Skylab (space station) 1:43; 16:2170
smog 10:1305; 19:2612
*SOHO (Solar and Heliospheric
  Observatory)* (space probe)
  15:2046, 2119, *2158*, 2159;
  17:2381–2
soil
  contaminated 15:*2110*
    treatment 7:901
  fertilizer application to 6:845
  high salt level, and desertification
    9:*1207*
  pH 12:*1693*
  see also land reclamation
Sojourner (space vehicle) 15:2158
solar energy, solar panels, on satellites 15:*2028*, 2117
*Solar and Heliospheric Observatory see
  SOHO*
Solar Maximum Mission (Solar Max)
  satellite 2:173; 15:2029; 16:2169
Solar System 5:696; **15:2118–23**
  eclipses in 5:710
  formation 5:698; 15:2118
  see also asteroids; comets; planetary
    science; Sun; and under names
    of the planets
solar wind, and auroras 14:*1899*,
  1900
space debris 12:1600; **15:2150–1**
Space Interferometry Mission (SIM)
  2:177; 17:2382
Spacelab (space module) 16:2171–2
Spacenet 1 (satellite) 15:*2025*
space probes **15:2156–60**
  design 15:2156–7
  fuel cells 7:936
  instruments 15:*2157*, 2158–9
  landers 15:2157–8
  orbits 12:1600
  propulsion
    ionic propulsion units 9:*1184*;
      14:1995
    and the slingshot effect 14:1996
    solar sailing 14:1996; **15**:*2159*

radio-controlled 14:*1913*
solar panels 15:2156
and the space race 1:42
stabilization 15:2157
and telemetry 17:2365
to monitor space debris 15:2150–1
to survey planets 12:1707; 17:2337
see also Mariner space probes;
  Pioneer space probes; Surveyor
  space probes; Voyager space
  probes
space shuttles 1:*41*, 43; 9:*1201*;
  12:*1620*; 16:**2165–9**, 2170–1
  accidents and disasters 6:815;
    16:2166, 2168
  air locks used in 1:*85*
  boosters 14:1994; 16:2166
  fuel cells 6:795
  heat-resistant tiles 1:44; 3:*427*;
    16:2166
  and the Hubble Space Telescope
    16:2168–9; 17:*2381*
  photography from 1:35
  remote handling by 14:*1955*, 1956;
    15:*2056*; 16:2168, 2169
  and satellites 15:*2024*, 2026;
    16:*2165*, 2168
  and space debris 15:2151
  and space probes 16:2168
  and space stations 14:*1955*, 1956;
    16:2169, 2172–3
  space suits 16:2177–8
  and telemetry 17:*2364*
  virtual reality practice for 19:*2604*
  *see also Atlantis; Challenger;
    Columbia; Discovery; Endeavour;
    Enterprise*
space simulation chambers 5:592
space station remote manipulator
  system (SSRMS) 14:1956
space stations 1:43; **16:2170–5**
  solar panels 15:2150–1
  space walks from 16:2178
  see also International Space Station;
    Mir; Salyut; Skylab; Spacelab
space suits 13:1862; **16:2176–8**
  breathing apparatus 3:*322*
space walks 16:2176
  from space shuttles 16:2169, 2177,
    2178
Sputnik I (satellite) 15:2024
Starlight mission 17:2382
stars 2:267
  binary 2:268–9
    and supernovas 17:2315, *2316*
  Cepheid variables 4:573
  electromagnetic radiation 6:*739*
  moving away from Earth 5:*672*
  neutron 17:2315, *2316*; 19:2724
  newborn 2:*176*
  nuclear fusion 6:764; 7:947
  origin of elements 6:*763*, 764
  parallax 2:178
  physical observing methods 2:178
  red giants 17:2315, *2316*
  shining 2:178–9
  shooting *see* meteors and
    meteorites
  stellar occultation 5:710
  temperature 17:2396
  T-Tauri 13:1758
  white dwarfs 14:1954; 17:2315,
    2316
  X rays from 2:174
  see also pulsars; Sun
Stormfury, Project 8:1096
subduction 13:1778, 1779
Sun 13:1758; **15**:2118–19; 17:2317
  corona 5:709; 17:2396
  eclipse 5:709, *710*
  electromagnetic radiation 6:*739*,
    740

infrared 6:742
energy 15:2114
formation 13:1758; 17:2317
and helioseismology 15:2046
magnetic loops 15:2119
neutrinos from 2:181
nuclear fusion 7:947; 10:*1361*;
  15:2114
solar spectrum 16:*2194, 2196*
space probes to 15:2046, 2118–19,
  2158, 2159; 17:2382
temperature 17:2396
and tides 17:2436–7, 2440
Sundra Trench 13:1779
supercontinents, Pangaea 5:699
supernovas 2:267; **17:2315–17**
  1987A 2:173, 179–80, *181*;
    17:2317
  for distance measurement 4:573
  and the formation of elements
    6:*763*
  gamma rays from 2:173
  and gravity waves 8:1022
  hypernovas 17:2317
  remnants 14:*1912*; 17:2316
  Type Ia 17:2315
  Type Ib 17:2316
  Type II 17:2315
surveying, other planets 12:1707;
  17:2337
Surveyor space probes 15:2157, 2159

T

telecommunications, satellite links
  4:540, *541*, 542; 15:*2025*, 2027,
  2029; 17:2359
telescopes
  space 15:2029; **17:2381–2**
    hydrostatic bearings 2:232
    infrared 2:177; 17:2382
    Next Generation Space
      Telescope (NGST) 2:177;
      17:2382
    observatories 11:1561
    ultraviolet 2:175–6
    see also Hubble Space Telescope;
      SOHO
Terrestrial Planet Finder (TPF)
  17:2382
Thames, River, pollution 13:*1799*;
  19:2648
thunderstorms **17:2428–31**
  lightning 4:555; 6:725;
    17:2428–30, 2431
  thunder 17:2431
  thunder clouds (cumulonimbus)
    9:1250; 10:*1399*, 1401; 17:2428,
    2429
  virtual reality simulations 4:*534*
tides 17:2436–7, **2439–40**
  and docks 5:668
  Earth tides 17:2440
  gravitation and 5:696–7; 8:*1022*;
    11:1521
    on moons 11:*1520*; 17:2440
  and marine salvage 15:2023
  the Moon and 5:696–7; 8:*1022*;
    11:1521; 17:2436–7, 2439, *2440*
  planetary 17:2440
  the Sun and 17:2436–7, 2440
  tidal flooding 7:891
Titan (moon) 15:2122, 2160
TOPEX/Poseidon (satellite) 11:1569
tornadoes 8:1094, *1095*, 1097–9
TransHab (space module) 16:2172
trenches, ocean floor 5:699; 11:1566;
  13:1778
tropopause 1:62
troposphere 1:62; 6:746; 10:1396,
  1399

tsunamis 5:707; **18:2509–11**
Tunguska event 10:1394
typhoons 8:1094

U

Uhuru (satellite) 19:2724
ultraviolet radiation, from space
  2:174–6
Ulysses (space probe) 15:2121
undersea habitats **18:2537–40**
Universe, thermodynamics and
  17:2416
Uranus 13:1757, 1758, 1761;
  15:2118, 2122, *2123*
  rings around 5:710; 15:*2123*

V

Van Allen belts 14:1899–1900
Vela supernova remnant 14:*1912*
Venera 15 and 16 (spacecraft)
  12:1707
vents, hydrothermal 10:1333;
  11:1567; 13:*1780*
Venus (planet) 13:1757; **15**:2118,
  2119–20, *2121*
  mapping 12:1707; 17:2337
  traveling to 12:1600
Viking space missions, and life on
  Mars 4:*446*
volcanoes 5:*696*
  formation 5:699
  and plate tectonics 13:1778
Voyager space probes 2:217; **15**:2156
  Voyager 2 15:2118
    and Iapetus (moon) 3:*393*
    and Neptune 5:710; 15:2118

W

water
  in the atmosphere 10:1396
  on Earth, source 13:1761
waves (oceanic) 19:2672, 2674
  tidal (tsunamis) **18:2509–11**
weather, study of *see* meteorology
weathering 7:981
Wegener, Alfred 5:707; 13:1777
wells, oil, set ablaze 6:806
Westar VI (satellite) 15:2029; 16:2169
white dwarves 14:1954; 17:2315,
  2316
Wide-Field Planetary Cameras
  2:176; **15**:2155
  Wide Field Camera 2 (WFC2)
    17:2381, *2382*
  Wide Field Camera 3 (WFC3)
    15:*2154*, 2155
Wilson, J. T. 13:1777, 1780
wind power, and land reclamation
  9:1206, 1208; 19:2695
winds
  Earth's surface 8:*1097*
    see also hurricanes and tornadoes
  erosion by 6:816–17, 819
  lunar 17:2440
  trade 14:1931, 2009
World Meteorological Organization
  (WMO) 10:1397
World Ocean Circulation
  Experiment 11:1568

Y

years 5:696; 17:2441
Yucatan peninsula, Chicxulub crater
  7:989
Yucca Mountain 11:*1547*

Electrical Engineering

A

acoustics, engineering 1:26
ADF (automatic direction-finding) equipment 1:66, 67
aircraft
control *see* aircraft-control engineering
wiring used in 3:346
aircraft-control engineering 1:65–8
altimetry 1:68
autopilot 1:67–8; 15:2057
electronics *see* avionics
head-up displays 8:1039–40
and landing 1:68; 14:1895
radar 1:67, 68; 14:1894, 1898
servomechanisms 15:2057
air-traffic control (ATC), transponders 1:67
alarms
burglar *see* burglar alarms
fire 2:239; 15:2045
alternators *see* generators, alternating current
ammeters 10:1402
Ampère, André 6:726
amperes (amps) 6:727
ampere turns 10:1313
amplifiers 1:124–6
audio 1:126
distortion 14:1903
avoidance 1:126
with feedback 1:126; 6:838–9
frequency response of 8:1072, 1073
for the hard of hearing 1:22
in hi fi systems 8:1071, 1074–5
integrated 1:126
intermediate frequency (IF) 17:2393
multistage 1:125
operational (op-amps) 1:125–6
preamplifiers 1:126
radio frequency (RF) 17:2393
radio telescope 14:1911
semiconductor 1:124; 18:2481
telephone 1:22
vacuum-tube 1:124; 6:751; 18:2565
amplitude distortion 8:1073
amps (amperes) 6:727
analog-to-digital converters (ADCs) 1:127, 128–9; 2:189
antitheft devices 3:341
arcing, in fuses 7:943
assemblers 10:1420
Atari 2600 (games console) 7:952
automatic direction-finding (ADF) equipment 1:66, 67
automobiles
electrical systems
alternator 2:201
battery 2:201, 227–8; 6:799
dynamo 7:972
voltage regulator 19:2618–19
electronics systems 2:202–4
air-pressure sensors 10:1418
diagnostic systems 2:202
engine-control module (ECM) 2:204
exhaust-gas analysis 2:203
fuel injection system 2:200, 203; 10:1426
ignition *see* ignition systems, automobile
microprocessors 2:202, 204; 10:1420, 1426
sensors 2:203–4
substations 2:203

autopilot 1:67–8; 15:2057
avionics (aviation electronics) 1:44, 66–7
and aircraft engines 1:78

B

balances, electronic 2:214–15
bandwidth 1:126
bar codes 3:401; 8:1082; 12:1624; 13:1803
for letters 10:1322
scanners *see* scanners, bar-code
for stock control 10:1341
Barkhausen effect 10:1315
batteries 2:225–9; 6:726, 799
alkaline 2:227; 6:799
automobile 2:201, 227–8; 6:799
battery-powered delivery vehicles 2:228
"button" 2:229
in calculators 3:360–1
dry 2:226–7
gas 7:935
lead-acid 2:227–8; 6:799
lithium alloy-iron sulfide 6:799
mercury cells 2:227; 10:1372
nickel-cadmium 2:229; 6:799
nickel-metal hydride 6:795
NiFe cells 2:228–9
rechargeable 1:99; 6:799
sodium-sulfur 2:229; 6:794–5, 799; 9:1287
voltaic piles 6:726
see also fuel cells
BCS theory 17:2311–12
bells, electric 2:239
bicycles, as stationary power units 7:903
biofuels 2:258–60; 6:794
Bloch walls 10:1315, 1316
blood pressure, monitors 6:757–8
Braun tubes 12:1607
breakdown 6:728; 9:1163
brushes 5:717
BSCCO superconductors 17:2313, 2314
bugging devices 6:759–61
buildings, intelligent 3:338
burglar alarms 2:239; 3:340–1; 5:672; 15:2043
buzzers, electric 2:239

C

cables
antitheft 3:341
between computers 4:539
coaxial 3:354; 4:539
power 3:344–6; 4:556; 6:729; 13:1833, 1836–7
insulation 3:345
superconducting 17:2314
submarine (undersea), power cables 3:349
calculators 3:359–61
capacitors (condensers) 3:386–7; 6:730; 14:1960–1
fixed, electrolytic and nonelectrolytic 3:387
in microphones 10:1424
as part of defibrillators 6:757
variable 3:387; 6:730
tuning and trimmer 3:387
Cardan, Jerome 6:725
cash registers 3:399–401
Castner-Kellner cells 6:738

cathode rays
are electrons 6:767
and vacuum tubes 5:657
cathode-ray tubes (CRTs) 3:408–10; 6:751; 10:1302; 12:1647–8
for computer monitors 3:409; 4:532
for electron microscopes 10:1431–2
in radar displays 14:1897–8
in television receivers 3:409; 12:1647–8; 17:2392, 2393
cat's whisker devices 6:752
charge, electrostatic *see* electrostatic charge
chimes, two-tone 2:239
circuit boards, printed *see* printed circuits
circuit breakers *see* fuses and circuit breakers
circuits, electrical *see* electrical circuits
clipping 8:1074
clocks
electric 4:486; 6:734
quartz 4:486–8; 17:2442, 2445–6
commutators 5:717
generating interference 6:745
condensers (electric components) *see* capacitors
conduction, electrical 4:554–6; 6:728
in metals 4:550, 556; 17:2417–18
see also insulators, electric; semiconductors; superconductivity
Cooper pairs 17:2312
copper, electrical properties 4:568
corotrons 12:1701
corposants 17:2431
Coulomb, Charles 6:725; 12:1727
Coulomb's law 6:725, 727
Crookes' dark space 5:656

D

Data Encryption Standard (DES) 5:594; 6:762
DECCA (navigation system) 7:872–3; 11:1511–12
decoders, satellite-TV 1:141
defibrillators 6:757
depletion layer (p-n junction) 5:654; 6:752; 15:2053, 2116–17; 18:2481
depolarizers 2:226
diathermy, surgical 6:758
dielectric constants 3:386
dielectrics 3:386; 9:1162, 1163
dielectric heating 11:1447–8
digital audio tape (DAT) players, amplifiers 1:126
digital displays 1:127; 5:646–8
digital-to-analog converters (DACs) 1:127
diodes 5:653–4; 14:1937
avalanche 19:2621
light-emitting (LEDs) 15:2054
in calculators 3:361; 5:654
in cameras 3:367
and fiber optics 3:355
in matrix displays 5:646, 647
in optoisolators 6:757
in planar displays 5:648
in watches 19:2650
semiconductor 5:653–4; 6:752; 15:2053–4; 18:2481–2
vacuum-tube (valves) 5:653; 6:750–1; 18:2480, 2563–4
zener 19:2619–21

see also discharge tubes; thyristors
dipoles (electrical) 4:554; 9:1163
induced 9:1163
discharge tubes 5:655–8; 9:1184
in greenhouses 8:1088–9
krypton 11:1529
mercury vapor 5:658; 14:1980; 18:2533
neon 4:555; 5:656, 657; 17:2392
sodium, street lights 1:101; 5:658; 14:1980
xenon 8:1077–8; 11:1529; 16:2285
distance-measuring equipment (DME) 1:67
distortion, sound, types of 8:1073–4
distributors, automobile 2:202–3; 8:1124–5
DME (distance-measuring equipment) 1:67
dopants 4:552; 6:752; 15:2116; 18:2481, 2482
drills 5:678–9
dental 2:233; 5:621–2
drums
drum machines 12:1670
electronic drum kits 12:1670
dry cells 2:226–7
dynamometers 10:1403
Regnier's 13:1825
dynamos 7:972; 13:1827; 19:2618–19
dynodes 12:1717, 1718

E

ECM (electrochemical machining) 6:735–6; 10:1310
ECMs (engine-control modules) 2:204
eddy currents 8:1140, 1141
Edison, Thomas 2:228; 6:730
and the incandescent lamp 3:394; 9:1244
electrets 5:715–16; 17:2369
transducers 5:715, 716; 18:2475–6
electrical circuits
bistable 4:487
capacitors in 3:386–7
resonance 12:1606; 14:1966
see also fuses and circuit breakers; resistors; switches
electrical engineering 5:717–20
electricity 6:725–30
circuits *see* electrical circuits
conductors *see* conduction, electrical
current 6:725–6, 727
alternating (AC) 6:729; 14:1937
direct (DC) 14:1937
and electrochemical cells 6:727
and power loss 6:729
see also electrochemistry
early experiments 6:725
and the electron 6:726, 727
and electrostatic charge 6:727
and the environment 5:720
for executions 6:730
from fish 6:730
generation *see* energy resources, renewable; power plants
insulators *see* insulators, electric
light converted into *see* photoelectric cells and photometry
meters 10:1404–5; 19:2704, 2705
and power 6:728–9
measurement 10:1403
resistance *see* resistance, electrical
static 6:725
storage

electricity, storage (*cont.*)
  in superconducting rings
    17:2314
  supply *see* power supply
  triboelectricity **6**:*725, 727, 728*
  see also batteries; electromagnet-
    ism; induction; semiconductors;
    superconductivity; transformers
electric motors **6**:731–4; **10**:1318
  commutator
    AC- **6**:734
    DC- **6**:*732*, 733–4
  commutatorless in **5**:717
  controls **6**:731
  in electric drills **5**:678
  hysteresis **6**:734
  induction **6**:*731*, 732–3; **9**:1252
  linear **6**:732; **9**:**1252–6**
  magnetic and electromagnetic
    6:731–2
  outboard **10**:1337; **12**:**1614–15**
  reluctance **5**:717, *718*; **6**:734
    magnetic micromotors **5**:718
  repulsion **6**:731
  reversible **6**:731
  for small marine craft **10**:1337
  stepping **6**:734
  in submarines **10**:1336–7
  synchronous **6**:733
  three-phase **6**:*734*
  universal **6**:734
  see also starter motors
electrochemical cells **6**:727
electrochemical deposition **10**:1418
electrochemical machining (ECM)
  6:**735–6**; **10**:1310
electrochemistry **4**:464; **6**:727
  see also electrolysis
electrodischarge machining (EDM;
  spark erosion; spark machining)
  6:735, 736; **10**:1364, *1366*
electrolysis **6**:**737–8**; **9**:1184
  Castner-Kellner cells **6**:738
  Faraday's laws **6**:737–8
  of sodium chloride **1**:25; **4**:450,
    452; **6**:737; **8**:1118; **9**:1184
  uses
    anodic stripping/cathodic
      polishing **2**:160
    in electrochemical machining
      6:735, 736
    electrolytic capacitors **3**:387
    for marine salvage **15**:2022–3
    metal plating *see* electroplating
    to conserve metals **2**:160
    to extract alkali metals **1**:99
    to extract aluminum **1**:110–11;
      6:738
    to extract metals **6**:738; **10**:1378
electrolytes, in batteries **2**:225–6
electromagnetic force compensation
  2:214
electromagnetic interference (EMI)
  6:745–6
electromagnetism **6**:726, **747–9**;
  12:1727–8
  Maxwell's equations **6**:748
  mediated by elementary particles
    6:770–1
  superconducting electromagnets
    5:718, 719–20; **9**:1256; **17**:2310,
    2314
  use
    in bone regeneration **2**:256
    in clutches **4**:492
    in electric bells **2**:239
    in electric motors **6**:731, 732,
      733
    in flowmeters **7**:896–7
    in loudspeakers **9**:1284, *1285*
    in magnetohydrodynamics
      (MHD) **10**:1318–19

  in seismographs **15**:2047
  in solenoids **15**:2124–5
  see also maglev (magnetic-levita-
    tion) vehicles
  see also induction
electromechanical coupling constant
  13:1744
electromotive force (emf) **6**:748;
  10:1313
  and magnetohydrodynamics
    10:1318
  see also voltage
electron guns **3**:408
electronics **6**:**750–5**
  automobile *see* automobiles, elec-
    tronics systems
  aviation *see* avionics
  circuits **6**:750
  components *see* capacitors; diodes;
    thyristors; transistors; triodes
  computer **6**:754–5
    see also integrated circuits
  and farm machinery **1**:50–1
  in medicine **6**:**756–8**
  miniaturization **6**:754–5
  optoelectronics **6**:755
  see also transducers and sensors
electronic surveillance **6**:**759–62**
electrons
  in batteries **2**:225
  discovery **2**:182; **3**:408; **6**:726, 763,
    767
  and electricity **6**:726
electroplating **6**:738; **17**:2323–4
  with chromium **4**:473
  with nickel **4**:473; **11**:1523
  preparation before **1**:17
  and waste disposal **19**:*2641*
electropults **9**:1254
electroscopes **6**:725
electrostatic charge **6**:727; **12**:1727
  and electrets **5**:715
  and electrostatic loudspeakers
    9:*1284*, 1285
  and microwave ovens **11**:*1449*
electrostatic generators **12**:*1648*
electrostatic precipitators **13**:1800
electrostatic spraying **13**:1824;
  16:2228
electrostriction **18**:2530
energy resources **6**:**790–7**
  fossil fuels **2**:258; **3**:391; **6**:790, 791
  hydrogen **6**:795–6
  nuclear energy **6**:796; **11**:1542–3
  renewable **6**:790, 791–7
    from the temperature gradient
      in the sea **6**:793, 795; **8**:1054
    geothermal **6**:*790*, 793
    see also biofuels; hydroelectric
      power; solar energy; tidal power;
      wave power; wind power
engine-control modules (ECMs)
  2:204
enthalpy **18**:2517
  stagnation **18**:2517
equalizers **8**:1073; **15**:2138
escalators and moving walkways
  6:**820–1**
Essen rings **4**:487–8
Evinrude, Ole **12**:1614
Evinrude portable motor **12**:*1615*

F

Faraday, Michael
  and electromagnetism **6**:726, *749*;
    8:1139; **10**:1313
  laws of electrolysis **6**:737–8
Faraday boxes **17**:2431
Faraday dark space **5**:656
FDDI (fiber-optic digital device

  interface) **4**:539
feedback **6**:**838–9**; **9**:1277
  in amplifiers **1**:126; **6**:838–9
  in oscillators **6**:754
  positive and negative **6**:839
  in transistors **6**:754
ferroelectrics **18**:2530
fiber-optic digital device interface
  (FDDI) **4**:539
Fizeau, A. H. L. **8**:1139; **9**:1240
flachenblitz (rocket lightning)
  17:2431
flash tubes, electronic **3**:365
Fleming, John Alexander **18**:2563
flux, magnetic **6**:748
flux pinning **17**:2310–11, 2314
flywheels **7**:**902–3**; **8**:1143
forward bias **5**:653; **18**:2482
Franklin, Benjamin **6**:725; **9**:1250;
  17:2428–9
frequency hopping **5**:596; **6**:762
frequency response **8**:1072; **10**:1424
fuel cells **6**:795–6, 799; **7**:**935–6**
  aluminum-air **7**:*936*
  nuclear, examination for surface
    defects **8**:*1082*
  solid-oxide **6**:795
  uses **7**:936
    in electric vehicles **5**:720;
      9:1287, 1288
    to detect alcohol **5**:686
Full Authority Digital Electronic
  Control (FADEC) **1**:78
fuses and circuit breakers **7**:**943–5**
  circuit breakers (CBs) **7**:943,
    944–5; **13**:1837
    miniature (MCBs) **7**:943, 945
    residual current (RCCBs) **7**:945
  in domestic wiring systems
    19:2705–7
  fuse boxes **19**:2705, *2708*
  fuses **7**:943–4; **13**:1837
fuzzy logic **2**:171; **9**:1277
  washing machines and **3**:431;
    19:2635–6

G

gain **6**:754
galvanometers **10**:1402–3
games consoles **7**:952
games machines **7**:**949–52**
gases, conduction in **4**:555
Geissler, Heinrich **5**:655
Geissler tubes **5**:*658*; **17**:2403
generators **6**:**971–2**; **10**:1318
  alternating-current (alternators)
    6:729; **7**:971–2; **19**:2619
    ambulance **1**:113
    automobile **2**:201
    power plant **13**:1827, 1829–30
  direct-current (dynamos) **7**:972;
    13:1827; **19**:2618–19
  superconductors used in **17**:2314
  voltage regulators for **19**:2618–19
germanium **6**:752; **18**:2481
Gray code **6**:731
grounding fault circuit interrupters
  (GFCIs) **19**:2707

H

Hall effect **10**:1320
harmonica bugs **6**:761
harmonic distortion **8**:1073, 1074
  total (THD) **8**:1074
hearing aids **8**:1043–4; **12**:1612
heart pacemaker **8**:**1048**
  external **8**:1048
  implantable **2**:257; **8**:1048

heat, detectors (firefighting) **6**:863
heaters
  in dishwashers **5**:659
  storage heaters **6**:800
heat sinks **17**:*2432*
henry (H) **8**:1139
hi-fi systems **1**:26–7; **8**:**1071–6**;
  13:1739
  see also loudspeakers
hum **8**:1074
hydroelectric power (HEP) **6**:786,
  792; **8**:**1112–15**; **13**:1820, 1827
  dams for **5**:605; **8**:1112
  high-head and low-head projects
    8:1112
  pumped-storage schemes **6**:798;
    8:1112, *1115*; **13**:*1827*; **18**:2520
  turbines **8**:1112–13; **18**:2520
  see also tidal power; wave power
HydroGen 1 (fuel cell) **7**:936
hysteresis loops **10**:1314–15; **18**:2478

I

ignition systems, automobile **2**:200,
  202–3; **8**:**1124–7**; **17**:*2445*
  distributor **2**:202–3; **8**:1124–5
  ignition coil (induction coil)
    8:1124, 1140
  spark plugs **2**:203; **8**:1125, 1126,
    1127; **9**:*1170*
ILSs *see* instrument landing systems
impedance **8**:1075; **14**:1960
incineration, plasma-arc **5**:720
induction **6**:729; **8**:**1138–41**; **12**:1727
  induction coils **8**:1139, *1141*
    see also transformers
  mutual-inductance **8**:1138, 1139
  self-inductance **8**:1138–9
  and Tesla coils **8**:1140; **17**:2403
inductive loops **14**:1985
instrument landing systems (ILSs)
  1:68, 88, 95, 96; **11**:1513
insulators, electric **3**:426; **4**:555, 556;
  6:728; **9**:**1162–3**
  and breakdown **9**:1163
  in power cables **3**:345
integrated circuits (silicon chips;
  microchips) **2**:169–70; **6**:750,
  754–5; **9**:**1164–8**
  in calculators **3**:359–60
  in cell phones **3**:416
  complexity
    large scale integration (LSI)
      2:169; **3**:359; **4**:525; **6**:755
    medium-scale integration (MSI)
      4:525; **6**:755
    ultra-large-scale integration
      (ULSI) **4**:525; **6**:755
    very-large-scale integration
      (VLSI) **2**:169; **3**:416; **4**:525;
      6:755; **10**:1426
  in computers **4**:*524*, 525; **9**:1165,
    1277
    latch circuits **9**:1277, 1279
  copper **4**:*524*
  switches **4**:552
  in watches **19**:2650
interference, electromagnetic (EMI)
  6:745–6
intermodulation distortion **8**:1073–4
International Thermonuclear
  Experimental Reactor (ITER)
  6:797
isolators **13**:1837

J

JET (Joint European Torus) **7**:947–8
jets (atmospheric phenomena)
  17:2431

Johnson 3.6 GT (motor) **12**:*1614*
Joint European Torus (JET) **7**:947–8
Josephson junctions **17**:*2312*, 2313, 2314

K

Kamerlingh Onnes, Heike **17**:2309
keypads, itemized **3**:*400*–1
kilowatt-hours **19**:*2704*
klystrons **6**:741, *745*, 751; **14**:1895–6

L

lambda sensors **2**:203
large-scale integration (LSI) *see* integrated circuits
leaders, upward (streamers) **9**:1250
Leclanché cells **2**:226–7; **4**:486
LEDs *see* diodes, light-emitting
Lenz's law **8**:1138
Leyden jars **6**:725
lighting, circuits, domestic **19**:2707–8
lightning **4**:555; **6**:725; **17**:2428–30
ball **17**:2431
lightning conductors **9**:1250–1
linear motors **6**:732; **9**:*1252*–6
tubular **9**:1253
see also maglev (magnetic-levitation) vehicles
liquids, electrical conduction **6**:728
Lissajous patterns **12**:1608
load cells **2**:215
lock-and-block signaling **14**:1924
logic, fuzzy *see* fuzzy logic
loudspeakers **9**:*1284*–5
electrostatic **9**:*1284*, 1285
flat-panel **9**:1285
hi-fi **8**:1071–2, *1074*
moving-coil **9**:1284, *1285*
public-address **1**:*126*
ribbon **9**:1285
LSI *see* integrated circuits

M

maglev (magnetic-levitation) vehicles
passenger links **5**:719; **10**:1349
trains **5**:*717*, 719; **7**:934; **9**:*1252*, *1254*, 1255–6; **10**:1349, *1363*, 1364–5; **14**:*1928*; **17**:2310, 2314
magnetic flux **6**:748
magnetometers **2**:156–7; **7**:992; **10**:*1320*; **11**:1571
fluxgate **10**:1320
Hall effect **10**:1320
proton **7**:992; **10**:1320
magnetomotive force (mmf) **6**:748; **7**:971; **10**:1313; **18**:2477
magnetostatic energy **10**:1316
magnetostriction **18**:2530
energy **10**:1316
magnetrons **6**:741, 751
in microwave ovens **11**:1448–9
and radar transmission **14**:1895, 1896
mats, pressure **3**:340
maximum demand indicators (MDIs) **10**:1405
Maxwell's equations **6**:748
medium-scale integration (MSI) *see* integrated circuits
Meissner, Walter **17**:2310
Meissner effect **17**:2310
mercury (metal), superconducting **17**:2309, 2314
microbalances **2**:214, 215
microchips *see* integrated circuits

microelectromechanical systems (MEMS) **17**:2446
micromachines and nanotechnology **10**:*1416–20*
micromotors **10**:*1416*, 1418–19
magnetic **5**:718
microphones **10**:*1423*–5; **13**:1745
for bugging **6**:759–60
carbon **10**:1423
as computer input devices **4**:527
condenser **10**:1424
crystal **10**:1424
directional **10**:1425
unidirectional **10**:*1423*, 1425
electret **5**:*715*, 716
frequency response of **10**:1424
long-range **10**:1425
moving-coil and ribbon **10**:1423–4
and the obstacle effect **10**:1424–5
output signals **1**:128
solar-powered **10**:*1423*
microprocessors **6**:755; **10**:*1426–9*; **15**:2054
on automobiles **2**:202, 204
on farm machinery **1**:51
for "intelligent prostheses" **2**:254
logic operations **9**:1277; **10**:*1427*–8
and optoelectronics **6**:755
see also integrated circuits
microwaves **6**:741–2
generation **6**:741, 745, 751
uses
movement sensors **3**:340, *341*; **15**:*2042*, 2043
to make logs pliable **7**:*924*
waveguides and **19**:2668–71
midi systems **8**:1075–6
Motogodille (motor) **12**:1614
MOSFETs **9**:1165; **10**:1426
motors, electric *see* electric motors
multichannel physiological recorders (MCPRs) **6**:758
music
digitally encoded **1**:*26*; **8**:1076
reproduction *see* hi-fi systems

N

nanotechnology *see* micromachines and nanotechnology
nanotubes, carbon **10**:*1420*
NES (Nintendo Entertainment System) **7**:952
NiFe cells **2**:228–9
niobium tin **3**:346; **17**:2312
Nixie tubes **5**:647
noise
of amplifiers **1**:126; **8**:1074–5
radio **14**:1903
reduction **1**:126, *129*
nuclear power **6**:729
nuclear reactors **11**:*1542*–6; **14**:*1907*
Cerenkov radiation **6**:*794*; **14**:*1907*
design **11**:1544–5
fast-breeder **7**:*877*; **11**:1546; **18**:*2547*
heat exchangers **8**:1054
nuclear emergencies **11**:**1535**–6, 1545
nuclear fission **6**:796; **7**:877; **11**:1543–6; **12**:*1728*; **13**:1832
MHD units used in **10**:1319
nuclear fuel cycle **11**:**1537**–9, 1546; **18**:*2547*–8
nuclear fusion **2**:248; **6**:796; **7**:947–8; **11**:*1545*
safety **11**:1535, 1545
thermal **11**:1545–6
boiling water reactors (BWRs) **11**:*1543*, 1545; **13**:1832;

18:2520
gas-cooled **2**:233; **11**:1546
heavy water reactors **11**:1545
pressurized-water reactors (PWRs) **11**:*1542*, *1543*, 1545; **13**:*1832*; **18**:2520
see also power plants, nuclear

O

obstacle effect **10**:1424–5
Oersted, Hans **6**:726, 747
Ohm, Georg **6**:726; **14**:*1960*
ohms **9**:1162
Ohm's law **6**:726, 728; **13**:1826; **14**:*1962*
op-amps (operational amplifiers) **1**:125–6
optoelectronics **6**:755
optoisolators **6**:757
oscillators **12**:1605–6
electrical circuits as **6**:754; **8**:1139; **12**:1606
oscilloscopes **12**:1607–8; **19**:*2617*
cathode-ray tubes **3**:409; **12**:1607
outboard motors **10**:1337; **12**:1614–15

P

pan pots **13**:1822
patient-monitoring systems **6**:*757*, 758
Peltier effect **17**:2417, 2418–19, *2420*
and thermography **17**:2421
permeability (magnetization) **10**:1315
photodiodes
and fiber optics **3**:355
silicon (SPDs), in exposure meters **3**:368
photoelectric cells and photometry **12**:*1704*–5
photoelectric cells (photocells) **1099**
in electric motors **6**:731
photoconductive cells **12**:*1704*, 1705
photoemissive cells **12**:1704–5
and photomultiplier tubes **12**:1717–18
photovoltaic *see* photovoltaic (PV) cells
and security systems **3**:340–1; **15**:*2043*
for streetlamp switches **14**:1980
photometry **12**:1705
see also solar energy, solar panels
photoelectric effect **9**:1241; **12**:1704
photoemissive cells **12**:1704–5
photometry **12**:1705
phototransistors **18**:2483
photovoltaic (PV) cells **2**:229; **4**:552; **6**:730, 792; **12**:*1704*, 1705
on bicycles **2**:244
in calculators **3**:361
photovoltaic effect **12**:1705
pickup, acoustic **13**:**1739–40**
piezoelectric constant **13**:1744
piezoelectric effect **13**:1744
piezoelectric material **5**:599; **10**:1364; **13**:**1744**–5
ceramics **3**:426; **13**:1745
quartz **5**:599; **12**:1606; **13**:1744, 1745
in clocks and watches **4**:487; **17**:2442, 2445–6; **19**:2650
as smart ceramics **10**:1352–3
as transducers **13**:1745, 1843; **18**:2474, 2529–30
use in ink-jet printers **4**:545

pixels **3**:432
plasma physics **5**:656; **10**:1362; **13**:**1762–3**
and nuclear fusion **7**:946–7; **10**:1319
in the Sun **10**:*1361*; **13**:1762
plasma-arc technology
for cutting metal **10**:1364, 1379–80
for waste incineration **5**:720
PMPO (peak music power output) **8**:1075
p-n junction (depletion layer) **5**:654; **6**:752; **15**:2053, 2116–17; **18**:2481
point-of-sale terminals, electronic (EPOS) **3**:401
polar diagrams **10**:1425
polarization (electrical) **3**:386; **9**:1163
in batteries **2**:226
in electrets **5**:715
Pong (electronic game) **7**:952
potential difference **4**:554; **6**:726, 728–9
potentiometers **8**:1071; **13**:**1821**–2; **18**:2474
carbon-track **13**:*1821*
panoramic **13**:1822
sliding-wire **13**:1821
pots (rheostats) **13**:1821, 1822
pan **13**:1822
power
electrical **6**:728–9, 729; **13**:1826
generation by thermopiles **17**:2420
measurement **10**:1403
power cables *see* cables, power
powerheads, outboard-motor **12**:1614
power plants **13**:1826, **1827–32**, *1834*
alternators **13**:1827, 1829–30
efficiency **6**:788
first public **13**:1827, 1833
gas turbines **13**:1832
natural gas-powered **7**:*967*; **13**:1828
hydroelectric *see* hydroelectric power
and nuclear fusion **2**:248
nuclear (nuclear fission) **7**:876; **12**:*1728*; **13**:1827–8, 1831–2
see also nuclear reactors
rated in power units **6**:790
solar **6**:792; **15**:2116
using carbon-based fuels **13**:1830–1
coal **13**:1827, 1831; **14**:1927
wood-burning **2**:258
power supply **13**:**1833–8**; **19**:2704–5
power cables *see* cables, power
and telemetry **17**:2364–5
preamplifiers (preamps) **1**:126
Priestley, Joseph **6**:725
printed circuits **13**:**1844–6**
public address systems **1**:*126*
public-key cryptosystems (PKCs) **6**:762
pylons, electricity **3**:344, *346*

Q

quadrophonic systems **8**:1072

R

radio tags **3**:341
record players **8**:1076
rectification **18**:2480
half- and full-wave **14**:1937

rectifiers 5:653; 6:750–1; **14:1937–8**; 15:2053
  mercury-arc 14:1937, 1938
  solid-state 14:1938
  see also diodes
relays 15:2124–5; 18:2480
resistance **14:1960–1**
  electrical 6:726, 728; 9:1162; 14:1960
    absence of *see* superconductivity
    in a capacitor 14:1960–1
    and Ohm's law 6:726, 728; 13:1826
    and resistivity of materials 6:728; 9:1162; 14:1960
    overcoming 14:1961
resistivity 6:728; 9:1162
resistors **14:1962–3**
  variable *see* potentiometers
resonance
  in electric circuits 12:1606; 14:1966
  and piezoelectric ultrasound sensors 13:1745
reverse bias 5:653; 18:2482
RGB displays 5:647
rheostats 13:1822
RMS (root-mean-square) value 8:1075
rolling roads 2:204

S

St. Elmo's fire 5:655; 17:2431
scan conversion tubes 3:410
scanners, bar-code 3:401; 8:1082, *1083*, *1150*; 10:1341
scoreboards, electronic 17:*2444*
Seebeck effect 17:2417, 2418, 2420
semiconductors 4:552, 555, 556; 6:728; 10:1361; **15:2052–4**
  intrinsic and extrinsic 15:2053
  lasers 9:1213, 1214; 15:2054
  p-n junction (depletion layer) 5:654; 6:752; 15:2053, 2116–17; 18:2481
  p-type and n-type 5:*653*, 654; 6:752; 15:2053; 18:2481–2
  silicon as 4:552; 5:599; 6:752; 15:2076
  uses 15:2053–4
    in calculators 3:359
    in CCDs 15:*2054*
    in electronic devices 6:752
    in pressure transducers 15:2054
    in rectifier applications 14:1938; 15:2053
    in refrigeration 17:2420
    in thyristors 17:2432
    in transistors 1:124; 6:753, 754; 15:*2053*, 2054; 18:2480–2, 2565
    see also integrated circuits; microprocessors
semimicrobalances 2:214
sensors *see* transducers and sensors
service panels 19:2705–7
servomechanisms 8:1017; **15:2055–7**
shaft encoders 6:731
shift registers 1:129
side flash 9:1251
signals
  electrical
    generation 12:1606
    sawtooth 12:1606
    square-wave 12:1606
    microwave 12:1606
signal-to-noise (S/N) ratio 8:1074–5
silicon chips *see* integrated circuits
smoke detectors 6:*863*
solar cells *see* photoelectric cells and photometry

solar energy 6:*729*, 791–2; 15:2054, **2114–17**
  for power plants 6:792; 15:2116
  solar panels 4:552; 6:*791*, 792; 8:1058
    on satellites 15:*2028*, 2117
    on space probes 15:2156
    on space stations 15:2150–1
  and Stirling engines 16:2269
solenoids 15:2124–5; 16:2241
Space Invaders (video game) 7:952
spark machining *see* electrodischarge machining
spark plugs 2:203; 8:1125, 1126, 1127; 9:*1170*
speakers *see* loudspeakers
sprites 17:2430
standard cells 13:1822
starter motors 15:*2125*; **16:2241**
  solenoid switches 15:2125; 16:2241
stereo systems 6:755; 8:1072
strain gauges 2:215; 18:2475
stratified charging 2:200
substations, electrical 13:1837
sulfating 2:228
superconducting tunnel junctions 3:*432*
superconductivity 4:550; **17:2309–14**
  applications 17:2313–14
    electromagnets 5:718, 719–20; 9:1256; 17:2310, 2314
    Josephson junctions 17:*2312*, 2313, 2314
    maglev trains 17:2310, 2314
  and the BCS theory 17:2311–12
  and cryogenics 5:589, *590*
  discovery 17:2309–10
  and flux pinning 17:2310–11
  and the Meissner effect 17:2310
  superconductors 4:553, 555, 556; 5:718; 6:728; 17:2312
    ceramics as 5:718; 17:2312–13
    high-temperature (HTSs) 17:2312–14
    type I and II 17:2311, 2312
surveillance, electronic *see* electronic surveillance
switches **17:2341**
  and Boolean algebra 9:1279
  contact 17:2341
  electronic, and reluctance motors 5:717, *718*
  eye-controlled 11:1470
  glass memory 4:552
  isolating 17:2341
  knife 17:2341
  load 17:2341
  photoelectrically-controlled 14:1980
  three-way 17:2341
  time 17:2444–5
    solar-dial 14:1980; 17:*2444*
  transistors as 18:2480
switch gear 13:1837
synchronization circuits (sync circuits) 12:1608

T

TACAN (tactical air navigation) 1:67
telemetry, electric 17:2364–5
Tesla, Nikola 13:*1834*; 17:2403
Tesla coils 8:1140; 17:**2403**
theodolites, electronic 2:157
thermionic emission 1:124; 5:657; 18:2563
thermocouples 1:65, 127; 13:1783; 17:*2395*, 2417, 2418, 2419, 2420

in engines 17:2423
thermoelectret forming process 5:715
thermoelectric devices 17:**2417–20**
  see also thermocouples
thermopiles 17:*2418*, 2420
Thomson effect 17:2417, 2419
thyratrons, gas 17:2432
thyristors 6:753; 14:1938; 17:2432–3
  bidirectional (triacs) 6:731; 17:2433
tidal power 6:792–3; 17:**2436–8**
  see also wave power
time-base circuitry 12:1608
timing devices 17:**2444–6**
  central-heating 8:1058; 17:2445
  in dishwashers 5:660
tokamaks 6:796; 7:947–8; 13:1763
toll charging, automatic 2:204
track-circuit signaling 14:1924
transducers and sensors 18:**2474–6**
  in automobiles
    fuel gauge 18:2474
    lambda sensors 2:203
    position 2:204
    pressure 2:203–4; 15:2054
    temperature 2:204
  sensors
    biosensors 14:1988
    in burglar alarms 3:340
    chemical 14:1988
    and robot senses 14:1988, 1989
  transducers
    in accelerometers 18:2476
    capacitative 18:2475
    displacement 18:2474
    electret 5:*715*, 716; 18:2475–6
    electrostrictive 18:2530
    feedback (fork balance) 18:2476
    inductive 18:2474–5
    linear variable differential (LVDTs) 18:2474–5
    load 18:*2476*
    magnetostrictive 18:*2530*
    piezoelectric materials as 13:1745, 1843; 18:2474, 2529–30
    pressure sensors 18:2474, 2510–11
    resonance 18:2476
    sonar 15:2126, 2128
    strain gauges 2:215; 18:2475
    see also pickup, acoustic
transformers 6:729, 747, 748, 749; 8:1139; 12:1728; 13:1835, *1838*; 18:**2477–9**
  air-cooled 18:2479
  autotransformers 18:*2478*
  design 18:2477–9
  distribution 18:2479
  eddy currents 8:1141
  generator 13:1830; 18:2479
  instrument 18:2479
  insulation in 9:*1163*; 18:2479
  in power plants 13:1830; 18:*2479*
  step-up and step-down 6:729; 18:2479
  transmission 18:2479
  unit 13:1830
transistors 6:752; 9:1164; 18:**2480–4**
  bipolar-junction 1:124–5; 6:753; 9:1164; 18:2482–3
  in calculators 3:359
  in computers 2:169; 4:524; 6:754
  "cut off" and "saturated" states 6:754
  logic gates 6:754
  field-effect (FETs) 1:125, 126; 6:753, 755; 18:2483
    ion-sensitive (ISFETs) 18:*2480*
    junction-gate (JFETs; JUGFETS) 18:2483–4

metal-oxide-semiconductor (MOSFETS; insulated gate FETs- IGFETS) 18:2484
  gain and feedback of 6:754
  modulating 18:2480
  phototransistors 18:2483
  point-contact 18:2481
  semiconductor 1:124; 6:753, 754; 15:*2053*, 2054; 18:2480–2, 2565
    CMOS 6:755
  transistor radios 18:2494
transmitters, infinity (harmonica bugs) 6:761
transverse flux motors (TFMs) 9:1254
triacs 6:731; 17:2433
triboelectricity 6:725, 727, *728*
trimmers, grass-cutting 8:1019
triodes, vacuum-tube (valves) 1:124; 6:751; 18:2480, 2564–5
turbogenerators 13:1830; 19:2639
tweeters 9:*1284*, 1285

U

ultra-large-scale integration (ULSI) *see* integrated circuits

V

vacuum tubes 1:124; 18:2480, **2563–5**
  in computers 2:169; 4:524; 6:754
  diodes 5:653; 6:750–1; 18:2480, 2563–4
  pentodes 18:2565
  tetrodes 18:*2564*, 2565
  and thermionic emission 1:124; 5:657; 18:2563
  triodes 1:124; 6:751; 18:2480, 2564–5
  see also cathode-ray tubes
valves, thermionic *see* vacuum tubes
van de Graaff generators 6:727
vector quantities, and electromagnetism 6:749
very-large-scale integration (VLSI) *see* integrated circuits
VHF omnidirectional ranging *see* VOR
video bugs 6:761
VLSI *see* integrated circuits
Volta, Alessandro 2:225; 6:726, 737
voltage 4:554; 6:748
  measuring *see* potentiometers
  see also electromotive force
voltage dividers 13:1821–2
voltage regulators 19:2618–21
voltaic piles 6:726
voltmeters 10:1402, 1403
VOR (VHF omnidirectional ranging) 1:67

W

watt meters 10:1403
watts 6:729
waveguides 19:2668–71
wave power 4:549; 19:2675–7
webers 10:1313
Weston standard cell 13:1822
Wheatstone, Charles 16:2195
Wheatstone bridges 13:*1822*
wheelchairs 11:1469–70
wind power 6:793; 19:2690–5
wiretapping 6:759
wiring systems 19:2704–8
woofers 9:*1284*, 1285
wow and flutter 8:1076

Fundamentals of Science

A

absolute zero **17**:2395, 2396
absorption **15**:2130
acceleration **3**:422; **5**:695
  angular **5**:695
  due to gravity **6**:789; **8**:1021
acoustics **1**:26–7
  architectural **1**:26, 27
  engineering **1**:26
  musical **1**:26
adhesion, surface **7**:934
adhesion tension **17**:2321
adsorption **15**:2129–30
aerodynamics **1**:36–9
  sailing and **14**:2010–11
air, density **5**:617
algebra **10**:1354, 1357
alpha decay **14**:1906–7
alpha particles **14**:1906
  and smoke detectors **6**:863
amplitude **12**:1605; **19**:2674
Anderson, Carl **2**:150; **6**:769
annihilation
  particle–antiparticle **2**:150, 151;
  6:769, 773
  radiation **6**:744, 745; **14**:1907
antihydrogen atoms **2**:151
antimatter **2**:150–1
  antiatoms **2**:151
  antiparticles **2**:150–1; **6**:768–9
    and annihilation **2**:150, 151;
    6:744, 773
    and black holes **2**:270
    of electrons (positrons) **2**:150,
    151; **6**:744, 769
    existence postulated **2**:150;
    14:1883
    and pair production **2**:151
  imbalance in the Universe **6**:773
antiprotons **2**:150
antiquarks **6**:772
Archimedes **5**:616; **8**:1100
Archimedes' principle **5**:616; **8**:1109;
  16:2245
arithmetic **10**:1354
astrophysics **2**:178–81
  astronomical spectroscopy **2**:178;
  16:2197
atmospheres **2**:222
atomic excitation **9**:1241–2
atomic number **14**:1905–6
atomic spectra **6**:768
atomic structure **2**:182–5
  Bohr model **2**:183; **14**:1881–2;
  16:2193
  Dalton's atomic theory **2**:182;
  4:461
  electrons **2**:183–5; **6**:767
    behaving as waves **2**:183–5, 184;
    6:767–8; **14**:1882
    binding energy (ionization
    potential) **2**:248
    discovery **2**:182; **3**:408; **6**:726,
    763, 767
    orbitals (shells; quantum energy
    levels) **2**:184, 185; **4**:442, 461,
    462; **9**:1209; **12**:1671–2;
    14:1881–2; **16**:2193, 2198
    and the periodic table
    12:1671–3
    s, p, d, and f states **2**:185–5;
    12:1671–3
  neutrons **2**:182, 183, 185; **14**:1906
  nucleus **2**:182, 183; **14**:1905–6
    binding energy **2**:248
    discovery **2**:183
    mass **2**:248
    model of proton and neutron

shells **6**:766
"plum pudding model" **2**:182–3
protons **2**:182, 183, 185; **6**:767;
  14:1905–6
  see also elementary particles
atomic weight **2**:182
auroras **14**:1899, 1900
  on Jupiter **14**:1900; **15**:2121
autocatalytic reactions **7**:879
average (mean) **16**:2246, 2248
Avogadro's Law **7**:961
axioms **10**:1357

B

Balmer, Johann **2**:183
bars **2**:222; **13**:1839
baryons **6**:770, 772
beats **19**:2673, 2674
Becquerel, Antoine Henri **14**:1905;
  18:2546
Bernoulli, Daniel **1**:37; **18**:2580
Bernoulli's effect **1**:70; **14**:2010,
  2011; **18**:2580–1
  Bernoulli's equation **1**:37;
  8:1109–10; **18**:2581
beta decay **6**:765, 771; **14**:1907
beta particles **14**:1907
  used for radiotherapy **14**:1922
Big Bang **4**:572, 573–4; **6**:773
binding energy **2**:248; **14**:1961
  nuclear **2**:248; **7**:876
biophysics **2**:261–2
Bohr, Niels **4**:461; **9**:1241
  the Copenhagen interpretation
  14:1883–4
  model of the atom **2**:183;
  14:1881–2; **16**:2193
Boltzmann, Ludwig **9**:1203
Bose–Einstein condensate (Bec)
  9:1214; **14**:1880
bosons **6**:770; **14**:1882
  gauge **6**:770–3
  Higgs **6**:767, 773
  W **2**:151; **6**:771
boundary layer **1**:37
Boyle's law **7**:960–1
bremsstrahlung **19**:2721, 2724
Broglie, Louis de **14**:1882
Brownian motion **9**:1203
bubble and cloud chambers **3**:333–4;
  12:1652
  bubble chambers **2**:183; **3**:333–4;
  6:768; **12**:1652, 1654; **17**:2313
  cloud chambers **2**:151; **3**:333
bulk modulus **5**:714
buoyancy force **5**:616; **8**:1109

C

calculus **10**:1356
caloric **6**:786
calories **6**:790
Cavendish, Henry **8**:1020–1
centrifugal force **3**:422
centripetal force **3**:422
CERN **12**:1652
  and antiatoms **2**:151
  bubble chamber **3**:333, 334
  L3 detector **6**:769
  Large Electron–Positron Collider
  (LEP) **6**:767
  Large Hadron Collider (LHC)
  6:767, 772; **12**:1648
Chadwick, James **6**:767; **14**:1905
chain reactions **7**:876, 877; **11**:1552
chaos theory **3**:430–1; **10**:1397

Charles's law **7**:960, 961
Clausius, Rudolf **17**:2415
cloud chambers see bubble and cloud
  chambers
combustion
  flame-retarding agents **7**:880–1
  slow **7**:879
  see also flames and ignition
condensed-matter physics **4**:550–3
conductivity, thermal, and vacuum
  measurement **18**:2559
conic sections, and planetary orbits
  12:1599
continuity equation **8**:1109
Coolidge, William **19**:2721
Coolidge tubes **19**:2721–2
cooling, law of **11**:1521
Cooper pairs **17**:2312
Copenhagen interpretation, the
  14:1883–4
Coriolis force **5**:699–700; **8**:1143;
  10:1399; **17**:2440
cosine waves **15**:2082
cosmic rays **6**:769; **7**:970
  detection **12**:1652
  and the Van Allen belts **14**:1900
cosmology **4**:572–6
  and microwave spectroscopy
  16:2199
  see also Universe
Coulomb, Charles **6**:725; **7**:933
Curie, Marie and Pierre **10**:1367;
  14:1905

D

damping, pendulums **12**:1605
dark matter **4**:575–6; **8**:1021
decibels (dB) **4**:513–14; **8**:1072
demagnetization, adiabatic **17**:2396
density **5**:616–17
  relative (specific gravity) **5**:616–17
dew point **8**:1123; **10**:1401; **19**:2665
diamagnetism **18**:2486
diffraction **5**:641; **19**:2672–3
  sound waves **15**:2133, 2134
dilatency **19**:2609–10
Dirac, Paul **2**:150; **6**:768–9; **14**:1883,
  1884
displacement **8**:1144
distance(s), and the velocity of light
  14:1950–1
domains (magnets) **10**:1316
domain theory, of ferromagnetism
  10:1315
Doppler effect (Doppler shift) **5**:672
  acoustic **5**:672; **14**:1897; **15**:2134
  and astrophysics **2**:178
  and blood flow **2**:280; **10**:1438
  and burglar alarms **3**:340, 341;
  5:672
  and lasers **9**:1214
  and radar
    search and surveillance **14**:1896,
    1897
    for space navigation **11**:1514
    to monitor the weather **10**:1397,
    1398; **14**:1898
    and traffic monitoring **14**:1985
  and radio astronomy **14**:1909
  and sonar **18**:2531
  and tornado detection **8**:1097–8
drag
  aircraft **1**:38–9, 66
  coefficient of **8**:1111
  ships' **8**:1111
dynamical variables **5**:694–5
dynamics **5**:694–5

E

Einstein, Albert
  and Brownian motion **9**:1203
  general theory of relativity (theory
  of gravity) **2**:269; **4**:572, 574–5;
  8:1021, 1143; **11**:1521
  and light **9**:1237, 1241
    stimulated emissions of photons
    9:1210; **12**:1704
  mass–energy equation **2**:150, 179,
  248; **7**:876; **14**:1953; **17**:2415
  and space–time **2**:269; **14**:1954
  special theory of relativity **2**:150,
  179, 180; **6**:788–9; **7**:876;
  14:1950–5; **17**:2442–3
Einstein rings **14**:1954
elasticity **5**:713–14; **10**:1361
  elastic collisions **9**:1202–3
  and springs **16**:2229
elastic modulus see Young's modulus
electricity **6**:725–30
  current **6**:725–6, 727
  and the electron **6**:726, 727
  and electrostatic charge **6**:727
  and power **6**:728–9
  static **6**:725
  triboelectricity **6**:725, 727, 728
electromagnetic pulse (EMP) energy
  6:746
electromagnetic radiation **6**:739–46,
  749; **9**:1237–8; **12**:1728
  blackbody radiation **6**:740
  from space **2**:173–7
  speed **6**:739, 749
  see also different components of the
  electromagnetic spectrum
electromagnetism **6**:726, 747–9
  and generators **7**:971, 972
  Maxwell's equations **6**:748
  mediated by elementary particles
  6:770–1
electrons
  beams, and electron microscopes
  10:1430
  behaving as waves **2**:183–5, 184;
  6:767–8; **14**:1882
  Cooper pairs **17**:2312
  discovery **2**:182; **3**:408; **6**:726, 763,
  767
  and electricity **6**:726
  and electromagnetic radiation
  6:739
  as leptons **6**:769, 770
  quantum number **6**:767–8
  spin **6**:768; **10**:1315–16; **14**:1882
  subatomic see atomic structure
electron volts **12**:1648
electroweak theory **6**:771, 773
elementary particles **6**:767–73;
  10:1362
  accelerated see particle accelerators
  antiparticles see antimatter, antiparticles
  baryons **6**:770, 772
  electrons
    quantum number **6**:767–8
    spin **6**:768; **10**:1315–16; **14**:1882
    see also atomic structure,
    electrons
  fermions **6**:770; **14**:1882
  and forces **6**:767, 770–3
  gauge **6**:770–3
  hadrons **6**:770, 773
  leaked by black holes **2**:270
  leptons **6**:769–70
  mesons **6**:770, 772
  motion observed see bubble and
  cloud chambers

elementary particles (*cont.*)
  spin (intrinsic angular momentum)
    6:768
  and unified field theories **6**:773
  see also bosons; cosmic rays; neutrons; photons; protons; quarks
energy breakeven **13**:1763
energy, mass, and weight **6:786–9**
  Einstein's mass–energy equation
    2:150, 179, 248; **6**:789; **14**:1953;
    17:2415
  energy **6**:786–8; **12**:1726
    binding **2:248**; **7**:876; **14**:*1961*
    chemical **6**:787
    conservation of **6**:786;
      12:1726–7; **17**:2414–15
    efficiency **6**:788
    electrical **6**:788
    electromagnetic **6**:788
    heat **6**:786, 787
    kinetic **5**:695; **6**:786, 787;
      10:1342; **12**:*1725*; **13**:1820;
      17:2415, *2416*
    mechanical **6**:786
    potential *see* potential energy
    sound **6**:787
    units of **6**:790
    see also entropy
  mass **5**:*695*; **6**:788, 789
  weight **6**:789
entropy **4**:463; **6**:788; **9**:1233;
    12:1727; **16**:2249; **17**:2415,
    2416
EPR paradox **14**:1884
equilibrant force **16**:2242
equilibrium, stable and unstable
    16:2243–4
Euclid **11**:1555, 1556
evaporation **18**:2569
exchange interaction **18**:2488
exponential functions **10**:1356–7

F

Faraday, Michael
  and electromagnetism **6**:726, *749*;
    8:1139; **10**:1313
  laws of electrolysis **6**:737–8
Fermat's last theorem **11**:1556
fermions **6**:770; **14**:1882
ferrimagnetism **10**:1316
ferromagnetism **10**:1314, 1315
Feynman, Richard **14**:1884
field synchronizing (field sync)
    signals **17**:2392–3
fission, nuclear **2**:248; **6**:796;
    7:876–7; **11**:1543–6; **12**:*1727*;
    13:1832
flames and ignition **7:878–9**; **13**:1745
  Bunsen burners **3:339**; **7**:878
flash point **7**:879
flow
  free molecular (Newtonian flow)
    1:38
  hypersonic **1**:38
  laminar **1**:38–9; **8**:1111; **19**:2610
  slip **1**:38
  supersonic **1**:37
  turbulent **1**:39; **8**:1111; **19**:2610
fluid dynamics *see* aerodynamics;
    hydrodynamics
fluids **10**:1359
  in equilibrium *see* hydrostatics
  Newtonian **19**:2609
  pressure in **1**:1839–40
    see also Venturi effect
  resistance in *see* viscosity
  thixotropic **19**:2609
  see also superfluids
flux density, magnetic **10**:1314–15
force(s) **11**:1520; **13**:1825; **16**:2242

equilibrant **16**:2242
fundamental **6**:767, 770–3;
    14:1880
  see also electromagnetism; gravity; strong nuclear force; weak nuclear force
  pressure and **13**:1839
  restoring **12**:1605
Foucault, Jean-Bernard-Léon
    8:1143; **12**:1665
Fourier analysis (harmonic analysis)
    19:2674
fractals **3**:430–1; **4**:*535*
fractions (numbers) **10**:1354
frequency
  natural **12**:1606; **13**:1745;
    14:1964–5
  of pendulums **12**:1605, 1606
  resonant **13**:1745; **14**:1964, 1966
  wave **6**:739; **19**:2672
frequency distributions **16**:2247–8
friction **7:933–4**; **14**:1961
  coefficient of **7**:933–4
  generating electricity **6**:725, 727,
    728
  sliding (dynamic friction) **14**:1961
Frisch, Otto **7**:876
fulcrums **9**:1231
functions, mathematical **10**:1355–6
fusion, latent energy of **4**:463
fusion, nuclear **1**:99; **2**:248; **6**:796–7;
    7:946–8; **11**:*1545*; **13**:1762–3
  inertial confinement **13**:1763
  magnetic confinement **13**:*1762*,
    1763
  in tokamaks **6**:*796*; **7**:947–8;
    13:1763
  in power plants **2**:248
  for rocket propulsion **14**:1996
  in stars and the Sun (hydrogen
    burning) **6**:764; **7**:947; **13**:1758;
    15:2114
  use of lasers in **7**:*946*, 947, 948;
    9:1214
  use of magnetohydrodynamics in
    experiments **10**:1319

G

Galilei, Galileo
  and gravity **8**:1021
  and mechanics **12**:1725
gamma rays **6**:744–5; **9**:1238;
    14:1907
  detection **6**:744–5
  from proton–antiproton interactions **2**:*151*
  from space **2**:173–4; **6**:745
    black holes **2**:268
  production **6**:744
  uses **6**:745
    food irradiation **6**:745; **7**:911
    lasers **9**:1214
  wavelength **6**:739–40, 744
gases **10**:1359, 1362
  dew point **8**:*1123*
  elasticity **5**:713
  energy distribution of molecules
    9:1203
  gas laws **4**:464; **7:960–1**; **10**:1362
  ideal **7**:960; **10**:1362
  kinetic theory of **7**:960–1; **9**:1203
  liquefaction **1**:63–4; **5**:590
  and pressure **7**:960–1; **13**:1840
  vapor density **5**:617
gauge bosons **6**:770–3
Gay-Lussac's law **7**:*960*, 961
Geiger, Hans **14**:1905
Gell-Mann, Murray **6**:770
geometry **10**:1354, 1357–8
g-forces **3**:*423*

gluons **6**:772
Goudsmit, Samuel **6**:768
gravitons **6**:773; **8**:1022
gravity **8:1020–2**; **12**:1726
  acceleration due to **6**:789; **8**:1021
  affecting light **8**:1021–2; **14**:1954
  and black holes **2**:269, 270;
    17:2443
  center of **16**:2243, 2244
  Einstein's general theory of relativity (theory of gravity) **2**:269;
    4:572, 574–5; **8**:1021, 1143;
    11:1521; **14**:1954
  gravitational lensing **14**:1954
  gravity-assisted projectiles **2**:217
  measuring **8**:1020–1
  mediated by gravitons **6**:773;
    8:1022
  Newton's law of gravitation **2**:269;
    8:1020, 1021; **11**:1520, 1521;
    12:1726
    and orbits **12**:1599
    and satellites **15**:2024–5
  the search for waves **2**:180; **8**:1022
  and the Theory of Everything
    8:1022
  and time **8**:1022; **17**:2443
  variations in **8**:1021–2
  waves **14**:1954
  zero **6**:789; **16**:*2176*
Grimaldi, Francesco **5**:641
Grossman, Marcel **14**:1954

H

hadrons **6**:770, *773*
Hahn, Otto **7**:876
harmonic analysis *see* Fourier analysis
Hawking, Stephen **2**:270
Hawking radiation **2**:270
heat
  differs from temperature **17**:2395
  a form of energy **6**:786, 787
  heat capacity **17**:2414
heat death **17**:2416
heat rays *see* infrared radiation
Heisenberg, Werner Karl **14**:1883
Heisenberg uncertainty principle
    6:770; **14**:1883; **16**:2249
hertz **6**:739
Hipparchus **10**:1355
histograms **16**:2248
Hooke's law **5**:713; **16**:2229
horsepower **13**:*1825*, 1826
Hubble constant **4**:572–3
Hubble's Law **4**:573
humidity
  measurement **8**:1123
  relative **8**:1123; **19**:2665
hydrodynamics **1**:36; **8:1109–11**
  hydrodynamic bearings **2**:231–2
  sailing and **14**:2011
hydrostatics **16**:2245

I

ice skaters, moment of inertia **8**:1143
ideal gas law **10**:1362
ignition **7**:879
impulse **9**:1203
inertia **8:1142–3**
  moment of **7**:902; **8**:1142, 1143
  rotational **8**:1030, 1142
infrared radiation **6**:740, 742; **9**:1237
  cosmic **4**:574, *575*
    and astronomy **2**:176–7; **6**:743
  detection **6**:742
infrasonic waves **15**:2134
integers **11**:1555
integration **9**:1201

interference **5**:641; **19**:2673, 2674
  constructive and destructive
    14:1934; **15**:2134
  and Newton's rings **9**:1243
  in rainbows **14**:1934
  sound waves **15**:2134; **19**:2673
International Practical Temperature
    Scale **17**:2420
ionization potential **2**:248
ions and ionization **9:1183–4**
  ionization
    chemical **9**:1183
    of gases **4**:555; **5**:655–6; **9**:1184;
      13:1762–3
    ionizing radiation **9**:*1183*, 1184
    to measure vacuums **18**:2559–60
    see also particle detectors; plasma physics
  ions
    in the atmosphere **9**:1184
    and electrolysis **6**:737; **9**:1184
    and electromagnetic fields
      9:1184
    molecular **4**:448; **10**:1344

J

Joliot, Frédéric **14**:1905
Joule, James **6**:786
joules **6**:790
Joule-Thomson Effect **1**:*64*
Julia sets **3**:431

K

Kamerlingh Onnes, Heike **14**:1947
Kelvin, Baron *see* Thomson, William
kinematics **5**:694
kinetics **9:1201–3**
  chemical reaction **4**:464; **9**:1202
  kinetic theory of gases **7**:960–1;
    9:1203
  see also momentum

L

Lavoisier, Antoine **4**:449; **6**:763, 788
leptons **6**:769–70
  tau **6**:769, 770
levers **9:1231**
lift **1**:38, 66, 70
line synchronizing (line sync) signals
    17:2392
liquids **10**:1359, 1361
  boiling point **18**:2569–70
  elasticity **5**:713
  electrical conduction **6**:728
  pressure applied to **8**:1109
  specific gravity **5**:616–17
  see also hydrodynamics; surface tension
load **13**:1825
logarithms **9:1275–6**; **10**:1357
Lorenz, Edward **3**:430
Lorenz attractor **3**:430
Lorenz transformations **14**:1952–3
Lucas-Lehmer test **11**:1556
Lyman, Theodore **2**:183

M

Mach, Ernst **8**:1143; **17**:2318
Mach numbers **1**:38; **17**:2318;
    19:2697, 2699
  cut-off **17**:2319
magnetism **10:1313–17**; **18**:2486–8
  diamagnetism **18**:2486
  Earth's **10**:1316–17; **13**:1777

of rocks in the past (paleomagnetism) 7:990, *991*, 992–3;
10:1317; **13**:1777
and the solar wind **14**:*1900*
and electron spin **10**:1315–16
ferromagnetism **10**:1314, 1315;
18:2486–8
hysteresis loops **10**:1314–15
magnetic circuits **10**:1313
paramagnetism **18**:2486
permanent magnets **10**:1313–14;
12:1727
magnetohydrodynamics (MHD)
10:**1318–19**
magnetomotive force (mmf) **6**:748;
7:971; **14**:1961; **18**:2477
Mandelbrot, Benoit **3**:430, 431
Mandelbrot sets **3**:*430*, 431
mass *see* energy, mass, and weight
mass defect **2**:248
mass–energy equation **2**:150, 179,
248; **7**:876; **14**:1953; **17**:2415
and nuclear mass **2**:248; **7**:876
mass number **14**:1906
mass ratio **14**:1991
mathematics **10**:**1354–8**
see also chaos theory; logarithms;
sine waves; statistics
matter
dark **4**:575–6; **8**:*1021*
law of conservation of **4**:449; **6**:788
properties of **10**:1359–62
wavelike properties **14**:1882;
19:2674
see also gases; liquids; plasma
physics; solids; superfluids
Maxwell, James Clerk **6**:739, 748;
9:1203, 1236
Maxwell–Boltzmann distribution
9:1203; **18**:2569
mean (average) **16**:2246
mechanical advantage **9**:1231
mechanics
dynamics **5**:**694–5**
classical **5**:694; **12**:1725–6
kinematics **5**:694
quantum *see* quantum theory,
quantum mechanics
static **5**:694; **16**:**2242–5**
statistical **4**:463; **12**:1728; **16**:2249;
17:2416
median **16**:2248
Meitner, Lise **7**:876
Mersenne numbers **11**:1556
mesons **6**:770, 772
mu *see* muons
Michelson, A. A. **9**:1240; **14**:1950
Minkowski universe **14**:1954
Möbius bands **10**:1358
mode **16**:2248
moments **16**:2243, *2244*
momentum **5**:694–5
angular **9**:1201
and torque **8**:1030
conservation of **12**:1726
linear **12**:1726
changes in **9**:1201
Morley, E.W. **9**:1240; **14**:1950
motion
circular and periodic **15**:*2081*
Newton's laws of *see* Newton,
Isaac, and Newton's laws
rotary **5**:695
M-theory **8**:1022; **14**:1954
muons **6**:769, 770; **14**:1952
music, scales **11**:**1507–9**

N

Navier, C.L.M.H. **1**:36
Navier-Stokes equations **1**:36
neutrinos **2**:180–1; **4**:575; **6**:769, 770
and expansion of the Universe
6:773
types, electron, muon, and tau
6:769
neutrons
albedo **14**:1899
and atomic structure **2**:*182*, 183,
185; **14**:1906
comprised of quarks **6**:770
decay **14**:1899
discovery **6**:763, 767
Newton, Isaac, and Newton's laws
11:**1520–1**
law of cooling **11**:1521
law of gravitation **2**:269; **8**:1020,
1021; **11**:1520, 1521; **12**:1726
and orbits **12**:1599
and satellites **15**:2024–5
laws of motion **5**:694; **11**:1520–1;
12:1725–6
first law **3**:422; **5**:695; **8**:1142;
11:1520; **12**:1725
second law **3**:422; **5**:695; **6**:789;
8:1144; **9**:1201; **11**:1520;
12:1725
third law **5**:695; **11**:1520;
12:1725; **14**:1991
and light **9**:1236, 1237, *1238*;
13:1853
and viscosity **19**:2610
Newtonian flow (free molecular
flow) **1**:38
nucleus, of the atom **2**:*182*, 183;
14:1905–6
numbers **9**:1275; **10**:1354–5
composite **11**:1555
Mersenne **11**:1556
number theory **11**:**1555–6**
perfect **11**:1555–6
prime **11**:*1555*
systems **10**:*1358*
number theory **11**:**1555–6**
nutcrackers, as levers **9**:1231

O

orbits **12**:**1599–1600**

P

pair production **2**:151; **6**:744
parallelogram law **16**:2242, 2244
paramagnetism **18**:2486
partial pressure, Dalton's law of **7**:961
particle accelerators **2**:*150*, 151;
3:*333*; **6**:769; **12**:**1647–50**;
13:1763; **17**:*2311*
circular
cyclotrons **12**:1649
synchrocyclotrons **12**:1649–50
synchrotrons **2**:261, 262;
12:1650
linear **6**:*765*; **12**:*1647*, 1648–9,
1726
for nuclear waste disposal
11:1550
Superconducting Super Collider
(SSC), siting **7**:986
uses **12**:1648
vacuums in **18**:2560
particle detectors **12**:**1651–4**
Cerenkov counters **12**:1654
drift chambers **12**:1654
Geiger–Müller tubes **6**:744; **7**:*970*;
12:1653
multiwire proportional chambers
(MPCs) **12**:1653
nuclear emulsions **6**:744; **12**:1652
scintillation counters **12**:*1653*,
1654, 1718
spark chambers **12**:1652–3
particles, elementary *see* elementary
particles
Pascal, Blaise **8**:1100
pascals **2**:222; **13**:1839
Pascal's Law **16**:2245
Pauli, Wolfgang **14**:1882
Pauli exclusion principle **14**:1882
pendulums **12**:**1664–5**; **14**:*1965*
compound **12**:1664
Foucault **8**:1030; **12**:1665
gridiron **12**:*1665*
and metronomes **10**:1408; **12**:1664
spherical **12**:1664
temperature-compensating
12:1664
torsion **12**:1665
use
in clocks **4**:*482*, 483–4; **12**:1664,
1665; **17**:2442
in oscillators **12**:1605
in seismographs **12**:1664–5;
15:2046–7
period **12**:1605; **19**:2672
permittivity **14**:1961
photons (quanta) **2**:151, 183;
6:743–4; **9**:1237, 1241; **12**:1728;
14:1880
antiparticles **6**:769
and electromagnetic interactions
6:770–1
energy **6**:788; **9**:1209; **14**:1880
interactions with matter
9:1209–10, 1241–2; **14**:1881
and photoemissive cells
12:1704–5
for laser and maser action **9**:1210
spontaneous and stimulated emissions **9**:1210
X-ray **4**:461–2, 551; **19**:2721, 2724
physics **12**:**1725–8**
astrophysics **2**:178–81
biophysics **2**:261–2
condensed-matter **4**:550–3
geophysics **7**:991–5
plasma *see* plasma physics
solid-state **4**:550
see also quantum theory
pions **12**:1652
pitch (sound) **1**:*65*, 70, 71; **15**:2132,
2134
of a string **16**:2283
unison **12**:1601
Planck, Max **2**:183; **9**:1237; **14**:1880
Planck's constant **6**:768; **9**:1202,
1209; **12**:1728; **14**:1880
plasma physics **5**:656; **10**:1362;
13:**1762–3**
and nuclear fusion **7**:946–7;
10:1319
in the Sun **10**:*1361*; **13**:1762
plasma temperature measurement
9:*1212*
Podolsky, Boris **14**:1884
Poincaré, Henri **3**:430; **14**:1950
poise, the **19**:2611
Poiseuille, Jean-Leonard-Marie
19:2610–11
positrons **2**:150; **6**:744, 769
emission **2**:151
potential energy **5**:695; **6**:786;
13:1820
electrostatic **6**:787, 788
gravitational **6**:787; **12**:*1725*;
13:1820; **17**:2415, *2416*
power **5**:695; **12**:1726; **13**:**1825–6**
electrical **6**:728–9; **13**:1826
measurement **10**:1403
powers, mathematical **9**:1275
pressure **13**:**1839–40**
air locks and **1**:85
atmospheric **1**:63; **10**:*1398*, 1399;
13:1840; **16**:2245; **18**:2558
measurement **2**:222–4; **13**:1840
autoclaves and **1**:85
dynamic **4**:521
in fluids **13**:1839–40
gases **7**:960–1; **13**:1840
and force **13**:1839
undersea diving and **2**:154;
5:666–7
probability theory **16**:2248–9
protons
and atomic structure **2**:*182*, 183,
185; **6**:767; **14**:1905–6
comprised of quarks **6**:770
discovery **6**:763, 767
proton–antiproton pairs **2**:151
Proust, Joseph **2**:182
Pythagoras
Pythagorean triplets **11**:1556
theorem **10**:1354–5; **15**:2082

Q

Quadratic equations **10**:1357
quantum chromodynamics (QCD)
6:772; **12**:1728; **14**:1884
see also quarks
quantum electrodynamics (QED)
14:1884
quantum numbers **6**:767–8
quantum theory **12**:1728; **14**:**1880–4**
Bohr model of the atom **2**:183;
14:1881–2; **16**:2193
Copenhagen interpretation
14:1883–4
electrons behaving as waves
2:183–5, *184*; **6**:767–8; **14**:1882
and light **9**:1241–2; **14**:1880;
16:2193
the photoelectric effect **9**:1241;
14:1881
Planck's constant **6**:768; **9**:1202,
1209; **12**:1728; **14**:1880
Planck's introduction of photons
(quanta) **2**:183; **14**:1880
polarized **14**:1883
wave–particle duality **14**:1881;
19:2673–4
Pauli exclusion principle **14**:1882
quantum mechanics **5**:694;
14:1882–3; **16**:2249; **17**:2416
and black holes **2**:270
and electron orbitals **4**:*442*, 461;
9:*1209*
and the EPR paradox **14**:1884
Heisenberg uncertainty principle **6**:770; **14**:1883; **16**:2249
and quantum chromodynamics
(QCD) **12**:1728; **14**:1884
and quantum electrodynamics
(QED) **14**:1884
and Schrödinger's cat **14**:1884
and wave functions of electrons
6:767–8
quarks **2**:*182*; **6**:770, 771; **14**:*1881*,
1884
charm and strange **6**:770
color charges **6**:772
quark-antiquark pairs **2**:*151*; **6**:772
top and bottom **6**:770
up and down **6**:770, 771

R

radiation
electromagnetic *see* electromagnetic radiation
ionizing **9**:*1183*, 1184
synchrotron **17**:2316

radiation (*cont.*)
thermal **17**:2421
radiation belts **14**:**1899–90**
radioactivity **14**:**1905–8**; **18**:2546
decay series **14**:1908
detection by Geiger–Müller tubes **7**:970
from igneous rocks **7**:995
and heat in the Earth's core **5**:698
modes of decay
alpha decay **14**:1906–7
beta decay **6**:765, 771; **14**:1907
electron capture **14**:1907
gamma rays emission **6**:744; **14**:1907
internal conversion **14**:1907
nuclear waste disposal **6**:796; **11**:1539, 1547–50; **18**:*2547*
radioactive fallout, protection against **7**:954
rates of decay **14**:1908
uses **14**:1908
in body scanning **2**:281; **3**:378; **14**:1917
radiocarbon dating **2**:157; **3**:393; **9**:1276; **14**:1908, 1916
radiotherapy **14**:1921
rainbow **14**:**1933–4**
redox reactions **12**:1616, 1617
redshift **2**:178; **5**:672; **14**:1954
reflection, sound waves **15**:2133
refraction, sound waves **15**:2133–4
relativity **14**:**1950–4**
general theory of (theory of gravity) **2**:269; **4**:572, 574–5; **8**:1021, 1143; **11**:1521; **14**:1954; **17**:2443
special theory of **2**:150, 179, 180; **6**:788–9; **7**:876; **14**:1950–5; **17**:2442–3
reproduction **14**:**1957–9**
resistance
in fluids *see* viscosity
magnetic **14**:1961
mechanical *see* friction
resonance **12**:1606; **14**:**1964–6**
acoustic **14**:1965
in electric circuits **12**:1606; **14**:1966
mechanical **14**:1964–5
and piezoelectric ultrasound sensors **13**:1745
tides and **17**:2439–40
reverberation time (RT) **15**:2133
Reynolds, Osborne **8**:1110–11
Reynolds numbers **8**:1111; **19**:2696–7
rigidity modulus (torsion modulus) **5**:714
roll **1**:70, 71
Röntgen, Wilhelm **10**:1367; **14**:1905; **19**:2721
Rosen, Nathan **14**:1884
rotation (mechanics) **12**:1726
and inertia **8**:1030, 1142
Rutherford, Ernest **6**:767; **11**:1525; **14**:1905

S

Salam, Abdus **6**:771
scalar quantities **5**:694, 695
Schrödinger, Erwin **2**:150, 183, 184; **4**:461; **14**:1883, 1884
Schrödinger equation **2**:183–5; **4**:462; **6**:726
Schrödinger's cat **14**:1884

Schwinger, Julian **14**:1884
scissors, as levers **9**:1231
shear modulus **5**:714
Shinichiro, Tomonaga **14**:1884
sine waves **15**:**2081–2**
siphons **15**:**2083**
and toilets **18**:2458–9
skin effect **8**:1116
Soddy, Frederick **14**:1905
solar wind
and auroras **14**:*1899*, 1900
measurement **15**:2159
solids **10**:1359–60
allotropes **10**:1360
elasticity **5**:713; **10**:1361
electrical properties **10**:1360–1
ionic **4**:443, 555–6; **9**:1163
magnetic properties **10**:1361
saturated vapor pressure **18**:2570
thermal properties **10**:1361
sonic booms **1**:37; **17**:2318–19
sorption **15**:**2129–30**
sound **15**:**2131–5**
and the atmosphere **1**:63
dispersion **5**:641
energy **6**:787
measured **11**:1530–1
frequency analysis **11**:1530
intensity **11**:1530
noise measurement **11**:**1530–2**
production and transmission **15**:2131
properties
loudness **15**:2132
timbre (tone) **3**:318; **15**:2132
see also pitch
science of *see* acoustics
speed of **1**:37–8, 63; **15**:2131–2; **17**:2318
waves **1**:26; **15**:2131, 2132–3; **19**:2672
diffraction **15**:*2133*, 2134
and the Doppler effect **5**:672; **14**:1897; **15**:2134
infrasonic **15**:2134
interference **15**:2134; **19**:2673
reflection and acoustics **15**:2133
refraction **15**:2133–4
standing waves **3**:318
ultrasonic **15**:2134–5; **18**:2528
specific gravity (relative density) **5**:616–17
speed **3**:422; **5**:694, *695*
springs **16**:**2229–30**; **17**:**2338–9**
standard deviation **16**:2247
standard model theory **6**:769
static mechanics (statics) **5**:694; **16**:**2242–5**
statistics **10**:1354; **16**:**2246–9**
statistical mechanics **4**:463; **12**:1728; **16**:2249; **17**:2416
Stokes, George **1**:36; **19**:2611
stoke, the **19**:2611
string theories **8**:1022; **14**:1954
strong nuclear force **6**:772, 773; **7**:876
subatomic particles *see* elementary particles
sundials **16**:**2301–2**; **17**:2441
superfluids **4**:550, 553; **5**:592; **7**:934; **10**:1362; **11**:1528–9
superstring theory **6**:773
surface tension **10**:*1359*, 1361–2; **17**:**2321**
detergents and **15**:*2108*
of mercury **10**:*1371*; **17**:2321
synchrotron radiation **17**:2316

T

temperature **17**:**2395–6**
critical **17**:2309; **18**:2569
effect on solids **10**:1361
ignition **7**:879
spontaneous **7**:879
inversion **17**:2419
low
absolute zero **17**:2395, 2396
and cryogenics **5**:589
neutral **17**:2419
scales **17**:2395–6, 2414
transition **4**:553; **10**:*1360*, 1362
Theory of Everything (TOE) **6**:767, 773; **8**:1022
thermodynamics **4**:463–4; **9**:1202; **12**:1727; **17**:**2413–16**
first law **6**:786; **12**:1727; **17**:2414–15
and heat capacity **17**:2414
and heat energy **17**:2413
and internal energy **17**:2413
second law **6**:788; **16**:2249; **17**:2415–16
life and **9**:1233
and statistical mechanics **17**:2416
and the Universe **17**:2416
thixotropy **19**:2609
Thomson, J. J. **2**:182; **3**:408; **6**:726, 767; **18**:2563
Thomson, William (*later* Baron Kelvin) **6**:786; **12**:1727; **17**:2395, 2414, 2419
thrust **1**:65
timbre (tone) **15**:2132
musical **3**:318
time **17**:**2441–3**
affected by gravity **8**:1022; **17**:2443
dilation **14**:1952
longitude and **9**:1215
and the special theory of relativity **17**:2442–3
Universal (UT) **17**:2442
tolerance **16**:2247
topology **10**:1358
torque **5**:695; **12**:1726
and angular momentum **8**:1030
torrs **18**:2558
torsion modulus (rigidity modulus) **5**:714
Townes, Charles **9**:1211, 1212
Triangle of Forces theorem **16**:2242
trigonometry **10**:1355–6; **15**:2082

U

Uhlenbeck, George **6**:768
ultraviolet radiation **6**:744; **9**:1237–8; **18**:2534
from space **2**:174–6
uses
fingerprinting **7**:916
food preservation **7**:908; **18**:2533
photolithography **10**:1417
stage lighting **16**:2234
to detect counterfeit banknotes **5**:584
water sterilization **19**:2666
uncertainty principle, Heisenberg **6**:770; **14**:1883; **16**:2249
unified field theories **6**:773; **14**:1880, 1954
Universe
age **4**:573

Big Bang **4**:572, 573–4; **6**:773
expanding **4**:573; **5**:672; **6**:773
missing mass in **4**:575–6
shape **4**:574–5

V

vacuum **18**:**2558–60**
applications **18**:2560
in cans **3**:381
distillation **5**:*661*, 663; **18**:2560
evaporation, of salt **14**:2016
measurement **18**:2559–60
partial **18**:2558
vacuum pumps **4**:522; **18**:2558
Van Allen belts **14**:1899–1900
vapor density **5**:617
vapor pressure **18**:**2569–70**
variance **16**:2247
vector quantities **5**:694–5; **16**:2242
and electromagnetism **6**:749
velocity **3**:422; **5**:694, *695*; **8**:1144
terminal **19**:2611
Venturi effect **18**:**2580–1**
see also Bernoulli's effect
viscosity **14**:1961; **19**:**2609–11**
coefficient of **19**:2609, 2610, 2611

W

Watt, James **13**:1826
wave functions, electron **6**:767–8
wavelength **6**:739; **19**:2672
of light **5**:641; **9**:1237
wave motion **19**:**2672–4**
diffraction **5**:641; **19**:2672–3
sound waves **15**:*2133*, 2134
and the Doppler effect **5**:672
and earthquakes **5**:707; **15**:2047–8
electromagnetic waves **6**:739–40
frequency **6**:739; **19**:2672
light waves **5**:641; **9**:1236; **14**:1880; **19**:2673–4
ocean waves **19**:2672, 2675
superposition of waves **19**:2674
velocity **19**:2672
wavelength **6**:739; **19**:2672
see also sound, waves
weak nuclear force **6**:771, 773
weight **12**:1725
weightlessness **6**:789
Weinberg, Steven **6**:771
work **5**:695; **12**:1726; **13**:1825

X

X rays **6**:744; **19**:2721
detection **6**:744
frequency **6**:739
sources **19**:2721–2
X-ray lasers **9**:1214

Y

yaw **1**:70, 71
Young, Thomas, and energy **6**:786
Young's modulus (elastic modulus) **5**:713; **15**:2131; **16**:2229

Z

Zweig, George **6**:770

Instrumentation and Analytical Technology

A

abney levels (surveying) 17:2336
absolute (Kelvin) temperature scale 17:2395, 2396, 2414
accelerator mass spectrometry (AMS) 2:157
accelerators see particle accelerators
accelerometers 2:208; 8:1144, 1145; 10:1420; 18:2476
accessibility aids 1:19–22
activation analysis 14:1907
neutron 2:158; 12:1659
alcohol, measured in the blood 5:684, 685–6; 7:918
altimetry 1:68; 2:178; 17:2337
ammeters 10:1402
anemometers 1:63, 130; 19:2699
archaeological technologies 2:156–60; 10:1386
armillary sundials 16:2301, 2302
asdic 15:2126, 2127
astrodomes 15:2063
astrolabes 15:2062
atomic absorption 2:157
audiometers 8:1041
autopsies (postmortems) 12:1658
reports 7:919
autoradiograms 7:973; 11:1477
AVIRISs (airborne visible/infrared imaging spectrometers) 17:2336

B

back staffs 15:2062
balances 2:214–15
see also weigh stations
ballistics 2:216–17
forensic 2:216; 7:916–17
balloons, scientific 2:220
barographs, aneroid 2:224
barometers 1:63; 2:222–4; 10:1372; 13:1840
Biological Integrated Detection System (BIDS) 4:441
biosensors 14:1988; 19:2606
blind, the, aids for see accessibility aids
blood, groups, typing 2:271–2, 273
blood-alcohol concentration (BAC) 5:685; 7:918
body scanners 2:278–82
BEAM 2:280; 3:312
CAT (CT) scans 2:278–9, 280; 14:1919; 19:2723
MRI 2:282; 3:312; 4:448; 5:718; 11:1540, 1541; 12:1657; 14:1966
positron emission tomography (PET) 2:151, 281; 3:312
radionuclide (scintigraphy) 2:281; 14:1917
thermographic 2:281, 282; 6:743; 17:2422
ultrasound see ultrasonics
xerography 2:281
bolometers 16:2198
Bourdon gauges 13:1840, 1842
Brabazon, J. T. C. Moore 1:33
Braille 1:19
micrometer calipers using 1:21–2
Brain Electric Activity Mapping (BEAM) 2:280; 3:312
breathalyzers 5:685–6
bubble and cloud chambers 3:333–4; 12:1652
bubble chambers 2:183; 3:333–4; 6:768; 12:1652, 1654; 17:2313

cloud chambers 2:151; 3:333
bullets, and forensic ballistics 2:216; 7:916

C

calorimeters, bomb 6:787
calorimetry 4:462–3
cameras, thermal-imaging (thermographs) 17:2421–2
canes, mobility aids 1:21
cannabis see marijuana
carbon, isotopes, and carbon dating 2:157; 3:393; 9:1276; 14:1908, 1916
Carlberg Automatic Transit Circle 2:178
CAT scanners see Computed Axial Tomography
Celsius (centigrade) temperature scale 17:2395, 2396
centigrade (Celsius) temperature scale 17:2395, 2396
centrifuges 3:422–3
Cerenkov counters 12:1654
CERN 12:1652
and antiatoms 2:151
bubble chamber 3:333, 334
L3 detector 6:769
Large Electron–Positron Collider (LEP) 6:767
Large Hadron Collider (LHC) 6:767, 772; 12:1648
Chandra (telescope) 17:2381
chart recorders see pen recorders
chemistry
analytical 4:445–8
drug and alcohol testing 5:684–6; 16:2226
chorionic villus sampling 11:1563, 1564
chromatography 2:251; 4:446, 469–71
column 1:109; 4:469
and forensic science 7:917–18
gas chromatography and mass spectrometry (GCMS) 4:471; 5:684; 10:1343
gas or gas-liquid (GC; GLC) 4:448, 470–1; 5:684; 10:1343
for blood alcohol content 7:918
and robot senses 14:1988
gel-permeation (GPC) 4:471
ion-exchange 4:471
liquid 4:470
high-performance (HPLC) 4:471; 5:684
paper 4:470, 471
thin-layer (TLC) 4:469, 470; 12:1686
Chronocal Speaking Clock 17:2348–9
chronometers 4:484; 9:1215, 1216; 11:1511
pocket 19:2651
clepsydrae (water clocks) 4:481, 488; 17:2441–2
clocks 4:481–8; 17:2441–2
alarm 4:481, 486
atomic 4:485, 488; 17:2349, 2443
electric 4:486
mechanical 4:481–6
jewel bearings 2:233
pendulum 4:482, 483–4; 12:1664, 1665; 17:2442
pneumatic 18:2567
quartz 4:486–8; 17:2442, 2445–6
radio-controlled 4:488

sundials 16:2301–2; 17:2441
talking 17:2348–9
water 4:481, 488; 17:2441–2
see also chronometers; watches
cloud chambers see bubble and cloud chambers
colorimetry 4:447, 510–12
Compton Observatory 2:173–4
Computed Axial Tomography (CAT; CT) scans 2:278–9, 280; 14:1919; 19:2723
computer voice-stress analyzers (CVSAs) 13:1808
coring tubes 7:987, 989
corpses, and forensic science 7:919–20; 8:1083
creatine, supplements, testing for 5:685
crops, aerial photography 1:34
cryobots 7:998
cryostats 11:1446
CT scanners (CAT scanners) see Computed Axial Tomography
cyclotrons 12:1649

D

dating, archaeological 2:157–8
death, time of 7:919–20
defibrillators 1:113
dendrochronology 4:478
densitometers 16:2195
reflection 4:512
detectors see particle detectors
diatoms, in the blood 7:919
diffraction, X-ray 2:261, 262; 4:462, 551; 5:598–9, 641; 12:1689; 19:2724
disabled, the, aids for see accessibility aids; mobility aids
distance(s), measuring 17:2333–4, 2337
distillation and sublimation 5:661–4
distillation 4:445; 5:661
sublimation 5:664; 18:2570
dye 6:834
DNA (deoxyribonucleic acid), analysis in archaeology 2:158
dosimeters 11:1531
drift chambers 12:1654
Drift Tube Linear Accelerator 12:1726
drug and alcohol testing 5:684–6
alcohol 5:684, 685–6
drugs 5:684, 685; 16:2226
drugs, illegal, and forensic science 7:917–18
dynamometers 10:1403
Regnier's 13:1825

E

EEGs (electroencephalograms) 3:312; 6:756, 758
and sleep 15:2099–2100
electrocardiographs (EKGs) 6:756–7; 8:1046; 12:1666
electromagnetic force compensation 2:214
electronic distance measurement (EDM) 17:2334, 2336
electron microprobes 12:1680
electrophoresis 2:251; 7:973, 976
gel 11:1480
erythropoietin (EPO), abuse, detecting 5:684
exposure metering 3:368; 12:1705

F

Farenheit temperature scale 17:2395, 2396
FBI (Federal Bureau of Investigation), Latent Fingerprint Section 7:916
Fermilab 14:1881
antiproton source 12:1649
collider detector 6:769; 12:1651
Tevatron particle accelerator 12:1648, 1649; 13:1763
Fermi National Accelerator Laboratory see Fermilab
fingerprinting 7:915–16, 917; 16:2249
DNA (genetic fingerprinting) 7:920, 978; 16:2249; 19:2736
flow cytometry 10:1333
flowmeters 7:896–7; 18:2475, 2581
for anesthetic gases 1:132
differential pressure meters 7:896
electromagnetic 7:896–7
gas meters 10:1406
positive displacement (PD) meters 7:896; 10:1406
rotary 10:1406
turbine 7:896, 897; 10:1406
variable area (rotameters) 7:897
vortex 7:897
capacitance 7:897
full bore 7:896
flow-nozzle meters 7:896
fluxgates 1:66
forensic science 7:915–20; 8:1083; 16:2197
forensic ballistics 2:216; 7:916–17
forensic pathology 7:919–20; 12:1658–9
forensic photography 12:1716
and poisons 7:918–19; 13:1792
see also fingerprinting
freeze etching 5:592; 14:1945

G

galvanographs 13:1807
galvanometers 10:1402–3
gamma rays, and radionuclide scanning (scintigraphy) 2:281
Geiger–Müller tubes 6:744; 7:970; 12:1653
genetic fingerprinting see fingerprinting, DNA
geodimeters 10:1328
geophones 11:1571
geo-radar equipment 2:157
global positioning systems (GPSs) 7:1006–8; 11:1512
and automobiles 2:204; 6:813
for mapmaking 10:1331
for missile guidance 11:1466, 1468
Navstar 7:1006; 11:1514; 15:2026
for space navigation 11:1514
for surveying 17:2336–7
to study plate tectonics 13:1780
gravimeters 7:992; 11:1571
gravimetric analysis 4:446
gravity meters 15:2048
gyrocompasses 8:1028–9; 11:1510
gyroscopes 8:1030–1
in gyrocompasses 8:1028
in hydrofoils 8:1117
in inertial guidance systems 8:1145; 11:1513
in missiles 8:1144; 11:1466
in monorails 11:1481–2
in satellites 15:2028

gyroscopes (*cont.*)
Schlick **16**:2232
scientific **8**:1029
for stabilization of ships **8**:1030–1; **15**:2072; **16**:2231–2
in wheelchairs **11**:1470

H

hair, and forensic science **7**:916
Harrison, John **4**:484; **9**:*1215*, 1216; **19**:*2652*
helioscopes **18**:2544
helixometers **7**:917
Hubble Space Telescope (HST) **2**:176, 177; **11**:*1560*, 1561; **15**:2029, 2118, 2122–3; **17**:2381
cameras **2**:176; **15**:*2154*, 2155; **17**:*2381*
charge-coupled devices **3**:432
hit by space debris **15**:2151
pictures by **2**:*175*; **4**:*572*; **17**:*2382*
space shuttle missions to **16**:2168–9; **17**:*2381*
hydrometers **5**:616–17
hydrophones **15**:2126
hygrometers **1**:63; **8**:1123

I

image intensifiers **8**:1128–31; **17**:2379
infrared radiation **6**:740, 742
cosmic **4**:574, *575*
and astronomy **2**:176–7; **6**:743
detection **6**:742
uses **6**:742–3
aerial photography **1**:35; **2**:*159*; **5**:*707*; **6**:*741*; **7**:986
in alcohol detectors **5**:686
burglar alarms **3**:340–1; **15**:2043
in computer mice **11**:1490, 1491
fire-detection **6**:864
heating **6**:742
thermography **2**:281, *282*; **7**:*995*; **17**:*2421–2*
interferometry **2**:177; **8**:1022; **9**:1214
holographic **8**:1083
schlieren **15**:2031
Twyman–Green **12**:1727
isotherms **17**:2422

K

Kelvin (absolute) temperature scale **17**:2395, 2396, 2414

L

lie detection **13**:1807–8
linear accelerators *see* particle accelerators, linear

M

McLeod gauges **10**:1326
magnetic resonance imaging (MRI) **2**:282; **3**:312; **4**:448; **5**:718; **11**:1540, *1541*; **12**:1657; **14**:*1966*
magnetism, and dating pottery **2**:*159*
magnetometers **2**:156–7; **7**:992; **10**:1320; **11**:1571
fluxgate **10**:1320
Hall effect **10**:1320
proton **7**:992; **10**:1320
magnifying mechanisms **13**:1843

manometers **10**:1326; **13**:1840; **16**:2211
sphygmomanometers **10**:1326; **16**:2211
marijuana (cannabis), identification **7**:917–18
Mars Orbiting Laser Altimeter (MOLA) **12**:1707
mass spectrometry **4**:*445*, 448; **9**:1184; **10**:1342–4
accelerator (AMS) **2**:157
gas chromatography and mass spectrometry (GCMS) **4**:471; **5**:684; **10**:1343
ICP-MS (inductively coupled plasma-mass spectrometry) **7**:982
ion-trap **4**:441
and nuclear mass **2**:248
uses **10**:1344
for isotope identification **10**:1344
to study rocks **12**:1680
medicine, forensic **7**:919
metal detectors **10**:1385–6
meters
electrical **10**:1402–3
electricity **10**:1404–5; **19**:*2704*, 2705
gas **10**:1406
parking **10**:1407
metronomes **10**:1408; **12**:1664
microanalyzers, electron probe **10**:1434
microarrays, DNA **11**:1480
microbalances **2**:214, 215
micrometers **10**:1421–2; **18**:2582
microprobes, electron **12**:1680
microscopes
acoustic **15**:*2135*; **18**:*2529*
scanning laser acoustic microscopy (SLAM) **15**:2135
atomic-force (AFMs) **4**:552; **6**:839; **10**:1417
binocular
for operations **12**:*1589*, 1590
for picture restoration **13**:*1743*
cutting sections for *see* microtomes
electron **2**:262; **10**:1430–2
cutting sections for **11**:1445, 1446
and freeze-etching **14**:*1945*
scanning electron microscopes **10**:1431–2; **12**:*1655*, *1715*
scanning-probe (SPMs) **10**:1417, 1419, 1420
scanning transmission electron microscopes (STEMs) **10**:1432
scanning tunneling microscopes (STMs) **4**:551–2, *553*; **10**:1417
transmission electron microscopes **10**:1431; **12**:*1659*
for examining rocks **7**:987
for micromachines and nanotechnology **10**:1416, 1417, *1419*
optical (compound microscopes) **2**:261; **10**:1433–5; **12**:*1715*
comparison microscopes **7**:917
cutting sections for **11**:1445, 1446
dark-field microscopy **10**:*1434*, 1435
fluorescence microscopy **10**:*1433*, 1435
interference microscopy **10**:1435
phase-contrast microscopy **10**:1435
polarizing microscopy **10**:1435; **12**:1680
slit lamp **12**:1589
stereoscopic microscopy

10:1434–5
surgical **10**:1437, 1440; **12**:*1589*, 1590
vernier gauges on **18**:*2582*
photography through *see* photomicrography
scanning laser acoustic (SLAMs) **3**:427
microtomes **11**:1445–6; **12**:*1656*
molecular biology **11**:1477–80
monochromators **16**:2198
Mount Palomar Sky Survey **17**:2380
MRI *see* magnetic resonance imaging
multiwire proportional chambers (MPCs) **12**:1653

N

narcotics, testing for **5**:684
neutron activation analysis **2**:158; **12**:1659
Next Generation Space Telescope (NGST) **2**:177; **17**:2382
noise measurement **11**:1530–1
nuclear emulsions **6**:744; **12**:1652
nuclear magnetic resonance (NMR) **4**:448; **5**:718; **11**:1540–1; **16**:*2195*

O

odometers **2**:245; **16**:2209–10
odontology, forensic **7**:919
ophthalmoloscopes **12**:1591
optometry **12**:1596–8
orifice plates **7**:896
oscilloscopes **12**:1607–8; **19**:*2617*
cathode-ray tubes **3**:409; **12**:1607

P

paints, and forensic science **7**:918
pantographs **15**:2066
particle accelerators **2**:*150*, 151; **3**:333; **6**:769; **12**:*1647–50*; **13**:*1763*; **17**:*2311*
circular
cyclotrons **12**:1649
synchrocyclotrons **12**:1649–50
synchrotrons **2**:261, 262; **12**:1650
linear **6**:765; **12**:*1647*, 1648–9, *1726*
for nuclear waste disposal **11**:1550
Superconducting Super Collider (SSC), siting **7**:986
uses **12**:1648
vacuums in **18**:2560
particle detectors **12**:1651–4
Cerenkov counters **12**:1654
drift chambers **12**:1654
Geiger–Müller tubes **6**:744; **7**:*970*; **12**:1653
multiwire proportional chambers (MPCs) **12**:1653
nuclear emulsions **6**:744; **12**:1652
scintillation counters **12**:*1653*, 1654, 1718
spark chambers **12**:1652–3
see also bubble and cloud chambers
pathology, forensic **7**:919–20
PCR (polymerase chain reaction) **7**:*974*
PD (positive displacement) meters **7**:896
pen recorders **12**:**1666**
PET *see* positron-emission tomography

pH
pH meters **12**:1692–3
titration and **4**:446
photoelastic analysis **9**:*1237*; **13**:1796
photoengraving **9**:1166; **11**:1517
photogrammetry **10**:1329; **12**:1706–7; **17**:2334
photomicrography **12**:1715–16
photomultiplier tubes (PMTs) **6**:745; **12**:1717–18
poisons **16**:2197
and forensic science **7**:918–19
polarimeters **13**:1793, 1796
polygraphs **13**:1807–8
polymerase chain reaction (PCR) **7**:*974*
positron-emission tomography (PET) **2**:151, 281; **3**:312
potentiometers **8**:1071; **13**:1821–2; **18**:2474
pottery, dating **2**:*159*
pressure, measurement *see* barometers; manometers; pressure gauges
pressure gauges **13**:1842–3
vacuum **18**:2559–60
see also barometers; manometers
propellers, propeller anemometers **1**:130
proton-induced X-ray emission (PIXE) **2**:158
psychrometers **8**:1123
pusher centrifuges **3**:423
pycnometers **5**:617

Q

quadrants **15**:2062

R

radar **14**:1893–8
side-looking airborne radar (SLAR) pictures **1**:35; **7**:990
to map planets **12**:1707
use in archaeology **2**:156, 157
use in seismology **7**:994–5
radioactive in-situ hybridization **11**:*1480*
radiocarbon dating **2**:157; **3**:393; **9**:1276; **14**:1908, 1916
radio-frequency analyzers **10**:1343
radiography **19**:2722–3
see also X-ray imaging
radioisotopic dating **14**:1916
carbon dating **2**:157; **3**:393; **9**:1276; **14**:1908, 1916
of rocks **7**:995; **14**:1916
radiology **14**:1917–19
see also body scanners; X-ray imaging, of the body
radionuclide scanning *see* scintigraphy
radiosondes **10**:*1396*, 1399
Rankine temperature scale **17**:*2395*, 2396
recorders, pen **12**:**1666**
remote sensing **7**:986
resonant mass detectors **8**:1022
rifling, and forensic ballistics **7**:916
rocks, analysis **7**:987
rotameters **7**:*896*, 897; **18**:2581

S

saccharimeters **13**:1793
Saccharomyces cerevisiae **2**:236
scales *see* balances
scanners, body *see* body scanners

scintigraphy (radionuclide scanning) 2:281; 14:1917
scintillation counters 12:*1653*, 1654, 1718
scintillators 6:745
search units, metal-detector 10:1385–6
seismology, seismographs 5:708; 12:1664–5; 15:2046–7
seismometers 11:1571
semimicrobalances 2:214
separators (centrifuges) 3:423
serology, forensic 7:919
sextants 11:1511, *1513*; 15:2062–3
on periscopes 12:1675
side-looking airborne radar (SLAR) 1:35
skulls
identifying people from 7:920
reconstruction of faces from 7:*915, 916*
SLAM (scanning laser acoustic microscopy) 15:2135
SOHO (Solar and Heliospheric Observatory, space probe) 15:2046, 2119, *2158, 2159*; 17:2381–2
solvent extraction 4:446
sonar 14:1894; 15:*2126–8*, 2135
use
in archaeology 2:157
by fishing vessels 7:872
guiding torpedoes 1:27
for marine salvage 15:2022
to detect submarines 8:1070; 15:*2127*, 2128
sound
and mobility aids 1:21
for underground detection 2:157
see also ultrasonics
Space Infrared Telescope Facility (SIRTF) 2:177
spark chambers 12:1652–3, *1654*
spectrometry 4:447; 16:2194
airborne visible/infrared imaging spectrometers (AVIRISs) 17:2336
atomic emission 2:158; 4:447
direct spectrometers 16:2195–6
Fourier spectrometers 16:2199
Gamma-Ray Spectrometer (GRS) 15:2160
inductively coupled plasma emission (ICPS) 2:158
infrared 4:448; 16:2199
MRI *see* magnetic resonance imaging
NMR *see* nuclear magnetic resonance
Stark-modulated spectrometers 16:2199
use in archaeology 2:157, 158
wavelength spectrometers 16:2194
X-ray fluorescence (XRF) 2:158; 4:447; 12:1680; 16:2196–7, *2199*; 19:2724
see also mass spectrometry; spectroscopy
spectrophotometry 4:512; 6:743; 16:2197, 2198–9
spectroscopy 16:*2193–9*
absorption 16:2194, 2198
infrared 12:1680
astronomical 2:178; 16:2197–8
atomic 2:183
and electron orbitals 4:461; 16:*2193*, 2197, 2198
emission 2:158; 16:2194
imaging 17:2336
laser-induced breakdown spectroscopy 4:441
mass *see* mass spectrometry

microwave 16:2199
molecular 4:462; 16:2199
near-infrared (NIR) 16:2249
Raman 16:2199
spectrochemical analysis 16:2194–7
spectrographs and spectrograms 16:2195–6
spectrophotometry 4:512; 6:743; 16:2197, 2198–9
use in archaeology 2:158
X-ray fluorescence (XRF) 2:158; 4:447; 12:1680; 16:2196–7, *2199*; 19:2724
see also spectrometry
speech disabilities, aids for 1:22
speedometers and tachographs 16:2209–10; 18:2508
tachometers 2:203; 16:*2209*, 2210; 18:2508
"standing-wave technique," seismic 2:157
Stereotoners 1:20
Stratospheric Observatory for Far Infrared Astronomy (SOFIA) 2:177
stress analysis (on materials)
holographic interferometry 8:1083
photoelastic 9:*1237*; 13:1796
sublimation *see* distillation and sublimation
sundials 16:2301–2; 17:2441
Superconducting Super Collider (SSC), siting 7:986
surveying 17:2333–7
aerial surveys 1:35; 11:*1571*; 17:2336
mapmaking 10:1329, *1330*
angular measurement 17:2336
cadastral 17:2333
engineering surveys 17:2333
geodetic and plane 17:2333
gravimetric 11:1571
ground surveys, mapmaking 10:1328–9
hydrographic 17:2333; 18:2531
laser reflectors 14:1944
linear measurement 17:2336
magnetometric 11:1571
other planets 12:1707; 17:2337
satellite 11:1571; 17:2337, 2422
seismic 7:*992*, 993–4; 11:1570–1
topographic 17:2333
using the global positioning system 17:2336–7
using lasers 9:1214
synchrocyclotrons 12:1649–50
synchrotrons 2:261, 262; 12:1650

T

tachometers *see* speedometers and tachographs
talking clocks 17:*2348–9*
taximeters 17:*2355*
telemeters, self-reducing 17:*2336*
telescopes
astronomical 17:*2377*
mirrors 11:1464
polarimeters attached to 13:1793
optical 11:1561; 17:*2376–80*
Galilean 17:*2377*, 2379
magnification 17:2376–7
mercury mirrors 11:1464; 17:2380
observatories 11:1560–1
reflector telescopes 11:1561–2; 17:*2376*, 2378–9
refractor telescopes 11:1561;

17:2377–8
Schmidt (wide-field) telescopes and cameras 11:1562; 17:2379–80
spectrographs attached to 16:2195
radio 11:1562; 14:1909
amplifiers 14:1911
antennas 14:1909–10
output devices 14:1911
Very Large Arrays (VLAS) 14:*1909*, 1910–11
space 15:2029; 17:2381–2
hydrostatic bearings 2:232
infrared 2:177; 17:2382
Next Generation Space Telescope (NGST) 2:177; 17:2382
observatories 11:1561
ultraviolet 2:175–6
see also Hubble Space Telescope; *SOHO*
tellurometers 10:1328; 14:1898
temperature, measurement *see* thermocouples; thermometry
Tevatron particle accelerator 12:1648, *1649*; 13:1763
theodolites 8:1031; 17:*2335*, 2336, *2337*
electronic 2:157; 17:2336
thermocouples 1:65, 127; 13:1783; 17:*2395, 2417, 2418, 2419*, 2420
in engines 17:2423
thermograms and thermography 17:*2421–2*
airscan thermographs 1:35
of the body 2:281, *282*; 6:743; 17:2422
thermoluminescent dating 2:157–8; 7:995
thermometry 1:63; 17:2395, **2423–4**
analog-display 1:127
clinical thermometers 17:2423–4
Galileo 5:*616*; 17:2423
gas thermometers 17:2395, 2424
LCD thermometers 9:*1259*
meteorological thermometers 17:2424
resistance thermometers 13:1783; 17:2424
Six's thermometers 17:2424
thermoscopes 17:2423
time-depth indicators (TDIs) 10.*1332*
timing devices 17:**2444–6**
central-heating 8:1058; 17:*2445*
in dishwashers 5:660
titration 4:446–7
tomography
positron-emission (PET) 2:151, 281; 3:312
seismic 15:2046
see also Computed Axial Tomography
tourbillons 19:2653
toxicology 16:2197
forensic 7:918–19; 13:1792
traffic, monitoring 14:1984–5
tree rings, study of 4:478
trees, dating 2:160
tunnels, wind *see* wind tunnels

U

ultracentrifuges 3:423
ultramicrotomes 11:1445, 1446
ultrasonics
uses
body scans 2:279–80, *282*; 12:1657; 18:2531
brain exploration 18:2532

dentistry 5:622
scans during pregnancy 11:*1564*; 18:2531, *2586*
security systems 3:340; 15:2043
therapy 18:2532, *2550*
urine, tests 5:*684, 685*

V

venturi meters 7:896
vernier scales (vernier gauges) 18:2582
viscometers 19:2611
VO₂Max machines 16:*2225*
voice-stress analysis 13:1808
voltmeters 10:1402, 1403
vortex shedding 7:897

W

watches
electronic 19:**2649–50**
LCD displays 5:646; 19:*2649*, 2650
LED displays 19:2650
radio-controlled 19:2650
tuning-fork watches 19:2649–50
TV watches 19:2650
mechanical 4:483; 19:*2651–3*
automatic 19:2653
jewel bearings 2:233; 19:2653
see also clocks
watt meters 10:1403
weigh stations 19:2682
weighting circuits, noise-measurement 11:1531
well logging 7:991
Wild photogrammetric instruments 10:1329
wind speed, measurement 1:63, 130
wind tunnels 1:*37, 38*; 19:**2696–9**
to test air flow over trucks 18:*2506*
to test bridges 3:327
to test sails and rigging 14:2012
World Weather Watch 1:35
Wyatt, John 19:2682

X

xerography, body scans using 2:281
X-ray fluorescence (XRF) 2:158; 4:447; 12:1680; 16:2196–7, *2199*; 19:2724
X-ray imaging 19:**2721–4**
baggage 1:89; 19:2724
of the body 12:1657; 14:1917; 19:*2721*, 2722–3, *2724*
of animals 18:2584
dental 5:619
fractures 3:*300*
see also Computed Axial Tomography
of bombs 3:295
of fake statues and artwork 5:584
fluoroscopy 8:1052; 19:2723–4
use in archaeology 2:158
xerography 2:281
X-ray astronomy 19:2724
and black holes 2:268, *270*; 19:2724
and the Chandra telescope 17:2381
and stars 2:174; 19:2724
X-ray crystallography, X-ray diffraction 2:261, 262; 4:462, 551; 5:598–9, 641; 12:1689; 19:2724
see also spectroscopy, X-ray fluorescence
XRF *see* X-ray fluorescence

Light, Optics, and Photography

A

Abbe, Ernst **10**:1430, 1433, 1434
Advanced Camera for Surveys (ACS)
    15:*2155*; **17**:*2382*
aerial photography **1**:33–5
    and archaeology **2**:156, *159*
    and geology **7**:990
    infrared **1**:35; **2**:*159*; **5**:707; **6**:*741*;
        7:986
    for maps and plans **10**:1329, *1330*;
        12:1706–7
    oblique and vertical **1**:34
    rocket camera **3**:369
    for surveying **17**:2334
afterglow **12**:1607
Alexander of Aphrodisias **14**:1933
Alexander's dark band **14**:1933, 1934
angstroms **6**:739
aperture size, camera **3**:363
Archer, Frederick Scott **12**:1708
archiving, holographic **8**:1083
Argand burners **9**:1247
astigmatism **6**:832

B

backscatter **18**:*2542*, 2543
Balmer series **16**:*2197*
Bartholinus, Erasmus **13**:1794
binoculars **2**:*249–50*
    binocular microscopes
        for operations **12**:*1589*, 1590
        for picture resoration **13**:*1743*
    binocular periscopes **12**:1674–5
    prisms **2**:249, 250; **13**:1853
birefringence **9**:1239; **13**:1794
black-level adjustment **17**:2388
blooming **9**:1230
blue-screen effects **16**:2187–8;
    17:2388–90
Brewster angle **13**:1796
brighteners, optical **5**:632, 693;
    10:1302

C

cadmium sulfide (CdS) cells **3**:368
California Extremely Large
    Telescope (CELT) **17**:2379
calotype process **12**:1708
camcorders **18**:2592
cameras **3**:363–9
    3-D **9**:1230
    35mm **3**:364–5, 368–9
    Advanced Photo System (APS)
        3:*367*
    aerial **1**:33, 34–5
    autofocus **3**:364
    automatic and semiautomatic
        3:369
    digital **1**:35; **3**:370–2
        combined with instant pictures
            9:1159
        and desktop publishing **5**:628
        for photomicrography **12**:1716
    and exposure control **3**:368, 369
    high-speed **8**:1078–9
    infrared **8**:*1128*
        with image intensifiers **8**:*1129*,
            1131
    instant-picture **9**:*1157–9*
    lenses **3**:363, 364, 367–9; **9**:1228
        of movie cameras **11**:1495
    microfilmers **10**:1415
    movie **11**:*1493–6*, 1498
        for optical soundtracks

15:2146–7
    multiband **1**:35
    reflex **3**:366–7
        single-lens (SLR) **3**:*366*, 367,
            368–9
        viewfinder displays **8**:1039
        twin-lens **3**:366–7
    rocket **3**:369
    roll-film **3**:365–6
    rotating-mirror **8**:*1078*
    Schmidt **17**:2379–80
    in sewers **19**:2648
    shutters **3**:363; **15**:*2074–5*
        speed **2**:205; **3**:363; **15**:*2075*;
            17:*2446*
        and Timetrack **16**:2190
    space, free-floating **15**:*2154*, 2155
    speed cameras **14**:1977, 1985
    stereo **16**:*2263*
    traffic-monitoring **14**:1977
    underwater **18**:*2541*, 2542, 2543
    video *see* video cameras
    video-bug **6**:761
    see also movie cameras; photo-
        graphy; television cameras
candlepower **12**:1705
cascade tubes **8**:1129
Cascariolo, Vincenzo **10**:1301
Cassegrain reflector **17**:2378
cataracts **6**:806, 832
cathodoluminescence **10**:1302
CCDs *see* charge-coupled devices
channel plate intensifiers **8**:1130–1
charge-coupled devices (CCDs)
    3:432
    and astrophysics **2**:178; **3**:432;
        15:*2054*
    in cameras **3**:*370*, 371, 432; **6**:761;
        8:1079
        television **17**:2385, 2386
        video **3**:432; **18**:*2590*, 2591–2
    in image intensifiers **8**:1131
    in optical scanners **12**:1592, 1593
    for space photography **15**:2155
chemiluminescence **10**:1302
chromakey **18**:2495
    see also blue-screen effects
chromatic aberration **9**:1229;
    11:1561; **17**:2377
CinemaScope **11**:1494
cinématographes **13**:1854
Cinerama film **11**:*1494*
CMOS (complementary metal oxide-
    silicon) technology **8**:1079;
    18:2590, 2592
coherent radiation **9**:1210–11, *1239*
collodion **12**:1708
color **4**:510
    monochromatic light **9**:1237
    subtractive and additive **4**:*511, 512*
colorimetry **4**:447, 510–12
color-reversal effects **17**:2388
color-reversal intermediaries (CRIs)
    11:1500
coma effect **9**:1229
CompactFlash **3**:370
Compton effect **9**:1241
contact image sensor (CIS) system
    12:1592
contact lenses **4**:560–3
    see also optometry

D

depth of field **3**:363; **9**:1227
Descartes, René **14**:1933
diamonds, identity patterns **9**:1243
diaphragm, camera **3**:*364*

dichroism **13**:1794–5
dichromate-gelatin (DCG) systems
    8:1082
diffraction **5**:641; **9**:1238
diffraction gratings **5**:641
Digistar digital projectors **13**:1756
discharge tubes **5**:655–8; **9**:1184
    in greenhouses **8**:1088–9
    krypton **11**:1529
    mercury vapor **5**:658; **14**:1980;
        18:2533
    neon **4**:555; **5**:*656*, 657; **17**:2392
    sodium, street lights **1**:101; **5**:658;
        14:1980
    xenon **8**:1077–8; **11**:1529; **16**:2285
DX coding **3**:369
dynodes **8**:1129

E

Eagle (night-vision device) **8**:*1131*
Eddystone lighthouse **9**:1248
Edison, Thomas
    and the incandescent lamp **3**:394;
        9:1244
    and movie film **11**:1494
Einstein, Albert
    and light **9**:1237, 1241
        stimulated emissions of photons
            9:1210; **12**:1704
electroluminescence **10**:1302
electrophotography **12**:1701
electrostatic focusing **8**:1129–30
endoscopes **6**:783–5, 856;
    17:2330–1, 2332
erbium-doped fiber amplifiers
    (EDFAs) **6**:856
ether (hypothetical medium) **9**:1236;
    14:1950; **19**:2673
exposure metering **3**:368; **12**:1705
    and space photography **15**:2154
extreme dynamic range (EDR)
    8:1079
eyeglasses *see* spectacles
eyes **6**:830–2
    and color vision **4**:510
    compound **6**:832
    contact lenses **4**:560–3
    defects **6**:832
    refractive state **12**:1596–8

F

Faint Object Camera (FOC) **2**:176;
    15:*2155*; **17**:*2381*
fiber optics **6**:854–6
    optical fibers **6**:855
        and holography **8**:1082
        low-attenuation **6**:856
        types **6**:*855*, 856
        as waveguides **19**:2671
    uses **6**:856
        in cable networks **3**:354–5;
            4:539, 542; **6**:856; **17**:2356–7,
            2371
        in endoscopes **6**:783–4, 856
        in image intensifiers **8**:1129–30
        in laser surgery **6**:*856*
        in submarine (undersea) cables
            3:349; **17**:2357
fibers, optical *see* fiber optics
film, photographic *see* photographic
    films and processing
filters
    optical **6**:857–8
        absorption **6**:857
        dichroic (interference filters;

dielectric filters) **6**:857–8;
    16:*2194*
    television-camera **17**:2388
    theatrical lighting **17**:2411
flashguns **6**:730; **8**:1077–8; **15**:2075
floodlights **17**:2386, 2410
fluorescence **5**:658; **9**:1241–2;
    10:1301–2; **18**:2534
    fluorescent lamps **5**:*656*, 657–8;
        9:1245; **10**:1302
    sprays to identify people **11**:1532
f numbers *see* focal ratio
focal length **9**:1226
focal ratio (f-ratio; f numbers) **3**:363;
    9:1227
Foucault test **9**:1243; **15**:2031
f-ratio *see* focal ratio
Fraunhofer, Joseph von **16**:2193
Fraunhofer lines **16**:2193
Fresnel, Augustin **9**:1230
Fresnel spots **17**:2409

G

gelatin process **12**:1708
Gemini Multi-Object Spectrograph
    17:*2378*
gem-print method **9**:1243
glasses *see* spectacles
glass shots **16**:2186

H

Hale telescope **2**:232; **17**:2378
headlights, automobile **11**:1464
head-up displays (HUDs) **1**:68;
    8:1039–40, 1082
    in cars **6**:*813*; **8**:1040
Helmholtz, Herman von **12**:1591
Herschel Telescope **17**:*2380*
High Resolution Channel (HRC)
    15:2155
high-speed photography **8**:1077–9,
    1109; **15**:2075; **16**:2285–6
    digital **8**:1079
holography **8**:1080–3
    anticounterfeiting and forgery
        5:584
    and head-up displays **8**:1040, 1082
    laser **8**:1080, 1081, 1082, *1083*;
        9:1214
    for artificial limbs **2**:253
    recording a hologram **8**:1080,
        1081
Hood, David **9**:1247
Hooke, Robert **10**:1433
Hubble Space Telescope (HST)
    2:176, 177; **11**:*1560*, 1561;
        15:2029, 2118, 2122–3; **17**:2381
    cameras **2**:176; **15**:*2154*, 2155;
        17:2381
    charge-coupled devices **3**:432
    pictures by **2**:*175*; **4**:*572*; **17**:*2382*
    space shuttle missions to
        16:2168–9; **17**:*2381*
Huygens, Christiaan **9**:1236; **14**:1880
Hycam movie cameras **11**:*1495*
hyperstereoscopy **16**:2264

I

image intensifiers **8**:1128–31;
    17:2379
image point **11**:1463
incandescence **10**:1301
incoherent bundles **6**:856

incoherent radiation **9**:1210, 1211, *1239*
infrared radiation, uses, aerial photography **1**:35; **2**:*159*; **5**:*707*; **6**:*741*; **7**:*986*
instant-picture cameras **9**:**1157–9**
interference **5**:641; **19**:2673
  constructive and destructive **14**:*1934*; **15**:*2134*
  and Newton's rings **9**:1243
  in rainbows **14**:1934
interferometry **2**:177; **8**:1022; **9**:1214
  holographic **8**:1083
  schlieren **15**:2031
  space telescopes and **17**:2382
  for testing lenses **9**:1243
irisation **9**:*1240*
I-Zone cameras **9**:1159

K

Kirchhoff, G. R. **9**:1159
Kitson, Arthur **9**:1247
Köler illumination **12**:1716

L

lamps (lights)
  arc **9**:1247; **17**:2342
  cutoff **14**:*1980*
  filament **9**:1210
  fluorescent **5**:*656*, 657–8; **9**:1245; **10**:*1302*
  infrared **6**:743
  mercury vapor **5**:658; **14**:*1980*
  metal-halide **5**:658; **10**:1302
  neon **4**:555; **5**:*656*, 657; **11**:*1529*
  sodium **5**:*655*, 658; **6**:743–4; **10**:1302
  street lights **1**:*101*; **5**:658; **6**:*858*; **14**:*1980*
  surgical **11**:1583–4
  ultraviolet *see* ultraviolet lamps
  see also discharge tubes; lightbulbs
LANBYs (large navigational buoys) **9**:*1249*
Large Zenith Telescope (LZT) **11**:1464
lasers and masers **9**:**1209–14**
  lasers **9**:1237, *1239*
    argon gas **12**:*1590*; **17**:2332
    atom **9**:1214
    dye **9**:*1210*, 1213
    excimer **9**:1213; **10**:*1418*; **12**:*1590*
    and fingerprinting **7**:*917*
    gas **9**:1212–13
    and holography *see* holography, laser
    for interferometry **9**:1214
    ion **9**:1213
    laser anemometers **19**:2699
    laser scans of skulls **7**:920
    reflectors **14**:*1944*
    ring **8**:1146
    semiconductor **9**:1213, 1214; **15**:2054
    solid-state **9**:*1209*, 1212
    used in bar-code scanners **3**:401
    used for cutting grass **8**:1019
    used in flow cytometry **10**:1333
    used for gem identification **9**:1243
    used as machine tools **9**:*1213*, 1214; **10**:*1363*
    used in mobility aids **1**:21
    used in stage lighting **16**:2234
    used for surgery **6**:785, *856*; **9**:1214
    used in surveying **9**:1214;

12:1707; **17**:2337
    used for velocity or flow determination **9**:1214
    used for welding **10**:1383–4
  masers **9**:1209
    ammonia **9**:1211–12
lenses **9**:**1225–30**
  achromatic **17**:2377
  camera *see* cameras, lenses
  contact **4**:560–3
  focal length **9**:1226
  focal ratio (*f* numbers) **9**:1227
  Fresnel **9**:1240, 1248; **14**:*1983*; **17**:*2409*
  oil immersion **10**:1434
  in refractor telescopes **11**:1561
  slide projector **13**:1855
  spectacle **9**:*1230*; **16**:2192
  types
    anamorphic **11**:*1495*; **13**:*1855*
    compound **9**:1226
    concave (negative lenses) **9**:*1225*, 1226
    convex (positive lenses) **9**:*1225–6*
    planoconcave **9**:1226
    uncorrected **9**:*1241*
    video camera **18**:2589–90
LIDAR (light detection and ranging) **13**:*1797*
Liebig, Justus von **11**:1463
light *see* light and optics
lightbulbs **9**:**1244–6**
  fluorescent **5**:*656*, 657–8; **9**:1245; **10**:1302
  General Lighting Service (GLS) **9**:1245
    manufacture **9**:1246
  tungsten–halogen lamps (quartz–iodine bulbs) **9**:1245
  see also lamps (lights)
lighthouses and lightships **9**:**1247–9**; **11**:1514
lighting
  circuits, domestic **19**:2707–8
  stage (theatrical) **16**:*2233*, 2234; **17**:2409–11
  street *see* street lighting
  television-production **17**:2386, 2387
  theatrical **16**:*2233*, 2234; **17**:2409–11
light and optics **4**:510; **9**:**1236–43**
  light **12**:1728
    affected by gravity **8**:1021–2; **14**:*1954*
    amplification **8**:1128
    and the atmosphere **1**:63
    black **16**:2234; **18**:2534
    coherent and incoherent **9**:1210–11, *1239*
    diffraction **5**:641; **9**:1238
    dispersion **5**:641
    frequency **6**:739
    interaction with matter **9**:1209–10, 1241–2; **14**:1881
    monochromatic **9**:1237
    particle nature **9**:1236, 1237; **14**:1880
    polarized *see* polarization (light)
    pollution **13**:*1803*
    quanta *see* photons
    shortest pulse achieved **9**:1243
    speed of **5**:710; **6**:739, 788; **9**:1237, 1238, 1240–1; **14**:1950
    treatment of medical conditions using **12**:1723–4
    wavelength **5**:641; **9**:1237
    wavelike nature **5**:641; **9**:1236; **14**:1880; **19**:2673–4
    wave–particle duality **14**:1881
    white **9**:1237; **13**:1853

see also interference; reflection; refraction; vision
  optics **9**:1241–2
    geometric **9**:1241
    holographic **8**:1082
    manufacture of optical components **9**:1242–3
    physical **9**:1241
    quantum **9**:1241–2
  see also color; fiber optics; lenses; prisms
lights *see* lamps
lightships **9**:1249
Lippershey, Hans **11**:1560; **17**:2380
Lockyer, Norman **16**:2194–5
lumens **9**:1244
Lumière, Auguste and Jean **13**:1854
luminance meters **12**:1705
luminescence **10**:**1301–2**
  see also fluorescence; phosphorescence
luminous flux **12**:1705

M

Maddox, R. L. **12**:1708
magic lanterns **13**:1854
magnification **9**:1227
Maiman, Theodore **9**:1211, 1212
matte paintings **16**:2187
matte shots **16**:2186–7
Maurer variable-sequence cameras **15**:2152–3
Mavica (camera) **3**:*370*, 371
Maxwell, James Clerk **6**:739; **9**:1236
Méliès, Georges **16**:2185
microfiches **10**:1415
microfilm **10**:**1415**
micrographs **12**:1715
microprisms, in cameras **3**:367
microscopes
  acoustic **15**:*2135*; **18**:*2529*
    scanning laser acoustic microscopy (SLAM) **15**:2135
  atomic-force (AFMs) **4**:552; **6**:839; **10**:1417
  binocular
    for operations **12**:*1589*, 1590
    for picture restoration **13**:*1743*
  electron **2**:262; **10**:**1430–2**
    cutting sections for **11**:1445, 1446
    and freeze-etching **14**:*1945*
    scanning electron microscopes **10**:1431–2; **12**:*1655*, *1715*
    scanning-probe (SPMs) **10**:1417, 1419, 1420
    scanning transmission electron microscopes (STEMs) **10**:1432
    scanning tunneling microscopes (STMs) **4**:551–2, *553*; **10**:1417
    for examining rocks **7**:987
    for micromachines and nanotechnology **10**:1416, 1417, *1419*
  optical (compound microscopes) **2**:261; **10**:1433–5; **12**:1715
    comparison microscopes **7**:917
    cutting sections for **11**:1445, 1446
    dark-field microscopy **10**:*1434*, 1435
    fluorescence microscopy **10**:*1433*, 1435
    interference microscopy **10**:1435
    phase-contrast microscopy **10**:1435
    polarizing microscopy **10**:1435; **12**:1680
    slit lamp **12**:1589
    stereoscopic microscopy

10:1434–5
    surgical **10**:1437, 1440; **12**:*1589*, 1590
    vernier gauges on **18**:*2582*
    photography through *see* photomicrography
    scanning laser acoustic (SLAMs) **3**:427
mirrors **11**:**1463–4**
  concave **11**:1463, 1464
  convex **11**:1463
  dielectric, "perfect" mirrors **9**:*1236*, 1243
  liquid-mercury **11**:1464; **17**:2380
  one-way **11**:1463
  parabolic **11**:1464
  spherical **17**:2379
  in telescopes **11**:1464, 1561–2; **12**:*1727*; **17**:2378
monobath process **12**:1712
movie cameras (motion picture cameras) **11**:*1493–6*, 1498; **15**:2075
  in space **15**:2152–3
movie film **11**:1494, 1498; **13**:1856–7
movie projectors **13**:1854, 1856–7
  and digital sound systems **15**:2148

N

Near Infrared Camera and Multi-Object Spectrometer (NICMOS) **17**:2381
neon tubes (neon lamps) **4**:555; **5**:*656*, 657; **11**:*1529*
Newton, Isaac, and light **9**:1236, 1237, *1238*; **14**:*1880*; **16**:2193
Newtonian reflector **17**:2378
Newton's rings **9**:1243
Nicol prisms **13**:1795
Niépce, Claude **12**:1708
Nikonos underwater cameras **18**:*2541*, 2542, 2543

O

ophthalmology **12**:**1589–90**
ophthalmoscopes **12**:1591, 1598
optical fibers *see* fiber optics
optics *see* light and optics
optometry **12**:**1596–8**
Origins program **17**:2382
Overwhelmingly Large Telescope (OWL) **17**:2379

P

Panavision film **11**:*1494*
parallax **16**:2263
periscopes **12**:**1674–5**; **16**:2290
Philips SL lamps **5**:*656*
phosphorescence **9**:1241–2; **10**:1301–2
  and oscilloscope screens **12**:1607
photocells *see* photoelectric cells and photometry
photochemistry **4**:464
photoconductors **17**:2421
photocopiers **12**:**1701–3**
photo detectors, for thermal imaging **6**:864
photoelectric cells and photometry **12**:**1704–5**
  photoelectric cells (photocells) in electric motors **6**:731
    photoconductive cells **12**:*1704*, 1705
    photoemissive cells **12**:1704–5
    and photomultiplier tubes **12**:1717–18

photoelectric cells and photometry (*cont.*)
  photovoltaic *see* photovoltaic (PV) cells
  and security systems 3:340–1; 15:2043
  for streetlamp switches 14:1980
  photometry 12:1705
  see also solar energy, solar panels
photoelectric effect 9:1241; 12:1704; 14:1881
photoemissive cells 12:1704–5
photoemissive materials 8:1128–9
photogrammetry 10:1329; 12:1706–7; 17:2334
photographic editing software 4:534
photographic films and processing 12:1708–14
  automatic processing 12:1713
  copying 12:1713–14
  false-color imagery 1:35; 2:156; 6:742
  film 8:1036
    35mm 3:364–5
    color 8:1036; 12:1710–11
    color masking 12:1711–12
    direct-positive 12:1710, 1711
    DX coding 3:369
    infrared 6:742; 12:1709
    instant-picture film 9:1158–9
    and light quanta 6:744
    manufacture 12:1714
    monochrome (black-and-white) 12:1708–10
    movie film 11:1494, 1498; 13:1856–7
    orthochromatic 12:1709
    panchromatic 12:1709; 16:2194
    for photomicrography 12:1715–16
    roll film 3:365–6
    for space photography 15:2153
  lithographic development 12:1713
  photographic paper 10:1413, 1414
  printing process 12:1712–13
    enlarging images 12:1708, 1712
  see also microfilm
photographs, for desktop publishing 5:628
photography
  filters 6:858
  flash 3:365; 6:730; 8:1077–8; 15:2075
  forensic 12:1716
  schlieren 15:2031, 2133
  trick 16:2185, 2186
  see also aerial photography; cameras; high-speed photography; photographic films and processing; space photography; underwater photography
photoluminescence 10:1302
photometry 12:1705
photomicrography 12:1715–16
  fluorescence 3:414
photomultiplier tubes (PMTs) 6:745; 12:1717–18
  in optical scanners 12:1592–3
photons (quanta) 2:151, 183; 6:743–4; 9:1237, 1241; 12:1728; 14:1880
  antiparticles 6:769
  and electromagnetic interactions 6:770–1
  energy 6:788; 9:1209; 14:1880
  interactions with matter 9:1209–10, 1241–2; 14:1881
  and photoemissive cells 12:1704–5
  for laser and maser action 9:1210
  spontaneous and stimulated emissions 9:1210

photosensors *see* photoelectric cells and photometry
photovoltaic (PV) cells 2:229; 4:552; 6:730, 792; 12:1704, 1705
  on bicycles 2:244
  in calculators 3:361
photovoltaic effect 12:1705
pin spots 16:2234
Planck, Max 2:183; 9:1237; 14:1880
Planck's constant 6:768; 9:1202, 1209; 12:1728; 14:1880
planetarium projectors 13:1755–6
polarization (light) 5:648; 9:1239; 13:1794–6; 14:1883; 19:2673
  circular 13:1796
  dichroic polarizers 13:1794–5
  elliptical 13:1796
  filters for 6:858; 18:2573
  and LCDs 5:648; 9:1258
  uses 13:1796
    microscopy 10:1435; 12:1680
    photoelastic stress analysis 9:1237; 13:1796
    polarimetry 13:1793, 1796
polycarbonate, for lenses 9:1229
Porter, Edwin S. 16:2185
posterization 12:1659
presbyopia 6:832
prisms 13:1853
  in binoculars 2:249, 250; 13:1853
  in cameras 3:367
    rotating 8:1079
  Nicol 13:1795
  in periscopes 12:1674–5
  and white light 9:1237, 1238
projection
  back 16:2188; 17:2388
  front 16:2187, 2188; 17:2387–8
  reflex (front-axial projection) 17:2388
projectors
  movie and slide 13:1854–7
    and digital sound systems 15:2148
    and stage effects 16:2234–5
  overhead 13:1855
  planetarium 13:1755–6
proximity focusing 8:1129
pumping, optical 9:1210, 1211
Pythagoras, and vision 9:1236

Q

quanta, of light *see* photons

R

radiancy, spectral 9:1237
radioluminescence 10:1302
rainbows 9:1243; 14:1933–4
rangefinders
  camera 3:364
  laser 2:249, 250
  "red eye" 3:365
redshift 2:178; 5:672; 14:1954
reflection 9:1238–9
  specular 11:1463
  total internal 6:783, 854; 9:1239
reflectors 14:1944
refraction 6:854; 9:1225, 1237, 1238–9
  and clouds 9:1240
  double 9:1239; 13:1794
  index of 6:854; 7:917; 9:1225, 1239; 13:1853
  and schlieren techniques 15:2030, 2133
  and rainbows 14:1933
  refractive state of the eye 12:1596–8

and underwater photography 18:2541
refractors, automatic 12:1598
resolution 10:1430
resolving power (RP), in photomicrography 12:1716
retinoscopy 12:1597–8
retinulae 6:832
rods and cones 6:831
röntgenoluminescence 10:1302

S

scanners, bar-code 3:401; 8:1082, 1083
scatter, light 11:1464
schlieren techniques 15:2030–1, 2133, 2134
Schmidt cameras and telescopes 11:1562; 17:2379–80
selenium cells 3:368; 12:1705
ships, lightships 9:1249
shutters, camera 3:363; 15:2074–5
  speed 2:205; 3:363; 15:2075; 17:2446
  and Timetrack 16:2190
skiaskopy (retinoscopy) 12:1597–8
slides, projection 13:1854–5
SmartMedia 3:370
Snell, Willebrord 13:1853
Snell's law 9:1225, 1239
Solar Blind Camera (SBC) 15:2155
solar cells *see* photoelectric cells and photometry
solar energy
  solar panels 4:552; 6:791, 792; 8:1058
    on satellites 15:2028, 2117
    on space probes 15:2156
    on space stations 15:2150–1
solar halos 9:1242
Space Interferometry Mission (SIM) 2:177; 17:2382
space photography 15:2152–5, 2158–9
  Hubble Space Telescope cameras 2:176; 15:2154, 2155; 17:2381
spectacles 16:2191–2
  and eye-controlled switches 11:1470
  frames 16:2191
    construction 16:2192
  lenses 9:1230; 16:2192
  sunglasses 11:1463
  to aid the deaf 9:1243
  see also optometry
spectrum
  of colors 13:1853
  solar 16:2194, 2196
spectrum theory 16:2193–4
spherical aberration 9:1227–9; 17:2379
spontaneous emission 9:1210
spotlights 16:2233, 2234; 17:2409–10
spot meters 15:2154
Sprint cameras 15:2154, 2155
stereoscopy 8:1080; 16:2263–4
  and aerial photography and surveying 1:33; 16:2264
  exaggerated (hyperstereoscopy) 16:2264
  vision 6:831; 16:2263
  see also binoculars
stimulated emission 9:1210
street lighting 5:658; 14:1977, 1980, 1985
  sodium lamps 1:101; 5:658; 6:858; 14:1980
  switches 14:1980; 17:2444
stroboscopes 8:1078; 16:2234,

2285–6; 17:2411
Subalert safety devices 18:2543
sundogs 9:1242
sunglasses 11:1463
sunlamps 5:658; 18:2533–4
Super 8 (film) 11:1494
superimposed images 17:2388
supernumerary arcs 14:1934
Swan, Joseph 9:1244

T

Talbot, William Henry Fox 12:1708
Technicolor process 11:1500
telescopes
  astronomical 17:2377
    mirrors 11:1464
    polarimeters attached to 13:1793
  optical 11:1561; 17:2376–80
    Galilean 17:2377, 2379
    magnification 17:2376–7
    mercury mirrors 11:1464; 17:2380
    observatories 11:1560–1
    reflector telescopes 11:1561–2; 17:2376, 2378–9
    refractor telescopes 11:1561; 17:2377–8
    Schmidt (wide-field) telescopes and cameras 11:1562; 17:2379–80
    spectrographs attached to 16:2195
    see also binoculars
  space 15:2029; 17:2381–2
    hydrostatic bearings 2:232
    infrared 2:177; 17:2382
    Next Generation Space Telescope (NGST) 2:177; 17:2382
    observatories 11:1561
    ultraviolet 2:175–6
    see also Hubble Space Telescope
television cameras 17:2383–5, 2386, 2387
  closed-circuit (CCTV) 3:340; 15:2042, 2044
  on roads 14:1977
  color 6:857, 858; 17:2384, 2385
  underwater, uncrewed 16:2293
  video cameras for television 18:2591
Terrestrial Planet Finder (TPF) 17:2382
theatrical lighting 16:2233, 2234; 17:2409–11
THEMIS *see* Thermal Emission Imaging System
Theoderic of Freiburg 14:1933
Thermal Emission Imaging System (THEMIS) 15:2157, 2158, 2160
TOMS 10:1440
tone-reversal effects 17:2388
traveling mattes 16:2187; 18:2495

U

ultraviolet lamps 6:744; 18:2533–4
  sunlamps 5:658; 18:2533–4
underwater photography 3:369; 18:2541–3

V

Very Large Telescope (VLT) 17:2380
video cameras 18:2589–92
  charge-coupled devices 3:432; 18:2590, 2591–2

sound recording **15**:*2149*
videomicrographics **10**:1415
vision **6**:830–1; **9**:1240
  persistence of **12**:1607
  quantifying **6**:832
  stereoscopic **6**:831
  visual acuity **12**:1596

W

wavelength, of light **5**:*641*; **9**:*1237*
webcams **18**:2592
Wheatstone, Charles **16**:2263
Wide Field Planetary Cameras **2**:176;
  15:2155; **17**:2381, *2382*

Y

Young, Thomas **9**:1236; **13**:1794
  double-slit experiment **14**:1880,
  1882; **19**:2673
yttrium–aluminum garnet (YAG)
  9:1212

Z

zone plates **9**:1230
zoptics **16**:*2186*

Manufacturing and Industry

A

abrasives, made by crystal synthesis
  17:2347
Acceptable Quality Level (AQL)
  14:1878
acetates, fibers *see* cellulose acetate;
  cellulose triacetate
aciding **16**:2237
aerospace industry **1**:41–4
affination **16**:2296–7
agriculture
  agricultural science **1**:*52–5*
  biogas from wastes **2**:259
  farm animal veterinary work
    18:2585–6
  intensive **1**:*56–7*, 58
  machinery **1**:45–51
    see also elevators, grain; irriga-
    tion techniques
  organic **1**:*58–61*; **7**:907; **19**:2680
    see also biological control
  robots used in harvesting **14**:1989
  and soil management **15**:2112–13
    see also crops; horticulture; weed
    control
air
  liquefaction **1**:64; **5**:590
  separation **5**:589–90
aircraft
  design **1**:*69–71*
  and aerodynamics **1**:39
alcohol
  for beverages *see* beer and brewing;
    spirits; winemaking
  distillation **1**:*97, 98*; **5**:661;
    16:2215–18
  production **1**:98
alkali industry **4**:450
alkylation **11**:1576, 1579
alluvial deposits and mining
  diamonds **5**:637, 638
  gold **8**:1013
aluminum
  extraction **1**:*109*, 110; **6**:738;
    10:1378
  manufacture **1**:110–11; **10**:*1388*
  pipes and tubes **13**:1751, *1752*
  welding **1**:111; **11**:1529
ammonia, manufacture **1**:25, **115**;
  3:*405*, 407; **4**:451
ammonium phosphate, production
  14:*2014*
Anderton Shearer loader **4**:*493*
annealing **4**:507; **10**:1387–8; **13**:*1786*
anodizing **17**:2323
antibiotics, manufacture **6**:*840*
Appert, Nicholas **7**:905
aquaculture (fish farming) **2**:**152–3**;
  7:874–5
  see also fishing industry
aquatint **6**:803, 805
  sugar **6**:805
argon, separation from air **5**:590
Armagnac **16**:2217
armaments, mass production **10**:1338
aromatic compounds, from petroleum **4**:453

asbestos, manufacture **6**:847
aspirin, packaging **12**:*1624*
assembly lines **6**:815; **10**:1339–40
  automobile **2**:198; **6**:815; **10**:1339,
    1341; **14**:1987
  in canning and bottling factories
    3:*382*, 385
  hand tools **13**:1789
atomizers **2**:258; **16**:2227
austenite **1**:104
autoclaves **2**:190; **3**:382; **13**:1841
automated storage/retrieval systems
  (AS/RSs) **19**:2622–3, 2624
automatic letter facers (ALFs)
  10:1323
automation, mass production
  10:1340–1, *1365*
automobile factories, conveyors
  4:564–5

B

bacon, curing **7**:905
bagging **12**:1623
baking **6**:841
ballotini **12**:1630; **14**:1977
Barbie dolls **10**:1341
basic oxygen steel (BOS) process
  9:*1188*, 1189–90
beating **2**:238
beer and brewing **1**:98; **2**:**234–7**;
  3:*406*; **6**:841
  widgets in beer cans **3**:384
bellows **4**:518
bells **2**:238–9; **12**:1668
  made into coins **3**:332
beneficiation **4**:497
benzene, industrial uses **8**:1107
Bessemer process **9**:1188
Betts electrolytic process **9**:1220
biobricks **3**:324
biodiesel **2**:259; **6**:794; **7**:963
biological control **1**:58, 61; **12**:*1677*,
  1678
  in aquaculture **2**:153
  using parasites **12**:1645
  using pheromones **12**:1691
biomass, conversion to ethanol
  7:962–3
biomass gasification **7**:959
biotechnology **2**:**263–6**
  and agriculture **1**:52; **2**:265–6
  cloned animals **1**:52; **2**:264;
    7:*978*
  DNA probes **2**:265
  engineered bacteria **1**:55; **2**:263,
    264
  for food additives **7**:914
  and medicine **2**:263, *264*
    "anti-sense" drugs **2**:265
    bioengineered vaccines **2**:264–5,
      266
    monoclonal antibodies **2**:265
  to make new proteins **2**:266
  transgenic animals **2**:*264*, 265, 266
  see also agriculture, agricultural
    science; genetic engineering

biscuit ware **3**:426
bismuth, removal from lead **9**:1220–1
bits, drill **5**:678–9; **18**:2465
  masonry **5**:679
  for oil exploration **5**:*639*, 680, 683;
    11:1573
bitumen, mining for **11**:1461–2
blanching **3**:381
blast furnace gas **7**:959
blast furnaces *see* furnaces, blast
blasting techniques (surface treatment) **1**:17; **17**:2322, *2325*
blockboard **9**:1295
block caving **5**:637; **6**:846
blow molding, thermoplastic
  13:1774–5
blowtorches **7**:879; **13**:*1786*
boat building **2**:**274–7**
boiling water reactors (BWRs)
  11:*1543*, 1545; **13**:1832;
  18:2520
bonding, textiles **17**:2408
bone ash (calcium phosphate) **3**:*425*;
  4:465
bookbinding **3**:301–2
boreholes, for fluid mining
  11:1461–2
boring mills **10**:1310
BOS (basic oxygen steel) process
  9:*1188*, 1189–90
Bosch, Karl **1**:115
bottles, automatic filling **12**:1622–3
bottling **3**:385
Bouchon, Basile **9**:1281
bourbon **16**:*2215*, 2216–17
bows and arrows **3**:306–8
braces (tools) **18**:2465
brandy **5**:661; **16**:2217
brass
  manufacture **1**:102; **3**:316
  working **3**:316–17
bread making and baking **6**:841
  additives **7**:907–8
breathing apparatus **3**:321–2
brewing *see* beer and brewing
bricks, manufacture **3**:323–4, 426
brighteners, optical **5**:632, 693;
  10:1302
Brin process **12**:1618
bromine
  extraction from seawater **8**:1036
  uses **8**:1036
bronze, manufacture **3**:331
bruting **5**:640
bulk transport *see* freight handling
burins (gravers) **6**:803, *804*
butter **5**:601
butyl alcohol **6**:842

C

cable and rope manufacture **3**:**350–2**;
  10:*1387*; **13**:1806
calcining **19**:2729
calcium hydroxide (slaked lime; lime)
  production **1**:*25*
  uses **1**:*25*

calcium oxide (quicklime; lime), production **9**:1200
calendering **17**:2408
canals, irrigation **9**:1191–2
CANDU reactors **11**:1545
candy *see* confectionary
canning and bottling **3**:**381–5**; **7**:905,
  909
canoes **2**:274, 276
capillary tubes, manufacture **13**:1752
carbonation **3**:385
carbon dioxide
  liquid, as a cleaning solvent **5**:689
  and soft-drink dispensers **15**:2109;
    18:2576
carbon-in-pulp (CIP) process **8**:1015
carbonization, of coal **7**:957–8
carboxylic acids, production **1**:25
carburizing **10**:1388
cardboard, manufacture **12**:1640
carding **16**:2213
cartons
  automatic filling of **12**:1623
  cardboard **7**:908
carvels, construction **2**:274–5
casting **3**:**402–4**; **10**:1389
  bells **2**:238
  continuous **3**:*403*
  cylindrical casting of brass **3**:317
  die **3**:404; **10**:*1378*, 1389–90;
    19:*2732*
  evaporative **3**:404
  investment (lost-wax process)
    3:403–4
  sand **3**:402–3, *404*
  shell molding (Croning process)
    3:403
  slip **3**:402, *425*, 427; **4**:466–7
Castner cells **1**:100
Castner-Kellner cells **6**:738
cathode-ray tubes (CRTs), manufacture **3**:409–10
Caxton, William **13**:1848
cellophane **3**:390; **12**:1626
cell system (mass production)
  10:1340
cellulose acetate **3**:390; **5**:634; **6**:852
  dyeing **5**:692; **6**:852
cellulose triacetate **6**:852
cement
  asbestos **6**:846–7
  bulk handling by rail **14**:1927
  cementitious pipes **13**:1750
  manufacture **3**:**417–21**; **9**:1200
cementite **1**:104
centrifuges **3**:*316*, 422–3
cereals, processing **7**:912
chambering **5**:637
chamber process **1**:23–4; **4**:452
champagne **19**:2703
channeling machines, for quarrying
  14:1886
cheese **5**:600, *601*, 602; **7**:*904*
  waxed coverings **7**:908
Chernobyl nuclear disaster **11**:1536
china clay (kaolin), world production
  11:1458
china and porcelain **4**:**465–8**

extrusion 3:427
    pipes produced by 13:1752
    thermoplastic 13:1773, 1774

F

fabrics see textiles
farming see agriculture
fasteners, clothes 6:835
fermentation 1:98; 6:840–2; 16:2215
    acetic 6:842
    for baking 6:841
    for biofuels 2:258–9
    brewing and 2:234, 236–7; 3:406;
        6:841
    for protein production 7:914;
        13:1866
    for winemaking 6:840–1; 19:2700,
        2701–2, 2703
ferrite 1:104
fertilizers 6:843–5
    ammonium nitrate 4:450; 6:829,
        843, 844
    manufacture 6:843, 844–5
fiberglass, for insulation 9:1160–1
fiber optics, optical fibers, manufac-
    ture 6:855
fibers
    mineral 6:846–7
    natural 6:848–50; 17:2404
        see also cotton; silk; wool
    optical see fiber optics
    synthetic 4:490; 5:691–2; 6:851–3;
        17:2404–5
        dyes for 5:692; 6:852
        geotextiles 17:2408
    see also spinning
fields, draining salt-contaminated
    water from 9:1192
files (tools), manufacture 18:2461–2
fire setting 11:1458
firing
    bricks 3:324
    china and porcelain 4:467
    glost 4:468
fish, food preservation 7:905, 908,
    909–10
fish farming see aquaculture
fishing industry 7:871–5; 15:2039
    clothing 13:1861–2
    fish farming see aquaculture
    freezing fish at sea 14:1947
    purse-seine fishing 7:871
        and suction pumps 4:522
        and sonar 15:2126
    trawling 7:871–2
flame fusion process 17:2346
flax 6:848, 849, 850; 17:2405
flexible manufacturing systems
    (FMSs) 10:1340–1
flint, mining for 11:1457–8
float process 7:1000–1
float zoning 15:2076–7
flooding, for irrigation 9:1191, 1193
floor covering 7:892–5
flotation process, for lead extraction
    9:1219
flow wrapping 12:1625
fluidics (fluid logic) 7:898–9; 9:1277
fluidized beds 7:900–1; 19:2639
fluorine
    production 8:1034
    uses 8:1034
fondants 4:557
food preservation and packaging
    7:904–8
    packaging 7:908; 9:1205;
        12:1622–5
    preservation
        blanching 7:905
        by Native Americans 7:908

canning and bottling 3:381–5;
    7:905, 909
    curing (salting and smoking)
        7:905, 908, 909–10
    dehydration 7:905–6, 907,
        910–11
    food additives 7:907–8
    freezing 7:906, 911
    irradiation 6:745; 7:908, 911
    pasteurization 5:600, 601, 603;
        7:906–7, 911
    pickling 7:906–7, 911
    sterilization 7:912
    sugaring 7:912
food processing 7:909–14
    additives 7:914
        vitamins 7:914
    canning and bottling 3:381–5;
        7:905, 909
    cereal 7:912
    cocoa manufacture 4:499–500
    coffee 4:501–3; 7:910
    cooking 7:909
    curing 7:905, 908, 909–10
    dehydration 7:905–6, 907, 910–11
    fish, on board ships 7:872, 873
    pasteurization 5:600, 601, 603;
        7:906–7, 911
    pickling 7:906–7, 911
    sterilization 7:912
    sugaring 7:912
    synthetic foods 7:913
        from single-cell proteins 7:914
    see also dairy industry; slaughter-
        houses
Ford, Henry 2:198; 10:1338, 1341
Ford Model T, manufacture 10:1341
forestry 7:921–5
    see also deforestation; lumber
forging 10:1388–9
    sheet metal 15:2064
fossil fuels 2:258; 3:391; 6:790, 791
Fourdrinier machines 12:1639–40
fractionating columns 5:662–3;
    11:1575, 1576
Frasch process 11:1461
freeze drying 7:910–11; 14:1947
    coffee 4:503
    specimens for taxidermy 17:2354
freezing
    foods 7:906, 910, 911
    methods, desalination 5:623,
        624–5
freight handling 7:928–32
    by cranes 5:586, 588, 670; 7:931,
        932
    by rail 7:928, 929; 14:1927
        and railroad yards 14:1929, 1930
    by ships see ships, bulk-carrying
    of grain 6:776; 7:928, 930
French fries, frozen 7:910, 911
Fröhlich retarders 14:1930
furnaces 7:940–2; 9:1209
    basic oxygen 7:941
    blast 3:391, 392
        earliest 7:942
        for iron production 9:1186–7;
            10:1378; 12:1617
        for lead production 9:1219
        for brass manufacture 3:316
    electric 7:942
        electric arc 3:316; 7:941, 942;
            8:1061; 9:1190
        electric induction 7:942
        resistance furnaces 7:942
    glass 7:940
    heat-treatment 10:1388
    muffle 6:780
    open-hearth 7:940
    pot 7:940
    solar 15:2116
    see also kilns

G

galvanizing 4:571; 17:2322, 2323,
    2325–6; 19:2732
gas and dust masks 7:953–4
    industrial 7:954
gas industry 7:955–9
    coal gas 7:957–8
    natural gas 7:955–7
    oil gas 7:959
gears, cutting 7:969
genetic engineering 1:52; 7:973–8;
    11:1478
    of animals 1:52–3; 2:263–4; 7:978
    and horticulture 8:1089
    for insulin 7:978; 13:1733–4;
        19:2727
    of plants and crops (food) 1:53;
        3:303, 304; 7:978; 12:1676
    herbicide-tolerant crops
        19:2681
geothermal power 6:790, 793
gill nets 7:872
gin 5:663; 16:2217
glass 3:425–6; 4:493; 7:999–1001
    colored 6:858
    didymium 6:858
    etching 6:805
    glass mosaic (glass appliqué)
        16:2238
    heat-resistant 7:1001
    incising patterns on 1:17; 5:638
    laminated safety 1:30; 2:209
    light-sensitive 7:1001
    optical and ophthalmic 7:1001
        for optical filters 6:858
    patterned 7:1001
    powdered 6:779
    production 4:493; 7:999–1001
    recycling 14:1940, 1942
    safety 7:1001
    sculptures 16:2238
    slab (dalles de verre) 16:2238
    stained 6:858; 7:999; 16:2236–8
    wired 7:1001
    see also enamels, vitreous
glazing 4:467
goggles, industrial 13:1861
gold 8:1013–16
    alluvial 8:1013
    extraction 8:1013–15
    mining for 8:1013; 11:1460
    refining 8:1015
grain, bulk handling 6:776; 7:928,
    930
graphitization, of carbon fibers
    3:395; 17:2405
gravure 6:805
gravure processes, inks 8:1152
gray goods 17:2408
greenhouses 8:1088–9
    for hydroponics 8:1122; 9:1194
Griess process 1:135; 5:691
grinding machines 10:1309–10
grit blasting 1:17; 17:2322
gum running 9:1205
guns, spray 16:2227–8
Gutenberg, Johann 5:630; 13:1847,
    1848

H

Haber, Fritz 1:115; 3:407; 4:451
Haber (or Haber-Bosch) process
    1:25, 115; 4:451; 11:1525–6
    catalysts 3:405, 407
hacksaws 18:2463
halftone process 13:1850–1
Hall, Charles M. 10:1378
hammers
    manufacture 18:2461

riveting 13:1789
hardening (metalworking) 10:1388
high-speed dispersers (HSDs)
    12:1630
hipping (hot isostatic pressing) 3:404
Hoffmann kilns 9:1200
hollanders 12:1639
hollow bar 13:1752
honey 4:557
hook and loop tape (Velcro) 6:835
hops, drying 9:1199
horticulture 8:1088–9
hosiery and knitware manufacture
    8:1090–3
hot-dip process 17:2326
humidification, and desalination
    5:624
hump yards 14:1929
hydrapulpers 12:1638–9
hydrocarbons
    production 8:1106
    see also cracking
hydrochloric acid, production 1:25
hydrocracking 8:1119; 11:1576, 1578
hydrocyclones 5:638
hydrodesulfurization 3:406
hydroelectric power (HEP) 6:786,
    792; 8:1112–15; 13:1820, 1827
    dams for 5:605; 8:1112
    high-head and low-head projects
        8:1112
    pumped-storage schemes 6:798;
        8:1112, 1115; 13:1827; 18:2520
    turbines 8:1112–13; 18:2520
    see also tidal power; wave power
hydrofining 8:1119; 11:1580
hydrogen
    manufacture 8:1118
    uses
        ammonia manufacture 1:115;
            3:405
        cooling dynamos 8:1119
        cutting and welding 1:119
        hydrocracking 8:1119; 11:1578
        hydrofining 8:1119; 11:1580
        in nuclear fusion 7:946, 947
hydrogenation 3:406
hydrogen peroxide, manufacture
    12:1621
hydroponics 8:1120–2; 9:1194
hydrothermal synthesis 19:2729

I

illuminating gas (town gas) 7:957
Imperial Smelting Process (ISP)
    19:2731–2
inclinables, open-back 15:2065
incineration, municipal waste
    19:2638–9
Industrial Revolution
    and cotton 5:581
    and metals 10:1378
injection molding
    acrylic 13:1794
    reaction (RIM) 13:1776
    temperatures measured 17:2417
    thermoplastic 13:1773, 1774
    for thermosets 13:1775
intaglio processes 6:803
integrated circuits (silicon chips;
    microchips)
    manufacture 6:751, 752; 9:1166,
        1264; 10:1427, 1428; 13:1763
    testing 6:752; 9:1166–8;
        10:1341
International Thermonuclear
    Experimental Reactor (ITER)
    6:797
Intertype machines 13:1849
iodine, preparation 8:1035

iron and steel
  iron
    cast (pig iron) 9:1187–8
    pipes 13:1749
    production 9:1186–8
    ships carrying ore 5:671; 9:1190
    world production of ore 11:1458
    wrought 9:1187
  steel
    casting 3:403; 9:1190
    heat treatment of 1:104;
      10:1387
    high-tensile 13:1749
    history 9:1188–9
    mild 13:1749; 19:2640
    pipes 13:1749, 1751, 1753, 1754
    production 9:1188–90; 12:1617,
      1619
    refining 9:1189, 1190
    transportation 7:929
irrigation techniques 9:1191–4;
  18:2570
  causing desertification 9:1207
  see also hydroponics
ISO standards 14:1879
isostatic pressing 3:427
  hot (hipping) 3:404
ITER (International Thermonuclear
  Experimental Reactor) 6:797

J

Jacquard, Joseph Marie 4:523;
  9:1281–2
JET (Joint European Torus) 7:947–8
jewelry
  enameling 6:780
  gold 8:1016
  platinum and palladium 13:1783
  see also stone cutting
Joint European Torus (JET) 7:947–8
joints (mechanical)
  adhesive 1:28–9
  in plumbing pipework 13:1786,
    1787
Judson, Whitcomb 6:835
jute 6:849, 850

K

kaolin see china clay
Kay, John 16:2212
kenaf 6:848
kerfs 5:640
kilns 7:940; 9:1199–1200
  for brick manufacture 3:323, 324
  for cement manufacture 3:418–19;
    9:1200
  for china and porcelain manufac-
    ture 4:467
  continuous 3:323, 324; 9:1200
  low-temperature 9:1199–1200
kimberlite 5:637, 638
knitting
  cotton 5:582
  see also hosiery and knitware manu-
    facture
knives, utility 18:2464
König, Friedrich 13:1849
Koppers-Totzek process 7:956
krill 7:875

L

lacquers and varnishes 9:1204–5
  manufacture 9:1205
landfill 14:1939; 19:2640–2
  cleaning waste water from 12:1610
  reclamation 9:1207–8

lasers and masers
  lasers
    used as machine tools 9:1213,
      1214; 10:1363
    used in nuclear fusion 7:946,
      947, 948; 9:1214
    used in printing 9:1263;
      13:1850, 1852
    used for surface-alloy coatings
      1:107
    used to scan timber 9:1295
    used in uranium enrichment
      18:2548
laundry 9:1217–18
leaching, used in fluid mining
  11:1462
lead
  occurrence and extraction 9:1219
  refining 9:1219–21
  uses, pipes 13:1751, 1787
leather 9:1222–4
  aniline 9:1224
  chamois 9:1223
  dyeing 5:690; 9:1223–4
  patent 9:1224
  suede 9:1224
  tanning 4:473; 9:1223
Leblanc process 4:450
Leonids 10:1393
levels, spirit 18:2464–5
lifting wheels 5:638
light and optics, optics, manufacture
  of optical components 9:1242–3
lime see calcium hydroxide; calcium
  oxide
limestone, crushed 14:1885
Linde process 1:64
Linotype machines 5:630; 13:1849
liqueurs 5:661; 16:2217
liquid petroleum gas (LPG) 7:955,
  959
  from oil refining 11:1577
liquids, microencapsulated 10:1413
lithium, production 1:99–100
lithography 5:630; 9:1260–4;
  13:1849–50, 1851–2
  lithographic development of films
    12:1713
    offset 9:1263–4; 13:1847, 1848,
      1850, 1852
    web offset 9:1264; 11:1517–18;
      13:1850
    heat-set 13:1850
  see also photolithography; printing;
    stereolithography
lithos 4:468
lobsters, catching 7:874
logic, fluid see fluidics
longwall working 4:496–7
looms 9:1280–3
  Jacquard 4:523; 7:894; 9:1281–2
  rug and carpet 7:893; 9:1280
lost-wax process 3:403–4
lubrication 10:1289–92
  of bearings 2:231; 9:1289
  of dental drills 5:621
Ludlow system 13:1849
lumber 9:1293–6
  drying 9:1199–1200, 1295
  see also forestry
Lurgi process 7:957, 959

M

machining centers, CNC 18:2464
madeira 19:2703
magnox reactors 11:1546
mail-sorting machinery 10:1321–5
majolica ware 3:425
manganese, seafloor nodules, mining
  11:1462

mangles 9:1218
manipulators see remote handling
Mannesmann process 13:1751
margarine, manufacture 3:406
martensite 1:104
mass production 1:41–2; 10:1338–41
  of automobiles 10:1338, 1339,
    1341, 1380
  of clocks 4:486
  of clothes 4:489–90
  die casting 10:1389–90
  and ergonomics 6:815
  of glass 4:493
  using sewing machines 15:2061
  see also assembly lines; conveyors
matting 16:2237
mauveine (dye) 1:133, 134; 4:453
meat
  canned 7:912
  curing 7:905
mercerization 6:849
mercury (metal), extraction 10:1371
mercury cells, for preparation of
  chlorine 8:1035
merry-go-round system, for freight
  14:1927, 1929
metal cutting and joining
  10:1379–84
  brazing 10:1380–1
  cutting 10:1364
    electrochemical machining
      6:735–6; 10:1310
    electrodischarge machining
      (EDM; spark erosion; spark
      machining) 6:735, 736;
      10:1364, 1366
    flame 10:1379, 1380
    plasma-arc 10:1364, 1379–80
    powder 10:1379
    using lasers 9:1213, 1214;
      10:1363, 1364
    using thermic lances 17:2412
    water-jet 10:1364
  riveting 10:1379, 1384
  soldering 10:1381–2
  see also welding
metals
  drilling 5:678–9
  extraction 10:1377–8
    using electrolysis see electrolysis,
      uses
metalworking 10:1387–91
  brass working 3:316–17
  drawing 3:316; 10:1390–1
    sheet metal 15:2064
    tube 13:1751–2
  forging 10:1388–9
  heat treatment 10:1387–8;
    18:2462
  rolling 10:1391
  sheet metal 15:2064–6
  smoothing and polishing, using
    electrochemical machining 6:736
  tubular products 10:1391
  see also casting; coins and minting;
    metal cutting and joining; pipe
    and tube manufacture; tool
    manufacture
methane
  in coal mines 4:494
  for hydrogen production 8:1118
  liquefied, transportation 7:929
  see also natural gas
methanol (methyl alcohol; wood
  alcohol)
  engines powered with 2:258; 6:794
  production 1:98
methanolysis 13:1776
mezzotint 6:803, 804
MG (machine glazed) papermaking
  machines 12:1640
microencapsulation 10:1413–14

milk
  condensed and evaporated 5:600,
    602–3
  dried 5:603; 7:910; 11:1452
  homogenized 5:601
  hygienic quality tests 5:601
  milking machines 5:600–1;
    11:1451–2
  packaging 7:908; 12:1624–5
  pasteurized 5:600, 601, 603; 7:906,
    911
  processing 5:601
  production
    and biotechnology 2:264, 266
    in cows 1:57
  spoilage 7:905
  sterilized 5:601; 7:912
  UHT 5:601
  see also dairy industry
mill borers 10:1310
milling 19:2694
milling machines 10:1309, 1310
mining techniques 11:1457–62
  alluvial mining
    for diamonds 5:638
    for gold 8:1013
  development 11:1457–8
  fluid mining 11:1461–2
  marine mining 11:1462
  surface mining (opencast mining;
    strip mining) 1:109; 5:701;
    11:1457, 1458–60
    auger mining 4:495; 11:1460
    for coal 4:495–6, 564; 11:1460
    for diamonds 5:637
    open pits 11:1458–9
    placer mining 11:1460
    strip mining 11:1459
    for uranium 11:1457
  underground mining 11:1457,
    1459, 1460–1
    for coal 4:496–7; 11:1460–1
    for diamonds 5:637–8
    drift mines 11:1460, 1461
    for gold 11:1460
    ventilation 8:1059, 1060
minting see coins and minting
mirrors, production 11:1463–4
molasses, ethanol produced from
  7:963
molding
  blow 13:1774–5
  compression 13:1775
  contact lenses 4:562
  injection see injection molding
  rotational 13:1775
  shell (Croning process) 3:403
mollusks, harvesting 7:874
Mond carbonyl process 11:1523
monosodium glutamate, production
  7:914
mordanting 5:690–1
movie production 11:1497–1500
  animation 1:136–40; 4:536;
    16:2189–90
  soundtracks 15:2146–9
    music scores 11:1499, 1500;
      15:2149
  special effects 16:2185–90
  stereoscopic movies 16:2263–4
MOX reactors 11:1538, 1539
Murdock, William 7:955

N

napping 17:2408
National Water Carrier 9:1192
natural gas 3:391; 7:955–7
  for electricity generation 6:791
  and oil recovery 11:1573
  for power plants 7:967

storage 7:*955*, 957
sulfur from 16:2299
needles, hypodermic, manufacture
  13:*1752*
Newcomen, Thomas 11:1458
newspaper production 11:**1515–19**;
  13:1849
nickel, occurrence and extraction
  11:1522–3
nitric acid, preparation 1:24–5;
  4:451; 11:1525; 13:*1783*
nitrogen
  liquid 1:*62*; 5:591; 11:1525, *1527*;
    14:1927
  production 11:1525
nodding donkeys 5:683; 11:1573–4
North Sea, drilling for oil 5:682
nougat 4:557–8
nuclear fuel cycle 11:**1537–9**, 1546;
  18:2547–8
nuclear reactors 11:**1542–6**; 14:*1907*
  Cerenkov radiation 6:*794*; 14:*1907*
  design 11:1544–5
  fast-breeder 7:*877*; 11:1546;
    18:*2547*
  heat exchangers 8:1054
  nuclear emergencies 11:**1535–6**,
    1545
  nuclear fission 6:796; 7:*877*;
    11:1543–6; 12:*1728*; 13:1832
    MHD units used in 10:1319
  nuclear fuel cycle 11:**1537–9**,
    1546; 18:2547–8
  nuclear fusion 2:248; 6:796;
    7:*947–8*; 11:*1545*
  propulsion 11:1546; 15:*2073*
    for submarines 10:1336, 1366;
      11:*1542*, 1546; 16:*2290*
  safety 11:1535, 1545
  thermal 11:1545–6
    boiling water reactors (BWRs)
      11:*1543*, 1545; 13:1832;
      18:2520
    gas-cooled 2:233; 11:1546
    heavy water reactors 11:1545
    pressurized-water reactors
      (PWRs) 11:*1542*, *1543*, 1545;
      13:1832; 18:2520
  waste disposal from *see* nuclear
    waste disposal
  see also power plants, nuclear
nuclear waste disposal 6:796;
  11:1539, **1547–50**; 18:*2547*
numerical control systems 10:1340
nutrient film technique (NFT)
  8:1120–1
nylons
  for hosiery and knitwear 8:1090–1
  manufacture 6:852

O

oasts 9:1199
ocean floor, mining 11:1462
oil exploration and production 7:990;
  11:**1570–4**
  drill bits 5:*639*, 680
    turbine 5:683
  exploration 7:993–4; 11:1570–3
    using seismology 7:993–4;
      11:1570–1; 15:*2048*, 2135
  horizontal drilling 5:683
  oil drilling rigs 4:*548*; 5:**680–3**;
    11:*1570*
  oil pipelines 13:1753, *1754*
  oil recovery 11:1573–4
  see also petroleum (crude oil)
oil gas 7:959
oil refining 5:661, *662*, 663; 8:1106;
  11:**1575–80**
  cracking 4:453; 11:1575–6, 1578

catalytic 4:*459*; 11:1576
  hydrocracking 11:1576, 1578
  thermal 11:1578
hydrofining 11:1580
and pollution 13:*1798*
products from 4:453; 5:663;
  11:1577–80
oil shale 11:1574
oilskins 13:1862
oils, vegetable
  for biodiesel 6:*794*; 7:963
  hydrogenation 3:406
open-hearth process 9:1189
optics *see* light and optics
ores, bulk handling 7:928
overlock machines 4:490
oxyacetylene welding 12:1620
oxygen
  manufacture 12:1618
  separation from air 5:590;
    12:1618–19
oysters 2:*153*; 7:875

P

packaging 7:908; 12:**1622–5**
  see also food preservation and
    packaging
packaging-wrap manufacture
  12:**1626**
paddocking 8:1013
paddy fields 9:1191
paints
  manufacture 12:1630
  spray guns for 16:2227–8
panning, for gold 8:1013
pantographs 15:2066
panty hose 8:1090, *1091*, 1092–3
paper
  manufacture 9:1296; 12:**1636–40**;
    13:1847
    for banknotes 5:583
    cotton used in 5:582
    wastes for food production
      7:914; 19:2727
  NCR (no carbon required)
    10:1413
  photographic 10:*1413*, 1414
  recycling 14:1939–40
paperback production 3:302
parachutes, manufacture 12:1642–3
Parkes process 9:1220; 15:2079
pasteurization 5:601, *603*; 7:906–7,
  911
patio process 15:2079
pearlite 1:104
perchloroethylene (perc) 5:687–9
petroleum (crude oil)
  bulk handling 7:928–9
  chemicals from 4:453; 5:663
  formation of reservoirs of 11:1572
  refining *see* oil refining
  synthetic, for cleaning textiles
    5:689
  see also bitumen; natural gas; oil
    exploration and production
phonography (records and vinyl
  discs), record manufacture
  12:1695–6
phosphors, manufacture 18:2487
phosphorus, manufacture 12:1698–9
photocomposition, newspaper
  11:1517
photoelectric profiling 10:1380
photoetching process 13:1845–6
photographic films and processing,
  film, manufacture 12:1714
photogravure 13:1852
photolithography 10:*1416*, 1417–18
photoresist 5:651
phototypesetting 5:630

pickers (spindle pickers), cotton
  5:582
pickling
  animal skins 9:1222
  foods 7:906–7, 911
  metals 2:223
Piermatics 5:640
pipelines 13:**1753–4**
  bulk-handling, at docks 7:929
  control systems 13:1754
  corrosion control and testing
    13:1754
  gas 13:1754
  oil 13:1753, *1754*
  pneumatic, valves 18:*2567*
  repairs, using freezing 5:591
  on tankers 17:2351
  and telemetry 17:2365
  water-intake
    antifouling techniques 2:149
    gas 7:*959*
pipe and tube manufacture
  13:**1749–52**, 1754
  pressure pipes, from asbestos
    6:847; 13:1750
pistols, captive bolt 15:2096
Pitot tubes 1:*65*
Pittsburgh process 7:1000
planers (machine tools) 10:1308,
  1309
planes, manufacture 18:2460–1
planks, production 9:1294–5, *1296*
plasma physics 13:**1762–3**
  plasma beat-wave accelerators
    13:1763
  plasma deposition 13:1763
  plasma welding 10:*1366*, 1383
plastic forming 3:426–7
plastics
  plating 17:*2324*
  processing 13:**1773–6**
platforming 11:1576
plating
  electroless 17:2324
  tools 18:*2464*
  see also electroplating
pliers, manufacture 18:2463–4
plywood 9:1295; 19:2709
  manufacture 19:2710–11
    adhesives used in 1:*30*; 19:2709
poling 4:567
polishing 17:2325
polyesters, production 6:853
polystyrene, plating 17:*2324*
polytetrafluoroethylene (PTFE;
  polytetrafluoroethene; Teflon),
  manufacture 13:1813–14
porcelain *see* china and porcelain
port (fortified wine) 19:2702
ports, bulk-handling *see* docks
potatoes
  dried 7:910
  frozen French fries 7:*910*, 911
pottery 3:424–5
powder coatings 13:**1823–4**
powder metallurgy 1:104–6, *107*;
  3:404
power plants 13:1826, **1827–32**,
  1834
  alternators 13:1827, 1829–30
  efficiency 6:788
  first public 13:1827, 1833
  gas turbines 13:1832
    natural gas-powered 7:967;
      13:1828
  hydroelectric *see* hydroelectric
    power
  and nuclear fusion 2:248
  nuclear (nuclear fission) 7:876;
    12:*1728*; 13:1827–8, 1831–2
    see also nuclear reactors
  rated in power units 6:790

solar 6:792; 15:2116
  using carbon-based fuels
    13:1830–1
  coal 13:1827, 1831; 14:1927
  wood-burning 2:258
pozzolana 3:417; 4:546
precipitation hardening 1:104
presses
  dome 18:2578
  drill 10:1310
  machine 10:1306, 1310
  for sheet metal 15:2064–5
  vacuum 18:2578
  veneer 18:2578; 19:2711
pressing, clothes 4:490
pressure cookers, industrial 13:1841
pressurized-water reactors (PWRs)
  11:*1542*, *1543*, 1545; 13:1832;
  18:2520
printing 13:**1847–52**
  banknotes 5:583
  collotype 13:1852
  colorimeters used in 4:*512*
  fabric 5:*692*, 693; 6:**833–4**;
    17:2408
  gravure 9:*1263*; 13:1850, 1851–2
  history 13:1847–50
  illustrations 13:1850–1
  inks used for 8:1152
  letterpress 9:*1263*; 11:1517;
    13:1849, *1850*, 1851, 1852
  lithographic *see* lithography
  maps 10:1329–30
  newspapers 11:1517–18; 13:1849
  offset *see* lithography, offset
  print identification 13:1851
  reprographic 13:1852
  resist 6:834
  roller 6:833, 834
  screen 6:833–4; 13:1852
    for circuit boards 13:1845
  transfer 6:834
  web offset *see* lithography, web
    offset
  see also engraving and etching
producer gas (Siemen's gas) 7:*956*,
  958
promoters, catalyst 3:407
prospecting, mineral, using spectrochemical analysis 16:2196–7
protective clothing 13:**1860–3**
  fire-resistant 6:*847*
  see also breathing apparatus; gas
    and dust masks
proteins
  manufacture
    single-cell protein (SCP) foods
      6:810; 7:914; 13:*1866*
    using genetic engineering 7:978
    vegetable, artificial meats from
      7:913–14
PTFE *see* polytetrafluoroethylene
pug mills 3:*425*
pulleys, wooden, mass production
  10:1341
pultrusion 13:*1774*
pulverised fuel ash (PFA) 13:1831
pumping stations, gas 13:1754
punches 18:2465
Purbeck stone 14:*1886*
purple dye 5:693
pusher centrifuges 3:423
pyrolysis 13:1776

Q

qanaats 9:1192
quality management 14:**1877–9**
  sampling 14:1878; 16:*2249*
quarrying 14:**1885–6**
quicklime *see* calcium oxide

R

radiography, industrial uses **19**:2723
railroad systems **4**:475–6; **10**:1364–5;
    14:*1923–8*
    and freight **7**:928, 929; **14**:1927,
        1929
    tracks **3**:*403*; **14**:1923
        testing **14**:*1878*; **18**:*2530*
railroad yards **14**:**1929–30**
rapiers **9**:1283
rasps **18**:2461
rayon
    dyeing **5**:691–2
    manufacture **3**:390; **6**:851
records (discs) *see* phonography
recycling **14**:**1939–43**; **19**:2640
    automobiles **10**:*1364*, 1366
    glass **14**:*1940*, 1942
    metals **14**:1940–1
    oils **14**:1942
    paper **14**:1939–40
    plastics **10**:1366; **12**:1625;
        13:1776; **14**:1941
    wastes
        hazardous **14**:1942
        organic **14**:1942, 1943
reducing machines **4**:507
reforming **4**:453; **11**:1576, 1579
refractories **3**:425
refrigeration **14**:**1945–7**
    dilution refrigerators **5**:*591*
    in space program flights **5**:592
    thermoelectric **17**:2420
    use in boring tunnels **18**:2516
    using liquid nitrogen **5**:591
remote handling **14**:**1955–6**
    of radioactive substances **14**:1955
        nuclear fuels **14**:*1905*
    of space cameras **15**:*2154*, 2155
rennet **5**:602
Resazurin test **5**:601
resin-in-pulp (RIP) process **8**:1015
resistors, manufacture **14**:1962–3
retting **6**:850
rice, growing **9**:1191
ring diffusers **16**:2296
riveting **10**:1384
rivet sets **18**:2465
Robocarriers **10**:*1338*
rolling (metalworking) **10**:1391
Root, Elisha **10**:1338
ropes, manufacture *see* cable and rope
        manufacture
rotational molding, thermoplastic
    13:1775
roving process **16**:2214
rum **5**:661; **16**:2217

S

sake (rice wine) **19**:2726
salt *see* sodium chloride
sampling, quality-control **14**:1878;
    16:*2249*
sandblasting **1**:17; **17**:2322, *2325*
sandstone **14**:1885
saponification **1**:25; **15**:2107
sawing, planks **9**:1295
saws, manufacture **18**:2462–3
scaifes **5**:640
scrap recovery, using cryogenics
    5:591
screwdrivers, manufacture **18**:*2462*,
    2463
screws, manufacture **15**:**2032–4**
seafloor *see* ocean floor
seasoning, timber **9**:1295
seeding
    agricultural **1**:48–9
    horticultural **8**:1089

Sellafield (Windscale) **11**:1535
Senefelder, Alois **9**:*1260*; **13**:1849–50
separators (centrifuges) **3**:423
serigraphy *see* printing, screen
sets, television **17**:2386–7
sewage, treatment *see* wastewater
        treatment
sewing machines, industrial **15**:2061
shadufs **9**:*1192*, 1231
shapers (machine tools) **10**:1308–9
sheet forming **4**:562
sheet metal **15**:**2064–6**
shell molding (Croning process)
    3:*403*
sherardizing **17**:2323
sherry **19**:2702–3
shingles (asbestos) **6**:846
ships
    bulk-carrying **7**:928–32; **9**:1190;
        15:*2071–2*
        see also tankers
    construction **15**:2073
    container ships **7**:932; **15**:*2067*,
        2069–70
    fishing and whaling
        factory ships **7**:*872*; **19**:2686
        see also fishing industry; trawlers
    industrial **15**:2073
    refrigeration **14**:1945
        reefer (refrigerated transport)
            ships **15**:2071
shot blasting **17**:2322
shrink fitting **5**:591
shrink-wrapping **7**:908; **12**:1624
shuttles **9**:1280–1
    flying **9**:1283; **16**:2212
Siemen's gas (producer gas) **7**:*956*,
    958
silicon
    production **15**:2076
        manufacture of crystals **5**:599;
            15:2076–7
silk **6**:849, *850*; **17**:2404, 2405, 2408
    artificial **3**:390; **6**:851
silkworms **6**:849
    bioengineered **2**:266
silver, extraction **9**:1220; **15**:2079–80
sintering **1**:105
    reaction **3**:427
sisal **6**:*849*, 850
slate **14**:1885
slaughterhouses **15**:**2096–8**
slopers **4**:489
smelting **12**:1617, 1620
soaps **6**:837; **15**:2107
    flakes **5**:632; **15**:*2107*
    manufacture **5**:632; **6**:837;
        15:**2107–8**
        soap-based washing powders
            5:632; **15**:2108
    shaving **15**:2108
    soft **15**:2108
sodium carbonate (soda; soda ash),
    manufacture **4**:450
sodium chloride (salt)
    electrolysis **1**:25; **4**:450, *452*;
        6:737; **8**:1118
    in food processing *see* curing
    production **14**:**2016**
        from evaporation **11**:1569;
            14:2016
        mining **11**:1462; **14**:2016
sodium cyanide, preparation **1**:100–1
sodium hydroxide (caustic soda),
    preparation **1**:25; **6**:738
soil, management **15**:2112–13
solar energy **6**:*729*, 791–2; **15**:2054,
    2114–17
    for power plants **6**:792; **15**:2116
soldering **10**:1381–2
Solvay process **4**:450
sorbants, use in fluidized beds **7**:901

spark plugs, manufacture **3**:427
spectacles, frames, construction
    16:2192
spinnerets
    for artificial meats **7**:913
    for synthetic fibers **6**:851, 852
spinning **16**:2212–14
    cotton **5**:581, 582; **16**:2212–13
spinning wheels **16**:2212
spirits **1**:*97*; **5**:661, *663*; **6**:841;
    16:**2215–18**
    poteen **5**:664
spray guns **16**:**2227–8**
spraying, electric-arc **17**:2323
springs, manufacture **16**:2230
stained glass **6**:858; **7**:*999*;
    16:**2236–8**
stapling machines **13**:1789
starch **3**:390
steam digesters **13**:1841
stereolithography **10**:1366
stills **5**:661, *663*; **16**:2215
    molecular **5**:664
stock control **10**:1341
stockings, manufacture **8**:1090–3
Stoddard solvent **5**:687
stone
    crushed **14**:1885, 1886
    dimension **14**:1885, 1886
stone cutting **16**:**2270–2**
storage/retrieval (S/R) systems
    automated (AS/RSs) **19**:2622–3,
        2624, 2625
    in process **19**:2624–5
stretch forming **2**:277
stretch wrapping **12**:1624
stripping, cotton **5**:581, 582
sugar
    and confectionary **4**:557
    refining **4**:557; **16**:**2295–7**
        quality-control **13**:1793
sulfur
    mining for **11**:1461
    occurrence and extraction **16**:2299
sulfuric acid, industrial manufacture
    1:23–4; **4**:452
surface treatments **17**:**2322–6**
    coatings **17**:2323
        surface-alloy **1**:107
        see also galvanizing
    polishing **17**:2325
    using water jets **17**:2322–3
    see also abrasives; electroplating
sweeteners, food **7**:914
sweetening, of crude oil **11**:1580
switchyards **14**:1929, 1930

T

tankers **17**:**2350–2**
    liquefied gas vessels **17**:2352
    oil **5**:671; **15**:2072
        supertankers (very large crude
            carriers) **7**:928–9; **11**:*1577*
    ore-carrying **9**:1190
    safety **17**:2352
    see also ships, bulk-carrying
tanning **4**:*473*; **9**:1223
tar, distillation **11**:1575
tar sands, oil from **11**:1574
Teflon *see* polytetrafluoroethylene
television production **17**:**2386–91**
    interactive television **17**:2391
    teleprompters **17**:2373–5
tempering **1**:104; **10**:1388; **18**:*2462*
tentering **17**:2408
terracotta **4**:467
Tetra Paks **7**:908; **12**:1624–5
textiles **17**:**2404–8**
    fabrics **17**:2406–8
        nonwoven **17**:2408

optical brighteners for **5**:632,
    693; **10**:1302
printing **5**:*692*, 693; **6**:833–4;
    17:2408
see also dyes
water-repellent finishes
    19:2659–60
woven **17**:2405–6
see also weaving
finishing processes **17**:2408
see also fibers, natural; fibers,
    synthetic
thermoforming, vacuum **13**:*1773*,
    1775
thread rolling **15**:2034
Three Mile Island **11**:1535–6
tidal power **6**:792–3; **17**:**2436–8**
    see also wave power
tiles, manufacture **3**:427
timber
    drying **9**:1199–1200, 1295
    see also lumber
tin
    mining for **11**:1462; **17**:*2448*
    occurrence and production
        17:2447
    prospecting for **16**:*2199*
tires, manufacture **18**:2453–5
Tokaimura, nuclear incident at
    11:1536
tokamaks **6**:796; **7**:947–8; **13**:1763
tool manufacture **18**:**2460–5**
    see also screws, manufacture
total color transfer process **4**:468
town gas (illuminating gas) **7**:*957*
Toxiplex system **13**:1803
transfer machines, cold-heading
    15:2034
transuranic waste **11**:1548
trass **3**:417
trawlers **7**:871–3, *874*
treadmills **9**:1194
trees *see* forestry; lumber
trichloroethylene **5**:687
trunk deck vessels **17**:2350–1
tubes, capillary, manufacture **13**:1752
tubes, metal **10**:1391
tumbling, barrel **17**:2322
typesetting **5**:630
Tyrian purple dye **5**:693

U

UHT (ultra-high temperature)
    processes **7**:912
ULCCs (Ultra Large Crude
    Carriers) **17**:*2350*, 2351
ultracentrifuges **3**:423
Ultra Large Crude Carriers
    (ULCCs) **17**:*2350*, 2351
ultrasonics **15**:2134–5; **18**:**2528–32**
    sources and detectors **18**:2529–30
    piezoelectric transducers
        13:1745; **18**:2529–30
    uses
        cavitation **18**:2532
        cleaning **13**:1745
        cutting and machining **10**:1310;
            18:*2528*, 2532
        nondestructive testing **14**:*1878*;
            18:*2529, 2530, 2531, 2532*
        sonar **18**:2531
        underwater surveying **18**:2531
        welding **1**:111; **10**:1384
ultrasound machining (USM)
    10:1310
Uperization **5**:601
uranium
    isotopes, separation (enrichment)
        3:423; **11**:1537–8, 1544;
        18:2548

mining for 11:*1457*, *1462*, 1537
  disposal of wastes 11:1547
ore refining process 11:1537
reprocessing 11.1538–9, 1549
reprocessing of spent fuel
  11:1538–9, 1549
use in nuclear reactors 6:796;
  11:1537–9; 13:1831
waste disposal 11:1547, 1550

V

vacuum arc remelting furnaces
  9:*1189*
vacuum forming, thermoplastic
  (vacuum thermoforming)
  13:*1773*, 1775
vapor deposition
  chemical (CVD) 5:639; 10:1418
  using vacuums 18:2560
varnishes *see* lacquers and varnishes
Vaucanson, Jacques de 9:1281
Velcro 6:835
veneers 18:2578–9; 19:2710–11
Very Large Crude Carriers (VLCCs)
  17:2351
vinegar 6:842; 7:911
viscose 3:390; 6:851
vitrification 4:467
vitrification plants 11:1550
VLCCs (Very Large Crude Carriers)
  17:2351
vodka 5:661; 16:2217
von Patera process 15:2079
vulcanization 14:1997, 2001; 18:2454

W

warehousing 19:2622–5
washing pans, rotary 5:638

waste disposal 19:2637–42
  burning in fluidized beds 7:901;
    19:2639
  composting 6:843; 10:1411;
    19:2640
  exportation 6:809
  incineration 19:2638–9
  nuclear 6:796; 11:1539, 1547–50;
    18:*2547*
  packaging waste 12:1625
  refuse dumps 19:*2637*
  removal 19:2637–40
  special and hazardous waste
    19:2641, *2647*
  subsurface waste, detection 7:994
  transfer stations 19:2642
  using bacteria 10:1411
  using reverse osmosis 12:1610
  using yeast 19:2727
  waste as a source of energy 6:797;
    10:1411
  see also landfill; recycling; waste-
    water treatment
Waste Isolation Pilot Project (WIPP)
  11:1548
wastewater treatment (sewage treatment) 19:2643–8
  ceramic diffusion plates 9:*1199*
  fertilizers from 6:844
  in fluidized beds 7:901
  and septic tanks 5:*674*; 19:2648
  using algae 8:1108; 13:1803;
    19:*2645*
  using water hyacinths 13:1803
water, jets, for cleaning 17:2322–3
water cannons, use in mining
  11:1461
water gas process 7:959
watermarks 5:583
water mills 19:2657
water supply 4:476; 13:1786–7;
  19:2661–7

wells 19:2683–4
  see also wastewater treatment
water wheels 9:1192
waterworks 19:2662
Watt, James 11:1458; 15:2055;
  16:2256
wave power 4:549; 19:2675–7
weaving 17:2405–6
  cotton 5:581, 582; 9:*1283*
  rugs and carpets 7:*893*, 894
  see also looms
web-offset printing 9:1264;
  11:1517–18; 13:1850
weed control 19:2678–81
welding 10:*1381*
  aluminum 1:111; 11:1529
  arc 1:*111*; 3:336; 8:1119;
    10:1382–3; 11:*1528*, 1529
  electron-beam 1:111; 10:1383
  friction welding 7:*934*; 10:1384
  gas 10:1382
  laser 10:1383–4
  oxyacetylene 12:1620
  plasma 10:*1366*, 1383
  pressure 10:1384
  ultrasonic 1:111; 10:1384
Well's counterrotating turbine
  19:2676
wet cleaning 5:689
whaling 19:2685–8
wheat, puffed 7:912
whey 5:601, 603
whey, cheese, concentration 12:1610
whiskey 1:*97*; 5:661; 16:2215–17
Whitney, Eli 10:1338
widgets 3:384
Wilkinson, John 13:1826
winding mechanisms, at pit heads
  4:*494*
windmills *see* wind power
wind power 6:793; 13:1826;
  19:2690–5

Windscale (Sellafield) 11:1535
winemaking 1:98; 6:840–1;
  19:2700–3
wire, insulated copper, scrap recovery
  5:591
Wohlwill process 8:1015
wood alcohol *see* methanol
woodworking 19:2716–18
wool 6:848–9, 850
  spinning 16:2214
wrapping
  packaging-wrap manufacture
    12:1626
  shrink 7:908; 12:1624
  stretch 12:1624
wrenches, manufacture 18:2462

Y

yarn 17:2405
  for stockings 8:1090–1
  synthetic, preparation 6:853
  see also spinning
yeast 6:840; 10:1409–10; 19:2725–7
  food yeast 19:2726–7
  and protein production 6:810;
    7:914; 13:*1866*; 19:2726–7
  industrial uses 19:2727
yogurt 5:603; 7:904

Z

zeolites
  as catalysts 3:406; 19:2730
  synthesis 19:2729
zinc, production 19:2731–2
zippers 6:835
  insertion of 4:490
zone refining 17:2347
zubrowka 16:2218

Mechanical Engineering

A

accumulators (hydraulics) 8:1102–3
actuators (jacks) 8:1101, 1103;
  15:2064; 16:*2245*
  servomechanisms and 15:2056,
    2057
aerosols 1:*40*
afterburning 1:65, 76; 7:*965*, 966
agriculture
  machinery 1:45–51
air conditioning 8:1058, 1060–2,
  1063, 1064
aircraft
  control *see* aircraft-control
    engineering
  engines *see* aircraft engines
aircraft-control engineering 1:65–8
aircraft engines 1:72–8
  bypass principle and ratio 1:77, 78
  coolant injection 1:76; 7:966
  cooling 1:72–3
  development(s) 1:72–6
    new 1:78
  gas turbine 1:75, 77
  in-line 1:72
  jet 1:73, 75–6, 77; 7:965–6
    propfan 1:*44*, 78
    propulsive efficiency 1:77
    ramjets and pulse jets (athodyds)
      1:76; 7:967
    scramjet 1:78; 17:2320
    turbofan (fanjet) 1:65, 74, 75,

  76–8; 7:966
    turbojet 1:65; 7:965
    turboprop 1:*72*, 76; 7:966–7
    turboramjets 1:76; 7:967
    turboshaft 1:76; 7:967; 8:1067
  radial 1:72–3, 75
  rotary 1:72
  steam-powered 1:75; 2:210–11
  supercharged 1:74; 16:2303
  turbochargers 1:74, 75; 7:965
  V-formation 1:72
air-cushion vehicles (ACVs; hovercraft; ground-effect machines)
  1:79–81
Anderton Vertical Lift 3:376
apple-picking machines 1:*51*
arms, mechanical 8:*1101*
athodyds 1:76; 7:967
augers 15:2032
  grain elevators 6:776
  for mining 11:1460
  in screw conveyors 4:565
automobiles
  engine 2:198, 199–200
    adhesives used in 1:*29*
    camshafts 2:200
    cooling systems 6:801–2
    crankshaft bearings 2:231
    cylinders 2:199–200, 202
    fan 6:802
    flywheels 7:*902*, 903; 8:1143
    fuel injection 2:200, 203;
      9:*1176*; 10:1426

  fuel pump 4:521
  ignition *see* ignition systems,
    automobile
  lubrication 9:1291–2
  oil filters 9:1292
  oil pan 9:1291–2
  oil pump 2:231; 4:521; 9:1292
  starter motor 16:2241
  and tachometers 2:203
  testing 16:*2285*
  virtual models 19:*2607*
  see also carburetors; internal
    combustion engines
  transmission 2:200; 18:2489–92
    automatic 2:200; 4:492; 7:903;
      8:1104; 18:*2490–1*, 2492
    clutch 2:200; 4:491–2
    constant-mesh 18:2490
    continuously variable (CVT)
      18:*2492*
    differentials 18:2491–2
    flywheels 7:903; 8:1143
    manual 2:200; 4:491, *492*;
      18:2489–90
    semiautomatic 7:903
    synchromesh 18:*2489*, 2490–1

B

Barber, John 7:964
Barker's mill 18:2517
bearings and bushings 2:230–3

bearings
  air 9:1290
  ball 2:230–1
  bicycle 2:243
  in clocks and watches 2:233;
    19:2653
  fluid-film 2:231–3; 9:1289
  magnetic 17:2314
  rolling-element 2:230–1
  rubbing 2:233
  bushings 2:230, *232*
Bendix–Weiss joints 18:2545
bicycles, as stationary power units
  7:903
Birfield-Rzeppa joints 18:*2544*, 2545
boat lifts 3:376
boilers, steam-engine 16:2257
boring mills 10:1310
Bosch, Robert 7:937
Bosch common-rail high-pressure
  injection system 9:*1176*
Bosch K Jetronic injection system
  7:*939*
Brown, Samuel 9:1169
bushings 2:230, *232*
bypass principle and ratio 1:77, 78

C

cams 3:*362*
  cam chains 3:*429*
camshafts 2:200

carburetors **2**:200, 203; **3**:*396–7*; **9**:1171

Carnot cycle **8**:1053; **17**:2414, 2415
  reverse **8**:1063

catalytic converters **2**:205; **3**:405, *407*; **13**:1782, 1802; **15**:*2130*
  zeolite traps **19**:2729

chain drive **3**:*428–9*

chip breakers **10**:*1309*

choke (venturi) **3**:396

Clam (wave-energy device) **19**:*2675–6*

clocks, mechanical **4**:*481–8*

clutches **2**:200; **4**:*491–2*
  dog **18**:2490, 2491
  electromagnetic **4**:492

Cockerell, Christopher **1**:80

Cockerell's rafts **19**:2677

cold heading **15**:*2033–4*

combine harvesters **1**:*45*, 49, 51

common-rail fuel injection systems **9**:*1176*

compressors and pumps **4**:**518–22**
  compressors **4**:518, 519–20
    centrifugal **1**:76; **16**:2303
    compressed air line apparatus **3**:322
    as energy storage **6**:*798–9*
    in jet engines **1**:77
    reciprocating **4**:518, 519
    rotary **4**:519
    rotary vane **4**:519
    screw **4**:519
    for spray guns **16**:*2228*
    superchargers **1**:74
    two-stage **4**:518
  pumps **4**:520
    for aviation fuel **1**:88
    bicycle **4**:518
    Bolsena **4**:520, 521
    centrifugal **4**:521
    cryopumps **5**:592; **18**:2559
    cylinder **8**:1102
    in dishwashers **5**:659
    double-action **4**:*520–1*
    electromagnetic **4**:522; **9**:1254
    filter **18**:2581
    gear **8**:1102
    high-pressure **4**:522
    hydraulic **4**:521; **8**:1101, 1102
    jack (nodding donkeys) **5**:683; **11**:*1573–4*
    jet **4**:522
    for oil recovery **5**:683; **11**:*1573–4*
    peristaltic **4**:521, *522*; **13**:1752
    positive-displacement **4**:*520–1, 522*
    reciprocating **4**:*520–1*
    rotary **4**:*520*, 521; **7**:903; **18**:*2558–9*
    self-priming **4**:*521–2*
    sorption **18**:2559
    sublimation **18**:2559
    sucker-rod **11**:1573
    vacuum **4**:522; **18**:2558
    vane **5**:659
    vapor-diffusion **18**:2559
    water for irrigation **9**:1192
    windmill **19**:2695

conveyors **4**:*564–5*
  baggage, at airports **1**:89, 90

coolant injection **1**:76

cryopumps **5**:592; **18**:2559

cultivators **1**:*47–8*, 51

D

die hobbing **15**:2066

dies, for sheet metal **15**:2064, 2065, 2066

Diesel, Rudolf **7**:937; **9**:1174

diesel engines **7**:937–8, 939; **9**:1171, 1174–5
  common-rail fuel injection systems **9**:*1176*
  soundproofing **15**:*2141*
  in submarines **10**:*1336–7*; **16**:2290, 2291
  in trucks **18**:2506
  turbocharged **9**:1174

die sinking **15**:2066

differentials **18**:*2491–2*

dishwashers **5**:*659–60*
  see also washing machines

drill presses **10**:1310; **19**:2718

drills
  pneumatic **13**:*1788, 1789*
  see also drill presses

dynamos **7**:972; **13**:1827; **19**:*2618–19*

E

E3 (energy-efficient engine) **3**:427

ejectors, air **4**:522

electric motors **6**:**731–4**; **10**:1318
  commutator
    AC- **6**:734
    DC- **6**:*732*, 733–4
  commutatorless in **5**:717
  controls **6**:731
  in electric drills **5**:678
  hysteresis **6**:734
  induction **6**:731, 732–3; **9**:1252
  linear **6**:732; **9**:*1252–6*
  magnetic and electromagnetic **6**:*731–2*
  outboard **10**:1337; **12**:**1614–5**
  reluctance **5**:717, *718*; **6**:734
    magnetic micromotors **5**:718
  repulsion **6**:731
  reversible **6**:731
  for small marine craft **10**:1337
  squirrel-cage **6**:*731, 733*
  stepping **6**:734
  in submarines **10**:*1336–7*
  synchronous **6**:733
  three-phase **6**:*734*
  universal **6**:734
  see also starter motors

electrodischarge machining (EDM; spark erosion; spark machining) **6**:735, 736; **10**:1364, *1366*

elevators (vertical transport), grain **6**:776; **7**:930

engines
  aircraft *see* aircraft engines
  automobile *see* automobiles, engine
  cooling systems **6**:*801–2*; **8**:*1055*
  internal combustion *see* internal combustion engines
  jet
    E3 (energy-efficient engine) **3**:427
    see also aircraft engines, jet
  tank **2**:167

escalators and moving walkways **6**:**820–1**

external combustion engines **8**:1053
  Stirling engines **16**:**2266–9**
  see also steam engines

F

FADEC servomechanisms **15**:*2055*

fanjets *see* turbofans

flypresses **7**:903

flywheels **7**:**902–3**; **8**:1030

fruit machines (slot machines) **7**:*949–50*

fuel injection **2**:200, 203; **7**:**937–9**

G

games machines **7**:**949–52**

gas turbines **7**:**964–7**; **18**:*2517*
  blades **1**:106; **6**:736; **7**:964; **11**:*1522*
  heat exchangers **8**:1055
  and helicopter engines **8**:1067
  for marine propulsion **10**:1336; **13**:*1858*
    hovercraft **1**:*80*
  in power plants **7**:967; **13**:1828, 1832
  soundproofing **15**:*2140*
  see also aircraft engines, jet

gears **7**:**968–9**
  automobile **2**:200; **18**:*2489–92*
  bicycle **2**:*241–2*
  functions **7**:968
  micromachine **10**:*1416*

governors **8**:1017; **15**:*2055–6*

grass-cutting equipment **8**:*1018–9*

Great Britain, SS **3**:428

grinding machines **10**:*1309–10*

ground-effect machines *see* air-cushion vehicles

H

heat engines **8**:1053
  Carnot cycle **8**:1053; **17**:2414, 2415
  Nitinol **1**:107

heat exchangers **8**:*1054–5*, 1064; **11**:*1524*

heating and ventilation systems **8**:**1056–62**
  air conditioning **8**:1058, 1060–2, *1063*, 1064
  heating systems **8**:*1056–8*
    corrosion inhibitors **4**:571
    and heat pumps **8**:1064
    solar energy **6**:792; **8**:1058; **15**:*2115–16*
    storage heaters **6**:800
  ventilation systems **8**:1056, 1058–60

heat pumps **8**:*1060*, **1063–4**
  geothermal **6**:800

Hispano-Suiza engines **1**:72

hovercraft *see* air-cushion vehicles

hunting **15**:2056, 2057; **17**:2426

hydraulics **8**:**1100–4**
  braking systems **3**:*314–5*
  excavators **5**:704; **8**:*1100*
  hydraulic pumps **4**:521
  hydraulic springs **16**:2230
  power-steering systems **16**:*2261–2*
  for tunneling **18**:*2512*, 2513, *2514*
  see also water rams

hydrostatics, hydrostatic bearings **2**:*232–3*

I

ignition systems, automobile **2**:200, 202–3; **8**:**1124–7**; **17**:*2445*
  distributor **2**:*202–3*; **8**:*1124–5*
  ignition coil (induction coil) **8**:1124, 1140
  spark plugs **2**:203; **8**:1125, 1126, 1127; **9**:*1170*

impellers **4**:521

inclined planes, on canals **3**:376

intercooling **16**:2304; **18**:2506

internal combustion engines **9**:**1169–76**
  cooling systems **6**:*801–2*; **8**:*1055*
  crankshaft **9**:1173; **18**:2489
  cylinder configuration **9**:*1172–3*

design **9**:*1172–4*
development of **9**:*1169–71*
  future **9**:1176
diesel *see* diesel engines
emission-control systems **9**:1176
four-stroke **9**:1169, 1170, 1171
fuel injection **7**:*937–9*; **9**:*1171–2*
fuel pumps **7**:*937–8*
gasoline **7**:938, 939; **9**:1176
invention **2**:198
for marine propulsion **10**:1336
  inboard and outboard **16**:2206, *2208*
starter motor **15**:*2125*; **16**:2241
stratified-charge **9**:1176
and transmission systems **18**:2489
two-stroke **9**:1170, 1171, 1292
  motorcycle **11**:1489
valves **9**:*1173–4*
  and cams **3**:362
  exhaust **18**:2568
  manufacture **1**:101
Wankel **9**:1170–1, *1173*, 1175–6
see also automobiles, engine; gas turbines; superchargers and turbochargers

J

jacks *see* actuators

jigsaws **19**:2717

jointers **19**:*2717–8*

K

key-cutting machines **9**:1198

L

lathes **10**:*1306–8*; **19**:2716
  automatic **10**:1308; **15**:2032
  CNC **18**:*2465*
  diamond **5**:639
  geometric **5**:583
  jewelers' **10**:1308
  for making screws **15**:2032
  turret **10**:1307; **15**:2032
  vertical **2**:*238*

Lenoir, J. J. Étienne **2**:198; **9**:1169

Limpet (wave-energy device) **19**:2676

M

machine presses **10**:1306, 1310

machine tools **10**:**1306–10**, 1338
  and cam systems **3**:362
  clutches in **4**:492
  cutters used in **18**:2465
  diamond **5**:639
  drill presses **10**:1310
  electrochemical machining **6**:*735–6*; **10**:1310
  flypresses **7**:903
  grinding machines **10**:*1309–10*
  jig borers **10**:1310
  lasers as **9**:*1213*, 1214; **10**:*1363*
  machine presses **10**:1306, 1310
  mechanical machining **6**:735; **10**:*1306–10*
  milling machines **10**:1309, *1310*
  surfacing tools **10**:*1308–9*
  ultrasound machining **10**:1310
  see also lathes; woodworking

magnetos **8**:1124, 1127
  flywheel **8**:1125

manifolds **2**:205

Manly, Charles **1**:72

marine engineering 10:1365–6
mechanical engineering 10:1363–6
metal cutting and joining
  10:1379–81
  brazing 10:1380–1
  cutting 10:1364
    electrochemical machining
      6:735–6; 10:1310
    electrodischarge machining
      (EDM; spark erosion; spark
      machining) 6:735, 736;
      10:1364, 1366
    flame 10:1379, 1380
    plasma-arc 10:1364, 1379–80
    powder 10:1379
    using lasers 9:1213, 1214;
      10:1363, 1364
    using thermic lances 17:2412
    water-jet 10:1364
  riveting 10:1379, 1384
  soldering 10:1381–2
  see also welding
mill borers 10:1310
milling machines 10:1309, 1310
minimum torque indication (MTI)
  system 13:1789
modeling, three-dimensional
  10:1366
Morley, Samuel 9:1169
mortisers 19:2718
motors
  air 13:1788
  electric see electric motors
  gear 8:1103–4
  hydraulic 8:1103–4
  piston 13:1788
  turbine 13:1788
  vane 8:1104
    positive-displacement 13:1788
  see also internal combustion
    engines
Motronic injection system 7:939
mowers, grass 8:1018–19
MTI (minimum torque indication)
  system 13:1789
mufflers 2:205; 15:2141

N

nodding donkeys 5:683; 11:1573–4

O

oil coolers 9:1292
oil filters 9:1292
oscillating water column (OWC)
  systems 19:2676, 2677
Otto, Nicolaus 2:198

P

Parsons, Charles 7:964
Pelamis (wave power system)
  19:2677
Pelton wheels 8:1113; 18:2519
pistons, reciprocating 13:1789
planers (machine tools) 10:1308,
  1309; 19:2717
plows 1:46–7, 49, 51
  mole 5:674
  underwater cable-laying 3:349
pneumatic tools 13:1788–9
presses
  drill 10:1310
  machine 10:1306, 1310

for sheet metal 15:2064–5
propfans 1:44, 78
prototypes 10:1366
PS Frogs 19:2677
pulleys 13:1869, 1872
pulse jets 7:967
pumps see compressors and pumps
pyramids 13:1870–2

R

radiators
  central-heating, thermostatic
    valves 17:2427
  engine 6:801; 8:1054, 1055
rafts, Cockerell's 19:2677
ramjets 1:76; 7:967
rapid prototyping (RP) 10:1366
regenerators, in Stirling engines
  16:2267
Rochas, Alphonse Beau de 9:1169
Rocket (steam engine) 16:2259
Roots blowers 16:2303, 2304
routers 19:2718

S

Salter Duck 19:2675
sanding machines 1:17; 19:2718
saws 18:2460; 19:2716–17
scavenging, two-stroke engine
  9:1171
Scotch mill 18:2517
scramjets 1:78; 17:2320
screws
  machine 15:2032
  manufacture 15:2032–4
  screw jacks 15:2033
  self-tapping 15:2033
  wood 15:2032
servo, brake-assisted 2:201
servomechanisms 8:1017; 15:2055–7
servomotors 1:66; 2:204
shapers (machine tools) 10:1308–9;
  19:2718
slot machines (one-armed bandits;
  fruit machines) 7:949–50
smokejacks 7:964
spark erosion see electrodischarge
  machining
spark machining see electrodischarge
  machining
spark plugs 2:203; 8:1125, 1126,
  1127; 9:1170
splitters 18:2506–7
starter motors 15:2125; 16:2241
steam engines 9:1169; 16:2256–9
  aircraft 1:75; 2:210–11
  automobile 2:198; 16:2259
  governors 15:2055–6
  for marine propulsion 10:1335;
    16:2258
  for mining 11:1458
  see also traction engines
steam turbines see turbines, steam
Stephenson, George, Rocket 16:2259
stereolithography 10:1366
Stirling engines 16:2266–9
stoichiometric ratio 16:2303
stone monuments 16:2273–5
superchargers and turbochargers
  16:2303–4
  intercooling 16:2304; 18:2506
  superchargers 9:1172; 16:2303,
    2304
    aircraft engine 1:74; 16:2303

vane 16:2303
turbochargers 16:2303, 2304
  aircraft engine 1:74, 75; 7:965
  automobile 2:200
  in diesel engines 9:1174;
    18:2506
  in power plants 7:971
  in racing car engines 14:1889
suspension systems 17:2338–40
synchromesh 18:2489, 2490–1

T

TAPCHAN (tapered channel)
  systems 19:2676
thermic lances 17:2412
thread rolling 15:2034
threads, screw 15:2032–3
threshing machines 1:49–50
throttles 1:65; 3:396
tidal fences 17:2438
torque
  control 13:1789
  converters 8:1104
torque-controlled motor system
  13:1789
traction engines 16:2256; 18:2472–3
transfer machines, cold-heading
  15:2034
transmission, automobile see automobiles, transmission
Trevithick, Richard 16:2256;
  18:2472
turbines 18:2517–20
  blade erosion 18:2520
  gas see gas turbines
  reaction 8:1113, 1115; 18:2517–18
  steam 7:964; 8:1053; 18:2517,
    2518, 2519, 2520
    aircraft 1:75
    centrifugal governors 8:1017
    impulse 18:2519
    for marine propulsion
      10:1335–6
    in power plants 13:1827;
      18:2520
  water 18:2517–18, 2519–20
    Deriaz turbines 18:2518,
      2519–20
    Francis turbines 18:2518,
      2519–20
    in hydroelectric plants
      8:1112–13; 18:2520
    impulse 8:1112–13; 18:2518–19
    Kaplan turbines 18:2518,
      2519–20
    Pelton wheels 8:1113;
      18:2519–20
    for tidal power 17:2437, 2438
    turbo impulse 18:2519
  wave 18:2520; 19:2676, 2677
  wind 6:793; 18:2520
turbochargers see superchargers and
  turbochargers
turbofans (fanjets) 1:65, 74, 75, 76–8;
  7:966
turboprops 1:72, 76; 7:966–7
turboramjets 1:76; 7:967
turboshafts 1:76; 7:967; 8:1067

U

ultrasound machining (USM)
  10:1310
Unified Thread series 15:2032–3
uniflow engines 16:2258

V

vacuum-servo braking systems 3:313,
  314–15
valves, mechanical 18:2566–8
  on aerosol cans 1:40
  ball 18:2568
  bileaflet disk 18:2568
  brass instrument 3:319
  butterfly 18:2568
  cut-out 8:1103
  demand valves, in aqualungs 2:154,
    155
  disk 18:2568
  gate 18:2567, 2568
  globe 18:2568
  heart 18:2568
  internal combustion engine
    9:1173–4
    and cams 3:362
    exhaust valves 18:2568
    manufacture 1:101
  lift 18:2568
  Medtronic-Hall 18:2568
  nonreturn (check valves) 8:1103;
    18:2567–8
    for respirators 3:321
    for taps 13:1787
  piston 16:2256
  poppet 18:2568
  relief 8:1103
  rotary 16:2262
  selector 8:1103, 1104
  single-stage 2:154
  sleeve 1:74; 18:2568
  slide 18:2568
  spool 18:2566–7
    axial 16:2262
  Starr-Edwards 18:2568
  stop 18:2568
  toilet 18:2457–8
ventilation systems see heating and
  ventilation systems
venturi (choke) 3:396

W

Wankel engines 9:1170–1, 1173,
  1175–6
washing machines 19:2634–6
  and chaos theory 3:431
  drums, polished 6:736
  fuzzy logic 3:431; 19:2635–6
  used by the laundry industry
    9:1217–18
  see also dishwashers
water-jet propulsion 10:1365
water mills 19:2657
water pumps 6:801
water rams 19:2658
wave power 4:549; 19:2675–7
welding 10:1381
  aluminum 1:111; 11:1529
  arc 1:111; 3:336; 8:1119;
    10:1382–3; 11:1528, 1529
  electron-beam 1:111; 10:1383
  friction welding 7:934; 10:1384
  gas 10:1382
  laser 10:1383–4
  oxyacetylene 12:1620
  plasma 10:1366, 1383
  pressure 10:1384
  ultrasonic 1:111; 10:1384
Whittle, Frank 1:75; 7:965
woodworking 19:2716–18
wrenches, pneumatic 13:1789

Military Technology

A

A-1 (rocket) 14:*1992*
A-6 Intruder (aircraft) 11:*1456*
A-10 (aircraft) 2:*284*
Aardvark (flailing machines) 3:*294*
Ack-pack (flame thrower) 7:*883*
ADAM (Area Denial Artillery
    Munition) 11:*1454*
advanced combat direction system
    (ACDS) 19:*2627*
Agents Blue, Orange, and White
    4:*438*
Aggregat rocket series 14:*1992*
airborne warning and control
    systems (AWACS) 14:*1895*
aircraft
    ejection seats 5:**711–12**; 8:*1038*
    naval mines deployed from
        11:*1456*
    pilotless 13:**1747–8**; 14:*1913*
    radio and radar jamming equip-
        ment 16:*2250*, 2252–3, *2254*
    refueling (in-flight) 14:**1948–9**
    STOL 1:*71, 77*; 18:*2551*
    swing-wing (variable geometry)
        1:*70, 71*
    with upright fins 1:*39*
    wings, variable-geometry 17:*2319*
aircraft carriers 19:*2626, 2627,*
    2629–30
    aircraft
        arresting mechanisms for
            19:*2632–3*
        steam catapults for 19:*2628,*
            2630–1
air-cushion vehicles (ACVs; hover-
    craft; ground-effect machines),
    military 1:*80, 81, 123*
airships
    zeppelins 1:*91–2*
    carrying bombs 2:*283*
air-traffic control (ATC), military
    1:*93*
American Civil War
    naval mines 11:*1454*
    torpedoes 18:*2467*
ammunition 1:**116–20**
    cartridges 1:*118*; 8:*1024*
    see also armor; ballistics
amphibious vehicles, military
    1:*122–3*; 2:*168*
Amtrack vehicles 1:*122*
anthrax, as a biological weapon
    4:*437, 438, 441*
antiaircraft guns (AA guns) 1:**143–4**
antisatellite weapons (ASATs)
    16:*2181*
antitank weapons
    bazookas 11:*1487*
    mines 11:*1453–4, 1455*
    recoilless guns 11:**1485–7**
APDS (armor-piercing discarding
    sabot) shells 1:*119*; 2:*167*
Area Denial Artillery Munition
    (ADAM) 11:*1454*
Ark Royal, HMS 19:*2630*
armaments, tank 2:*166*
armor
    armor-piercing bombs 2:*286*
    body 2:**161–3**; 13:*1860*
    tank 2:*167*
armored vehicles and tanks 2:**164–8**
    armored vehicles 2:*164, 166, 168*;
        14:*1972*
        tracked 18:*2471*
    tanks 2:*166–8*
        armaments 2:*166*
        and armor-piercing shells

1:*119–20*
    bullet splash inside 2:*162*
    crossing water 1:*122*; 2:*168*
    history 2:*162, 164–6*
    light and main battle 2:*165–6*
    suspension system 18:*2469–70*
    see also antitank weapons
armor-piercing discarding sabot
    (APDS) shells 1:*119*; 2:*167*
arrows 14:*1967*
Arwen 37 (rifle) 11:*1533*
ASATs (antisatellite weapons)
    16:*2181*
assault ships 19:*2629*
asteroids, and space weapons 16:*2184*
Atlas (missile) 11:*1466*
automatic weapons and machine
    guns 2:**193–7**; 8:*1025*
    blowback 2:*194–5, 197*
    early automatic weapons 2:*193*
    gas-operated 2:*194*
    machine guns 8:*1025*
        assault rifles 2:*196*
        general-purpose (GPMGs)
            1:*116*; 2:*196*
        light (automatic rifles) 1:*118*;
            2:*196*; 8:*1025*; 14:*1968*
        motor-driven 2:*197*
        recoil 2:*193–4*
        tracer 2:*217*
    self-loading 2:*193*
        self-loading pistols 2:*196–7*
    submachine guns (machine pistols;
        machine carbines) 2:*195–6, 197*;
        8:*1025*
AV-8 (aircraft) 18:*2551, 2553*
    see also British Aerospace Harrier
AWACS (airborne warning and con-
    trol systems) 14:*1895*

B

B-2 stealth bombers 1:*69*; 16:*2254*
Ballistic Missile Defense
    Organization (BMDO) 16:*2183*
ballistics 2:**216–17**
    forensic 2:*216*; 7:*916–17*
    terminal 2:*216–17*
    see also ammunition
baton rounds 11:*1533*
Battle Management/Command,
    Control, and Communications
    (BM/C3) 16:*2182*, 2184
battlewagons 2:*168*
bazookas 11:*1487*
beam-riding guidance 11:*1468*
Bergmann Maschinenpistole (sub-
    machine gun) 2:*195*
BGM-109 Tomahawk *see* Tomahawk
biowarfare *see* chemical and bio-
    logical warfare
blowback weapons 2:*194–5, 197*
boats, patrol 19:*2633*
bombards 11:*1484*
bombs 2:**283–6**
    aiming devices 2:*284, 285,* **287–8**
    bomb and mine disposal 3:**293–6**;
        5:*591*; 14:*1956*; 18:*2471*
        clothing for 2:*163*; 3:*295*
    cluster 2:*286*
    flying 2:*286*
    gas-generating 2:*286*
    incendiary 2:*286*; 12:*1699*
    nuclear *see* nuclear weapons
    "smart" 2:*288*
    smoke 2:*286*
    terrorist 3:*293–5*
    see also explosives; missiles

bombsights 2:*287–8*
box launchers, for missiles 11:*1467*
bridges, amphibious bridging rigs
    1:*123*
British Aerospace Harrier 1:*71*;
    13:*1826*; 18:*2553*
    cockpit controls 1:*66*
    engine 1:*75, 78*
    inertial guidance platform 8:*1144*
    see also AV-8
Browning guns 2:*194*
brucellosis, as a biological weapon
    4:*438*
bullets 1:*118–19*
    aerodynamic properties 2:*216*
    rubber 11:*1533*; 14:*1973*
bullet splash 2:*162*
Bushnell's keg 11:*1454*

C

Captor (mine) 18:*2468*
Carl Gustav M2 (antitank gun)
    11:*1485*
cartridges (ammunition) 1:*118*;
    8:*1024*
    shotgun 14:*1970*
catapults, steam, on aircaft carriers
    19:*2628, 2630–1*
cellulose nitrate 3:*390*
Ch-46 Sea Knight helicopters
    19:*2629*
chaff 16:*2253–4*
chemical and biological warfare
    4:**437–41**
Chemical Weapons Convention
    (CWC) 4:*437*, 439
chlorine, as a chemical weapon 4:*437,*
    438; 8:*1036*
ciphers 5:*594*
clothing, protective *see* protective
    clothing
CN gas (Mace) 11:*1532*; 14:*1972*
comint 16:*2255*
convertiplanes 18:*2552*
cordite 3:*390*; 6:*842*
crossbows 3:*308*
cryptology 5:**593–6**
CS gas 4:*437*; 11:*1532*

D

DarkStar (aircraft) 16:*2255*
Davids (submarine) 16:*2288*
Davis guns 11:*1486*
deep submergence rescue vessels
    (DSRVs) 16:*2293*
defoliating agents 4:*438*
Desert Storm, Operation 11:*1468*;
    16:*2250*
destroyers, guided-missile (GMDs)
    19:*2627–9, 2631*
digital scene-matching area correla-
    tor (DSMAC) 11:*1468*
dioxin 4:*438*
discarding sabot principle 2:*216*
dogs, sniffer 3:*296*
drogues 5:*711*; 12:*1641, 1642,* 1643
drones, target 13:*1747–8*

E

ECCMs (electronic countercounter-
    measures) 16:*2254–5*
ECMs (electronic countermeasures)
    16:*2250–3*

Edelmann, Geoff 16:*2253*
effect geschoss bullets 1:*118–19*
ejection seats 5:**711–12**; 8:*1038*
electric shock devices (weapons)
    11:*1534*
Enigma machine 5:*593*, 595–6
exoatmospheric kill vehicles (EKVs)
    16:*2179*, 2181, 2184
explosive ordnance disposal (EOD)
    3:*293*
    suits 2:*163*; 3:*295*
explosives 3:*390*; 6:**826–9**
    in ammunition 1:*116*, 117
    detonation 6:*826–7*
    high and low 1:*116*; 6:*826–7*
    in torpedoes 18:*2468*
    see also bombs; mines, explosive;
        missiles
Extended Performance Hydrofoil
    (EPH) 8:*1117*

F

F-4 Phantom (aircraft) 16:*2250*
F-15B (aircraft) 17:*2318*
F-86 Sabre (aircraft) 17:*2319*
F-100 Super Sabre (aircraft) 17:*2319*
F/A 18 Hornet (aircraft) 11:*1456*;
    19:*2631*
Falklands War
    antipersonnel mines 6:*829*
    bomb disposal after 3:*295*
    bombs 2:*284*
    grenades 12:*1700*
    troopships 15:*2073*
FASCAM (FAmily of SCAttereable
    Mines) system 11:*1454*
Fiedler, Richard 7:*882*
fin-stabilized discarding sabot
    (FSDS) projectiles 1:*119*
fission, nuclear, and nuclear weapons
    11:*1551–3*
flailing machines 3:*294*
flame throwers 7:**882–3**
flintlocks 2:*193*; 8:*1024*
flying boats 2:*212, 213*; 13:*1747*;
    15:*2036*
fog sprays 11:*1532*
frigates 19:*2627, 2629*
    hybrid 8:*1117*
FSDS (fin-stabilized discarding
    sabot) projectiles 1:*119*
Fulton, Robert 16:*2288*
fuses and circuit breakers
    fuses
        ammunition 1:*117–18, 119*
        bomb 2:*285*
fusion, nuclear, and nuclear weapons
    11:*1553–4*

G

gamma rays, uses, lasers 9:*1214*
gas and dust masks 7:**953–4**
    military 7:*954*
Gatling guns 2:*193*
gelignite 1:*116*
GEMSS (Ground Emplacement
    Mine Scattering System)
    11:*1454*
Greek fire 7:*869, 882*
grenade launchers 14:*1972*
grenades 1:*120*
    chemical 4:*438*; 11:*1532*; 12:*1700*
    light and noise 11:*1533*
    smoke 14:*1972*
Grumman X29 (aircraft) 1:*43*

Gulf War
 aircraft **16:**2250
 missiles **11:**1468
 oil well fires after **6:**806
guncotton **3:**390
gunpowder **4:**449; **6:**826, 829
 black **1:**101, 120
guns **8:1023–7**
 ammunition **1:**116
 antiaircraft **1:**143–4
 antitank **1:**119; **11:**1485
 and armor **2:**162
 cartridges **1:**118; **8:**1024
 naval **8:**1023, 1026
 silencers **8:**1027
 see also automatic weapons and
  machine guns; ballistics; mortars, bazookas, and recoilless
  guns; rifles and shotguns

H

Harpoon antiship weapon **16:**2291
Harrier *see* British Aerospace Harrier
Hawkeye aircraft **14:**1893
head-mounted displays (HMDs), and
 augmented reality **19:**2608
head-up displays (HUDs)
 8:1039–40, 1082
Heckler and Koch G11 (rifle)
 14:1968–9
Heckler and Koch G36 (rifle)
 14:1969
helicopters **8:1065–70**; **18:**2551–2
 midair recovery systems (MARS)
  13:1748
 military **8:**1067–8, 1070; **19:**2629
 torpedoes **18:**2468
 unpiloted **13:**1748
 use of sonar devices **15:**2128
Hercules (aircraft) **14:**1948
Herstal XM303 (weapons system)
 11:1533–4
HESH (high explosive squash head)
 1:120
Hexogen *see* RDX
high explosive squash head (HESH)
 1:120
HiMAT (Highly Maneuverable
 Aircraft Technology) **1:**65
Hiroshima, atomic bomb used on
 11:1551, 1552, 1554; **14:**1908
Holland, John **16:**2288
Hotchkiss guns **2:**194
hovercraft *see* air-cushion vehicles
Hughes Chain Guns **2:**197
Hydrofoil Collision Avoidance and
 Tracking System (HYCATS)
 8:1117
hydrofoils, military **8:**1117
hydrophones **15:**2126
 and underwater stealth communication **16:**2253

I

ICBMs *see* intercontinental ballistic
 missiles
image intensifiers **8:1128–31**
Individual Weapon, 5.56mm **2:**195
inertial guidance **8:1144–6**; **11:**1468,
 1512, 1513
in-flight interceptor communications
 system (IFICS) **16:**2184
Ingram MII (submachine gun) **2:**196
intercontinental ballistic missiles
 (ICBMs) **11:**1465–6, 1468
 defense against **16:**2180, 2182–4
Iran–Iraq War, chemical weapons
 4:439

J

jamming techniques
 active **16:**2250–3
 passive **16:**2253–4

K

KA-1 Power Staf (nonlethal weapon)
 11:1534
Kalashnikov AK47 (machine gun)
 2:196
 ammunition **2:**216
kinetic energy (KE) attack **1:**119
Knickebein system **16:**2250
Korean War
 defoliants used in **4:**438
 napalm **7:**883
Krupp guns **8:**1027

L

L1A2 image intensifiers **8:**1130
landing vehicles, tracked (military)
 1:123
LARC-60 vehicles **1:**123
lasers and masers
 lasers
  and antiaircraft guns **1:**144
  as anti-ballistic weapons
   16:2183
  as antisatellite weapons
   16:2181–2
  laserguide rangefinders **2:**249,
   250
  as nonlethal weapons **11:**1534
  to guide bombs **2:**284
  to guide missiles **11:**1468
LEASATs (satellites) **15:**2029
Leopard tanks **18:**2470
Little Boy (atomic bomb) **11:**1552
Little David (mortar) **11:**1484
Lockheed F-104 Starfighter (aircraft)
 17:2319
Lockheed SR-71 Blackbird (aircraft)
 17:2319
longbows **3:**306–8
LVTP-7 (Amtrack) vehicles **1:**122

M

M2 (antitank gun) **11:**1485
M3 (half-tracked vehicle) **18:**2471
M9E1-7 (flame thrower) **7:**883
M16 (automatic rifle) **2:**196; **14:**1969
M60 (machine gun) **2:**196
M65 (gun) **8:**1027
M132 (flame thrower) **7:**883
M202A2 (flame thrower) **7:**883
M224 (mortar) **11:**1485
Mace (CN gas) **11:**1532; **14:**1972
machine carbines *see* submachine
 guns
machine guns *see* automatic weapons
 and machine guns
machine pistols *see* submachine guns
Manhattan Project **11:**1554
Martin P.6M Seamaster (aircraft)
 15:2036
matchlocks **2:**193; **8:**1024
Maxim, Hiram, and the Maxim gun
 2:193–4
Maynard tape **8:**1024
MG42 (machine gun) **2:**196
microwaves, uses, as nonlethal
 weapons **11:**1534
midair recovery system (MARS),
 helicopter **13:**1748
MiG-25 (aircraft) **17:**2319

Mine Eyes (mine detectors) **3:**293
Mine-Guzzlers (demining machines)
 3:294
mines, explosive **3:**293; **6:**829;
 11:1453–6
 antiarmor **11:**1453–4
 antipersonnel **11:**1453, 1454,
  1455, 1456
 disposal *see* bombs, bomb and mine
  disposal
 naval **11:**1454–6; **19:**2633
 space mines **16:**2181
minesweepers **19:**2633
Minuteman (missile) **11:**1466;
 16:2179, 2181
MIRVs (multiple independently targetable reentry vehicles)
 11:1468
missiles **11:1465–8**
 antiaircraft **1:**143, 144
  surface-to-air (SAMs) **1:**144
 antiradar (ARMs) **16:**2254
 ballistic **11:**1465, 1468
  defense against **16:**2180, 2182–4
  intercontinental ballistic missiles
   (ICBMs) **11:**1465–6, 1468
  submarine-launched (SLBMs)
   16:2182
 cruise **11:**1465, 1466, 1467, 1468;
  16:2291
 guided **1:**143; **6:**742; **11:**1465,
  1487
 "smart" **11:**1467–8
 stealth (Sea Skuas) **16:**2251
 strategic **11:**1465, 1468
 warheads **11:**1468
 see also bombs; explosives
Mk 46 torpedoes **18:**2468
Mk 48 ADCAP torpedoes **18:**2467–8
Morse code **5:**593
mortars, bazookas, and recoilless
 guns **11:1484–7**
 bazookas **11:**1487
 mortars **11:**1484–5
 recoilless guns **11:**1485–7
moving target indication (MTI)
 5:672; **14:**1898
MRVs (multiple reentry vehicles)
 11:1468
MTI (moving target indication)
 5:672; **14:**1898
multiple independently targetable
 reentry vehicles (MIRVs)
 11:1468
multiple reentry vehicles (MRVs)
 11:1468
mustard gas, as a chemical weapon
 4:437, 438; **7:**953; **8:**1036
MX (missiles) **14:**1993

N

Nagasaki, atomic bomb used on
 11:1551, 1553; **14:**1908
napalm **2:**284; **7:**883
national missile defense (NMD)
 system **16:**2181, 2182, 2183–4
nerve gases **4:**437, 438–9
night, binoculars **2:**250
nitrocellulose **3:**390
nitroglycerine **3:**390
nonlethal weapons **11:1532–4**;
 14:1972
 tear gases **4:**437; **11:**1532, 1534;
  14:1972
 water cannons **11:**1533, 1534;
  14:1972
Northrop B-2 bomber **1:**69; **16:**2254
nuclear weapons **11:1551–4**
 bombs
  atomic (A-bombs) **2:**286; **7:**877;

 11:1551, 1552–4; **14:**1906, 1908
 fission-fusion-fission (Triple-F)
  11:1554
 hydrogen **2:**286; **7:**947; **11:**1551
 neutron **11:**1551, 1554
 missiles with nuclear warheads
  11:1468

O

oleoresin capsicum (OC) **11:**1532,
 1533
optical range finders **1:**143–4
organ guns **2:**193

P

P-3 Orion (aircraft) **11:**1456
Panavia Tornado (aircraft), weapons
 1:117
parachutes **12:1641–3**
 ballistic **18:**2527
 drogue **5:**711; **12:**1641, 1642, 1643
Paris gun **8:**1026
patrol boats **19:**2633
payload launch vehicles (PLVs)
 16:2184
PBX (plastic-bonded explosive)
 18:2468
Peacekeeper (missile) **11:**1465, 1466
pentaerythritol tetranitrate (PETN)
 1:116; **6:**827, 828
pepper sprays **11:**1532–3; **14:**1972
percussion locks **8:**1024
phosgene (carbonyl chloride), as a
 chemical weapon **4:**437, 438;
 7:953; **8:**1036
pilotless aircraft **13:1747–8**; **14:**1913
pistols
 air **8:**1025
 automatic **2:**196–7
 machine *see* submachine guns
poison gas **4:**437
pontoons **3:**328; **15:**2023
PPSh-41 (submachine gun) **2:**195–6
predictors **1:**143–4
propellants, ammunition **1:**116–17
protective clothing
 against chemical weapons **4:**439,
  440
 see also armor, body
proximity-fusing **11:**1485
psychochemicals **4:**437

Q

Q fever, as a biological weapon **4:**438
quinuclidinyl benzilate (BZ) **4:**437

R

radar **14:1893–8**
 and antiaircraft guns **1:**144
 and early-warning defense systems
  14:1893, 1895–6, 1897
 ground-penetrating (GPR)
  14:1898
 IFF (Interrogation Friend or Foe)
  1:144
 for mine detection **3:**293
 and MTI (moving target indication) **5:**672; **14:**1898
 search **14:**1898
 and stealth technologies
  jamming techniques **16:**2251–2
  radar-avoidance aircraft **1:**69,
   144; **10:**1350; **16:**2254
 used in "smart" missiles **11:**1467–8

radar (cont.)
　X-band (XBR), to track missiles
　　16:2184
railway guns **8**:1026, 1027
rangefinders, laser **2**:*249*, *250*
range-gate stealing **16**:2252
Rasura radar packs **14**:1898
RDX (Hexogen; Cyclonite) **1**:116;
　6:828
reconnaissance
　by radio-controlled aircraft
　　14:1913
　by remotely piloted vehicles
　　(RPVs) **13**:1747
　electronic **16**:2255
refueling, in-flight **14**:*1948–9*
Remote Antiarmor Mine System
　(RAAMS) **11**:1454
remote handling, bomb- and mine-
　disposal robots **3**:294, 295, *296*;
　14:*1956*; **18**:2471
remotely piloted vehicles (RPVs)
　13:1747–8
revolvers **8**:1025–6
　fitted with riot-control hardware
　　14:*1972*
ricin **4**:438
rifles and shotguns **14**:**1967–70**
　rifles **14**:1967
　　antitank **1**:119
　　assault **2**:196
　　automatic (light machine guns)
　　　1:118; **2**:196; **8**:1025; **14**:*1968*
　　bolt-action **14**:1967–8
　　breech- and muzzle-loading
　　　14:1967
　　self-loading **14**:1968
　　semiautomatic **8**:1025
　shotguns **14**:1967, 1969–70
　　double-barreled **14**:*1969*, 1970
riot control **14**:**1971–2**
robotics, for remote handling, bomb
　and mine disposal **3**:294, 295,
　296; **14**:*1956*; **18**:2471
rockets and space propulsion
　rockets
　　antitank **7**:883; **11**:1487
　　for missile propulsion **11**:1466,
　　　1487; **14**:*1991*
Rockwell B-1 bomber **1**:*70*
rounds, baton **11**:1533
RPVs (remotely piloted vehicles)
　13:1747–8

S

S-3 Viking (aircraft) **11**:1456
SAMs (surface-to-air missiles) **1**:144
Sarin **4**:437, 439, *441*; **12**:1700
satellites, artificial
　military, as targets for space
　　weapons **16**:2180–2
　as space mines **16**:2181
Saunders Roe SR-A1 (aircraft)
　15:2036
saxitoxin **4**:438
SBIRS (High) **16**:2184
Schwarzlose machine guns **2**:194
Sealab program **18**:2538, 2539
search and rescue (SAR) operations
　15:2038
Sea Skuas (missiles) **16**:*2251*
semiactive homing **11**:1468
shells
　antiaircraft-gun **1**:143–4
　armor-piercing **1**:119–20

carrying chemical weapons **4**:*441*
chemical-energy (CE) **1**:119–20
ships
　naval mines deployed from
　　11:1456
　radio and radar jamming equip-
　　ment **16**:2253
　warships **19**:2626–33
Short Sutherland (aircraft) **15**:2036
shotguns *see* rifles and shotguns
silencers, gun **8**:1027
SLBMs (submarine-launched
　ballistic missiles) **16**:2182
sleep guns **11**:1534
Soman **4**:437; **12**:1700
sonar
　use **15**:2128–9
　　guiding torpedoes **1**:27; **18**:2468
　　to detect submarines **8**:1070;
　　　15:*2127*, 2128
SOSUS (Sound Surveillance System)
　15:2128
space mines **16**:2181
space weapons **16**:**2179**–*4*
Spearfish torpedoes **18**:2468
SR.N5 (air-cushion vehicle) **1**:*80*
Star Wars (Strategic Defense
　Initiative; SDI) **16**:2183, 2184
stealth technologies **16**:**2250–5**
　electronic countermeasures
　　18:2550–3
　stealth aircraft **1**:*69*, 144; **10**:*1350*;
　　16:2254
Sterling submachine guns **2**:*197*
"sticky foam" **11**:*1532*
Stinger (missile) **1**:144; **11**:1487
Stingray torpedoes **18**:2468
Stokes, Sir Wilfred **11**:1484
STOL aircraft **1**:71, 77; **18**:2551
Strategic Defense Initiative (SDI;
　Star Wars) **16**:2183, 2184
"stun guns" **11**:1534
submachine guns (machine pistols;
　machine carbines) **2**:195–6, *197*;
　8:1025
submarine-launched ballistic missiles
　(SLBMs) **16**:2182
submarines **16**:**2287–91**
　air locks used in **1**:85
　armaments **16**:2182, *2288*, *2289*,
　　2290, 2291
　concrete used in **4**:549
　design **10**:1366; **16**:2288
　detection, by sonar **8**:1070;
　　15:*2127*, 2128
　diving **16**:2288–9
　early **16**:2287–8
　helicopters towed behind **8**:1070
　hunters, helicopter **8**:1070
　navigation **16**:2290–1
　periscopes **12**:1674–5; **16**:2290
　power **10**:1336–7; **16**:2289–90
　　diesel engines **10**:1336–7;
　　　16:2290, 2291
　　nuclear propulsion **10**:1336,
　　　1366; **11**:1542, 1546; **16**:2290,
　　　2291
　　steam **16**:2289–90
　　Stirling engines **16**:*2266*, 2269
　rescuing **15**:*2023*
　and sonar **8**:1070; **15**:*2127*, 2128
　underwater stealth communication
　　16:2253
　see also torpedoes
Subroc (antisubmarine weapon)
　16:2291
surface-effect vehicles **1**:122, 123

surface-to-air missiles (SAMs) **1**:144
SURTASS (Surveillance Towed
　Array) **15**:2128
surveillance, using thermography
　17:2422

T

tabun **4**:437; **12**:1700
tactical missile systems (TACMs)
　11:1466
tanks *see* armored vehicles and tanks
target-augmentation techniques
　13:1748
Tasers **11**:1534
tear gases **4**:437; **11**:1532, *1534*;
　14:*1972*
telint **16**:2255
TERCOM (terrain contour match-
　ing system) **11**:1468
terminal guidance systems (TGSs)
　2:288
tetryl **1**:116
Thompson Model 1928 (submachine
　gun) **2**:195
TNT *see* trinitrotoluene
Tomahawk (missile) **11**:1466, *1467*,
　1468; **16**:2291
　antiship **11**:*1466*
topex **18**:2468
torpedoes **1**:27; **16**:2291; **18**:**2467–8**
Tortoise (tracked armored vehicle)
　18:2471
toss-bombing **2**:*287*
total-containment vessels (TCVs)
　3:296
tracked vehicles **18**:**2469–71**
　half-tracks **18**:2470–1
　tanks **2**:167–8; **18**:2469–70, 2471
Trident missiles **16**:*2289*, 2291
trinitrotoluene (TNT) **1**:116; **6**:828
Turtle (submarine) **16**:2287–8
typhoid, as a biological weapon **4**:*437*

U

Uzi (submachine gun) **2**:196

V

V1 (bomb) **2**:286
V-2s (rocket missiles) **8**:1144;
　14:*1992*
V/STOL (VTOL) aircraft **1**:71, 77,
　78; **18**:**2551–3**
　convertiplanes **8**:1069; **18**:2552
　see also helicopters
V agents **4**:437
Vietnam War
　chemical weapons **4**:438
　napalm **7**:883
　helicopters **8**:1068
Villar Perosa (submachine gun) **2**:195
Vulcan Air Defence System, Vulcan
　Gatling guns **1**:144; **2**:197

W

warheads, torpedo **18**:2468
warships **19**:2626–33
water cannons, law-enforcement
　11:*1533*, 1534; **14**:*1972*
weapons, nonlethal *see* nonlethal

weapons
　Webley Tempest (air pistol) **8**:1025
Wheelbarrow (robot) **3**:296; **14**:*1956*;
　18:2471
wheel locks **8**:1024
Whitehead, Robert **18**:2467
wire guidance
　missile **11**:1466–7
　torpedo **18**:2468
Wombat (recoilless gun) **11**:1486
World War I
　aerial photography **1**:33
　aircraft **1**:41–2; **2**:212
　airships **1**:92
　body armor **2**:162
　bombsights **2**:287
　chemical weapons **4**:437, 438;
　　8:1036
　flame throwers **7**:882
　gas masks **7**:953
　guns **8**:*1023*, 1026
　parachutes **12**:1641
　periscopes **12**:1674
　tanks **2**:162, 164, 168
World War II
　aerial photography **1**:34
　aircraft **1**:41; **2**:213; **15**:*2023*
　balloons **2**:218
　flight recorders **7**:884
　flying boats **15**:2036
　fuel-injection systems **7**:937
　ammunition **1**:118
　　antitank guns **1**:119
　　white phosphorus used in
　　　12:1700
　automatic rifles **8**:1025
　body armor **2**:162–3
　bombs **2**:284, 286; **3**:293
　　atomic **11**:1551, 1552, 1553,
　　　1554
　　disposal **3**:293
　bombsights **2**:287–8
　chemical weapons **4**:437, 438
　computers **4**:523
　cryptology **5**:593, 595–6
　flame throwers **7**:882, 883
　guns **8**:1027
　　naval **8**:*1023*
　kamikaze speedboats **16**:2208
　military bridges **3**:328
　motorcycles **11**:1489
　naval mines **11**:1454–5
　radio jamming **16**:2250
　radio receivers **14**:1904
　radio transmitters, power **17**:2420
　submarines, helicopters towed
　　behind **8**:1070
　tanks **2**:164
　torpedoes **18**:2467
　V-2 missiles **8**:1144; **14**:1992

X

X-ray imaging, of bombs **3**:295
X rays
　anti-ballistic weapons **16**:2183
　X-ray lasers **9**:1214

Y

yellow fever, as a biological weapon
　4:438

Transportation and Leisure

A

ABS (antilock braking system) **2**:201, 204, 206; **3**:315
Ackermann steering **16**:2260, *2262*
ACVs *see* air-cushion vehicles
Advanced Light Rapid Transit (ALRT) system **10**:1349
Advanced Passenger Trains (APTs) **14**:1928
advance traffic information (ATI) **14**:1926
Aerotrains **11**:1482; **14**:1928
ailerons **1**:66, 71
airbags **2**:209; **10**:*1417*
Airbus 320 (aircraft) **2**:213
Airbus Industrie A380 **1**:*83*
aircraft
  aerodynamics **1**:38–9, 69
  ambulance **1**:113; **8**:1067, *1070*
  at airports **1**:87–8
  autopilot **1**:67–8; **15**:2057
  axes of rotation (pitch, roll and yaw) **1**:*70*, 71
  braking systems **3**:314, 315
  for container traffic **7**:932
  control surfaces **1**:65–6, 71
  delta **1**:70–1
  design **1**:69–71
    and aerodynamics **1**:39
  drag **1**:38–9, 66
  ejection seats **5**:711–12; **8**:1038
  engines *see* aircraft engines
  firefighting from **6**:861; **8**:1067; **15**:*2035, 2036*
  flight recorders **1**:67; **7**:884–5
  fly-by-wire **1**:44, 66; **2**:213
  flying wing **1**:69–70
  fuel-level sensors and indicators **18**:*2484*
  fuselage **1**:69–70
  high-altitude **10**:*1401*; **12**:1620
  jet
    fuel **11**:1579
    jetliners **1**:83–4; **2**:213
    V/STOL **18**:*2552*
    wings **1**:70
  landings **1**:66, 68, 88–9, 94, 95, 96; **11**:1513
    blind **1**:96
  lift **1**:38, 66, 70
    center of **1**:69
  navigation *see* navigation, aircraft
  pilotless **13**:1747–8; **14**:1913
  pressure transducers **18**:*2474*
  pressurized air cabins **1**:82–3
  propellers *see* propellers, aircraft
  radio-controlled **14**:1913
  refueling (in-flight) **14**:1948–9
  rudders **1**:66, 71; **14**:2004; **15**:2057
  seaplanes and amphibians **1**:69; **15**:2035–7
  sound and the Doppler effect **5**:672
  stalling **1**:70
  STOL **1**:71, 77; **18**:2551
  STOVL **18**:2553
  subsonic **1**:70
  sunken, recovery **15**:2022–3
  supersonic *see* supersonic flight
  swing-wing (varible geometry) **1**:*70*, 71
  tail **1**:69
  thrust **1**:65
  tires **18**:*2456*
  toilets **18**:*2458*, 2459
  transonic **17**:2319
  turning **1**:*71*
  ultralight **8**:1038; **18**:2524–7

  undercarriage, retractable **18**:2535–6
  with upright fins **1**:*39*
  used for pesticide application **12**:*1676*, 1677
  V/STOL **18**:2551–3
  vectored-thrust **1**:71, 77; **18**:2552–3
  wings **1**:*43*, 44, 70–1
    aerodynamics **1**:38–9
    and schlieren techniques for sections of **15**:2031
    supersonic-speed **17**:2319
    variable-geometry **17**:2319
  see also airliners
aircraft engines **1**:72–8
  bypass principle and ratio **1**:77, 78
  coolant injection **1**:76; **7**:966
  cooling **1**:72–3
  development(s) **1**:72–6
    new **1**:78
  gas turbine **1**:75, 77
  in-line **1**:72
  jet **1**:*73*, 75–6, 77; **7**:965–6
    propfan **1**:*44*, 78
    propulsive efficiency **1**:77
    ramjets and pulse jets (athodyds) **1**:76; **7**:967
    scramjet **1**:78; **17**:2320
    turbofan (fanjet) **1**:65, *74*, 75, 76–8; **7**:966
    turbojet **1**:65; **7**:965
    turboprop **1**:*72*, 76; **7**:966–7
    turboramjets **1**:76; **7**:967
    turboshaft **1**:76; **7**:967; **8**:1067
  radial **1**:72–3, 75
  rotary **1**:72
  steam-powered **1**:*75*; **2**:210–11
  supercharged **1**:*74*; **16**:2303
  turbochargers **1**:74, 75; **7**:965
  V-formation **1**:72
air-cushion vehicles (ACVs; hovercraft; ground-effect machines) **1**:79–81; **2**:233; **10**:1337
  military **1**:*80*, 81, 123
airfoils **10**:1335
  and racing cars **14**:1889–90
  and sail design **14**:*2009*
  in wind tunnels **19**:*2698*
airliners **1**:82–4
  at airports **1**:*88*
  early development **1**:42, 82
  jetliners **1**:83–4; **2**:213
  using head-up displays **8**:1040
airports **1**:86–90
  firefighting at **1**:89; **6**:860, 862
  maglev links **5**:719
  noise from **15**:2141
  runways **1**:87, 88, *94*
  stacked aircraft over **1**:*96*
  see also air-traffic control
airships **1**:91–2; **2**:218
  Hindenberg **8**:1119; **9**:1288
  see also balloons
air-traffic control (ATC) **1**:93–6; **11**:1513
  radar **1**:88, 94–5; **3**:410; **14**:1895–6, *1897*
  virtual reality and **19**:*2608*
airways **1**:93
all-terrain vehicles (ATVs) **1**:121
ALRVs (Articulated Light Rail Vehicles) **16**:*2278*
Alvin (submersible) **11**:*1568, 1569*; **16**:2294
ALWEG systems **11**:1482
ambulances **1**:112–13
amphibians (seaplanes) **15**:2035, 2037

amphibious vehicles **1**:121–3
Amphicats **1**:121
Amsterdam, metro system **10**:1349
Amtrack vehicles **1**:*122*
antiroll tanks **16**:2231
Antwerp, port **9**:1266
Aquarius (ocean laboratory) **18**:*2538, 2539*, 2540
Ariane launch vessels **1**:43
armored vehicles and tanks **2**:164–8
Arun class lifeboats **15**:2040
astrodomes **15**:2063
astrolabes **15**:2062
astronavigation **11**:1511
Atlantis (space shuttle) **1**:*85*; **2**:*173*; **16**:*2169, 2174*
ATVs (all-terrain vehicles) **1**:121
autogiros (gyroplanes) **2**:*212*; **8**:1065, 1067, 1069–70
  pilotless **13**:*1747*
automatic radar-plotting aid (ARPA) **11**:1514
automatic train protection **14**:1925–6
automation, mass transit and subway **10**:1348
automobiles **2**:198–201
  air bags **2**:209; **10**:*1417*
  alarms **3**:340; **12**:*1664*
  alternative power sources **2**:200; **5**:720
    alcohol-based (biofuels) **2**:258, 259; **6**:794
    electric cars **2**:200, 201; **5**:720; **6**:794–5; **9**:1286–7
    hybrid-drive cars **5**:720; **9**:1288; **16**:2269
    hydrogen **2**:200; **8**:1119; **9**:1287–8
    liquid propane gas **7**:959
    ZLEV cars **2**:201
  bearings and bushings **2**:*232*
  body **2**:199
    aerodynamics **1**:36, *37*; **2**:199, *200*, 209
    corrosion resistance **2**:199; **4**:*570*
    powder coatings **13**:*1823*
    and safety **2**:207
  braking systems **2**:201, 206; **3**:314–15
    antilock (ABS) **2**:201, 204, 206; **3**:315
    disk-type and drum-type **2**:201; **3**:313–14
    parking brake **3**:314
  collisions **2**:*206, 207*, 208
  combustion **2**:200
  cooling system **8**:*1054*
    radiator **8**:1054, *1055*
  cooling systems, thermostats **17**:*2426, 2427*
  customized **10**:1341
  decorative and protective coatings **17**:2324
  design, using wind tunnels **19**:*2696, 2699*
  development of **2**:198–9
  for disabled drivers **11**:1471
  electrical systems
    alternator **2**:201
    battery **2**:201, 227–8; **6**:799
    dynamo **7**:972
    voltage regulator **19**:2618–19
  electronics systems **2**:202–4
    air-pressure sensors **10**:*1418*
    diagnostic systems **2**:202
    engine-control module (ECM) **2**:204
    exhaust-gas analysis **2**:203

  fuel injection system **2**:200, 203; **10**:*1426*
    ignition **8**:1125–6
    microprocessors **2**:202, 204; **10**:*1420*, 1426
    sensors **2**:203–4
  engine **2**:198, 199–200
    camshafts **2**:200
    cooling systems **6**:801–2
    crankshaft bearings **2**:231
    cylinders **2**:199–200, 202
    fan **6**:802
    flywheels **7**:*902*, 903; **8**:1143
    fuel injection **2**:200, 203; **9**:*1176*; **10**:1426
    fuel pump **4**:521
    lubrication **9**:1291–2
    oil filters **9**:1292
    oil pan **9**:1291–2
    oil pump **2**:231; **4**:521; **9**:1292
    starter motor **16**:2241
    and tachometers **2**:203
    testing **16**:*2285*
    virtual models **19**:*2607*
    see also carburetors
  exhaust system **2**:205
    catalytic converters **2**:205; **3**:405, *407*; **13**:*1782, 1802*; **15**:*2130*
    chromium-plated tailpipes **4**:570
    mufflers **2**:205; **15**:2141
  four-wheel drive **2**:200
  front-wheel drive (FWD) **2**:200; **18**:2544–5
  fuel tank **2**:207
  headlights **11**:1464
  head-up displays **6**:*813*; **8**:1040, *1129*
  instrument panel (dashboard displays) **6**:755, *813*, 814
    fuel gauge **18**:2474
    odometers **16**:2209–10
    oil gauge **9**:1292
    speedometers **16**:2209, *2210*
    tachometers **16**:2210
  "intelligent" **10**:*1420*
  interior design **6**:814
  lightning and **17**:2431
  manufacture
    mass production **10**:1338, 1339, 1341, *1380*; **14**:1987; **15**:*2066*
    sheet-metal working **15**:*2064*, 2065
  model, radio-controlled **14**:1915
  noise reduction **15**:2141
  odometers **2**:245
  radio antennas **6**:740
  recyclable **10**:*1364*, 1366
  reflectors **14**:1944
  safety **2**:199, 206–9
  sealants used in **1**:32
  steam cars **2**:198; **16**:2259
  steering **2**:201, 207; **16**:2260–2
    levers **11**:1471
    steering columns **2**:207, *209*; **16**:2260
  suspension **2**:201; **16**:2229
    active **2**:201, 204, 206–7; **17**:2339
    hydropneumatic **2**:201; **17**:2339
    independent **2**:201
    pneumatic **17**:2339
    shock absorbers **10**:1353; **16**:2229
    see also suspension systems
  tires **2**:201, 206; **17**:2338
  transmission **2**:200; **18**:2489–92
    automatic **2**:200; **4**:492; **7**:903; **8**:1104; **18**:*2490–1*, 2492

transmission (*cont.*)
  clutch **2**:200; **4**:491–2
  constant-mesh **18**:2490
  continuously variable (CVT) **18**:2492
  differentials **18**:2491–2
  flywheels **7**:903; **8**:1143
  manual **2**:200; **4**:491, *492*; **18**:2489–90
  semiautomatic **7**:903
  synchromesh **18**:*2489*, 2490–1
  transport, as rail freight **14**:1927
  trim **4**:*472*, 473
  wheels, camber angles **16**:2261
  windshields **1**:30; **7**:1001
  see also racing cars and dragsters
autorotation **8**:1066–7
aviation
  electronics (avionics) **1**:44, 66–7, 78
  flight simulators **7**:**886**–7; **11**:1501; **19**:2603–4
  history of **2**:**210**–13
    aircraft engines **1**:72–6; **2**:213
    airships **1**:91–2
    balloons **2**:*210*, 218
    gliders **2**:210; **7**:1004
    passenger aircraft and airliners **1**:82, 83–4; **2**:213
    World War I **1**:41–2; **2**:212
    World War II **1**:41; **2**:213; **15**:*2023*
    Wright brothers **1**:72, 77; **2**:211; **19**:2696
axles **17**:2339–40

B

baggage handling, at airports **1**:89–90
ballonets **1**:91
balloons **2**:**218–21**; **7**:961; **13**:*1839*
  parachuting from **12**:1643
  see also airships
balls
  golf **16**:2220–1
  tennis **16**:2219–20
baseball
  equipment **13**:1862; **16**:*2223*, 2224
  pitching baseballs **5**:*694*
basketball, clothing **13**:1862
bathyscaphes **16**:2292–3
bathyspheres **10**:1333; **16**:2292
Bell XP-59 **2**:213; **7**:965
Benz, Karl **2**:198
Berlin, subways **10**:1349
Bertin Hovertruck **1**:81
bicycles **2**:**240–4**; **16**:2222
  aerodynamics **2**:*243*, 244
    cyclists **1**:*39*
  amphibious **1**:122
  bicycle pumps **4**:518
  brakes **2**:242–3
  frames **2**:243–4
  freewheeling **2**:242
  racing **2**:*241*, 244
  recumbent **1**:*39*; **2**:*242*, 244
  riding **8**:1030
  tires and wheels **2**:241, 243, 244; **17**:2338
  transmission systems **2**:241–2
    chain drive **2**:241, 242; **3**:428
    gears **2**:241–2
    using computers **2**:244
"Big Boys" (locomotives) **9**:1274
biplanes **2**:211, 212
  Hiperlight **18**:2525
blimps **1**:91
Bluebird (speedboat) **16**:2208
boats
  fireboats **6**:861

flying *see* flying boats
  ice **14**:2013
  jet **16**:2208
  lifeboats **15**:2038–40, 2050–1
  model, radio-controlled **14**:1914–15
  see also self-righting boats; speedboats
Boeing 247 **1**:82; **2**:213
Boeing 314 Clipper (seaplane) **15**:2035
Boeing 707 **1**:84; **2**:213
Boeing 747 **1**:84, 89; **2**:*212*
Boeing 767-200 **1**:82–3
Boeing Chinook **8**:1067, 1068
Boeing jetfoil **8**:1117
Boeing Sonic Cruiser **1**:71
Boeing Stratoliner **1**:82–3
Boneshakers **2**:240
"bow thrusters" **15**:2068
boxing, clothing **13**:1863
braking systems **3**:**313–15**; **7**:933
  air brakes **3**:315
    on gliders **7**:1005
    on trucks **18**:2507
  aircraft **3**:314, 315
  antilock (ABS) **2**:201, 204, 206; **3**:315
  automobile *see* automobiles, braking systems
  band **3**:313
  bicycle **2**:242–3
  block **3**:314
  cable car **3**:356
  disk **2**:201; **3**:314; **7**:*933*
  drum **2**:201; **3**:313–14
  dual **3**:315
  electric **3**:315
  hydraulic **3**:314–15
  power brakes **3**:*313*, 314–15
  regenerative **3**:315; **9**:1287; **10**:1346
  rheostatic **10**:1346
  train **3**:314, 315; **10**:1346; **14**:1925, 1926
  truck **18**:2507
Breitling Orbiter 3 (balloon) **2**:220, 221
buses (transport) **3**:**342–3**
  brakes **3**:315
  electric **9**:1286
  flywheel-driven **8**:1030
  hydrogen-powered **8**:1119; **9**:1288
    fuel-cells **7**:936; **9**:1288
  rear-window lenses **9**:1230

C

cable cars
  aerial **3**:358
  streetcar **16**:2276–7
cables, for launching gliders **7**:1004
cable transport systems **3**:**356–8**
cableways **3**:*357*
camber **16**:2261
canals **3**:**373–6**
  locks **3**:373, 375–6; **9**:**1265–6**
  capstans **19**:2689
  caravels **14**:2010
carburetors **2**:200, 203; **3**:**396–7**; **9**:1171
cargo handling
  at airports **1**:89
  cableways **3**:*357*
cars, electric **2**:200, 201; **5**:720; **6**:794–5; **9**:1286–7
catamarans **10**:1365; **16**:*2205*, 2206, *2207*
Cayley, Sir George **2**:210; **7**:1004; **8**:1065
chain drives **3**:**428–9**

bicycle **2**:241, 242; **3**:428
chairlifts **3**:*357*
Challenger (space shuttle) **15**:2029; **16**:2168
  and space debris **12**:1600
Channel Tunnel, rail link through **4**:476
clay-pigeon shooting **14**:1970; **16**:2224
cliff railways **3**:356–7
Cobras (helicopters) **8**:*1067*
cog railways **4**:**506**
  funiculars **3**:357–8
Columbia (space shuttle) **1**:43; **16**:2166, 2167; **17**:*2364*
compasses, magnetic **11**:1510, *1514*
Concorde (aircraft) **1**:84; **2**:213; **17**:2319–20
  engine **1**:65
  Kevlar fuel-tank linings **13**:1806
conduit systems, for streetcars **16**:2277, 2278
Conshelf (submersibles) **18**:2538–9
containers **7**:931; **15**:2069
  air containerization **7**:932
  container ships **7**:932; **15**:2067, 2069–70
  docks **5**:669–70
  handling **7**:930–2
    cranes **5**:*586*, 588, 670; **7**:931, *932*
  rail transport **14**:1927
convertiplanes **8**:1069; **18**:2552
Cook, James **15**:2062
Cugnot, Nicolas Joseph **2**:198; **16**:2259
cyclists *see* bicycles

D

Daimler, Gottlieb **2**:198; **16**:2204
day-color-light signals **14**:1924
Day, J. **16**:2287
"dead man's handle" **14**:1926
dead reckoning (DR) **11**:1511
De Havilland Comet **1**:83–4
dimethylether (DME) fuel **3**:343
dinghies
  capsized **15**:2050
  inflatable, inshore-rescue **15**:2041
dirigibles *see* airships
dirt-car racing **14**:1891
Discovery (space shuttle) **9**:*1201*; **15**:*2024*
Docklands Light Railway **10**:1348; **14**:1925; **16**:2278
Douglas DC aircraft
  DC-1, DC-2, and DC-3 **1**:82
  DC-7 **2**:213
  DC-8 **1**:84
drag racing *see* racing cars and dragsters
Drebbel, Cornelius van **16**:2287
drogues **5**:711; **12**:1641, *1642*, 1643
DUKW vehicles **1**:*121*, 122–3
dummies, crash-test **2**:208
Dunlop, John Boyd **17**:2338; **18**:2453
Dusenbergs (racing cars) **14**:1892

E

Eagle (microlight aircraft) **18**:*2524*
electropults **9**:1254
elevators (aerodynamic surface), controlling flight **1**:66, 71, 91
elevators (vertical transport) **6**:774–5; **15**:2095
  freefalling, and weight **6**:*789*
  paternoster **6**:775

elevons **1**:71
Endeavour (space shuttle) **14**:*1955*; **16**:*2165*, 2168, 2169; **17**:*2359*
Enterprise (space shuttle) **16**:2166–7
Eurostar trains **9**:*1273*
Extended Performance Hydrofoil (EPH) **8**:1117

F

fencing (sport) **16**:*2224*
Ferrari T4 racing car **8**:*1124*
ferries
  propulsion **10**:1365
  roll-on roll-off **5**:670; **15**:*2069*, 2070
fireboats **6**:861
firefighting, appliances **6**:*859*, 860–1
fission, nuclear
  and marine propulsion **10**:1336
  and rocket propulsion **14**:1995–6
flight *see* aviation
flight plans **1**:93–4
flight simulators **7**:**886**–7; **11**:1501; **19**:2603–4
floatplanes **15**:2035, 2037
flume stabilizers **16**:2231
fly-by-wire (FBW) systems **1**:44, 66; **2**:213
Flyer I (aircraft) **2**:211
flying boats **2**:212, 213; **13**:*1747*; **15**:2035, 2036
Fokke Fa330 ("Water Wagtail") **8**:1070
Fokker f-28 Fellowship **1**:*31*
football, clothing **13**:1862; **16**:*2226*
Ford, Henry **2**:198; **10**:1338, 1341
Ford Model T **2**:198; **11**:1575
  manufacture **10**:1341
Ford Trimotor ("Tin Goose") **1**:82
Ford UFO vehicles **9**:1176
forklifts **7**:**926–7**
Formula 1 cars **14**:1888
Frahm antiroll tanks **16**:2231
Freedom Ship **15**:*2072*, 2073
freewheeling **2**:242
Friendship 7 (rocket) **14**:*1991*
funiculars **3**:357–8

G

Gagarin, Yuri **1**:42
Garnerin, André-Jacques **12**:1641
gates, miter (locks) **9**:1266
Germany, Transrapid system **5**:719; **9**:*1256*; **10**:1349
Giffard, Henri **1**:91
gliders **7**:**1004–5**
  history **2**:210; **7**:1004
  gliding angle **7**:1005
global positioning systems (GPSs), and automobiles **2**:204; **6**:*813*
Gloster Meteor **7**:965
Gloster-Whittle E 28/39 **7**:965
golf balls **16**:2220–1
golf carts, air-cushion-assisted **1**:81
golf clubs **16**:2223–4
Gordon Bennett races **2**:218
Grand Canal (China) **3**:376
Grand Prix racing **14**:1887–9, 1890, 1892
  scale models **14**:1915
gravity assist (slingshot effect) **14**:1996
ground-effect machines *see* air-cushion vehicles
GT racing **14**:1891
  scale models **14**:1915
gum shields **13**:1863
gyroplanes *see* autogiros

H

hang gliders 8:**1037–8**
Harrison, John 4:484; 9:*1215*, 1216
Heinkel He 178 (aircraft) 2:213;
  7:*965*
helicopters *see* **1065–70**; 18:*2551–2*
  amphibious operations 15:2037
  convertiplanes 8:1069
  engines 8:1067
    servomechanisms 15:*2055*
  midair recovery systems (MARS)
    13:*1748*
  military 8:1067–8, 1070; 19:*2629*
  model, radio-controlled 14:1914,
    1915
  smart rotor system 10:*1352*
  uses 8:1067–8
    ambulances 1:113; 8:1067, *1070*
    firefighting 6:861; 8:1067
    sea rescue 15:2038, 2039
  see also autogiros
Helios (aircraft) 14:1913; 15:*2114*,
  2117
helmets, sports 13:1862
High Speed Civil Transport (HSCT)
  17:2320
Hindenberg (airship) 8:1119; 9:1288
Hiperlight biplanes 18:2525
hobbyhorses 2:240
Hong Kong, mass transit system
  10:1346, *1347*; 14:*1927*
hopper cars 7:929
horse cars 16:2276
hot rod racing 14:1891
hovercraft *see* air-cushion vehicles
hovertrains, monorail 11:1482
Hughes Transportation Management
  Systems (HTMS) 19:2682
hulls
  damaged 15:2021
  Kevlar 13:*1771, 1804*
  planing 8:1116
  speedboat 16:2204, 2205–6
hydrofoils 8:**1116–17**
hydroplanes 10:*1336*; 16:2205, 2208
  stepped 16:2208
Hyper-X hypersonic flight development program 13:*1748*
HyShot project 17:2320

I

ice boats 14:2013
icebreakers 15:2073
ice hockey, clothing 13:1863
inertial guidance 8:**1144–6**; 11:1468,
  1512, 1513
integrated transport network 3:343
Inter City Express (ICE) trains
  9:1274

J

jet cars 14:1892
jetfoils 8:1117
jetliners 1:83–4; 2:213
jet skis 10:*1334*
Joides Resolution (ship) 11:1568
joints (mechanical)
  universal 18:**2544–5**
    constant-velocity 18:2544–5
"jumbo" jets 1:84; 2:*212*, 213
junks 14:2009–10

K

Kamov Ka 26 8:1067
knots 11:1510–11

L

Lake Buccaneer (aircraft) 15:2037
LARC-60 vehicles 1:123
Lartigue, C. F. M. T. 11:1481, 1482
Lartigue lines 11:1481
LASH (lighter aboard ship) vessels
  15:2070–1
latitude and longitude 9:**1215–16**
  see also sextants
launch vehicles 14:1991
Leonardo da Vinci
  bicycle 2:240
  lock gates 3:373; 9:1266
lifeboats 15:2038–40, 2050–1
  inshore 15:2040–1
life rafts 15:*2040*
lighter aboard ship (LASH) vessels
  15:2070–1
light-rail systems 16:2278
  Docklands Light Railway 10:1348;
    14:1925; 16:2278
light, rapid, comfortable (LRC)
  trains 9:1255
light rapid transit systems 16:2278
Lilienthal, Otto 2:210
Lindbergh, Charles 2:213
liquid petroleum gas (LPG), a vehicle
  fuel 2:200; 3:343
Listowel and Ballybunion monorail
  11:1482
loading gauge 14:1923
Locher track 4:506
lock-and-block signaling 14:1924
Lockheed L-1011 Tristar, undercarriage 18:*2535*
Lockheed-Martin X-35 (aircraft)
  18:*2553*
Lockheed Starliner 2:213
locks (in waterways)
  at docks 5:668, 669; 9:1266
  canal 3:373, 375–6; 9:**1265–6**
locomotives and power cars
  9:**1270–4**
  diesel locomotives 9:1272
  electric locomotives 9:1273
  gas turbine powered 9:1273
  steam locomotives 9:1270–2, 1274
  trolley locomotives, in coal mines
    4:*494*
  see also traction engines; trains
London, underground (subway;
  "tube") 10:1346–7, 1349
longitude 9:1215–16; 11:1511;
  15:2062
long ships, Norse 14:2009
loran (long-range-navigation system)
  11:1511–12
  for aircraft 1:67
  for fishing vessels 7:872–3
Lotus 38 (racing car) 14:1892
low-emission road vehicles 9:**1286–8**
  electric 2:200, 201; 5:720; 6:794–5;
    9:1286–7
  hybrid-powered vehicles 5:720;
    9:1288
  hydrogen-powered 2:200; 8:1119;
    9:1287–8
  zero-level emission vehicles
    (ZLEVs) 2:201
  see also automobiles, alternative
    power sources
LRC (light, rapid, comfortable)
  trains 9:1255
LVTP-7 (Amtrack) vehicles 1:*122*

M

McDonnell Douglas DC-9 1:84
MacPherson struts 16:*2229*
maglev (magnetic-levitation) vehicles

passenger links 5:719; 10:1349
trains 5:*717*, 719; 7:934; 9:*1252*,
  1254, 1255–6; 10:1349, *1363*,
  1364–5; 14:1928; 17:2310, 2314
magnetohydrodynamics (MHD),
  propulsion using 5:719–20;
  10:1319, 1337
marine propulsion 10:**1334–7**,
  1365–6
  propellers 10:1337; 13:1858, 1859
  torpedoes 18:2467–8
  using magnetohydrodynamics
    5:719–20; 10:1319, 1337
Martin P.6M Seamaster (aircraft)
  15:2036
Mary Rose (ship) 15:*2022*
mass transit and subways 10:**1345–9**
  subways 10:1346–7, 1349
    signaling 14:1924–5
    ventilation in 8:1060
  see also maglev vehicles, trains;
    streetcars
Maxim, Hiram, and powered flight
  2:211
Mecalifts 11:1471
meters, parking 10:*1407*
microlights 8:1038; 15:2037;
  18:*2525–7*
  paraplanes 12:1643
microwave landing systems (MLSs)
  1:96
midget-car racing 14:1888, 1891
Miss America II (speedboat) 16:2208
Miss America X (speedboat) 16:2208
MLX01 (train) 9:1256
mobility aids 11:**1469–72**
monorail systems 10:1345;
  11:**1481–3**
Moon, and the Apollo program 1:42
mopeds 11:1489
Moto Guzzi Le Mans Mark III
  11:*1488*
motorcycles 11:**1488–9**
  model 14:1915
motorcyclists 8:*1142*
Motor Lifeboats (MLBs) 15:2040
motor racing *see* racing cars and
  dragsters
mountaineering, clothing 13:*1863*
mouth guards 13:1862

N

nautical miles 11:1511
Nautilus (submarine) 11:1542
navigation 11:**1510–14**
  aircraft 1:66–7; 8:*1028*; 11:1513
    collision avoidance 11:1513
    using head-up displays 8:1040
    using sextants 15:2063
    see also air-traffic control
  gyrocompasses 8:**1028–9**; 11:1510
  history 7:1006; 11:1510
  inertial guidance systems
    8:**1144–6**; 11:1468, 1512, 1513
  marine 15:2068
    collision avoidance 11:1514
    dead reckoning (DR) 11:1511
    echo sounders 11:1512;
      15:2126–7
    fishing vessels 7:872–3
    and Harrison's chronometer
      4:484; 9:*1215*, 1216; 11:1511
    knots 11:1510–11
    radio and radar 11:1511–12,
      1514
    using gyroscopes 8:1028, *1031*
    using sextants 11:1511, *1513*;
      15:2062–3
  radio 7:1006; 11:1511–2
  satellite systems

and seismology 7:994
see also global positioning
  systems
space 11:1514
using compasses (magnetic)
  11:1510, *1514*
New Wave human-powered vehicles
  2:*243*
New York City, mass transit system
  10:1345–6
nuclear power, for marine propulsion
  10:1336

O

Oakley self-righting system
  15:2050–1
oars 10:1334
O-bahn 3:343
octants, reflecting 15:2062
off-road vehicles, models, racing
  14:1915
Olympic Games, drug testing at
  16:*2225*
Omega system 11:1511–12
onkers 19:*2695*
Orion, Project 14:1995
ornithopters 2:210
Ortho Kinetics Travel Chairs
  11:1472
outriggers 16:2206
overdrachs 3:376

P

paddles 10:1334
Panama Canal 9:*1265*, 1266; 11:1514
pantographs 9:1286; 16:*2277–8*
parachutes 12:**1641–3**
  airframe (whole-frame parachutes)
    12:1643
  drogue 5:711; 12:1641, *1642*, 1643
Paraguay (ship) 14:1945
Paraplanes 12:1643
Paris, metro (subway) 10:1348
park-and-ride 10:1345
paved concrete track (PACT), railroad 14:1923
PCCs (streetcars) 16:2278
"Pendolino" trains 9:1274
Piccard, Auguste 16:2292–3
pilotless aircraft 13:**1747–8**
Pisces class submersibles 11:*1566*
plenum chamber vessels 1:80
propellers 13:**1858–9**
  aircraft 1:74; 13:1858–9
    propfan 1:*44*, 78
    thrust and balance 1:65;
      13:1858–9
  marine-propulsion 10:1337;
    13:1858, 1859; 15:2068
    and cavitation 13:1859
    speedboat 16:2206–7
  outboard-motor 12:1614
protective clothing, sports 16:2224,
  2226
pump escapes (triple-combination
  pumpers) 6:860

Q

quadrants 15:2062
Queen Elizabeth II (ship) 15:*2070*

R

racing, motor *see* racing cars and
  dragsters
racing cars and dragsters 14:**1887–92**

racing cars and dragsters (cont.)
  drag racing 14:1890, 1891–2
  racing cars 14:1887–91
    engines 7:903; 14:1889
    speedway 14:1891
    sports car (GT) racing 14:1891
    tires 14:1888, 1890; 18:2454,
      2455–6
rack-and-pinion railway systems
  3:357; 4:506
rackets
  squash and badminton 16:2222
  tennis 16:2221–3
radar
  for navigation 11:1510, 1513, 1514
  plan-position 14:1894
radomes 1:69
rafts, life 15:2040
railroad systems 4:475–6; 10:1364–5;
  14:1923–8
  casting of components 3:402, 403
  and freight 7:928, 929; 14:1927,
    1929
  tracks 3:403; 14:1923
    testing 14:1878; 18:2530
  tunnels 18:2512
  weigh stations 19:2682
  see also mass transit and subways;
    railways; trains
railways
  cliff 3:356–7
  cog 4:506
  funicular 3:357–8
  monorail systems 10:1345;
    11:1481–3
  see also mass transit and subways;
    railroad systems; trains
rapid transit systems see mass transit
  and subways
reaching (sailing) 14:2009
Refrigorifique (ship) 14:1945
refueling, in-flight 14:1948–9
Renault, Louis 2:198
Rhine-Main-Danube canal 9:1266
Rideau Canal 9:1266
roads
  arrester beds alongside 14:1981
  construction 5:701; 14:1973–7,
    1981
  crash barriers 14:1979–81
  drainage 5:675; 14:1975, 1981
  markings 14:1976–7, 1982
  signs 14:1982–4
road signs, reflective 14:1944
road systems and traffic control
  14:1978–85
road trains 9:1175; 18:2505
roadways, world's oldest 4:477, 478
Rocket (steam engine) 16:2259
rocket cars 14:1892
rockets and space propulsion
  14:1990–6
  boosters 14:1994; 16:2166
  propulsion 12:1620; 14:1993–6
    ionic (solar-electric) propulsion
      9:1184; 14:1995
  rockets
    construction 14:1996
    ejection seat 5:711
    launch 14:1996
    sounding 14:1991
    and the Venturi effect 18:2580
  scramjet engines 1:78; 17:2320
roll-on roll-off systems 15:2070
  for cargo 7:932
  ferries 5:670; 15:2070
Royal George (steam engine) 9:1274
rudders 14:2002–4
  aircraft 1:66, 71; 14:2004; 15:2057
  ships' 14:2002–4; 15:2068
  trim 12:1615
runways, airport 1:87, 88, 94

S

SACEM 10:1348
SAFEGE (monorail system) 11:1483
safety belts 2:207–9; 18:2476
sailboards 14:2006–7
sailing 14:2008–13
sailplanes see gliders
sails 10:1334–5; 14:2013
  lateen 14:2010
  sailboard 14:2007
San Francisco, streetcars 3:356, 358;
  16:2277, 2278
Saturn V (launch vehicle) 14:1995,
  1996
Saunders Roe Princess (aircraft)
  15:2036
Saunders Roe SR-A1 (aircraft)
  15:2036
SB-11s (gliders) 7:1005
Schneider Trophy races 15:2035
schooners 14:2010
Schwarz, David 1:91
scooters 11:1489
  powered-wheelchair 11:1469
Seadog (submersible) 18:2471
seaplanes and amphibians 1:69;
  15:2035–7
  flying boats 2:212, 213; 13:1747;
    15:2035, 2036
sea rescue 15:2038–41
  lifeboats 15:2038–40, 2050–1
  inshore 15:2040–1
sea sleds 16:2206
Seawise Giant (ship) 7:928
security trucks 2:168
self-righting boats 15:2050–1
  lifeboats 15:2040, 2050–1
semaphore signals, railway 14:1924
semitrailers 18:2505
sextants 11:1511, 1513; 15:2062–3
  on periscopes 12:1675
Shepard, Alan, Jr. 1:42
Shin Aitoku Maru (ship) 14:2013
shin guards 13:1862
Shinkai 6500 (submersible) 16:2292
Shinkansen ("bullet" trains) 3:328;
  9:1274; 14:1927–8
ships 15:2067–73
  antifouling coatings 2:149
  braking 15:2068
  bulk-carrying 7:928–32; 9:1190;
    15:2071–2
  see also tankers
  cable-laying 3:347, 348, 349;
    17:2356
  centers of buoyancy and gravity
    15:2069
  construction 15:2073
  container ships 7:932; 15:2067,
    2069–70
  electromagnetic propulsion
    10:1319
  fishing and whaling
    factory ships 7:872; 19:2686
    see also trawlers
  grounded 15:2021, 2039
  icebreakers 15:2073
  industrial 15:2073
  LASH (lighter aboard ship) vessels
    15:2070–1
  life rafts 15:2040
  motor, sail-assisted 14:2013
  navigation 15:2068
    using gyroscopes 8:1028, 1031
    see also navigation, marine
  parts of 15:2067–8
  passenger 15:2072–3
  propellers see propellers, marine-
    propulsion
  radio-controlled model 14:1915
  refrigeration 14:1945

reefer (refrigerated transport)
  ships 15:2071
residence 15:2072, 2073
ro-ro see roll-on roll-off systems
rudders 14:2002–4; 15:2068
search radar used on 14:1898;
  15:2069
speed 11:1510–11; 15:2069–70
stability 15:2069
  see also stabilizers, ship
sunken, salvaged 15:2021–3
tonnage 15:2068
towed 15:2021
warships 19:2626–33
wind pumps on 19:2695
see also boats; hydrofoils; marine
  propulsion; warships
shock absorbers 10:1353; 16:2229;
  17:2339, 2340
Short Sarafand (aircraft) 15:2035
Short Sutherland (aircraft) 15:2036
short takeoff and landing (STOL)
  1:71, 77; 16:2251
signaling, railway 14:1924–6
Sikorsky, Igor 8:1065
skiing and snowboarding 5:714
  skin suits 16:2224
  skis and snowboards 15:2084–6
sky divers 12:1641, 1643
Skyhawk (aircraft) 14:1948
Skylab (space station) 1:43; 16:2170
slingshot effect (gravity assist)
  14:1996
slipways, greasing 9:1290
snowboards and skis 15:2084–6
snow vehicles, tracked 18:2470, 2471
soccer, clothing 13:1863
Solar Challenger (aircraft) 2:213;
  15:2117
solar sailing 14:1996; 15:2159
Sojourner (space vehicle) 15:2158
"sonic cruisers" 1:84
spacecraft
  navigation 11:1514
  orbits 12:1599–1600
space probes, and the space race 1:42
space race 1:42; 14:1993
space shuttles 1:41, 43; 9:1201;
  12:1620; 16:2165–9, 2170–1
  accidents and disasters 6:815;
    16:2166, 2168
  air locks used in 1:85
  boosters 14:1994; 16:2166
  dietary needs in 11:1558
  fuel cells 6:795
  heat-resistant tiles 1:44; 3:427;
    16:2166
  and the Hubble Space Telescope
    16:2168–9; 17:2381
  photography from 1:35
  remote handling by 14:1955, 1956;
    15:2056; 16:2168, 2169
  and satellites 15:2024, 2026;
    16:2165, 2168
  and space debris 15:2151
  and space probes 16:2168
  and space stations 14:1955, 1956;
    16:2169, 2172–3
  space suits 16:2177–8
  space walks 16:2169, 2176, 2178
  and telemetry 17:2364
  virtual reality practice for 19:2604
  see also Atlantis; Challenger;
    Columbia; Discovery; Endeavour;
    Enterprise
speedboats 16:2204–8
speedometers and tachographs
  16:2209–10
  tachometers 2:203; 16:2209, 2210;
    18:2508
speedway racing 14:1891
Sperry, Elmer 13:1747; 16:2232

Spirit of St. Louis (aircraft) 2:213
sponsons 16:2208
sports car racing 14:1891
sports equipment 16:2219–24
  clothing 13:1862–3; 16:2224, 2226
sprint-car racing 14:1891
Sprite (unpiloted helicopter) 13:1748
SR.N1 (air-cushion vehicle) 1:80–1
SR.N4 (air-cushion vehicle) 1:80, 81
SR.N5 (air-cushion vehicle) 1:80
stabilizers, ship 16:2231–2
  antiroll tanks 16:2231
  bilge keels 16:2232
  flume 16:2231
  gyroscopic 8:1030–1; 15:2072;
    16:2231–2
  oscillating weights 16:2232
  stabilizer fins 16:2231, 2232
steamboats, paddle 10:1335
steamships 10:1335–6
steering systems 16:2260–2
  Ackermann 16:2260, 2262
  automobile steering columns
    2:207, 209; 16:2260
  power steering 16:2260, 2261–2
  tracked-vehicle 18:2469
  variable-ratio 2:207
stock-car racing 14:1891
streetcars 10:1345, 1348, 1349;
  16:2276–8
  San Francisco 3:356, 358; 16:2277,
    2278
struts, MacPherson 16:2229
submarine inertial navigation system
  (SINS) 16:2290
submarines
  air locks used in 1:85
  concrete used in 4:549
  design 10:1366; 16:2288
  diving 16:2288–9
  early 16:2287–8
  helicopters towed behind 8:1070
  hunters, helicopter 8:1070
  navigation 16:2290–1
  periscopes 12:1674–5; 16:2290
  power 10:1336–7; 16:2289–90
    diesel engines 10:1336–7;
      16:2290, 2291
    nuclear propulsion 10:1336,
      1366; 11:1542, 1546; 16:2290,
      2291
    steam 16:2289–90
    Stirling engines 16:2266, 2269
  rescuing 15:2023
  and sonar 8:1070; 15:2127, 2128
  underwater stealth communication
    16:2253
submersibles 10:1333; 11:1569;
  16:2292–4
  Alvin 11:1568, 1569; 16:2294
  for marine salvage 15:2023
  Pisces class 11:1566
  tracked 18:2471
  see also submarines
subways see mass transit and subways
supersonic flight 1:37; 7:966;
  17:2318–20
  cloud production 18:2570
  sonic booms 1:37; 17:2318–19
  supersonic aircraft 1:70–1, 84;
    17:2318, 2319
  tested in wind tunnels 19:2698–9
supertankers 7:928–9; 11:1577
surface-effect craft 1:122
suspension systems 17:2338–40
  automobile see automobiles,
    suspension
  racing car 14:1890–1
  tank 2:168
  tracked-vehicle 18:2469–70
swamp buggies 1:121–2
swap bodies 14:1927

T

tachometers *see* speedometers and
tachographs
tacking (sailing) **14**:2009
tankers **17**:2350–2
docks **5**:671; **7**:929
liquefied gas vessels **17**:2352
oil **5**:671; **15**:2072
hydraulics used in **8**:1104
supertankers (very large crude
carriers) **7**:928–9; **11**:*1577*
ore-carrying **9**:1190
pipelines and pumps **17**:2351–2
safety **17**:2352
see also ships, bulk-carrying
taxicabs, taximeters **17**:*2355*
tennis
balls **16**:2219–20
rackets **16**:2221–3
Tereshkova, Valentina **1**:42
Terex Titan 33-19 (dump truck)
9:1176
TGV (Train á Grand Vitesse) **1**:*36*;
4:476; **9**:1255, 1274; **14**:1928
Thompson, Robert **17**:2338
Thomson, R.W. **18**:2453
tires **18**:2453–6
bicycle **2**:241, 243; **17**:2338
cross-ply (bias) **18**:2453, 2454–5,
2456
manufacture **18**:2453–5
neutral contour (NCTs) **18**:2456
P8 **18**:2456
pneumatic **2**:243; **17**:2338;
18:2453
racing car **14**:*1888*, 1890; **18**:*2454*,
2455–6
radial-ply **2**:201, 206; **18**:2453,
2454–5, 2456
rib-tread **14**:1890
rubber **14**:1998, 2001
run-flat **2**:206
safety **18**:2455
scrap recovery schemes **5**:591
self-repairing **2**:206
sealants in **1**:32
slick **14**:1890; **18**:*2454*
TRX **18**:2456
toll charging, automatic **2**:204
"Tom Thumb" (locomotive) **9**:1274
TOPS (total operations processing
systems) **14**:1926
torsion bars **17**:2338–9
total operations processing systems
(TOPS) **14**:1926
Toyota Prius **9**:1288

track-circuit signaling **14**:1924
tracked vehicles **5**:703; **18**:**2469–71**
half-tracks **18**:2470–1
tanks **2**:167–8; **18**:2469–70, 2471
traction engines **16**:*2256*; **18**:**2472–3**
traffic
monitoring **14**:1984–5
road *see* road systems and traffic
control
signs *see* road signs
Train á Grand Vitesse *see* TGV
trains
brakes **3**:314, 315; **10**:1346;
14:1925, 1926
electric
brakes **3**:315; **10**:1346
externally-powered **9**:1286
high-speed **9**:1255, *1256*, 1274;
14:1927–8
Eurostar **9**:*1273*
Japanese Shinkansen ("bullet"
trains) **3**:328; **9**:1274; **14**:1927–8
maglev (magnetic-levitation)
5:717, 719; **7**:934; **9**:*1252*,
1254, 1255–6; **10**:1349, *1363*,
1364–5; **14**:1928; **17**:2310,
2314
tilting trains **9**:1273–4; **14**:1928
Train á Grand Vitesse (TGV)
1:*36*; **4**:476; **9**:1255, 1274;
14:1927
mass transit and subway **10**:1346–7
rubber-tired **10**:1346
see also locomotives and power
cars; railroad systems; railways
trams *see* streetcars
transmission, automobile *see* automobiles, transmission
Transrapid system **5**:719; **9**:1256;
10:1349
trawlers **7**:871–3, *874*
tricycles **2**:240, *241*
Trieste (submersible) **11**:1569;
16:2293
trimarans **16**:2206
trim tabs **1**:66
trollers **16**:2277
trolleybuses **3**:343
trolley locomotives, in coal mines
4:*494*
trucks **18**:2505–8
brakes **3**:315; **18**:2507
dump **5**:703
world's largest **9**:1176
engine **18**:2506
firefighting **6**:861
forklift *see* forklifts

haulage **7**:929
instrumentation **18**:2508
power steering **16**:*2260*
reach **7**:927
road trains **9**:*1175*; **18**:2505
security **2**:*168*
steam **18**:2473
tank **18**:2506
trailers **18**:2505–6
transmission **18**:2490, 2506–7
turret **7**:927
"vibroseis" **11**:1571
trunk deck vessels **17**:2350–1
tugs, salvage **15**:2021
tunnels, ventilation in **8**:1060
Turbinia (ship) **10**:1335–6; **16**:2204
Tyne class lifeboats **15**:2040

U

Ultra Large Crude Carriers
(ULCCs) **17**:*2350*, 2351
ultralight aircraft **8**:1038; **18**:2524–7
see also microlights
undercarriage, retractable **18**:2535–6
universal joints **18**:2544–5
Ust-Kamenogorsk, lock at **9**:1266

V

V-22 Osprey (aircraft) **18**:2552
V/STOL (VTOL) aircraft **1**:71, 77,
78; **18**:**2551–3**
convertiplanes **8**:1069; **18**:2552
see also helicopters
Vaderland (ship) **17**:2350
Vancouver, Advanced Light Rapid
Transit (ALRT) **10**:1349
VariEze (aircraft) **18**:*2526*
VASIs (visual approach slope indica-
tors) **1**:88
VC-400 (aircraft) **18**:2552
Very Large Crude Carriers (VLCCs)
17:2351
visual approach slope indicators
(VASIs) **1**:88
VOR (VHF omnidirectional rang-
ing), beacons **1**:88
VS-316A (helicopter) **8**:1065

W

walkers, swivel **11**:1470–1
walking frames **11**:1472

warehouses, driverless transport in
19:2624
warships **19**:**2626–33**
Washington D.C., mass transit and
subways **10**:*1348*
water bombers **15**:*2035, 2036*
water-jet propulsion **10**:1365
water skiing **2**:231
water tenders **6**:861
"Water Wagtail" **8**:1070
weirs, navigation weirs **9**:1265
Welbikes **11**:1489
Westland Sea King helicopters
8:1070
wheelchairs **11**:1469–70
windshields
automobile **1**:30; **7**:1001
bicycle **2**:*243*
windsurfing **13**:*1840*; **14**:2013
wings *see* aircraft, wings
World, The (ship) **15**:2073
Wright, Orville and Wilbur **1**:72, 77;
2:211
wind tunnel built by **19**:2696

X

X-15 (aircraft) **17**:2319
X-43 (aircraft) **13**:1748; **17**:2320
X-wing project **8**:1070

Y

yachts **14**:*2008*, 2009
for wheelchair-users **11**:*1469*
Yamato-1 (ship) **5**:719–20; **10**:1319;
17:2314
Year Book of Automobile Sport (Yellow
Book) **14**:1887–8

Z

Zeppelin, Ferdinand von **1**:91
zeppelins **1**:91–2
carrying bombs **2**:283
zero-level emission vehicles (ZLEVs)
2:201
Zimmer frames **11**:*1472*
ZLEVs (zero-level emission vehicles)
2:201

General Index

A

A-1 (rocket) **14**:1992
Abbe, Ernst **10**:1430, 1433, 1434
ABE (Autonomous Benthic Explorer) **16**:2294
abney levels **17**:2336
abrasives **1**:17–18; **17**:2322
　aluminum oxide **1**:17, 18, *111*
　diamond **1**:18; **5**:*638*
　made by crystal synthesis **17**:2347
　used in grinding machines **10**:1309–10
ABS (acrylonitrile-butadiene-styrene) rubber **13**:1772; **14**:2001
ABS (antilock braking system) **2**:201, 204, 206; **3**:315
abscesses, dental (gumboils) **5**:619
abscisic acid **3**:305
absolute (Kelvin) temperature scale **17**:2395, 2396, 2414
absolute zero **17**:2395, 2396
absorption **15**:2130
accelerated graphics port (AGP) **4**:534–5
acceleration **3**:422; **5**:695
　angular **5**:695
　due to gravity **6**:789; **8**:1021
accelerator mass spectrometry (AMS) **2**:157
accelerators *see* particle accelerators
accelerometers **2**:208; **8**:1144, *1145*; **10**:1420; **18**:*2476*
Acceptable Quality Level (AQL) **14**:1878
accessibility aids **1**:19–22
　see also mobility aids
accretion **2**:270; **13**:1759
　accretion disks **2**:268; **10**:*1362*
accumulators (hydraulics) **8**:1102–3
accumulators (storage registers) **10**:1428
acetates, fibers *see* cellulose acetate; cellulose triacetate
acetic acid, and sodium acetate **12**:1693
acetic anhydride **6**:852
Acetobacter **7**:911
acetone *see* propanone
acetylcholine **3**:413, 414; **11**:1506
　organophosphates and **12**:1700
　in plants **3**:305
　receptors **3**:*414*
acetylcholinesterase **4**:437
acetyl coenzyme A (acetyl CoA) **10**:1374, 1375
acetylene *see* ethyne
acetylsalicylic acid *see* aspirin
Acheson, Edward **1**:18
acid rain **1**:*25*; **13**:1798; **16**:2300
acids and alkalis **1**:23–5
　acids
　　Lewis acids **1**:23
　　organic **1**:23
　　poisoning from **13**:1791
　　protonic **1**:23
　alkalis **1**:23
　see also pH
Ackermann steering **16**:2260, *2262*
Ack-pack (flame thrower) **7**:*883*
acoustics **1**:26–7
　architectural **1**:26, 27
　engineering **1**:26
　musical **1**:26
　see also noise measurement
Acrilan *see* polyacrylonitrile

acromegaly **6**:782
acrylamide (propenamide) **13**:1771
acrylic acid (propenoic acid) **12**:1629
acrylic fibers **6**:853
acrylic resins **1**:30–1; **12**:1629
acrylics **13**:1771
acrylonitrile (propenonitrile) **7**:880; **14**:1999
　polymers of **6**:853; **13**:1771
actinides **6**:765; **12**:1673; **18**:2485, 2487
actinium **18**:2485
actinomycetes **10**:1409
activation analysis **14**:1907
　neutron **2**:158; **12**:1659
activation energy **9**:1202
active galactic nuclei (AGNs) **2**:174
actuators (jacks) **8**:1101, 1103; **15**:2064; **16**:*2245*
　servomechanisms and **15**:2056, 2057
ACVs *see* air-cushion vehicles
Ada, Countess of Lovelace **4**:523
ADAM (Area Denial Artillery Munition) **11**:1454
addiction, drug **12**:1685
adenine **7**:973–4; **11**:1477, 1478
adenosine diphosphate (ADP) **10**:1373–6; **12**:1700
adenosine monophosphate (AMP) **10**:1373, 1376
adenosine triphosphate (ATP) **9**:1234; **10**:1373–6; **12**:1700
ADF (automatic direction-finding) equipment **1**:66, 67
adhesion, surface **7**:934
adhesion tension **17**:2321
adhesives and sealants **1**:28–32
　anaerobic **1**:32
　thermoplastic and thermosetting **1**:30
　wood **19**:2718
adipose tissue **6**:836
adits **11**:1460
Adobe Pagemaker **11**:1518
Adobe PhotoShop **12**:1594
ADP *see* adenosine diphosphate
adrenal glands **6**:781; **8**:1086
adrenaline *see* epinephrine
ADSLs (asymmetric digital subscriber lines) **11**:1476, 1517; **17**:2358
adsorption **15**:2129–30
Advanced Camera for Surveys (ACS) **15**:2155; **17**:*2382*
advanced combat direction system (ACDS) **19**:*2627*
advanced intelligent tape (AIT) **10**:1312
Advanced Light Rapid Transit (ALRT) system **10**:1349
Advanced Passenger Trains (APTs) **14**:1928
Advanced Research Projects Agency (ARPA) **11**:1501
advance traffic information (ATI) **14**:1926
adzes **18**:2460
aerial photography **1**:33–5
　and archaeology **2**:156, 159
　and geology **7**:990
　infrared **1**:*35*; **2**:*159*; **5**:*707*; **6**:*741*; **7**:*986*
　for maps and plans **10**:1329, *1330*; **12**:1706–7
　oblique and vertical **1**:34
　rocket camera **3**:369

for surveying **17**:2334
aerials *see* antennas
aerodynamics **1**:36–9
　sailing and **14**:2010–11
aeronomy **10**:1401
aerosols **1**:40
aerospace industry **1**:41–4
Aerotrains **11**:1482; **14**:1928
affination **16**:2296–7
afterburning **1**:65, 76; **7**:*965*, 966
Agenda 21 **6**:808–9
aggregate **4**:546
　for lightweight concrete **4**:549
Aggregat rocket series **14**:1992
aging, study of *see* gerontology
agonists **2**:252
agriculture
　agricultural science **1**:52–5
　　computerized farming **1**:55
　　see also biotechnology; genetic engineering
　biogas from wastes **2**:259
　erosion prevention **6**:817–18, 819
　farm animal veterinary work **18**:2585–6
　intensive **1**:56–7, 58
　machinery **1**:45–51
　　see also elevators (vertical transport), grain; irrigation techniques
　organic **1**:58–61; **7**:907; **19**:2680
　　see also biological control
　robots used in harvesting **14**:1989
　soil management **15**:2112–13
　see also crops; horticulture; weed control
AIDS (acquired immunodeficiency syndrome) **6**:811–12; **8**:1137; **10**:*1368*, 1369–70
　anti-HIV therapy **12**:1688
　virus *see* HIV
ailerons **1**:66, 71
air **1**:62–4
　composition **1**:62
　density **5**:617
　liquefaction **1**:64; **5**:590
　origins **1**:62–3
　separation **5**:589–90
　uses for gases **1**:64
　see also atmosphere
airbags **2**:209; **10**:*1417*
airborne warning and control systems (AWACS) **14**:1895
air brushes **2**:258
air conditioning **8**:1058, 1060–2, *1063*, 1064
aircraft
　adhesives used in **1**:*31*
　aerodynamics **1**:38–9, 69
　ambulance **1**:113; **8**:1067, *1070*
　at airports **1**:87–8
　autopilot **1**:67–8; **15**:2057
　axes of rotation (pitch, roll, and yaw) **1**:*70*, 71
　braking systems **3**:314, 315
　for container traffic **7**:932
　control *see* aircraft-control engineering
　control surfaces **1**:65–6, 71
　delta **1**:70–1
　design **1**:69–71
　　and aerodynamics **1**:39
　drag **1**:38–9, 66
　ejection seats **5**:711–12; **8**:1038
　engines *see* aircraft engines

firefighting from **6**:861; **8**:1067; **15**:*2035, 2036*
flight recorders **1**:67; **7**:884–5
fly-by-wire **1**:44, 66; **2**:213
flying wing **1**:69–70
fuselage **1**:69–70
high-altitude **10**:*1401*; **12**:1620
jet
　engines *see* aircraft engines, jet
　fuel **11**:1579
　jetliners **1**:83–4; **2**:213
　V/STOL **18**:2552
　wings **1**:70
landings **1**:66, 68, 88–9, 94, 95, 96; **11**:1513
lift **1**:38, 66, 69,70
materials **1**:*43*, 44
navigation *see* navigation, aircraft
pilotless **13**:1747–8; **14**:1913
pressure transducers **18**:*2474*
pressurized air cabins **1**:82–3
propellers *see* propellers, aircraft
radio-controlled **14**:1913
radio and radar jamming equipment **16**:*2250*, 2252–3, *2254*
refueling (in-flight) **14**:1948–9
rivets **10**:*1379*
rudders **1**:66, 71; **14**:2004; **15**:2057
seaplanes and amphibians **1**:69; **15**:*2035–7*
sound and the Doppler effect **5**:672
stalling **1**:70
STOL **1**:71, 77; **18**:2551
STOVL **18**:2553
subsonic **1**:70
sunken, recovery **15**:2022–3
supersonic *see* supersonic flight
swing-wing (variable geometry) **1**:*70*, 71
tail **1**:69
thrust **1**:65
tires **18**:*2456*
toilets **18**:*2458*, 2459
transonic **17**:2319
turning **1**:*71*
ultralight **8**:1038; **18**:2524–7
undercarriage, retractable **18**:2535–6
used for pesticide application **12**:*1676*, 1677
V/STOL **18**:2551–3
vectored-thrust **1**:71, 77; **18**:2552–3
wings **1**:*43*, 44, 70–1
　aerodynamics **1**:38–9
　supersonic-speed **17**:2319
　variable-geometry **17**:2319
wiring used in **3**:346
see also airliners
aircraft carriers **19**:2626, *2627*, 2629–30
　aircraft
　　arresting mechanisms for **19**:2632–3
　　steam catapults for **19**:*2628*, 2630–1
aircraft-control engineering **1**:65–8
　altimetry **1**:68
　autopilot **1**:67–8; **15**:2057
　electronics *see* avionics
　head-up displays **8**:1039–40
　and landing **1**:68; **14**:*1895*
　radar **1**:67, 68; **14**:1894, 1898
　servomechanisms **15**:2057
aircraft engines **1**:72–8
　bypass principle and ratio **1**:77, 78

coolant injection **1**:76; **7**:966
cooling **1**:72–3
development(s) **1**:72–6, 78
  gas turbine **1**:*75, 77*
  in-line **1**:72
  jet **1**:73, 75–6, 77; **7**:965–6
    propfan **1**:*44*, 78
    propulsive efficiency **1**:77
    ramjets and pulse jets (athodyds) **1**:76; **7**:967
    scramjet **1**:78; **17**:2320
    turbofan (fanjet) **1**:65, *74, 75,* 76–8; **7**:966
    turbojet **1**:65; **7**:965
    turboprop **1**:72, 76; **7**:966–7
    turboramjets **1**:76; **7**:967
    turboshaft **1**:76; **7**:967; **8**:1067
  radial **1**:72–3, 75
  rotary **1**:72
  steam-powered **1**:75; **2**:210–11
  supercharged **1**:74; **16**:2303
  turbochargers **1**:74, 75; **7**:965
  V-formation **1**:72
air-cushion vehicles (ACVs; hover-craft; ground-effect machines) **1**:**79–81**; **2**:233; **10**:1337
  military **1**:*80*, 81, 123
airfoils **10**:1335
  and racing cars **14**:1889–90
  and sail design **14**:*2009*
  in wind tunnels **19**:*2698*
air hammers **13**:1746
airliners **1**:**82–4**
  at airports **1**:88
  early development **1**:*42*, 82
  jetliners **1**:83–4; **2**:213
  using head-up displays **8**:1040
air locks **1**:85
airports **1**:**86–90**
  firefighting at **1**:89; **6**:*860*, 862
  maglev links **5**:719
  noise from **15**:2141
  runways **1**:87, 88, *94*
  tensile structures at **17**:2400, 2401, 2402
  see also air-traffic control
Air Rescue Service **1**:113
airships **1**:**91–2**; **2**:218
  Hindenberg **8**:1119; **9**:1288
  zeppelins **1**:91–2, **2**:283
  see also balloons
airstreams **10**:1400
air-traffic control (ATC) **1**:**93–6**; **11**:1513
  military **1**:*93*
  radar **1**:88, 94–5; **3**:410; **14**:1895–6, *1897*
  transponders **1**:67
  virtual reality and **19**:*2608*
airways **1**:93
Akashi Kaikyo Bridge **4**:474
alarms
  burglar *see* burglar alarms
  fire **2**:239; **15**:2045
albinism **7**:*979*, 980
albumin **2**:*264*, **14**:1918
alburnum **9**:1294
alchemy **4**:449; **5**:661
alcohol **1**:**97–8**
  for beverages *see* beer and brewing; spirits; winemaking
  as a biofuel **2**:258–9; **6**:794
  distillation **1**:*97, 98*; **5**:661; **16**:2215–18
  industrial **6**:842
  measured in the blood **5**:684, 685–6; **7**:918
  production **1**:98
  surface tension **17**:2321
aldehydes **4**:456
aldosterone **6**:781; **8**:1085, 1086
aldrin **12**:1676

Aldrin, Edwin, Jr. **15**:*2152*, 2154
alembics **5**:661
Alexander of Aphrodisias **14**:1933
Alexander's dark band **14**:1933, 1934
algae **12**:*1719*
  algal blooms **19**:2663
  blue-green **5**:*700*; **6**:823; **10**:1412
  used in pollution control **13**:1803
  used in sewage treatment **8**:1108; **13**:1803; **19**:2645
algebra **10**:1354, 1357
  Boolean **9**:1277, 1279
alicyclic compounds **4**:455
alignments **16**:2273
aliphatic compounds **8**:*1105*
alkali industry **4**:450
alkali metals **1**:**99–101**; **12**:1673
alkaline earth metals **12**:1673
alkaloids **12**:1686–7; **13**:*1790*
alkanes (paraffins) **4**:454, 456; **8**:1105, 1106
alkenes (olefins) **4**:454–5, 456; **8**:1105, 1107
  catalytic hydrogenation **15**:2129, 2130
  fibers derived from **6**:853
alkoxide ions **4**:456
alkylation **11**:1576, 1579
alkylbenzine sulfonate (NSD) **5**:631, 632
alkyl phenol polyethylene oxide **5**:631
alkynes **4**:454, 455, 456; **8**:1105, 1107
allergies **8**:1135
  asthma and **10**:1305
  to food additives **7**:907
alloys **1**:**102–7**; **10**:1387
  amorphous (metallic glasses) **1**:107
  dental amalgams **5**:619; **10**:1371; **15**:2080
  fusible **1**:106
  heat treatment of steel **1**:104; **10**:1387
  intermetallic compounds **1**:104; **10**:*1351*
  multiphase **1**:103
  powder metallurgy **1**:104–6
  precipitation hardening **1**:104
  shape-memory **5**:622; **10**:1351–2, 1363
    Nitinol **1**:106–7; **10**:1351–2, 1363
  solid solutions **1**:103
  superconductivity **17**:2312
  uses **1**:105–7
    aircraft construction **1**:44, 106; **10**:1363
    bioengineering **2**:256
    coins **4**:*507*
    superplastic forming **10**:1363
  see also names of individual alloys
all-terrain vehicles (ATVs) **1**:121
alluvial deposits and mining
  diamonds **5**:637, 638
  gold **8**:1013
alpha decay **14**:1906–7
alpha particles **14**:1906
  and smoke detectors **6**:*863*
ALRVs (Articulated Light Rail Vehicles) **16**:*2278*
alternators *see* generators, alternating current
altimetry **1**:68; **2**:178; **17**:2337
altitude sickness **10**:1305
alumina *see* aluminum oxide
aluminum **1**:**108–11**
  alloys **1**:106, *108*, 109–10; **3**:332
  compounds, uses **1**:109–10
  corrosion resistance **4**:570
  discovery **4**:449
  extraction **1**:*109*, 110; **6**:738; **10**:1378

foil **1**:109
  manufacture **1**:110–11; **10**:*1388*
  occurrence **1**:109
  pipes and tubes **13**:1751, *1752*
  powdered **1**:108–9
  properties **1**:108
  recycling **14**:1940–1
  uses **1**:108–10
    bicycle frames **2**:243
    boat building **2**:277
    in buildings **3**:336
    cans **3**:385
    in paints **12**:1628
    in power cables **3**:344
  welding **1**:111; **11**:1529
aluminum bronze **3**:332
aluminum chloride **12**:1616
  hydrated (aluminum chloro-hydrate) **1**:110
aluminum hydroxide **1**:109; **19**:2664
aluminum oxide (alumina) **1**:109, 110
  aluminum manufactured from **1**:110–11
  forming gemstones **5**:599
  melting point **3**:424
  uses **3**:426
    abrasives **1**:*17*, 18, *111*
    in ammonia synthesis plants **3**:407
    in batteries **2**:229
aluminum silicate **15**:2077
aluminum sulfate **1**:109
alums **1**:109
ALUs (arithmetic and logic units) **4**:528; **10**:1428
Alvarez, Luis Walter **7**:989; **12**:1648
alveoli **10**:1303, *1304*
  and cancer **12**:*1655*
Alvin (submersible) **11**:*1568*, 1569; **16**:2294
Alzheimer's disease **3**:414; **7**:*996*, 997; **13**:*1865*
AM *see* amplitude modulation
amalgams **1**:106; **10**:1372
  dental **5**:619; **10**:*1371*; **15**:2080
Amazon Basin, deforestation **15**:*2113*
amber **6**:725
ambulances **1**:**112–13**
  aircraft **1**:113; **8**:1067, *1070*
americium **6**:765
amides **4**:457; **11**:1527
amine oxides **6**:851
amines **11**:1527
amino acids **1**:114; **2**:*251*; **4**:458; **7**:974; **13**:*1864*, 1866
  essential **11**:1557; **13**:1866
aminobenzene *see* aniline
aminophenols **8**:1108
ammeters **10**:1402
ammonia
  manufacture **1**:25, 115; **3**:*405*, 407; **4**:451; **11**:1525–6
  uses **11**:1526–7
    for maser action **9**:1211–12
    refrigeration **14**:1946
ammonites **7**:989; **12**:*1633*
ammonium chloride (ammoniac) **11**:1527
ammonium dihydrogen phosphate (ADP) **13**:1744–5
ammonium hydrogen sulfate, electrolysis **12**:1621
ammonium ions **14**:2015
ammonium nitrate
  explosive **6**:827, 829
  fertilizer **4**:*450*; **6**:829, 843, 844
ammonium nitrate fuel-oil mixture (ANFO) **6**:828
ammonium perchlorate **14**:1994
ammonium phosphate, production **14**:*2014*
ammonium salts **14**:2014–15

ammonium sulfate, fertilizer **6**:844
ammonium thioglycolate **8**:1032
ammunition **1**:**116–20**
  cartridges **1**:118; **8**:1024
  see also armor; ballistics
amniocentesis **11**:1564
amnioscopes **6**:785
amoebas
  binary fission **14**:1957
  detection of chemicals **15**:2105
  digestion by **5**:645
amosite **6**:846
Ampère, André **6**:726
amperes (amps) **6**:727
ampere turns **10**:1313
amphetamines **12**:1681, 1682
amphibians (animals)
  evolution **6**:824
  reproduction **14**:*1957*, 1958–9
amphibians (seaplanes) **15**:2035, 2037
amphibious vehicles **1**:**121–3**
  military **1**:122–3; **2**:168
amphiboles **6**:846
amplification, measured **9**:*1275*
amplifiers **1**:**124–6**
  audio **1**:126
  distortion **14**:1903
    avoidance **1**:126
  with feedback **1**:126; **6**:838–9
  frequency response of **8**:1072, 1073
  for the hard of hearing **1**:22
  in hi-fi systems **8**:1071, 1074–5
  integrated **1**:126
  intermediate frequency (IF) **17**:2393
  multistage **1**:125
  operational (op-amps) **1**:125–6
  preamplifiers **1**:126
  radio frequency (RF) **17**:2393
  radio telescope **14**:1911
  semiconductor **1**:124; **18**:2481
  telephone **1**:22
  turbulence (fluidic devices) **7**:899
  vacuum-tube **1**:124; **6**:751; **18**:2565
amplitude **12**:1605; **19**:2674
amplitude distortion **8**:*1073*
amplitude modulation (AM) **11**:1473; **14**:1902–3
amps (amperes) **6**:727
Amsterdam, metro system **10**:1349
Amtrack vehicles **1**:*122*
amylase **5**:642, 643
amyotrophic lateral sclerosis (ALS) **19**:*2615*
anabolism **6**:810; **10**:1376
analgesics **12**:1681, 1683
analog and digital systems **1**:**127–9**
  analog audio **4**:513–14; **8**:1071, 1076; **15**:2144–5
  analog-to-digital converters (ADCs) **1**:127, 128–9; **2**:189
  in cell phones **3**:416
  computers **1**:127
  digital audio **8**:1076; **15**:2145
  digital computer animation **1**:138
  digital encryption **5**:594; **6**:762
  digital imaging (image intensifiers) **8**:1131
  digitally-encoded sound **1**:26; **6**:755
    on compact discs (CDs) **4**:514–15
  digital mapping **10**:1330–1
  digital radio **6**:755; **14**:1904
  digital television *see* television broadcasting, digital TV
  digital-to-analog converters (DACs) **1**:127
  digital video (DV) **19**:2602

analog and digital systems (*cont.*)
  displays
    analog 1:*127*
    digital *see* digital displays
  signals 1:128
analog-to-digital converters (ADCs) 1:*127*, 128–9; 2:189
anastomoses 10:1437, 1438, *1440*
anatase 5:599
Anderson, Carl 2:150; 6:769
Anderton Vertical Lift 3:376
androids 14:1989
anechoic chambers 1:*26*; 15:*2131*, *2133*
anemia 11:1558
  sickle-cell 7:980
anemometers 1:63, 130; 19:2699
anencephaly 12:1660
anesthetics 1:**131–2**; 10:1368; 11:1582, *1583*; 12:1681; 17:2328–9
  for dentistry 5:618
  epidural 1:132
  inhalation 1:131–2; 12:1620, *1621*
  liquid 1:131
  local 1:132; 5:618; 17:2328
  pressure measurement 13:*1843*
  see also surgery
ANFO (ammonium nitrate fuel-oil mixture) 6:828
angina pectoris 8:1052
angiograms, nuclear 14:1919
angioplasty, balloon 8:1052
angledozers 5:705
angle grinders 1:*17*
angstroms 6:739
aniline (phenylamine; aminobenzene) 1:*133*; 4:453, 457, 498; 8:1107
  steam distillation 5:663
aniline and azo dyes *see* dyes
animals
  cells 3:411–12
  cloned 1:52; 2:264; 7:*978*
  cold-blooded and warm-blooded 6:836–7
  experimental (for pathology) 12:1656
  eyes 6:832
  feedstuffs for 6:810; 7:914; 13:*1866*
  genetically-engineered 1:52–3; 2:263–4
    transgenic 2:*264*, 265, 266
  intensively-reared livestock 1:56–7
  smell used by 15:2105
  study of (zoology) 19:**2733–6**
  tracking 19:2734, *2736*
  see also veterinary science and medicine
animation 1:**136–40**; 4:536; 16:2189–90
anime cartoons 1:140
anisometropia 4:560
anisotropy 9:1257–8
ankylosing spondylitis 10:1369
annealing 4:507; 10:1387–8; 13:*1786*
annihilation
  particle–antiparticle 2:150, 151; 6:769, *773*
  radiation 6:744, 745; 14:1907
anodizing 17:2323
anorexics (diet pills) 12:1682
antagonists 2:252
Antarctic 11:*1566*
  maps 10:1330
  ozone layer over 4:480; 6:806
  pollution monitoring in 13:*1800*
  sub-ice lake 7:998; 9:1235
antenna complexes 12:1719
antennas 1:**141–2**
  automobile 6:740
  cell phone 3:415, 416

dish 1:*141*, 142
  microwave 1:*141*, *142*; 6:741–2, *744*
  monopole and dipole 1:142
  radio 1:141–2; 6:741; 14:1904
  receiving 1:141–2
  satellite-tracking 15:2057
  television 1:142; 19:*2671*
  transmitting 1:141, *142*
  radar 14:*1897*
anthracene 4:498
anthracite (hard coal) 4:494
anthraquinones 5:691
anthrax
  as a biological weapon 4:*437*, 438, 441
  vaccines 18:2555
antiaircraft guns (AA guns) 1:**143–4**
antibiotics 12:1681, 1687
  discovery 10:1368
  manufacture 6:*840*
  penicillin 6:*841*
  testing 10:*1411*
antibodies (immunoglobulins) 2:264; 8:1133–5, *1137*
  and cancer 3:*380*
  monoclonal 2:265, 266
    manufacture 8:1137
    for radiotherapy 14:1922
  resistance to 10:1411
anticyclones 10:1399; 14:1932
antidepressants 12:1681; 13:1868
antidiuretic hormone (ADH) 6:781; 8:1085
antifouling techniques 2:149
antifreeze 1:73, 97; 6:802
antigenic drift and shift 18:2556–7
antigens 8:1133
  manufacture 7:978
antihistamines 12:1682, 1689
antihydrogen atoms 2:151
antihypertensives 12:1682
anti-inflammatory drugs 12:1682
antimatter 2:**150–1**
  antiatoms 2:151
  antiparticles 2:150–1; 6:768–9
  and annihilation 2:150, 151; 6:744, *773*
    and black holes 2:270
    of electrons (positrons) 2:150, 151; 6:744, 769
    existence postulated 2:150; 14:*1883*
    and pair production 2:151
  imbalance in the Universe 6:773
antimony, alloys with lead 9:1221
antioxidants 16:2225
antiprotons 2:*150*
antiquarks 6:772
antiroll tanks 16:2231
antisatellite weapons (ASATs) 16:2181
antisepsis 17:2328
antitank weapons
  bazookas 11:1487
  mines 11:1453–4, *1455*
  recoilless guns 11:1485–7
antitheft devices 3:341
alpha-1 antitrypsin 2:266
ants
  pheromones 12:1690
  slaves 12:1644
anxiety 10:1369
anxiolytic antidepressants 12:1681
APDS (armor-piercing discarding sabot) shells 1:119; 2:167
aperture size, camera 3:363
aphelion 12:1599
aphids, alfalfa 12:1678
Apligraf 18:2500
Apollo missions
  fuel cells 7:936

photography 15:2152
  space suits 16:2177
appendix 5:644
Appert, Nicholas 7:905
apple-picking machines 1:*51*
application service providers (ASPs) 9:1182
aquaculture (fish farming) 2:152–3; 7:874–5
  see also fishing industry
aqualungs 2:154–5; 5:666; 10:1333
aquamarines 16:2272
aquaplaning 2:231; 14:1981
aqua regia 1:25; 13:1782
Aquarius (ocean laboratory) 18:*2538*, *2539*, 2540
aquatint 6:803, 805
  sugar 6:805
aqueous humor 6:830, 831; 9:1240
Aracon 2:160
aragonite 16:2240
aramids 6:852; 13:1805, 1806; 17:2405
  see also Kevlar
arcade games *see* games machines
Archaebacteria 10:1412
archaeoastronomy 16:2274–5
archaeological technologies 2:156–60; 10:1386
Archaeopteryx 6:823, 825; 12:1635
arches, and dam construction 5:607
Archimedes 5:616; 8:1100
Archimedes principle 5:616; 8:1109; 16:2245
Archimedes' screws 4:565; 9:1192; 15:2032; 19:2695
architecture
  capsule 3:338
  see also building techniques; vault construction
archiving, holographic 8:1083
arcing, in fuses 7:943
Arctic, pollution monitoring in 13:*1800*
Area Denial Artillery Munition (ADAM) 11:1454
Arecibo, radio telescopes 14:1910, *1911*
Argand burners 9:1247
Argentinosaurus 12:1635
argon 11:*1528*, 1529
  separation from air 5:590
Ariane (rocket) 1:43, 15:2151
Aricept 7:997
ARISE satellite 14:*1910*, 1911
Aristotle 2:182; 5:661; 9:1277; 14:1933
  and gravity 8:1021
arithmetic 10:1354
arithmetic and logic units (ALUs) 4:528; 10:1428
Ark Royal, HMS 19:*2630*
Armagnac 16:2217
armaments
  mass production 10:1338
  tank 2:166
Armillaria 12:1645
armillary sundials 16:*2301*, 2302
armor
  armor-piercing bombs 2:286
  body 2:161–3; 13:1860
  tank 2:167
armored vehicles and tanks 2:**164–8**
  armored vehicles 2:164, 166, 168; 14:*1972*
    tracked 18:*2471*
  tanks 2:166–8
    armaments 2:166
    and armor-piercing shells 1:119–20
    crossing water 1:122; 2:168
    history 2:162, 164–6

light and main battle 2:165–6
  suspension system 18:2469–70
  see also antitank weapons
armor-piercing discarding sabot (APDS) shells 1:119; 2:167
arms
  artificial 2:254–5
  mechanical 8:*1101*
  reattachment 13:1765–6
  robotic 14:1986, 1987, *1988*; 15:*2056*; 16:2169
Armstrong, Neil 15:*2152*, 2154
Arnel 6:852; 13:1769
aromatic compounds 4:455; 8:1106, 1107–8
  aromatic rings as functional groups 4:456
  from petroleum 4:453
ARPANET 9:1178
arrowheads, Neolithic 7:*1000*
arrows 3:306-8, 14:1967
arsenic
  in groundwater 7:*981*
  poisoning 12:1659
arteries
  blocked using radiology 14:*1918*
  cerebral, blocked 10:*1438*
  coronary 8:1046
    and heart disease 8:1046–7, 1052
  nanorobots in 10:*1419*
arthritis 10:1369; 19:*2721*
arthroscopy 10:1437, 1439–40
artificial insemination, in cows 1:52
artificial intelligence 2:**169–72**
  and computer games 11:1503
  and personal computers 4:531
  and reading devices 1:20
  see also robotics
artificial reality (projected reality) 19:2604
Arun class lifeboats 15:2040
Arwen 37 (rifle) 11:1533
ASATs (antisatellite weapons) 16:2181
asbestos 6:846–7; 7:*953*; 15:2077
  diseases related to 6:847; 10:1305
  manufacture 6:847
asbestosis 6:847
Ascaridia galli 12:1645
ASCII 2:247; 4:529
ascorbic acid *see* vitamins, C
asdic 15:2126, *2127*
asepsis 10:1367–8; 17:2327, 2329
aspartame 7:914
Aspergillus niger 19:2727
Aspergillus oryzae 19:2726
asphalt
  as a fuel 6:797
  liquid, transportation 7:929
aspiration, fluid 2:280
aspirin 8:1047; 12:1686
  mode of action 12:1683
  packaging 12:*1624*
  in plants 3:305
  various effects 12:1681
ASPs (application service providers) 9:1182
assault ships 19:2629
assembler programs 4:530
assemblers 10:1420
assembly language 4:530
assembly lines 6:815; 10:1339–40
  automobile 2:198; 6:815; 10:1339, 1341; 14:1987
  in canning and bottling factories 3:*382*, 385
  hand tools 13:1789
astatine 8:1036
asteroids 5:698; 13:*1761*; 15:2123
  and extinction of the dinosaurs 7:989

and source of water on Earth **13**:1761
and space weapons **16**:2184
asthma **10**:1305
drugs for **2**:252
astigmatism **6**:832; **9**:*1241*; **12**:1597, 1598
astroarchaeology **16**:2274–5
astrobiology (exobiology) **9**:1235
astrolabes **15**:2062
astronauts
dietary needs **11**:*1558*, 1559
and *g*-forces **3**:*423*
suits *see* space suits
weightlessness **8**:*1020*
astronavigation **11**:1511
astronomy **2**:173–7
eclipses **5**:709–10
observatories **11**:1560–2
radio **14**:1909–12
X ray **19**:2724
and black holes **2**:268, *270*; **19**:2724
and the Chandra telescope **17**:2381
and stars **2**:174; **19**:2724
see also astrophysics; telescopes
astrophysics **2**:178–81
astronomical spectroscopy **2**:178; **16**:2197
see also astronomy
Aswan High Dam **5**:608; **6**:819; **9**:1191
asymmetric digital subscriber lines (ADSLs) **11**:1476, 1517; **17**:2358
Atari 2600 (games console) **7**:952
atherosclerosis **6**:837; **8**:1046; **11**:1559
coronary artery **8**:1046–7, 1052
treatment, using phototherapy **12**:1723–4
athodyds **1**:76; **7**:967
Atlantic Ocean, relief map **7**:*991*
Atlantis (space shuttle) **1**:*85*; **2**:*173*; **16**:*2169*, *2174*
Atlas (missile) **11**:1466
atmosphere **5**:699–700
corrosion in **4**:571
creation **5**:700
depressions **10**:1399
and tides **7**:891
ions in **9**:1184
levels **1**:*62, 63*
oxygen *see* oxygen, atmospheric
pollution *see* pollution, atmospheric
and solar radiation **10**:1396
vapor pressure **18**:2570
water in **10**:1396; **18**:2570; **19**:*2655, 2665*
see also air
atmospheres **2**:222
atmospheric windows **6**:743
atomic absorption **2**:*157*
atomic excitation **9**:1241–2
atomic mass, relative **6**:763, 764
atomic number **14**:1905–6
atomic spectra **6**:768
atomic structure **2**:182–5
Bohr model **2**:183; **14**:1881–2; **16**:2193
Dalton's atomic theory **2**:182; **4**:461
electrons **2**:183–5; **6**:767
behaving as waves **2**:183–5, 184; **6**:767–8; **14**:1882
binding energy (ionization potential) **2**:248
discovery **2**:182; **3**:408; **6**:726, 763, 767
orbitals (shells; quantum energy

levels) **2**:184, 185; **4**:442, 461, 462; **9**:1209; **12**:1671–2; **14**:1881–2; **16**:2193, *2198*
and the periodic table **12**:1671–3
s, p, d, and f states **2**:184, 185, **12**:1671–3
neutrons **2**:*182*, 183, 185; **14**:1906
nucleus **2**:*182*, 183; **14**:1905–6
binding energy **2**:248
discovery **2**:183
mass **2**:248
model of proton and neutron shells **6**:766
"plum pudding model" **2**:182–3
protons **2**:*182*, 183, 185; **6**:767; **14**:1905–6
see also elementary particles
atomic weight **2**:182
atomizers **2**:258; **16**:2227
ATP *see* adenosine triphosphate
atrioventricular node **8**:1046
atropine **12**:1686–7; **13**:1792
ATVs (all-terrain vehicles) **1**:121
audiometers **8**:*1041*
audio and video recording **1**:129; **2**:186–9; **4**:513–14; **15**:2143–4
compact discs (CDs) **4**:514–15
magnetic tape **2**:186–7; **10**:1311, 1312; **15**:2144–5
see also digital audio tapes
for movie production **11**:1498–9
multitrack **10**:1312
records **12**:1694–5, 1697
video cassettes **2**:187–8; **10**:1312; **19**:2600–2
compared with DVDs **5**:652
see also phonography; sound effects and sampling; sound mixing; sound reproduction; video cameras; video recorders
auditoriums, design **1**:26, 27
auditory tubes (Eustachian tubes) **8**:1042
augers **15**:2032
grain elevators **6**:776
for mining **11**:1460
in screw conveyors **4**:565
augmented reality (AR; mixed reality) **19**:2608
auroras **14**:*1899*, 1900
on Jupiter **14**:*1900*; **15**:2121
austenite **1**:104; **10**:*1387*
Australia, Great Artesian Basin **9**:1194; **19**:2684
autism **18**:2556
autocatalytic reactions **7**:879
autoclaves **2**:190; **3**:382; **13**:1841
see also pressure cookers
autogiros (gyroplanes) **2**:*212*; **8**:1065, 1067, 1069–70
pilotless **13**:*1747*
autoimmunity **8**:1135; **10**:1369
automata, hydraulic **8**:1104
automated storage/retrieval systems (AS/RSs) **19**:2622–3, 2624
automatic direction-finding (ADF) equipment **1**:66, 67
automatic radar-plotting aid (ARPA) **11**:1514
automatic teller machines (ATMs) **2**:191–2
automatic train protection **14**:1925–6
automatic weapons and machine guns **2**:193–7; **8**:1025
blowback **2**:194–5, *197*
early automatic weapons **2**:193
gas-operated **2**:194
machine guns **8**:1025
assault rifles **2**:196
general-purpose (GPMGs) **1**:*116*; **2**:196

light (automatic rifles) **1**:118; **2**:196; **8**:1025; **14**:*1968*
motor-driven **2**:197
recoil **2**:193–4
tracer **2**:*217*
self-loading **2**:193
self-loading pistols **2**:196–7
submachine guns (machine pistols; machine carbines) **2**:195–6, *197*; **8**:1025
automation
mass production **10**:1340–1, *1365*
mass transit and subway **10**:1348
automobiles **2**:198–201
airbags **10**:*1417*; **2**:209
alarms **3**:340; **12**:*1664*
alternative power sources **2**:200; **5**:720
alcohol-based (biofuels) **2**:258, 259; **6**:794
electric cars **2**:200, 201; **5**:720; **6**:794–5; **9**:1286–7
hybrid-drive cars **5**:720; **9**:1288; **16**:2269
hydrogen **2**:200; **8**:1119; **9**:1287–8
liquid propane gas **7**:959
ZLEV cars **2**:201
bearings and bushings **2**:*232*
body **2**:199
aerodynamics **1**:36, *37*; **2**:199, *200*, 209
corrosion resistance **2**:199; **4**:*570*
powder coatings **13**:*1823*
and safety **2**:207
braking systems **2**:201, 206; **3**:314–15
antilock (ABS) **2**:201, 204, 206; **3**:315
disk-type and drum-type **2**:201; **3**:313–14
parking brake **3**:314
collisions **2**:*206, 207*, 208
combustion **2**:200
cooling system **8**:*1054*
radiator **8**:1054, *1055*
cooling systems, thermostats **17**:*2426*, 2427
customized **10**:1341
decorative and protective coatings **17**:2324
design, using wind tunnels **19**:*2696, 2699*
development of **2**:198–9
for disabled drivers **11**:1471
electrical systems
alternator **2**:201
battery **2**:201, 227–8; **6**:799
dynamo **7**:972
voltage regulator **19**:2618–19
electronics systems **2**:202–4
air-pressure sensors **10**:*1418*
diagnostic systems **2**:202
engine-control module (ECM) **2**:204
exhaust-gas analysis **2**:203
fuel injection system **2**:200, 203; **10**:1426
ignition **8**:1125–6
ignition *see* ignition systems, automobile
microprocessors **2**:202, 204; **10**:*1420*, 1426
sensors **2**:203–4
engine **2**:198, 199–200
camshafts **2**:200
cooling systems **6**:801–2
crankshaft bearings **2**:231
cylinders **2**:199–200, 202
fan **6**:802
flywheels **7**:*902*, 903; **8**:1143

fuel injection **2**:200, 203; **9**:*1176*; **10**:1426
fuel pump **4**:521
ignition *see* ignition systems, automobile
lubrication **9**:1291–2
oil filters **9**:1292
oil pan **9**:1291–2
oil pump **2**:231; **4**:521; **9**:1292
starter motor **16**:2241
tachometers **2**:203
see also carburetors; internal combustion engines
exhaust system **2**:205
catalytic converters **2**:205; **3**:405, *407*; **13**:1782, 1802; **15**:*2130*
chromium-plated tailpipes **4**:570
mufflers **2**:205; **15**:2141
four-wheel drive **2**:200
front-wheel drive (FWD) **2**:200; **18**:2544–5
fuel tank **2**:207
headlights **11**:1464
head-up displays **6**:*813*; **8**:1040, *1129*
instrument panel (dashboard displays) **6**:*755, 813*, 814
fuel gauge **18**:*2474*
odometers **16**:2209–10
speedometers **16**:2209, *2210*
tachometers **16**:2210
"intelligent" **10**:*1420*
interior design **6**:814
manufacture
mass production **10**:1338, 1339, 1341, *1380*; **14**:1987; **15**:2065, *2066*
model, radio-controlled **14**:1915
noise reduction **15**:2141
odometers **2**:245
radio antennas **6**:740
recyclable **10**:*1364*, 1366
reflectors **14**:1944
safety **2**:199, **206–9**
sealants used in **1**:32
steam cars **2**:198; **16**:2259
steering **2**:201, 207; **16**:2260–2
levers **11**:1471
steering columns **2**:207, *209*; **16**:*2260*
suspension **2**:201; **16**:2229
active **2**:201, 204, 206–7; **17**:2339
hydropneumatic **2**:201; **17**:2339
independent **2**:201
pneumatic **17**:2339
shock absorbers **10**:1353; **16**:2229
see also suspension systems
tires **2**:201, 206; **17**:2338
transmission **2**:200; **18**:2489–92
automatic **2**:200; **4**:492; **7**:903; **8**:1104; **18**:*2490–1*, 2492
clutch **2**:200; **4**:491–2
constant-mesh **18**:2490
continuously variable (CVT) **18**:2492
differentials **18**:2491–2
flywheels **7**:903; **8**:1143
manual **2**:200; **4**:491, *492*; **18**:2489–90
semiautomatic **7**:903
synchromesh **18**:*2489*, 2490–1
trim **4**:*472*, 473
wheels, camber angles **16**:2261
windshields **1**:30; **7**:1001
see also racing cars and dragsters
Autonomous Benthic Explorer (ABE) **16**:2294
autopilot **1**:67–8; **15**:2057
autopsies (postmortems) **12**:1658

autoradiograms **7**:*973*; **11**:*1477*
autorotation **8**:1066–7
autotransformers **18**:*2478*
auxins, and weed control **19**:2679
AV-8 (aircraft) **18**:*2551*, 2553
see also British Aerospace Harrier
avatars **11**:1503
average (mean) **16**:2246, 2248
aviation
  electronics (avionics) **1**:44, 66–7, 78
  flight simulators **7**:**886–7**; **11**:1501; **19**:2603–4
  history of **2**:**210–13**
    aircraft engines **1**:72–6; **2**:213
    airships **1**:91–2
    balloons **2**:*210*, 218
    gliders **2**:210; **7**:1004
    passenger aircraft and airliners **1**:82, 83–4; **2**:213
    World War I **1**:41–2; **2**:212
    World War II **1**:41; **2**:213; **15**:*2023*
    Wright brothers **1**:72, 77; **2**:211; **19**:2696
avionics (aviation electronics) **1**:44, 66–7
  and aircraft engines **1**:78
AVIRISs (airborne visible/infrared imaging spectrometers) **17**:2336
Avogadro's Law **7**:961
AWACS (airborne warning and control systems) **14**:1895
axes **18**:2460
axioms **10**:1357
axles **17**:2339–40
aye-ayes **19**:2736
azathioprine **18**:2499
azeotropes **5**:663

B

B-2 stealth bombers **16**:2254
Babbage, Charles **2**:*171*; **4**:523
babies
  congenital defects, heart **8**:1046, 1051; **12**:1660
  crib deaths **12**:1661
  crying **16**:2200
  premature **12**:1661
  Rhesus **2**:272
  skeleton **3**:*297*
  sleep **15**:*2099*
  "test tube" **7**:980; **11**:1564
Babylonians
  cities **15**:2113
  numbers **10**:*1358*
  ziggurats **11**:1560
Bach, J. S. **12**:1602
backcrosses **1**:53
backscatter **18**:*2542*, 2543
backup storage **5**:609
backward chaining **2**:171
bacon, curing **7**:905
Bacon, Roger **6**:826
bacteria **10**:1409
  at temperature extremes **9**:1232
  corrosion-inducing **4**:571
  effect on iron **7**:982
  and food spoilage **7**:904–5
  and genetic engineering **7**:977
  gold-depositing **10**:1412
  and human health **10**:1410–11
  immune response to **8**:1136
  mesophilic **7**:904
  and the origins of life **10**:1412
  photosynthetic, fossils **7**:988
  proteolytic **7**:905
  psychrophilic **7**:904
  spores **7**:904

affecting canning and bottling **3**:381
  "superbugs" 440-1 **10**:1411
  symbiotic **10**:1333
  thermophilic **7**:904
  used by man **10**:1411–12
    as animal feedstuff **10**:1412
    as biological weapons **4**:438
    methane production **2**:259–60; **10**:1411
    waste management **10**:1411; **13**:1802–3
bacteriophages **10**:1410, *1412*
  and genetic engineering **7**:977
Baekeland, Leo **13**:1770
baffles **2**:205
baggage handling, at airports **1**:89–90
bags, plastic **13**:1774
Baird, John Logie **17**:2383, 2392; **19**:2597
Bakelite **8**:1108; **9**:1162; **13**:1770, 1773; **17**:2370
baking **6**:841
balance **8**:1043
balances **2**:**214–15**
  electronic **2**:214–15
  see also weigh stations
Ballistic Missile Defense Organization (BMDO) **16**:2183
ballistics **2**:**216–17**
  forensic **2**:*216*; **7**:916–17
  terminal **2**:216–17
  see also ammunition
balloons **2**:**218–21**; **7**:961; **13**:*1839*
  carrying bombs **2**:283
  hang-gliding from **8**:1038
  in the logging industry **9**:1296
  meteorological **2**:220; **10**:*1396*, 1401
  parachuting from **12**:1643
  scientific **2**:220
  see also airships
ballotini **12**:1630; **14**:1977
balls
  golf **16**:2220–1
  tennis **16**:2219–20
Balmer, Johann **2**:183
Balmer series **16**:*2197*
bandwidth **1**:126
banknotes, counterfeiting **5**:583–4; **8**:*1130*
Barber, John **7**:964
Barbie dolls **10**:1341
barbiturates **12**:1682
  poisoning **13**:1791
bar codes **3**:401; **8**:1082, *1083*; **12**:1624; **13**:*1803*
  for letters **10**:1322
  scanners *see* optical scanners, bar-code; scanners, bar-code
  for stock control **10**:1341
Bardeen, John **18**:2481
barite **16**:2299
barium oxide **12**:1618
barium peroxide **12**:1618
barium sulfate **19**:2723
barium titanate **3**:426; **13**:1745
Barkhausen effect **10**:1315
Barnard, Christiaan **18**:2501
barographs, aneroid **2**:224
barometers **1**:63; **2**:**222–4**; **10**:*1372*; **13**:1840
barrages, tidal **17**:2437–8
Barrer, Richard **19**:2728, 2729
barriques **19**:2702
Barron, Robert **9**:1268
bars **2**:222; **13**:1839
Bartholinus, Erasmus **13**:1794
baryons **6**:770, 772
baseball
  equipment **13**:1862; **16**:*2223*, 2224

Basic Metabolic Rate (BMR) **8**:1085
basic oxygen steel (BOS) process **9**:*1188*, 1189–90
basketball, clothing **13**:1862
bathing aids, for the disabled **11**:1472
bathrooms, plumbing **13**:*1787*
bathyscaphes **16**:2292–3
bathyspheres **10**:1333; **16**:2292
baton rounds **11**:1533
bats (animal) **18**:*2532*
batteries **2**:**225–9**; **6**:726, 799
  alkaline **2**:227; **6**:799
  automobile **2**:201, 227–8; **6**:799
  battery-powered delivery vehicles **2**:*228*
  "button" **2**:229
  in calculators **3**:360–1
  dry **2**:226–7
  gas **7**:935
  lead–acid **2**:227–8; **6**:799
  lithium alloy–iron sulfide **6**:799
  mercury cells **2**:227; **10**:1372
  nickel–cadmium **2**:229; **6**:799
  nickel–metal hydride **6**:795
  NiFe cells **2**:228–9
  pneumatic **6**:799
  rechargeable **1**:99; **6**:799
  sodium–sulfur **2**:229; **6**:794–5, 799; **9**:1287
  voltaic piles **6**:726
  see also fuel cells
Battle Management/Command, Control, and Communications (BM/C3) **16**:*2182*, 2184
Baudot, Jean-Maurice-Emile **3**:354; **11**:1474
baud rate **3**:354; **4**:541; **11**:1474
bauxite **1**:109, 110; **10**:1378
Bayer, Adolf von **13**:1770
Bayliss, Sir William **8**:1084
bazookas **11**:1487
BBICs *see* biointegrated circuits
BCS theory **17**:2311–12
beaches, erosion **6**:818–19
beam-riding guidance **11**:1468
beans, baked **7**:909
bearings and bushings **2**:**230–3**
  bearings
    air **9**:1290
    ball **2**:230–1
    bicycle **2**:243
    in clocks and watches **2**:233; **19**:2653
    fluid-film **2**:231–3; **9**:1289
    magnetic **17**:2314
    rolling-element **2**:230–1
    rubbing **2**:233
  bushings **2**:230, *232*
beats **19**:2673, 2674
Becquerel, Antoine Henri **14**:1905; **18**:2546
beer and brewing **1**:98; **2**:**234–7**; **3**:*406*; **6**:841
  widgets in beer cans **3**:384
beetle banks **1**:55
beetles
  Colorado **3**:303; **12**:1676
  ladybug **12**:1677, 1678
  and past climates **4**:477, *478*
behavior therapy **13**:1868
Bell, Alexander Graham **12**:1694; **17**:2368–9
bellows **4**:518; **13**:1843
bells **2**:**238–9**; **12**:1668
  electric **2**:239
  made into coins **3**:332
  tubular **12**:*1669*
Bell Telephone Laboratories **18**:2480–1
Belusov-Zhabotinski reaction **4**:*463*
benchmarks **17**:2335
Bendix–Weiss joints **18**:2545

bends, the **2**:155; **5**:667; **11**:1528; **16**:2292; **18**:2537
  and saturation diving **18**:2537–8
beneficiation **4**:497
benthic species **10**:1332
Benz, Karl **2**:198
benzene **4**:455, 498; **8**:1105–6
  bonds in **4**:444; **8**:1105–6
  from oil refining **11**:1578–9
  industrial uses **8**:1107; **11**:1578–9
  ring structure **8**:*1106*, 1108
benzine **5**:687
benzol **4**:498
benzoyl peroxide **1**:100; **13**:1771, 1810
Bergmann Maschinenpistole (sub-machine gun) **2**:195
Berg, Paul **7**:977
berkelium **6**:765
Berlin, subways **10**:1349
Bérliner, Emile **12**:1694
Berners-Lee, Timothy **8**:1147; **9**:1178; **11**:1502
Bernoulli, Daniel **1**:37; **18**:2580
Bernoulli's effect **1**:70; **14**:2010, 2011; **18**:2580–1
  Bernoulli's equation **1**:37; **8**:1109–10; **18**:2581
Bertin Hovertruck **1**:81
beryllium, atomic structure **2**:*182*
Berzelius, J. J. **15**:2076
Bessemer process **9**:1188
beta carotene **11**:1558–9
beta decay **6**:765, 771; **14**:1907
beta particles **14**:1907
  used for radiotherapy **14**:1922
Betts electrolytic process **9**:1220
bezoar stones **13**:1792
BGM-109 Tomahawk *see* Tomahawk
Bible, printing **13**:1848
bicycles **2**:**240–4**; **16**:*2222*
  aerodynamics **2**:*243*, 244
  cyclists **1**:*39*
  amphibious **1**:122
  bicycle pumps **4**:518
  brakes **2**:242–3
  frames **2**:243–4
  freewheeling **2**:242
  racing **2**:*241*, 244
  recumbent **1**:*39*; **2**:*242*, 244
  riding **8**:1030
  as stationary power units **7**:903
  tires and wheels **2**:241, 243, 244; **17**:2338
  transmission systems **2**:241–2
    chain drive **2**:241, 242; **3**:428
    gears **2**:241–2
    using computers **2**:244
Big Bang **4**:572, 573–4; **6**:773
"Big Boys" (locomotives) **9**:1274
Big Muskie (earthmoving machine) **5**:702
bile **5**:643
bimetallic strips **15**:2045
  thermometers **17**:*2423*, 2424
  in thermostats **17**:2426–7
  in watches **19**:2652
binary fission **14**:1957
binary system **1**:128; **2**:**245–7**
  and computers **2**:246; **4**:524, 529
  and digital audio recording **4**:514–15
  and digital audio tapes **2**:189
binding energy **2**:248; **14**:*1961*
  nuclear **2**:248; **7**:876
binoculars **2**:**249–50**
  binocular microscopes
    for operations **12**:*1589*, 1590
    for picture restoration **13**:*1743*
  binocular periscopes **12**:1674–5
  prisms **2**:249, 250; **13**:1853
biobricks **3**:324

Biocam **2**:242
biochemistry **2**:251–2
bioconversion **2**:258
biodiesel **2**:259; **6**:794, **7**:963
biodiversity **2**:262, 266
 in forests **7**:922
biodynamics **1**:58
bioengineering (biomedical engineering; bionics) **2**:253–7
   heart pacemakers **2**:257; **8**:1048
   prosthetic eyes **12**:1613; **13**:1767
bioethanol **2**:259
biofuels **2**:258–60; **6**:794
biogas **2**:259–60
 for buses **3**:343
bioinorganic chemistry **4**:452
biointegrated circuits (biolumines-
  cent bioreporter integrated
  circuits; BBICs) **9**:1168
biological control **1**:58, 61; **12**:1677,
  1678
 in aquaculture **2**:153
 using parasites **12**:1645
 using pheromones **12**:1691
Biological Integrated Detection
  System (BIDS) **4**:441
biology
 astrobiology (exobiology) **9**:1235
 botany **3**:303–5
 cell **2**:251; **3**:411–14
 marine *see* marine biology
 microbiology **10**:1409–12
 molecular **11**:1477–80
 zoology **19**:2733–6
 see also biotechnology
bioluminescence **10**:1301, 1302
biomass, conversion to ethanol
  7:962–3
biomass gasification **7**:959
biomes, in the Eden Project **7**:984
biomineralization **10**:1412
biophysics **2**:261–2
biopsies **2**:280; **3**:378; **12**:1657
bioreactors **3**:406
bioremediation **10**:1411; **13**:1802–3
BIOS (basic input-output system)
  9:1167
biosensors **14**:1988; **19**:2606
biosphere **5**:700
biosteel **2**:163
biosynthesis *see* anabolism
biotechnology **2**:263–6
 and agriculture **1**:52; **2**:265–6
  cloned animals **1**:52; **2**:264;
   7:978
 DNA probes **2**:265
 engineered bacteria **1**:55; **2**:263,
  264
 for food additives **7**:914
 and medicine **2**:263, 264
  "anti-sense" drugs **2**:265
  bioengineered vaccines **2**:264–5,
   266
  monoclonal antibodies **2**:265
 to make new proteins **2**:266
 transgenic animals **2**:264, 265, 266
 see also agriculture, agricultural
  science; genetic engineering
biotecture **3**:338
biotin **19**:2613
biowarfare *see* chemical and biological warfare
biplanes **2**:211, 212
 Hiperlight **18**:2525
bipolar disorder **4**:452
birds
 brood parasitism **12**:1644
 droppings (guano) **12**:1698, 1700
 migratory **11**:1514; **19**:2734
 reproduction **14**:1959
 salt glands **8**:1087
 song **16**:2200

birefringence **9**:1239; **13**:1794
Birfield-Rzeppa joints **18**:2544, 2545
Biro, Lazlo and Georg **12**:1663
biscuit ware **3**:426
bismuth, removal from lead **9**:1220–1
bisphenol **13**:1772
Biston betularia **6**:823
bitmaps **4**:533; **12**:1594, 1595
bits (computer)
 named **8**:1148
 parity (check bits) **4**:541–2; **5**:612;
  8:1148
bits, drill **5**:678–9; **18**:2465
 masonry **5**:679
 for oil exploration **5**:639, 680, 683;
  11:1573
bitumen **1**:30; **5**:663; **6**:817
 from oil refining **11**:1575, 1579
 mining for **11**:1461–2
blackbody radiation **6**:740; **15**:2114
"black box" flight recorders *see* FDRs
black holes **2**:174, 180, **267–70**;
  8:1021–2; **17**:2315
 annihilation radiation from **6**:745
 and radio astronomy **14**:1912
  the ARISE satellite **14**:1910
 and time **17**:2443
black-level adjustment **17**:2388
black smokers **13**:1780
blacktop (tarmacadam) **1**:30;
  14:1973, 1975
 and paving machines **14**:1976
bladder, operations on **18**:2550
blanching **3**:381; **7**:905
blast furnace gas **7**:959
blast furnaces *see* furnaces, blast
blasting techniques (surface treatment) **1**:17; **17**:2322, 2325
blast lamps **3**:339
blastocysts **6**:777, 778
blazars **2**:267
bleaches, ingested **13**:1791
blimps **1**:91
blind, the
 aids for *see* accessibility aids
 helped to see **2**:257
blind spot **9**:1240
blinking **6**:830
Bloch walls **10**:1315,1316
blockboard **9**:1295; **19**:2710
block caving **5**:637; **6**:846
block diagrams **9**:1278
block and tackle **13**:1869
blood **2**:271–3
 artificial **2**:272–3
 calcium levels **6**:782
 carbon dioxide level **10**:1305
 cells
  counts **12**:1656–7
  freeze etching **5**:592
  red **3**:413
 circulation discovered **13**:1733
 clots **8**:1047
 flow detected **2**:280; **10**:1438;
  18:2531
 glucose, testing for **12**:1657
 groups **2**:271; **17**:2328
  typing **2**:271–2, 273
 plasma **12**:1657
 of porphyria victims **12**:1724
 substitutes **13**:1733
 testing **12**:1656–7
 transfusions **2**:272, 273; **17**:2328
blood-alcohol concentration (BAC)
  5:685; **7**:918
blood pressure
 measuring
  automated monitors **6**:757–8
  sphygmomanometers **10**:1326;
   16:2211
 monitors **6**:757–8
 regulation **3**:413–14

blood pumps, external **4**:520
bloodsucking animals **5**:645
blood vessels
 joined using microsurgery
  10:1437, 1438, 1440
 see also arteries; veins
blooming **9**:1230
blowback weapons **2**:194–5, 197
blow molding, thermoplastic
  13:1774–5
blowout preventers (BOPs) **5**:682
blowtorches **7**:879; **13**:1786
blubber **6**:836
blue-baby syndrome **8**:1046
Bluebird (speedboat) **16**:2208
blue-screen effects **16**:2187–8;
  17:2388–90
boat building **2**:274–7
 see also ships
boat lifts **3**:376
boats
 fireboats **6**:861
 flying *see* flying boats
 ice **14**:2013
 ice boats **14**:2013
 jet **16**:2208
 lifeboats **15**:2038–40, 2050–1
 model, radio-controlled
  14:1914–15
 patrol **19**:2633
 see also self-righting boats;
  speedboats
bodies, and cryogenics **5**:592
body scanners **2**:278–82**
 BEAM **2**:280; **3**:312
 CAT (CT) scans **2**:278–9, 280;
  14:1919; **19**:2723
 MRI **2**:282; **3**:312; **4**:448; **5**:718;
  11:1540, 1541; **12**:1657;
  14:1966
 positron emission tomography
  (PET) **2**:151, 281; **3**:312
 radionuclide (scintigraphy) **2**:281;
  14:1917
 thermographic **2**:281, 282; **6**:743;
  17:2422
 ultrasound *see* ultrasonics
 xerography **2**:281
Boehm, Theobald **19**:2715
Boeing 247 **1**:82; **2**:213
Boeing 314 Clipper (seaplane)
  15:2035
Boeing 707 **1**:84; **2**:213
Boeing 747 **1**:84, 89; **2**:212
Boeing 767-200 **1**:82–3
Boeing Chinook **8**:1067, 1068
Boeing jetfoil **8**:1117
Boeing Sonic Cruiser **1**:71
Boeing Stratoliner **1**:82–3
bohrium **6**:766
Bohr, Niels **4**:461; **9**:1241
 the Copenhagen interpretation
  14:1883–4
 model of the atom **2**:183;
  14:1881–2; **16**:2193
boilers, steam-engine **16**:2257
boiling water reactors (BWRs)
  11:1543, 1545; **13**:1832;
  18:2520
bolometers **16**:2198
Boltzmann, Ludwig **9**:1203
Boltzmann distribution **4**:463;
  12:1728; **17**:2416
bombards **11**:1484
bombs **2**:283–6**
 aiming devices **2**:284, 285, **287–8**
 bomb and mine disposal **3**:293–6;
  5:591; **14**:1956; **18**:2471
 clothing for **2**:163; **3**:295
 cluster **2**:286
 flying **2**:286
 gas-generating **2**:286

incendiary **2**:286; **12**:1699
 nuclear *see* nuclear weapons
 "smart" **2**:288
 smoke **2**:286
 terrorist **3**:293–5
 see also explosives; missiles
bombsights **2**:287–8
bonding, textiles **17**:2408
bond polarization **4**:459
bonds, chemical *see* chemical bonding
  and valency
bone
 DNA analysis **2**:158
 grafts **13**:1766; **18**:2504
 necrosis **5**:667
 scans **14**:1917–18
bone ash (calcium phosphate) **3**:425;
  4:465
bone marrow **3**:298–9
 transplants **3**:380; **18**:2499, 2502,
  2503–4
bone meal **6**:844
bones, and fracture treatment
  3:297–300**
 see also joints (body parts)
Boneshakers **2**:240
bookbinding **3**:301–2
books
 anti-theft devices **15**:2044
 ISBNs **8**:1149
 library classification system **8**:1149
 talking **1**:19
Boole, George **9**:1277
boranes **4**:451
borax (sodium borate) **1**:100; **12**:1709
borazon **11**:1527
boreholes
 for fluid mining **11**:1461–2
 for well logging **7**:991
bores, tidal **17**:2440
boring mills **10**:1310
boron carbide **1**:18
boron hydrides **4**:451
boron nitride **2**:163; **11**:1527;
  17:2347
borosilicate glass **11**:1549–50
Borrelly (comet) **15**:2123
BOS (basic oxygen steel) process
  9:1188, 1189–90
Bosch, Karl **1**:115
Bosch, Robert **7**:937
Bosch common-rail high-pressure
  injection system **9**:1176
Bosch K Jetronic injection system
  7:939
Bose–Einstein condensate (Bec)
  9:1214; **14**:1880
bosons **6**:770; **14**:1882
 gauge **6**:770–3
 Higgs **6**:767, 773
 W **2**:151; **6**:771
botany **3**:303–5
 paleobotany **12**:1634
 see also crops; plants
bottles
 automatic filling **12**:1622–3
 plastic, for recycling **14**:1941
bottling **3**:385
Bouchon, Basile **9**:1281
boundary layer **1**:37
bourbon **16**:2215, 2216–17
Bourdon gauges **13**:1840, 1842
bovine somatotropin (BST) **1**:57
bovine spongiform encephalopathy
  (BSE) **18**:2587
bows and arrows **3**:306–8**
 "bow thrusters" **15**:2068
boxing, clothing **13**:1863
box launchers, for missiles **11**:1467
Boyle, Robert **4**:449; **6**:763; **7**:960;
  12:1671
Boyle's apparatus **1**:131–2

Boyle's law 7:960–1
Brabazon, J. T. C. Moore 1:33
braces (tools) 18:2465
brachiation 9:*1234*
Braille 1:19
  micrometer calipers using 1:*21–2*
brain 3:**309–12**
  Alzheimer's disease 13:*1865*
  dangers from cell phones? 3:416
  death, defined 18:2498
  drug entry into 12:1683–5
  olfactory lobe 15:2103, *2104*
  scans 6:*756*
    BEAM 2:*280*; 3:312
    CAT (CT) 2:278–9, *280*; 3:*311*
    EEG 3:312; 6:756, *758*;
     15:2099–2100
    MRI 3:312; 7:*996*
    PET 2:281; 3:312
    ultrasound 18:2532
    X-ray fluoroscopy 19:*2724*
  and sleep 15:2099, *2100*
  and speech/language 3:310;
   16:2201
  surgery 10:*1438*, 1440; 17:*2328*,
   2329, 2330
Brain Electric Activity Mapping
  (BEAM) 2:*280*; 3:312
braking systems 3:**313–15**; 7:933
  air brakes 3:315
    on gliders 7:1005
    on trucks 18:2507
  aircraft 3:314, 315
  antilock (ABS) 2:201, 204, 206;
   3:315
  automobile *see* automobiles,
   braking systems
  band 3:313
  bicycle 2:242–3
  block 3:314
  cable car 3:356
  disk 2:201; 3:314; 7:*933*
  drum 2:201; 3:313–14
  dual 3:315
  electric 3:315
  hydraulic 3:314–15
  power brakes 3:*313*, 314–15
  regenerative 3:315; 9:1287;
   10:1346
  rheostatic 10:1346
  train 3:314, 315; 10:1346; 14:1925,
   1926
  truck 18:2507
Bramah, Joseph 9:1268
Brand, Hennig 12:1698
brandy 5:661; 16:2217
brass 1:106, 107; 3:**316–17**; 19:2731
  manufacture 1:102; 3:316
  working 3:316–17
brass instruments 3:**318–20**; 14:1965
Braun tubes 12:1607
Bravais lattices 5:598
bread making and baking 6:841
  additives 7:907–8
breakdown 6:728; 9:1163
breasts, cosmetic surgery 13:1764–5;
  15:*2078*
breathalyzers 5:685–6
breathing 10:1303–5
breathing apparatus 3:**321–2**
  aqualungs 2:**154–5**; 5:666;
   10:1333
breeches-buoy equipment 15:2039
breeding
  plant 1:*52*, 53–4; 8:1089
  selective breeding of livestock 1:56
Breitling Orbiter 3 (balloon) 2:220,
  221
bremsstrahlung 19:2721, 2724
Brenner, Sydney 7:975
brewing *see* beer and brewing
Brewster angle 13:1796

bricks 3:336
  insulating 9:1161
  manufacture 3:323–4, 426
  recording Earth's magnetism
   10:1317
bridges 3:**325–30**; 4:474
  adhesives used in 1:*29*
  amphibious bridging rigs 1:*123*
  erection 3:330; 4:549; 14:*1977*
  materials 3:329–30
    plastic 4:476
  natural frequency 14:1964–5
  support columns, protection
   14:1981
  tensioned steel bars in 17:2402
  types
    arch 3:327–8
    Bailey 3:328
    bascule 3:*325*
    beam 3:325; 17:*2402*
    box girder 3:325, *329*
    cable-stayed 3:326, 327, *329*;
     4:474–5, 476
    cantilever and suspended-span
     3:325
    lifting 3:*327*
    suspension 3:325–7; 4:474
brighteners, optical 5:632, 693;
  10:1302
brimstone 16:2298
Brin process 12:1618
British Aerospace Harrier 1:71;
  13:*1826*; 18:2553
  cockpit controls 1:*66*
  engine 1:*75*, 78
  inertial guidance platform 8:*1144*
  see also AV-8
broadband ISDN 11:1476
brocade 17:*2405*, 2406–7
Broglie, Louis de 14:1882
bromine 8:1036
  compounds, flame-retarding 7:881
  extraction from seawater 8:1036;
   11:1569
  uses 8:1036
bromochlorodifluoromethane (BCF)
  8:1034
bromoethane 4:459
bromomethane 4:459
bronchi 10:1303
bronchioles 10:1303
bronchitis, chronic 10:1305
bronchoscopes 6:785; 17:2331
bronze 1:106; 3:**331–2**
  bells cast in 2:238
  manufacture 3:331
Bronze Age, furnaces 7:940
brookite 5:599
Brownian motion 9:1203
Browning guns 2:194
Brown, Samuel 9:1169
brucellosis, as a biological weapon
  4:438
Brunel, Marc Isambard 10:1341;
  18:2512
brushes 5:717
bruting 5:640
BSE (bovine spongiform
  encephalopathy) 18:2587
bubble and cloud chambers 3:**333–4**;
  12:1652
  bubble chambers 2:*183*; 3:333–4;
   6:*768*; 12:1652, *1654*; 17:2313
  cloud chambers 2:151; 3:333
Buckminster Fuller, Richard 7:983;
  17:2402
buckminsterfullerenes (buckyballs)
  4:451; 10:1360
budding 14:1957
  yeasts 19:2726, 2727
buffers, chemical
  in living cells 1:114
  solutions 12:1693

bugging devices 6:759–61
bugles 3:319
buildings
  heat loss detected 17:2422
  insulation *see* insulation, thermal
  intelligent 3:338
  building techniques 3:**335–8**
    in earthquake zones 5:707–8
    tensile structures 3:338;
     17:2397–402
  vault construction 18:2571–4
  see also cranes; geodesic structures;
   skyscrapers
bulimia nervosa 12:1658
bulk modulus 5:714
bulk transport *see* freight handling
bulldozers 5:705; 18:2471
  tracks 18:2470
bullets 1:118–19
  aerodynamic properties 2:216
  and forensic ballistics 2:216; 7:916
  rubber 11:1533; 14:1973
Buna rubbers 13:1771; 14:1999
Bundesmann test 19:*2660*
Bunsen, R. W. 16:2193
Bunsen burners 3:339; 7:878
buoyancy force 5:616; 8:1109
buoys
  with radar devices 11:1514
  sonar 8:1070; 15:2128
burbling 14:2002
burglar alarms 2:239; 3:**340–1**;
  5:672; 15:2043
burins (gravers) 6:803, *804*
burns 2:281
buses (data paths) 10:1428
buses (transport) 3:**342–3**
  brakes 3:315
  electric 9:1286
  flywheel-driven 8:1030
  hydrogen-powered 8:1119; 9:1288
  fuel-cells 7:936; 9:1288
  rear-window lenses 9:1230
bushings 2:230, *232*
Bushnell's keg 11:1454
but-1-ene 13:1770; 15:*2129*
but-2-ene 4:455; 8:1105
butadiene 4:460; 8:1106; 13:1771;
  14:1999–2001
butane 4:454; 5:625; 7:955, 959
  from oil refining 11:1577
  liquefied 8:1106
butanone 11:1579
butter 5:601
butterflies, monarch 19:2733
butyl alcohol 6:842
Buys Ballot law 10:1399
buzzers, electric 2:239
bycatch 7:871
bypass principle and ratio 1:77, 78
bytes 5:610

C

cable cars
  aerial 3:358
  streetcar 16:2276–7
cablenets 17:2397–8, 2400
cable networks 3:**353–5**
  see also telecommunications
cable and rope manufacture 3:**350–2**;
  10:*1387*; 13:1806
cables
  antitheft 3:341
  between computers 4:539
  for bridges 3:326, 327, *329*
  coaxial 3:354; 4:539
  for launching gliders 7:1004
  polymer, for fiber optics 6:856
  power 3:344–6; 4:*556*; 6:729;
   13:*1833*, 1836–7
    installation 3:346

insulation 3:345
  superconducting 17:2314
  submarine (undersea) 3:**347–9**;
   18:2471
    manufacture 3:348, *350*
    power cables 3:349
  telephone 3:347; 17:2356, *2357*,
   2371; 18:2471
  in tensile structures 17:2397–8,
   2399, 2400
  see also cable and rope manufacture
cable transport systems 3:**356–8**
cabochons 16:2270, 2272
caching 9:1167
cadmium, poisoning 13:1801
cadmium sulfide (CdS) cells 3:368
caecum 5:644
Caenorhabditis elegans 11:1480
caesium, in atomic clocks 4:485, 488
caissons 1:85; 15:2091
calciferol 19:2613
calcining 19:2729
calcite 16:2239, 2240
calcitonin 8:1086
calcium 18:2486
  in the blood 6:782
  calcium carbide, action of water on
   8:1107
  calcium carbonate
   in toothpaste 18:2466
   see also limestone
  calcium chloride, electrolysis 6:738
  calcium hydroxide (slaked lime; lime)
   production 1:*25*
   uses 1:*25*; 3:*417*; 19:2656
  calcium magnesium silicate 15:2077
  calcium oxide (quicklime; lime),
   production 9:1200
  calcium phosphate 3:298
calculators 3:**359–61**
calculus 10:1356
calendars 17:2441
calendering 17:2408
calico 17:2407
California Extremely Large
  Telescope (CELT) 17:2379
californium 6:765
  isotopes 14:1907
Callisto (moon) 15:2121
calluses 3:299
caloric 6:786
calories 6:790
calorimetry 4:462–3
calotype process 12:1708
Calvin cycle 12:1720–1
camber 16:2261
camcorders 18:2592
  tapes 2:187
cameras 3:**363–9**
  3-D 9:1230
  35mm 3:364–5, 368–9
  Advanced Photo System (APS)
   3:*367*
  aerial 1:33, 34–5
  autofocus 3:364
  automatic and semiautomatic
   3:369
  digital 1:35; 3:**370–2**
   combined with instant pictures
    9:1159
   and desktop publishing 5:628
   for photomicrography 12:1716
  and exposure control 3:368, 369
  gamma 14:1917, 1919
  high-speed 8:1078–9
  infrared 8:*1128*
   with image intensifiers 8:*1129*,
    1131
  instant-picture 9:**1157–9**
  lenses 3:363, 364, 367–9; 9:1228
   of movie cameras 11:1495
  microfilmers 10:1415

movie 11:1493–6, 1498
  for optical soundtracks
    15:2146–7
  multiband 1:35
  reflex 3:366–7
    single-lens (SLR) 3:366, 367,
      368–9
    viewfinder displays 8:1039
    twin-lens 3:366–7
  rocket 3:369
  roll-film 3:365–6
  rotating-mirror 8:1078
  Schmidt 17:2379–80
  in sewers 19:2648
  shutters 3:363; 15:2074–5
    speed 2:205; 3:363; 15:2075;
      17:2446
    and Timetrack 16:2190
  space, free-floating 15:2154, 2155
  speed cameras 14:1977, 1985
  stereo 16:2263
  thermal-imaging (thermographs)
    17:2421–2
  traffic-monitoring 14:1977
  underwater 18:2541, 2542, 2543
  video see video cameras
  video-bug 6:761
  see also movie cameras; photo-
    graphy; television cameras
Campbell, John 15:2062
cams 3:362
  cam chains 3:429
camshafts 2:200
Canadarm 2 (robotic arm) 16:2169,
  2173, 2174
canals 3:373–6
  irrigation 9:1191–2
  locks 3:373, 375–6; 9:1265–6,
    1266
  tunnels 18:2512
cancer
  breast 2:282; 7:997; 12:1687
  and calcium levels in the blood
    6:782
  causes 2:252; 3:377, 378; 11:1479
  cervical 17:2331
  childhood 12:1661
  detection
    using scintigraphy 14:1917
    using thermography 2:281, 282
  diagnosis 3:378
  formation 3:377
  head and neck 13:1767
  holographic visualization 8:1083
  immunity 3:378; 8:1137
  lung 3:378; 6:847; 10:1305;
    11:1529; 12:1655
  skin 6:806; 15:2089
  throat 12:1613
  treatment 3:377–80
    antibody-directed drug therapy
      3:380
    anti-sense drugs 2:265
    bone marrow transplants 3:380
    chemotherapy 3:377, 379, 380;
      12:1685, 1687
    gene therapy 3:380
    hormone therapy 3:379–80
    internal phototherapy 12:1723,
      1724
    photodynamic therapy (PDT)
      3:380
    platinum drugs 13:1783
    radiotherapy 3:378, 379, 380;
      14:1920–2; 19:2723
    surgery 3:378–9, 380; 17:2331
    use of growth factors 2:273
    using lasers 17:2331
  vaccines 2:265; 3:380
  see also leukemia
candlepower 12:1705
CANDU reactors 11:1545

candy see confectionary
cannabis see marijuana
canning and bottling 3:381–5; 7:905,
  909
canoes 2:274, 276
capacitors (condensers) 3:386–7;
  6:730; 14:1960–1
  fixed, electrolytic and nonelec-
    trolytic 3:387
  in microphones 10:1424
  as part of defibrillators 6:757
  variable 3:387; 6:730
  tuning and trimmer 3:387
Cape Canaveral, vehicle assembly
  building 8:1062; 14:1996
capillary tubes, manufacture 13:1752
caprolactam 13:1804, 1811
capsaicin 11:1532
capstans 19:2689
captive breeding 18:2588; 19:2736
caravels 14:2010
carbamates, pesticides 12:1677
carbohydrates 3:388–90; 11:1557
  metabolism 8:1085–6
carbolic acid 10:1367
carbolic oil 4:498
carbon 3:391–3
  activated 3:322; 4:476
  allotropes 3:392; 10:1360
  bonds 3:393; 4:454
  inorganic compounds 4:449
  isotopes 2:157; 3:393; 6:763;
    9:1276; 14:1906
    and carbon dating 2:157; 3:393;
      9:1276; 14:1908, 1916
  nanotubes 10:1420
  organic compounds see chemistry,
    organic
  phase diagrams of 10:1362
  "sinks" 6:807–8
carbonation 3:385
carbon black 10:1311; 12:1628, 1696
carbon cycle 9:1233
carbon dating 2:157; 3:393; 9:1276;
  14:1908, 1916
carbon dioxide
  and anesthesia 1:132
  atmospheric, from ice-core
    samples 13:1800
  blood levels 10:1305
  cycle 1:64
  in fire extinguishers 6:863
  a greenhouse gas 4:477, 479;
    6:807; 7:998
  lasers using 9:1213
  liquid 18:2569
    as an explosive 6:829
    as a cleaning solvent 5:689
    and soft-drink dispensers 15:2109;
      18:2576
  solid 5:664; 18:2570
carbon disulfide 4:464
carbon fiber 3:394–5; 17:2405
  manufacture 3:394–5
carbon-in-pulp (CIP) process 8:1015
carbonization, of coal 7:957–8
carbon monoxide
  molecules 4:462
  poisoning 13:1792; 18:2488
carbon tetrachloride 8:1106
carbonyl chloride see phosgene
Carborundum see silicon carbide
carboxylic acids 1:25; 4:457
  production 1:25
carburetors 2:200, 203; 3:396–7;
  9:1171
carburizing 10:1388
cardboard, manufacture 12:1640
carding 16:2213
cardiology, nuclear 14:1919
cardiopulmonary bypass 8:1049
  see also heart-lung machines

cardiovascular drugs 12:1682
cards
  for automatic teller machines
    2:191
  CD business cards 4:515
  credit and debit 3:401
    transaction-recording devices
      3:400
  identity 3:341
  memory (PC cards) 5:615
  plug-in 4:539
  punched, for data input 5:609
cargo handling
  at airports 1:89
  at docks see docks, bulk handling
    methods
caries, dental 5:618–19
carillons 2:239
carnauba wax 5:716
Carnivore (surveillance system) 6:762
carnivores 5:644
Carnot cycle 8:1053; 17:2414, 2415
  reverse 8:1063
carotene 5:602
Carothers, Wallace 13:1804
carpets 7:893–5, 14:1999
carrier frequency 14:1901; 15:2144
  processing 10:1331
cars, electric 2:200, 201; 5:720;
  6:794–5; 9:1286–7
cartography see maps, mapmaking
  techniques
cartons
  automatic filling of 12:1623
  cardboard 7:908
cartoons, animated 1:136, 137–8, 140
cartridges (ammunition) 1:118;
  8:1024
  shotgun 14:1970
carvels, construction 2:274–5
car washes 3:398
cascade tubes 8:1129
Cascariolo, Vincenzo 10:1301
casein 5:600; 9:1224
cash dispensers see automatic teller
  machines
cash registers 3:399–401
Cassegrain reflector 17:2378
cassettes
  audio 2:186; 10:1312
  video 2:187–8; 10:1312
Cassini (space probe) 15:2122, 2160
cassiterite 17:2447
caster 16:2261
casting 3:402–4; 10:1389
  air-pressure, for artificial limbs
    2:253
  bells 2:238
  continuous 3:403
  cylindrical casting of brass 3:317
  die 3:404; 10:1378, 1389–90;
    19:2732
  evaporative 3:404
  investment (lost wax process)
    3:403–4
  sand 3:402–3, 404
  shell molding (Croning process)
    3:403
  slip 3:402, 425, 427; 4:466–7
Castner cells 1:100
Castner-Kellner cells 6:738
catabolism 6:810; 10:1373–5
catalysts 3:402–7; 4:452, 464
  biological see enzymes
  chiral 4:458
  and fluidized beds 7:901
  transition-metal 3:405; 4:452;
    18:2488
catalytic converters 2:205; 3:405,
  407; 13:1782, 1802; 15:2130
  zeolite traps 19:2729
catamarans 10:1365; 16:2205, 2206,

2207
cataplexy 15:2102
catapults, steam, on aircaft carriers
  19:2628, 2630–1
cataracts 6:806, 832; 12:1589
catechol 8:1108
catheterization, cardiac 8:1052
cathode rays
  are electrons 6:767
  and vacuum tubes 5:657
cathode-ray tubes (CRTs) 3:408–10;
  6:751; 10:1302; 12:1647–8
  for computer monitors 3:409;
    4:532
  for electron microscopes
    10:1431–2
  manufacture 3:409–10
  in oscilloscopes 3:409; 12:1607
  in radar displays 14:1897–8
  in television receivers 3:409;
    12:1647–8; 17:2392, 2393
cathodic protection 4:571; 13:1754;
  19:2732
cathodoluminescence 10:1302
cats, veterinary medicine and
  18:2583–5, 2588
CAT scanners see Computed Axial
  Tomography
cat's eyes 14:1982
cat's whisker devices 6:752
cattle
  beef and veal production 1:57
  dairy see cows
  growth hormones 18:2588
  slaughtering 15:2096, 2098
caustic potash see potassium
  hydroxide
caustic soda see sodium hydroxide
CAVE (cave automatic virtual environment) 11:1503, 19:2604
Cavendish, Henry 8:1020–1
caves, stalactites and stalagmites
  16:2239–40
cavitation 8:1111; 13:1745; 15:2135;
  18:2520, 2532
  marine propellers and 13:1859
Caxton, William 13:1848
Cayley, Sir George 2:210; 7:1004;
  8:1065
CCDs see charge-coupled devices
CCTV (closed-circuit television)
  3:340; 14:1977; 15:2042, 2044
CD-ROMs see compact discs
CDs see compact discs
cell biology 2:251; 3:411–14
cell membrane 3:411
cellophane 3:390; 12:1626; 13:1769
cellos 16:2280
cell system (mass production)
  10:1340
cellular telephones (cell phones)
  3:415–16; 17:2358–9
  answering service 17:2367
  Internet access via 4:540; 8:1147
  traffic monitoring using 14:1985
Celluloid 3:390; 13:1768
cellulose 3:389–90; 6:852
  adhesive 1:29–30; 3:390
  and cellophane manufacture
    12:1626; 13:1769
  combustion 7:881
  digestion 5:644
  paper made from 12:1636–7
  plastics derived from 13:1768–9
  regenerated, for textiles 6:851;
    13:1769
cellulose acetate 3:390; 5:634; 6:852;
  12:1609–10; 13:1769; 16:2191
  dyeing 5:692; 6:852
cellulose nitrate 3:390; 13:1768–9;
  16:2191
cellulose triacetate 6:852

cellulose triethanoate 13:1769
cellulose xanthate 6:851
Celsius (centigrade) temperature
    scale 17:2395, 2396
cement 3:335; 4:546
    asbestos 6:846–7
        pipes 13:1750
    bulk handling by rail 14:1927
    cementitious pipes 13:1750
    cold-setting acrylic (dental
        cement) 2:256
    dental 5:619
    early 3:417
    hydraulic 1:31
    macro-defect-free (MDF) 3:421
    manufacture 3:417–21; 9:1200
    reinforced 3:421; 4:546
        glass-reinforced (GRC) 7:1003
    see also concrete
centigrade (Celsius) temperature
    scale 17:2395, 2396
central heating 8:1056–8, 1064
    thermostats 17:2426–7
    timing devices 8:1058; 17:2445
central nervous system (CNS), drugs
    acting on 12:1683–5
central processing units (CPUs)
    10:1416–17
    and caching 9:1167
    in calculators 3:360
    in computers 4:527, 528, 529, 530;
        10:1428–9
    in mobile phones 3:416
    see also microprocessors
centrifugal force 3:422
centrifuges 3:316, 422–3
centripetal force 3:422
centromere (kentochore) 7:980
cephalosporin 12:1687
Cepheid variables 4:573
ceramics 3:424–7; 10:1340
    piezoelectric 3:426; 13:1745
    smart 10:1352–3
    structural 3:336
    superconducting 5:718;
        17:2312–13
    uses
        in bulletproof jackets 2:163
        as insulators 3:346; 9:1162
ceramides 8:1033
cereals, processing 7:912
cerebellum 3:310
cerebrospinal fluid 3:310
Cerenkov counters 12:1654
Cerenkov radiation 6:794; 14:1907
cerium 18:2485
CERN 12:1652
    and antiatoms 2:151
    bubble chamber 3:333, 334
    L3 detector 6:769
    Large Electron-Positron Collider
        (LEP) 6:767
    Large Hadron Collider (LHC)
        6:767, 772; 12:1648
cervix, cancer 17:2331
cesium 1:99, 101
    and atomic clocks 17:2443
    isotopes 14:1921
CFCs see chlorofluorocarbons
chabazite 19:2728
Chadwick, James 6:767; 14:1905
chaff 16:2253–4
chain drives 3:428–9
    bicycle 2:241, 242; 3:428
chain mail 2:161, 162
chain reactions 7:876, 877; 11:1552
chairlifts 3:357
chalcopyrite 16:2299
Challenger (space shuttle) 15:2029;
    16:2168
    and space debris 12:1600
chambering 5:637

chamber process 1:23–4; 4:452
champagne 19:2703
Chandra X-ray Observatory 2:174,
    17:2381
channel plate intensifiers 8:1130–1
Channel Tunnel 4:475; 7:1008
    rail link through 4:476
chaos theory 3:430–1; 10:1397
chaperonins 2:252
Chappe, Ignace and Claude 17:2360,
    2361
chaptalization 19:2702
charcoal
    activated 7:953; 13:1791; 15:2130
    fuel 2:258; 3:391
Chardonnet, Hilaire de 6:851
charge, electrostatic see electrostatic
    charge
charge-coupled devices (CCDs)
    3:432
    and astrophysics 2:178; 3:432;
        15:2054
    in cameras 3:370, 371, 432; 6:761;
        8:1079
        television 17:2385, 2386
        video 3:432; 18:2590, 2591–2
    in image intensifiers 8:1131
    in optical scanners 12:1592, 1593
    for space photography 15:2155
Charles's law 7:960, 961
Charon (moon) 15:2122
chart recorders see pen recorders
charts, weather 10:1398–1400
checks, sorting by MICR 12:1595
cheese 5:600, 601, 602; 7:904
    waxed coverings 7:908
chemical and biological warfare
    4:437–41
chemical bonding and valency
    4:442–4; 6:787
    coordinate bonds 4:444
    covalent bonds 4:442, 443; 5:597
    hydrogen bonds 4:444; 5:597;
        19:2654–5
    ionic bonds 4:442–3; 5:597
    metallic bonding 4:442, 444; 5:597
    polar bonds 4:444
    van der Waals forces 5:598;
        15:2129
chemical reactions
    exothermic and endothermic 4:464
    kinetics 4:464; 9:1202
    oxidation and reduction
        12:1616–17
chemicals, carcinogenic 3:378
chemical vapor deposition (CVD)
    5:639; 10:1418
Chemical Weapons Convention
    (CWC) 4:437, 439
chemiluminescence 10:1302
chemisorption 15:2129–30
chemistry
    analytical 4:445–8
        drug and alcohol testing
            5:684–6; 16:2226
    inorganic 4:449–52
    organic 4:453–8
        see also hydrocarbons
    organometallic 4:459–60
    physical 4:461–4
chemotherapy 3:377, 379, 380;
    12:1685, 1687
Chek Lap Kok Airport 4:474; 5:677
Chernobyl nuclear disaster 11:1536
chess, played on computers 2:169,
    171
chiasma 3:309
Chicago, sewage from 19:2648
Chicago Tribune Tower 15:2092
Chichén Itzá 16:2275
chickens 1:56–7
    parasites of 12:1645

slaughtering 15:2098
Chicxulub crater 7:989
Chile saltpeter see sodium nitrate
chimes, two-tone 2:239
chimneys 8:1056
chimpanzees 19:2733, 2734
China, ancient
    earthquake detection 15:2046
    explosives 6:826
    kilns 9:1200
    lodestones 10:1314; 11:1510
    natural gas 6:797
    paper manufacture 12:1636
    printing 13:1852
china clay (kaolin) 1:109; 3:424;
    4:466
    world production 11:1458
china and porcelain 4:465–8
    bone china 3:425; 4:465
    porcelain 3:427; 4:468
    soft-paste 4:468
China Syndrome 11:1536
chintz 17:2407
chipboard 19:2709
    manufacture 19:2709–10
chip breakers 10:1309
chirality (optical activity) 4:457
chiral synthesis 4:458
Chiron (asteroid) 15:2123
chiropractic 10:1370; 12:1611
chisels 18:2465
chlorine 8:1034–5
    compounds 8:1035–6
    manufacture 4:452; 8:1035
    uses 8:1035
        as a chemical weapon 4:437,
            438; 8:1036
    in the water supply 4:476
chloroacetophenone 8:1036; 11:1532
chlorobutadiene (chloroprene)
    14:2001
chloroethene (vinyl chloride) 7:880,
    892–3; 8:1035, 1107
    copolymer 12:1696
chlorofluorocarbons (CFCs) 1:40;
    4:480; 6:806, 807; 8:1034;
    13:1798
    as refrigerants 8:1062
chloroform 8:1036; 10:1368
    poisoning 13:1791
chloromethane 4:459
    chlorine isotopes in 10:1344
chlorophyll 3:412; 12:1719–20, 1722
chloroplasts 3:412, 413; 12:1719,
    1721, 1722
chloroprene (chlorobutadiene)
    14:2001
chloroxylenol 8:1108
chocolate 4:499, 558–9
    see also cocoa manufacture
choke (venturi) 3:396
cholecystokinin 5:643
cholera 6:811; 19:2648
    chicken 18:2554–5
    vaccine 18:2556, 2557
cholesterol 6:837; 8:1046, 1052;
    11:1558, 1559
cholesteryl benzoate 9:1257
cholinesterase, inhibitors 7:997
Chomsky, Noam 16:2201
chondrites 10:1392
    carbonaceous 3:393
chondrules 10:1392
chordae tendinae 8:1045
chorionic villus sampling 11:1563,
    1564
choroid 6:830
Christmas disease 7:980
Christmas Trees 5:682; 11:1573
chromakey 18:2495
    see also blue-screen effects
chromatic aberration 9:1229;

11:1561; 17:2377
chromatography 2:251; 4:446,
    469–71
    column 1:109; 4:469
    and forensic science 7:917–18
    gas chromatography and mass
        spectrometry (GCMS) 4:471;
        5:684; 10:1343
    gas or gas-liquid (GC; GLC)
        4:448, 470–1; 5:684; 10:1343
        for blood alcohol content 7:918
        and robot senses 14:1988
    gel-permeation (GPC) 4:471
    ion-exchange 4:471
    liquid 4:470
        high-performance (HPLC)
            4:471; 5:684
    paper 4:470, 471
    thin-layer (TLC) 4:469, 470;
        12:1686
chromic oxide 4:472
chromite ore, extraction 4:472
chromium 4:472–3; 18:2486
    extraction 4:472
    powder 1:105
    uses 4:472, 473
chromizing 4:473
chromolithographic process 9:1264
chromosomes 3:411, 412–13; 6:823;
    7:979, 980
    sex (X and Y) 3:412–13
    and genetic disorders 7:980
    in situ hybridization 7:980
    see also DNA; genes; genetics
chromosphere 11:1528
chronic fatigue syndrome 13:1868
Chronocal Speaking Clock
    17:2348–9
chronometers 4:484; 9:1215, 1216;
    11:1511, 19:2651
Chrysler Building 15:2092
chrysoberyl 16:2270
chrysotile (white asbestos) 6:846
Chubb, Jeremiah 9:1268
chuck, drill 5:678
chyme 5:643
cigarette smoke, lung damage
    10:1305
ciliary body 6:830
ciliary muscles 9:1240
CinemaScope 11:1494
cinématographes 13:1854
Cinerama film 11:1494
cinnabar 10:1371; 16:2299
ciphers 5:594
circuit aging 9:1168
circuit boards, printed see printed
    circuits
circuit breakers see fuses and circuit
    breakers
circuits, electrical see electrical
    circuits
cire perdu (lost-wax process) 3:403–4
cirrhosis 18:2532
citric acid 19:2727
citric acid cycle see Krebs cycle
civil engineering 4:474–6
    see also bridges; dams; geodesic
        structures; railroad systems;
        roads, construction; tunneling;
        water supply
Clam (wave-energy device)
    19:2675–6
clarinets 19:2714, 2715
classification, plant and animal
    12:1632–3
clathrate compounds 11:1529
claudication, intermittent 19:2613
Clausius, Rudolf 17:2415
Claus process 16:2299
clavichords 13:1735
Clavinets, Hohner 13:1740

clay **15**:2077
  and brick manufacture **3**:323–4
  china see china clay
  heavy **3**:*424*
  pipes **13**:*1750*, 1751
  in soil **15**:2110, 2111–12
clay-pigeon shooting **14**:1970;
  16:2224
clean-room technology
  clothing **13**:*1860*
  for surgery **11**:1582–3
clear-cutting, forests **7**:921–2
cleft lip and palate **13**:1766–7
clepsydrae (water clocks) **4**:481, 488;
  17:2441–2
cliff railways **3**:356–7
climatology **4**:*477–80*
  Earth's climatic divisions **14**:*1932*
  El Niño **4**:478–9; **15**:2029
  global warming **4**:479–80;
    6:807–8; **7**:922; **13**:*1800*
  past climates **4**:477–8; **7**:998;
    11:1568
  see also meteorology; ozone layer
cling film **12**:1626
clinker, cement **3**:419
clip art **4**:*533*
clippers, hair **14**:*1935*, 1936
clipping **8**:1074
clocks **4**:*481–8*; **17**:2441–2
  alarm **4**:481, 486
  atomic **4**:485, 488; **17**:2349, 2443
  electric **4**:486; **6**:734
  mechanical **4**:481–6
    jewel bearings **2**:233
    pendulum **4**:*482*, 483–4;
      12:1664, *1665*; **17**:2442
  pneumatic **18**:2567
  quartz **4**:486–8; **17**:2442, 2445–6
  radio-controlled **4**:488
  sundials **16**:*2301–2*; **17**:2441
  talking **17**:*2348–9*
  water **4**:481, 488; **17**:2441–2
  see also chronometers; watches
clock speeds **10**:1429
cloning, animals **1**:52; **2**:264; **7**:*978*
Clostridium
  acetobutylicum **6**:842
  botulinum **7**:905, 911
clothing
  bulletproof **2**:163; **13**:1806
  protective see protective clothing
clothing, manufacture **4**:*489–90*
  hosiery and knitwear **8**:1090–3
  industrial sewing machines
    15:2061
  see also fasteners, clothes; fibers,
    natural; fibers, synthetic; textiles
cloud chambers see bubble and cloud
  chambers
clouds **19**:*2665*
  classification **10**:1400–1
  formation **10**:1401; **14**:1931–2;
    18:2570
  ionization **17**:2429–30
  nacreous **9**:*1240*
  noctilucent **9**:*1240*
  seeding **8**:1096; **18**:2570
  thunder (cumulonimbus) **9**:1250;
    10:1399, 1401; **17**:2428, 2429
  wave patterns **19**:*2673*
clozapine **13**:1868
clutches **2**:200; **4**:*491–2*
  dog **18**:2490, 2491
  electromagnetic **4**:492
CMOS (complementary metal
  oxide–silicon) technology
  8:1079; **18**:2590, 2592
CNC (computer numerical control)
  10:1340; **18**:*2464*, *2465*
CN gas (Mace) **11**:1532; **14**:1972
coacervation **10**:1413, *1414*

coal **2**:258; **3**:391
  as an engine fuel **7**:937
  burned in fluidized beds **7**:900
  coal gas from **7**:957–8
  destructive distillation of **5**:664
  formation **6**:824
  mining **4**:493–7; **11**:1460–1
  "seacoal" **4**:497
  types **4**:494
  world production **11**:1458
coal gas **7**:957–8
coal tar **4**:453, **498**
  aniline dyes from **1**:133–4
Coanda effect (wall attachment
  effect) **7**:898–9
Coanda, Henri **7**:898
coasts
  continental coastlines **7**:990
  erosion of **6**:818–19
  length of British coastline **3**:431
cobalt, isotopes **7**:911; **14**:1921
cobalt (II) chloride **14**:*2015*
COBE (Cosmic Background
  Explorer) **4**:*573*
Cobras (helicopters) **8**:*1067*
cocaine **5**:618; **12**:1687
cochlea **15**:2132
cochlear implants **8**:1044; **12**:1612
Cockerell, Christopher **1**:80
Cockerell's rafts **19**:2677
cocoa manufacture **4**:*499–500*
  see also chocolate
coconut fiber **6**:850
codeine **12**:1687; **16**:2226
codons **7**:975; **11**:1478
coefficient of performance **8**:1063–4
coelacanths **12**:*1632*
coffee **4**:*501–3*; **7**:910
coffee-making equipment **4**:*504–5*
cognac **16**:2217
cognitive therapy **13**:1868
cog railways **4**:*506*
  funiculars **3**:357–8
coherent radiation **9**:1210–11, *1239*
coil coating process **12**:1630
coins and minting **4**:*507–9*
  bronze coins **3**:332
  coin handling in slot machines
    7:950
  coin validation in vending
    machines **4**:509; **18**:2575
  counterfeit coins **5**:584
  gold coins **8**:*1015*
coir **6**:850
coke **4**:494
coke oven gas **7**:959
coking (thermal cracking) **11**:1578
coking, on catalysts **3**:406
cold heading **15**:2033–4
coliform count **19**:2662
collagen **3**:298; **19**:2614
collimators, multileaf **14**:1922
collodion **3**:390, **12**:1708
colon **5**:644
  and endoscopy **6**:784, 785
color **4**:510
  monochromatic light **9**:1237
  subtractive and additive **4**:*511*, *512*
colorants, hair **8**:*1032*, 1033
color blindness **4**:510; **12**:1598
colorimetry **4**:447, **510–12**
color mapping **4**:533–4
color-register encoding **4**:534
color-reversal effects **17**:2388
colostomy **3**:379
Columbia Basin Project **5**:605
Columbia (space shuttle) **1**:*43*;
  16:*2166*, 2167; **17**:*2364*
  crystal growth experiment **19**:*2729*
coma effect **9**:1229
combined heat and power (CHP)
  plants **19**:2639

combine harvesters **1**:*45*, 49, 51
combing, yarns **16**:2213
combustion **12**:1617, 1620
  flame-retarding agents **7**:880–1;
    13:1771
  fluidized-bed **7**:900
  slow **7**:879
  see also flames and ignition
comets **15**:2123
  Halley's **10**:1393
  orbits **12**:1599
  Shoemaker-Levy 9 **2**:176; **15**:2121
common-rail fuel-injection systems
  9:*1176*
communication
  animal **19**:2733
    by smell **15**:2104–5
commutators **5**:717
  generating interference **6**:745
COMPAC network **3**:348
compact discs (CDs)
  audio **1**:129; **4**:*513–17*; **5**:650
    amplifiers **1**:126; **4**:*514*
    CD jukeboxes **9**:1197
    CD players **4**:*517*; **5**:650
  CD-ROMs **5**:614, 650; **6**:*754*
    drives **4**:527
    multimedia **11**:1502
    rewritable **5**:614
  manufacture **5**:*614*, 651
  trucks **18**:2507
  see also digital versatile discs
    (DVDs)
compacters **5**:703
compasses, magnetic **11**:1510, *1514*
compensation curbs **19**:2652
complement **8**:1132
composites **10**:1353
  for aircraft **1**:*43*, 44
  carbon fibers used in **3**:395
  for prostheses **2**:255
  smart **10**:1353
composting **6**:843; **10**:1411; **19**:2640
compounds, intermetallic **1**:104;
  10:*1351*
compressibility effects **17**:2318
compression **5**:714
compression molding **13**:1775
compression techniques **15**:2145
  computer **4**:533, 534
  and DVDs **5**:651
compressors and pumps **4**:*518–22*
  compressors **4**:518, 519–20
    centrifugal **1**:*76*; **16**:2303
    compressed air line apparatus
      3:322
    as energy storage **6**:798–9
    in jet engines **1**:77
    reciprocating **4**:518, 519
    rotary **4**:519
    rotary vane **4**:519
    screw **4**:519
    for spray guns **16**:*2228*
    superchargers **1**:74
    two-stage **4**:518
  pumps **4**:520
    for aviation fuel **1**:88
    Bolsena **4**:520, 521
    centrifugal **4**:521
    cryopumps **5**:592; **18**:2559
    cylinder **8**:1102
    double-action **4**:520–1
    electromagnetic **4**:522; **9**:1254
    filter **18**:2581
    gear **8**:1102
    high-pressure **4**:522
    hydraulic **4**:521; **8**:1101, 1102
    jack (nodding donkeys) **5**:683;
      11:1573–4
    jet **4**:522
    for oil recovery **5**:683;
      11:1573–4

    peristaltic **4**:521, *522*; **13**:1752
    positive-displacement **4**:520–1,
      522
    reciprocating **4**:520–1
    rotary **4**:*520*, 521; **7**:903;
      18:*2558–9*
    self-priming **4**:521–2
    sorption **18**:2559
    sublimation **18**:2559
    sucker-rod **11**:1573
    vacuum **4**:522; **18**:2558
    vane **5**:659
    vapor-diffusion **18**:2559
    water for irrigation **9**:1192
    windmill **19**:2695
Compton effect **9**:1241
Compton Observatory **2**:173–4
Computed Axial Tomography (CAT;
  CT) scans **2**:278–9, *280*;
  14:*1919*; **19**:2723
computer-aided design (CAD) **4**:532;
  6:814–15; **10**:*1364*, 1365
  and aerodynamic shapes **1**:*37*
  and chip circuitry **6**:*750*
  and clothing manufacture **4**:489
  and electrodischarge machining
    6:736
  see also computer graphics;
    ergonomics
computer-aided manufacture (CAM)
  4:532; **10**:1365
computer-assisted retrieval (CAR)
  systems **10**:1415
computer generated images (CGIs)
  7:887; **16**:2190
computer graphics **1**:138, 139;
  4:*532–6*
  of chemicals **4**:*464*; **5**:*599*
  of protein structure **13**:*1864*, 1866
  of shoe designs **6**:*814*
  of voiceprints **16**:*2200*
  of zeolites **4**:*464*; **19**:*2730*
  see also computer-aided design
computer output microfilmers
  (COMs) **10**:1415
computer printers **4**:528, *543–5*
  dot-matrix **19**:2720
  ink-jet **1**:40; **4**:*544–5*; **19**:2720
    bubble-jet **4**:544
    nozzles **15**:2077
  laser **4**:528, 543; **19**:2720
  line **4**:545
    barrel printers **4**:*545*
    train and chain printers **4**:545
  plotters **4**:528
  printing photographs **3**:*372*
computers **4**:*523–31*
  analog and digital **1**:127; **4**:523
  and animated movies **1**:137–8, 139,
    140
  at airports **1**:*88*
  in aviation **1**:44
  and the binary system **2**:246;
    4:524, 529
  chess-playing **2**:*169*, 171
  components **4**:*527*, 528
    CPU see central processing units
    drives see data storage
    power supply unit (PSU) **4**:529
    see also integrated circuits
  customized **10**:1341
  development of **2**:*171*; **4**:523–4
  and digital cameras **3**:370
  electronics **6**:754–5
  in engineering **10**:1365
  fluidic digital **7**:899
  future of computing **4**:531
  graphical user interfaces (GUIs)
    4:531; **8**:1147; **11**:1490, 1501
  graphics cards (video cards;
    adapters) **4**:527
  and the hexadecimal system

computers, and the hexadecimal
system (*cont.*)
2:246–7
languages 4:530; 10:1428
high-level 2:*246*; 4:530
laptop 4:526; 19:2720
logic functions 9:1277–9
machine code 10:1428
mainframe 4:526
making components for 3:404
memory 5:609; 9:1167
optical 9:*1213*
random access *see* RAM
read-only (ROM) 5:609
minicomputers 4:525, 526
monitors (VDUs; visual display
units) 3:409; 4:527; 5:599
color 4:532, 533
liquid crystal display (LCD)
4:532; 9:1259
monochrome 4:533
multimedia 4:525, 534–5
and music 17:2345
networks 4:526, **537–42**; 8:1150
and epidemiology 6:*812*
infrared 19:2707
local-area (LANs) 4:526, 537,
538–9, 541
peer-to-peer 4:538
power-line 19:2707
wide-area (WANs) 4:537,
539–40, 542
notebook 11:*1491*
operating systems 4:525, 530
output devices 4:527–8
palmtop 4:526
personal organizers 4:*530*
personal (PCs) 4:*523*, 525, 526–7
desktop 4:*526*
future developments 4:531
input devices 4:527
output devices 4:527–8
parity-bit checking 4:542
printers *see* computer printers
programming and software 4:523,
529–30; 8:1148
image-manipulation software
5:629
photographic editing software
4:534
spreadsheets 8:1150
see also databases; word
processors
scanners *see* optical scanners
security 4:530–1
and data interception 6:761–2
serial- and parallel processing
2:172
stereoscopic images 16:2264
see also artificial intelligence; data
storage; mice and pointing
devices; modems and ISDN
computer-to-plate systems 9:1263
computer voice-stress analyzers
(CVSAs) 13:1808
concert halls *see* auditoriums
conching 4:558–9
Concorde (aircraft) 1:84; 2:213;
17:2319–20
engine 1:65
Kevlar fuel-tank linings 13:1806
concrete 3:417; 4:**546–9**
blocks and walls, splitting 17:2412
bonding sections together 1:*29*
corrosion 4:571
lightweight 4:549
aerated 4:*547*, 549
polymer-impregnated (PIC) 4:549
precast 4:547–8
prestressed 3:329–30, 335;
4:548–9; 13:1750
reinforced 3:329–30, 335, 420;

4:547; 13:1750
sealants over 1:32
uses
boat building 2:277
for bridges 3:329–30; 17:*2402*
for buildings 3:335, 338
pipes 13:1750
roads 14:1975–6
see also cement
condensation nuclei 14:1931
condensed-matter physics 4:**550–3**
condensers (distillation), Liebig
5:662
condensers (electric components) *see*
capacitors
condors, Californian 18:2587–8;
19:*2733*, 2735–6
conduction, electrical 4:554–6; 6:728
in metals 4:550, 556; 17:2417–18
see also insulators, electric; semiconductors; superconductivity
conductivity, thermal, and vacuum
measurement 18:2559
conduit systems, for streetcars
16:2277, 2278
confectionery 4:**557–9**
conformational therapy 14:1922
congenital defects 12:1660
heart 8:1046, 1051; 12:1660
Congreve, Sir William 14:1991
conic sections, and planetary orbits
12:1599
conservation, animal 19:2734–6
consonance 11:1507
constantan 4:568
construction
earthmoving machinery 5:701
see also building techniques
contact image sensor (CIS) system
12:1592
contact lenses 4:**560–3**
manufacture 4:562–3
see also optometry
contact process 1:23, 24; 4:452
containers 7:931; 15:2069
air containerization 7:932
container ships 7:932; 15:*2067*,
2069–70
docks 5:669–70
handling 7:930–2
cranes 5:*586*, 588, 670; 7:931,
932
rail transport 14:1927
continental drift 4:478; 7:990;
13:1777
see also plate tectonics
continental shelves 11:1566
continuity equation 8:1109
contraceptives 13:1818
from cotton 5:*581*
oral 12:1682; 13:1818
control question tests (CQTs)
13:1808
convection currents, and plate
tectonics 5:699
convertiplanes 8:1069; 18:2552
conveyors 4:**564–5**; 10:1339–40
baggage, at airports 1:89, 90
convulsants, poisoning 13:1791
Cooke, William 17:2360
cooking, food 7:909
microwave 11:1448
Cook, James 15:2062
coolant injection 1:76
Coolidge, William 19:2721
Coolidge tubes 19:2721–2
cooling, law of 11:1521
cooperite (platinum sulfide) 13:1781
Cooper pairs 17:2312
coordinated universal time (UTC)
17:2349
coordination 18:2488

copal 13:1741, 1742–3
Cope, Edward Drinker 12:1633
Copenhagen interpretation, the
14:1883–4
copolymers 13:1812
self-polishing (SPCs) 2:149
synthetic rubber 14:1999–2001
vinyl acetate 12:1696; 13:1771
copper 4:**566–8**
alloys 1:102; 4:568; 15:2080
blister 4:567
electrical properties 4:568
electrolytic 4:568
etched copper printed circuit
boards 13:1845–6
extraction 4:566–7
mining 11:1459
oxygen-free 4:568
patina 4:571
pipes 13:1751
scale 13:1787
powder 1:105
refined 4:567–8
refining 4:567; 6:738
tough-pitch 4:568
see also brass; bronze
copper arsenate, chromated (CCA)
9:1295
copper ferrocyanide 12:1609
copper (I) oxide (cuprous oxide)
2:149
copper (II) oxide (cupric oxide) 2:149
copper phosphide 3:332
copper phthalocyanine 12:1628
copper sulfate (blue vitriol) 4:566
copper sulfide 4:566
corals, digestion by 5:645
cor anglais 19:2715
cordite 3:390; 6:842
coring tubes 7:987, *989*
Corinth Canal 3:*374*
Coriolis effect, and hurricanes
8:1094
Coriolis force 5:699–700; 8:1143;
10:1399; 17:2440
cork
floor tiles 7:893
production 7:925
corn
breeding 1:*52*, 53
genetically-engineered 3:303
cornea 6:830; 9:1240
and laser surgery 12:1590
coronagraphs 5:*709*
coronary arteries, dilating 17:2330
coronary-artery bypass graft (CABG)
surgery 8:1052
coronary sinus 8:1045
corotrons 12:1701
corposants 17:2431
corpses, and forensic science
7:919–20; 8:1083
corpus callosum 3:309
corrosion 12:1617
prevention 4:**569–71**
in cars 2:199
in pipelines 13:1754
corticosterone 8:1085
cortisol 6:781; 8:1086
cortisone 2:186; 12:1682
corundum 1:18, 109; 16:2270
Corynebacterium glutamicam 7:914
cosine waves 15:2082
cosmetic surgery 13:1764–5
Cosmic Background Explorer
(COBE) satellite 4:*573*
cosmic rays 6:769; 7:970
detection 12:1652
and the Van Allen belts 14:1900
cosmology 4:**572–6**
and microwave spectroscopy
16:2199

see also Universe
cotton 5:**581–2**; 6:848, 849; 17:2404,
2405
flame-resistant 7:881; 13:*1862*
weaving 5:581, 582; 9:*1283*
cotton gins 5:581
Cotton, William 8:1092
Coulomb, Charles 6:725; 7:933;
12:1727
Coulomb's law 6:725, 727
counterfeiting and forgery 5:**583–4**;
8:*1130*
countries, developing 7:985–6
Courtelle 6:853
Cousteau, Jacques 2:155; 10:1333;
18:2538–9
cowpox 8:*1134*
cows
artificial insemination of 1:52;
18:2585
and biotechnology 2:266
hormones and 1:52, 57
improving herds 1:52
veterinary work and 18:2585–6,
2588
see also dairy industry; milk
Crab nebula 17:2316, 2317
cracking 4:453; 11:1575–6, 1578
catalytic 4:*459*; 11:1576
hydrocracking 8:1119; 11:1576,
1578
thermal 11:1578; 13:1776
cranequins 3:308
cranes 5:**585–8**
bridge 5:585–6
for containers 5:*586*, 588, 670;
7:931, *932*
crawler 5:585
floating 5:588, 669, *671*; 15:2022
gantry 5:585, 586, 670
goliath 5:586, 588
jib (derrick cranes) 5:586–8
telescoping boom 5:587
tower 5:*585*, 587, 588
in warehouses 19:2624
on wharfs and docks 5:588, *668*,
669, 671
craniofacial surgery 13:1767
crash barriers, road 14:1979–81
C-reactive protein 13:1866
cream 5:601
creosote oil 4:498
crepe 17:2407
cresols 8:1108
cretonne 17:2407
Creutzfeldt-Jakob disease (CJD),
new-variant 18:2587
Crick, Francis 7:973, 975
critical mass 7:877
crocidolite (blue asbestos) 6:846
Croning process (shell molding)
3:403
Crookes, Sir William 12:*1671*
Crookes dark space 5:656
crops
aerial photography 1:34
biowarfare against 4:441
and computerized farming 1:*55*
fuel from 2:260
genetically-engineered 1:53, 55;
3:303; 7:907
grown in water (hydroponics)
8:1120–2; 9:1194
herbicide-tolerant 19:2680–1
irrigation 9:**1191–4**
leguminous 15:2113
for manure 6:844
root 15:2113
rotation 1:60–1; 6:844; 12:1676
in forestry 7:924
and the soil 15:2113
trees as 7:923, 924

see also horticulture; pest control
crossbows 3:308
cross breeding 1:*52*
cross-linkers 12:1628–9
crowd control 14:1971–2
crowns, dental 5:*619*
crude oil *see* petroleum
crumhorns 19:2714
cryobots 7:998
cryogenics 1:64; 5:589–92
  see also refrigeration
cryolite 6:738
cryopumps 5:592; 18:2559
cryostats 5:*590, 591*; 11:1446
cryosurgery 5:591; 17:2330
cryptology 5:593–6
  see also security systems
crystals and crystallography 4:550;
  5:597–9
  birefringence of crystals 9:1239;
    13:*1794*
  bonds 5:597–8
  cleavage planes 5:598
  covalent crystals 5:597
  crystal formation 5:599
  crystals in industry 5:599
  impurities 5:599
  ionic crystals 4:443; 5:597
  liquid crystals 4:551; 9:**1257–9**;
    10:1352, 1362
  metallic crystals 5:597
  periodic structures 5:598
  synthetic crystals 17:2346–7
  unit cells 5:598; 10:1359; 13:1744
  X-ray crystallography, X-ray dif-
    fraction 2:261, 262; 4:462, 551;
    5:598–9, 641; 12:1689; 19:2724
  see also gemstones
CS gas 4:437; 11:1532
ctenophores 10:*1301*
CT scanners (CAT scanners) *see*
  Computed Axial Tomography
cuckoos 12:1644
Cugnot, Nicolas Joseph 2:198;
  16:2259
cuirasses 2:162
Cullen, William 14:1945
cullet 14:1942
cultivators 1:47–8, 51
cuprammonium process 6:851
cupronickels 4:568; 11:1523
cuprophan 5:634
curare 12:1687; 13:*1791*
Curie, Marie and Pierre 10:1367;
  14:1905
Curie point 13:1745
curing, food 7:905, 908, 909–10
curium 6:765
currency, printing 6:805
currents, ocean 5:700; 11:1568–9
customization, mass 10:1341
cuttings, and road construction
  14:1974
CVRs (Cockpit Voice Recorders)
  7:884, 885
Cyana (submersible) 13:1780
cyanates 11:1527
cyanide(s) 11:1527
  detection in blood 12:*1657*
  poisoning 13:1792
cyanoacrylates 1:31–2
cyanocobalamin 19:2613
cyclamates 7:914
cyclic-AMP 2:251; 8:1087
cycloalkenes 4:455
cycloalkynes 4:455
cyclohexane 4:455; 8:1107; 11:1579
cyclone extractors 12:1638
cyclones (depressions) 14:1932
cyclones (storms) *see* hurricanes
Cyclonite *see* RDX
cyclononyne 4:455

cyclopropane 4:455; 8:1106; 12:1681
cyclopropene 4:455
cyclosporin 18:2499, 2503
cyclotrons 12:1649
Cygnus Loop (supernova) 17:*2315*
Cygnus X-1 2:269; 19:2724
cymbals 12:1667–8, *1669*
cysteine 13:1864
cystic fibrosis 7:980; 12:1660
cytochromes 13:1865
cytokinins 3:305
cytological specimens, for cancer
  investigations 3:378
cytoplasm 3:411, 413
cytosine 7:973–4; 11:1477, 1478
Czochralski method 15:2077;
  17:2347

D

2,4-D 19:2679
Dacron 3:350; 6:853; 13:1772
Daimler, Gottlieb 2:198; 16:2204
dairy industry 5:600–3
  mechanized 1:50
  milking machines 11:**1451–2**
Dalton, John 2:182; 4:461; 6:763;
  12:*1671*
DAM-ATOLL ocean energy conversion system 4:549
dammar 13:*1741, 1742–3*
damping, pendulums 12:1605
dams 5:604–8
  and beach erosion 6:819
  circular 17:2438
  coffer 5:608
  earth-fill 5:605–6
  and flooding 7:888–9, 891; 9:1191
  homogenous 5:605
  hydropower 5:605; 8:1112
  and irrigation 9:1191, 1192
  multiple-arch 5:607
  rock-fill 5:606
  solid-masonry arch 5:607
  solid-masonry gravity 5:606–7
  spillways in 7:888–9
  steel and timber 5:608
  see also barrages, tidal
daphnia 12:*1716*
dark matter 4:575–6; 8:*1021*
DART (Deep Ocean Assessment and
  Reporting of Tsunamis) 18:2511
Darwin, Charles 6:822, 823, *825*;
  12:1633
databases 8:1148–50
  security, for riot prevention
  14:1971
Data Encryption Standard (DES)
  5:594; 6:762
data gloves 11:1503; 19:2603–6
data rate 5:612
data storage 5:609–15
  on digital cameras 3:370–2
  floppy disks 5:609, 612
  hard disk drives 5:609, 610–12;
    9:1167
  magneto-optical discs 5:*613,*
    614–15
  memory cards (PC cards) 5:615
  microfilm 10:**1415**
  optical systems
    CD-ROMs *see* compact discs
    DVDs *see* digital versatile discs
    WORM drives 5:614
  tape drives 5:612–13
    digital audio tapes (DATs) 1:129;
      2:189; 5:612, *615*
  using scanning tunneling micro-
    scopes (STMs) 4:552
  Zip drives and disks 4:527; 5:612
dating, archaeological 2:157–8
DATs *see* digital audio tapes

Davis guns 11:1486
Davy, Sir Humphry 1:100; 4:449;
  8:1034
day-color-light signals 14:1924
days 5:696, 697; 17:2441
dB-A scale 11:1531
DDT 1:61; 12:1676, 1678
"dead man's handle" 14:1926
dead reckoning (DR) 11:1511
deaeration 3:381
deafness, aids for 1:22
  bionic ears 2:257
  cochlear implants 8:1044; 12:1612
  hearing aids 8:1043–4
  spectacles to aid deaf people
    9:1243
death
  definition of 9:1232
  time of 7:919–20; 12:1658–9
DECCA (navigation system)
  7:872–3; 11:1511–12
decibels (dB) 4:513–14; 8:1072
decoders, satellite-TV 1:*141*
decompression chambers 2:155
decompression sickness *see* bends, the
decongestants 12:1682
Deep Sea Drilling Project 11:1568;
  13:1777
Deep Space 1 (space probe) 14:*1994,*
  1995; 15:2123
Deep Space Network 15:2156–7
deep submergence rescue vessels
  (DSRVs) 16:2293
defibrillators 1:113; 6:757; 8:1047
deflashing 5:591
defoliating agents 4:438
deforestation 6:809; 7:921–2, 985,
  986; 15:2112, *2113*
degradation, chemical, of toxic
  agents 4:440
De Havilland Comet 1:83–4
dehydration, osmotic 12:1610
Delta Project 7:*890*, 891; 9:1206
demagnetization, adiabatic 17:2396
dementia, senile 14:1919
Demikar, Vladimir 18:2500
demodulation 11:1473
dendrimers 13:1812
dendrites 3:300
dendrochronology 4:478
denim 17:2407
densitometers 16:2195
  reflection 4:*512*
density 5:616–17; 10.1359
  relative (specific gravity) 5:616–17
dentine 18:2466
dentistry 5:618–22; 13:*1782*
  amalgams 5:619; 10:1371; 15:2080
  drills 2:233; 5:621–2
  holographic dental records 8:1083
  sealants 1:32
  see also teeth; toothpaste
depletion layer (p-n junction) 5:654;
  6:752; 15:2053, 2116–17;
  18:2481
depolarizers 2:226
depth of field 3:363; 9:1227
dermabrasion 13:1767
dermatitis (eczema) 15:2089
dermis 15:2087, *2088*
derricks
  crane *see* cranes, jib
  oil rig 5:680
desalination (desalting) 5:623–5, 662
  reverse osmosis for 5:625;
    12:1610; 19:*2666*
  using solar energy 5:624; 15:2116
descaling 2:223
Descartes, René 14:1933
deserts
  formation 9:*1207*
  reclamation 9:1207

Desert Storm, Operation 11:1468;
  16:*2250*
design *see* computer-aided design;
  ergonomics
desktop publishing (DTP) 5:626–30;
  19:*2720*
destroyers, guided-missile (GMDs)
  19:2627–9, *2631*
detectors *see* particle detectors
detergents
  manufacture 5:631–2
  in toothpaste 18:2466
  zeolites and 19:2730
deuterium 7:947; 8:1118; 19:2655
  in hydrogen bombs 11:1553
deuterium hydrogen oxide 19:2655
deuterium oxide (heavy water)
  11:1553; 19:2655–6
  in nuclear reactors 11:1545
deuterons 7:946
dew, for irrigation 9:1193–4; 18:2570
Dewar flasks (thermos bottles)
  17:2425
Dewey Decimal Classification 8:1149
dew point 8:1123; 10:1401; 19:2665
dextrin 3:390; 6:842
dhows 2:276
diabetes 3:414; 6:782; 8:1085–6;
  10:1375
  blood tests 12:1657
  and exercise 16:2225
  immune system and 8:1136
  insulin injections 18:*2557*
  recent developments in research
    13:1733–4
  and sight 12:*1590*
diaglycerol 2:252
dialysis machines 5:633–6; 12:1609;
  18:2549–50
dialyzers 5:634–5
diamagnetism 18:2486
1,4-diaminobenzene (*p*-phenylene-
  diamine) 12:1710
1,6-diaminohexane 13:1806
diamond-anvil cells 12:1680;
  15:2049
diamonds 5:*637*, 637–40, 640;
  10:1360; 12:1679
  covalent crystals 3:*393*; 4:443;
    5:597
  cutting and polishing 5:*637*, 640;
    16:*2270, 2271, 2272*
  diamond coatings 13:1763
  as gemstones 5:*637, 638*
  identity patterns 9:1243
  mining 5:637–8
  properties 3:*391*, 392; 5:639
    melting point 3:393
  screening 5:638
  synthetic (industrial) 1:18; 3:392;
    5:599, 637, 639; 17:2346
  uses in industry 5:*638*, 639, 680
diaphragm, camera 3:*364*
diastase 6:842
diastole 8:1045
diathermy, surgical 6:758; 17:2329
diatoms, in the blood 7:919
diazepam (Valium) 12:1682; 13:1791
dicalcium orthophosphate 12:1699
dicalcium phosphate 12:1699
1,1-dichloroethene 7:880
dichloromethane 8:1106
dichroism 13:1794–5
dichromate-gelatin (DCG) systems
  8:1082
didgeridoos (didjeridus) 19:2715
dieldrin 12:1676
dielectric constants 3:386
dielectrics 3:386; 9:1162, *1163*
  dielectric heating 11:1447–8
dies, for sheet metal 15:2064, 2065,
  2066

Diesel, Rudolf 7:937; 9:1174
diesel engines 7:937–8, 939; 9:1171, 1174–5
 common-rail fuel injection systems 9:*1176*
 soundproofing 15:*2141*
 in submarines 10:1336–7; 16:2290, 2291
 in trucks 18:2506
 turbocharged 9:1174
die sinking 15:2066
diet *see* nutrition and food science
diethylamine 4:456
diethyl ether *see* ethoxyethane
"diet pills" 12:1682
diets
 and health 7:996; 8:1047
 low-fat 6:837
Difference Engine 2:*171*; 4:523
differentials 18:2491–2
diffraction 5:641; 9:1238; 19:2672–3
 sound waves 15:*2133*, 2134
 X-ray 2:261, 262; 4:462, 551; 5:598–9, 641; 12:1689; 19:2724
diffraction gratings 5:641
diffusion 5:633
digestive system 5:642–5
diggers 5:703
Digistar digital projectors 13:1756
digital audio broadcasting (DAB) 14:1904
digital audio tape (DAT) players, amplifiers 1:126
digital audio tapes (DATs) 1:129; 2:189; 5:612, *615*
digital displays 1:127; 5:646–8
digital linear tape (DLT) 10:1312
digital mapping 10:1330–1
digital scene-matching area correlator (DSMAC) 11:1468
digital subscriber lines (DSLs) 4:540; 17:2358
 asymmetric (ADSLs) 11:1476, 1517; 17:2358
digital systems *see* analog and digital systems
digital-to-analog converters (DACs) 1:127
digital versatile discs (DVDs) 1:129; 3:354; 5:614, 649–52; 8:1148; 11:1500
 multimedia 11:1502
 recording on 5:652
digital video discs *see* digital versatile discs
digital video (DV) 19:2602
digitizers *see* graphics tablets
digits, replacement 10:1439
dihexylamine nitrate 4:571
dilatency 19:2609–10
dimethylbenzene *see* xylene
2,3-dimethylbuta-1,3-diene, polymerization 14:1999
2,2-dimethylbutane 4:*454*
dimethylether (DME) fuel 3:343
dinghies
 capsized 15:2050
 inflatable, inshore-rescue 15:2041
dinosaurs 6:825; 12:1635
 extinction 7:989; 10:1395; 11:1568
 fossils 12:*1631, 1634*, 1635
diodes 5:653–4; 14:1937
 avalanche 19:2621
 light-emitting (LEDs) 15:2054
  in calculators 3:361; 5:*654*
  in cameras 3:367
  and fiber optics 3:355
  in matrix displays 5:*646*, 647
  in optoisolators 6:757
  in planar displays 5:648
  in watches 19:2650
 semiconductor 5:653–4; 6:752;

15:2053–4; 18:2481–2
 vacuum-tube (valves) 5:653; 6:750–1; 18:2480, 2563–4
 zener 19:2619–21
 see also discharge tubes; thyristors
dioxins 4:438
 decomposition of 5:720
 elimination from soil 7:901
dipoles (antennas) 1:142
 half-wave 6:740
dipoles (electrical) 4:*554*; 9:1163
 induced 9:1163
Dirac, Paul 2:150; 6:768–9; 14:1883, 1884
dirigibles *see* airships
dirt-car racing 14:1891
disabled, the, aids for *see* accessibility aids; mobility aids
disaccharides 3:389
discarding sabot principle 2:216
discharge tubes 5:655–8; 9:1184
 in greenhouses 8:1088–9
 krypton 11:1529
 mercury vapor 5:658; 14:1980; 18:2533
 neon 4:555; 5:*656*, 657; 17:2392
 sodium, street lights 1:101; 5:658; 14:1980
 xenon 8:1077–8; 11:1529; 16:2285
Discovery (space shuttle) 9:*1201*; 15:*2024*
discrete multitone (DMT) 17:2358
diseases
 bacteria and 10:1410–11
 from animals (zoonoses) 18:2586–7
 inherited 12:1660–1
 notifiable 6:811
 skin 15:2089
 study of *see* epidemiology; pathology
dishwashers 5:659–60
 see also washing machines
Disney, Walt 1:136
displacement 8:1144
distance-measuring equipment (DME) 1:67
distance(s)
 measuring 1:67; 17:2333–4, *2337*
 and the velocity of light 14:1950–1
distillation and sublimation 5:661–4
 distillation 4:445; 5:661
  alcohol 1:*97, 98*; 5:661; 16:2215–18
  at reduced pressure (vacuum distillation) 5:*661*, 663; 18:2560
  azeotropic 5:663
  continuous 16:2215
  destructive 5:664
  fractional 5:662–3; 11:1576
  molecular 5:664
  of petroleum (crude oil) 5:661; 11:1576, 1577–9
  steam 5:663
  of water 5:623–5; 15:2116
 sublimation 5:664; 18:2570
  dye 6:834
distortion, sound, types of 8:1073–4
distress signals 7:870
distributed processing 4:538
distributors, automobile 2:202–3; 8:1124–5
ditches 5:674, 675
dithering 4:533–4
diuretics 12:1682
diving, undersea
 dangers 2:155; 11:1528
 gases for respiration 5:667; 11:1528; 12:1620
 see also aqualungs; diving suits
diving suits 5:665–7; 13:1862
 atmospheric (ADSs) 5:666–7

 see also aqualungs
dizziness 8:1043
DNA (deoxyribonucleic acid) 1:114; 3:412; 6:823; 7:973, 979; 9:*1233*
 analysis in archaeology 2:*158*
 automated synthesizers 11:*1478*
 fingerprinting (genetic fingerprinting) 7:920, 978; 16:2249; 19:2736
 and genetic engineering 7:977–8
 lambda 7:977
 microarrays 11:1480
 probes 12:1657
 and protein synthesis 7:974–5; 11:1477–8; 12:1657
 recombinant 7:977; 18:2556
 redundant and "junk" 11:1478
 repair, using nanorobots 14:*1989*
 replication 7:975
 sequencing 7:975–6; 11:*1480*
 structure 2:261; 7:973–4; 11:1477
 to test for genes ("DNA probes") 2:265
 see also chromosomes; genes
DNA polymerase 7:*974*, 978; 11:1478
Docklands Light Railway 10:1348; 14:1925; 16:2278
docks 5:668–71
 bulk handling methods 7:929–31
 cranes 5:588, *668*, 669; 7:931, *932*
 grain 6:776; 7:928, 930
 container 5:669–70
 dry 5:671
 firefighting at 6:861
 floating 5:*668*, 671
 locks at entrances to 5:668, 669; 9:1266
 pipelines 7:929
docosahexaenoic acid (DHA) 11:1559
documents, forged 5:584
dodecyl benzene 8:1107
dogs
 microchipped 18:2588
 veterinary medicine and 18:2583–5, 2588
Dolby systems 15:2147–8
 Dolby Digital 5:652; 15:2148
Dolly the sheep 2:264
dolmen 16:2273
dolomite, uses 7:901
dolphins 19:2733
domain names 9:1180
domains (magnets) 10:1316
 on hard disks 5:610
domain theory, of ferromagnetism 10:1315
domes, geodesic 1:*108*; 3:*336*; 7:983–4; 16:2245; 17:*2400*
L-dopa 12:1684
dopamine 12:1684
dopants 4:552; 6:752; 15:2116; 18:2481, 2482
doping 9:1164, 1166; 10:*1427*; 15:2053
Doppler effect (Doppler shift) 5:672
 acoustic 5:672; 14:1897; 15:2134
 and astrophysics 2:178
 and blood flow 2:280; 10:1438
 and burglar alarms 3:340, *341*; 5:672
 and lasers 9:1214
 and radar
  search and surveillance 14:1896, 1897
  for space navigation 11:1514
  to monitor the weather 10:1397, 1398; 14:1898
  and traffic monitoring 14:1985
 and radio astronomy 14:1909

 and sonar 18:2531
 and tornado detection 8:1097–8
dosimeters 11:1531
double basses 16:2280
Douglas DC aircraft
 DC-1, DC-2, and DC-3 1:82
 DC-7 2:213
 DC-8 1:84
Down's syndrome, testing for 11:1564
doxorubicin 12:1687
dozers, tracks 18:*2469*, 2471
drag
 aircraft 1:38–9, 66
 coefficient of 8:1111
 ships' 8:1111
draglines 5:703
drag racing *see* racing cars and dragsters
drainage 5:673–5
Dralon 6:853
DRAM (dynamic random-access memory) 6:*753*; 9:1167
drawframes 16:2213
drawing (metalworking) 3:316; 10:1390–1
 sheet metal 15:*2064*
 tube 13:1751–2
dreaming 15:2100–1
dredgers (dredges) 5:676–7
drift chambers 12:1654
Drift Tube Linear Accelerator 12:*1726*
drill (fabric) 17:2407
drilling, directional 3:346
drilling rigs
 oil 4:*548*; 5:680–3; 11:*1570*
 see also oil exploration and production
drill presses 10:1310; 19:2718
drills 5:678–9
 bow 18:2460
 dental 2:233; 5:621–2
 hand 18:2465
 pneumatic 13:*1788, 1789*
 twist 18:2465
 use in mining 11:*1458*, 1459
 use in tunneling 18:2513
 see also drill presses
drinks
 bottling 3:385
 carbonation 3:385
 dispensing machines 15:2109; 18:2575–6
drives, computer 4:527, 528; 5:610–15
drizzle 19:2665
drogues 5:711; 12:1641, *1642*, 1643
drones, target 13:1747–8
drop hammers 13:1746
Drosophila 6:778
drossing 9:1219–20
drought 13:*1819*
drug and alcohol testing 5:684–6
 alcohol 5:684, 685–6
 drugs 5:684, *685*; 16:2226
drugs, illegal, and forensic science 7:917–18
drugs, medical *see* pharmaceuticals; pharmacology
drums 12:1668–70
 drum machines 12:1670; 17:2344–5
 synthesizers 17:2344
dry cells 2:226–7
dry cleaning 5:687–9
dry ice 18:2570
drying
 food 7:905–6, 910–11
 supercritical 2:159–60
dry-pressing 3:427
dry spinning 6:852

DSLs *see* digital subscriber lines
DSM (*Diagnostic and Statistical Manual of Mental Disorders*) **13**:1867
DTaP vaccine **18**:2556
DTS (Digital Theater Systems) process **15**:2148
dubbing **11**:1500
dubnium **6**:765
ducted installations, of power cables **3**:346
DUKW vehicles **1**:*121*, 122–3
dulcin **8**:1108
dummies, crash-test **2**:208
Dunlop, John Boyd **17**:2338; **18**:2453
duodenum **5**:643
Duralumin **1**:106, 109
duramen **9**:1294
Dusenbergs (racing cars) **14**:1892
dust storms **6**:819
DVDs *see* digital versatile discs
dwarfism **6**:781; **8**:1086
DX coding **3**:369
dyes **4**:*498*
    aniline and azo **1**:133–5; **5**:690–1
    disperse **5**:691–2; **6**:852
    dyeing process **5**:690–3
        Griess process **1**:135; **5**:691
        for plastics **13**:*1775*
    fading in sunlight **4**:464
    fastness **5**:693
    and medicine **1**:135
    natural **5**:690
    reactive **5**:691
    structures **1**:134
    sulfur **5**:691
    synthetic **5**:690–1
    triarylmethane **1**:134–5
    uses
        carpets **7**:894
        fabric printing **6**:834
        hosiery and knitwear **8**:1093
        as laser media **9**:1213
        optical filters **6**:858
        synthetic fibers **5**:692; **6**:852
        textiles **17**:2408
    vat **5**:691
Dynabooks **11**:1501
dynamical variables **5**:694–5
dynamics **5**:694–5
dynamite **6**:827
    manufacture **6**:828
dynamometers **10**:1403
    Regnier's **13**:*1825*
dynamos **7**:972; **13**:1827; **19**:2618–19
    cooling **8**:1119
dynodes **8**:1129; **12**:*1717*, 1718
Dyson, James **18**:2561–2
dysprosium **18**:2486

E

E3 (energy-efficient engine) **3**:427
ear, nose, and throat (ENT) *see* otolaryngology
ears **8**:1041–3; **15**:2131, 2132
    bionic **2**:*257*
Earth **5**:696–700; **13**:1757
    age **5**:698; **6**:824; **13**:1757–8
    climatic divisions **14**:1932
    development of life on **1**:62–3; **5**:700; **6**:823; **9**:1234–5; **10**:1412; **12**:1633–4
    "free oscillations" **5**:708
    interior tides (Earth tides) **17**:2440
    layers, detection **15**:2048
    light pollution **13**:*1803*
    orbit **15**:2114
    origin **5**:698; **6**:764
    precession **5**:696
    radiation belts **14**:1899–90

    rotation **8**:1143
        gyrocompasses and **8**:1028–9
        pendulums and **12**:1665
    source of water on **13**:1761
    structure **5**:697; **15**:2048
        core **5**:697; **15**:2048, 2049
        tilt **5**:696
    see also atmosphere; geology; plate tectonics
earthenware **3**:425; **4**:465
earthmoving machinery **5**:701–5; **14**:1974
earthquakes **5**:706–8; **7**:*993*; **15**:2049
    and dams **5**:608
    detection using fiber optics **6**:856
    plate tectonics and **5**:*706*, 707; **13**:*1777*, *1780*
    scales of intensity
        Mercalli scale **15**:2049
        Richter scale **9**:1276; **15**:2049
    and the soil **15**:2113
    and tsunamis **18**:2509, 2510
    see also seismology
Earth Summit (1992) **6**:807–8
eating disorders, bulimia nervosa **12**:1658
Ebola virus **4**:440–1
Echelon **6**:762
echo sounders, ships' **7**:871–2, 875; **11**:1512; **15**:2126–7
    and geology **7**:990
eclipses **5**:709–10
ECM (electrochemical machining) **6**:735–6; **10**:1310
E. coli see *Escherichia coli*
*Eco*RI (restriction enzyme) **11**:1478
ectoderm **6**:777
ectoparasites **12**:1644
cczcma (dermatitis) **15**:2089
eddy currents **8**:1140, 1141
Eddystone light **9**:1248
Eden Project **7**:984; **13**:*1768*
Edison, Thomas **2**:228; **6**:730
    and the incandescent lamp **3**:394; **9**:1244
    and movie film **11**:1494
    and sound recording **2**:186; **4**:513; **12**:1694
    and the telegraph **3**:353
editing, television productions **17**:2390–1; **18**:2495
EEGs (electroencephalograms) **3**:312; **6**:756, *758*
    and sleep **15**:2099–2100
EEPROMs (electrically erasable-programmable read-only memories) **9**:1167
EFTPOS (electronic funds transfer at point of sale) **3**:401
Egyptians, ancient
    dams **9**:1191, 1206
    dentistry **5**:618
    dyes **5**:693
    glass **7**:999, 1002
    knitting **8**:1090
    locks (security) **9**:1267
    numbers **10**:*1358*
    quarrying **14**:1885
    raising water **9**:1192
    ships **15**:2067
    surgery **17**:2327
    tools **18**:2460
Ehrlich, Paul **1**:135
eicosapentanoic acid (EPA) **11**:1559
Einstein, Albert
    and the atomic bomb **11**:1554
    and Brownian motion **9**:1203
    general theory of relativity (theory of gravity) **2**:269; **4**:*572*, 574–5; **8**:1021, 1143; **11**:1521
    and light **9**:1237, 1241
        stimulated emissions of photons

        9:1210; **12**:1704
    mass–energy equation **2**:150, 179, 248; **7**:876; **14**:1953; **17**:2415
    and space–time **2**:269; **14**:1954
    special theory of relativity **2**:150, 179, 180; **6**:788–9; **7**:876; **14**:1950–5; **17**:2442–3
einsteinium **6**:765
Einstein rings **14**:*1954*
ejection seats **5**:711–12; **8**:1038
ejectors, air **4**:522
EKGs *see* electrocardiographs
elasticity **5**:713–14; **10**:1361
    elastic collisions **9**:1202–3
    and springs **16**:2229
elastic limit **5**:713; **16**:2229
elastic modulus *see* Young's modulus
Elastic Rebound Theory **5**:707
elastic region **5**:713
elastomeric fibers **6**:853
elastomers **15**:2078
elbows, prosthetic **2**:255
electrets **5**:715–16; **17**:2369
    transducers **5**:*715*, 716; **18**:2475–6
electrical circuits
    bistable **4**:487
    capacitors in **3**:386–7
    resonance **12**:1606; **14**:1966
    see also fuses and circuit breakers; resistors; switches
electrical engineering **5**:717–20
electricity **6**:725–30
    circuits *see* electrical circuits
    conductors *see* conduction, electrical
    current **6**:725–6, 727
        alternating (AC) **6**:729; **14**:1937
        direct (DC) **14**:1937
        and electrochemical cells **6**:727
        and power loss **6**:729
        see also electrochemistry
    early experiments **6**:725
    and the electron **6**:726, 727
    and electrostatic charge **6**:727
    and the environment **5**:720
    for executions **6**:730
    from fish **6**:730
    generation *see* energy resources, renewable; power plants
    insulators *see* insulators, electric
    light converted into *see* photo-electric cells and photometry
    meters **10**:1404–5; **19**:*2704*, 2705
    and power **6**:728–9
        measurement **10**:1403
    resistance *see* resistance, electrical
    static **6**:725
    storage
        in superconducting rings **17**:2314
        see also capacitors
    supply *see* power supply
    triboelectricity **6**:725, 727, *728*
    see also batteries; electromagnet-ism; induction; semiconductors; superconductivity; transformers
electric motors **6**:731–4; **10**:1318
    commutator
        AC- **6**:734
        DC- **6**:732, 733–4
    commutatorless in **5**:717
    controls **6**:731
    in electric drills **5**:678
    hysteresis **6**:734
    induction **6**:*731*, 732–3; **9**:1252
    linear **6**:732; **9**:1252–6
    magnetic and electromagnetic **6**:731–2
    outboard **10**:1337; **12**:1614–15
    reluctance **5**:717, *718*; **6**:734
        magnetic micromotors **5**:718
    repulsion **6**:731

    reversible **6**:731
    for small marine craft **10**:1337
    squirrel-cage **6**:*731*, 733
    stepping **6**:734
    in submarines **10**:1336–7
    synchronous **6**:733
    three-phase **6**:*734*
    universal **6**:734
    see also starter motors
electric shavers **14**:1936
electric shock devices (weapons) **11**:1534
electrocardiographs (EKGs) **6**:756–7; **8**:*1046*; **12**:1666
electrochemical cells **6**:727
electrochemical deposition **10**:1418
electrochemical machining (ECM) **6**:735–6; **10**:1310
electrochemical series (electromotive series) **17**:2324
electrochemistry **4**:464; **6**:727
    see also electrolysis
electroconvulsive therapy (ECT) **13**:1868
electrodialysis **5**:623, 625
electrodischarge machining (EDM; spark erosion; spark machining) **6**:735, 736; **10**:1364, *1366*
electroluminescence **10**:1302
electrolysis **6**:737–8; **9**:1184
    Castner-Kellner cells **6**:738
    Faraday's laws **6**:737–8
    of sodium chloride **1**:25; **4**:450, *452*; **6**:737; **8**:1118; **9**:1184
    uses
        aniodic stripping/cathodic polishing **2**:160
        in electrochemical machining **6**:735, 736
        electrolytic capacitors **3**:387
        in gold refining **8**:1015
        for marine salvage **15**:2022–3
        metal plating *see* electroplating
        to conserve metals **2**:160
        to extract alkali metals **1**:99
        to extract aluminum **1**:110–11; **6**:738
        to extract metals **6**:738; **10**:1378
        to extract zinc **19**:2731
electrolytes, in batteries **2**:225–6
electromagnetic force compensation **2**:214
electromagnetic interference (EMI) **6**:745–6
electromagnetic pulse (EMP) energy **6**:746
electromagnetic radiation **6**:739–46, 749; **9**:1237–8; **12**:1728
    blackbody radiation **6**:740
    from space **2**:173–7
    speed **6**:739, 749
    see also different components of the electromagnetic spectrum
electromagnetism **6**:726, 747–9; **12**:1727–8
    and generators **7**:971, 972
    Maxwell's equations **6**:748
    mediated by elementary particles **6**:770–1
    superconducting electromagnets **5**:718, 719–20; **9**:1256; **17**:2310, 2314
    use
        in bone regeneration **2**:256
        in clutches **4**:492
        in electric bells **2**:239
        in electric motors **6**:731, 732, 733
        in flowmeters **7**:896–7
        in loudspeakers **9**:1284, *1285*
        in magnetohydrodynamics (MHD) **10**:1318–19

electromagnetism, use (*cont.*)
  in seismographs 15:2047
  in solenoids 15:2124–5
  see also maglev (magnetic-
    levitation) vehicles
  see also induction
electromotive force (emf) 6:748;
  10:1313
  and magnetohydrodynamics
    10:1318
  see also voltage
electron avalanche 7:970
electron guns 3:408
electronic countercountermeasures
  (ECCMs) 16:2254–5
electronic countermeasures (ECMs)
  16:2250–3
electronic distance measurement
  (EDM) 17:2334, 2336
electronic news gathering (ENG)
  17:2389; 18:2592
electronics 6:750–5
  automobile *see* automobiles, elec-
    tronics systems
  aviation *see* avionics
  circuits 6:750
  components *see* capacitors; diodes;
    thyristors; transistors; triodes
  computer 6:754–5
    see also integrated circuits
  and farm machinery 1:50–1
  in medicine 6:756–8
  miniaturization 6:754–5
  optoelectronics 6:755
  see also transducers and sensors
electronic surveillance 6:759–62
electron microprobes 12:1680
electrons
  in batteries 2:225
  beams, and electron microscopes
    10:1430
  behaving as waves 2:183–5, 184;
    6:767–8; 14:1882
  Cooper pairs 17:2312
  discovery 2:182; 3:408; 6:726, 763,
    767
  and electricity 6:726
  and electromagnetic radiation
    6:739
  as leptons 6:769, 770
  quantum number 6:767–8
  spin 6:768; 10:1315–16; 14:1882
  subatomic *see* atomic structure
  transfer, in oxidation and reduction
    12:1616
electron volts 12:1648
electrophoresis 2:251; 7:973, 976
  gel 11:1480
electrophotography 12:1701
electroplating 6:738; 17:2323–4
  with chromium 4:473
  with nickel 4:473; 11:1523
  preparation before 1:17
  and waste disposal 19:2641
electropolishing 17:2325
electropults 9:1254
electrorheological fluids 10:1353
electroscopes 6:725
electroslag refining (ESR) 9:1190
electrostatic charge 6:727; 12:1727
  and electrets 6:715
  and electrostatic loudspeakers
    9:1284, 1285
  and microwave ovens 11:1449
electrostatic focusing 8:1129–30
electrostatic generators 12:1648
electrostatic precipitators 13:1800
electrostatic spraying 13:1824;
    16:2228
electrostriction 18:2530
electroweak theory 6:771, 773
electrum 4:507

elementary particles 6:767–73;
    10:1362
  accelerated *see* particle accelerators
  antiparticles *see* antimatter,
    antiparticles
  baryons 6:770, 772
  electrons
    quantum number 6:767–8
    spin 6:768; 10:1315–16; 14:1882
  fermions 6:770; 14:1882
  and forces 6:767, 770–3
  gauge 6:770–3
  hadrons 6:770, 773
  leaked by black holes 2:270
  leptons 6:769–70
  mesons 6:770, 772
  motion observed *see* bubble and
    cloud chambers
  spin (intrinsic angular momentum)
    6:768
  and unified field theories 6:773
  see also bosons; cosmic rays; neu-
    trons; photons; protons; quarks
elements, chemical 6:763–6
  abundance 10:1377
  atomic number 14:1905–6
  classifications 6:764
  elements 110 to 112, synthesis
    6:766
  elements beyond 112 6:766
  mass number 14:1906
  origins of 6:763, 764
  synthetic 6:764–6
  theories and discoveries of 4:449;
    6:763
  transition *see* transition elements
  see also isotopes; periodic table
elephants 19:2733, 2734, 2735
elevators (aerodynamic surface), controlling flight 1:66, 71, 91
elevators (vertical transport)
    6:774–5; 15:2095
  freefalling, and weight 6:789
  grain 6:776; 7:930
  paternoster 6:775
elevons 1:71
ELISA (enzyme-linked immunosorbent assay) 6:811; 18:2584
El Niño 4:478–9; 15:2029
Eloner's reaction 8:1015
ELVES 17:2431
e-mail 4:537; 9:1179; 10:1325;
    17:2363
  addresses 9:1180
  attachments 9:1182
  interception systems 6:762
  newsletters via 11:1519
  and viruses 4:531
  see also mail sorting machinery
embankments, and road construction
    14:1974
embolisms, pulmonary 14:1918
embryology 6:777–8
embryos 6:777
  gene testing in 7:980
emeralds 4:472, 17:2346
emery 1:18, 109
emphysema, drugs for 2:264, 266
Empire State Building 3:337;
    15:2092, 2094
  elevators 15:2095
  lights at the top of 9:1243
enamels
  stoving 12:1629–30
  vitreous (porcelain enamel)
    6:779–80
enantiomers 4:457, 458, 12:1689
encapsulation technology, microencapsulation 10:1412–13
encephalins 3:311
Encephalitis lethargica (sleepy sickness)
    12:1684

encephalograms 3:312
encoding, electronic 5:596
Endeavour (space shuttle) 14:1955;
    16:2165, 2168, 2169; 17:2359
endocrinology 6:781–2
endoderm 6:777
endometrium, removal 11:1563–4
endoparasites 12:1644
endoplasmic reticulum 3:411
endoprostheses 2:255–6
endorphins 3:311
endoscopes 6:783–5, 856;
    17:2330–1, 2332; 18:2550
  in veterinary medicine 18:2584
energy breakeven 13:1763
energy, mass, and weight 6:786–9
  Einstein's mass–energy equation
    2:150, 179, 248; 6:789; 14:1953;
    17:2415
  energy 6:786–8; 12:1726
    binding 2:248; 7:876; 14:1961
    chemical 6:787
    conservation of 6:786;
      12:1726–7; 17:2414–15
    efficiency 6:788
    electrical 6:788
    electromagnetic 6:788
    heat 6:786, 787
    kinetic 5:695; 6:786, 787;
      10:1342; 12:1725; 13:1820;
      17:2415, 2416
    for living organisms 10:1373
    mechanical 6:786
    potential *see* potential energy
    sound 6:787
    units of 6:790
    see also entropy
  mass 5:695; 6:788, 789
  weight 6:789
energy resources 6:790–7
  fossil fuels 2:258; 3:391; 6:790, 791
  hydrogen 6:795–6
  nuclear energy 6:796; 11:1542–3
  renewable 6:790, 791–7
    from the temperature gradient
      in the sea 6:793, 795; 8:1054
    geothermal 6:790, 793
    nuclear energy 6:796; 11:1542–3
    see also biofuels; hydroelectric
      power; solar energy; tidal power;
      wave power; wind power
energy storage 6:798–800
  compressed-air and -gas systems
    6:798–9
  geothermal energy 6:800
  pumped storage 6:798; 8:1112,
    1115; 13:1827; 18:2520
  thermal storage 6:800
  see also batteries; capacitors
engines
  aircraft *see* aircraft engines
  automobile *see* automobiles, engine
  cooling systems 6:801–2; 8:1055
  internal combustion *see* internal
    combustion engines
  jet
    E3 (energy-efficient engine)
      3:427
    see also aircraft engines, jet
  tank 2:167
engraving and etching 6:803–5
ENIAC computers 4:524
Enigma machine 5:593, 595–6
ENT (ear, nose, and throat) *see*
  otolaryngology
Enterococcus faecium 10:1411
enterogastrone 5:643
enterokinase 5:643
Enterprise (space shuttle) 16:2166–7
enthalpy 18:2517
  stagnation 18:2517
entomology, forensic 7:919–20

entropy 4:463; 6:788; 9:1233;
    12:1727; 16:2249; 17:2415,
    2416
environmental science 6:806–9
  ozone depletion 4:480; 5:687;
    6:806–7; 13:1798; 14:1947
  see also geography; global warming;
    pollution
enzyme-linked immunosorbent assay
  (ELISA) 6:811; 18:2584
enzymes 1:114; 6:810
  are catalysts 3:406, 407; 6:810;
    13:1865
  denatured 6:810
  in detergents 5:632
  digestive 5:642–3
  and food spoilage 7:905
  from transgenic animals 2:264, 266
  and ligands 2:252
  pacemaker 10:1376
  restriction 7:975, 976; 11:1478
  structure 2:251, 252
  used in brewing 1:98; 3:406
  in yeast 6:841–2
epicenters, earthquake 5:706, 707
epidemics 6:811; 13:1816
epidemiology 6:811–12
epidermis 15:2087, 2088
epiglottis 10:1303
epinephrine (adrenaline) 6:781;
    8:1085, 1108
  receptors 8:1087
epitaxy 17:2347
EPR paradox 14:1884
equalizers 8:1073; 15:2138
equilibrant force 16:2242
equilibrium, stable and unstable
    16:2243–4
erbium 18:2486
erbium-doped fiber amplifiers
  (EDFAs) 6:856
ergonomics 6:813–15
  see also computer-aided design
Erlich, Paul 10:1368
Eros (asteroid) 15:2123
erosion 6:816–19
  tectonic 13:1778
erythropoietin (EPO) 2:273; 18:2549
  abuse, detecting 5:684; 16:2226
escalators and moving walkways
    6:820–1
escapement, deadbeat 4:484
Escherichia coli (*E. coli*) 10:1409
  and genetic engineering 2:263;
    7:977, 978; 10:1409
    for blood substitutes 13:1733
  infection by viruses 10:1410, 1412;
    11:1480
  and water quality 19:2662
esophagus 5:642
Essen rings 4:487–8
esters 4:457
  as biofuels 2:259
estradiol 8:1086
estriol 8:1086
estrogen(s) 8:1086; 12:1687
  the menopause and 7:997
  in plants 3:305
estrus 14:1959
etching *see* engraving and etching
ETFE (ethyltetrafluoroethylene)
    7:984
ethanal, production 3:407
ethane 1:97, 98; 4:454; 8:1105, 1106
ethanediol *see* ethylene glycol
ethanoate ions 4:457; 14:2015
ethanoic acid (acetic acid) 1:23; 4:457
  manufacture 1:25
ethanol (ethyl alcohol) 1:97, 98;
    4:456
  as an automobile fuel 6:794;
    7:962–3

as a biofuel **2**:259
in gasoline **6**:842
for petroleum-like hydrocarbons **4**:458
production **1**:98; **5**:663; **8**:1107
from biomass **7**:962–3
ethene *see* ethylene
ethene dichloride **8**:1107
ethenyl ethanoate *see* vinyl acetate
ether
anesthesia using **10**:1368; **17**:2327–8
evaporation **5**:592
ether (hypothetical medium) **9**:1236; **14**:1950; **19**:2673
Ethernet **4**:539, 541
ethers, crown **4**:458
ethoxyethane (diethyl ether) **4**:456
ethyl alcohol *see* ethanol
ethylamine **4**:456
ethyl chloride **8**:1106
ethylene (ethene) **4**:454, 456; **8**:1105, 1107
hydration of **1**:98
polymerization **13**:1810; **18**:2488
ethylene bromide **8**:1036
ethylene glycol (ethanediol) **1**:73, 97, *98*; **6**:802; **8**:1107
ethylene oxide **8**:1107
ethyltetrafluoroethylene (ETFE) **7**:984
ethyne (acetylene) **4**:455; **8**:1105, 1107
hydrogenation of **8**:*1107*
oxyacetylene welding **12**:1620
ethynyl radicals **10**:1419
Euclid **11**:1555, 1556
eukaryotes **6**:823; **9**:1235; **10**:1412
Europa (moon) **15**:2120, 2160
European Center for Weather Forecasting **10**:*1400*, 1401
Eurostar trains **9**:*1273*
Eustachian tubes **8**:1042
eutrophication **12**:1700
evaporation **5**:661; **18**:2569
event horizon **2**:267, *269*, 270
Evinrude portable motor **12**:*1615*
evolution **6**:822–5; **12**:*1633*, 1634–5
language **16**:2200
smell and **15**:2106
excavators
hydraulics **5**:704; **8**:*1100*
steam-powered **5**:701
see also earthmoving machine
exchange interaction **18**:2488
executions, use of electricity **6**:730
exercise **7**:997; **16**:2225–6
exoatmospheric kill vehicles (EKVs) **16**:*2179*, 2181, 2184
exobiology (astrobiology) **9**:1235
expectorants **12**:1682
expert systems **2**:170–1
Explorer 1 (satellite) **14**:1899
explosive ordnance disposal (EOD) **3**:293
suits **2**:163; **3**:295
explosives **3**:390; **6**:826–9
in ammunition **1**:116, 117
detonation **6**:826–7
high and low **1**:116; **6**:826–7
in torpedoes **18**:2468
used in mining **11**:1461
used in quarrying **14**:*1885*
see also bombs; mines, explosive; missiles
exponential functions **10**:1356–7
exposure metering **3**:368; **12**:1705
and space photography **15**:2154
Extended Performance Hydrofoil (EPH) **8**:1117
external combustion engines **8**:1053
Stirling engines **16**:2266–9

see also steam engines
extinction **12**:1635
dinosaurs **7**:989; **10**:1395; **11**:1568
extinguishers, fire **6**:862–3
Extravehicular Mobility Units (EMUs) **13**:1862; **16**:2176, *2178*
extreme dynamic range (EDR) **8**:1079
Extreme Ultraviolet Explorer (EUVE) **2**:175
extrusion **3**:427
pipes produced by **13**:1752
thermoplastic **13**:*1773*, 1774
Exxon Valdez oil spill **10**:1411
eyes **6**:830–2
and color vision **4**:510
compound **6**:832
contact lenses **4**:560–3
defects **6**:832
diseases and disorders **12**:1589–90, 1598
in animals **18**:2584
refractive state **12**:1596–8
surgery **12**:*1589*, 1590; **17**:2329
plastic surgery **13**:*1764*
using lasers **9**:1213, 1214; **12**:1590; **17**:*2330*

F

F-4 Phantom (aircraft) **16**:*2250*
F-15B (aircraft) **17**:*2318*
F/A 18 Hornet (aircraft) **11**:1456; **19**:*2631*
fabrics *see* textiles
fabric softeners **5**:632
facsimile transmission (faxes) **10**:1325; **17**:2357, 2363
factories, noise **15**:2141
Factor VIII **7**:978
FADEC (Full Authority Digital Electronic Control) **1**:78, **15**:*2055*
FADH₂ **10**:1373, 1374, 1375
Faint Object Camera (FOC) **2**:176; **15**:2155; **17**:2381
Falklands War
antipersonnel mines **6**:829
bomb disposal after **3**:295
bombs **2**:*284*
grenades **12**:1700
troopships **15**:*2073*
fallopian tubes **6**:777
families, and the aging population **13**:1819
fanjets *see* turbofans
fans **13**:*1745*
in air-conditioning systems **8**:1061
in ventilation systems **8**:1059, *1060*
Faraday, Michael
and electromagnetism **6**:726, *749*; **8**:1139; **10**:1313
laws of electrolysis **6**:737–8
Faraday boxes **17**:2431
Faraday cages **6**:746
Faraday dark space **5**:656
Farenheit temperature scale **17**:*2395*, 2396
farming *see* agriculture
farsightedness *see* hyperopia
Far Ultraviolet Spectroscopic Explorer (FUSE) **2**:*174*, 175–6; **17**:2382
fascicular repair **10**:1437
fasteners, clothes **6**:835
fatigue, driver **18**:2508
fat(s) **4**:457; **6**:836–7; **11**:1557
and detergents **5**:631–2
saturated and unsaturated **6**:836, 837; **11**:1557
storage in the body **6**:836
see also oils
fatty acids **6**:836; **11**:1557

faults, geological **5**:707
radar interferometry **7**:*993*
transform faults **13**:1780
faxes **10**:1325; **17**:2357, 2363
FBI (Federal Bureau of Investigation), Latent Fingerprint Section **7**:916
FDDI (fiber-optic digital device interface) **4**:539
FDRs (Flight Data Recorders) **7**:884–5
feedback **6**:838–9; **9**:1277
in amplifiers **1**:126; **6**:838–9
in oscillators **6**:754
positive and negative **6**:839
in transistors **6**:754
Fehlings solution **16**:2295
feldspar **1**:109
felt **17**:2404
fences, perimeter **15**:2042
Fermat's last theorem **11**:1556
fermentation **1**:98; **6**:840–2; **16**:2215; **19**:2725
acetic **6**:842
for baking **6**:841
for biofuels **2**:258–9
brewing and **2**:234, 236–7; **3**:*406*; **6**:841
for protein production **7**:914; **13**:1866
for winemaking **6**:840–1; **19**:2700, 2701–2, *2703*
Fermilab (Fermi National Accelerator Laboratory) **14**:*1881*
antiproton source **12**:*1649*
collider detector **6**:*769*; **12**:*1651*
Tevatron particle accelerator **12**:1648, *1649*; **13**:1763
fermions **6**:770; **14**:1882
fermium **6**:765
Ferrari T4 racing car **8**:*1124*
ferric chloride **9**:1188
ferric oxide *see* iron (III) oxide
ferries
propulsion **10**:1365
roll-on roll-off **5**:670; **15**:*2069*, 2070
ferrimagnetism **10**:1316
ferrite **1**:104
ferrocene **4**:*459*, 460
ferroelectrics **18**:2530
ferromagnetism **10**:1314, 1315
fertilization, in-vitro ("test tube baby" method) **7**:980; **11**:1564
fertilizers **6**:843–5
ammonium nitrate **4**:*450*; **6**:829, 843, 844
manufacture **6**:843, 844–5
organic **1**:61
manures **6**:843–4
phosphorus **6**:844–5; **12**:*1698*, 1699, 1700
and water pollution **6**:845; **12**:1700
fetuses **6**:777
and fetal stethoscopes **16**:2265
screening **11**:*1563*, 1564; **18**:2531
fever **6**:810
Feynman, Richard **10**:1416, 1417; **14**:1884
fiberboard **19**:2711
fiberglass, for insulation **9**:1160–1
fiber-optic digital device interface (FDDI) **4**:539
fiber optics **6**:854–6
optical fibers **6**:855
and holography **8**:1082
low-attenuation **6**:856
manufacture **6**:855
types **6**:*855*, 856
as waveguides **19**:2671
uses **6**:856

in cable networks **3**:354–5; **4**:539, 542; **6**:856; **17**:2356–7, 2371
in endoscopes **6**:783–4, 856
in image intensifiers **8**:1129–30
in laser surgery **6**:*856*
in submarine (undersea) cables **3**:349; **17**:*2357*
fibers
mineral **6**:846–7
natural **6**:848–50; **17**:2404
see also cotton; silk; wool
nonwoven fabrics **17**:2404
optical *see* fiber optics
synthetic **4**:490; **5**:691–2; **6**:851–3; **17**:2404–5
cellulose-derived **6**:851–2; **13**:1768–9
dyes for **5**:692; **6**:852
flammability **7**:880
geotextiles **17**:2408
see also spinning
Fibonacci series **11**:*1555*
fibrillation, ventricular **8**:1047
fibroblasts **3**:*300*
fibroin **6**:849
fibroplasia, retrolentral **19**:2613
field synchronizing (field sync) signals **17**:2392–3
files (data) **5**:612
files (tools), manufacture **18**:2461–2
fillings, dental **5**:618, 619; **10**:1371
film, photographic *see* photographic films and processing
film formers **12**:1627
films, animated *see* animation
filters
HEPA **7**:954
odor, in air-conditioning units **8**:1061
optical **6**:857–8
absorption **6**:857
dichroic (interference filters; dielectric filters) **6**:857–8; **16**:*2194*
television-camera **17**:2388
fingerprinting **7**:915–16, *917*; **16**:2249
DNA (genetic fingerprinting) **7**:920, 978; **16**:*2249*; **19**:2736
fin-stabilized discarding sabot (FSDS) projectiles **1**:119
fireboats **6**:861
firefighting **6**:859–64
appliances **6**:*859*, 860–1
at airports **1**:89; **6**:*860*, 862
detectors **6**:863–4; **15**:2045
extinguishers and sprinklers **6**:862–3, 864
fire-resistant clothing **6**:*847*
foam generation **6**:862
from aircraft **6**:861; **8**:1067; **15**:*2035*, *2036*
from fireboats **6**:861
hazards **6**:864
and thermal imaging **6**:864
in warehouses **19**:2622–4
fireflies **10**:1301
fires
forest **6**:809, 863; **7**:924–5
fighting **6**:861; **7**:925
movie special effects **16**:2189
oil well **6**:806
pyrotechnic stage effects **16**:*2233*, 2235
see also firefighting
fire setting **11**:1458
fireworks and flares **7**:869–70
firing
bricks **3**:324
china and porcelain **4**:467
glost **4**:468

fish
  depleted stocks 6:809
  evolution 6:824
  food preservation 7:905, 908,
    909–10
  parasitic 12:1645
  puffer fish poison 13:1792
  reproduction 14:1958
  taxidermy 17:2354
fish farming see aquaculture
fishing industry 7:871–5; 15:2039
  clothing 13:1861–2
  fish farming see aquaculture
  freezing fish at sea 14:1947
  purse-seine fishing 7:871
    and suction pumps 4:522
  and sonar 15:2126
  trawling 7:871–2
fission, nuclear 2:248; 6:796;
    7:876–7; 11:1543–6; 12:1727;
    13:1832
  and marine propulsion 10:1336
  and nuclear weapons 11:1551–3
  and rocket propulsion 14:1995–6
  see also nuclear reactors; power
    plants, nuclear
fistulae, arterio-venous (A-V) 5:635
FIV (feline immunodeficiency virus)
    18:2588
Fizeau, A. H. L. 8:1139; 9:1240
FLAG (fiber optic link around the
    globe) 3:355
flailing machines 3:294
flame fusion process 17:2346
flame retarding agents 7:880–1;
    13:1771
flames and ignition 7:878–9; 13:1745
  Bunsen burners 3:339; 7:878
flame throwers 7:882–3
flannel 17:2407
flares see fireworks and flares
flashguns 6:730; 8:1077–8; 15:2075
flashing 5:623–4
flash point 5:687; 7:879; 9:1291
flash tubes, electronic 3:365
Flatiron Building 15:2092, 2094
flax 6:848, 849, 850; 17:2405, 2406,
    2408
Fleming, Alexander 10:1368
Fleming, John Alexander 18:2563
flexible manufacturing systems
    (FMSs) 10:1340–1
flies
  and forensic entomology 7:919
  fruit 6:778
  photomicrograph of 12:1715
flight see aviation
flight plans 1:93–4
flight recorders 1:67; 7:884–5
flight simulators 7:886–7; 11:1501;
    19:2603–4
flintlocks 2:193; 8:1024
floatplanes 15:2035, 2037
float process 7:1000–1
float zoning 15:2076–7
flocculation 19:2656
flood control 7:888–91
flooding
  behind dams 5:608
  chemical, fire, or steam, for oil
    recovery 5:683
  for irrigation 9:1191, 1193
floodlights 17:2386, 2410
floor coverings 7:892–5
  carpets 7:893–5; 9:1280
  cork 7:893
  linoleum 7:892, 894
  rubber 7:893
  vinyl 7:892–3
floppy disks 5:609, 612
flotation process, for lead extraction
    9:1219

flow
  free molecular (Newtonian flow)
    1:38
  hypersonic 1:38
  laminar 1:38–9; 8:1111; 19:2610
  plastic see plastic deformation
  slip 1:38
  supersonic 1:37
  turbulent 1:39; 8:1111; 19:2610
flow cytometry 10:1333
flowmeters 7:896–7; 18:2475, 2581
  for anesthetic gases 1:132
  differential pressure meters 7:896
  electromagnetic 7:896–7
  gas meters 10:1406
  positive displacement (PD) meters
    7:896; 10:1406
  rotary 10:1406
    turbine 7:896, 897; 10:1406
  variable area (rotameters) 7:897
  vortex 7:897
    capacitance 7:897
    full bore 7:896
flow-nozzle meters 7:896
flow wrapping 12:1625
fluid dynamics see aerodynamics;
    hydrodynamics
fluidics (fluid logic) 7:898–9; 9:1277
fluidized beds 7:900–1; 19:2639
  fluidized-bed catalytic crackers
    (FCCs) 11:1578
fluids 10:1359
  in equilibrium see hydrostatics
  Newtonian 19:2609
  pressure in 13:1839–40
    see also Venturi effect
  resistance in see viscosity
  thixotropic 19:2609
  see also superfluids
fluorescein 10:1302
fluorescence 5:658; 9:1241–2;
    10:1301–2; 18:2534
  fluorescent lamps 5:656, 657–8;
    9:1245; 10:1302
  sprays to identify people 11:1532
fluorescent multilayer discs (FMDs)
    5:652
fluoride, and teeth 5:620; 8:1034,
    1036; 18:2466; 19:2666
fluorine 4:442; 8:1034
  production 8:1034
  uses 8:1034
fluorocarbons 19:2660
fluoroscopy 8:1052; 19:2723
  television 19:2723–4
flurane anesthetics 1:131
flush tanks 15:2083
flutes 19:2712–13, 2714, 2715
flux, magnetic 6:748
flux density, magnetic 10:1314–15
fluxes 10:1382
fluxgates 1:66
flux pinning 17:2310–11, 2314
fly-by-wire (FBW) systems 1:44, 66;
    2:213
Flyer I (aircraft) 2:211
flying boats 2:212, 213; 13:1747;
    15:2035, 2036
flying-spot scanners 17:2384
flypresses 7:903
flywheels 7:902–3; 8:1030, 1143
FM see frequency modulation
f numbers see focal ratio
foam
  firefighting 6:862, 863
  plastic 13:1772, 1776
  "sticky" 11:1532
focal length 9:1226
focal ratio (f-ratio; f numbers) 3:363;
    9:1227
fog 10:1401; 18:2570
  monitors on roads 14:1977

fog sprays 11:1532
foil, aluminum 1:109
Foley techniques 15:2136, 2137
folic acid 19:2613
foliot weights 4:482
follicle-stimulating hormone (FSH)
    6:782; 8:1086
fondants 4:557
fonts 5:627
food
  additives 7:914
  carbohydrates 3:388, 389, 390
  energy from 12:1617
  genetically-modified 1:53; 3:303,
    304; 7:978; 12:1676
  organic 1:58, 61
  slimming foods 3:390
  spoilage 7:904–5
  sterilization 5:601; 7:912; 18:2533
  synthetic
    artificial meats 7:913–14
    from single-cell proteins 7:914;
      13:1866
food poisoning 7:904
  Clostridium botulinum 7:905
food preservation and packaging
    7:904–8
  packaging 7:908; 9:1205;
    12:1622–5
  preservation
    blanching 7:905
    canning and bottling 3:381–5;
      7:905, 909
    curing (salting and smoking)
      7:905, 908, 909–10
    dehydration 7:905–6, 907,
      910–11
    food additives 7:907–8
    freezing 7:906, 911
    irradiation 6:745; 7:908, 911
    pasteurization 5:600, 601, 603;
      7:906–7, 911
    pickling 7:906–7, 911
    sterilization 7:912
    sugaring 7:912
food processing 7:909–14
  additives 7:914
    vitamins 7:914
  canning and bottling 3:381–5;
    7:905, 909
  cereal 7:912
  cocoa manufacture 4:499–500
  coffee 4:501–3; 7:910
  cooking 7:909
  curing 7:905, 908, 909–10
  dehydration 7:905–6, 907, 910–11
  fish, on board ships 7:872, 873
  pasteurization 5:600, 601, 603;
    7:906–7, 911
  pickling 7:906–7, 911
  sterilization 7:912
  sugaring 7:912
  synthetic foods 7:913
    artificial meats 7:913–14
    from single-cell proteins 7:914
  see also dairy industry; slaughter-
    houses
food science see nutrition and food
    science
football, clothing 13:1862; 16:2226
footings, spread 15:2091
foot and mouth disease 2:261;
    18:2587
force(s) 11:1520; 13:1825; 16:2242
  equilibrant 16:2242
  fundamental 6:767, 770–3;
    14:1880
    see also electromagnetism; grav-
      ity; strong nuclear force; weak
      nuclear force
  pressure and 13:1839
  restoring 12:1605

Ford, Henry 2:198; 10:1338, 1341
Ford Model T 2:198; 11:1575
  manufacture 10:1341
forensic science 7:915–20; 8:1083;
    16:2197
  forensic ballistics 2:216; 7:916–17
  forensic pathology 7:919–20;
    12:1658–9
  forensic photography 12:1716
  and poisons 7:918–19; 13:1792
  see also fingerprinting
forestry 7:921–5
  see also deforestation; lumber
forging 10:1388–9
  sheet metal 15:2064
forklifts 7:926–7
formic acid see methanoic acid
Formula 1 cars 14:1888
forward bias 5:653; 18:2482
forward chaining 2:171
fossil fuels 2:258; 3:391; 6:790, 791
fossils 6:822, 823, 825; 7:987–8;
    12:1631–5
  ammonites 7:989; 12:1633
  coelacanth 12:1632
  microfossils 12:1634
Foucault, Jean-Bernard-Léon
    8:1143; 12:1665
Foucault test 9:1243; 15:2031
foundations, on clay soils 15:2112
Fourcault process 7:1000
Fourdrinier machines 12:1639–40
Fourier analysis (harmonic analysis)
    19:2674
fovea 6:831; 9:1240
fractals 3:430–1; 4:535
fractionating columns 5:662–3;
    11:1575, 1576
fractions (numbers) 10:1354
fractures, bone, treatment 3:299–300
fragrances, microencapsulated
    10:1414
frameworks, structural 16:2244–5
francium 1:99, 101
Franklin, Benjamin 6:725; 9:1250;
    17:2428–9
Franklin, Rosalind 7:973
Frasch, Herman 16:2299
Frasch process 11:1461
f-ratio see focal ratio
Fraunhofer, Joseph von 16:2193
Fraunhofer lines 16:2193
free radicals 11:1559; 16:2225
freewheeling 2:242
freeze drying 7:910–11; 14:1947
  coffee 4:503
  specimens for taxidermy 17:2354
freeze etching 5:592; 14:1945
freezing
  foods 7:906, 910, 911
  methods, desalination 5:623,
    624–5
freight handling 7:928–32
  by cranes 5:586, 588, 670; 7:931,
    932
  by rail 7:928, 929; 14:1927
    and railroad yards 14:1929, 1930
  by ships see ships, bulk-carrying
    of grain 6:776; 7:928, 930
  see also containers; docks; forklifts
Frei, Otto 17:2399, 2400
French fries, frozen 7:910, 911
French horns 3:318
freons 8:1036, 1062; 14:1947
frequency
  natural 12:1606; 13:1745;
    14:1964–5
  of pendulums 12:1605, 1606
  resonant 13:1745; 14:1964, 1966
  wave 6:739; 19:2672
frequency distributions 16:2247–8
Frequency Division Multiple Access

(FDMA) **3**:416
frequency hopping **5**:596; **6**:762
frequency modulation (FM) **11**:1473
 and electronic organs **12**:1603–4
 and mobility aids **1**:21
 and television receivers **17**:2393
 and video recorders **19**:2599–600
frequency response **8**:1072; **10**:1424
frequency shift keying **11**:1474
Fresnel spots **17**:2409
Freud, Sigmund **13**:1867
friction **7**:933–4; **14**:1961
 coefficient of **7**:933–4
 counteracted in machines *see*
  bearings and bushings
 generating electricity **6**:725, 727,
  728
 kinetic **7**:933
 laws of **7**:933–4
 limiting **7**:933
 rolling **7**:934
 sliding (dynamic friction) **14**:1961
 static **7**:933
frigates **19**:2627, *2629*
 hybrid **8**:1117
Frisch, Otto **7**:876
frogs
 calls **19**:2733
 curare from **13**:*1791*
 reproduction **14**:*1957*, 1958–9
fronts, weather **10**:*1397*, *1398*, 1400
Froude number **8**:1111
fructose **3**:389
fructose-1,6-diphosphate **10**:1374
fructose-6-phosphate **10**:1374
fruit machines (slot machines)
 7:949–50
fruits
 dehydration **12**:1610
 dietary **11**:1558
 premature ripening **1**:55
FSDS (fin-stabilized discarding
  sabot) projectiles **1**:119
fuchsin, basic (dye) **1**:134, 135
fudge **4**:557
fuel cells **6**:795–6, 799; **7**:935–6
 aluminum-air **7**:*936*
 nuclear, examination for surface
  defects **8**:*1082*
 solid-oxide **6**:795
 uses **7**:936
  in electric vehicles **5**:720;
   9:1287, 1288
  to detect alcohol **5**:686
fuel injection **2**:200, 203; **7**:937–9
Fujita tornado scale **8**:1099
fulcrums **9**:1231
Full Authority Digital Electronic
  Control (FADEC) **1**:78
fullerenes **4**:451, *455*
 buckminsterfullerenes (buckyballs)
  4:451; **10**:1360
fumaroles **9**:1235
functional groups **4**:456–7
functions, mathematical **10**:1355–6
Fundy, Bay of **17**:2438, 2440
fungi **10**:1409–10
 infections in animals **18**:2585
 parasitic **12**:1644–5
 reproduction **14**:*1958*
 use in pest control **12**:1645
 see also yeast
fungicides, microencapsulated
  10:1414
funiculars **3**:357–8
furnaces **7**:940–2; **9**:*1209*
 basic oxygen **7**:*941*
 blast **3**:391, *392*, **7**:942
  for iron production **9**:1186–7;
   10:1378; **12**:1617
  for lead production **9**:1219
  for brass manufacture **3**:316

construction **7**:940–1
 electric **7**:942
  electric arc **3**:316; **7**:*941*, 942;
   8:*1061*; **9**:1190
  electric induction **7**:942
  resistance furnaces **7**:942
 glass **7**:*940*
 heat-treatment **10**:1388
 muffle **6**:*780*
 open-hearth **7**:*940*
 pot **7**:940
 solar **15**:2116
 see also kilns
FUSE (Far Ultraviolet Spectroscopic
  Explorer) **2**:174, 175–6; **17**:2382
fuses and circuit breakers **7**:943–5
 circuit breakers (CBs) **7**:943,
  944–5; **13**:1837
  miniature (MCBs) **7**:943, 945
  residual current (RCCBs) **7**:945
  in domestic wiring systems
   19:2705–7
 fuse boxes **19**:2705, *2708*
 fuses **7**:943–4; **13**:1837
  ammunition **1**:117–18, *119*
  bomb **2**:285
fusion, latent energy of **4**:463
fusion, nuclear **1**:99; **2**:248; **6**:796–7;
  7:946–8; **11**:*1545*; **13**:1762–3
 inertial confinement **13**:1763
 magnetic confinement **13**:1762,
  1763
  in tokamaks **6**:796; **7**:947–8;
   13:1763
 and nuclear weapons **11**:1553–4
 in power plants **2**:248
 for rocket propulsion **14**:1996
 in stars and the Sun (hydrogen
  burning) **6**:764; **7**:947; **13**:1758;
  15:2114
 use of lasers in **7**:*946*, 947, 948;
  9:1214
 use of magnetohydrodynamics in
  experiments **10**:1319
fuzzy logic **2**:171; **9**:1277
 washing machines and **3**:431;
  19:2635–6

G

gabbards **5**:588
gabions **9**:1206–7
gadolinium **11**:1549; **12**:1724,
  18:2486
Gagarin, Yuri **1**:42
Gagnan, Emil **2**:*154*, 155
gain **6**:754
galactose **3**:389
Galapagos Islands **6**:825
galaxies
 accretion disks **10**:*1362*
 active **14**:1912
 black holes in **2**:268, 269, 270;
  17:2443
 Cartwheel **2**:*179*
 Centaurus A **2**:*269*
 distance estimated **2**:178
 and gravitational lensing **4**:*572*
 M87 **10**:*1362*; **17**:*2443*
 NGC 628 **17**:*2378*
 our *see* Milky Way
 polar-ring **8**:*1021*
 and radio astronomy **14**:1912
 receding **4**:573
 Seyfert **2**:174, 267
 "starburst" **2**:177
 "ultra-faint" **2**:174
galena **9**:1219; **16**:2299
Galilei, Galileo **2**:222
 clock **4**:*482*
 and gravity **8**:1021
 and mechanics **12**:1725

telescope **11**:1561
 thermoscope **17**:2423
Galileo (spacecraft) **15**:2120, 2121,
  2123
gallbladder, removal **17**:2331
gallic acid **12**:1708
gallium arsenide **9**:1213; **15**:2116
gallium indium phosphide **15**:2116
galls **12**:1646, 1659
gallstones **6**:784
 removal **6**:785
galvanic skin response (GSR)
  13:1807
galvanizing **4**:571; **17**:2322, 2323,
  2325–6; **19**:2732
galvanographs **13**:1807
galvanometers **10**:1402–3
games, computer **4**:536
 Majestic **11**:1503
games consoles **7**:952
games machines **7**:949–52
gamma-ray bursts **17**:2317
gamma rays **6**:744–5; **9**:1238;
  14:1907
 dangers of **6**:745
 detection **6**:744–5
 from space **2**:173–4; **6**:745
  black holes **2**:268
 gamma-camera scans of the body
  14:1917, 1919
 production **6**:744
 and radionuclide scanning (scintigraphy) **2**:281
 uses **6**:745
  food irradiation **6**:745; **7**:911
  lasers **9**:1214
 wavelength **6**:739–40, 744
gantries, crane **5**:585, 586
Ganymede (moon) **9**:*1235*; **15**:2121
garnets **1**:18; **7**:*982*; **16**:2271
gas and dust masks **7**:953–4
 civil defense masks **4**:*440*
 industrial **7**:954
 military **7**:954
 see also respirators
gases **10**:1359, 1362
 atmospheric **1**:62
 conduction in **4**:555
 dew point **8**:*1123*
 elasticity **5**:713
 energy distribution of molecules
  9:1203
 gas laws **4**:464; **7**:960–1; **10**:1362
  ideal **7**:960; **10**:1362
 kinetic theory of **7**:960–1; **9**:1203
 liquefaction **1**:63–4; **5**:590
 and pressure **7**:960–1; **13**:1840
 vapor density **5**:617
gas industry **7**:955–9
 coal gas **7**:957–8
 natural gas **7**:955–7
 oil gas **7**:959
gas oil **11**:1579
gasoline **8**:1106
 biofuel replacements **2**:258, 259;
  6:794
 containing alcohol **6**:842; **7**:962
 containing lead **9**:1221
 from oil refining **11**:1576, 1580
 and the greenhouse effect **6**:794
 lead-free **8**:1036; **11**:*1578*
 octane numbers **8**:1106; **11**:*1578*
 straight-run **11**:1577
 synthetic **7**:962–3
 tetraethyl lead additive **4**:459;
  13:1802
gastroscopes **6**:785; **17**:2331
gas turbines **7**:964–7; **18**:*2517*
 blades **1**:106; **6**:736; **7**:964;
  11:*1522*
 heat exchangers **8**:1055
 and helicopter engines **8**:1067

for marine propulsion **10**:1336;
  13:1858
 hovercraft **1**:*80*
 in power plants **7**:967; **13**:1828,
  1832
 soundproofing **15**:*2140*
 see also aircraft engines, jet
gates, miter **9**:1266
gateways **4**:541
Gatling guns **2**:193
Gay-Lussac's law **7**:*960*, 961
gears **7**:968–9
 automobile **2**:200; **18**:2489–92
 bicycle **2**:241–2
 cutting **7**:969
 functions **7**:968
 micromachine **10**:*1416*
Geiger, Hans **14**:1905
Geiger–Müller tubes **6**:744; **7**:970;
  12:1653
Geissler, Heinrich **5**:655
Geissler tubes **5**:*658*; **17**:2403
gelatin
 blasting **6**:827
 for optical filters **6**:857, 858
gelatin process **12**:1708
gelignite **1**:116
gels, polyelectrolyte **10**:1353
Gemini, Project **15**:2152
Gemini 5 (spacecraft) **7**:936
Gemini Multi-Object Spectrograph
  17:*2378*
gemstones **5**:598
 coloration **4**:472
 cutting **16**:2270–2
 diamonds **5**:*637*, 638
 polished **1**:18
 synthetic **17**:2346, *2347*; **18**:*2487*
generators **7**:971–2; **10**:1318
 alternating-current (alternators)
  6:729; **7**:971–2; **19**:2619
  ambulance **1**:113
  automobile **2**:201
  power plant **13**:1827, 1829–30
 direct-current (dynamos) **7**:972;
  13:1827; **19**:2618–19
 superconductors used in **17**:2314
 voltage regulators for **19**:2618–19
genes **3**:412; **6**:823; **7**:973, 979–80;
  11:1477
 and aging **7**:996
 banks **8**:*1120*; **11**:1478–9
 in development **6**:778
 dominant and recessive **6**:823;
  7:980
 intermediate **7**:980
 isolation **11**:1478
 jumping (transposons) **3**:*303*
 libraries **11**:1478
 mutated *see* mutations
 polygenic **7**:980
 selector (homeotic genes) **6**:778
 see also chromosomes; DNA;
  genetics
gene therapy **3**:380; **7**:978
genetic engineering **1**:52; **7**:973–8;
  11:1478
 of animals **1**:52–3; **2**:263–4; **7**:978
 and biological weapons **4**:440
 for blood substitutes **13**:*1733*
 gene therapy **3**:380; **7**:978
 and horticulture **8**:1089
 for insulin **7**:978; **13**:1733–4;
  19:2727
 of plants and crops (food) **1**:53;
  3:303, 304; **7**:978; **12**:1676
 herbicide-tolerant crops
  19:2681
 and transplants **13**:1734
 see also biotechnology; DNA
genetic fingerprinting *see* fingerprinting, DNA

2851

genetics **7:979–80**
  definition of life **9**:1233
  genetic disorders **7**:980
  high-tech plant breeding **1**:53–4
  see also chromosomes; DNA; genes
genome **7**:976; **11**:1478
  mapping **1**:53–4; **7**:980;
    11:1479–80
    Human Genome Project **7**:976,
      980; **11**:1479–80
genus **12**:1632
geochemistry **7:981–2**
geodesic structures **7:983–4**
  domes **1**:*108*; **3**:*336*; **7**:983–4;
    16:2245; **17**:*2400*
geographical information systems
  7:*985*, 986
geography **7:985–6**
  see also environmental science
geologic traps **11**:1572
geology **7:987–90**
  economic **7**:989–90
  geologic timescale **6**:824–5; **7**:988
  radioisotopic dating **7**:995;
    14:1916
  see also fossils; plate tectonics
geometry **10**:1354, 1357–8
geophones **11**:1571
geophysics **7:991–5**
  gravimeters **7**:992; **11**:1571
  oil and gas exploration **7**:993–4
  see also paleomagnetism; plate
    tectonics; seismology
geo-radar equipment **2**:157
geostationary Earth orbits (GEOs)
  space debris **15**:2150, *2151*
  see also satellites, artificial, orbits
geotextiles **17**:2408
geothermal power **6**:790, 793
germanium **6**:752; **15**:2052; **18**:2481
germ theory **10**:1367
gerontology **7:996–7**
geysers **5**:*700*
g-forces **3**:*423*
ghost illusions **16**:*2234*
"ghosts" (false frequencies) **15**:2145
gibberellic acid **3**:305
GIF (graphics image format) **4**:534;
  12:1594
gigantism **6**:781; **8**:1086
Gigantosaurus **12**:1635
Gilbert, William **6**:725, 747
gill nets **7**:872
gin **5**:*663*; **16**:2217
gingivitis **5**:619–20
Giotto (spacecraft) **15**:2123
glaciology **7:998**
glands
  endocrine **6**:781–2; **8**:1084
  see also hormones
glass **3**:425–6; **4**:493; **7:999–1001**;
  10:1360
  borosilicate **11**:1549–50
  colored **6**:858
  cutting **16**:2237
  didymium **6**:858
  etching **6**:805
  and forensic science **7**:917
  glass mosaic (glass appliqué)
    16:2238
  heat-resistant **7**:1001
  incising patterns on **1**:17; **5**:*638*
  laminated safety **1**:30; **2**:209
  light-sensitive **7**:1001
  optical and ophthalmic **7**:1001
    for optical filters **6**:858
  patterned **7**:1001
  photochromatic **16**:2192
  powdered **6**:779
  production **4**:493; **7**:999–1001
  recycling **14**:*1940*, 1942
  safety **7**:1001

sculptures **16**:2238
  slab (*dalles de verre*) **16**:2238
  stained **6**:858; **7**:*999*; **16**:**2236–8**
  wired **7**:1001
  see also enamels, vitreous; glass
    fibers
glasses see spectacles
glass fibers **7:1002–3**
  GRPs see plastics, glass-reinforced
  manufacture **7**:1002–3
  Teflon-coated glass fiber fabric
    17:2399, 2400, 2401
  see also fiberglass
glass-reinforced plastic (GRPs) see
  plastics, glass-reinforced
glass-reinforced polyester (GRP)
  3:337
Glauber, Johann Rudolf **11**:1525
glaucoma **17**:2332
glazing **4**:467
gliders **7:1004–5**
  history **2**:210; **7**:1004
gliding angle **7**:1005
Global Climate Model **4**:*477*
Global Climate Observing System
  (GCOS) **4**:479
global positioning systems (GPSs)
  7:1006–8; **11**:1512
  and automobiles **2**:204; **6**:*813*
  for mapmaking **10**:1331
  for missile guidance **11**:1466, 1468
  Navstar **7**:1006; **11**:1514; **15**:2026
  for space navigation **11**:1514
  for surveying **17**:2336–7
  to study plate tectonics **13**:1780
global system for mobile communications (GSM) **3**:416
global warming **4**:479–80; **6**:807–8;
  7:922; **13**:*1800*
glockenspiels **12**:1668, *1669*
Gloster Meteor **7**:965
glowworms **10**:1301, *1302*
glucagon **10**:1375; **13**:1792
  receptors **8**:1087
glucocorticoids **8**:1086
glucose **3**:389
glucose-6-phosphate **10**:1374
glucose tolerance tests **12**:1657
glue **1**:29
  marine **1**:30
  superglue **1**:30
  surgical **1**:31
  see also adhesives
gluons **6**:772
glutamate **3**:414
glyceraldehyde-3-phosphate **10**:1374
glycerine see glycerol
glycerol (glycerine) **1**:97, 98; **4**:457;
  6:836, 837
glyceryl monothioglycolate **8**:1032
glycogen **3**:389, 390; **8**:1085
glycolysis **10**:1374, 1376
glyphosate (Roundup) **19**:2681
GM-CSF **2**:*263*, 265, 273
  and gene therapy **3**:380
gnotobiotic environments **8**:*1133*
Goddard, Robert **14**:1993
go devils (pigs) **13**:1754
goggles
  industrial **13**:1861
  virtual-reality **4**:532, **19**:2603–6
goiter **8**:1036, *1087*
gold **8:1013–16**
  alloys **8**:1016
  alluvial **8**:1013
  deposited by bacteria **10**:1412
  extraction **8**:1013–15
  isotopes **14**:1921
  jewelry **8**:1016
  mining for **8**:1013; **11**:1460
  refining **8**:1015
  rolled **16**:2191

uses **8**:*1013*, 1016
Golden Gate Bridge **3**:329
golf balls **16**:2220–1
golf clubs **16**:2223–4
Golgi apparatus **3**:411; **8**:1084
gonads **6**:781
Gondwanaland **7**:990
gongs **12**:1668, *1669*
Gordon Bennett races **2**:218
Gore-Tex **13**:1861, *1863*
Goudsmit, Samuel **6**:768
governors **8**:1017; **15**:2055–6
grabs
  cactus **4**:*496*
  clamshell **5**:704
graders (scrapers) **5**:703; **14**:1974
graft versus host disease (GVHD)
  18:*2499*, 2503
Graham, Thomas **12**:1609
grain, bulk handling **6**:776; **7**:928,
  930
gramophones **12**:1694
Grand Canal (China) **3**:376
Grand Coulee Dam **5**:605
Grand Prix racing **14**:1887–9, 1890,
  1892
  scale models **14**:1915
granite **7**:981
granulocytes **3**:*413*
grapes, and winemaking **19**:2700–1
graphical user interfaces (GUIs)
  4:*531*; **8**:1147; **11**:1490, 1501
graphics, computer see computer
  graphics
graphics cards (video cards; adapters)
  4:527
graphics image format (GIF) **4**:534;
  12:1594
graphics tablets (digitizers) **4**:535;
  11:1492
graphite **3**:392, *393*, 395; **9**:1289;
  10:1360–1; **12**:1679
  diamonds created from **17**:2346
graphitization, of carbon fibers
  3:395; **17**:2405
graphophones **12**:1694
grass-cutting equipment **8:1018–19**
gravimeters **7**:992; **11**:1571
gravimetric analysis **4**:446
gravitons **6**:773; **8**:1022
gravity **8:1020–2**; **12**:1726
  acceleration due to **6**:789; **8**:1021
  affecting light **8**:1021–2; **14**:1954
  and black holes **2**:269, 270;
    17:2443
  center of **16**:2243, 2244
  Einstein's general theory of relativ-
    ity (theory of gravity) **2**:269;
    4:572, 574–5; **8**:1021, 1143;
    11:1521; **14**:1954
  gravitational lensing **14**:1954
  gravity-assisted projectiles **2**:217
  measuring **8**:1020–1
  mediated by gravitons **6**:773;
    8:1022
  Newton's law of gravitation **2**:269;
    8:1020, 1021; **11**:1520, 1521;
    12:1726
    and orbits **12**:1599
    and satellites **15**:2024–5
  the search for waves **2**:180; **8**:1022
  and the Theory of Everything
    8:1022
  and time **8**:1022; **17**:2443
  variations in **8**:1021–2
  waves **14**:1954
  zero **6**:789; **16**:*2176*
gravity assist (slingshot effect)
  14:1996
gravity meters **15**:2048
gravure **6**:805
gravure processes, inks **8**:1152

gray goods **17**:2408
gray-scale imaging **4**:533
Great Artesian Basin **9**:1194; **19**:2684
Great Belt see Store Baelt
Great Pyramid of Cheops **13**:*1870*,
  1871–2
Greek fire **7**:869, 882
Greeks, ancient
  cement **3**:417
  dentistry **5**:618
  and gravity **8**:1020, 1021
  numbers **10**:*1358*
  sundials **16**:2302
  theater **8**:1104
  theories of matter **2**:182; **6**:763
  and vision **9**:1236
Green Bank Telescope (GBT)
  14:1909–10
greenhouse gases **4**:477, 479; **6**:794,
  807; **7**:998
greenhouses **8**:1088–9
  for hydroponics **8**:1122; **9**:1194
Greenwich mean time (GMT)
  17:2442
grenade launchers **14**:1972
grenades **1**:120
  chemical **4**:*438*; **11**:1532; **12**:1700
  light and noise **11**:*1533*
  smoke **14**:1972
Griess process **1**:135; **5**:691
Grigg-Skjellerup (comet) **15**:2123
Grimaldi, Francesco **5**:641
grinding machines **10**:1309–10
grit blasting **1**:17; **17**:2322
Ground Emplacement Mine
  Scattering System (GEMSS)
  11:1454
grounding fault circuit interrupters
  (GFCIs) **19**:2707
groundwater
  analysis **7**:982
  arsenic in **7**:981
  pollution from nitrates **1**:54
  as a water supply **19**:2661
growth factors **2**:273
growth hormone(s)
  and aging **7**:997
  for farm animals **1**:52, 57; **18**:2588
  human (HGH) **2**:263; **6**:781, 782;
    7:997; **8**:1086; **16**:2226
  rat **2**:*265*
groynes **6**:818, 819
Gruinard Island **4**:438, 441
GT racing **14**:1891
  scale models **14**:1915
guanine **7**:973–4; **11**:1477, 1478
guano **12**:*1694*, 1700
guitars **16**:2282, *2283*
  pickup **13**:1739–40; **16**:2282
  synthesizers **17**:2344
Gulf Stream **11**:*1568*
Gulf War
  aircraft **16**:*2250*
  missiles **11**:1468
  oil well fires after **6**:806
gum arabic **1**:30
gum disease **5**:619–20
gum shields **13**:1863
gums, plant, adhesive **1**:29–30
guncotton **3**:390; **6**:827
gunmetals **3**:331
gunpowder **4**:449; **6**:826, 829
  black **1**:101, 120
guns **8:1023–7**
  ammunition **1**:116
  antiaircraft **1**:143–4
  antitank **1**:119; **11**:*1485*
  and armor **2**:162
  cartridges **1**:118; **8**:1024
  naval **8**:*1023*, 1026
  silencers **8**:1027
  spray **16**:2227–8

see also automatic weapons and machine guns; ballistics; mortars, bazookas, and recoilless guns; rifles and shotguns
Gutenberg, Johann **5**:630; **13**:1847, 1848
gynecology and obstetrics **11**:**1563–4**
gypsum **3**:417; **16**:2240, 2299
gyrocompasses **8**:**1028–9**; **11**:1510
gyroplanes *see* autogiros
gyroscopes **8**:**1030–1**
  in gyrocompasses **8**:1028
  in hydrofoils **8**:1117
  in inertial guidance systems **8**:1145; **11**:1513
  in missiles **8**:1144; **11**:1466
  in monorails **11**:1481–2
  in satellites **15**:2028
  Schlick **16**:2232
  scientific **8**:1029
  for stabilization of ships **8**:1030–1; **15**:2072; **16**:2231–2
  in wheelchairs **11**:1470

H

Haber, Fritz **1**:115; **3**:407; **4**:451
Haber (*or* Haber-Bosch) process **1**:25, 115; **4**:451; **11**:1525–6
  catalysts **3**:*405*, 407
hacksaws **18**:2463
hadrons **6**:770, 773
hafnium **18**:2485
Hagelin, Boris **5**:*596*
hagfish **12**:1645
Hahn, Otto **7**:876
hair **15**:2087
  beard **14**:1935
  and forensic science **7**:916
  lanugo **14**:1935
  structure **1**:10
  treatment **8**:**1032–3**
hair clippers **14**:*1935*, 1936
Hale telescope **2**:232; **17**:*2378*
Hale, William **14**:1991
half-life **11**:1547
halftone process **13**:1850–1
halite **14**:2016
Hall, Charles M. **10**:1378
Hall effect **10**:1320
hallmarking, gold **8**:1016
haloalkanes **4**:456, 459
halogens **8**:**1034–6**
halothane **1**:131
hammers
  manufacture **18**:2461
  riveting **13**:1789
Hamming, Richard **8**:1148
Hamming code **8**:1148
handoff **3**:415
hands
  artificial **2**:254–5
  transplants **10**:1439; **18**:2504
  virtual **17**:2332
handshaking **4**:541
handwriting, and optical character recognition **12**:1595
hang gliders **8**:**1037–8**
hapticity **4**:460
harbors
  lighthouses **9**:1247
  see also docks
hardening (metalworking) **10**:1388
hardness
  Moh's scale of **1**:17
  scale of **7**:987
harmonica bugs **6**:761
harmonic analysis *see* Fourier analysis
harmonic distortion **8**:1073, 1074
  total (THD) **8**:1074
harmonics **3**:318; **16**:2284
Harpoon antiship weapon **16**:2291

harpoons **19**:2685, 2686
harps **16**:2280–2
  automatic **16**:2284
harpsichords **13**:1735–6
  electric **17**:2342
Harrier *see* British Aerospace Harrier
Harrison, James **14**:1947
Harrison, John **4**:484; **9**:*1215*, 1216; **10**:1408; **19**:2652
Harvey, William **10**:1367; **13**:1733
hassium **6**:766
Haversian canals **3**:298, *299*
Hawking, Stephen **2**:270
  and voice synthesis **19**:*2615*, 2617
Hawking radiation **2**:270
hayfever **8**:1135
head-coupled displays (HCDs) **19**:2605
headlights, automobile **11**:1464
head-mounted displays (HMDs) **19**:2604–5, 2606
  and augmented reality **19**:2608
head-up displays (HUDs) **1**:68; **8**:**1039–40**, 1082
  in cars **6**:*813*; **8**:1040, *1129*
hearing **8**:**1041–4**, 1072; **9**:1284; **11**:1530; **15**:2142
  damage **11**:*1530*
  the ears and **8**:1041–3; **15**:2131, 2132
hearing aids **1**:22; **8**:**1043–4**; **12**:1612
heart **8**:**1045–7**
  artificial **2**:256–7; **8**:*1047*
  disorders **8**:1046–7
    cardiovascular drugs **12**:1682
    congenital defects **8**:1046, 1051; **12**:1660
    monitoring
      electrocardiographs (EKGs) **6**:756–7; **8**:*1046*; **12**:1666
      ultrasound scans **2**:282
    muscle **11**:1504, 1505–6
    pacemaker *see* heart pacemaker
    radiological scans **14**:1919
    surgery on *see* heart surgery
    transplants *see* transplants, heart
    see also stethoscopes
heart attack (myocardial infarction) **6**:837; **8**:1047, 1052; **10**:1305; **11**:1559
heart block **8**:1047
heart disease, coronary **8**:1046–7; **10**:1305; **11**:1559
heart failure, congestive **8**:1047
heart-lung machines **8**:1049, 1050, 1051, 1052; **18**:*2501*
heart pacemaker **8**:**1048**
  external **8**:1048
  implantable **2**:257; **8**:1048
  natural **2**:257; **11**:1506
heart surgery **8**:**1049–52**
  see also heart pacemaker
heat
  detectors (firefighting) **6**:863
  differs from temperature **17**:2395
  a form of energy **6**:786, 787
  heat capacity **17**:2414
heat adsorption **7**:881
heat capacity **4**:463; **12**:1728
heat engines **8**:**1053**
  Carnot cycle **8**:1053; **17**:2414, 2415
heaters
  in dishwashers **5**:659
  storage heaters **6**:800
heat exchangers **8**:**1054–5**, 1064; **11**:*1524*
heating and ventilation systems **8**:**1056–62**
  air conditioning **8**:1058, 1060–2, *1063*, 1064
  heating systems **8**:1056–8

corrosion inhibitors **4**:571
  and heat pumps **8**:1064
  solar energy **6**:792; **8**:1058; **15**:2115–16
  storage heaters **6**:800
  ventilation systems **8**:1056, 1058–60
heat pumps **8**:**1060**, **1063–4**
  geothermal **6**:800
heat rays *see* infrared radiation
heat sinks **17**:*2432*
heavy water *see* deuterium oxide
Heckler and Koch (rifles) **14**:1968–9
Heisenberg, Werner Karl **14**:1883
Heisenberg uncertainty principle **6**:770; **14**:*1883*; **16**:2249
Helicobacter pylori **10**:*1367*, 1411
helicopters **8**:**1065–70**; **18**:2551–2
  amphibious operations **15**:2037
  convertiplanes **8**:1069
  engines **8**:1067
    servomechanisms **15**:*2055*
  midair recovery systems (MARS) **13**:1748
  military **8**:1067–8, 1070; **19**:*2629*
  model, radio-controlled **14**:1914, *1915*
  smart rotor system **10**:*1352*
  torpedoes **18**:*2468*
  unpiloted **13**:1748
  uses **8**:1067–8
    ambulances **1**:113; **8**:1067, *1070*
    firefighting **6**:861; **8**:1067
    sea rescue **15**:2038, 2039
    use of sonar devices **15**:2128
  see also autogiros
Helios (aircraft) **14**:1913; **15**:*2114*, 2117
helioscopes **18**:2544
helioseismology **15**:2046
helium **11**:1528–9
  atomic structure **2**:*182*
  in balloons and airships **1**:91, 92; **2**:219
  isotopes **11**:1528–9
  liquid **5**:591–2; **11**:1529
  nucleus, binding energy **2**:248
  produced by the Big Bang **4**:573–4
  superfluidity **4**:553; **5**:592; **7**:934; **10**:1362; **11**:1528–9
  and underwater diving **5**:667; **11**:1528; **18**:2538
helium burning **6**:764
helixometers **7**:917
helmets, sports **13**:1862
Helmholtz, Herman von **12**:1591
hematite **9**:1186
hematoporphyrin derivative (HPD) **12**:*1613*
hemodialysis *see* dialysis machines
hemoglobin **1**:134; **9**:1188; **13**:1865; **18**:2488
  synthetic **13**:*1733*
hemolysis, and heart-lung machines **8**:1050
hemophilia **7**:978, 980
hemorrhage, gastrointestinal **6**:785
hemp **3**:350
henry (H) **8**:1139
heparin **8**:1050
hepatitis **18**:2532
  hepatitis B **10**:1369; **12**:*1659*
  vaccine **2**:266; **18**:2555, 2556
herbicides **19**:2679–80
  microencapsulated **10**:1414
herbivores **8**:644
Hercules (aircraft) **14**:*1948*, **15**:2036
heredity *see* genetics
hermaphrodites, hydras **14**:1958
Héroult, Paul-Louis-Toussaint **10**:1378
Herschel, William **6**:742; **11**:1560

Herschel Telescope **17**:*2380*
Herstal XM303 (weapons system) **11**:1533–4
hertz **6**:739
Hertz, Heinrich **14**:1893
HESH (high explosive squash head) **1**:120
heuristics **2**:171, 172
hex-1-ene **13**:1770
hexacyanoferrate ions **18**:2488
hexadecimal system **2**:246–7
hexane **4**:*454*, 459; **11**:1579
  isomerization **11**:1578
Hexogen *see* RDX
hibernation **10**:1376
hi-fi systems **1**:26–7; **8**:**1071–6**; **13**:1739
  see also loudspeakers
high explosive squash head (HESH) **1**:120
high pressure nervous syndrome **5**:667
High Resolution Channel (HRC) **15**:2155
High Speed Civil Transport (HSCT) **17**:2320
high-speed dispersers (HSDs) **12**:1630
high-speed photography **8**:**1077–9**, *1109*; **15**:2075; **16**:2285–6
  digital **8**:1079
highways
  major **14**:1979
  monitoring **14**:1985
Himalayas **5**:699
Hindenberg (airship) **8**:1119; **9**:1288
Hiperlight biplanes **18**:2525
hip joints
  artificial **2**:254, *255*, *256*; **10**:1352; **14**:1917–18
  dysplasia, in dogs **18**:2584
Hipparchus **10**:1355
hipping (hot isostatic pressing) **3**:404
Hippocrates **10**:1367
Hiroshima, atomic bomb used on **11**:1551, 1552, 1554; **14**:*1908*
Hispano-Suiza engines **1**:72
histograms **16**:2248
histopathology **12**:*1655*
HIV (human immunodeficiency virus) **10**:1369–70
  and anti-HIV therapy **12**:1688
  tracking **6**:811–12
  vaccine **18**:2555
  see also AIDS
HLA (human leukocyte antigen) system **18**:2498
hoarseness **12**:1613
hobbyhorses **2**:240
Hodgkin's disease **3**:379
Hoffmann, August **1**:133–4
Hoffmann kilns **9**:1200
Hohmann transfer ellipses **12**:1600
hoists, for the disabled **11**:1471
Holland, John **16**:2288
Hollerith, Herman **4**:523
holmium **18**:2486
holography **8**:**1080–3**
  acoustic **15**:2135
  anticounterfeiting and forgery **5**:584
  and head-up displays **8**:1040, 1082
  laser **8**:1080, 1081, 1082, *1083*; **9**:1214
    for artificial limbs **2**:253
  recording a hologram **8**:1080, *1081*
honey **4**:557
honeybees **10**:1317
Hong Kong **15**:*2092*
  Chek Lap Kok Airport **4**:474; **5**:677

Hong Kong (*cont.*)
 harbor, tunnel under **18**:*2513, 2516*
 mass transit system **10**:1346, *1347*; **14**:1927
Hooke, Robert **10**:1433; **18**:2544; **19**:2651
Hooke's law **5**:713; **16**:2229
hook and loop tape (Velcro) **6**:835
hooks, split (hand substitutes) **2**:255
Hoover Dam **5**:608; **18**:2520
hopper cars **7**:929
hops, drying **9**:1199
hormone replacement therapy (HRT) **3**:298; **6**:782; **7**:997
hormones **2**:251; **3**:413; **6**:781–2; **8**:*1084–7*
 and aging **7**:997
 for cancer treatment **3**:379–80
 growth *see* growth hormone(s)
 as medicines **12**:1687
 plant **3**:305
 sex **8**:1086–7
 see also endocrinology
horologiums **4**:481
horsepower **13**:*1825*, 1826
horticulture **8**:*1088–9*
hosiery and knitware manufacture **8**:*1090–3*
hospitals, waste disposal **19**:2641
Hotchkiss guns **2**:194
hot-dip process **17**:2326
hotels, underwater **18**:2540
hot rod racing **14**:1891
hours **4**:481
hovercraft *see* air-cushion vehicles
hovertrains, monorail **11**:1482
HRT (hormone replacement therapy) **3**:298; **6**:782; **7**:997
HTML (hypertext markup language) **9**:*1179*; **11**:1502
http (hypertext transfer protocol) **9**:1177
Hubble constant **4**:572–3
Hubble's Law **4**:573
Hubble Space Telescope (HST) **2**:176, 177; **11**:*1560*, 1561; **15**:2029, 2118, 2122–3; **17**:2381
 cameras **2**:176; **15**:*2154*, 2155; **17**:2381
 charge-coupled devices **3**:432
 hit by space debris **15**:2151
 space shuttle missions to **16**:2168–9; **17**:*2381*
hubs, computer-network **4**:*539*
hulls
 damaged **15**:2021
 Kevlar **13**:*1771, 1804*
 planing **8**:1116
 speedboat **16**:2204, 2205–6
hum **8**:1074
Human Exploration and Development of Space (HEDS) **16**:2174
Human Genome Project (HGP) **7**:976, 980; **11**:1479–80
humans
 cloning **2**:266
 energy requirements **6**:791
 evolution **6**:825; **12**:*1633*
  language **16**:2200
  origins **12**:1635
  pheromones **12**:*1691*
 preserved
  in ice **4**:477, *478*
  in peat **2**:160; **4**:477
Humber Bridge **3**:329; **4**:474
humidification
 in air-conditioning systems **8**:1061
 and desalination **5**:624
humidity
 measurement **8**:1123

relative **8**:1123; **19**:2665
hummingbirds, migration **19**:2733
hump yards **14**:1929
hunting **15**:2056, 2057; **17**:2426
Huntington's chorea **3**:414; **7**:980
hurricanes and tornadoes **8**:*1094–9*
 hurricanes **8**:1094–6, *1098*; **15**:*2028*
  and tsunamis **18**:2510
 tornadoes **8**:1094, *1095*, 1097–9
Huygens (space probe) **15**:2122
Huygens, Christiaan **4**:*482*, 483, 486; **9**:*1236*; **12**:1664; **14**:1880; **19**:2651
hybridization, and agriculture **1**:*52*
hybridomas **2**:*265*; **8**:1137
hydras **14**:1957, 1958
hydraulics **8**:*1100–4*
 braking systems **3**:314–15
 excavators **5**:704; **8**:*1100*
 hydraulic pumps **4**:521
 hydraulic springs **16**:2230
 power-steering systems **16**:2261–2
 for tunneling **18**:*2512*, 2513, *2514*
 see also water rams
hydrazine **11**:1527
hydrazoic acid **11**:1527
hydrocarbons **8**:*1105–8*
 production **8**:1106
 saturated and unsaturated **8**:1105
 see also cracking
hydrocephalus **12**:1660
hydrochloric acid **1**:2, 23, 25
 in the stomach **5**:642
hydrochlorofluorocarbons **14**:1947
hydrocracking **8**:1119; **11**:1576, 1578
hydrocyclones **5**:638
hydrodesulfurization **3**:406
hydrodynamics **1**:36; **8**:*1109–11*
 hydrodynamic bearings **2**:231–2
 sailing and **14**:2011
hydroelectric power (HEP) **6**:786, 792; **8**:*1112–15*; **13**:1820, 1827
 dams for **5**:605; **8**:1112
 pumped-storage schemes **6**:798; **8**:1112, *1115*; **13**:*1827*; **18**:2520
 turbines **8**:1112–13; **18**:2520
 see also tidal power; wave power
hydrofining **8**:1119; **11**:1580
hydrofluoric acid **6**:805
hydrofluorocarbons **14**:1947
hydrofoils **8**:*1116–17*
hydrogen **8**:*1118–19*
 bonds **4**:444; **5**:597; **19**:2654–5
  in molecular hydrogen **4**:443
 ions, and pH measurement **12**:1692
 isotopes **7**:946; **8**:1118; **13**:1763
 liquid **1**:64; **6**:795; **9**:1287
 manufacture **8**:1118
 monoatomic **10**:1317
 uses **8**:1119
  ammonia manufacture **1**:115; **3**:*405*
  in balloons and airships **1**:91, 92; **2**:219
  in bubble chambers **3**:334
  cooling dynamos **8**:1119
  cutting and welding **1**:119
  in fuel cells **6**:795; **7**:935; **9**:1288
  hydrocracking **8**:1119; **11**:1578
  hydrofining **8**:1119; **11**:1580
  in nuclear fusion **7**:946, 947
  vehicle fuel **8**:1119; **9**:1287–8
hydrogenation **3**:406; **13**:1782; **15**:2107
hydrogen bromide **7**:881; **8**:1119
hydrogen burning **6**:764
hydrogen chloride **8**:1035, 1119; **9**:1163
hydrogen cyanide **8**:1119
hydrogen fluoride **8**:1034, 1119

hydrogen iodide **8**:1119
hydrogen peroxide **8**:1119; **12**:1621
 manufacture **12**:1621
hydrogen sulfide **7**:956; **16**:2299, 2300
hydrographs, flood **7**:888
Hydrolab (underwater laboratory) **18**:2539
hydrolases **6**:810
hydrolysis **7**:962–3
hydrometers **5**:616–17
hydrophones **15**:2126, **16**:2253
hydroplanes **10**:*1336*; **16**:2205, 2208
 stepped **16**:2208
hydroponics **8**:*1120–2*; **9**:1194
hydroquinone **12**:1713
hydrostatics **16**:2245
 hydrostatic bearings **2**:232–3
hydrothermal vents **10**:1333; **11**:1567; **13**:1780
hydroxyl ions **12**:1692
hygrometers **1**:63; **8**:*1123*
hyperglycemia **12**:1657
hypermetropia *see* hyperopia
hypernovas **17**:2317
hyperopia (hypermetropia; farsightedness) **6**:832; **12**:1597; **16**:2191
hyperparasitism **12**:1644
hypertension, pulmonary **18**:2502
hypertext markup language (HTML) **9**:*1179*; **11**:1502
hypertext transfer protocol (http) **9**:1177
hyperthyroidism **8**:1085
hyphae, fungal **12**:1644–5
hypnotherapy **10**:1370
hypnotics **12**:1682
 poisoning **13**:1791
hypocausts, Roman **8**:1056
hypothalamus **3**:310
hypothermia, for heart surgery **8**:1049–51
hypothyroidism **8**:1085
hysteresis loops **10**:1314–15; **18**:2478
hysteria **13**:1868

I

Iapetus (moon) **3**:393
iBOTs (wheelchairs) **11**:1470
ibuprofen **4**:458; **12**:1682
ICBMs *see* intercontinental ballistic missiles
ice **10**:*1360*, 1361; **19**:*2665*
 forms of **19**:2655
 glacial, investigations **7**:998
 humans preserved in **4**:477, *478*
ice ages **4**:478; **6**:809
icebergs
 fresh water from **19**:2667
 radio tagging **14**:*1904*
ice boats **14**:2013
icebreakers **15**:2073
ice cores **6**:809; **13**:*1800*
ice hockey, clothing **13**:1863
icehouses **19**:2667
ice skaters, moment of inertia **8**:1143
ichthyosaurs **6**:825
iconoscope cameras **17**:2383, 2384
ideal gas law **10**:1362
identity cards **3**:341
idiophones **12**:1667–8
ignition **7**:879
ignition systems, automobile **2**:200, 202–3; **8**:*1124–7*; **17**:*2445*
 distributor **2**:202–3; **8**:1124–5
 ignition coil (induction coil) **8**:1124, 1140
 spark plugs **2**:203; **8**:1125, 1126, 1127; **9**:*1170*
IJssel Lake (IJsselmeer) **9**:1208
ileum **5**:642, 643

illuminating gas (town gas) **7**:*957*
illustrator programs **5**:629
image intensifiers **8**:*1128–31*; **17**:2379
image-manipulation software **5**:629
images
 and computer graphics **1**:139; **4**:536
 viewed on computer screens **9**:*1257*
immunity **8**:1132–5
immunization **8**:1135
 active and passive **8**:1137
 see also vaccines
immunodeficiency
 AIDS **8**:1137
 feline **18**:2588
 see also AIDS
immunoglobulins *see* antibodies
immunology **8**:*1132–7*
 and cancer **3**:378; **8**:1137
 see also vaccines
immunostimulation **8**:1137
immunosuppression **8**:1137; **18**:2499
impedance **8**:1075; **14**:1960
impellers **4**:521
Imperial Smelting Process (ISP) **19**:2731–2
impulse **9**:1203
incandescence **10**:1301
incineration
 of chemical weapons **4**:440
 municipal waste **19**:2638–9
 plasma-arc **5**:720
inclined planes, on canals **3**:376
incoherent bundles **6**:856
incoherent radiation **9**:1210, 1211, *1239*
indigestion **5**:645
indole-acetic acid **3**:305
induction **6**:729; **8**:*1138–41*; **12**:1727
 induction coils **8**:1139, *1141*
  see also transformers
 mutual-inductance **8**:1138, 1139
 self-inductance **8**:1138–9
 and Tesla coils **8**:1140; **17**:2403
inductive loops **14**:1985
industrial aids, for the blind/partially sighted **1**:21–2
Industrial Revolution
 building techniques **3**:335
 and cotton **5**:581
 dams **5**:604–5
 earthmoving operations **5**:701
 and metals **10**:1378
inertia **8**:*1142–3*
 moment of **7**:902; **8**:1142, 1143
 rotational **8**:1030, 1142
inertial guidance **8**:*1144–6*; **11**:1468, *1512*, 1513
infertility, in animals **18**:2584
influenza **8**:1135
 monitoring **6**:811
 vaccines **18**:2556–7
information technology **8**:*1147–50*
information theory **8**:1148
Infrared Astronomical Satellite (IRAS) **2**:176–7
infrared radiation **6**:740, 742; **9**:1237
 cosmic **4**:574, *575*
 and astronomy **2**:176–7; **6**:743
 detection **6**:742
 uses **6**:742–3
  aerial photography **1**:35; **2**:*159*; **5**:*707*; **6**:*741*; **7**:986
  in alcohol detectors **5**:686
  burglar alarms **3**:340–1; **15**:2043
  in computer mice **11**:1490, 1491
  fire-detection **6**:864
  heating **6**:742
  thermography **2**:281, *282*; **7**:*995*; **17**:2421–2

infrasonic waves **15**:2134
inhalers **1**:40
injection molding
    acrylic **13**:*1794*
    reaction (RIM) **13**:*1776*
    temperatures measured **17**:*2417*
    thermoplastic **13**:*1773*, 1774
    for thermosets **13**:1775
ink **8**:**1151–2**
    for banknotes **5**:583, 584
    electronic **10**:*1413*, 1414
    for gravure processes **8**:1152
inositol triphosphate **2**:252
insects **19**:2736
    hormones **8**:1087
    reproduction **14**:1958
insemination, artificial **1**:52
insomnia **15**:2101–2
instant-picture cameras **9**:**1157–9**
instrument landing systems (ILSs)
    1:68, 88, 95, 96; **11**:1513
instruments, musical *see* music, musi-
    cal instruments
insulation
    thermal **9**:**1160–1**
        glass fibers for **7**:1002; **9**:1160–1
        vacuums and **17**:2425; **18**:2560
insulators, electric **3**:*426*; **4**:555, 556;
    6:728; **9**:**1162–3**
    and breakdown **9**:1163
    in power cables **3**:345
insulin **2**:263; **5**:643; **8**:1085–6;
    10:1375
    from genetic engineering **7**:978;
        13:1733–4; **19**:2727
    injections **18**:*2557*
    receptors **8**:1087
intaglio processes **6**:803
integers **11**:1555
integrated circuits (silicon chips;
    microchips) **2**:169–70; **6**:*750*,
    754–5; **9**:**1164–8**
    in calculators **3**:359–60
    in cell phones **3**:416
    complexity
        large scale integration (LSI)
            2:169; **3**:359; **4**:525; **6**:755
        medium-scale integration (MSI)
            4:525; **6**:755
        ultra-large-scale integration
            (ULSI) **4**:525; **6**:755
        very-large-scale integration
            (VLSI) **2**:169; **3**:416; **4**:525;
            6:755; **10**:1426
    in computers **4**:*524*, 525; **9**:1165,
        1277
    latch circuits **9**:1277, 1279
    copper **4**:*524*
    manufacture **6**:751, 752; **9**:1166,
        1264; **10**:1427, *1428*; **13**:*1763*
    testing **6**:752; **9**:1166–8;
        10:*1341*; **14**:*1879*
    metal oxide–silicon (MOS) **3**:*361*
    in sewing machines **15**:2060
    switches **4**:552
    to monitor animals **18**:2588
    in watches **19**:2650
    see also microprocessors
integrated thermal meteoroid
    garments (ITMGs) **16**:2177
integrated transport network **3**:343
integration **9**:1201
Intel, landmark processors **10**:1429
Intelsat VI (satellite) **15**:*2027*;
    16:*2165*; **17**:*2359*
intensive care units **11**:1584
Inter City Express (ICE) trains
    9:1274
intercontinental ballistic missiles
    (ICBMs) **11**:1465–6, 1468
    defense against **16**:2180, 2182–4
intercooling **16**:2304; **18**:2506

intercostal muscles **10**:1303
interest, compound **9**:1276
interfacing **5**:646
interference **5**:641; **19**:2673, 2674
    constructive and destructive
        14:1934; **15**:2134
    electromagnetic (EMI) **6**:745–6
    and Newton's rings **9**:1243
    in rainbows **14**:1934
    sound waves **15**:2134; **19**:2673
interferometry **2**:177; **8**:1022; **9**:1214
    holographic **8**:1083
    schlieren **15**:2031
    space telescopes and **17**:2382
    for testing lenses **9**:1243
    Twyman-Green **12**:1727
interferon **2**:263; **3**:380; **7**:*977*;
    8:1133, 1137
    computer graphics model **5**:*599*
intergalactic medium (IGM) **2**:175
interleukin-2 **3**:380
intermetallic compounds **1**:104;
    10:*1351*
intermodulation distortion **8**:1073–4
internal combustion engines
    9:**1169–76**
    cooling systems **6**:801–2; **8**:*1055*
    crankshaft **9**:1173; **18**:2489
    cylinder configuration **9**:1172–3
    design **9**:1172–4
    development of **9**:1169–71
    future **9**:1176
    diesel *see* diesel engines
    emission-control systems **9**:1176
    four-stroke **9**:1169, 1170, 1171
    fuel injection **7**:**937–9**; **9**:*1171–2*
    fuel pumps **7**:937–8
    gasoline **7**:938, 939; **9**:1176
    invention **2**:198
    for marine propulsion **10**:1336
        inboard and outboard **16**:2206,
            2208
    starter motor **15**:*2125*; **16**:2241
    stratified-charge **9**:1176
    and transmission systems **18**:2489
    two-stroke **9**:1170, 1171, 1292
        motorcycle **11**:1489
    valves **9**:1173–4
        and cams **3**:*362*
        exhaust **18**:2568
        manufacture **1**:101
    Wankel **9**:1170–1, *1173*, 1175–6
    see also automobiles, engine; gas
        turbines; superchargers and
        turbochargers
international date line **9**:1215
International Space Station (ISS)
    1:43; **14**:*1955*, 1956; **15**:*2056*,
    2153
    construction **16**:2169, 2173
    detected for damage **15**:2155
    science programs **16**:2174–5
    and telemetry **17**:*2364*
International Ultraviolet Explorer
    (IUE) **2**:174
Internet **4**:537, 539–40; **9**:**1177–82**
    in 3-D **11**:1503
    addresses **9**:1180
    animation on **1**:140
    browers **9**:1180–1
    future **9**:1182
    history of **9**:1178–9
    Internet microwaves **11**:1450
    newspaper production and
        11:1516–17, 1519
    and riot control **14**:1971
    search engines **2**:170–1; **9**:*1180*,
        1181, 1279
    via cable networks **3**:*354*
    and viruses **4**:531
    webcams and **18**:2592
    see also e-mail; World Wide Web

Internet service providers (ISPs)
    4:526; **9**:1178–9, 1180; **10**:1325
    and e-mail interception **6**:762
    modems and **11**:1474
    protocols **11**:1475
intestines
    large **5**:644–5
    small **5**:*642*, 643–4
intrauterine devices (IUDs) **13**:1818
Invar **1**:106; **11**:1524
inversion (hydrolysis of sucrose)
    16:2295
inversion (molecular motion) **9**:1212
invertase **5**:643; **6**:841
invertebrates, paleontology
    12:1634–5
invert syrup **3**:389
in-vitro culturing **2**:266
in-vitro fertilization ("test tube baby"
    method) **7**:980; **11**:1564
Io (moon) **11**:*1520*; **15**:2121
iodine **8**:1036
    isotopes **8**:1036; **14**:1907, 1908,
        1921
    preparation **8**:*1035*
    sublimation **5**:*664*
ion channels **3**:413
ion exchange
    chromatography **4**:471
    for desalination **5**:625
    for lens surfaces **9**:*1225*
    to soften water **19**:2656
ionic materials
    solids **4**:443, 555–6; **9**:1163
    solutions **4**:556
ionic propulsion units **9**:*1184*
ionization detectors, in smoke detec-
    tors **6**:863
ionization potential **2**:248
ionizers **9**:1184
ionosphere **1**:62; **9**:*1183*
ions and ionization **9**:**1183–4**
    ionization
        chemical **9**:1183
        of gases **4**:555; **5**:655–6; **9**:1184;
            13:*1762–3*
        ionizing radiation **9**:*1183*, 1184
        to measure vacuums **18**:2559–60
        see also particle detectors; plasma
            physics
    ions
        in the atmosphere **9**:1184
        and electrolysis **6**:737; **9**:1184
        and electromagnetic fields
            9:1184
        molecular **4**:448; **10**:1344
Iran–Iraq War, chemical weapons
    4:439
iridium **10**:1395; **13**:1781, 1782
    isotopes **14**:1921
iris **6**:830; **9**:1240
    recognition **2**:192; **9**:1269
iron *see* iron and steel
iron (II) chloride (ferrous chloride)
    12:1616
iron (III) chloride (ferric chloride)
    9:1188
iron disulfide (iron pyrite) **8**:1024
iron (III) oxide (ferric oxide) **9**:1188;
    12:1628
    hydrated (rust) **4**:570; **9**:1188;
        12:1617, 1621; **17**:2325–6
    inks **5**:584
    on magnetic tapes **10**:1311
    and thermic lances **17**:2412
iron and steel **9**:**1185–90**
    corrosion **4**:569, 570; **12**:1621
        prevention **4**:571
    iron
        burning in oxygen **12**:1617
        cast (pig iron) **1**:106; **7**:942;
            9:*1185*, 1187–8; **17**:2448

compounds **9**:1188
    effect of bacteria on **7**:982
    manufacture **3**:391, *392*
    ores **9**:1185–6; **11**:1458
    physical properties **9**:1185
    pipes **13**:*1749*
    powder **1**:105
    production **9**:1186–8
    recycling **14**:1940
    ships carrying ore **5**:671; **9**:1190
    world production of ore **11**:1458
    wrought **9**:1187
steel **1**:106; **9**:1188
    abrasion of **1**:*18*
    austenitic **13**:1830
    for boat building **2**:277
    bridges **3**:329, 330
    in buildings **3**:335–6, 337;
        15:2091, 2095
    in bulletproof jackets **2**:163
    cans **3**:382, 383
    carbon content **9**:1189
    casting **3**:*403*; **9**:1190
    chromium **4**:473
    heat treatment of **1**:104;
        10:1387
    high-tensile **13**:1749
    history **9**:1188–9
    mild **13**:1749; **19**:*2640*
    pipes **13**:1749, *1751*, 1753, 1754
    plastic coated **17**:*2322*
    production **9**:1188–90; **12**:*1617*,
        1619
    recycling **14**:1940
    refining **9**:*1189*, 1190
    for reinforced concrete **3**:329,
        420; **4**:547
    stainless **4**:473, 570; **11**:1523–4
    tin-free (TFS) **3**:383
    tin-plated **3**:382, 383; **4**:571
    tool **4**:507–8
    transportation **7**:929
irrigation techniques **9**:**1191–4**;
    18:2570
see also hydroponics
ISDN *see* modems and ISDN
islands of stability **6**:766
isobars **10**:1399
isobutylene (methylpropene)
    14:2001
isocyanides **11**:1527
isoflurane **1**:132
isolators **13**:1837
isomerases **6**:810
isomerism
    alcohols **1**:98
    geometric **4**:455
    polarimeters and **13**:*1793*
isoprene, polymers **14**:1997, 2001
ISO standards **14**:1879
isostatic pressing **3**:427
    hot (hipping) **3**:*404*
isotherms **17**:2422
isotopes **6**:763–4
    carbon *see* carbon, isotopes
    and mass spectrometry **10**:1344
    radioactive **11**:1547
    scanning using **2**:281; **3**:378
    to label organic compounds **2**:251
    uranium *see* uranium, isotopes
ISPs *see* Internet service providers
item coding **3**:401
ITER (International Thermonuclear
    Experimental Reactor) **6**:797

J

jackets, flak **2**:163
jackhammers **9**:1195; **13**:*1840*
jacks *see* actuators
Jacquard, Joseph Marie **4**:523;
    9:1281–2

jamming techniques **16**:2250–3
　active **16**:2250–3
　passive **16**:2253–4
Jansky, Karl **14**:1909
Janssen, Pierre **11**:1528
jaundice **6**:784
　neonatal **12**:1724
jejunum **5**:643
Jenner, Edward **8**:1132; **18**:2554
jersey **8**:1091
JET (Joint European Torus) **7**:947–8
jet cars **14**:1892
jetfoils **8**:1117
jetliners **1**:83–4; **2**:213
jets (atmospheric phenomena) **17**:2431
jet streams, balloons in **2**:221
jewelry
　enameling **6**:780
　gold **8**:1016
　platinum and palladium **13**:1783
　see also stone cutting
jigsaws **19**:2717
Joides Resolution (ship) **11**:1568
jointers **19**:2717–18
Joint European Torus (JET) **7**:947–8
Joint Photographic Experts Group
　(JPEG) **4**:534; **12**:1594
joints (body parts)
　artificial **2**:254, 255–6; **10**:1352;
　　17:2332; **18**:2504
　examined by endoscopes *see*
　　arthroscopy
　movement **3**:297–8
　shoulder **9**:*1234*
joints (mechanical)
　adhesive **1**:28–9
　Hooke **18**:2544
　in plumbing pipework **13**:*1786*,
　　1787
　universal **18**:2544–5
　　constant-velocity **18**:2544–5
　woodworking **19**:*2716*
Joliot, Frédéric **14**:1905
Josephson junctions **17**:*2312*, 2313,
　2314
Joule, James **6**:786
joules **6**:790
journalism, electronic **17**:2389
joysticks, computer **4**:535; **11**:1492
JPEG (Joint Photographic Experts
　Group) **4**:534; **12**:1594
Judson, Whitcomb **6**:835
juke boxes **9**:**1196–7**
Julia sets **3**:431
jumbo jets **1**:84; **2**:*212*, 213
junks **14**:2009–10
Jupiter **13**:1757, 1758, 1760;
　15:2118, 2121
　auroras **14**:*1900*; **15**:2121
　moons **9**:*1235*; **11**:*1520*; **14**:*1900*;
　　15:2121–2
　eclipses **5**:710
jute **6**:849, 850

K

Kalashnikov AK47 (machine gun)
　2:196
　ammunition **2**:*216*
kaolin *see* china clay
kapok **6**:849
karats **8**:1016
Kariba Dam **19**:*2667*
Kay, John **16**:*2212*
keels **2**:274
　bilge **16**:2232
keelsons **2**:274
Kekulé, Friederich A. **8**:1108
Kelvin, Baron *see* Thomson, William
Kelvin (absolute) temperature scale
　17:2395, 2396, 2414

Kennedy Space Center **12**:1600
Kepler, Johannes **8**:1020; **15**:2157;
　16:2301
　and planetary orbits **12**:1599
　third law **11**:1521
keratin **15**:2087
keratinocytes **15**:2087, 2089
keratoconus **4**:560
kerogen **11**:1572
kerosene **5**:687; **8**:1106; **11**:1575,
　1579
ketones **4**:456
Kevlar **1**:44; **2**:220; **6**:852; **7**:880;
　13:1805, 1806; **17**:2405
　uses **13**:*1805*, 1806
　　on boat hulls **13**:*1771*, *1804*
　　clothing and textiles **2**:163;
　　　3:295; **13**:1806, 1860
　　in sailboards **14**:2006
keyboards
　computer **4**:527, 535
　piano or organ **11**:1507
　synthesizer **17**:2344
key-cutting machines **9**:**1198**
keypads, itemized **3**:400–1
keystones **18**:2574
kidneys
　artificial (dialyzers) **5**:634–5
　failure **5**:633; **18**:2549
　functions **5**:633, *634*
　radiological tests **14**:1918–19
　removal **17**:2332
　stones **18**:2532, 2549, *2550*
　structure **5**:*634*
　transplants **6**:782; **18**:2498, 2499
　see also dialysis machines
kieselguhr **6**:827
kilns **7**:940; **9**:**1199–1200**
　for brick manufacture **3**:323, 324
　for cement manufacture **3**:418–19;
　　9:1200
　for china and porcelain manufac-
　　ture **4**:467
　continuous **3**:323, 324; **9**:1200
　low-temperature **9**:1199–1200
kimberlite **5**:637, 638
kinases **2**:251
kinematics **5**:694
kinetic energy (KE) attack **1**:119
kinetics **9**:**1201–3**
　chemical reaction **4**:464; **9**:1202
　kinetic theory of gases **7**:960–1;
　　9:1203
　see also momentum
Kirchhoff, G. R. **9**:1159
klystrons **6**:741, *745*, 751; **14**:1895–6
knitting
　cotton **5**:582
　see also hosiery and knitware
　　manufacture
knots **11**:1510–11
Koch, Robert **10**:1367, 1409
Köler illumination **12**:1716
König, Friedrich **13**:1849
Koppers-Totzek process **7**:956
Krebs cycle (citric acid cycle; TCA
　cycle) **10**:1374, 1375, 1376
krill **7**:875
Krupp guns **8**:1027
krypton **11**:1529
krypton difluoride **11**:1529
Kuiper Belt **2**:176; **13**:1761
Kyoto Protocol **6**:807, 808

L

laboratories
　hospital, electronic apparatus
　　6:758
　underwater **18**:*2538*, 2539–40
lacquers and varnishes **9**:**1204–5**

lacquers **9**:1204, 1205
　manufacture **9**:1205
　varnishes **9**:1204, *1205*
　　manufacture **9**:1205
　　on paintings **13**:1741, 1742–3
　　solvents **13**:1823
　　uses **3**:385; **9**:1205
lactic acid
　chirality **4**:457
　and fermentation **6**:842
　in milk **7**:905
　in muscles **6**:840
Lactobacillus bulgaricus **5**:603; **7**:904
lactoferrin **1**:131; **2**:266
lactose **3**:389; **5**:600, 602
ladybugs **12**:1677, 1678
Laënnec, René **16**:2265
Lamarck, Jean Baptiste de **6**:822;
　12:1633, 1634
lambda (virus) **11**:1480
lambda sensors **2**:203
lampreys **12**:1645
lamps (lights)
　arc **9**:1247; **17**:2342
　cutoff **14**:1980
　filament **9**:1210
　fluorescent **5**:*656*, 657–8; **9**:1245;
　　10:1302
　infrared **6**:743
　mercury vapor **5**:658; **14**:1980
　metal-halide **5**:658; **10**:1302
　neon **4**:555; **5**:*656*, 657; **11**:*1529*
　semicutoff **14**:1980
　sodium **5**:*655*, 658; **6**:743–4;
　　10:1302
　　street lights **1**:101; **5**:658; **6**:858;
　　　14:1980
　surgical **11**:1583–4
　ultraviolet *see* ultraviolet lamps
　see also discharge tubes; lightbulbs
land, drainage **5**:673–4; **19**:2695
landfill **14**:*1939*; **19**:2640–2
　cleaning waste water from **12**:1610
　reclamation **9**:1207–8
land reclamation **9**:**1206–8**; **19**:2695
Landsat satellites **1**:35; **6**:*743*;
　10:1330; **17**:2337
landslides **5**:707; **6**:*816*
Landsteiner, Karl **17**:2328
Langerhans, islets of **10**:1375;
　13:1734
language *see* speech and language
La Niña **4**:479; **15**:2029
LANs (local-area networks) **4**:526,
　537, 538–9, 541
lanthanides (rare earth elements)
　12:1673; **18**:2487, 2488
lanthanum **18**:2485, 2487
laparoscopy **6**:785; **17**:2331–2;
　18:2549
laptops (laptop computers) **4**:526;
　19:2720
Large Magellanic Cloud **2**:180;
　17:*2316*
large-scale integration (LSI) *see* inte-
　grated circuits
Large Zenith Telescope (LZT)
　11:1464
Lartigue, C. F. M. T. **11**:1481, 1482
laryngophones **1**:22
larynx **10**:1303
　endoscopic surgery **12**:*1612*, 1613
　papillomata **12**:1613
Laserdisc (video disc) **5**:649, 650
　manufacture **5**:651
lasers and masers **9**:**1209–14**
　lasers **9**:1237, *1239*
　　and antiaircraft guns **1**:144
　　as anti-ballistic weapons
　　　16:2183
　　as antisatellite weapons
　　　16:2181–2

argon gas **12**:1590; **17**:2332
atom **9**:1214
and chemical bonds **4**:*461*
and compact discs (CDs)
　4:515–16
and digital versatile discs (DVDs)
　5:650
excimer **9**:1213; **10**:1418;
　12:1590
and fiber optics **4**:542; **9**:1214;
　17:2371
and fingerprinting **7**:*917*
gas **9**:1212–13
and holography *see* holography,
　laser
for interferometry **9**:1214
ion **9**:1213
laserguide rangefinders **2**:*249*,
　250
and magneto-optical discs **5**:613,
　614–15
as nonlethal weapons **11**:1534
reflectors **14**:1944
ring **8**:1146
semiconductor **9**:1213, 1214;
　15:2054
solid-state **9**:*1209*, 1212
to guide bombs **2**:284
to guide missiles **11**:1468
used in bar-code scanners **3**:401
used for cancer treatment
　12:*1613*
used for dentistry **5**:622
used in flow cytometry **10**:1333
used for gem identification
　9:1243
used as machine tools **9**:*1213*,
　1214; **10**:*1363*
used in nuclear fusion **7**:*946*,
　947, 948; **9**:1214
used in printing **9**:*1263*;
　13:*1850*, *1852*
used in stage lighting **16**:2234
used in surgery **6**:785, *856*;
　9:1214; **11**:1564; **12**:1590,
　1613; **13**:1767; **17**:2330, 2332
used in surveying **9**:1214;
　12:1707; **17**:*2337*
used in tunneling **18**:2516
used in uranium enrichment
　18:2548
used in velocity or flow deter-
　mination **9**:1214
used in welding **10**:1383–4
masers **9**:1209
　ammonia **9**:1211–12
　rubies used in **5**:599; **9**:1211, 1212
laterite **15**:2112
latex **14**:1997, 1998
lathes **10**:1306–8; **19**:2716
　automatic **10**:1308; **15**:2032
　CNC **18**:*2465*
　diamond **5**:639
　geometric **5**:583
　jewelers' **10**:1308
　for making screws **15**:2032
　turret **10**:1307; **15**:2032
　vertical **2**:*238*
latitude and longitude **9**:**1215–16**
　see also sextants
latrines **18**:2457
laughing gas (nitrous oxide) **1**:131;
　11:1527
launch vehicles **14**:1991
laundry **9**:**1217–18**
Lavoisier, Antoine **4**:449; **6**:763, 788;
　12:1618; **15**:2076
lawrencium **6**:765
L-dopa **12**:1684
leaching, used in fluid mining
　11:1462
lead **9**:**1219–21**

alloys 9:1221
compounds 9:1221
and health 9:1221
occurrence and extraction 9:1219
properties 9:1221
red 9:1221; 12:1628
refining 9:1219–21
uses 9:1221
pipes 13:1751, 1787
roofing 9:1220
white 12:1628
lead azide 6:827; 9:1221; 11:1527
lead carbonate 9:1221
lead chromate 9:1221
lead sulfide 9:1219, 1220
lead tetraethyl see tetraethyl lead
lead–tin–antimony alloys 1:104
lead zirconate titanate (PZT) 3:426;
10:1352, 1364; 13:1745
leather 9:1222–4; 13:1860
aniline 9:1224
chamois 9:1223
dyeing 5:690; 9:1223–4
patent 9:1224
suede 9:1224
tanning 4:473; 9:1223
leaves, structure 12:1719, 1721
Leblanc process 4:450
lecithin 4:500
Leclanché cells 2:226–7; 4:486
Leclerc, Georges-Louis 12:1633
LEDs see diodes, light-emitting
Leeuwenhoek, Antonie van 10:1367,
1434; 13:1733
legs
artificial 2:253–4
bone transplants 18:2504
leishmaniasis 8:1136
Lenoir, J. J. Étienne 2:198; 9:1169
lens-cleaning cloths 6:853
lenses 9:1225–30
achromatic 17:2377
camera see cameras, lenses
contact 4:560–3
eye 6:830, 832; 9:1240
uncorrected 9:1241
focal length 9:1226
focal ratio (f numbers) 9:1227
Fresnel 9:1240, 1248; 14:1983;
17:2409
"gravitational" 4:572, 576
oil immersion 10:1434
in refractor telescopes 11:1561
slide projector 13:1855
spectacle 9:1230; 16:2192
types
anamorphic 11:1495; 13:1855
compound 9:1226
concave (negative lenses)
9:1225, 1226
convex (positive lenses)
9:1225–6
planoconcave 9:1226
uncorrected 9:1241
video camera 18:2589–90
Lenz's law 8:1138
Leonardo da Vinci
bicycle 2:240
clock 4:483
and fossils 12:1632–3
and friction 7:933
hygrometer 8:1123
Last Supper restored 13:1741,
1742, 1743
lathes 19:2716
lock gates 3:373; 9:1266
looms 9:1280–1
Leonids 10:1393
leprosy, treatment 18:2555
leptons 6:769–70
tau 6:769, 770
leukemia 2:273; 3:379; 12:1661

treatment 12:1687; 13:1866;
14:1920
leveling 17:2335–6
levels, spirit 18:2464–5
lever escapement mechanism 4:483
levers 9:1231
Leyden jars 6:725
ley lines 16:2275
libraries 8:1149, 1150
robotics in 5:612
LIDAR (light detection and ranging)
13:1797
Liebig, Justus von 11:1463
lie detection 13:1807–8
life 9:1232–5
conditions artificially created
9:1235
definitions 9:1232–3
development on Earth 1:62–3;
5:700; 6:823; 9:1234–5;
10:1412; 12:1633–4
extraterrestrial? 4:446; 9:1235;
15:2121
lifeboats 15:2038–40, 2050–1
inshore 15:2040–1
life expectancy 13:1819
lifejackets, adjustable buoyancy 5:666
life rafts 5:712; 15:2040
life-support systems, in submersibles
16:2293–4
lift 1:38, 66, 70
lifting wheels 5:638
ligands 2:251, 252
ligases 6:810
ligatures 17:2329
light see light and optics
lightbulbs 9:1244–6
fluorescent 5:656, 657–8; 9:1245;
10:1302
manufacture 9:1246
tungsten–halogen lamps
(quartz–iodine bulbs) 9:1245
see also lamps (lights)
lighthouses and lightships 9:1247–9;
11:1514
lighting
circuits, domestic 19:2707–8
stage (theatrical) 16:2233, 2234;
17:2409–11
street see street lighting
television-production 17:2386,
2387
lightning 4:555; 6:725; 17:2428–30
ball 17:2431
lightning conductors 9:1250–1
light and optics 4:510; 9:1236–43
light 12:1728
affected by gravity 8:1021–2;
14:1954
amplification 8:1128
and the atmosphere 1:63
black 16:2234; 18:2534
coherent and incoherent
9:1210–11, 1239
diffraction 5:641; 9:1238
dispersion 5:641
frequency 6:739
interaction with matter
9:1209–10, 1241–2; 14:1881
monochromatic 9:1237
particle nature 9:1236, 1237;
14:1880
polarized see polarization (light)
pollution 13:1803
quanta see photons
shortest pulse achieved 9:1243
speed of 5:710; 6:739, 788;
9:1237, 1238, 1240–1; 14:1950
treatment of medical conditions
using 12:1723–4
wavelength 5:641; 9:1237
wavelike nature 5:641; 9:1236;

14:1880; 19:2673–4
wave–particle duality 14:1881
white 9:1237; 13:1853
see also interference; reflection;
refraction; vision
optics 9:1241–2
geometric 9:1241
holographic 8:1082
manufacture of optical components 9:1242–3
physical 9:1241
quantum 9:1241–2
see also color; fiber optics; lenses;
prisms; quantum theory, and light
light pens 4:535; 11:1492
light-rail systems 16:2278
Docklands Light Railway 10:1348;
14:1925; 16:2278
lights see lamps
lightships 9:1249
lignite 4:494
Lilienthal, Otto 2:210
limbs
artificial 2:253–5
reattachment 10:1439; 13:1765–6
transplanting 10:1439; 18:2504
lime see calcium hydroxide; calcium
oxide
limestone
cave decorations 16:2239
crushed 14:1885
uses 7:901
limonite 9:1186
Limpet (wave-energy device)
19:2676
Lindane 12:1676
Lindbergh, Charles 2:213
Lindow Man 4:477
linear accelerators see particle accelerators, linear
linear motors 6:732; 9:1252–6
tubular 9:1253
see also maglev (magnetic-
levitation) vehicles
linen 17:2404, 2408
flame-resistant 7:881
line synchronizing (line sync) signals
17:2392
Linnaeus, Carl 12:1632
linoleum (lino) 7:892, 894
Linotype machines 5:630; 13:1849
linseed oil 9:1204
and linoleum 7:892
in paints 12:1628
lipases 5:643; 6:836
liposuction 13:1767
Lippershey, Hans 11:1560; 17:2380
lips, cleft lip and palate 13:1766–7
liquefaction
of gases 1:63
air 1:64; 5:590
liquefied petrolem gas 2:200
liqueurs 5:661; 16:2217
liquid cooling garments (LCGs)
16:2177
liquid crystal displays (LCDs) 5:647,
648; 9:1258–9
uses 9:1259
in calculators 3:361
in projectors 13:1855
for screens and monitors 4:532;
9:1259
in watches 5:646; 19:2649, 2650
liquid crystals 4:551; 9:1257–9;
10:1352, 1362
see also liquid crystal displays
liquid petroleum gas (LPG) 7:955,
959; 8:1106
from oil refining 11:1577
a vehicle fuel 2:200; 3:343
liquid propane gas, a vehicle fuel
7:959

liquids 4:550; 10:1359, 1361
boiling point 18:2569–70
elasticity 5:713
electrical conduction 6:728
microencapsulated 10:1413
pressure applied to 8:1109
specific gravity 5:616–17
see also hydrodynamics; surface
tension
Lissajous patterns 12:1608
Lister, Sir Joseph 10:1367; 17:2328
litharge 9:1221
lithium 1:99–100
lithium-6 11:1553, 1554
in stars 13:1761
lithium-7 2:182
production 1:99–100
lithium carbonate 1:99; 4:452
lithium chloride 8:1123
lithium deuteride 11:1554
lithium hydride 1:99; 8:1119
lithium tantalate, piezoelectric 5:599
lithography 5:630; 9:1260–4;
13:1849–50, 1851–2
lithographic development of films
12:1713
offset 9:1263–4; 13:1847, 1848,
1850, 1852
web offset 9:1264; 11:1517–18;
13:1850
heat-set 13:1850
see also photolithography; printing;
stereolithography
lithosphere 5:697; 13:1777, 1778–9
lithotripsy 18:2549, 2550, 17:2330
litmus 12:1692
Little Boy (atomic bomb) 11:1552
liver transplants 18:2498
from animals 13:1734
lividity 12:1659
load 13:1825
load cells 2:215
loading gauge 14:1923
local-area networks (LANs) 4:526,
537, 538–9, 541
lock-and-block signaling 14:1924
Lockheed F-104 Starfighter (aircraft)
17:2319
Lockheed-Martin X-35 (aircraft)
18:2553
Lockheed SR-71 Blackbird (aircraft)
17:2319
locks (in waterways)
at docks 5:668, 669; 9:1266
canal 3:373, 375–6; 9:1265–6
construction 9:1266
locks (security) 9:1267–9
safe 14:2005
locomotives and power cars
9:1270–4
diesel locomotives 9:1272
electric locomotives 9:1273
gas turbine powered 9:1273
steam locomotives 9:1270–2, 1274
see also traction engines; trains
lodestones 10:1314; 11:1510, 1514
logarithms 9:1275–6; 10:1357
logic 9:1277–9
fluid see fluidics
fuzzy see fuzzy logic
in microprocessors 9:1277;
10:1427–8
logic gates 6:754
London, underground (subway;
"tube") 10:1346–7, 1349
London dispersion forces 4:444
longbows 3:306–8
longitude 4:488; 9:1215–16; 11:1511;
15:2062
longwall working 4:496–7
looms 9:1280–3
Jacquard 4:523; 7:894; 9:1281–2

looms (*cont.*)
    rug and carpet **7**:893; **9**:*1280*
loran (long-range-navigation system)
    11:1511–12
    for aircraft **1**:67
    for fishing vessels **7**:872–3
Lorenz, Edward **3**:430
Lorenz attractor **3**:430
Lorenz transformations **14**:1952–3
lost-wax process **3**:403–4
Lotus 38 (racing car) **14**:1892
loudspeakers **9**:**1284–5**
    electrostatic **9**:*1284*, 1285
    flat-panel **9**:1285
    hi-fi **8**:1071–2, *1074*
    moving-coil **9**:1284, *1285*
    public-address **1**:*126*
    ribbon **9**:1285
Love waves **15**:2048
low-emission road vehicles **9**:**1286–8**
    electric **2**:200, 201; **5**:720; **6**:794–5;
      9:1286–7
    hybrid-powered vehicles **5**:720;
      9:1288
    hydrogen-powered **2**:200; **8**:1119;
      9:1287–8
    zero-level emission vehicles
      (ZLEVs) **2**:201
    see also automobiles, alternative
      power sources
low-energy electron diffraction
    (LEED) **15**:2129
LP (long-playing) records **12**:1696
LSD (lysergic acid diethylamide)
    4:437
lubrication **9**:**1289–92**
    of bearings **2**:231; **9**:1289
    of dental drills **5**:621
lumber **9**:**1293–6**
    drying **9**:1199–1200, 1295
    see also forestry
lumens **9**:1244
Lumière, Auguste and Jean **13**:1854
luminance meters **12**:1705
luminescence **10**:**1301–2**
    see also fluorescence; phosphores-
      cence
luminous flux **12**:1705
Luna space probes **15**:2157
lungs **10**:**1303–5**
    cancer **3**:*378*; **6**:847; **10**:1305;
      11:1529; **12**:*1655*
    radiological tests **14**:1918
    transplants **18**:2499
Lurgi process **7**:*957*, 959
luteinizing hormone (LH) **8**:1086
lutes **16**:2282
lutetium **18**:2487
lutetium texaphyrin **12**:1723–4
lyases **6**:810
Lycra **6**:853
Lyell, Sir Charles **6**:822; **7**:987
Lyman, Theodore **2**:183
lymph nodes **3**:377, 378
lymphocytes **8**:*1132*, 1133, 1134–5,
    1136, *1137*
    and graft versus host disease
      18:2503
lyre family **16**:2283
lysosomes **3**:411
lysozyme **8**:1132, 1136

M

M16 (automatic rifle) **2**:196; **14**:1969
M60 (machine gun) **2**:196
M87 (galaxy) **10**:*1362*; **17**:*2443*
Maas River, damming of **7**:891
MacAdam, John **14**:1973
McDonnell Douglas DC-9 **1**:84
Mace (CN gas) **11**:1532; **14**:1972
Mach, Ernst **8**:1143; **17**:2318

machine code **10**:1428
machine guns *see* automatic weapons
    and machine guns
machine pistols *see* submachine guns
machine presses **10**:1306, 1310
machine tools **10**:**1306–10**, 1338
    and cam systems **3**:362
    clutches in **4**:492
    cutters used in **18**:2465
    diamond **5**:639
    drill presses **10**:1310
    electrochemical machining
      6:**735–6**; **10**:1310
    flypresses **7**:903
    grinding machines **10**:1309–10
    jig borers **10**:1310
    lasers as **9**:*1213*, 1214; **10**:*1363*
    machine presses **10**:1306, 1310
    mechanical machining **6**:735;
      10:1306–10
    milling machines **10**:1309, *1310*
    surfacing tools **10**:1308–9
    ultrasound machining **10**:1310
    see also lathes; woodworking
Mach numbers **1**:38; **17**:2318;
    19:*2697*, 2699
    cut-off **17**:2319
McLeod gauges **10**:1326
macronutrients **11**:1557
macrophages **8**:1132
macula **6**:831; **12**:1589
Maddox, R.L. **12**:1708
madeira **19**:2703
Magellan (spacecraft) **15**:2119–20,
    2121; **17**:2337
magic lanterns **13**:1854
magic numbers **6**:766
maglev (magnetic-levitation) vehicles
    passenger links **5**:719; **10**:1349
    trains **5**:717, 719; **7**:934; **9**:*1252*,
      1254, 1255–6; **10**:1349, *1363*,
      1364–5; **14**:1928; **17**:2310, 2314
magma **12**:1680
magnesia *see* magnesium oxide
magnesium
    burning in air **12**:1617
    extraction **6**:738; **10**:1378
    and flash photography **3**:365
    reaction with chlorine **12**:1616
magnesium oxide (magnesia) **3**:424,
    426
magnesium sulfate, hydrated (Epsom
    salts) **5**:*598*
magnetic flux **6**:748
magnetic resonance imaging (MRI)
    2:282; **3**:312; **4**:448; **5**:718;
    11:1540, *1541*; **12**:1657;
    14:*1966*
magnetic tapes and films **2**:186–7;
    10:**1311–12**
    for computers **5**:612–13
    digital **1**:129
    DATs *see* digital audio tapes
    materials **10**:1311
    video tape **10**:1312
magnetism **10**:**1313–17**; **18**:2486–8
    and dating pottery **2**:159
    diamagnetism **18**:2486
    Earth's **10**:1316–17; **13**:1777
      of rocks in the past (paleomag-
        netism) **7**:990, *991*, 992–3;
        10:1317; **13**:1777
      and the solar wind **14**:*1900*
    and electron spin **10**:1315–16
    ferromagnetism **10**:1314, 1315;
      18:2486–8
    hysteresis loops **10**:1314–15
    magnetic circuits **10**:1313
    paramagnetism **18**:2486
    permanent magnets **10**:1313–14;
      12:1727
magnetite, in humans **16**:2275

magnetohydrodynamics (MHD)
    10:**1318–19**
    propulsion using **5**:719–20;
      10:1319, 1337
magnetometers **2**:156–7; **7**:992;
    10:1320; **11**:1571
    fluxgate **10**:1320
    Hall effect **10**:1320
    proton **7**:992; **10**:1320
magnetomotive force (mmf) **6**:748;
    7:971; **10**:1313; **14**:1961;
    18:2477
magneto-optical discs **5**:*613*, 614–15
magnetorheological fluids **10**:1353
magnetos **8**:1124, 1127
    flywheel **8**:1125
magnetosphere **14**:1899, 1900
magnetostatic energy **10**:1316
magnetostriction **18**:2530
    energy **10**:1316
magnetrons **6**:741, 751
    in microwave ovens **11**:1448–9
    and radar transmission **14**:1895,
      1896
magnification **9**:1227
magnifying mechanisms **13**:1843
magnox reactors **11**:1546
mail-sorting machinery **10**:**1321–5**
Maiman, Theodore **9**:1211, 1212
malaria **18**:2555
    spread **12**:*1644*, 1646
malathion **12**:1700
malnutrition **10**:1370; **11**:1558
maltase **1**:98; **5**:643; **6**:810, 842
maltose **3**:389; **6**:842
mammals
    evolution **6**:825
    pheromones **12**:1691
    reproduction **14**:1959
Mandala machines **19**:2604
Mandelbrot, Benoit **3**:430, 431
Mandelbrot sets **3**:*430*, 431
M-and-E (music and effects) tracks
    11:1500
manganate (VII) salts **4**:443
manganese
    oxidation numbers **12**:1616
    seafloor nodules, mining **11**:1462
manganese carbonyl **18**:2488
manganese dioxide **3**:324
Manhattan Project **11**:1554
manifolds **2**:205
manipulators *see* remote handling
Manly, Charles **1**:72
Manned Maneuvering Unit (MMU)
    16:2169, 2178
Mannesmann process **13**:*1751*
manometers **10**:1326; **13**:1840;
    16:2211
    sphygmomanometers **10**:1326;
      16:**2211**
mantle, Earth's **5**:697
manures **6**:843–4
    excess nitrates from **1**:54
    green **6**:844
maps
    geochemical **7**:982
    geological **7**:989–90
    mapmaking techniques
      10:**1327–31**
      photogrammetry **10**:1329
      12:*1706–7*; **17**:2334
      see also surveying
    ocean floor **7**:*991*; **11**:1565;
      15:*2127*, 2128; **18**:2531
    weather **10**:*1398*
    see also charts
marble **7**:981
Marconi, Guglielmo **1**:142; **11**:1511;
    17:2392; **18**:2493
Marianas Trench **1**:69; **10**:1333;
    11:1566

pressure at **11**:1568
marijuana (cannabis), identification
    7:917–18
marine biology **10**:**1332–3**; **11**:1567,
    1569; **18**:2540
    and sonar **15**:*2126*, 2128
    see also oceanography
marine engineering **10**:1365–6
marine propulsion **10**:**1334–7**,
    1365–6
    propellers **10**:1337; **13**:1858, 1859
    torpedoes **18**:2467–8
    using magnetohydrodynamics
      5:719–20; **10**:1319, 1337
Mariner space probes **15**:2156, 2159
    Mariner 9 **15**:2159
marine salvage **15**:**2021–3**
marquetry **18**:2578–9
Mars **13**:1757; **15**:2118, 2120–1
    future bases on? **16**:*2171*
    life on? **4**:*446*; **9**:1235; **15**:2121
    mapping **12**:1707; **17**:2337
    rovers on **15**:2158
Mars Global Surveyor (MGS)
    12:1707; **15**:2120
Mars Odyssey (space probe) **15**:*2156*,
    2157, 2158, 2160; **17**:2337
Mars Orbiting Laser Altimeter
    (MOLA) **12**:1707
marsupials **14**:1958
martensite **1**:104; **10**:1351, 1388
mass *see* energy, mass, and weight
mass–energy equation **2**:150, 179,
    248; **7**:876; **14**:1953; **17**:2415
    and nuclear mass **2**:248; **7**:876
mass number **14**:1906
mass production **1**:41–2; **10**:**1338–41**
    of automobiles **10**:1338, 1339,
      1341, *1380*
    of clocks **4**:486
    of clothes **4**:489–90
    die casting **10**:1389–90
    and ergonomics **6**:815
    of glass **4**:493
    using sewing machines **15**:2061
    see also assembly lines; conveyors
mass ratio **14**:1991
mass spectrometry **4**:*445*, 448;
    9:1184; **10**:**1342–4**
    accelerator (AMS) **2**:157
    gas chromatography and mass
      spectrometry (GCMS) **4**:471;
      5:684; **10**:1343
    ICP-MS (inductively coupled
      plasma-mass spectrometry)
      7:982
    ion-trap **4**:441
    and nuclear mass **2**:248
    uses **10**:1344
      for isotope identification
        10:1344
      to study rocks **12**:1680
mass transit and subways **10**:**1345–9**
    subways **10**:1346–7, 1349
      signaling **14**:1924–5
      ventilation in **8**:1060
    see also maglev (magnetic levita-
      tion) vehicles, trains; streetcars
master-slave systems **14**:1956
matches **12**:1700
matchlocks **2**:193; **8**:1024
materials science **10**:**1350–3**
    see also petrology
mathematics **10**:**1354–8**
    see also binary system; calculators;
      chaos theory; hexadecimal system;
      logarithms; sine waves; statistics
matrix displays **5**:646
    using light-emitting diodes
      (LEDs) **5**:*646*, 647
      full-color video displays (RGB
        displays) **5**:647

matrixing **15**:2148
matte paintings **16**:2187
matter
   dark **4**:575–6; **8**:*1021*
   law of conservation of **4**:449; **6**:788
   properties of **10**:*1359–62*
   wavelike properties **14**:1882;
     19:2674
   see also gases; liquids; plasma
     physics; solids; superfluids
matte shots **16**:2186–7
matting **16**:2237
Mauna Kea, telescopes on **11**:*1561*
Maurer variable-sequence cameras
   15:2152–3
mauveine (dye) **1**:133, 134; **4**:453;
   5:690
Maxim, Hiram
   and the Maxim gun **2**:193–4
   and powered flight **2**:211
Maxwell, James Clerk **6**:739, 748;
   9:1203, 1236
Maxwell's equations **6**:748
Maxwell–Boltzmann distribution
   9:1203; **18**:2569
Mayans
   astronomy **16**:2275
   numbers **10**:*1358*
   pyramids **11**:1560; **16**:2275
MDF (medium density fiberboard)
   19:2711
mean (average) **16**:2246, 2248
meat
   artificial **7**:913–14
   canned **7**:912
   curing **7**:905
mechanical advantage **9**:1231
mechanical engineering **10**:1363–6
mechanics
   dynamics **5**:694–5
     classical **5**:694; **12**:1725–6
     kinematics **5**:694
   quantum *see* quantum theory,
     quantum mechanics
   static **5**:694; **16**:*2242–5*
   statistical **4**:463; **12**:1728; **16**:2249;
     17:2416
mechanochemistry **10**:1420
median **16**:2248
medicine **10**:1367–70
   "alternative" **10**:1370
   electronics in **6**:756–8
   forensic **7**:919
   sports **16**:*2225–6*
   see also veterinary science and
     medicine
medicines *see* pharmaceuticals (medical drugs); pharmacology
medicine wheels **16**:2275
medium density fiberboard (MDF)
   19:2711
medium-scale integration (MSI) *see*
   integrated circuits
megaliths **16**:2273, 2274–5
meiosis **3**:*412*
Meissner, Walter **17**:2310
Meissner effect **17**:2310
meitnerium **6**:766
Meitner, Lise **7**:876
melamine-formaldehyde polymers
   13:1773
melanin **15**:2088
   in hair **8**:1033
melanocytes **15**:2088, *2089*
melanoma **6**:806
Méliès, Georges **16**:2185
Mellotron **17**:2344
membranes, semipermeable **12**:1609
membranophones **12**:1668–70
memory (personal) **3**:310
memory
   devices **9**:1167

modules **9**:1167
   see also computers, memory
memory cards (PC cards) **5**:615
Mendel, Gregor **6**:823; **7**:979
mendelevium **6**:765
Mendeleyev, Dmitri **4**:449; **12**:1671;
   18:2485
Ménière's disease **8**:1043
menopause **7**:997
menstrual disorders, sports and
   16:2226
Mercalli scale **15**:2049
Mercator, Gerardus **10**:1327
mercerization **6**:849
mercuric chloride **2**:226; **13**:1801
mercuric sulfate **10**:1372; **13**:1801
mercuric sulfide **10**:1371
Mercury (planet) **13**:1757; **15**:2118,
   2119
mercury (metal) **10**:1371–2
   alloys *see* amalgams
   extraction **10**:1371
   occurrence **10**:1371
   superconducting **17**:2309, 2314
   surface tension **10**:*1371*; **17**:2321
   toxicity **10**:1372; **12**:1659;
     13:1801; **16**:2197
   uses **10**:1371–2; **13**:1801
     in barometers **2**:222–3; **10**:*1372*
     in batteries **2**:227; **10**:1372
     in dental fillings **5**:620; **10**:1371
     in discharge lamps **5**:658;
       10:*1372*; **14**:1980; **18**:2533–4
     in liquid-mercury telescopes
       11:1464; **17**:2380
mercury cells, for preparation of
   chlorine **8**:1035
mercury fulminate (mercury II iso-
   cyanate) **6**:827; **8**:1024
meridian, prime **9**:1215
MERLIN (multi-element radio link
   interferometer network)
   14:1910
mesoderm **6**:777
mesons **6**:770, 772
   mu *see* muons
mesophyll, palisade and spongy
   12:1719, *1721*
mesothelioma **6**:847; **10**:1305
metabolic rate, and body size **2**:262
metabolism **6**:810; **10**:1373–6
   anabolism **6**:810; **10**:1376
   catabolism **6**:810; **10**:1373–5
metal cutting and joining
   10:1379–84
   brazing **10**:1380–1
   cutting **10**:1364
     electrochemical machining
       6:735–6; **10**:1310
     electrodischarge machining
       (EDM; spark erosion; spark
       machining) **6**:735, 736;
       10:*1364*,*1366*
     flame **10**:1379, 1380
     plasma-arc **10**:1364, 1379–80
     powder **10**:1379
     using lasers **9**:*1213*, 1214;
       10:*1363*, 1364
     using thermic lances **17**:2412
     water-jet **10**:1364
   riveting **10**:*1379*, 1384
   soldering **10**:1381–2
   see also welding
metal detectors **10**:1385–6
metallic glasses (amorphous alloys)
   1:107
metals **10**:1377–8
   alkali *see* alkali metals; alkaline
     earth
   bonds **4**:442, 444
   conserving **2**:160
   crystal structure **1**:102, *103*

drilling **5**:678–9
electrical conduction **4**:550, 556;
   17:2417–18
extraction **10**:1377–8
heavy **13**:1801
joints **1**:29
melting point, casting and **3**:404
rare earth *see* lanthanides
recycling **14**:1940–1
tests for, qualitative and quantitative **4**:446
transition *see* transition elements
see also alloys
metalworking **10**:1387–91
   brass working **3**:316–17
   drawing **3**:316; **10**:1390–1
     sheet metal **15**:*2064*
     tube **13**:1751–2
   forging **10**:1388–9
   heat treatment **10**:1387–8;
     18:2462
   rolling **10**:1391
   sheet metal **15**:*2064–6*
   smoothing and polishing, using
     electrochemical machining **6**:736
   tubular products **10**:1391
   see also casting; coins and minting;
     metal cutting and joining; pipe
     and tube manufacture; tool
     manufacture
Meteor Crater (Arizona) **10**:*1392*,
   1394
meteoroids **10**:1392
meteorology **10**:1396–1401
   thermometers for **17**:2424
   upper atmosphere studies **10**:1401
   weather
     fronts **10**:*1397, 1398*, 1400
     mapping and forecasting **6**:746;
       10:*1397–1400*, 1401; **14**:1898;
       15:*2028*
     modeling **3**:430
     observations **10**:1396–7
     records **4**:477
     virtual reality **4**:*534*
     see also clouds
   see also barometers; climatology;
     hurricanes and tornadoes; rain
     and rainfall; thunderstorms
meteors and meteorites **10**:1392–5;
   11:1568
   carbon-rich **3**:393
   craters **10**:*1392, 1393*, 1394, 1395
   from Mars **9**:1235; **15**:2121
meters
   electrical **10**:1402–3
   electricity **10**:1404–5; **19**:*2704*,
     2705
   gas **10**:1406
   parking **10**:1407
methacrylate esters **13**:1771
methacrylic acid (2-methylpropenoic
   acid) **12**:1629; **13**:1771
methane **4**:454; **8**:1105, 1106
   a biogas **2**:259–60
   bonding in **4**:*442*, 455
   in coal mines **4**:494
   in fuel cells **7**:936
   for hydrogen production **8**:1118
   induced dipoles **9**:1163
   as landfill gas **14**:*1939*
   liquefied, transportation **7**:929
   and the ozone layer **13**:1798
   reaction with oxygen **6**:787; **7**:878
   see also natural gas
methanoic acid (formic acid) **1**:25
methanol (methyl alcohol; wood
   alcohol) **1**:97; **16**:2215
   engines powered with **2**:258; **6**:794
   in fuel cells **7**:936
   for petroleum-like hydrocarbons
     4:458

production **1**:98
methanolysis **13**:1776
methyl alcohol *see* methanol
methylamine **4**:444
methylchloride **15**:2078
methyl orange **12**:1692
methylpropene (isobutylene)
   14:2001
2-methylpropenoic acid (methacrylic
   acid) **12**:1629
methyl salicylate (oil of wintergreen)
   1:98
metronomes **10**:1408; **12**:1664
mezzotint **6**:803, 804
MG42 (machine gun) **2**:196
micafill *see* vermiculite
micas **15**:2077
   muscovite **15**:*2075*, 2077
   in paints **12**:1628
mice and pointing devices **4**:535;
   11:1490–2
   mice **4**:527, 535; **11**:1490–1
Michelson, A.A. **9**:1240; **14**:1950
microanalyzers, electron probe
   10:1434
microarrays, DNA **11**:1480
microbalances **2**:214, 215
microbiology **10**:1409–12
   see also bacteria; fungi; microorgan-
     isms; protozoa; viruses
microchips *see* integrated circuits
microcomputers *see* computers,
   personal
microencapsulation **10**:1413–14
microfiches **10**:1415
microfilm **10**:1415
microfiltration **12**:1610
micrographs **12**:1715
microlenses **17**:2330
microlights **8**:1038; **15**:*2037*;
   18:*2525–7*
micromachines and nanotechnology
   10:1416–20
micrometeorites **10**:1392
micrometers **10**:*1421–2*; **18**:2582
micromotors **10**:*1416*, 1418–19
   magnetic **5**:718
micronutrients **11**:1557–8
   see also minerals; vitamins
microorganisms
   affecting canning and bottling
     3:381, 382, 385
   and fermentation **6**:840
   influencing corrosion **4**:571
   see also bacteria; viruses
micropaleontology **12**:1634
microphones **10**:1423–5; **11**:1531;
   13:1745
   for bugging **6**:759–60
   carbon **10**:1423
   as computer input devices **4**:527
   condenser **10**:1424
   crystal **10**:1424
   directional **10**:1425
     unidirectional **10**:*1423*, 1425
   electret **5**:*715*, 716
   frequency response of **10**:1424
   long-range **10**:1425
   moving-coil and ribbon **10**:1423–4
   and the obstacle effect **10**:1424–5
   output signals **1**:128
microprobes, electron **12**:1680
microprocessors **6**:755; **10**:1426–9;
   15:2054
   on automobiles **2**:202, 204
   on farm machinery **1**:51
   for "intelligent prostheses" **2**:254
   logic operations **9**:1277;
     10:1427–8
   and optoelectronics **6**:755
   see also central processing units;
     integrated circuits

microscopes
  acoustic **15**:*2135*; **18**:*2529*
    scanning laser acoustic
      microscopy (SLAM) **15**:2135
  atomic-force (AFMs) **4**:552; **6**:839;
    10:1417
  binocular
    for operations **12**:*1589*, 1590
    for picture restoration **13**:*1743*
  cutting sections for *see* microtomes
  electron **2**:262; **10**:*1430–2*
    cutting sections for **11**:*1445*,
      1446
    scanning electron microscopes
      10:1431–2; **12**:*1655*, *1715*
    scanning-probe (SPMs)
      10:1417, 1419, 1420
    scanning transmission electron
      microscopes (STEMs) **10**:1432
    scanning tunneling microscopes
      (STMs) **4**:551–2, *553*; **10**:1417
    transmission electron micro-
      scopes **10**:1431; **12**:*1659*
  for examining rocks **7**:987
  for micromachines and nanotech-
    nology **10**:1416, 1417, *1419*
  optical (compound microscopes)
    2:261; **10**:*1433–5*; **12**:*1715*
    comparison microscopes **7**:917
    cutting sections for **11**:*1445*,
      1446
    dark-field microscopy **10**:*1434*,
      1435
    fluorescence microscopy
      10:*1433*, 1435
    interference microscopy
      10:1435
    phase-contrast microscopy
      10:1435
    polarizing microscopy **10**:1435;
      12:1680
    slit lamp **12**:1589
    stereoscopic microscopy
      10:1434–5
    surgical **10**:1437, 1440; **12**:*1589*,
      1590
    vernier gauges on **18**:*2582*
  scanning laser acoustic (SLAMs)
    3:427
Microsoft
  Internet Explorer **9**:1180, 1181
  operating systems
    Windows **4**:525, 539
microsurgery **10**:*1436–40*;
  13:*1765–6*
  on the eye **12**:1590
  limb reattachment **10**:1439;
    13:1765–6
  skin grafts **10**:1438–9
  see also plastic surgery
microtomes **11**:*1445–6*; **12**:*1656*
microtunneling machines **18**:2516
microwave landing systems (MLSs)
  1:96
microwave ovens **11**:*1447–50*
microwaves **6**:741–2
  antennas **1**:*141*, *142*; **6**:741–2, *744*
  communications **6**:746; **17**:2359
  cosmic **4**:574
  danger to health **11**:1450
  generation **6**:741, 745, 751
  uses
    in computer networks **4**:542
    microwave ovens **11**:*1447–50*
    movement sensors **3**:340, *341*;
      15:*2042*, 2043
    as nonlethal weapons **11**:1534
    to make logs pliable **7**:*924*
  waveguides and **19**:2668–71
  see also radar
Mid-Atlantic Ridge **10**:1333;
  11:*1565*

MIDI (Musical Instrument Digital
  Interface) **12**:1604; **17**:2345
midi systems **8**:1075–6
Mies van der Rohe, Ludwig **15**:2093
MiG-25 (aircraft) **17**:2319
migration **19**:2733–4
  birds' **11**:1514; **19**:2734
Milankovitch cycles **4**:478
milk
  condensed and evaporated **5**:600,
    602–3
  dried **5**:*603*; **7**:910; **11**:*1452*
  as a food **5**:600
  from genetically-modified animals
    7:977
  homogenized **5**:601
  hygienic quality tests **5**:601
  milking machines **5**:600–1;
    11:*1451–2*
  packaging **7**:908; **12**:1624–5
  pasteurized **5**:600, 601, *603*; **7**:906,
    911
  processing **5**:601
  production
    and biotechnology **2**:*264*, 266
    in cows **1**:57
  spoilage **7**:905
  sterilized **5**:601; **7**:912
  UHT **5**:601
  see also dairy industry
Milky Way **2**:270; **5**:696
  annihilation radiation from **6**:745
Millennium Bridge, London
  14:*1964*, 1965
Millennium Dome, London **3**:*337*,
  338; **17**:2401–2
milling **19**:2694
milling machines **10**:1309, *1310*
Minamata disease **13**:1801
mineral oils, for lubrication **9**:1289,
  1290–1
minerals
  dietary **11**:1557, 1558
  hardness **7**:987
  oldest **7**:988
mineral wools **9**:1161
mines, explosive **3**:293; **6**:829;
  11:*1453–6*
  antiarmor **11**:1453–4
  antipersonnel **11**:1453, *1454*,
    1455, 1456
  disposal *see* bombs, bomb and
    mine disposal
  naval **11**:1454–6; **19**:2633
  space mines **16**:2181
minesweepers **19**:2633
minicomputers **4**:525, 526
Mini Moogs **17**:2342
mining techniques **11**:*1457–62*
  alluvial mining
    for diamonds **5**:638
    for gold **8**:1013
  development **11**:1457–8
  fluid mining **11**:1461–2
  marine mining **11**:1462
  surface mining (opencast mining;
    strip mining) **1**:*109*; **5**:701;
    11:1457, 1458–60
    auger mining **4**:495; **11**:1460
    for coal **4**:495–6, *564*; **11**:1460
    for diamonds **5**:637
    open pits **11**:1458–9
    placer mining **11**:1460
    strip mining **11**:1459
    for uranium **11**:*1457*
  underground mining **11**:1457,
    1459, 1460–1
    for coal **4**:496–7; **11**:1460–1
    for diamonds **5**:637–8
    drift mines **11**:1460, 1461
    for gold **11**:1460
    theodolites used in **8**:1031

ventilation **8**:*1059*, 1060
    see also tunneling
Minkowski, Hermann **14**:1954
Minkowski universe **14**:1954
minting *see* coins and minting
Minuteman (missile) **11**:1466;
  16:*2179*, 2181
Mir (space station) **1**:43; **15**:*2150*,
  2151; **16**:2172
mirrors **11**:*1463–4*
  concave **11**:1463, 1464
  convex **11**:1463
  dielectric, "perfect" mirrors
    9:*1236*, 1243
  liquid-mercury **11**:1464; **17**:2380
  one-way **11**:1463
  parabolic **11**:1464
  production **11**:1463–4
  spherical **17**:2379
  in telescopes **11**:1464, 1561–2;
    12:*1727*; **17**:2378
MIRVs (multiple independently
  targetable reentry vehicles)
  11:1468
missiles **11**:**1465–8**
  antiaircraft **1**:143, 144
    surface-to-air (SAMs) **1**:144
  antiradar (ARMs) **16**:2254
  ballistic **11**:1465, 1468
    defence against **16**:2180, 2182–4
    intercontinental ballistic missiles
      (ICBMs) **11**:1465–6, 1468
    submarine-launched (SLBMs)
      16:2182
  cruise **11**:1465, 1466, 1467, 1468;
    16:2291
  guided **1**:143; **6**:742; **11**:1465,
    1487
  "smart" **11**:1467–8
  stealth (Sea Skuas) **16**:2251
  strategic **11**:1465, 1468
  warheads **11**:1468
  see also bombs; explosives
mistletoe **12**:1644
mites
  harvest **18**:2585
  red spider **12**:1677
mitochondria **3**:411, *413*, *414*;
  10:1375, 1412
mitosis **3**:*412*, 413
mixed reality (augmented reality; AR)
  19:2608
mixing desks **15**:2138–9
  video **17**:*2390*
MMR vaccine **18**:2556
MMX processors **10**:1428
mobile phones *see* cellular telephones
mobility aids **1**:20–1; **11**:*1469–72*
Möbius bands **10**:1358
mode **16**:2248
modeling
  molecular **12**:1688–9
  three-dimensional **10**:1366
models
  computer *see* computer models
  small-scale
    for movie special effects
      16:*2185*, *2187*, 2188
    of rivers **7**:890–1
  virtual **19**:*2607*, 2608
modems and ISDN **11**:**1473–6**
  ISDN **4**:540; **11**:1476, 1517;
    17:2357–8
    broadband **11**:1476
    and newspaper production
      11:1519
  modems **1**:129; **4**:540; **8**:1148;
    11:1473–5, 1476; **17**:2357
    cable **11**:*1475*, 1476; **17**:2358
    protocols **11**:1475–6
  see also ADSLs
Moh's scale of hardness **1**:17

molasses **16**:2297
  blackstrap **16**:2296, 2297
  ethanol produced from **7**:963
molding
  blow **13**:1774–5
  compression **13**:1775
  contact lenses **4**:562
  injection *see* injection molding
  rotational **13**:1775
  shell (Croning process) **3**:403
molds (fungi), and food spoilage
  7:905
molecular biology **11**:*1477–80*
  molecular biophysics **2**:261
  see also DNA; genetic engineering;
    genetics
molecular sieving **19**:2729–30
molecules
  computer graphics **4**:*534*
  custom-built, using nanotech-
    nology **10**:1419
  and quantum physics **12**:1728
  rotational and vibrational energy
    9:1209
  structure established **4**:462
moles (machines) **18**:2516
molybdenum disulfide **9**:1289
moments **16**:2243, *2244*
momentum **5**:694–5
  angular **9**:1201
    and torque **8**:1030
  conservation of **12**:1726
  linear **12**:1726
    changes in **9**:1201
momochromatism **4**:510
Mond carbonyl process **11**:1523
monkeys, vervet **19**:2733
monoamine-oxidase inhibitors
  (MAOIs) **12**:1681–2; **13**:1868
monoamines **3**:311
monobath process **12**:1712
monochromators **16**:2198
monomethylhydrazine **15**:2029
monopoles **1**:142
monorail systems **10**:1345;
  11:**1481–3**
monosaccharides **3**:388–9
monosodium glutamate **7**:907
  allergy to **7**:907
  production **7**:914
Monte Carlo modeling **2**:172;
  10:1401
Montgolfier, Jean **13**:1847
months **17**:2441
Montreal Protocol **6**:807
Moog, Robert **17**:2342, 2343
Moon
  and the Apollo program **1**:42
  Earth's gravitational pull on
    11:1521
  eclipse **5**:709–10
  lasers bounced off **9**:1214; **14**:1944
  photography on **15**:*2152*, 2154
  Surveyor craft landing on **15**:2157
  and tides on Earth **5**:696–7;
    8:*1022*; **11**:1521; **17**:2436–7,
    2439, *2440*
  and tsunamis **18**:*2511*
moons, tidal effects on **11**:*1520*
mopeds **11**:1489
mordanting **5**:690–1
Morley, E. W. **9**:1240; **14**:1950
Morley, Samuel **9**:1169
morphine **12**:1685, 1687
morphogens **6**:778
Morse, Samuel **3**:353; **17**:2361
Morse code **5**:593
Morse system **5**:593; **17**:2357, 2361
  and paper-tape **17**:2361–2
mortar **3**:417
mortars, bazookas, and recoilless
  guns **11**:**1484–7**

MOSFETs **9**:1165; **10**:1426
mosquitoes **10**:1367; **12**:*1644*, 1646
　weapons against **12**:1678
moths
　codling **19**:2736
　control of prickly pear using
　　19:2679
　peppered **6**:823; **13**:*1799*
　pheromones **12**:1690–1; **19**:2736
motion
　circular and periodic **15**:*2081*
　Newton's laws of *see* Newton,
　　Isaac, and Newton's laws
　rotary **5**:695
motion sensors *see* movement sensors
motorcycles **11**:**1488–9**
　model **14**:1915
motorcyclists **8**:*1142*
Motor Lifeboats (MLBs) **15**:2040
motor neurone disease **13**:1734
motor racing *see* racing cars and
　dragsters
motors
　air **13**:1788
　electric *see* electric motors
　gear **8**:1103–4
　hydraulic **8**:1103–4
　piston **13**:1788
　turbine **13**:1788
　vane **8**:1104
　　positive-displacement **13**:1788
　see also internal combustion
　　engines
mountains, formation **5**:699; **11**:1565
Mount Palomar Sky Survey **17**:2380
mouse, computer *see* mice and point-
　ing devices
mouth **5**:642
mouth guards **13**:1862
movement sensors **3**:340, *341*;
　15:*2042*, 2043
movie cameras (motion picture cam-
　eras) **11**:*1493–6*, 1498; **15**:2075
　in space **15**:2152–3
movie film **11**:1494, 1498; **13**:1856–7
movie production **11**:**1497–1500**
　animation **1**:136–40; **4**:536;
　　16:2189–90
　soundtracks **15**:**2146–9**
　　music scores **11**:1499, 1500;
　　　15:2149
　special effects **16**:**2185–90**
　stereoscopic movies **16**:2263–4
movie projectors **13**:1854, 1856–7
　and digital sound systems **15**:2148
moving target indication (MTI)
　5:672; **14**:1898
mowers, grass **8**:1018–19
MOX reactors **11**:1538, 1539
MPEG (Moving Picture Experts
　Group) **18**:2497
　MPEG-2 process **5**:651
MRI *see* magnetic resonance imaging
MRSA (methicillin-resistant
　Staphylococcus aureus) **10**:1411
MRVs (multiple reentry vehicles)
　11:1468
M-theory **8**:1022; **14**:1954
MTSOs (mobile telephone switching
　offices) **17**:2359
mufflers **2**:205; **15**:2141
mulching **19**:2680
　stubble **6**:817
multifrequency tone (MFT) dialing
　17:2371
multimedia **11**:**1501–3**
　see also flight simulators; virtual
　　reality
multiple reentry vehicles (MRVs)
　11:1468
multiple sclerosis, mobility aids for
　11:1471

multiplexing **4**:535, 542; **17**:2356
　time-division (TDM) **1**:129;
　　17:2356, 2365
muons **6**:769, 770; **14**:1952
Murdock, William **7**:955
muriatic acid **2**:160
muscle relaxants **12**:1682
muscles **11**:**1504–6**
　cells **3**:411; **11**:1505–6
　movement at the molecular level
　　2:262
muscovite **15**:*2075*, 2077
muscular dystrophy
　Duchenne's **7**:980
　mobility aids for **11**:1470–1
museums
　multimedia technology **11**:*1502*
　virtual **11**:1503
music
　atonal **11**:1509
　digitally encoded **1**:26; **8**:1076
　movie scores **11**:1499, 1500;
　　15:2149
　musical instruments
　　brass **3**:**318–20**; **14**:1965
　　organs **12**:**1601–4**; **14**:1965
　　percussion **12**:**1667–70**
　　stringed **16**:**2279–84**
　　woodwind **14**:1965; **19**:**2712–15**
　　see also synthesizers
　reproduction *see* compact discs;
　　digital audio tapes; hi-fi systems
　scales **11**:**1507–9**
muslin **5**:582, **17**:2407
mustard gas **3**:379
　as a chemical weapon **4**:437, 438;
　　7:953; **8**:1036
mutations **6**:778, 823; **9**:1233;
　　11:1479
　deletion, detected **11**:1479
　induced in plants **1**:54
　somatic **8**:1134, 1135
mutes, brass instrument **3**:320
MX (missiles) **14**:*1993*
Mycoderma aceti **6**:842
myeloid cells **8**:1133
myocardial infarction *see* heart attack
myocarditis **8**:1047
myofibrils **11**:1505
myopia (nearsightedness) **6**:832;
　　9:*1213*; **12**:1596–7
　laser surgery and **12**:1590
myosin **13**:1865

N

NADH **10**:1373, 1374, 1375
Nagasaki, atomic bomb used on
　　11:1551, 1553; **14**:*1908*
nanofiltration **12**:1610
nanotechnology *see* micromachines
　　and nanotechnology
nanotubes, carbon **10**:1420
napalm **2**:*284*; **7**:883
naphtha **11**:1575, 1577–9
naphthalene **4**:455, 498
napping (fabrics) **17**:2408
narcolepsy **15**:2102
narcotics
　poisoning **13**:1791
　testing for **5**:684
national missile defense (NMD)
　　system **16**:2181, *2182*, 2183–4
Native Americans
　food preservation **7**:908
　medicine wheels **16**:2275
natrolite **19**:2728
natural gas **3**:391; **7**:955–7
　for electricity generation **6**:791
　and oil recovery **11**:1573
　for power plants **7**:967
　storage **7**:*955*, 957

sulfur from **16**:2299
natural-language processing **2**:172
　see also voice recognition and
　　synthesis
natural selection **6**:822
nautical miles **11**:1511
Nautilus (submersible) **16**:2288
Nautilus (submarine) **11**:1542
Navier, C. L. M. H. **1**:36
Navier-Stokes equations **1**:36
navigation **11**:**1510–14**
　aircraft **1**:66–7; **8**:*1028*; **11**:1513
　　collision avoidance **11**:1513
　　using head-up displays **8**:1040
　　using sextants **15**:2063
　　see also air-traffic control
　gyrocompasses **8**:1028–9; **11**:1510
　history **7**:1006; **11**:1510
　inertial guidance systems
　　8:**1144–6**; **11**:1468, *1512*, 1513
　marine **15**:2068
　　collision avoidance **11**:1514
　　dead reckoning (DR) **11**:1511
　　echo sounders **11**:1512;
　　　15:2126–7
　　fishing vessels **7**:872–3
　　and Harrison's chronometer
　　　4:484; **9**:*1215*, 1216; **11**:1511
　　knots **11**:1510–11
　　radio and radar **11**:1511–12,
　　　1514
　　using gyroscopes **8**:1028, *1031*
　　using sextants **11**:1511, *1513*;
　　　15:2062–3
　radio **7**:1006; **11**:1511–2
　satellite systems
　　and seismology **7**:994
　　see also global positioning
　　　systems
　space **11**:1514
　using compasses (magnetic)
　　11:1510, *1514*
Navstars **7**:1006; **11**:1514; **15**:2026
Near Infrared Camera and Multi-
　　Object Spectrometer (NIC-
　　MOS) **17**:2381
Near-Shoemaker (space probe)
　　15:2123
nearsightedness *see* myopia
nebulas
　Eagle **2**:176
　Eskimo **2**:*175*, 176
　Horsehead **17**:*2382*
　Hourglass **2**:*248*
　Orion **2**:177
needles, hypodermic, manufacture
　　13:1752
Negev Desert, for irrigation
　　9:1193–4
nematodes, parasitic **12**:*1644*, 1645
neodymium **5**:622; **9**:1212
neon **4**:442; **11**:1529
neon tubes (neon lamps) **4**:555;
　　5:*656, 657*; **11**:*1529*
neoprene **13**:1771–2, 1862; **14**:2001
Neptune **13**:1757, 1758, 1761;
　　15:2118, 2122
　discovery (eighth planet) **5**:694
　rings around **5**:710
neptunium **6**:764–5
nerve cells *see* neurons
nerve gases **4**:437, 438–9
NES (Nintendo Entertainment
　　System) **7**:952
Netherlands
　flood control **7**:*890*, 891
　land reclamation **9**:1206, 1208;
　　19:2695
Netscape **9**:1180
networks, computer *see* computers,
　　networks
neural tube defects **12**:1660

neurochemistry **3**:311
neurology **3**:312
neurons (nerve cells) **3**:411
　in the brain **3**:309, 311
　　diaphorase neurons **3**:414
neurotransmitters **3**:311, 413–14;
　　11:1506
　and parkinsonism **12**:1684
neutrinos **2**:180–1; **4**:575; **6**:769, 770
　and expansion of the Universe
　　6:773
　types, electron, muon, and tau
　　6:769
neutron activation analysis **2**:158;
　　12:1659
neutrons
　albedo **14**:1899
　and atomic structure **2**:182, 183,
　　185; **14**:1906
　comprised of quarks **6**:770
　decay **14**:1899
　discovery **6**:763, 767
　neutron-scattering experiments
　　5:*591*
Newcomen, Thomas **11**:1458
news gathering, electronic (ENG)
　　17:2389
newspapers
　inks **8**:1152
　production **11**:**1515–19**; **13**:1849
Newton, Isaac, and Newton's laws
　　11:**1520–1**
　law of cooling **11**:1521
　law of gravitation **2**:269; **8**:1020,
　　1021; **11**:1520, 1521; **12**:1726
　　and orbits **12**:1599
　　and satellites **15**:2024–5
　laws of motion **5**:694; **11**:**1520–1**;
　　12:1725–6
　　first law **3**:422; **5**:695; **8**:*1142*;
　　　11:1520; **12**:1725
　　second law **3**:422; **5**:695; **6**:789;
　　　8:1144; **9**:1201; **11**:1520;
　　　12:1725
　　third law **5**:695; **11**:1520;
　　　12:1725; **14**:1991
　and light **9**:1236, 1237, *1238*;
　　13:1853; **14**:1880; **16**:2193
　and viscosity **19**:2610
Newtonian flow (free molecular
　　flow) **1**:38
Newtonian reflector **17**:2378
Newton's rings **9**:1243
New York City, mass transit system
　　10:1345–6
Next Generation Space Telescope
　　(NGST) **2**:177; **17**:2382
niacin **19**:2613
Nichrome **14**:1963
nickel **11**:**1522–4**
　alloys **4**:568; **10**:*1390*; **11**:*1522*,
　　1523–4
　　cupronickels **4**:568; **11**:1523
　　Elinvar **1**:106; **11**:1524
　　Invar **1**:106; **11**:1524
　　nickel silver (German silver)
　　　3:317; **4**:568; **11**:1523
　　Nimonic (superalloys) **1**:106;
　　　4:473; **11**:*1523*, 1524
　　in steels and cast irons
　　　11:1523–4
　　see also Nitinol
　catalysts **18**:2488
　corrosion **4**:569
　occurrence and extraction
　　11:1522–3
　plating **6**:738
　powder **1**:105
nickel carbonyl **11**:1523; **12**:1616;
　　18:2488
nickel oxide **4**:569; **11**:1523
nickel sulfide **11**:1523

Nicol prisms 13:1795
nictitating membrane 6:832
Niépce, Claude 12:1708
NiFe cells 2:228–9
night, binoculars 2:250
nightmares 15:2102
Nile River
    Aswan High Dam 5:608; 6:819;
        9:1191
    flooding 7:891; 9:1191, 1206
Nimonic alloys (superalloys) 1:106;
    4:473; 11:1523, 1524
niobium 3:404
    alloys 3:346; 17:2312
niobium tin 3:346; 17:2312
niobium titanium 17:2312, 2314
Nitinol, and shape memory 1:106–7;
    10:1351–2, 1363
nitric acid 1:24
    bonds in 4:444
    preparation 1:24–5; 4:451;
        11:1525; 13:1783
    uses 1:25
nitric oxide, biological roles
    3:413–14
nitrobenzene 1:133
nitrocellulose 3:390; 6:827; 13:1768
nitrogen 11:1525–7
    atmospheric 1:62
        fixed by bacteria 6:843; 11:1526
    bonds in 4:442
    compounds 11:1525–6
    cycle 11:1526
    isotopes 11:1525
    liquid 1:62; 5:591; 11:1525, 1527;
        14:1927
        transport 14:1927
    production 11:1525
    uses 1:64; 11:1525
nitrogen narcosis 2:155; 18:2538
nitrogen tetroxide 15:2029
nitroglycerine 3:390; 6:827
nitromethanol 14:1891, 1892
nitrous oxide 11:1527
    anesthetic (laughing gas) 1:131;
        11:1527
    bonds in 4:444
Nixie tubes 5:647
NOAA (National Oceanic and
    Atmospheric Administration)
    10:1398
    satellites 8:1096
nobelium 6:765
noble-gas configurations 4:442;
    9:1183
noble gases 4:442; 11:1528–9;
    12:1672
    see also helium; krypton; neon;
        radon; xenon
nodding donkeys 5:683; 11:1573–4
nodules, metal-bearing, seafloor
    11:1462
noise
    of amplifiers 1:126; 8:1074–5
    radio 14:1903
    reduction 1:126, 129
noise measurement 11:1530–1
    see also soundproofing
Nomex 7:880; 13:1806, 1860
nonlethal weapons 11:1532–4;
    14:1972
    tear gases 4:437; 11:1532, 1534;
        14:1972
    water cannons 11:1533, 1534;
        14:1972
nonsteroidal anti-inflammatory
    drugs (NSAIDs) 12:1682
norepinephrine (noradrenaline)
    3:414; 6:781
    in plants 3:305
North Sea
    drilling for oil 5:682

natural gas from 7:956
nose
    cancer 12:1613
    plastic surgery 13:1764, 1765
    and smell 15:2103, 2105–6
    see also sinuses, nasal
notebook computers 11:1491
notes, fundamental 3:318
nougat 4:557–8
Novocain 1:132
novocaine 12:1681
NSAIDs (nonsteroidal anti-inflam-
    matory drugs) 12:1682
NTSC system 17:2394
nuclear emulsions 6:744; 12:1652
nuclear fuel cycle 11:1537–9, 1546;
    18:2547–8
nuclear magnetic resonance (NMR)
    4:448; 5:718; 11:1540–1;
    16:2195
    see also magnetic resonance
        imaging
nuclear power 6:729
    for marine propulsion 10:1336
nuclear reactors 11:1542–6; 14:1907
    Cerenkov radiation 6:794; 14:1907
    design 11:1544–5
    fast-breeder 7:877; 11:1546;
        18:2547
    heat exchangers 8:1054
    nuclear emergencies 11:1535–6,
        1545
    nuclear fission 6:796; 7:877;
        11:1543–6; 12:1728; 13:1832
        MHD units used in 10:1319
    nuclear fuel cycle 11:1537–9,
        1546; 18:2547–8
    nuclear fusion 2:248; 6:796;
        7:947–8; 11:1545
    propulsion 11:1546; 15:2073
        for submarines 10:1336, 1366;
            11:1542, 1546; 16:2290
    safety 11:1535, 1545
    thermal 11:1545–6
        boiling water reactors (BWRs)
            11:1543, 1545; 13:1832;
            18:2520
        gas-cooled 2:233; 11:1546
        heavy water reactors 11:1545
        pressurized-water reactors
            (PWRs) 11:1542, 1543, 1545;
            13:1832; 18:2520
    waste disposal from see nuclear
        waste disposal
    see also power plants, nuclear
nuclear stability 6:765, 766
nuclear waste disposal 6:796;
    11:1539, 1547–50; 18:2547
nuclear weapons 11:1551–4
    bombs
        atomic (A-bombs) 2:286; 7:877;
            11:1551, 1552–4; 14:1906, 1908
        fission-fusion-fission (Triple-F)
            11:1554
        hydrogen 2:286; 7:947; 11:1551
        neutron 11:1551, 1554
    missiles with nuclear warheads
        11:1468
nucleic acid 7:973
    hybridization 12:1657
nucleoside analogs 12:1688
nucleotides 7:973
    as probes 10:1333
nucleus
    of the atom 2:182, 183; 14:1905–6
    cell 3:411, 413
numbers 9:1275; 10:1354–5
    composite 11:1555
    Mersenne 11:1556
    number theory 11:1555–6
    perfect 11:1555–6
    prime 11:1555

numerical control systems 10:1340
nutrient film technique (NFT)
    8:1120–1
nutrition and food science
    11:1557–9
    milk 5:600
    and sports medicine 16:2225–6
    see also vitamins
nylons 6:852; 13:1769, 1804–5, 1811,
    1812; 17:2404
    for hosiery and knitwear 8:1090–1
    manufacture 6:852; 17:2405
    uses
        in bulletproof jackets 2:163
        parachute material 12:1643
        ropes 3:350–1
        in tires 18:2456
Nyquist's theorum 15:2145

O

Oakley self-righting boat system
    15:2050–1
oak trees, galls 12:1646
oars 10:1334
oasts 9:1199
O-bahn 3:343
obelisks 4:481
Oberth, Hermann 14:1993
obesity 6:837
oboes 19:2713
observatories 11:1560–2
obstacle effect 10:1424–5
obstetrics and gynecology 11:1563–4
Ocean Drilling Program 11:1568
ocean floor
    geological samples 7:989
    hydrothermal vents 10:1333;
        11:1567; 13:1780
    life on 11:1567
    maps 7:991; 11:1565; 15:2127,
        2128; 18:2531
    mining 11:1462
    ocean ridges 7:995; 10:1317, 1333;
        11:1565
    spreading 7:995; 11:1565; 13:1777
    temperature 17:2396
oceanography 11:1565–9
    satellites and 11:1569; 15:2029
    see also marine biology; ocean floor;
        oceans; sea levels; submersibles;
        undersea habitats
oceans
    currents 5:700; 11:1568–9
    density 11:1566
    energy from the temperature
        gradient of 6:793, 795; 8:1054
    pressure beneath 11:1568
    resources 11:1569
    salinity 11:1566
    temperature 11:1566
Ocean Thermal Energy Conversion
    (OTEC) 6:795; 8:1054
octane numbers, gasoline 8:1106;
    11:1578
octants, reflecting 15:2062
octaves 11:1507
oculists (ophthalmologists) 12:1589,
    1596
odometers 2:245; 16:2209–10
odontology, forensic 7:919
Oersted, Hans 6:726, 747
off-road vehicles, models, racing
    14:1915
Ohio Bridge 3:329
Ohm, Georg 6:726; 14:1960
ohms 9:1162
Ohm's law 6:726, 728; 13:1826;
    14:1962
oil coolers 9:1292
oil exploration and production 7:990;
    11:1570–4

drill bits 5:639, 680
    turbine 5:683
exploration 7:993–4; 11:1570–3
    using seismology 7:993–4;
        11:1570–1; 15:2048, 2135
horizontal drilling 5:683
oil drilling rigs 4:548; 5:680–3;
    11:1570
oil pipelines 13:1753, 1754
oil recovery 11:1573–4
    see also petroleum (crude oil)
oil filters 9:1292
oil gas 7:959
oil length 9:1204
oil refining 5:661, 662, 663; 8:1106;
    11:1575–80
    cracking 4:453; 11:1575–6, 1578
        catalytic 4:459; 11:1576
        hydrocracking 11:1576, 1578
        thermal 11:1578
    hydrofining 11:1580
    and pollution 13:1798
    products from 4:453; 5:663;
        11:1577–80
"oil rig" (mnemonic) 12:1616
oil rigs see drilling rigs
oils
    in paints 12:1628
    recycling 14:1942
    see also fat(s)
oil shale 11:1574
oilskins 13:1862
oil spills 10:1411
oils, vegetable
    for biodiesel 6:794; 7:963
    hydrogenation 3:406
oil of wintergreen (methyl salicylate)
    1:98
olefins see alkenes
oleoresin capsicum (OC) 11:1532,
    1533
oleum 1:24
olfactory system 15:2103, 2105–6
oligonucleotides 11:1479
olivine 10:1392
Olympic Games
    drug testing at 16:2225
    Munich, tensile structures 17:2402
omnivores 5:644–5
oncogenes, ras 2:252
oncology, radiation see radiology
oNLine System (NLS) 11:1501
op-amps (operational amplifiers)
    1:125–6
open-hearth process 9:1189
operating rooms 6:758; 11:1581–4;
    17:2327, 2329, 2332
    patient surveillance units 6:757
    polygraphs 13:1808
    see also anesthetics; surgery
operating systems, computer 4:525,
    530
ophthalmology 12:1589–90
    ophthalmologists (oculists)
        12:1589, 1596
    ophthalmoscopes 12:1591, 1598
opium 13:1791
optical character recognition (OCR)
    systems 1:20; 4:527; 5:626;
        12:1593, 1594–5
    mail-sorting 10:1323, 1324
    in newspaper production 11:1518
optical fibers see fiber optics
optical range finders 1:143–4
optical scanners 4:527, 535; 5:626;
    12:1592–5
    bar-codes 3:401; 8:1082, 1083,
        1150; 10:1341
    are 1-bit scanners 12:1593
        on microwave ovens 11:1450
    color 12:1593
    drum 12:1592–3

flatbed **5**:628; **12**:1592, 1593
image resolution **12**:1593–4
magnetic-ink-character-recognition (MICR) **12**:1595
OCR *see* optical character recognition (OCR) systems
optical mark recognition (OMR) machines **12**:1595
sensors **12**:1592–3
storing images **12**:1594
opticians
dispensing **12**:1596
ophthalmic **12**:1596
optic nerve, damage to **12**:1589–90
optics *see* light and optics
optoelectronics **6**:755
optoisolators **6**:757
optometrists **12**:1589
optometry **12**:1596–8
orbits **12**:1599–1600
spacecraft **12**:1599–1600
and monitoring space debris **15**:2150–1
see also satellites, artificial, orbits
ores, bulk handling **7**:928
organophosphates **12**:1677, 1700
organs (body parts), artificial creation of **6**:778
organs, musical **12**:1601–4; **14**:1965
Hammond **13**:1740
orifice plates **7**:896
Orionids **10**:1393
Orion nebula **13**:1760
orreries, projection **13**:1756
orthicons **17**:2383, 2384
image **17**:2384
orthodontics **5**:618, 622
orthophosphoric acid **12**:1699
oscillating water column (OWC) systems **19**:2676, 2677
oscillators **12**:1605–6
electrical circuits as **6**:754; **8**:1139; **12**:1606
oscilloscopes **12**:1607–8; **19**:*2617*
cathode-ray tubes **3**:409; **12**:1607
osmium **13**:1781, 1782
osmosis **12**:1609–10
and kidney dialysis **5**:633
reverse **12**:1609–10
for desalination **5**:*625*; **12**:1610; **19**:*2666*
osteoarthritis **10**:1369
osteocytes **3**.*300*
osteopathy **10**:1370; **12**:1611
osteoporosis **3**:298; **7**:997
OTEC (Ocean Thermal Energy Conversion) **6**:795; **8**:1054
otolaryngology **12**:1612–13
Otto, Nicolaus **2**:198
outboard motors **10**:1337; **12**:1614–15
outriggers **16**:2206
ovens, microwave **11**:1447–50
overlock machines **4**:490
overtones **16**:2283–4
Overwhelmingly Large Telescope (OWL) **17**:2379
OWC (oscillating water column) systems **19**:2676, 2677
owls, eyes **6**:830
oxazolidinones **10**:1411
oxidation numbers **12**:1616
oxidation and reduction **12**:1616–17
oxidation state **4**:443
oxides **12**:1620–1
oxidoreductases **6**:810
oxyacetylene welding **12**:1620
oxygen **12**:1618–21
atmospheric **1**:62–3; **12**:1620, 1719
in ancient times **6**:823, 824; **7**:988

discovery **12**:1618
liquid **5**:591; **14**:1927
manufacture **12**:1618
separation from air **5**:590; **12**:1618–19
oxides **12**:1620–1
synthesis in stars **6**:*763*
uses **1**:64; **12**:1619–20
see also ozone
oxygen-fuel lances **17**:2412
oxyhemoglobin **9**:1188
oxytocin **6**:781–2
oysters **2**:*153*; **7**:875
ozone **12**:1621
used in water treatment **19**:2664–6
ozone layer **1**:62; **4**:479; **6**:806, 824; **7**:988; **12**:1621
depletion **4**:480; **6**:806–7; **13**:1798
dry-cleaning solvents and **5**:687
refrigerants and **14**:1947
research planes **10**:*1401*

P

pacemakers, cardiac *see* heart pacemaker
packaging **7**:908; **12**:1622–5
see also food preservation and packaging
packaging-wrap manufacture **12**:1626
packet switching **4**:541
paddles **10**:1334
paddocking **8**:1013
paddy fields **9**:1191
paintings
cave **12**:1627
fake **5**:584
oil **13**:1741
restoration **13**:1741–3
paints **12**:1627–30
acrylic **12**:1629
alkyd **12**:1628–9
antifouling **2**:149
emulsion (latex) **12**:1629
and forensic science **7**:918
luminescent **10**:1302
manufacture **12**:1630
metallic **12**:1628
oil **12**:1628
pearlescent **12**:1628
pigments **12**:1627–8, 1630
solvents **13**:1823
reduction **12**:1630
spray guns for **16**:2227–8
stoving enamels **12**:1629–30
pair production **2**:151; **6**:744
paleobotany **12**:1634
paleomagnetism **7**:990, *991*, 992–3; **10**:1317; **13**:1777
paleontology **12**:1631–5
invertebrate **12**:1634–5
see also evolution; fossils
palladium **13**:1781, 1783; **15**:2130; **18**:2485
PAL (phase alternating line) system **17**:2394
palynology **12**:1634
Panama Canal **9**:*1265*, 1266; **11**:1514
Panavia Tornado (aircraft), weapons **1**:*117*
Panavision film **11**:*1494*
pancreas **5**:643; **6**:781
artificial **13**:1734
cancer **6**:784
endoscopy **6**:784
transplants **6**:782
cells **13**:1734
Pandora (moon) **12**:*1599*
Pangaea **5**:699
panharmonicons **17**:2342
panning, for gold **8**:1013

pan pots **13**:1822
pan and scan **5**:652
pantographs **9**:1286; **15**:2066; **16**:2277–8
pantothenic acid **19**:2613
panty hose **8**:1090, *1091*, 1092–3
paper
flash **16**:2235
litmus **12**:*1692*
manufacture **9**:1296; **12**:1636–40; **13**:1847
for banknotes **5**:583
cotton used in **5**:582
wastes for food production **7**:914; **19**:2727
NCR (no carbon required) **10**:1413
photographic **10**:*1413*, 1414
recycling **14**:1939–40
paperback production **3**:302
papyrus **12**:1636
parachutes **12**:1641–3
airframe (whole-frame parachutes) **12**:1643
ballistic **18**:2527
drogue **5**:711; **12**:1641, *1642*, 1643
manufacture **12**:1642–3
paraffins *see* alkanes
Parafil rope **13**:1806
parallax **16**:2263
parallelogram law **16**:2242, 2244
parallel processing **4**:526
paramagnetism **18**:2486
paramecia **14**:*1958*
paramedics **1**:112
paraplanes **12**:1643
paraquat **7**:918; **19**:2679
pararosaniline chloride **1**:134–5
parasitology and parasites **12**:1644–6
parathyroid gland **6**:781
parathyroid hormone (parathormone) **6**:781, 782; **8**:1085
Paré, Ambroise **13**:1764; **17**:2327
Paris gun **8**:1026
parity checking **4**:541–2; **5**:612
park-and-ride **10**:1345
Parkesine **13**:1768
Parkes process **9**:1220; **15**:2079
parkinsonism **12**:1684
Parkinson's disease **12**:1684
treatment **3**:414; **5**:592
parquetry **18**:2579
parthenogenesis **14**:1957
partial pressure, Dalton's law of **7**:961
particle accelerators **2**:*150*, 151; **3**:333; **6**:769; **12**:1647–50; **13**:1763; **17**:2311
circular
cyclotrons **12**:1649
synchrocyclotrons **12**:1649–50
synchrotrons **2**:261, 262; **12**:1650
linear **6**:765; **12**:*1647*, 1648–9, *1726*
for nuclear waste disposal **11**:1550
Superconducting Super Collider (SSC), siting **7**:986
uses **12**:1648
vacuums in **18**:2560
particle detectors **12**:1651–4
Cerenkov counters **12**:1654
drift chambers **12**:1654
Geiger–Müller tubes **6**:744; **7**:970; **12**:1653
multiwire proportional chambers (MPCs) **12**:1653
nuclear emulsions **6**:744; **12**:1652
scintillation counters **12**:*1653*, 1654, 1718
spark chambers **12**:1652–3
see also bubble and cloud chambers

particles, elementary *see* elementary particles
Pascal, Blaise **8**:1100
pascals **2**:222; **13**:1839
Pascal's Law **16**:2245
passwords, computer **4**:530–1
pasteurization **5**:601, *603*; **7**:906–7, 911
milk **5**:600, 601, *603*; **7**:906–7, 911
Pasteur, Louis **6**:840; **7**:906; **10**:1367, 1409; **17**:2328; **18**:2554–5
and fermentation **19**:2725
Pathfinder (space probe) **15**:2158
pathology **12**:1655–9
clinical **12**:1655, 1656–7
comparative **12**:1655–6
forensic **7**:919–20; **12**:1655, 1658–9
plant **12**:1659
patient-monitoring systems **6**:757, 758
patina, of copper **4**:571
patrol boats **19**:2633
Pauling, Linus **19**:2614
Pauli, Wolfgang **14**:1882
Pauli exclusion principle **14**:1882
paved concrete track (PACT), railroad **14**:1923
paving machines **14**:1976
pay-and-display, ticket machines **10**:1407
payload launch vehicles (PLVs) **16**:2184
PBX (plastic-bonded explosive) **18**:2468
PBXs (private branch exchanges) **17**:2372
PCMCIA modems **11**:1475
PCR (polymerase chain reaction) **11**:1479
PCs *see* computers, personal
PD (positive displacement) meters **7**:896
Peacekeeper (missile) **11**:*1465*, 1466
pearlite **1**:104; **10**:1387
peat **6**:824
preservation in **2**:160; **4**:477
pectin **7**:911, 912
pediatrics **12**:1660–1
Pelamis (wave power system) **19**:2677
pellagra **19**:*2614*
Peltier effect **17**:2417, 2418–19, *2420*
and thermography **17**:2421
Pelton wheels **8**:1113; **18**:2519
pemmican **7**:908
"Pendolino" trains **9**:1274
pendulums **12**:1664–5; **14**:*1965*
compound **12**:1664
Foucault **8**:1030; **12**:1665
gridiron **12**:*1665*
and metronomes **10**:1408; **12**:1664
spherical **12**:1664
temperature-compensating **12**:1664
torsion **12**:1665
use
in car alarm systems **12**:*1664*
in clocks **4**:*482*, 483–4; **12**:1664, *1665*; **17**:*2442*
in oscillators **12**:1605
in seismographs **12**:1664–5; **15**:2046–7
penicillin **6**:*841*; **8**:1108; **10**:1409
Penicillium spp. **12**:*1682*
for cheesemaking **5**:602
for penicillin production **6**:*841*
peninsula of stability **6**:766
pen recorders **12**:1666
pens **12**:1662–3
ballpoint **12**:1663
ink **8**:1151–2; **12**:1663

pens (*cont.*)
   felt and fiber-tip **12**:1663
      to detect counterfeit banknotes
         5:584
   fountain **12**:1662
   ink **8**:1151–2
pentaerythritol tetranitrate (PETN)
      1:116; **6**:827, 828
pentane **4**:454; **9**:1161; **17**:2424
Pentium processors **10**:1429
pentoses **3**:389
pepper sprays **11**:1532–3; **14**:1972
peptide bonds **13**:1864
perchloroethylene (perc) **5**:687–9;
      8:1036
percussion instruments **12**:**1667–70**
percussion locks **8**:1024
perfluorocarbons **2**:273
performance, coefficient of **8**:1063–4
peridontal disease **5**:619–20
perihelion **12**:1599
period **12**:1605; **19**:2672
periodic structures **5**:598
periodic table **4**:449; **6**:764;
      12:**1671–3**
   oxidizing and reducing agents
      12:1616
   see also elements, chemical
periosteum **3**:298
periscopes **12**:**1674–5**; **16**:2290
peristalsis **5**:642, 643
Perkin, William **1**:134; **4**:*498*; **5**:690
perlite **8**:1122
permeability (magnetization)
      10:1315
permittivity **14**:1961
personal organizers **4**:*530*
Perspex **4**:560; **13**:1770
pest control **12**:**1676–8**
   biological *see* biological control
   in forests **7**:925
   pest avoidance **1**:61
   pesticides **6**:*844*; **12**:1676–8
      applying **12**:*1676*, 1677
      microencapsulated **10**:1414
      organic **1**:58, *59*
      organochlorine **12**:1676–7
      organophosphorus **12**:1677
      resistance to **12**:1678
      synthetic **1**:54–5, 61
pesticides *see* pest control, pesticides
PET *see* polyethylene terephthalate;
      positron-emission tomography
petrochemicals *see* hydrocarbons
petroleum (crude oil) **3**:391
   alternatives from fermentation
      4:458; **6**:842
   bulk handling **7**:928–9
   chemicals from **4**:453; **5**:663;
      11:1577–80
   compositions **11**:1577
   formation of reservoirs of **11**:1572
   oil spills **10**:1411
   refining *see* oil refining
   sulfur content **11**:1577, 1580;
      16:2300
   synthetic, for cleaning textiles
      5:689
   see also bitumen; natural gas; oil
      exploration and production
petrology **12**:**1679–80**
pewter **9**:1221; **17**:2448
   conservation **2**:160
pH
   measurement **12**:**1692–3**
   pH meters **12**:1692–3
   titration and **4**:446
phage vectors **7**:977
phagocytosis **8**:*1132*, 1133
pharmaceuticals (medical drugs)
      12:**1681–5**
   administration **12**:1683

anticancer *see* chemotherapy
   for asthma **2**:252
   combinations **12**:1685
   cytotoxic **18**:2499
   dependency **12**:1685
   design, using computer graphics
      4:*534*; **12**:1689
   development of **3**:414
   dosage **12**:1682–3
   drug distribution **12**:1683–5
   encapsulated **10**:1413, 1414
   from biotechnology **2**:263
      "anti-sense" drugs **2**:265
      from transgenic plants and
         animals **2**:*264*, 266
   immunosuppressive **18**:2499
   inhalers for **1**:40
   mode of action **12**:1683, 1687–8
   molecular modeling **12**:1688–9
   pain relief **12**:1683
   receptors **12**:1687–8
   resistance **12**:1685
   side effects **12**:1685, 1689
   targeting **12**:1689
   testing of new **12**:*1685*, 1689
   trials **6**:*811*
   types **12**:1681–2
      sulphonamide **1**:135
   see also anesthetics; antibiotics
   see also pharmacology; vaccines
pharmacology **12**:**1686–9**
   see also pharmaceuticals
pharynx **10**:1303
phase diagrams **10**:*1360*, 1362;
      12:1680
phases, of matter **10**:1362
phase-shift keying (PSK) **11**:1475
PHB (polyhydroxybutyrate) **3**:303
phenacetin **8**:1108
phenakistoscopes **1**:136
phenol **4**:457, 498; **8**:1107, 1108
phenolase **7**:905
phenolics, as adhesives **1**:30
phenolphthalein **12**:1692
phenols, polyhydric **8**:1108
phenylamine *see* aniline
phenylethene *see* styrene
phenylmercuric acetate **10**:1372
pheromones **12**:**1690–1**; **15**:2105;
      19:2736
   traps **12**:1678, 1691
phobias **10**:1369
phonographs **4**:513
phonography (records and vinyl
      discs) **4**:513–14; **8**:1076;
      12:**1694–7**; **15**:2144
   record manufacture **12**:1695–6
phosgene (carbonyl chloride)
      13:1772
   as a chemical weapon **4**:437, 438;
      7:953; **8**:1036
phosphine **12**:1700
phosphoenolpyruvate (PEP) **10**:1374
3-phosphoglycerate **12**:1720
phosphoinositide system **2**:252
phosphor bronze **3**:332; **16**:2230
phosphorescence **9**:1241–2;
      10:1301–2
   and oscilloscope screens **12**:1607
phosphoric acid **1**:23
phosphors **5**:599; **10**:1302
   manufacture **18**:2487
phosphorus **12**:**1698–1700**
   allotropes **3**:392; **12**:1698
   compounds **12**:1699–1700
   fertilizers **6**:844–5; **12**:*1698*, 1699,
      1700
   manufacture **12**:1698–9
   sources **12**:*1698*, 1700
   uses **12**:1699
phosphorus pentachloride
      12:1699–1700

phosphorus sesquisulfide **12**:*1700*
phosphorus trichloride **8**:1034;
      12:1699–1700
photocells *see* photoelectric cells and
      photometry
photochemistry **4**:464; **9**:1202
photochemotherapy **12**:1724
photocomposition, newspaper
      11:1517
photoconductors **17**:2421
photocopiers **12**:**1701–3**
photo detectors, for thermal imaging
      6:864
photodiodes
   and fiber optics **3**:355
   silicon (SPDs), in exposure meters
      3:368
photodynamic therapy (PDT) **3**:380
photoelastic analysis **9**:*1237*; **13**:1796
photoelastic material **17**:*2398*
photoelectric cells and photometry
      12:**1704–5**
   photoelectric cells (photocells)
      in electric motors **6**:731
      photoconductive cells **12**:*1704*,
         1705
      photoemissive cells **12**:1704–5
      and photomultiplier tubes
         12:1717–18
      photovoltaic *see* photovoltaic
         (PV) cells
      and security systems **3**:340–1;
         15:2043
      for streetlamp switches **14**:1980
   photometry **12**:1705
   see also solar energy, solar panels
photoelectric effect **9**:1241; **12**:1704;
      14:1881
photoemissive cells **12**:1704–5
photoemissive materials **8**:1128–9
photoengraving **9**:1166; **11**:1517
photoetching process **13**:1845–6
photogrammetry **10**:1329;
      12:*1706–7*; **17**:2334
photographic editing software **4**:534
photographic films and processing
      12:**1708–14**
   automatic processing **12**:1713
   copying **12**:1713–14
   false-color imagery **1**:35; **2**:156;
      6:742
   film **8**:1036
      35mm **3**:364–5
      color **8**:1036; **12**:1710–11
      color masking **12**:1711–12
      direct-positive **12**:*1710*, 1711
      DX coding **3**:369
      infrared **6**:742; **12**:1709
      instant-picture film **9**:1158–9
      and light quanta **6**:744
      manufacture **12**:1714
      monochrome (black-and-white)
         12:1708–10
      movie film **11**:1494, 1498;
         13:1856–9
      orthochromatic **12**:1709
      panchromatic **12**:1709; **16**:*2194*
      for photomicrography
         12:1715–16
      roll film **3**:365–6
      for space photography **15**:2153
   lithographic development **12**:1713
   photographic paper **10**:*1413*, 1414
   printing process **12**:1712–13
      enlarging images **12**:*1708*, 1712
   see also microfilm
photographs, for desktop publishing
      5:628
photography
   filters **6**:858
   flash **3**:365; **6**:730; **8**:1077–8;
      15:2075

forensic **12**:1716
   schlieren **15**:2031, *2133*
   trick **16**:2185, 2186
   see also aerial photography; cam-
      eras; high-speed photography;
      photographic films and process-
      ing; space photography; under-
      water photography
photogravure **13**:1852
photolithography **10**:*1416*, 1417–18
photoluminescence **10**:1302
photometry **12**:1705
photomicrography **12**:**1715–16**
   fluorescence **3**:*414*
photomultiplier tubes (PMTs) **6**:745;
      12:**1717–18**
   in optical scanners **12**:1592–3
photon drive **14**:1996
photons (quanta) **2**:151, 183;
      6:743–4; **9**:1237, 1241; **12**:1728;
      14:1880
   antiparticles **6**:769
   and electromagnetic interactions
      6:770–1
   energy **6**:788; **9**:1209; **14**:1880
   interactions with matter
      9:1209–10, 1241–2; **14**:1881
   and photoemissive cells
      12:1704–5
   for laser and maser action **9**:1210
   spontaneous and stimulated
      emissions **9**:1210
   X-ray **4**:461–2, 551; **19**:2721, 2724
photoresist **5**:651
photosensors *see* photoelectric cells
      and photometry
photosetting machines **11**:1517
photosynthesis **1**:62; **3**:389, 412;
      5:645; **10**:1373; **12**:**1719–22**
photosystems I and II **12**:1722
phototherapy (photodynamic
      therapy) **12**:**1723–4**
phototransistors **18**:2483
phototypesetting **5**:630; **9**:1261
photovoltaic (PV) cells **2**:229; **4**:552;
      6:730, 792; **12**:*1704*, 1705
   on bicycles **2**:244
   in calculators **3**:361
photovoltaic effect **12**:1705
phthalic acid **11**:1628
physics **12**:**1725–8**
   astrophysics **2**:**178–81**
   biophysics **2**:**261–2**
   condensed-matter **4**:**550–3**
   geophysics **7**:**991–5**
   plasma *see* plasma physics
   solid-state **4**:550
   see also quantum theory
physiology **13**:**1733–4**
   definition of death **9**:1232
phytoplankton **10**:1332
pianolas **13**:1738
pianos **13**:**1735–8**
   electromechanical **17**:2342
   electronic **17**:*2343*
   keyboards **11**:1507
   player **13**:1738
Piccard, Auguste **16**:2292–3
piccolos **19**:2715
pickers (spindle pickers), cotton
      5:582
pickling
   animal skins **9**:1222
   foods **7**:906–7, 911
   metals **2**:223
pickup, acoustic **13**:**1739–40**
picric acid (trinitrophenol) **6**:827,
      828; **8**:1108; **11**:1527
picture restoration **13**:**1741–3**
piezoelectric constant **13**:1744
piezoelectric effect **13**:1744
piezoelectric material **5**:599;

10:1364; **13**:1744–5
  ceramics **3**:426; **13**:1745
  quartz **5**:599; **12**:1606; **13**:1744,
    1745
    in clocks and watches **4**:487;
      17:2442, 2445–6; **19**:2649, 2650
  as smart ceramics **10**:1352–3
  as transducers **13**:1745, 1843;
    18:2474, 2529–30
  use in ink-jet printers **4**:545
pigments
  in butter **5**:602
  in paint **12**:1627–8, 1630
pigs (go devils) **13**:1754
pigs (animals)
  cloned **7**:*978*
  intensively-reared **1**:*56*, 57
  organically-reared **1**:*61*
  organs, for transplants **18**:2504
  slaughtering **15**:2096–7, 2098
  transgenic **18**:2504
  and truffles **12**:*1690*
  veterinary work and **18**:2586
pile drivers **13**:1746
piles
  and building techniques **3**:338
  sheet and bearing **13**:1746
pill, contraceptive **13**:1734, 1818
pilotless aircraft **13**:1747–8; **14**:1913
Pinatubo, Mount **6**:806–7
pinball machines **7**:951
pinning, bone fractures **3**:300
Pioneer space probes **12**:1707;
  15:2156
  Pioneer 10 **14**:1913
pions **12**:1652
pipelines **13**:1753–4
  bulk-handling, at docks **7**:929
  control systems **13**:1754
  corrosion control and testing
    13:1754
  gas **13**:1754
  oil **13**:1753, *1754*
  pneumatic, valves **18**:*2567*
  repairs, using freezing **5**:591
  on tankers **17**:2351
  and telemetry **17**:2365
  water-intake
    antifouling techniques **2**:149
    gas **7**:*959*
pipelining, and microprocessor
  performance **10**:1429
pipes
  domestic plumbing **13**:*1786*
    scale **13**:1787
  underground, for drainage **5**:674,
    675
  pipe and tube manufacture
    13:1749–52, 1754
  pressure pipes, from asbestos
    6:847; **13**:1750
Pisces class submersibles **11**:*1566*
pistols
  air **8**:1025
  automatic **2**:196–7
  captive bolt **15**:2096
  machine *see* submachine guns
  Very **7**:870
pistons, reciprocating **13**:1789
pitch (material) **4**:498; **10**:1359
pitch (sound) **1**:65, *70*, 71; **15**:2132,
  2134
  of a string **16**:2283
  unison **12**:1601
pitchblende **18**:2487
Pitot tubes **1**:*65*
pitting **4**:569
Pittsburgh process **7**:1000
pituitary gland **6**:781–2; **8**:1085, *1086*
  cell culture, and insulin production
    13:1733–4
pixels **3**:432; **4**:532, 533

and video cameras **18**:2590–1
placebos **12**:1689
placenta, hormones **6**:782
plague **6**:811
planar displays **5**:648
Planck, Max **2**:183; **9**:1237, **14**.1880
Planck's constant **6**:768; **9**:1202,
  1209; **12**:1728; **14**:1880
planers (machine tools) **10**:1308,
  1309; **19**:2717
planes, manufacture **18**:2460–1
planetarium projectors **13**:1755–6
planetars **13**:1760
planetary science **13**:1757–61
  planets
    age **13**:1757–8
    chaotic bombardment of
      13:1759
    and eclipses **5**:710
    extrasolar **13**:1759–60; **14**:1912
    and extraterrestrial life **4**:*446*;
      9:1234
    formation **13**:1758–9
    free-floating **13**:1760
    gaseous (gas giants; outer
      planets) **13**:1757, 1758,
      1760–1; **15**:2118
    habitable **13**:1761
    migration **13**:1761
    orbits **12**:1599; **13**:1761
    and planetarium projectors
      13:1755–6
    relief mapping **12**:1707
    terrestrial (inner planets)
      13:1757, 1759; **15**:2118
    see also Solar System; space probes
planetesimals **13**:1758, 1759
planks, production **9**:1294–5, *1296*
plankton **10**:1332, 1333
plan position indicators (PPIs) **1**:94;
  14:1898
plants
  and the atmosphere **1**:*62*, 63
  carnivorous **5**:645
  cells **3**:412, *413*
  communication between **3**:304–5
  evolution **7**:988
  fat-reducing **6**:837
  genetically-engineered *see* genetic
    engineering
  grown in water (hydroponics)
    8:1120–2; **9**:1194
  high-tech breeding **1**:53–4
  in-vitro culturing **2**:*200*
  leguminous **11**:*1526*
  natural fibers from **6**:849–50
  and nickel **11**:1524
  parasitic **12**:1644
  photosynthesis **1**:62; **3**:389, 412;
    5:645; **10**:1373; **12**:1719–22
  reproduction **14**:1958
  sense of touch **3**:303–4, *305*
  size and metabolic rate **2**:262
  transgenic **19**:2681
plaque
  arterial **8**:1046–7, 1052
  dental **5**:619
plasma physics **5**:656; **10**:1362;
  13:1762–3
  and nuclear fusion **7**:946–7;
    10:1319
  in the Sun **10**:*1361*; **13**:1762
plasma-arc technology
  for cutting metal **10**:1364,
    1379–80
  for waste incineration **5**:720
plasma beat-wave accelerators
  13:1763
plasma deposition **13**:1763
plasma temperature measurement
  9:*1212*
plasma welding **10**:*1366*, 1383

plasmids **1**:53; **2**:263, *264*; **7**:977
plasmolysis **12**:1609
plaster, gypsum **3**:417
plaster casts **3**:300
plastic deformation (plastic flow)
  1:102; **5**:713
plastic flow *see* plastic deformation
plastic forming **3**:426–7
plastics **13**:1768–72
  cellulosic **13**:1768–9
  epoxies **13**:1772
  from plants **3**:303
  glass-reinforced (GRPs) **7**:1003
    in boat building **2**:274, 276–7
    in bows **3**:307, 308
    for mannequins **13**:*1772*
    for pipes **5**:675; **13**:1750, 1751
    in trucks **18**:2507
  plating **17**:2324
  polyalkenes **13**:1770–1
    see also polyethylene; polypropy-
      lene
  polyamide *see* polyamides
  polycarbonates **9**:1229; **13**:1768,
    1772
  polyester *see* polyesters
  polyurethane *see* polyurethanes
  processing **13**:1773–6
  PTFE *see* polytetrafluoroethylene
  recycling **10**:1366; **12**:1625;
    13:1776; **14**:1941
  reinforced, with asbestos **6**:847
  synthetic **13**:1769–70
    see also polychloroethene; poly-
      styrene
  thermosets **13**:1750
  uses
    batteries **2**:229
    bearings **2**:233
    bicycle frames **2**:243
    in buildings **3**:337, *337*
    contact lenses **4**:560
    food and drink containers **3**:382,
      385; **12**:1625
    pipes **13**:1750–1, 1787
    see also fibers, synthetic
  see also thermoplastics
plastic surgery **13**:1764–7
  on gums **5**:620
  limb reattachment **13**:1765–6
  see also microsurgery; skin, grafts
plate tectonics **5**:698–9; **7**:990, 995;
  11:1565, 1568; **13**:1777–80
  and earthquakes **5**:*706*, 707,
    13:1777, *1780*
  see also continental drift
platforming **11**:1576
platforms, oil-drilling **5**:680, 681,
  682–3; **11**:*1574*
plating
  electroless **17**:2324
  tools **18**:2464
  see also electroplating
platinum **10**:*1377*; **13**:1781
  as a catalyst **3**:406; **13**:1782;
    15:*2129*
  in resistance thermometers
    17:2424
platinum diarsenide (sperrylite)
  13:1781
platinum metals **13**:1781–3; **18**:2485
platinum sulfide (cooperite) **13**:1781
plenum chamber vessels **1**:80
Plexiglas **4**:560; **13**:1770; **16**:2191,
  2192
  and triboelectricity **6**:*728*
pliers, manufacture **18**:2463–4
plotters **4**:528
plowing **15**:2113
  contour **6**:817, *819*
  for weed control **19**:2678, 2680
plows **1**:46–7, *49*, 51

mole **5**:674
  underwater cable-laying **3**:349
plumbing **13**:1784–7
Pluto **15**:2118, 2122–3
  moon **15**:2122–3
  orbit **13**:1761
plutonium **14**:1906–7
  in heart pacemakers **8**:1048
  isotopes **7**:877; **11**:1544, 1547
  and nuclear fission **11**:1538, 1539,
    1546; **13**:1831
    nuclear weapons **11**:1552–3
  recovery **6**:766
plutonium dioxide **11**:1539
plutonium nitrate **11**:1539
plutonium nitride **11**:1538
plywood **9**:1295; **19**:2709
  manufacture **19**:2710–11
    adhesives used in **1**:30; **19**:2709
  uses
    boatbuilding **2**:275–6
    for buildings **3**:336
pneumatic tools **13**:1788–9
  jackhammers **9**:1195; **13**:*1840*
  see also pile drivers
pneumographs **13**:1807
pneumonia, vaccine **18**:2557
p-n junction (depletion layer) **5**:654;
  6:752; **15**:2053, 2116–17;
  18:2481
Podolsky, Boris **14**:1884
Poincaré, Henri **3**:430; **14**:1950
point radiation **17**:2334
points, railroad **14**:1924
point-to-point protocol (PPP)
  11:1475–6
Poiseuille, Jean-Léonard-Marie
  19:2610–11
poison gas **4**:437
poisons **13**:1790–2; **16**:2197
  and forensic science **7**:918–19;
    13:*1792*
polar diagrams **10**:1425
polarimeters **13**:1793, 1796
polarization (electrical) **3**:386; **9**:1163
  in batteries **2**:226
  in electrets **5**:715
polarization (light) **5**:648; **9**:1239;
  13:1794–6; **14**:1883; **19**:2673
  circular **13**:1796
  dichroic polarizers **13**:1794–5
  elliptical **13**:1796
  filters for **6**:858; **18**:*2573*
  and LCDs **5**:648; **9**:*1258*
  uses **13**:1796
    microscopy **10**:*1435*; **12**:*1680*
    photoelastic stress analysis
      9:*1237*; **13**:1796
    polarimetry **13**:1793, 1796
polarization (radio transmission)
  6:741
polders **9**:1206, 1208
poling **4**:567; **13**:1745
polio, vaccines **18**:2555, 2556
polishing **17**:2325
pollen **10**:*1431*; **14**:1958
  and archaeology **2**:159
pollution
  acid rain **1**:*25*; **13**:1798; **16**:2300
  atmospheric **13**:1797–8
    and corrosion **4**:571
    emission control **13**:1800–2
    from forest fires **6**:*808*
    from oil-well burning **6**:806
  effects on the lungs **10**:1305
  and free radicals **11**:1559
  light **13**:1802, *1803*
  monitoring and control
    13:1797–1803
    from automobiles **2**:205;
      13:1802
  natural remedies **10**:1411;

pollution, natural remedies (cont.)
13:1802–3
using LIDAR 13:1797
see also wastewater treatment
noise 13:1802
soil 15:2113
transport-related 5:720
visual 5:647
water 13:1798, 1799, 1802
from crude oil 6:806
from fertilizers 6:845; 12:1700
from tankers 17:2352
in the water supply 4:476
polonium 1:1276
polyacrylonitrile (PAN; Acrilan)
3:394, 395; 6:853; 13:1771
gels 10:1353
polyalkenes (polyolefins) 6:853;
13:1770
see also polyethylene; polypropylene
polyamides 13:1772, 1804–6, 1811
aromatic see aramids
Nomex 7:880; 13:1806, 1860
polyimides 13:1804, 1806
uses, car washes 3:398
see also Kevlar; nylons
polybutadiene 4:460
polycarbonates 13:1768, 1772
for lenses 9:1229
polychlorinated biphenyls 7:901
polychloroethene (polyvinyl chloride; PVC) 7:880, 893; 8:1035;
13:1769–70, 1771; 17:2448
baton rounds 11:1533
and cling film 12:1626
plasticized 12:1696; 13:1770, 1771
polydimethylsiloxane (PDMS)
15:2078
polyelectrolyte gels 10:1353
polyesters 6:853; 13:1772
dyeing 5:692, 693
glass-reinforced (GRP) 3:337
as membranes on tensile structures
17:2398
for powder coatings 13:1823–4
production 6:853; 13:1811
recycling 13:1776
for rope making 3:350–1
polyethene see polyethylene
polyethylene (polyethene; polythene)
6:853; 13:1770, 1773
chlorinated (CPE) 14:1941
formation 13:1810
low- and high-density 13:1770–1
strengthening 6:745
uses 2:255; 13:1770–1
car washes 3:398
cling film 12:1626
food packaging 7:908; 12:1676;
13:1770–1
polyethylene glycol 2:159, 160
polyethylene terephthalate (PET)
6:853; 12:1622; 13:1772;
14:1941
polygraphs 13:1807–8
polyhydroxybutyrate (PHB) 3:303
polyhydroxyethylmethacrylate 4:561
polyimides 13:1804, 1806
polyisobutene 14:1994
polyisocyanurate 9:1161
polyisoprene 13:1771
polymerase chain reaction (PCR)
7:974; 11:1479
polymers and polymerization
13:1809–12
polymerization
processes 13:1809–12
reactions 13:1809
polymers
architecture 13:1812
for batteries 2:229

coatings see powder coatings
cyanoacrylate 1:32
for fiber-optic cables 6:856
"living" 4:460
shape-memory 10:1352;
12:1624
smart 10:1352
see also copolymers; plastics;
polyamides
polymethylmethacrylate 4:560;
13:1770
polyolefins see polyalkenes
polyols 1:98
polypeptides 13:1864–5
polypropene see polypropylene
polypropylene (polypropene)
13:1770, 1809
biaxially oriented 12:1626
uses 3:384; 4:546; 6:853; 13:1769
polyps, colon 6:784, 785
polysaccharides 3:389–90
polysiloxanes see silicones
polystyrene 8:1108; 9:1161; 13:1770,
1772, 1775
expanded (Styrofoam) 13:1776
plating 17:2324
polytetrafluoroethylene (PTFE;
polytetrafluoroethene; Teflon)
8:1034; 13:1769, 1771, 1813–15
manufacture 13:1813–14
uses 2:233; 3:337; 9:1289; 13:1771,
1814–15
Teflon-coated glass fiber fabric
17:2399, 2400, 2401
tubing 13:1752
polythene see polyethylene
polyurethane rubbers 14:2001
polyurethanes (PUs) 13:1772
for filling wall cavities 9:1161
foams 13:1772, 1776; 15:2023,
2051
uses
for baton rounds 11:1533
for filling wall cavities 9:1161
for marine salvage 15:2023
polyvinyl acetate (PVA) 4:546
adhesives based on 1:30; 19:2718
polyvinyl chloride see polychloroethene
polyvinylidene chloride 13:1744
Pong (electronic game) 7:952
pontoons 3:328; 15:2023
population 13:1816–19
control see contraceptives
population inversion 9:1210, 1213
porcelain see china and porcelain
porphyria 12:1724
porphyrins 12:1723
port (fortified wine) 19:2702
Portable Life Support Systems
(PLSSs) 16:2177, 2178
portraits, computer 7:920
ports, bulk-handling see docks
position-control mechanisms
15:2057
positron-emission tomography
(PET) 2:151, 281; 3:312
positrons 2:150; 6:744, 769
emission 2:151
postcards, 3-D 16:2263
postmortems (autopsies) 12:1658
POSTNET 10:1322
post-traumatic stress disorder
(PTSD) 13:1867
potassium 1:99, 101
electron orbitals 2:185
fertilizers 6:845
potassium alum 1:109
potassium aluminum sulfate 14:2015
potassium bromide 1:101; 12:1708,
1711
potassium carbonate 1:100, 101

potassium chloride 1:101; 6:845
potassium dichromate 2:226;
12:1711
potassium hexacyanoferrate 12:1711;
14:2015
potassium hydroxide (caustic potash)
1:23, 101
in batteries 2:227
in fuel cells 7:936
preparation 1:25
and soap manufacture 15:2107
potassium iodide 1:101
potassium nitrate (saltpeter) 8:1024;
11:1525
potassium sodium tartrate (Rochelle
salt) 13:1744–5
potassium sulfate 6:845
potatoes 12:1693
dried 7:910
frozen French fries 7:910, 911
genetically-engineered 3:303, 304
potential difference 4:554; 6:726,
728–9
potential energy 5:695; 6:786;
13:1820
electrostatic 6:787, 788
gravitational 6:787; 12:1725;
13:1820; 17:2415, 2416
potentiometers 8:1071; 13:1821–2;
18:2474
carbon-track 13:1821
panoramic 13:1822
sliding-wire 13:1821
pots (rheostats) 13:1821, 1822
pan 13:1822
pottery 3:424–5
dating 2:159
powder coatings 13:1823–4
powder lances 17:2412
powder metallurgy 1:104–6, 107;
3:404
power 5:695; 12:1726; 13:1825–6
electrical 6:728–9, 729; 13:1826
generation by thermopiles
17:2420
measurement 10:1403
power blocks 7:873
power cables see cables, power
powerheads, outboard-motor
12:1614
power plants 13:1826, 1827–32,
1834
alternators 13:1827, 1829–30
efficiency 6:788
first public 13:1827, 1833
gas turbines 13:1832
natural gas-powered 7:967;
13:1828
hydroelectric see hydroelectric
power
and nuclear fusion 2:248
nuclear (nuclear fission) 7:876;
12:1728; 13:1827–8, 1831–2
see also nuclear reactors
rated in power units 6:790
solar 6:792; 15:2116
using carbon-based fuels
13:1830–1
coal 13:1827, 1831; 14:1927
wood-burning 2:258
powers, mathematical 9:1275
power supply 13:1833–8; 19:2704–5
power cables see cables, power
and telemetry 17:2364–5
power supply units (PSUs) 4:529
pozzolana 3:417; 4:546
Prandtl, Ludwig 1:37
praseodymium 18:2485, 2488
preamplifiers (preamps) 1:126
precession 5:696
precipitates, and qualitative analysis
4:446

precipitation hardening 1:104
Precision Positioning Service (PPS)
7:1008
predictors 1:143–4
prednisone 18:2499
prefabricated building components
3:338
pregnancy 11:1563–4; 14:1958
ectopic 6:785
medical drugs taken during
12:1685
nutrition during 8:1047
preterm delivery 12:1661
rubella during 12:1589
tests during 8:1135; 11:1563, 1564
tests for 2:265
see also in-vitro fertilization;
obstetrics and gynecology
prehension 2:255
presbyopia 6:832; 16:2191
presses
dome 18:2578
drill 10:1310
hydraulic 8:1100–1
machine 10:1306, 1310
for sheet metal 15:2064–5
vacuum 18:2578
veneer 18:2578; 19:2711
pressing, clothes 4:490
pressure 13:1839–40
air locks and 1:85
atmospheric 1:63; 10:1398, 1399;
13:1840; 16:2245; 18:2558
measurement 2:222–4; 13:1840
autoclaves and 1:85
dynamic 4:521
in fluids 13:1839–40
gases 7:960–1; 13:1840
and force 13:1839
measurement see barometers;
manometers; pressure gauges
undersea diving and 2:154;
5:666–7
pressure cookers 2:190; 13:1841
industrial 13:1841
see also autoclaves
pressure gauges 13:1842–3
vacuum 18:2559–60
see also barometers; manometers
pressurized-water reactors (PWRs)
11:1542, 1543, 1545; 13:1832;
18:2520
Priestley, Joseph 6:725; 12:1618;
15:2109
primates, evolution 6:825
Principia (Newton) 8:1020
printed circuits 13:1844–6
printers, computer see computer
printers
printing 13:1847–52
banknotes 5:583
collotype 13:1852
colorometers used in 4:512
and desktop publishing 5:630
fabric 5:692, 693; 6:833–4;
17:2408
gravure 9:1263; 13:1850, 1851–2
history 13:1847–50
illustrations 13:1850–1
inks used for 8:1152
letterpress 9:1263; 11:1517;
13:1849, 1850, 1851, 1852
lithographic see lithography
maps 10:1329–30
newspapers 11:1517–18; 13:1849
offset see lithography, offset
print identification 13:1851
reprographic 13:1852
resist 6:834
roller 6:833, 834
screen 6:833–4; 13:1852
for circuit boards 13:1845

transfer **6**:834

web offset *see* lithography, web offset

see also computer printers; engraving and etching; photocopiers

prisms **13**:*1853*

in binoculars **2**:249, 250; **13**:1853

in cameras **3**:367

rotating **8**:1079

Nicol **13**:1795

in periscopes **12**:1674–5

and white light **9**:1237, *1238*

probability theory **16**:2248–9

proctoscopes **17**:2331

producer gas (Siemen's gas) **7**:*956*, 958

progesterone **12**:1687

program counters **10**:1428

programmable logic controllers (PLCs) **10**:1365

programming, computer *see* computers, programming and software

prohormones **8**:1084

projected reality (artificial reality) **19**:2604

projection

back **16**:2188; **17**:2388

front **16**:*2187*, 2188; **17**:2387–8

reflex (front-axial projection) **17**:2388

projections, mapmaking **10**:1327

projectors

movie and slide **13**:*1854–7*

and digital sound systems **15**:2148

and stage effects **16**:2234–5

overhead **13**:*1855*

planetarium **13**:*1755–6*

prokaryotes **6**:823; **9**:1235

prolactin **8**:1087

promoters, catalyst **3**:407

PROMs (programmable read-only memories) **9**:1167

propanal **4**:456

propane **3**:334; **4**:454; **7**:*955*, 959; **8**:1105

from oil refining **11**:1577

liquefied **8**:1106

propanol **1**:*98*

propanone (acetone) **4**:456

propellants, ammunition **1**:116–17

propellers **13**:*1858–9*

aircraft **1**:74; **13**:1858–9

propfan **1**:*44*, 78

thrust and balance **1**:65; **13**:1858–9

marine-propulsion **10**:1337; **13**:1858, 1859; **15**:2068

and cavitation **13**:1859

speedboat **16**:2206–7

outboard-motor **12**:1614

propeller anemometers **1**:130

propenamide (acrylamide) **13**:1771

propene (propylene) **4**:454; **8**:1105

polymers **13**:1812

see also polypropylene

propenoic acid (acrylic acid) **12**:1629; **13**:1771

propenonitrile *see* acrylonitrile

propfans **1**:*44*, 78

proplyds (protoplanetary disks) **13**:1759–60

prop washes **15**:2023

propyne **4**:455; **8**:1105

prospecting, mineral, using spectrochemical analysis **16**:2196–7

prostaglandins **12**:1683

in plants **3**:305

prostate gland, operations on **18**:2550

prostheses **2**:253–7; **13**:1764, 1767

eye **12**:*1613*; **13**:1767

see also bioengineering

protective clothing **13**:*1860–3*

against chemical weapons **4**:*439, 440*

fire-resistant **6**:*847*

sports **16**:*2224, 2226*

see also armor, body; breathing apparatus; diving suits; gas and dust masks; space suits

proteins **2**:261; **13**:*1864–6*

chiral **4**:458

complete and incomplete **11**:1557

dietary **11**:1557; **13**:*1866*

fibrous **13**:1865

functions **13**:1865

see also enzymes

globular **13**:1865

manufacture

single-cell protein (SCP) foods **6**:810; **7**:914; **13**:*1866*

using genetic engineering **7**:978

structure **2**:261; **13**:*1864–5*

from computer graphics **13**:*1864*, 1866

synthesis **7**:974–5; **11**:1477–8; **12**:1657

uses **13**:1865–6

see also amino acids

protocols **4**:537

modem **11**:1475–6

proton-induced X-ray emission (PIXE) **2**:158

protons

and atomic structure **2**:*182*, 183, 185; **6**:767; **14**:1905–6

comprised of quarks **6**:770

discovery **6**:763, 767

proton-antiproton pairs **2**:151

protoplanetary disks (proplyds) **13**:1759–60

prototypes **10**:1366

protozoa, immune response to **8**:1136

Proust, Joseph **2**:182

proximity caching **11**:1503

Prozac (fluoxetine) **12**:1682; **13**:1868

Pseudomonas spp. **9**:1168; **10**:1411

PSK (phase-shift keying) **11**:1475

psoralen compounds **12**:1723; **18**:*2533*

psoriasis **12**:*1724*; **15**:2089; **18**:*2533*

PSUs (power supply units) **4**:529

psychiatry **13**:*1867–8*

psychoacoustics **1**:26–7

psychoanalysis **13**:1867

psychochemicals **4**:437

psychology, sports **16**:2226

psychrometers **8**:1123

PTFE *see* polytetrafluoroethylene

ptyalin **5**:642

public address systems **1**:*126*

public-key cryptosystems (PKCs) **6**:762

publishing, desktop *see* desktop publishing

pug mills **3**:*425*

pulleys **13**:*1869*, 1872

wooden, mass production **10**:1341

pulsars **17**:2316–17

and radio astronomy **14**:1912

X-ray **17**:*2316*; **19**:2724

pulse-code modulation (PCM) **1**:128–9

and electronic organs **12**:1603

pulse jets **7**:967

pulse meters **16**:2224

pulverised fuel ash (PFA) **13**:1831

pumice **1**:17, 18

pumped-storage projects **6**:798; **8**:1112, *1115*; **13**:1827; **18**:2520

pump escapes (triple-combination pumpers) **6**:860

pumping, optical **9**:1210, 1211

pumping stations, gas **13**:1754

pumps *see* compressors and pumps

punchballs **16**:2224

punches **18**:2465

pupils, eye **6**:830, *831*; **9**:1227

purifiers **3**:322

purpura (dye) **1**:133

pusher centrifuges **3**:423

PVC (polyvinyl chloride) *see* polychloroethene

pycnometers **5**:617

pylons, electricity **3**:344, *346*

pyramids **13**:*1870–2*

Mayan **11**:1560; **16**:2275

pyrethrum **12**:*1676*, 1677

pyridine **4**:455

pyridoxine **19**:2613

pyrite **16**:2299

pyrolysis **13**:1776

pyrotechnic effects **16**:*2233*, 2235

pyroxene **10**:1392

Pythagoras

musical scale **11**:1508

Pythagorean triplets **11**:1556

theorem **10**:1354–5; **15**:2082

and vision **9**:1236

Q

Q fever, as a biological weapon **4**:438

quadrants **15**:2062

quadratic equations **10**:1357

quadrophonic systems **8**:1072

quality management **14**:*1877–9*

sampling **14**:1878; **16**:*2249*

quanta, of light *see* photons

quantum chromodynamics (QCD) **6**:772; **12**:1728; **14**:1884

see also quarks

quantum electrodynamics (QED) **14**:1884

quantum numbers **6**:767–8

quantum theory **12**:1728; **14**:*1880–4*

Bohr model of the atom **2**:183; **14**:1881–2; **16**:2193

Copenhagen interpretation **14**:1883–4

electrons behaving as waves **2**:183–5, *184*; **6**:767–8; **14**:1882

and light **9**:1241–2; **14**:1880; **16**:2193

the photoelectric effect **9**:1241; **14**:1881

Planck's constant **6**:768; **9**:1202, *1209*; **12**:1728; **14**:1880

Planck's introduction of photons (quanta) **2**:183; **14**:1880

polarized **14**:1883

wave–particle duality **14**:1881; **19**:2673–4

Pauli exclusion principle **14**:1882

quantum mechanics **5**:694; **14**:1882–3; **16**:2249; **17**:2416

and black holes **2**:270

and electron orbitals **4**:442, 461; **9**:1209

and the EPR paradox **14**:1884

Heisenberg uncertainty principle **6**:770; **14**:1883; **16**:2249

and quantum chromodynamics (QCD) **12**:1728; **14**:1884

and quantum electrodynamics (QED) **14**:1884

and Schrödinger's cat **14**:1884

and wave functions of electrons **6**:767–8

quarks **2**:*182*; **6**:770, 771; **14**:*1881*, 1884

charm and strange **6**:770

color charges **6**:772

quark–antiquark pairs **2**:*151*; **6**:772

top and bottom **6**:770

up and down **6**:770, 771

Quark Xpress **11**:1518

quarrying **14**:*1885–6*

quartz **7**:981; **15**:*2075*; **16**:*2270*

in clocks and watches **4**:486–8; **17**:*2442*, 2445–6; **19**:*2649*, 2650

in computer motherboards **4**:529

piezoelectric **5**:599; **12**:1606; **13**:1744, 1745

quasars **2**:174, 267, *270*; **14**:1904

Queen Elizabeth II (ship) **15**:*2070*

quicklime *see* calcium oxide

quinine **1**:134; **12**:1686

R

RAAMS (Remote Antiarmor Mine System) **11**:1454

rabies, vaccines **18**:2555, 2556

racing, motor *see* racing cars and dragsters

racing cars and dragsters **14**:*1887–92*

drag racing **14**:*1890*, 1891–2

racing cars **14**:1887–91

engines **7**:903; **14**:1889

speedway **14**:1891

sports car (GT) racing **14**:1891

tires **14**:*1888*, 1890; **18**:*2454*, 2455–6

rack-and-pinion systems **3**:357; **4**:506

rackets

squash and badminton **16**:2222

tennis **16**:2221–3

racketts **19**:*2713*, 2714

racon **11**:1514

radar **6**:742; **14**:*1893–8*

air traffic control **1**:88, 94–5; **3**:410; **14**:1895–6, *1897*

and antiaircraft guns **1**:144

displays **14**:*1897–8*

plan position indicators (PPIs) **1**:94; **14**:1898

Doppler **1**:68; **5**:672; **8**:1097–8; **14**:1897

search and surveillance **14**:*1896*, 1897

for space navigation **11**:1514

to monitor the weather **10**:1397, 1398; **14**:1898

and traffic monitoring **14**:1985

and early-warning defense systems **14**:*1893*, 1895–6, 1897

ground-penetrating (GPR) **14**:1898

"guns" **14**:*1893*

IFF (Interrogation Friend or Foe) **1**:144

for mine detection **3**:293

and MTI (moving target indication) **5**:672; **14**:1898

for navigation **11**:*1510*, 1513, 1514

plan-position **14**:1894

pulsed **14**:1894, *1896*

range and wavelength **14**:1895–6

and remote-sensing satellite pictures **7**:986

safety **14**:1898

search **14**:1898

secondary surveillance (SSR) **1**:94–5; **14**:1897

side-looking airborne radar (SLAR) pictures **1**:35; **7**:990

and stealth technologies

jamming techniques **16**:2251–2

radar-avoidance aircraft **1**:69, 144; **10**:*1350*; **16**:2254

synthetic aperture (SAR) **12**:1707; **17**:2337

to calculate altitude **1**:68

to map planets **12**:1707

tracking **14**:1896

radar (*cont.*)
  transmitters **14:**1895
  use in archaeology **2:**156, 157
  used in "smart" missiles **11:**1467–8
  use in seismology **7:**994–5
  X-band (XBR), to track missiles **16:**2184
radar-absorbent materials (RAMs) **10:***1350*
radiancy, spectral **9:**1237
radiation
  effects on the body
    cause of cancer **3:**378
    dangers from cell phones **3:**416
    from radiotherapy **14:**1921
    in space **16:***2175*
  electromagnetic *see* electromagnetic radiation
  ionizing **9:***1183*, 1184
  synchrotron **17:**2316
  thermal **17:**2421
radiation belts **14:1899–90**
radiators
  central-heating, thermostatic valves **17:**2427
  engine **6:**801; **8:**1054, *1055*
radio **6:**740–1; **14:1901–4**
  AM (amplitude modulation) **11:**1473; **14:**1902–3; **18:***2496*
  and diodes **18:**2564
  antennas **1:**141–2; **6:**741; **14:**1904
  broadcasting **18:**2493–4, 2495–6
  and cell phones **3:**415–16; **17:**2358–9
  communication **17:**2358
    see also cellular telephones
  digital **6:**755; **14:**1904
  distortion **14:**1903
  and feedback theory **6:**839
  FM (frequency modulation) **11:**1473; **14:**1903
  IF (intermediate frequency) **14:**1903
  long-wave **1:**142; **6:**739; **18:**2494
  medium-wave **1:**142; **18:**2494
  modulation **14:**1901
  noise **14:**1903
  short-wave **18:**2494
  speed of radio waves **14:**1894
  stereo broadcasting **15:**2144
  telemetry **17:**2365
  telescopes **11:**1562; **14:**1909
    amplifiers **14:**1911
    antennas **14:**1909–10
    output devices **14:**1911
    Very Large Arrays (VLAS) **14:***1909*, 1910–11
  transistor **18:**2494
  transmitters **6:**740
    to track animals **19:**2734
  tuning circuits **12:**1606; **14:**1966
  UHF **1:**142
  VHF **1:**142; **6:**739; **14:***1901*; **18:**2494
    and air-traffic control **1:**94, *95*
  VLF **6:**740
  see also radar
radioactivity **14:1905–8**; **18:**2546
  decay series **14:**1908
  detection by Geiger–Müller tubes **7:**970
  from igneous rocks **7:**995
  and heat in the Earth's core **5:**698
  modes of decay
    alpha decay **14:**1906–7
    beta decay **6:**765, 771; **14:**1907
    electron capture **14:**1907
    gamma rays emission **6:**744; **14:**1907
    internal conversion **14:**1907
  nuclear waste disposal **6:**796; **11:**1539, **1547–50**; **18:**2547

radioactive fallout, protection against **7:**954
rates of decay **14:**1908
  uses **14:**1908
    in body scanning **2:**281; **3:**378; **14:**1917
    radiocarbon dating **2:**157; **3:**393; **9:**1276; **14:**1908, 1916
    radiotherapy **14:**1921
    see also nuclear reactors; nuclear weapons
radio astronomy **14:1909–12**
radiocarbon dating **2:**157; **3:**393; **9:**1276; **14:**1908, 1916
radio control (RC) **14:1913–15**
radio-frequency analyzers **10:**1343
radio-frequency identification (RFID) tags **15:**2044–5
radiography **19:2722–3**
  industrial uses **19:**2723
  see also X-ray imaging
radioisotopes, of nitrogen **11:**1525
radioisotopic dating **14:1916**
  carbon dating **2:**157; **3:**393; **9:**1276; **14:**1908, 1916
  of rocks **7:**995; **14:**1916
radiology **14:1917–19**
  see also body scanners; X-ray imaging, of the body
radioluminescence **10:**1302
radionuclide scanning *see* scintigraphy
radiosondes **10:***1396*, 1399
radio tags **3:**341
radiotherapy **3:***378*, 379, 380; **14:1920–2**; **19:**2723
  conformational therapy **14:**1922
radon **5:**708; **11:**1529
  a health hazard **11:**1529
  isotopes **11:**1529
railroad systems **4:**475–6; **10:**1364–5; **14:1923–8**
  and freight **7:**928, 929; **14:**1927, 1929
  tracks **3:***403*; **14:**1923
  tunnels **18:**2512
  weigh stations **19:**2682
  see also mass transit and subways; railways; trains
railroad yards **14:1929–30**
railways
  cliff **3:**356–7
  cog **4:506**
  funicular **3:**357–8
  model **18:***2479*
  monorail systems **10:**1345; **11:1481–3**
  see also mass transit and subways; railroad systems; trains
rainbows **9:***1243*; **14:1933–4**
rain and rainfall **14:1931–2**; **19:**2665
  acid rain **1:**25; **13:**1798; **16:**2300
  generation **10:***1397*, 1398; **14:**1931–2
  weather fronts and **10:***1397*
  see also clouds; thunderstorms
RAM (random-access memory) **4:**528, 529; **5:**609; **9:**1167; **10:**1429
  dynamic (DRAM) **9:**1167
  static (SRAM) **5:**615; **9:**1167
ramjets **1:**76; **7:**967
RAM-ROM packs **12:**1604
Ramsay, Sir William **11:**1528, 1529
Rance barrage **17:**2437, *2438*
random-access memory *see* RAM
rangefinders
  camera **3:***364*
  laser **2:***249, 250*
Ranger space probes **15:**2157, 2159
Rankine temperature scale **17:***2395*, 2396

rapid prototyping (RP) **10:**1366
rapid transit systems *see* mass transit and subways
rare earths *see* lanthanides
rats, pest control of **12:**1677, 1678
Rayleigh waves **15:**2048
rayon **13:**1860
  dyeing **5:**691–2
  manufacture **3:**390; **6:**851
raytracing **4:**536
razors **14:1935–6**
RBMK reactors **11:**1536
RDAs (recommended dietary allowances) **11:**1558
RDX (Hexogen; Cyclonite) **1:**116; **6:**828
reading aids **1:**19–20
read-only memory *see* ROM
receptors, cell **3:**413
recognition systems **3:**341; **9:**1269; **15:**2043–4
  iris or retina **2:**192; **9:**1269
  voice *see* voice recognition and synthesis
reconnaissance
  by radio-controlled aircraft **14:**1913
  by remotely piloted vehicles (RPVs) **13:**1747
  electronic **16:**2255
recorders, pen **12:1666**
recorders (musical instruments) **19:**2713
recording studios **15:**2143–4
record players **8:**1076; **9:**1284; **12:**1697; **13:**1739
records (discs) *see* phonography
recrystallization **4:**445
rectification **18:**2480
  half- and full-wave **14:**1937
rectifiers **5:**653; **6:**750–1; **14:1937–8**; **15:**2053
  mercury-arc **14:**1937, 1938
  solid-state **14:**1938
  see also diodes
rectum **5:**644
recycling **14:1939–43**; **19:**2640
  automobiles **10:***1364*, 1366
  glass **14:***1940*, 1942
  metals **14:**1940–1
  oils **14:**1942
  paper **14:**1939–40
  plastics **10:**1366; **12:**1625; **13:**1776; **14:**1941
  wastes
    hazardous **14:**1942
    organic **14:**1942, 1943
red giants **17:**2315, *2316*
redox reactions **12:**1616, 1617
redshift **2:**178; **5:**672; **14:**1954
reduced-instruction-set computer (RISC) processors **4:**526; **10:**1428
reduction *see* oxidation and reduction
refinery gas **8:**1118
reflection **9:1238–9**
  sound waves **15:**2133
  specular **11:**1463
  total internal **6:**783, 854; **9:**1239
reflectors **14:**1944
reforming **4:**453; **11:**1576, 1579
refraction **6:**854; **9:**1225, 1237, 1238–9
  and clouds **9:***1240*
  double **9:**1239; **13:**1794
  index of **6:**854; **7:**917; **9:**1225, 1239; **13:**1853
  and schlieren techniques **15:**2030, *2133*
  and rainbows **14:**1933
  refractive state of the eye **12:**1596–8

sound waves **15:**2133–4
  and underwater photography **18:**2541
refractories **3:**425
refractors, automatic **12:**1598
refrigeration **14:1945–7**
  dilution refrigerators **5:**591
  in space program flights **5:**592
  thermoelectric **17:**2420
  use in boring tunnels **18:**2516
  using liquid nitrogen **5:**591
refuelling, in-flight **14:1948–9**
refuse-derived fuel (RDF) **19:**2638
regenerators, in Stirling engines **16:**2267
rehydration therapy, oral **10:**1370
relativity **14:1950–4**
  general theory of (theory of gravity) **2:**269; **4:**572, 574–5; **8:**1021, 1143; **11:**1521; **14:**1954; **17:**2443
  special theory of **2:**150, 179, 180; **6:**788–9; **7:**876; **14:**1950–5; **17:**2442–3
relays **15:**2124–5; **18:**2480
remote handling **14:1955–6**
  bomb- and mine-disposal robots **3:**294, 295, 296; **14:**1956; **18:**2471
  by space shuttles **14:***1955*, 1956; **15:**2056; **16:**2168, 2169
  of radioactive substances **14:**1955
    nuclear fuels **14:***1905*
  of space cameras **15:***2154*, 2155
remotely operated vehicles (ROVs) **14:**1987
  submersibles **15:**2023; **16:**2294
remotely piloted vehicles (RPVs) **13:**1747–8
remote sensing **7:**986
renal failure **5:**633
Renault, Louis **2:**198
renin **18:**2549
rennet **5:**602
rennin **5:**643
renograms **14:**1918–19
repeaters, submarine-cable **3:**347–9
repetitive strain injury (RSI) **11:**1491
replication **9:**1233
reproduction **14:1957–9**
reptiles, evolution **6:**824, 825
reservoirs **8:**1112
  and flood control **7:**888–90
  and pumped-storage projects **6:**798; **8:**1112, *1115*; **13:***1827*; **18:**2520
  siltation **5:**608
  for water supply **19:**2661–2, 2663
resins
  acrylate **10:***1419*
  acrylic **1:**30–1; **12:**1629
  alkyd **9:**1204; **12:**1628–9
  epoxy **1:**30; **13:**1772
  ion-exchange **15:**2130
  melamine-formaldehyde (MF) **12:**1629
  natural
    for adhesives **1:**30
    for varnishes **9:**1204; **13:**1742–3
  phenolic **13:**1775
  polyester **1:**31; **13:**1823
  synthetic **1:**30; **12:**1629; **13:**1743
  thermosetting **13:**1773, 1775
  urea-formaldehyde (UF) **12:**1629
  vinyl **1:**30
resistance **14:1960–1**
  electrical **6:**726, 728; **9:**1162; **14:**1960
    absence of *see* superconductivity
  in a capacitor **14:**1960–1
  and Ohm's law **6:**726, 728; **13:**1826

and resistivity of materials
  6:728; 9:1162; 14:1960
in fluids *see* viscosity
magnetic 14:1961
mechanical *see* friction
overcoming 14:1961
resistivity 6:728; 9:1162
resistors 14:1962–3
  manufacture 14:1962–3
  variable *see* potentiometers
resolution 10:1430
resolving power (RP), in photomicrography 12:1716
resonance 12:1606; 14:1964–6
  acoustic 14:1965
  in electric circuits 12:1606;
    14:1966
  mechanical 14:1964–5
  and piezoelectric ultrasound
    sensors 13:1745
  tides and 17:2439–40
resonance (in chemical bonding)
  4:444
resonance (planetary orbits) 13:1761
Resonance Theory 8:1043
respiration
  aerobic 6:840
  anaerobic 6:840
  see also lungs
respirators 3:321–2
restoration, picture 13:1741–3
retina 4:510; 6:830–1; 12:1589
  and color blindness 12:1598
  detached 12:1589
  repaired using lasers 12:1590
  retinitis pigmentosa 12:1589
retinitis pigmentosa 12:1589
retinol 19:2613
retinoscopy 12:1597–8
retrosynthesis 4:458
reverberation time (RT) 15:2133
  of auditoriums 1:27
reverse bias 5:653; 18:2482
reverse transcriptase 11:1478
revolvers 8:1025–6
Reynolds, Osborne 8:1110–11
Reynolds numbers 8:1111;
  19:2696–7
RGB displays 5:647
rheostats 13:1822
Rhesus (Rh) factor 2:271–2
Rhine-Main-Danube canal 9:1266
rhodamine 6G 9:1213
rhodium 13:1781, 1782, 1783
rhodopsin 6:831
riboflavin (vitamin B2) 5:600; 6:837;
  19:2613
ribosomes 3:411–12; 11:1477, 1478
ribulose 1,5-biphosphate 12:1720
rice 9:1191
  lysine in 3:303
Richter scale 9:1276; 15:2049
ricin 4:438; 13:1792
rickets 11:1558
rifampicin 6:812
rifles and shotguns 14:1967–70
  rifles 14:1967
    antitank 1:119
    assault 2:196
    automatic (light machine guns)
      1:118; 2:196; 8:1025; 14:1968
    bolt-action 14:1967–8
    breech- and muzzle-loading
      14:1967
    Heckler and Koch G11
      14:1968–9
    self-loading 14:1968
    semiautomatic 8:1025
  shotguns 14:1967, 1969–70
    double-barreled 14:1969, 1970
rifling 8:1023
  and forensic ballistics 7:916

rigor mortis 7:919; 12:1658–9
ring diffusers 16:2296
ringworm 18:2585
riot control 14:1971–2
RISC (reduced-instruction-set computer) processors 4:526; 10.1428
rivers
  erosion by 6:818
  flood control 7:888, 890–1
riveting 10:1384
rivet sets 18:2465
RMS (root-mean-square) value
  8:1075
RNA (ribonucleic acid) 7:973
  messenger (mRNA) 7:974, 975;
    11:1477; 12:1657
  transfer (tRNA) 11:1478
road haulage 7:928, 929
roads
  construction 5:701; 14:1973–7,
    1981
    earthmoving machinery 5:703
  crash barriers 14:1979–81
  drainage 5:675; 14:1975, 1981
  markings 14:1976–7, 1982
  signs 14:1982–4
road signs, reflective 14:1944
road systems and traffic control
  14:1978–85
road trains 9:1175; 18:2505
roadways, world's oldest 4:477, 478
robotics 2:172; 10:1366; 14:1986–9
  and agricultural machinery 1:51
  androids 14:1989
  arms 14:1986, 1987, 1988; 15:2056
    on space stations 15:2056;
      16:2169, 2173, 2174
  for bomb and mine disposal 3:294,
    295, 296; 14:1956; 18:2471
  continuous-path (CP) robots
    14:1987
  early robots 14:1886
  fractal shape-changing 9:1255
  industrial robots 14:1986–7
    for mass production 10:1339,
      1340, 1365; 15:2066
  in libraries 5:612
  linear motors used in 9:1255
  for milking cows 11:1452
  nanorobots 10:1420; 14:1989
    in blood vessels 10:1419
  point-to-point (PTP) robots
    14:1987–8
  for remote handling
    bomb and mine disposal 3:294,
      295, 296; 14:1956; 18:2471
    of nuclear fuel 14:1905
  second generation robots
    14:1987–8
  senses 14:1988–9
  submersible robots 16:2294
  for surgery 10:1440; 17:2331–2;
    19:2616
  vacuum cleaners 18:2562
  and voice recognition 14:1989;
    19:2616, 2617
  see also artificial intelligence; space
    probes
Rochelle salt 13:1744–5
Rocket (steam engine) 16:2259
rocket cars 14:1892
rockets and space propulsion
  14:1990–6
  propulsion 12:1620; 14:1993–6
    ionic (solar-electric) propulsion
      9:1184; 14:1995
  rockets
    antitank 7:883; 11:1487
    construction 14:1996
    demonstrating laws of motion
      11:1520–1
    distress 7:870

ejection seat 5:711
  launch 14:1996
  for missile propulsion 11:1466,
    1487; 14:1991
  sounding 14:1991
  and the Venturi effect 18:2580
scramjet engines 1:78; 17:2320
rocks
  analysis 7:987
  artificial 12:1679–80
  chemical composition 7:981–2
  magnetism 7:992
    in the past (paleomagnetism)
      7:990, 991, 992–3; 13:1777
  sedimentary, oil exploration and
    11:1571
  types 7:981–2, 987; 12:1679
  see also geochemistry; geology;
    petrology
Rockwell B-1 bomber 1:70
rock wool 9:1161
rods and cones 6:831; 9:1240
Roemer, Olaus 5:710; 9:1240
roll (aviation) 1:70, 71
rolling (metalworking) 10:1391
roll-on roll-off systems 15:2070
  for cargo 7:932
  ferries 5:670; 15:2070
Romans, ancient
  cement 3:417
  central heating 8:1056
  dams 5:604, 606–7
  dentistry 5:618
  distillation 5:661
  firefighting 6:859, 863
  glass 7:999
  land reclamation 9:1206
  lighthouses 9:1247
  numbers 10:1358
  roads 14:1973
  sundials 16:2302
  traffic congestion 10:1407
  use of lead 9:1219
  vaults 18:2571
ROM (read-only memory) 9:1167
  ROM cards 5:615
röntgenoluminescence 10:1302
Röntgen, Wilhelm 10:1367; 14:1905,
  19:2721
ropes, manufacture *see* cable and rope
  manufacture
ROSAT (satellite) 2:174
Rosen, Nathan 14:1884
rosins 10:1382
rotameters 7:896, 897; 18:2581
rotation (mechanics) 12:1726
  and inertia 8:1030, 1142
rotational molding, thermoplastic
  13:1775
rounds, baton 11:1533
routers 4:541; 19:2718
routing units 15:2138–9
rovers, on planets 15:2158
ROVs *see* remotely operated vehicles
RPVs (remotely piloted vehicles)
  13:1747–8
rubber
  for bearings 2:233
  elasticity 5:714
  high-hysteresis 17:2339
  natural 14:1997–8
    for adhesives 1:30
    synthetic 14:2001
    vulcanized 14:1997; 18:2454
  scrap recovery schemes 5:591
  synthetic 1:31; 13:1771–2;
    14:1999–2001
    ABS 13:1772
    flooring 7:893
    for tires 18:2454
rubella 12:1589
rubidium 1:99, 101

in atomic clocks 4:485
rubies 1:109; 4:472; 5:599; 16:2270,
  2271, 2272
  for jewel bearings 2:233
  for lasers and masers 5:599;
    9:1211, 1212
  synthetic 17:2346
rudders 14:2002–4
  aircraft 1:66, 71; 14:2004; 15:2057
  ships' 14:2002–4; 15:2068
  trim 12:1615
rum 5:661; 16:2217
rumen 5:644
ruminants 5:644
run-time engines 11:1502
runways, airport 1:87, 88, 94
rust 4:569, 570; 9:1188; 12:1617,
  1621; 17:2325–6
ruthenium 13:1781, 1782
Rutherford, Ernest 6:767; 11:1525;
  14:1905
rutherfordium 6:765
rutile 5:599; 12:1627

S

Sabin, Albert Bruce 18:2555
saccharimeters 13:1793
saccharin 7:914
Saccharomyces
  bailii 7:907
  cerevisiae 2:236; 7:963;
    10:1409–10; 19:2725
  sake 19:2726
sacrificial protection 4:571
SAD (seasonal affective disorder)
  12:1724
safes 9:1269; 14:2005
  see also locks (security)
safety belts 2:207–9; 18:2476
Saffir-Simpson scale 8:1095
Sagan, Carl 9:1234
Sahara Desert, water beneath
  19:2667
sailboards 14:2006–7
sailing 14:2008–13
sailplanes *see* gliders
sails 10:1334–5; 14:2013
  lanteen 14:2010
  sailboard 14:2007
St. Elmo's fire 5:655; 17:2431
St. Helens, Mount, eruption 7:925;
  17:2415
sake (rice wine) 19:2726
Salam, Abdus 6:771
salbutamol 2:232
salicylic acid 12:1686
  and plants 3:305
saliva 5:642
Salk, Jonas Edward 18:2555
Salmonella 7:906
salt *see* sodium chloride
saltdomes, sulfur in 16:2300
Salter Duck 19:2675
salt marshes 6:819
saltpeter *see* potassium nitrate
salts, chemical 14:2014–15
salvage, marine 15:2021–3
salvarsan (arsphenamine) 1:135;
  10:1368
Salyut (space station) 1:43; 16:2170
sampling, quality-control 14:1878;
  16:2249
sampling technology 15:2137
SAMs (surface-to-air missiles) 1:144
San Andreas fault 5:706, 707, 708
sand, as abrasive 1:18
sandblasting 1:17; 17:2322, 2325
sanding machines 1:17; 19:2718
sandpaper 1:17, 18
sands, in soil 15:2110, 2111
sandstone 7:981; 14:1885

San Francisco
  earthquakes 5:706
  streetcars 3:356, *358*; 16:2277,
    2278
saponification 1:25; 15:2107
sapphires 1:109; 5:599; 16:2271,
    2272
  for jewel bearings 2:233
  synthetic 17:2346
sapwood 9:1294
sarcolemma 11:1504–5
Sarin 4:437, 439, *441*; 12:1700
Sarracenia plants 15:*2105*
satellites, artificial 1:42–3;
    15:2024–9
  astronomical 2:173, 174, 176–7
    ARISE 14:*1910*, 1911
    COBE 4:*573*
    IRAS 2:176–7
    X-ray 19:2724
    see also telescopes, space
  attitude control 15:2028–9
  communications 4:540, *541*, 542;
    15:*2025*, 2029; 17:2359
  construction 15:2026–8
  and earthmoving machines 5:705
  electricity from 15:2117
  first 1:42
  and global positioning systems
    2:204; 7:1006–7
  launch techniques 15:2026
  and mapping 10:1330
  mechanics 15:2024–5
  military, as targets for space
    weapons 16:2180–2
  oceanographic 11:1569; 15:2029
  orbits 12:1599–1600; 15:2025–6;
    16:2180–1
    geostationary (parking orbits)
      8:1096; 10:1397; 12:1600;
      15:2025, 2150; 17:2359
  remote sensing 7:986, *995*;
    15:2029
    photography 1:*33*, 35; 2:156;
      6:*743*
    radar 7:986
    surveying for oil deposits
      11:1571
  as space mines 16:2181
  and telemetry 17:2365
  thermal cameras 17:2422
  to track animals 19:2735
  weather and climate 4:*479*; 7:986;
    8:1095–6, *1098, 1099*; 10:1397,
    1398; 15:*2028*, 2029
  working environment 15:2026
  working life 15:2029
Saturn 13:1757, 1758, 1761;
    15:2118, 2122
  moons 12:*1599*; 13:*1760*; 15:2122,
    2160
  rings 12:*1599*; 13:*1760*
Saturn V (launch vehicle) 14:1995,
    1996
sawing, planks 9:1295
saws 18:2460; 19:2716–17
  manufacture 18:2462–3
saxitoxin 4:438
saxophones 3:320; 19:*2712*, 2713
SBR (styrene-butadiene rubber)
    14:2001
SCADA (system control and data
    acquisition) systems 10:1340,
    1348; 19:2667
scalar quantities 5:694, 695
scales *see* balances
scandium 18:2485, 2487
scanners
  bar-code 3:401; 8:1082, *1083*,
    1150; 10:1341
  body *see* body scanners
  optical *see* optical scanners

scatter
  light 11:*1464*
  tropospheric 19:*2668*
scatterguns 8:1026
scavenging, two-stroke engine
    9:1171
SCBA (self-contained breathing
    apparatus) 3:322
Scheele, Carl Wilhelm 8:1034;
    11:1525; 12:1618, 1698
schistosomiasis 12:1646
schizophrenia 13:1868
Schizosaccharomyces pombe 10:1410;
    11:1479
schlieren techniques 15:2030–1,
    2133, 2134
Schmidt cameras and telescopes
    11:1562; 17:2379–80
Schneider Trophy races 15:2035
schooners 14:2010
Schrödinger, Erwin 2:150, 183, 184;
    4:461; 14:1883, 1884
Schrödinger equation 2:183–5;
    4:462; 6:726
Schrödinger's cat 14:1884
Schwarzschild, Karl 2:270
Schwarzschild radius 17:2443
scintigraphy (radionuclide scanning)
    2:281; 14:1917
scintillation counters 12:*1653*, 1654,
    1718
scintillators 6:745
sclera 6:830
scooters 11:1489
  powered-wheelchair 11:1469
scoreboards, electronic 17:*2444*
scramjets 1:78; 17:2320
scrapers (graders) 5:703; 14:1974
scrapie 18:2587
screens, movie and slide projector
    13:1855
screwdrivers, manufacture 18:*2462*,
    2463
screws
  Archimedes' 4:565; 9:1192;
    15:2032; 19:2695
  machine 15:2032
  manufacture 15:2032–4
  screw jacks 15:2033
  self-tapping 15:2033
  wood 15:2032
scuba diving, suits 5:665
scums 19:2656, 2666
scurvy 11:1558; 19:*2614*
Seaborg, Glen 12:1673
seaborgium 6:765, 766
SEACOM network 3:348
seafloor *see* ocean floor
Sealab program 18:2538, 2539
sealants 1:28, 32
sea levels
  and global warming 4:480; 6:807
  varying 11:1566; 13:1780
    measured 11:1569
seals, elephant 10:*1332*
seaplanes and amphibians 1:69;
    15:2035–7
  flying boats 2:212, 213; 13:1747;
    15:2035, 2036
search engines 2:170–1; 9:*1180*,
    1181, 1279
search and rescue (SAR) operations
    15:2038, 2040
search units, metal-detector
    10:1385–6
sea rescue 15:2038–41
  lifeboats 15:2038–40, 2050–1
  inshore 15:2040–1
Seasat (satellite) 8:*1097*; 11:1569
Sea Skuas (missiles) 16:*2251*
seasonal affective disorder (SAD)
    12:1724

seasoning, timber 9:1295
seasons 5:696
sea walls 6:819; 7:891
seawater, desalination (desalting)
    5:623–5, 662
sebaceous glands 15:2088
sebum 15:2088
seconds 17:2442, 2443
secretin 5:643
security systems 15:2042–5
  against data interception 6:761–2
  against intruders 15:2042–3
    burglar alarms 2:239; 3:340–1;
      5:672; 15:2043
    movement sensors 3:340, *341*;
      15:*2042*, 2043
  airport 1:87, *89*
  CCTV cameras 3:340; 15:2042,
    2044
  fire protection
    fire alarms 2:239; 15:2045
    fire detectors 6:863–4; 15:2045
  integrated 15:*2043*
  personal identification *see* recog-
    nition systems
  security guards 15:2042, 2043
  store detectives 15:2045
  tagging 15:2044–5
  see also cryptology; locks (security);
    safes
security trucks 2:*168*
sedatives 12:1682
sediment, ocean, cores 4:478
Seebeck effect 17:2417, 2418, 2420
seeding
  agricultural 1:48–9
  horticultural 8:1089
seersucker 17:2407
Segovia, Andrés 16:2282
seismology 7:991; 15:2046–9
  four-dimensional 7:994–5
  for oil and gas exploration 7:*992*,
    993–4; 11:1570–1; 15:*2048*,
    2135
  seismic sections 7:993–4
  seismographs 5:708; 12:1664–5;
    15:2046–7
  three-dimensional reflection 7:994
  and tsunamis 18:2510
  see also earthquakes
seismometers 11:1571
selective serotonin reuptake
    inhibitors (SSRIs) 12:1681–2;
    13:1868
selenium 7:982; 19:2727
selenium cells 3:368; 12:1705
self-contained breathing apparatus
    (SCBA) 3:322
self-polishing copolymer (SPC)
    2:149
self-righting boats 15:2050–1
  lifeboats 15:2040, 2050–1
Sellafield (Windscale) 11:1535
semaphore signals 17:2360, *2361*
  railway 14:1924
semen, bull, frozen 14:*1947*
semicircular canals 8:1042, 1043
semiconductors 4:552, 555, 556;
    6:728; 10:1361; 15:2052–4
  intrinsic and extrinsic 15:2053
  lasers 9:1213, 1214; 15:2054
  p-n junction (depletion layer)
    5:654; 6:752; 15:2053, 2116–17;
    18:2481
  p-type and n-type 5:*653*, 654;
    6:752; 15:2053; 18:2481–2
  silicon as 4:552; 5:599; 6:752;
    15:2076
  uses 15:2053–4
    in calculators 3:359
    in CCDs 15:*2054*
    in electronic devices 6:752

  in pressure transducers 15:2054
  in rectifier applications 14:1938;
    15:*2053*
  in refrigeration 17:2420
  in thyristors 17:2432
  in transistors 1:124; 6:753, 754;
    15:*2053*, 2054; 18:2480–2, 2565
  see also integrated circuits;
    microprocessors
semimicrobalances 2:214
semipermeable membranes 5:633,
    634
semitrailers 18:2505
Senefelder, Alois 9:1260; 13:1849–50
senility, blood flow and 14:1919
sensors *see* transducers and sensors
separators (centrifuges) 3:423
septic tanks 5:*674*; 19:2648
sequence homology 11:1478
sequencers 17:2344
serge 17:2407
Serial Line Internet Protocol (SLIP)
    11:1475–6
serigraphy *see* printing, screen
serology
  forensic 7:919
  veterinary 18:2584
serotonin, in plants 3:305
servers (in computer networks)
    4:526, 537, 538
service providers, Internet 4:540
servo, brake-assisted 2:201
servomechanisms 8:1017; 15:2055–7
servomotors 1:66; 2:204
sets, television 17:2386–7
Severe Combined Immune
    Deficiency (SCID) 8:*1133*
Severn tidal project 17:2438
sewage, treatment *see* wastewater
    treatment
sewers 5:*673*, 674–5
  concrete 4:*549*
  remote-controlled cameras in
    19:2648
sewing machines 4:490; 15:2058–61
  industrial 15:2061
sex-change operations 13:1765
sextants 11:1511, *1513*; 15:2062–3
  on periscopes 12:1675
shadufs 9:1192, 1231
shaft encoders 6:731
shampoos 8:1033
Shannon, Claude 8:1148
shantung 17:2407
shape-memory effect (SME)
    1:106–7; 10:1351
  polymers 10:1352
  see also alloys, shape-memory
shapers (machine tools) 10:1308–9;
    19:2718
shawms 19:2713
shear modulus 5:714
sheep
  cloned 2:264
  Judas 15:2096
  milk from transgenic ewes 2:*264*,
    266
  slaughtering 15:2096–7
  veterinary work and 18:2586
sheet forming 4:562
sheet metal 15:2064–6
sheet piles 1:207
Sheffield plate 15:2080
shellac 12:1696
shell molding (Croning process)
    3:403
shells
  antiaircraft-gun 1:143–4
  armor-piercing 1:119–20
  carrying chemical weapons 4:*441*
  chemical-energy (CE) 1:119–20
Shepard, Alan, Jr. 1:42

sherry **19**:2702–3
shingles (asbestos) **6**:846
Shinichiro, Tomonaga **14**:1884
Shinkansen ("bullet" trains) **3**:328; **9**:1274; **14**:1927–8
ships **15**:2067–73
  antifouling coatings **2**:149
  braking **15**:2068
  bulk-carrying **7**:928–32; **9**:1190; **15**:2071–2
    see also tankers
  cable-laying **3**:347, 348, 349; **17**:2356
  centers of buoyancy and gravity **15**:2069
  construction **15**:2073
  container ships **7**:932; **15**:2067, 2069–70
  electromagnetic propulsion **10**:1319
  fishing and whaling
    factory ships **7**:872; **19**:2686
    see also fishing industry; trawlers
  grounded **15**:2021, 2039
  icebreakers **15**:2073
  industrial **15**:2073
  LASH (lighter aboard ship) vessels **15**:2070–1
  lightships **9**:1249
  motor, sail-assisted **14**:2013
  naval mines deployed from **11**:1456
  navigation **15**:2068
    using gyroscopes **8**:1028, 1031
    see also navigation, marine
  parts of **15**:2067–8
  passenger **15**:2072–3
  propellers see propellers, marine-propulsion
  radio-controlled model **14**:1915
  radio and radar jamming equipment **16**:2253
  refrigeration **14**:1945
    reefer (refrigerated transport) ships **15**:2071
  residence **15**:2072, 2073
  ro-ro see roll-on roll-off systems
  rudders **14**:2002–4; **15**:2068
  search radar used on **14**:1898; **15**:2069
  speed **11**:1510–11; **15**:2069–70
  stability **15**:2069
    see also stabilizers, ship
  sunken, salvaged **15**:2021–3
  tonnage **15**:2068
  towed **15**:2021
  warships **19**:2626–33
  wind pumps on **19**:2695
  see also boat building; boats; hydrofoils; marine propulsion; warships
shock absorbers **10**:1353; **16**:2229; **17**:2339, 2340
Shockley, William **18**:2481
Shoemaker-Levy 9 (comet) **2**:176; **15**:2121
shooting stars see meteors and meteorites
short takeoff and landing (STOL) **1**:71, 77; **16**:2251
shot blasting **17**:2322
shotguns see rifles and shotguns
shovels, steam-powered **5**:701, 703
shrink-wrapping **7**:908; **12**:1624
shunts, arterio-venous (A-V) **5**:635, 636
shutters, camera **3**:363; **15**:2074–5
  speed **2**:205; **3**:363; **15**:2075; **17**:2446
shuttles **9**:1280–1, 1283; **16**:2212
sickle-cell disease **2**:273
side-looking airborne radar (SLAR) **1**:35

SIDS (sudden infant death syndrome) **12**:1661
Siemen's gas (producer gas) **7**:956, 958
signaling, railroad **14**:1924–6
signals
  distress **5**:712
  electrical
    generation **12**:1606
    sawtooth **12**:1606
    square-wave **12**:1606
    microwave **12**:1606
signal-to-noise (S/N) ratio **8**:1074–5
Sikorsky, Igor **8**:1065
silencers
  in air-conditioning units **8**:1061
  gun **8**:1027
silica (silicon dioxide) **15**:2076
  abrasive **1**:17, 18
  dust **7**:954
  gel **15**:2130
  see also quartz
silicates **15**:2077
silicon **4**:449; **15**:2076–7
  cantilevers **10**:1418
  compounds **15**:2077
  and photolithography **10**:1417–18
  production **15**:2076
    manufacture of crystals **5**:599; **15**:2076–7
  as a semiconductor **4**:552; **5**:599; **6**:752; **15**:2076
silicon carbide (Carborundum) **1**:18; **3**:426; **17**:2347
silicon chips see integrated circuits
silicones (polysiloxanes) **1**:32; **15**:2077, 2078
  sealants **1**:32
  silicone rubbers **14**:2001; **15**:2077
  and water-repellent textiles **19**:2660
silicon nitride **3**:426, 427
silk **6**:849, 850; **17**:2404, 2405, 2408
  artificial **3**:390; **6**:851
silkworms **6**:849
  bioengineered **2**:266
silt, in soil **15**:2110
siltation, of reservoirs **5**:608
silver **15**:2079–80, **18**:2485
  EPNS (electroplated nickel silver) **11**:1523; **15**:2080
  extraction **9**:1220; **15**:2079–80
  solid **15**:2080
  sterling **15**:2080
silver bromide **8**:1036; **12**:1652, 1709; **15**:2080
silver chloride **12**:1709; **15**:2080
silver iodide **8**:1096; **12**:1708, 1709
silver nitrate **12**:1708; **15**:2080
silver sulfide **15**:2079, 2080
simulators
  cab **19**:2603–4
  space simulation chambers **5**:592
  see also flight simulators
sine waves **15**:2081–2
singularities **2**:267
sinks, carbon **6**:807–8
sinoatrial node **8**:1046; **11**:1506
sintering **1**:105; **3**:427
sinuses, nasal **12**:1612–13
siphons **15**:2083
  and toilets **18**:2458–9
sisal **3**:350; **6**:849, 850
skeletons **3**:297
  and archaeology **2**:158
  identifying people from **7**:920
skiaskopy (retinoscopy) **12**:1597–8
skiing and snowboarding **5**:714
  skin suits **16**:2224
  skis and snowboards **15**:2084–6
skin **15**:2087–9
  animal **9**:1222

  artificial **15**:2087, 2088–9
  diseases **15**:2089
    in animals **18**:2585
    cancer **6**:806; **15**:2089
  galvanograph records **13**:1807
  grafts **10**:1438–9; **13**:1765, 1766; **15**:2087; **18**:2500
  resurfacing **13**:1767
  structure **15**:2087, 2088
skin effect **8**:1116
skull
  boring holes into **17**:2327
  X-ray image **19**:2724
skulls
  identifying people from **7**:920
  reconstruction of faces from **7**:915, 916
sky divers **12**:1641, 1643
Skylab (space station) **1**:43; **16**:2170
skyscrapers **15**:2090–5
  construction **15**:2093
    cranes used in **5**:588
    substructure **15**:2091–2
slaking **1**:25
SLAM (scanning laser acoustic microscopy) **15**:2135
slate **14**:1885
slaughterhouses **15**:2096–8
SLBMs (submarine-launched ballistic missiles) **16**:2182
sleep **15**:2099–2102
  deprivation **15**:2101
  disorders **15**:2101–2
sleep guns **11**:1534
sleeping sickness
  African trypanosomiasis **1**:135
  Encephalitis lethargica **12**:1684
sleepwalking **15**:2102
slides, projection **13**:1854–5
slingshot effect (gravity assist) **14**:1996
slip-form machines **14**:1976
SLIP (Serial Line Internet Protocol) **11**:1475–6
Slocum, Joshua **2**:276
slot machines (one-armed bandits; fruit machines) **7**:949–50
smallpox **10**:1368–9
  as a biological weapon **4**:437
  inoculation (variolation) **18**:2554
  vaccines **2**:264; **8**:1132, 1134; **18**:2554
smart materials **10**:1350–3, 1363–4
smell and taste **15**:2103–6
  smell **3**:310; **15**:2103–6
  taste **15**:2103–4, 2106
smelting **12**:1617, 1620
Smith, William **6**:822; **12**:1633
smog **10**:1305; **19**:2612
smoke detectors **6**:863
smokeless zones **13**:1802
smoking
  and free radicals **11**:1559
  and lung damage **10**:1305
snakes
  feeding **5**:645
  and infrared radiation **6**:742
  venom **13**:1792
Snell, Willebrord **13**:1853
Snell's law **9**:1225, 1239
snorkels (firefighting) **6**:861
snowboards and skis **15**:2084–6
snow vehicles, tracked **18**:2470, 2471
soaps **4**:457; **5**:631; **6**:837; **15**:2107
  flakes **5**:632; **15**:2107
  lithium **1**:99
  manufacture **5**:632; **6**:837; **15**:2107–8
    soap-based washing powders **5**:632; **15**:2108
  shaving **15**:2108
  soft **15**:2108

soda see sodium carbonate
soda ash see sodium carbonate
sodium **1**:99, 100; **4**:442
  production **1**:100
  reaction with water **1**:101
  uses **1**:100–1
sodium acid pyrophosphate **12**:1699
sodium alkyl sulphates **1**:101
sodium aluminate **1**:109
sodium azide **11**:1525
sodium borate (borax) **1**:100; **12**:1709
sodium carbonate (soda; soda ash) **1**:100; **12**:1709
  manufacture **4**:450
sodium cellulose xanthate **12**:1626
sodium chlorate **19**:2679
sodium chloride (salt) **1**:100
  bonds **4**:442–3; **5**:597, 598
  and corrosion **4**:570, 571
  electrical conduction **4**:555–6
  electrodialysis, for desalination **5**:625
  electrolysis **1**:25; **4**:450, 452; **6**:737; **8**:1118; **9**:1184
  and erosion **6**:819
  a food additive **7**:907
  in food processing see curing
  formation **9**:1183
  and health **7**:907; **8**:1035
  production **14**:2016
    from evaporation **11**:1569; **14**:2016
    mining **11**:1462; **14**:2016
  unit cells **10**:1359
sodium cyanide, preparation **1**:100–1
sodium fluoride **18**:2466
sodium hydroxide (caustic soda) **1**:23; **12**:1709
  preparation **1**:25; **6**:738
  and soap manufacture **15**:2107
sodium hypochlorite **1**:25
sodium laureth sulfate **8**:1033
sodium monofluorophosphate **18**:2466
sodium nitrate (Chile saltpeter) **1**:24–5, 100; **6**:826; **11**:1525
  use in curing **7**:905
sodium peroxide **1**:100
sodium salicylate **7**:869
sodium silicate (water glass) **1**:30
sodium sulfite **12**:1709
sodium thiosulfate **12**:1708
sodium tripolyphosphate **5**:631; **12**:1699
soft-drink dispensers **15**:2109; **18**:2576
software see computers, programming and software
SOHO (Solar and Heliospheric Observatory) (space probe) **15**:2046, 2119, 2158, 2159; **17**:2381–2
soil
  contaminated **15**:2110
    treatment **7**:901
  drainage **5**:673–4
  earthmoving affecting **5**:701
  effect of lightning on **6**:725
  engineering **15**:2110–12
  erosion, reduction **1**:61; **6**:816–18
  fertilizer application to **6**:845
  improvement, in forests **7**:924
  lateritic **15**:2112
  management **15**:2112–13
  pH **12**:1693
  profiles **15**:2112
  research **15**:2110–13
  tillage **1**:55
  see also earthmoving machinery; land reclamation
Sojourner (space vehicle) **15**:2158
Solar Blind Camera (SBC) **15**:2155

solar cells *see* photoelectric cells and
photometry
Solar Challenger (aircraft) **2**:*213*;
15:2117
solar energy **6**:*729*, 791–2; **15**:2054,
2114–17
for distillation of seawater **5**:624;
15:2116
for power plants **6**:792; **15**:2116
solar-heated balloons **2**:220
solar panels **4**:552; **6**:*791*, 792;
8:1058
on satellites **15**:*2028*, 2117
on space probes **15**:2156
on space stations **15**:2150–1
solar-powered vehicles **15**:2117
aircraft **2**:*213*; **15**:*2114*, 2117
bicycles **2**:244
and Stirling engines **16**:2269
storage **6**:792
for watches **19**:2650
water-heating systems **6**:792;
8:1058; **15**:2115–16
see also photoelectric cells and
photometry
solar halos **9**:*1242*
Solar and Heliospheric Observatory see
SOHO
Solar Maximum Mission (Solar Max)
satellite **2**:173; **15**:2029; **16**:2169
solar sailing **14**:1996; **15**:*2159*
Solar System **5**:696; **15**:**2118–23**
eclipses in **5**:710
formation **5**:698; **15**:2118
see also asteroids; comets; planetary
science; Sun; and under names
of the planets
solar wind
and auroras **14**:*1899*, 1900
measurement **15**:2159
soldering **10**:1381–2
solders **1**:31, 106; **10**:1381–2;
17:2448
solenoids **15**:2124–5; **16**:2241
solids **10**:1359–60
allotropes **10**:1360
amorphous **4**:*550*, 551
crystalline *see* crystals and crystallography
elasticity **5**:713; **10**:1361
electrical properties **10**:1360–1
ionic **4**:443, 555–6; **9**:1163
magnetic properties **10**:1361
saturated vapor pressure **18**:2570
thermal properties **10**:1361
solid solutions **1**:103
Solvay process **4**:450
solvent extraction **4**:446
solvent(s), water as a **19**:2655
Soman **4**:437; **12**:1700
somatoform disorder **13**:1867–8
somatotrophin **18**:2588
sonar **14**:1894; **15**:2126–8, 2135
use **15**:2128–9
in archaeology **2**:157
by fishing vessels **7**:872
guiding torpedoes **1**:27; **18**:2468
for marine salvage **15**:2022
to detect submarines **8**:1070;
15:*2127*, 2128
sonarbuoys **8**:1070
sonic booms **1**:37; **17**:2318–19
Sony's Dynamic Digital Sound
(SDDS) **15**:2148–9
soot, and corrosion **4**:571
sorbants, use in fluidized beds **7**:901
sorption **15**:2129–30
SOSUS (Sound Surveillance System)
15:2128
sound **15**:2131–5
and the atmosphere **1**:63
dispersion **5**:641

energy **6**:787
measured **11**:1530–1
frequency analysis **11**:1530
hearing **8**:1041–4
intensity **11**:1530
and mobility aids **1**:21
noise measurement **11**:1530–2
production and transmission
15:2131
properties
loudness **15**:2132
timbre (tone) **3**:318; **15**:2132
see also pitch
science of *see* acoustics
speed of **1**:37–8, 63; **15**:2131–2;
17:2318
see also supersonic flight
for underground detection **2**:157
waves **1**:26; **15**:2131, 2132–3;
19:2672
diffraction **15**:*2133*, 2134
and the Doppler effect **5**:672;
14:1897; **15**:2134
infrasonic **15**:2134
interference **15**:2134; **19**:2673
reflection and acoustics **15**:2133
refraction **15**:2133–4
standing waves **3**:318
ultrasonic **15**:2134–5; **18**:2528
see also hearing; sonar; ultrasonics
sound effects and sampling
15:2136–7
sound mixing **8**:*1071*; **13**:1822;
15:2138–9
soundproofing **15**:2140–1
see also noise measurement
sound reproduction **15**:2142–5
on DVDs **5**:652
quadraphonic **15**:2145
soundtracks **15**:2146–9
music scores **11**:1499, 1500;
15:2149
sousaphones **3**:320
soybeans **6**:837; **13**:*1865*
artificial meats from **7**:913–14
herbicide-tolerant **19**:2681
spacecraft
model, for movies **16**:*2185*
navigation **11**:1514
orbits **12**:1599–1600
space debris **12**:1600; **15**:2150–1
Space Infrared Telescope Facility
(SIRTF) **2**:177
Space Interferometry Mission (SIM)
2:177; **17**:2382
Spacelab (space module) **16**:2171–2
space mines **16**:2181
space photography **15**:2152–5,
2158–9
Hubble Space Telescope cameras
2:176; **15**:*2154*, 2155; **17**:2381
space probes **15**:2156–60
design **15**:2156–7
fuel cells **7**:936
instruments **15**:*2157*, 2158–9
landers **15**:2157–8
orbits **12**:1600
propulsion
ionic propulsion units **9**:*1184*;
14:1995
solar sailing **14**:1996; **15**:*2159*
radio-controlled **14**:*1913*
solar panels **15**:2156
stabilization **15**:2157
and telemetry **17**:2365
to monitor space debris **15**:2150–1
to survey planets **12**:1707; **17**:2337
space shuttles **1**:*41*, 43; **9**:*1201*;
12:*1620*; **16**:2165–9, 2170–1
accidents and disasters **6**:815;
16:2166, 2168
air locks used in **1**:*85*

boosters **14**:1994; **16**:2166
fuel cells **6**:795
heat-resistant tiles **1**:44; **3**:*427*;
16:2166
photography from **1**:35
remote handling by **14**:*1955*, 1956;
15:*2056*; **16**:2168, 2169
and space debris **15**:2151
and space stations **14**:*1955*, 1956;
16:2169, 2172–3
space suits **16**:2177–8
and telemetry **17**:*2364*
virtual reality practice for **19**:*2604*
space simulation chambers **5**:592
space stations **1**:43; **16**:2170–5
solar panels **15**:2150–1
space walks from **16**:2178
see also International Space Station;
Mir; Salyut; Skylab; Spacelab
space suits **13**:1862; **16**:2176–8
breathing apparatus **3**:*322*
space walks **16**:2176
from space shuttles **16**:2169, *2177*,
2178
space weapons **16**:2179–4
spark chambers **12**:1652–3, *1654*
spark machining *see* electrodischarge
machining
spark plugs **2**:203; **8**:1125, 1126,
1127; **9**:*1170*
manufacture **3**:427
speakers *see* loudspeakers
Spearfish torpedoes **18**:2468
special effects **16**:2185–90
see also animation
species **12**:1632
specific gravity (relative density)
5:616–17
specific impulse (I$_{sp}$) **14**:1993, 1994,
1995
spectacles **16**:2191–2
frames **16**:2191
construction **16**:2192
lenses **9**:*1230*; **16**:2192
mobility aids built into **1**:21
to aid the deaf **9**:1243
see also optometry
spectrometry **4**:447; **16**:2194
airborne visible/infrared imaging
spectrometers (AVIRISs)
17:2336
atomic emission **2**:158; **4**:447
direct spectrometers **16**:2195–6
Fourier spectrometers **16**:2199
gamma-ray spectrometer (GRS)
15:2160
inductively coupled plasma emission (ICPS) **2**:158
infrared **4**:448; **16**:2199
Stark-modulated spectrometers
16:2199
use in archaeology **2**:157, 158
wavelength spectrometers **16**:2194
X-ray fluorescence (XRF) **2**:158;
4:447; **12**:1680; **16**:2196–7,
2199; **19**:2724
see also mass spectrometry;
spectroscopy
spectrophotometry **4**:512; **6**:743;
16:2197, 2198–9
spectroscopy **16**:2193–9
absorption **16**:2194, 2198
infrared **12**:1680
astronomical **2**:178; **16**:2197–8
atomic **2**:183
and electron orbitals **4**:461;
16:2193, *2197, 2198*
emission **2**:158; **16**:2194
imaging **17**:2336
laser-induced breakdown spectroscopy **4**:441
mass *see* mass spectrometry

microwave **16**:2199
molecular **4**:462; **16**:2199
near-infrared (NIR) **16**:2249
Raman **16**:2199
spectrochemical analysis
16:2194–7
spectrographs and spectrograms
16:2195–6
spectrophotometry **4**:512; **6**:743;
16:2197, 2198–9
use in archaeology **2**:158
X-ray fluorescence (XRF) **2**:158;
4:447; **12**:1680; **16**:2196–7,
2199; **19**:2724
see also spectrometry
spectrum
of colors **13**:1853
solar **16**:*2194, 2196*
spectrum theory **16**:2193–4
speech disabilities, aids for **1**:22
speech and language **16**:2200–3;
19:2615
and the brain **3**:310; **16**:2201
see also voice recognition and
synthesis
speed **3**:422; **5**:694, *695*
speedboats **16**:2204–8
speedometers and tachometers
16:2209–10; **18**:2508
tachometers **2**:203; **16**:*2209*, 2210;
18:2508
speedway racing **14**:1891
sphalerite **9**:1219; **19**:2731
spherical aberration **9**:1227–9;
17:2379
Sphinx, restoration **6**:818
sphygmomanometers **10**:1326;
16:2211
Spider system **5**:596
spillways **5**:604
in dams **7**:888–9
spina bifida
mobility aids for **11**:1470–1
testing for **11**:1564
vitamin supplements and **19**:2614
spin dryers **3**:422
spinnerets
for artificial meats **7**:913
for synthetic fibers **6**:851, 852
spinning **16**:2212–14
cotton **5**:581, 582; **16**:2212–13
spinning wheels **16**:2212
spirits **1**:97; **5**:661, *663*; **6**:841;
16:2215–18
Spirit of St. Louis (aircraft) **2**:213
splints **3**:299
splitters **18**:2506–7
spondylitis, ankylosing **10**:1369
sponsons **16**:2208
spontaneous emission **9**:1210
spontaneous generation, refuted
10:1434
sports car racing **14**:1891
sports equipment **16**:2219–24
clothing **13**:1862–3; **16**:2224, *2226*
sports medicine **16**:2225–6
spotlights **16**:*2233*, 2234;
17:2409–10
spray guns **16**:2227–8
springs **16**:2229–30; **17**:2338–9
manufacture **16**:2230
sprinkler systems
fire fighting **6**:864
for irrigation **9**:1193
sprites **17**:2430
Sputnik I (satellite) **15**:2024
SRAM (static random access
memory) **5**:615; **9**:1167
SSRIs (selective serotonin reuptake
inhibitors) **12**:1681–2; **13**:1868
stabilizers, ship **16**:2231–2
antiroll tanks **16**:2231

bilge keels **16**:2232
flume **16**:2231
gyroscopic **8**:1030–1; **15**:2072; **16**:2231–2
oscillating weights **16**:2232
stabilizer fins **16**:2231, *2232*
stage effects **16**:2233–5
see also theatrical lighting
stained glass **6**:858; **7**:*999*; **16**:2236–8
stains, laboratory **1**:135
stalactites and stalagmites **16**:2239–40
stamens **14**:1958
stamps **10**:1321, 1323
standard deviation **16**:2247
standard model theory **6**:769
Standard Positioning Service (SPS) **7**:1008
standing-wave technique, seismic **2**:157
Staphylococcus aureus, methicillin resistant (MRSA) **10**:1411
stapling machines **13**:1789
starch **3**:389, 390
starches, adhesive **1**:29–30
stars **2**:267
binary **2**:268–9
and supernovas **17**:2315, *2316*
Cepheid variables **4**:573
electromagnetic radiation **6**:*739*
moving away from Earth **5**:*672*
neutron **17**:2315, *2316*; **19**:2724
newborn **2**:*176*
nuclear fusion **6**:764; **7**:947
origin of elements **6**:*763*, 764
parallax **2**:178
physical observing methods **2**:178
red giants **17**:2315, *2316*
shining **2**:178–9
shooting *see* meteors and meteorites
stellar occultation **5**:710
temperature **17**:2396
T-Tauri **13**:1758
white dwarves **14**:1954; **17**:2315, *2316*
X rays from **2**:174
see also pulsars; Sun
starter motors **15**:*2125*; **16**:2241
solenoid switches **15**:2125; **16**:2241
Star Wars (Strategic Defense Initiative; SDI) **16**:2183, 2184
static mechanics (statics) **5**:694; **16**:2242–5
statistics **10**:1354; **16**:2246–9
statistical mechanics **4**:463; **12**:1728; **16**:2249; **17**:2416
stealth technologies **16**:2250–5
electronic countermeasures **18**:2550–3
stealth aircraft **1**:*69*, 144; **10**:*1350*; **16**:2254
steamboats, paddle **10**:1335
steam digesters **13**:1841
steam engines **9**:1169; **16**:2256–9
aircraft **1**:75; **2**:210–11
automobile **2**:198; **16**:2259
governors **15**:2055–6
for marine propulsion **10**:1335; **16**:2258
for mining **11**:1458
see also traction engines
steamships **10**:1335–6
steam turbines *see* turbines, steam
steel *see* iron and steel
steering systems **16**:2260–2
Ackermann **16**:2260, *2262*
automobile steering columns **2**:207, *209*; **16**:2260
power steering **16**:2260, 2261–2

tracked-vehicle **18**:2469
variable-ratio **2**:207
stem cells **7**:997; **8**:1132
embryonic **3**:414; **6**:778
stents **8**:1052; **14**:*1918*
Stephenson, George, *Rocket* **16**:2259
stereolithography **10**:1366
stereophonic reproduction **15**:2142–3
onto records **12**:1697; **15**:2144
stereoradiography **16**:2264
stereoscopy **8**:1080; **16**:2263–4
and aerial photography and surveying **1**:33; **16**:2264
vision **6**:831; **16**:2263
see also binoculars
stereo systems **6**:755; **8**:1072
sterilization
in autoclaves **2**:190
food **5**:601; **7**:912; **18**:2533
of hospital laundry **9**:1218
using gamma rays **6**:745
sterilization (surgical) **13**:1818
Sterling submachine guns **2**:197
steroids **6**:781
drug testing for **16**:2226
in plants **3**:305
sterols, plant **6**:837
stethoscopes **16**:2265
stills **5**:661, *663*; **16**:2215
molecular **5**:664
stimulated emission **9**:1210
Stinger (missile) **1**:144; **11**:1487
Stingray torpedoes **18**:2468
Stirling engines **16**:2266–9
stock-car racing **14**:1891
stock control **10**:1341
stockings, manufacture **8**:1090–3
stoichiometric ratio **16**:2303
Stokes, George **1**:36; **19**:2611
Stokes, Sir Wilfred **11**:1484
STOL aircraft **1**:71, 77; **18**:2551
stomach **5**:642–3, *644*
stone
crushed **14**:1885, 1886
dimension **14**:1885, 1886
stone cutting **16**:2270–2
Stonehenge **11**:1560; **16**:2273–4
stone monuments **16**:2273–5
stop signals, road **14**:1983
storage/retrieval (S/R) systems
automated (AS/RSs) **19**:2622–3, 2624, 2625
in process **19**:*2624–5*
storm-water overflows **5**:675
strabismus (squint) **6**:832
strain **5**:713
strain gauges **2**:215; **18**:2475
Strategic Defense Initiative (SDI; Star Wars) **16**:2183, 2184
stratosphere **1**:62; **10**:1396
Stratospheric Observatory for Far Infrared Astronomy (SOFIA) **2**:177
streetcars **10**:1345, 1348, 1349; **16**:2276–8
San Francisco **3**:356, *358*; **16**:2277, 2278
street lighting **5**:658; **14**:1977, 1980, *1985*
sodium lamps **1**:101; **5**:658; **6**:858; **14**:1980
switches **14**:1980; **17**:*2444*
Streptococcus **12**:*1682*
thermophilus **5**:603; **7**:904
streptokinase **8**:1047
Streptomyces spp. **10**:1409; **12**:1687
stress (on materials) **5**:713, 714
analysis
holographic interferometry **8**:1083
photoelastic **9**:*1237*; **13**:1796

stringed instruments **16**:2279–84
string theories **8**:1022; **14**:1954
stripping, cotton **5**:581, 582
stroboscopes **8**:1078; **16**:2234, 2285–6; **17**:2411
strokes, vascular **3**:414; **10**:*1438*
stromatolites **5**:700; **7**:988
strong nuclear force **6**:772, 773; **7**:876
strontium-90 **17**:*2418*
Stuart Little (movie) **1**:*136*, 139
studios, recording **15**:2143–4
stun guns **11**:1534
styluses, record **12**:*1696*, 1697
styrene (phenylethene) **8**:1107; **12**:1629; **13**:1770, 1771, 1772; **14**:1999–2001
subatomic particles *see* elementary particles
subduction **13**:1778, 1779
sublimation *see* distillation and sublimation
submachine guns (machine pistols; machine carbines) **2**:195–6, *197*; **8**:1025
submarine inertial navigation system (SINS) **16**:2290
submarine-launched ballistic missiles (SLBMs) **16**:2182
submarines **16**:2287–91
air locks used in **1**:85
armaments **16**:2182, *2288*, 2289, *2290*, 2291
design **10**:1366; **16**:2288
detection, by sonar **8**:1070; **15**:*2127*, 2128
diving **16**:2288–9
hunters, helicopter **8**:1070
navigation **16**:2290–1
periscopes **12**:1674–5; **16**:2290
power **10**:1336–7; **16**:2289–90
diesel engines **10**:1336–7; **16**:2290, 2291
nuclear propulsion **10**:1336, 1366; **11**:1542, 1546; **16**:2290, 2291
steam **16**:2289–90
Stirling engines **16**:2266, 2269
rescuing **15**:2023
and sonar **8**:1070; **15**:2127, 2128
underwater stealth communication **16**:2253
see also torpedoes
submersibles **10**:1333; **11**:1569; **16**:2292–4
Alvin **1**:*1568*, 1569; **16**:2294
for marine salvage **15**:2023
tracked **18**:2471
see also submarines; undersea habitats
substations, electrical **13**:1837
subways *see* mass transit and subways
sucrose **3**:389, *390*
sudden infant death syndrome (SIDS) **12**:1661
sugar **3**:389
bonds in **5**:597
and confectionary **4**:557
in food **7**:907
refining **4**:557; **16**:2295–7
quality-control **13**:1793
sugar beet **16**:2295, 2296
sugarcane **16**:2295, 2296
as a biofuel source **7**:*962*
suicide **10**:1369
sulfa drugs **10**:1368
sulfanilamide **8**:1108
sulfur **13**:*1794*; **16**:2298–300
allotropes **16**:2298
amorphous **16**:2299
compounds **16**:2300
in crude oil (petroleum) **11**:1577,

1580; **16**:*2300*
from seawater **11**:1569
mining for **11**:1461
occurrence and extraction **16**:2299
oxidation numbers **12**:1616
plastic **16**:2298–9
sulfur dioxide **11**:1527
sulfur hexafluoride **9**:1162
sulfuric acid **1**:23
industrial manufacture **1**:23–4; **4**:452
uses **1**:24
in batteries **2**:225–6
Sun **13**:1758; **15**:2118–19; **17**:2317
corona **5**:709; **17**:2396
eclipse **5**:709, *710*
electromagnetic radiation **6**:*739*, 740
infrared **6**:742
energy **15**:2114
formation **13**:1758; **17**:2317
and helioseismology **15**:2046
magnetic loops **15**:2119
neutrinos from **2**:181
nuclear fusion **7**:947; **10**:*1361*; **15**:2114
solar spectrum **16**:*2194*, *2196*
space probes to **15**:2046, 2118–19, *2158*, 2159; **17**:2382
temperature **17**:2396
and tides **17**:2436–7, 2440
sundials **4**:*481*; **16**:2301–2; **17**:2441
sundogs **9**:*1242*
sunlamps **5**:658; **18**:2533–4
Super 8 (film) **11**:1494
"superbugs" **4**:440–1; **10**:1411
superchargers and turbochargers **16**:2303–4
intercooling **16**:2304; **18**:2506
superchargers **9**:1172; **16**:2303, *2304*
aircraft engine **1**:74; **16**:2303
vane **16**:2303
turbochargers **16**:2303, 2304
aircraft engine **1**:74, 75; **7**:965
automobile **2**:200
in diesel engines **9**:1174; **18**:2506
in power plants **7**:*971*
in racing car engines **14**:1889
supercomputers **4**:*525*, 526
superconductivity **4**:550; **17**:2309–14
applications **17**:2313–14
electromagnets **5**:718, 719–20; **9**:1256; **17**:2310, 2314
Josephson junctions **17**:*2312*, 2313, 2314
maglev trains **17**:2310, 2314
and the BCS theory **17**:2311–12
and cryogenics **5**:589, *590*
discovery **17**:2309–10
and flux pinning **17**:2310–11
and the Meissner effect **17**:2310
superconductors **4**:553, 555, 556; **5**:718; **6**:728; **17**:2312
ceramics as **5**:718; **17**:2312–13
high-temperature (HTSs) **17**:2312–14
type I and II **17**:2311, 2312
supercontinents, Pangaea **5**:699
supercooling **7**:999
superfluids **4**:550, 553; **5**:592; **7**:934; **10**:1362; **11**:1528–9
superglue **1**:30
supernovas **2**:267; **17**:2315–17
1987A **2**:173, 179–80, *181*; **17**:2317
for distance measurement **4**:573
gamma rays from **2**:173
and gravity waves **8**:1022
hypernovas **17**:2317
remnants **14**:*1912*; **17**:2316

supernumerary arcs **14**:1934
superphosphate, fertilizers **6**:844–5
supersonic flight **1**:37; **7**:966;
  17:2318–20
  cloud production **18**:2570
  sonic booms **1**:37; **17**:2318–19
  supersonic aircraft **1**:70–1, 84;
    17:*2318*, 2319
  tested in wind tunnels **19**:2698–9
superstring theory **6**:773
supertankers **7**:928–9; **11**:*1577*
surface-effect vehicles **1**:122, 123
surface tension **10**:*1359*, 1361–2;
  17:*2321*
  detergents and **15**:*2108*
  of mercury **10**:*1371*; **17**:2321
surface-to-air missiles (SAMs) **1**:144
surface treatments **17**:2322–6
  coatings **17**:2323
    surface-alloy **1**:107
    see also galvanizing
  polishing **17**:2325
  using water jets **17**:2322–3
  see also abrasives; electroplating
surfactants **5**:631, 632
surgery **17**:2327–32
  alternatives to **17**:2330
    see also body scanners
  aseptic **10**:1367; **17**:2327, 2329
  cold-probe **5**:592
  cryosurgery **5**:591; **17**:2330
  diagnostic **12**:1657–8
  endoscopes used in **6**:785;
    12:1613; **17**:2330–1, 2332
  eye **12**:*1589*, 1590
    using lasers **9**:1213, 1214;
      12:1590; **17**:*2330*
  heart (cardiovascular) **8**:**1049–52**
  history **17**:2327–8
  "keyhole" **18**:2549
  laser **6**:785, *856*; **9**:1214
  plastic, glues used in **1**:32
  preparation for **11**:1581–2;
    17:2328–9
  and robotics **10**:1440; **17**:2331–2;
    19:*2616*
  telesurgery **17**:2332
  veterinary **18**:2584–5
  virtual **17**:2332
  see also anesthetics; microsurgery;
    operating rooms
surveillance
  electronic see electronic surveil-
    lance
  Sentinel **6**:812
  using thermography **17**:2422
surveying **17**:2333–7
  aerial surveys **1**:35; **11**:*1571*;
    17:2336
    mapmaking **10**:1329, *1330*
  angular measurement **17**:2336
  cadastral **17**:2333
  engineering surveys **17**:2333
  geodetic and plane **17**:2333
  gravimetric **11**:1571
  ground surveys, mapmaking
    10:1328–9
  hydrographic **17**:2333; **18**:2531
  laser reflectors **14**:1944
  linear measurement **17**:2336
  magnetometric **11**:1571
  other planets **12**:1707; **17**:2337
  satellite **11**:1571; **17**:2337, 2422
  seismic **7**:*992*, 993–4; **11**:1570–1
  topographic **17**:2333
  using the global positioning system
    17:2336–7
  using lasers **9**:1214
Surveyor space probes **15**:2157, 2159
suspension systems **17**:2338–40
  automobile see automobiles,
    suspension

racing car **14**:1890–1
tank **2**:168
  tracked-vehicle **18**:2469–70
sustainable development **6**:808
sutures **17**:2329
swamp buggies **1**:121–2
sweat glands **15**:2105
sweeteners, food **7**:914
sweetening, of crude oil **11**:1580
switches **17**:2341
  and Boolean algebra **9**:1279
  contact **17**:2341
  electronic, and reluctance motors
    5:717, *718*
  eye-controlled **11**:1470
  fluid-operated see fluidics
  glass memory **4**:552
  isolating **17**:2341
  knife **17**:2341
  load **17**:2341
  photoelectrically-controlled
    14:1980
  three-way **17**:2341
  time **17**:2444–5
    solar-dial **14**:1980; **17**:*2444*
  transistors as **18**:2480
switches (intelligent hubs) **4**:539
switch gear **13**:1837
switchyards **14**:1929, 1930
symbiosis, parasitism **12**:1644
synapses **3**:309, *311*
  neuromuscular **3**:*414*; **11**:1506
synchrocyclotrons **12**:1649–50
synchromesh **18**:*2489*, 2490–1
synchronization circuits (sync
  circuits) **12**:1608
synchrotrons **2**:261, 262; **12**:1650;
  17:2316
synovial fluid **3**:297
synthesizers **17**:2342–5
  drum **12**:1670; **17**:2344–5
  in electronic organs **12**:1604
synthetic crystals **17**:2346–7
syphilis, treatment **1**:135
system control and data acquisition
  see SCADA
systole **8**:1045

T

tabun **4**:437; **12**:1700
TACAN (tactical air navigation) **1**:67
tachometers see speedometers and
  tachometers
Tacoma Narrows Bridge **3**:327;
  14:1965
tactical missile systems (TACMs)
  11:1466
taffeta **17**:2407
tagged image file format (TIFF) files
  12:1594
Talbot, William Henry Fox **12**:1708
talking clocks **17**:2348–9
tallows **15**:1382
tamoxifen **12**:1687
tankers **17**:2350–2
  docks **5**:671; **7**:929
  liquefied gas vessels **17**:2352
  oil **5**:671; **15**:2072
    hydraulics used in **8**:1104
    supertankers (very large crude
      carriers) **7**:928–9; **11**:*1577*
  ore-carrying **9**:1190
  pipelines and pumps **17**:2351–2
  safety **17**:2352
  see also ships, bulk-carrying
tanks see armored vehicles and tanks
tannin **8**:1151
tanning **4**:*473*; **9**:1223
tantalum **3**:404
TAPCHAN (tapered channel)
  systems **19**:2676

tar, distillation **11**:1575
tarmacadam see blacktop
tar sands, oil from **11**:1574
tartar, dental **5**:619–20
Tasers **11**:1534
taste **15**:2103–4
  taste buds **15**:2106
taxicabs, taximeters **17**:2355
taxidermy **17**:2353–4
taximeters **17**:2355
Tay-Sachs disease **7**:980
TB see tuberculosis
TBTO (tributyltin oxide) **2**:149
TCA cycle see Krebs cycle
TCP/IP (transmission control proto-
  col/Internet protocol) **9**:1178,
  1179–80
TDM (time-division multiplexing)
  1:129; **17**:2356, 2365
tear gases **4**:437; **8**:1036; **11**:1532,
  1534; **14**:1972
tear glands **6**:830
technetium, isotopes **14**:1907
Technicolor process **11**:1500
teeth **5**:642; **18**:2466
  of animals **5**:645
  decay **5**:618–19, *622*
  false **5**:*620*, 622
  fluoride and **5**:620; **8**:1034, *1036*;
    18:2466; **19**:2666
  identifying people from **7**:920
  replacement **5**:620
  structure **5**:618
  see also dentistry; toothpaste
Teflon see polytetrafluoroethylene
tektites **7**:989; **10**:1394–5
telecommunications **17**:2356–9
  cable networks **3**:353–5; **17**:2356
    data transmission **17**:2357
  fiber optics **3**:354–5; **4**:539, 542;
    6:856; **17**:2356–7, 2371
  submarine cables **3**:347–9;
    18:2471
  and data interception **6**:761–2
  high-speed data transfer
    17:2357–8
  operations centers **1**:*127*
  radio (earthbound) **17**:2358–9
    cell phones see cellular
      telephones
    signals **1**:129; **17**:2359
    see also radio
  satellite links **4**:540, *541*, 542;
    15:*2025*, 2027, 2029; **17**:2359
  using holography **8**:1082
  using microwaves **6**:746; **17**:2359
  see also modems and ISDN
teleconferencing **4**:525
  virtual reality (teleimmersion)
    19:2606
telegraph **17**:2357, **2360–3**
  cables **3**:347
  facsimile transmission **10**:1325;
    17:2363
  history **3**:353–4; **17**:2360–2
  telex network **17**:2357, 2362–3
  see also e-mail
teleimmersion **19**:2606
telemeters, self-reducing **17**:*2336*
telemetry **17**:2364–5
  electric **17**:2364–5
  multiplex **17**:2365
  pulse-rate **17**:2365
  radio **17**:2365
  space probe antennas **15**:2156
  uses **2**:257; **17**:2365
telephone answering machines
  17:2366–7
telephone systems **17**:2368–72
  cables **3**:347; **17**:2356, *2357*, 2371;
    18:2471
  cell phones see cellular telephones

cordless telephones **17**:2370
digital techniques **6**:755
and electronic surveillance **6**:759,
  760
exchanges **17**:2371–2
  answering services **17**:2367
  signaling **17**:2370–1
handsets **17**:2369–70
  and amplification **1**:22; **17**:2369
invention **17**:2368–9
IP (Internet protocol) telephony
  17:2370
local distribution **17**:2371
long-distance calls **17**:2372
"smart" telephones **17**:*2369*
and speaking clocks **17**:2348–9
third generation **3**:416
using fiber optics **6**:856
see also modems and ISDN
telepresence **19**:2604
teleprompters **17**:2373–5
telescopes
  astronomical **17**:*2377*
    mirrors **11**:1464
    polarimeters attached to
      13:1793
  optical **11**:1561; **17**:2376–80
    Galilean **17**:*2377*, 2379
    magnification **17**:2376–7
    mercury mirrors **11**:1464;
      17:2380
    observatories **11**:1560–1
    reflector telescopes **11**:1561–2;
      17:*2376*, 2378–9
    refractor telescopes **11**:1561;
      17:2377–8
    Schmidt (wide-field) telescopes
      and cameras **11**:1562;
      17:2379–80
    spectrographs attached to
      16:2195
    see also binoculars
  radio **11**:1562; **14**:1909
    amplifiers **14**:1911
    antennas **14**:1909–10
    output devices **14**:1911
    Very Large Arrays (VLAS)
      14:*1909*, 1910–11
  space **15**:2029; **17**:2381–2
    hydrostatic bearings **2**:232
    infrared **2**:177; **17**:2382
    Next Generation Space
      Telescope (NGST) **2**:177;
      17:2382
    observatories **11**:1561
    ultraviolet **2**:175–6
    see also Hubble Space Telescope;
      SOHO
telesurgery **17**:2332
teletherapy, cobalt **14**:1921
television broadcasting **6**:*741*;
  18:2494–6; **19**:*2671*
  cable television **3**:354; **17**:2356;
    18:*2494*, 2496–7
  digital TV (DTV; high-definition
    TV - HDTV) **6**:*754*, 755;
    11:1498; **17**:2385, *2392*;
    18:2497
  and editing **17**:2390–1; **18**:2495
  satellite **1**:*141*, 142; **3**:354; **18**:2497
television cameras **17**:2383–5, 2386,
  2387
  closed-circuit (CCTV) **3**:340;
    15:2042, 2044
  on roads **14**:1977
  color **6**:*857*, 858; **17**:2384, *2385*
television production **17**:2386–91
  interactive television **17**:2391
  teleprompters **17**:2373–5
  see also television cameras
television receivers **5**:599; **17**:2392–4
  antennas **1**:142

black-and-white 3:409
cable 3:354; 17:2356; 18:2496–7
cathode-ray tubes 3:409;
  12:1647–8; 17:2392, 2393
closed-circuit (CCTV) 3:340;
  14:1977; 15:2042, 2044
color 3:409; 4:511; 17:2385,
  2393–4
flat-screen 3:410
NTSC system 17:2394
PAL system 17:2394
picture reception 17:2392–3
plasma-technology 17:2394
signal decoding 17:2393
and sound 17:2393
widescreen 6:754
telex 17:2357, 2362–3
Telford, Thomas 3:374; 14:1973
tellurometers 10:1328; 14:1898
temperature 17:2395–6
  critical 17:2309; 18:2569
  effect on solids 10:1361
  ignition 7:879
  inversion 17:2419
  low
    absolute zero 17:2395, 2396
    and cryogenics 5:589
  measurement see thermocouples;
    thermometry
  neutral 17:2419
  regulation (body) 15:2087–8
  scales 17:2395–6, 2414
  transition 4:553; 10:1360, 1362
tempering 1:104; 10:1388; 18:2462
template matching 19:2615
Tencel 6:851; 13:1769
tendons 11:1504
tensile structures 3:338;
  17:2397–402
teratogenesis 12:1685
terephthalic acid 8:1107
terminal guidance systems (TGSs)
  2:288
terracing, hillside 6:817–18
terracotta 4:467
Terrestrial Planet Finder (TPF)
  17:2382
Terylene 8:1108
Tesla, Nikola 13:1834; 17:2403
Tesla coils 8:1140; 17:2403
testing, nondestructive, using sound
  waves 1:27
testosterone(s) 8:1087
  in plants 3:305
"test tube baby" procedure 7:900,
  11:1564
tetrachloromethane 4:462
tetraethyl lead 1:97, 101; 4:459;
  8:1036, 1106; 9:1221; 13:1802
tetrafluoroethene (tetrafluoroethylene) 13:1813, 1814
Tetra Paks 7:908; 12:1624–5
TEUs (twenty-foot equivalent units)
  15:2070
Tevatron particle accelerator
  12:1648, 1649; 13:1763
textiles 17:2404–8
  for the clothing industry 4:490
  fabrics 17:2406–8
    conservation 2:160
    fire-resistant 7:880, 881
    nonwoven 17:2408
    printing 5:692, 693; 6:833–4;
      17:2408
      see also dyes
    water-repellent finishes
      19:2659–60
    woven 17:2405–6
      see also weaving
  finishing processes 17:2408
  high-strength materials 17:2405
    see also carbon fiber; Kevlar

see also fibers, natural; fibers,
  synthetic
TGV (Train á Grand Vitesse) 1:36;
  4:476; 9:1255, 1274; 14:1928
thalidomide 12:1685
Thames, River
  pollution 13:1799; 19:2648
  tunnels under 18:2512–13
Thames Barrier 5:605; 7:888, 889,
  891
theatrical lighting 16:2233, 2234;
  17:2409–11
  see also stage effects
theodolites 8:1031; 17:2335, 2336,
  2337
  electronic 2:157; 17:2336
Theory of Everything (TOE) 6:767,
  773; 8:1022
thermic lances 17:2412
thermionic emission 1:124; 5:657;
  18:2563
thermocouples 1:65, 127; 13:1783;
  17:2395, 2417, 2418, 2419, 2420
  in engines 17:2423
thermodynamics 4:463–4; 9:1202;
  12:1727; 17:2413–16
  first law 6:786; 12:1727;
    17:2414–15
  and heat capacity 17:2414
  and heat energy 17:2413
  and internal energy 17:2413
  second law 6:788; 16:2249;
    17:2415–16
  and statistical mechanics 17:2416
  and the Universe 17:2416
thermoelectric devices 17:2417–20
  see also thermocouples
thermoforming, vacuum 13:1773,
  1775
thermograms and thermography
  17:2421–2
  airscan thermographs 1:35
  of the body 2:281, 282; 6:743;
    17:2422
thermoluminescent dating 2:157–8;
  7:995
thermometry 1:63; 17:2395, 2423–4
  analog-display 1:127
  clinical thermometers 17:2423–4
  gas thermometers 17:2395, 2424
  meteorological thermometers
    17:2424
  resistance thermometers 13:1783;
    17:2424
thermopiles 17:2418, 2420
thermoplastics
  pipes 13:1750
  powder coatings 13:1823–4
  processing of 13:1773, 1774–5
  recycling 14:1941
thermos bottles 17:2425
thermoscopes 17:2423
thermosets 13:1775
  for pipes 13:1750
  for powder coatings 13:1824
thermostats 17:2426–7
  automobile 17:2426, 2427
  central-heating 8:1058; 17:2426–7
  hot-water tank 13:1785
thiamine 19:2613
thiokol 14:2001
thixotropy 19:2609
Thomson, J. J. 2:182; 3:408; 6:726,
  767; 18:2563
Thomson, William (later Baron
  Kelvin) 6:786; 12:1727;
  17:2395, 2414, 2419
Thomson effect 17:2417, 2419
thorium 18:2487
  as a nuclear fuel 11:1539
thorium oxide 18:2487
threads, screw 15:2032–3

Three Gorges Dam 5:608; 8:1115
Three Mile Island 11:1535–6
threshing machines 1:49–50
throat surgery 12:1612, 1613
throttles 1:65; 3:396
throwing power 17:2323–4
thrust 1:65; 18:2573
thunderstorms 17:2428–31
  lightning 4:555; 6:725;
    17:2428–30, 2431
  thunder 17:2431
  thunder clouds (cumulonimbus)
    9:1250; 10:1399, 1401; 17:2428,
    2429
thymine 7:973–4; 11:1477, 1478
thymus 8:1134
thyristors 6:753; 14:1938; 17:2432–3
  bidirectional (triacs) 6:731;
    17:2433
thyroid gland 6:781; 8:1085, 1087
thyroxine 6:781; 8:1085
ticket machines 17:2434–5
  coin validation 4:509
  pay-and-display 10:1407; 17:2434
tidal fences 17:2438
tidal power 6:792–3; 17:2436–8
  see also wave power
tides 17:2436–7, 2439–40
  and docks 5:668
  Earth tides 17:2440
  gravitation and 5:696–7; 8:1022;
    11:1521
  on moons 11:1520; 17:2440
  the Moon and 5:696–7; 8:1022;
    11:1521, 17:2436–7, 2439, 2440
  planetary 17:2440
  the Sun and 17:2436–7, 2440
  tidal flooding 7:891
TIFF (tagged image file format) files
  12:1594
tillage, soil 1:55
timber
  for buildings 3:336
  drying 9:1199–1200, 1295
  see also lumber
timbre (tone) 15:2132
  musical 3:318
time 17:2441–3
  affected by gravity 8:1022; 17:2443
  dilation 14:1952
  equation of 16:2301
  longitude and 9:1215
  and the special theory of relativity
    17:2442–3
  Universal (UT) 17:2442
  see also clocks
time-base circuitry 12:1608
time-depth indicators (TDIs)
  10:1332
Time Division Multiple Access
  (TDMA) 3:416; 17:2359
time-division multiplexing (TDM)
  1:129; 17:2356, 2365
timing devices 17:2444–6
  central-heating 8:1058; 17:2445
  in dishwashers 5:660
tin 17:2447–8
  alloys 17:2448
    see also bronze; pewter; solders
  compounds 17:2448
  mining for 11:1462; 17:2448
  occurrence and production
    17:2447
  prospecting for 16:2199
  tin-plated steel 3:382, 383; 4:571
  uses, in canning 3:382, 383;
    17:2448
  white 17:2448
tin chloride 15:2080; 17:2448
tinnitus 8:1041

tinplate 17:2448
tires 18:2453–6
  bicycle 2:241, 243; 17:2338
  cross-ply (bias) 18:2453, 2454–5,
    2456
  manufacture 18:2453–5
  pneumatic 2:243; 17:2338;
    18:2453
  racing car 14:1888, 1890; 18:2454,
    2455–6
  radial-ply 2:201, 206; 18:2453,
    2454–5, 2456
  rib-tread 14:1890
  rubber 14:1998, 2001
  run-flat 2:206
  safety 18:2455
  scrap recovery schemes 5:591
  self-repairing 2:206
    sealants in 1:32
  slick 14:1890; 18:2454
tissue plasminogen activator 2:263
tissues, artificial creation of 6:778
tissue typing 18:2498
Titan (moon) 15:2122, 2160
titania 3:426
titanium 18:2486
  alloys 10:1351; 18:2485
    titanium–nickel 5:622; 10:1351
  uses 2:243, 256; 16:2191
titanium chloride 12:1627; 18:2488
titanium dioxide
  forms 5:599
  in paints 12:1627, 1628, 1630
  synthetic 5:599
titanium oxide 6:779
titration 4:446–7
TNT see trinitrotoluene
tobacco 3:304
  disease-resistant 1:55
tocophenol 19:2613
toilets 18:2457–9
Tokaimura, nuclear incident at
  11:1536
tokamaks 6:796; 7:947–8; 13:1763
tolerance 16:2247
Tollund Man 4:477
toluene 4:498; 5:617; 8:1107, 1108
  from oil refining 11:1578–9
Tomahawk (missile) 11:1466, 1467,
  1468; 16:2291
  antiship 11:1466
tomography
  positron-emission (PET) 2:151,
    281; 3:312
  seismic 15:2046
  see also Computed Axial
    Tomography
tone see timbre
tones and semitones 11:1508–9
tongue 15:2106
tool manufacture 18:2460–5
  see also screws, manufacture
toothpaste 1:17; 18:2466
topology 10:1358
torches, flame-cutting 10:1379
tornadoes 8:1094, 1097–9
torpedoes 1:27; 16:2291; 18:2467–8
torque 5:695; 12:1726
  and angular momentum 8:1030
  control 13:1789
  converters 8:1104
torque-controlled motor system
  13:1789
toss-bombing 2:287
total color transfer process 4:468
total-containment vessels (TCVs)
  3:296
total crop management 1:55
touch screens 11:1492
toxicology 16:2197
  forensic 7:918–19; 13:1792
trachea 10:1303

trackballs **4**:535; **11**:1492
track-circuit signaling **14**:1924
tracked vehicles **5**:703; **18**:*2469–71*
 half-tracks **18**:*2470–1*
 tanks **2**:167–8; **18**:*2469–70*, 2471
trackpads **4**:535; **11**:1492
traction **3**:300
traction engines **16**:*2256*; **18**:*2472–3*
tractors **1**:45–6; **8**:*1104*
 agricultural tracked **18**:2471
 crawler **5**:703
traffic monitoring **14**:1984–5
trains
 brakes **3**:314, 315; **10**:1346;
  14:*1925, 1926*
 electric
  brakes **3**:315; **10**:1346
  externally-powered **9**:1286
 high-speed **9**:1255, *1256*, 1274;
  14:1927–8
  Eurostar **9**:*1273*
  Japanese Shinkansen ("bullet"
   trains) **3**:328; **9**:1274; **14**:1927–8
  maglev (magnetic-levitation)
   5:717, 719; **7**:934; **9**:*1252,
   1254,* 1255–6; **10**:1349, *1363*,
   1364–5; **14**:1928; **17**:2310, 2314
  tilting trains **9**:1273–4; **14**:1928
  Train á Grand Vitesse (TGV)
   1:*36*; **4**:476; **9**:1255, 1274;
   14:1927
 mass transit and subway **10**:1346–7
 rubber-tired **10**:1346
 see also locomotives and power cars;
  railroad systems; railways
trams *see* streetcars
tranquilizers **12**:1682
transactinides **6**:765
Trans-Alaska pipeline **13**:1753
transducers and sensors **18**:2474–6
 in automobiles
  fuel gauge **18**:2474
  position **2**:204
  pressure **2**:203–4; **15**:2054
  temperature **2**:204
 sensors
  biosensors **14**:1988
  in burglar alarms **3**:340
  chemical **14**:1988
  and robot senses **14**:1988, 1989
 transducers
  in accelerometers **18**:2476
  capacitive **18**:2475
  displacement **18**:2474
  electret **5**:*715*, 716; **18**:2475–6
  electrostrictive **18**:2530
  feedback (fork balance) **18**:2476
  inductive **18**:2474–5
  linear variable differential
   (LVDTs) **18**:2474–5
  load **18**:*2476*
  magnetostrictive **18**:2530
  piezoelectric materials as
   13:1745, 1843; **18**:2474,
   2529–30
  pressure sensors **18**:2474,
   2510–11
  resonance **18**:2476
  sonar **15**:2126, 2128
  strain gauges **2**:215; **18**:2475
  see also pickup, acoustic
transesterification **2**:259
transformers **6**:729, 747, *748*, 749;
 8:1139; **12**:1728; **13**:1835, *1838*;
 18:2477–9
 air-cooled **18**:2479
 autotransformers **18**:*2478*
 design **18**:2477–9
 distribution **18**:2479
 eddy currents **8**:1141
 generator **13**:1830; **18**:2479
 instrument **18**:2479

insulation in **9**:*1163*; **18**:2479
 in power plants **13**:1830; **18**:*2479*
 step-up and step-down **6**:729;
  18:2479
transmission **18**:2479
 unit **13**:1830
transfusions, blood **2**:272, *273*;
 17:2328
transistors **6**:752; **9**:1164; **18**:2480–4
 bipolar-junction **1**:124–5; **6**:753;
  9:1164; **18**:2482–3
 in calculators **3**:359
 in computers **2**:169; **4**:524; **6**:754
 field-effect (FETs) **1**:125, 126;
  6:753, 755; **18**:2483
  ion-sensitive (ISFETs) **18**:*2480*
  junction-gate (JFETs;
   JUGFETS) **18**:2483–4
  metal-oxide-semiconductor
   (MOSFETS; insulated gate
   FETs–IGFETS) **18**:2484
 gain and feedback of **6**:754
 modulating **18**:2480
 phototransistors **18**:2483
 point-contact **18**:2481
 semiconductor **1**:124; **6**:753, 754;
  15:*2053*, 2054; **18**:2480–2, 2565
  CMOS **6**:755
 transistor radios **18**:2494
transition elements **12**:1673;
 18:2485–8
 as catalysts **3**:405; **4**:452; **18**:2488
 compounds **4**:*443*; **18**:2488
 see also platinum metals
Trans-Mediterranean pipeline **7**:*959*;
 13:1753
transmission, automobile *see* automobiles, transmission
transmission, broadcasting
 18:2493–7
 transmitting antennas **1**:141, *142*
transmit-receive (TR) cells **14**:1894,
 1896
transmutation
 artificial **11**:1525
 of nuclear waste **11**:1550
transpiration **19**:2665
transplants **18**:2498–504
 animal organs (xenotransplants)
  13:1734; **18**:2504
  bioprosthetic valves **18**:2500
 bone marrow **3**:380; **18**:*2499,
  2502,* 2503–4
 hand **10**:1439; **18**:2504
 heart **12**:1660; **18**:2498–9, 2500–2
  extra-heart operations **18**:2502
  heart-lung **12**:1660; **18**:*2499,
   2502*
  valves **18**:2499, 2500
  see also heart, artificial
 kidney **6**:782; **18**:2498
 limb **10**:1439; **18**:2504
 liver **13**:1734; **18**:2498
  microsurgery techniques
   10:1438–9
 pancreas **6**:782
 rejection **8**:1137
  drug control of **18**:2499
  graft versus host disease
   (GVHD) **18**:*2499*, 2503
 skin grafts **10**:1438–9; **13**:1765,
  1766; **15**:*2087*; **18**:2500
 spare-part surgery **18**:2499–2500,
  2503
  growing organs for **6**:778;
   18:2500
 tooth **5**:622
 see also joints (body parts), artificial
transposons (jumping genes) **3**:*303*
Transrapid system **5**:719; **9**:1256;
 10:1349
transuranic waste **11**:1548

transuranium (transuranic) elements
 6:764–5; **18**:2487
traveling mattes **16**:2187; **18**:2495
traveling-wave tubes **6**:741
traversing **17**:2334
trawlers **7**:871–3, *874*
TR (transmit-receive) cells **14**:1894,
 1896
treadmills **9**:1194
tree rings, study of **4**:478
trees
 dating **2**:*160*
 hardwood and softwood **9**:1293–4
 rubber **14**:1997
 see also forestry; lumber
trenches **5**:701
 cables laid in **3**:346
 ocean floor **5**:699; **11**:1566;
  13:1778
 for pipes **5**:674, 675, 703
trepanning **17**:2327
Trevira **6**:853
Trevithick, Richard **16**:*2256*;
 18:*2472*
triacs **6**:731; **17**:2433
Triangle of Forces theorem **16**:2242
triangles (musical instruments)
 12:1668, *1669*
triangulation **10**:1328, *1329*; **12**:1706
triboelectricity **6**:725, 727, *728*
tributyl phosphate (TBP) **11**:1539
tributyltin oxide (TBTO) **2**:149
tricarboxylic acid cycle (TCA) cycle
 see Krebs cycle
Tricel **6**:852; **13**:1769
trichloroacetic acid (TCA) **13**:1767
trichloroethylene **1**:131; **5**:687;
 8:1036
trichloromethane **13**:1769
tricycles **2**:240, *241*
tricyclic antidepressants **12**:1681;
 13:1868
Trident missiles **16**:*2289*, 2291
trigonometry **10**:1355–6; **15**:2082
trihalomethanes **4**:476
trilobites **6**:824; **12**:1634–5
trimarans **16**:2206
trim tabs **1**:66
trinitrophenol (picric acid) **6**:827,
 828; **8**:1108; **11**:1527
trinitrotoluene (TNT) **1**:116; **6**:828;
 8:1107, 1108; **11**:1527
triodes, vacuum-tube (valves) **1**:124;
 6:751; **18**:2480, 2564–5
tritium **1**:99; **7**:947; **8**:1118
 in hydrogen bombs **11**:1553
trolleybuses **3**:343
trolley locomotives, in coal mines
 4:*494*
trombones **3**:319
trophosomes **11**:1567
tropopause **1**:62
troposphere **1**:62; **6**:746; **10**:1396,
 1399
trucks **18**:2505–8
 brakes **3**:315; **18**:2507
 dump **5**:703
 engine **18**:2506
 firefighting **6**:861
 forklift *see* forklifts
 haulage **7**:929
 instrumentation **18**:2508
 power steering **16**:*2260*
 road trains **9**:*1175*; **18**:2505
 security **2**:*168*
 steam **18**:2473
 tank **18**:2506
 trailers **18**:2505–6
 transmission **18**:2490, 2506–7
 turret **7**:927
trumpets **3**:319
trunk deck vessels **17**:2350–1

trypanosomiasis **8**:1136
trypsinogen **5**:643
Tsing Ma Bridge **4**:474
Tsiolkovsky, Konstantin E. **14**:1991
tsunamis **5**:707; **18**:*2509–11*
tubas **3**:319, 320
tuberculosis (TB) **6**:811, 812;
 10:1305, *1370*
 in cattle **18**:2587
tubes, capillary, manufacture **13**:1752
tubes, metal **10**:1391
tube worms **10**:1333
tugs, salvage **15**:2021
tumors
 holographic visualization **8**:1083
 malignant and benign **3**:377
 see also cancer
tungsten **18**:2486
 for lightbulbs **9**:1244, 1245, 1246;
  13:1782–3; **14**:*1960*; **18**:2485
 thoriated **18**:2565
tungsten carbide, uses **5**:680
Tunguska event **10**:1394
tuning forks **12**:*1605*; **14**:1965
tunneling **4**:475; **18**:*2512–16*
 air locks used in **1**:85
 cut-and-cover method **10**:*1347*;
  18:2512
 machines **18**:*2512, 2514, 2515,
  2516*
 in mines **11**:*1461*
 New Austrian Tunneling Method
  4:475
tunnels
 lighting **14**:1980
 ventilation in **8**:1060
 wind *see* wind tunnels
tunnel shields **18**:2512–13
turbines **18**:2517–20
 blade erosion **18**:2520
 gas *see* gas turbines
 reaction **8**:1113, *1115*; **18**:2517–18
 steam **7**:964; **8**:1053; **18**:*2517,
  2518, 2519, 2520*
  aircraft **1**:75
  centrifugal governors **8**:1017
  impulse **18**:2519
  for marine propulsion
   10:*1335–6*
  in power plants **13**:1827;
   18:2520
 water **18**:2517–18, 2519–20
  Deriaz turbines **18**:2518,
   2519–20
  Francis turbines **18**:2518,
   2519–20
  in hydroelectric plants
   8:1112–13; **18**:2520
  impulse **8**:1112–13; **18**:2518–19
  Kaplan turbines **18**:2518,
   2519–20
  Pelton wheels **8**:1113;
   18:2519–20
  for tidal power **17**:*2437*, 2438
  turbo impulse **18**:2519
 wave **18**:2520; **19**:2676, *2677*
 wind **6**:793; **18**:2520
turbochargers *see* superchargers and
 turbochargers
turbofans (fanjets) **1**:65, *74, 75,* 76–8;
 7:966
turbogenerators **13**:1830; **19**:2639
turboprops **1**:72, 76; **7**:966–7
turboramjets **1**:76; **7**:967
turboshafts **1**:76; **7**:967; **8**:1067
turntables, record-player **12**:1697
turpentine **5**:661
tweeters **9**:*1284*, 1285
twenty-foot equivalent units (TEUs)
 15:2070
twill **17**:2406
Tycho's star **17**:2317

Tyne class lifeboats 15:2040
typefaces 5:627
typesetting 5:630
typewriters 18:2521–3; 19:2719
typhoid
    as a biological weapon 4:437
    vaccine 18:2557
typhoons 8:1094
typography 5:627
Tyrian purple dye 5:693

U

UHT (ultra-high temperature)
        processes 7:912
Uhuru (satellite) 19:2724
ulcers, stomach 10:1367, 1411
ULSI see integrated circuits
ultracentrifuges 3:423
ultrafiltration 5:633; 12:1610
Ultra Large Crude Carriers
        (ULCCs) 17:2350, 2351
ultra-large-scale integration (ULSI)
        see integrated circuits
ultralight aircraft 8:1038; 18:2524–7
    see also microlights
ultramicrotomes 11:1445, 1446
ultrasonics 15:2134–5; 18:2528–32
    sources and detectors 18:2529–30
        piezoelectric transducers
            13:1745; 18:2529–30
    uses
        body scans 2:279–80, 282;
            12:1657; 18:2531
        brain exploration 18:2532
        cavitation 18:2532
        cleaning 13:1745
        cutting and machining 10:1310;
            18:2528, 2532
        dentistry 5:622
        nondestructive testing 14:1878;
            18:2529, 2530, 2531, 2532
        scans during pregnancy 11:1564;
            18:2531, 2586
        security systems 3:340; 15:2043
        sonar 18:2531
        therapy 18:2532, 2550
        underwater surveying 18:2531
        welding 1:111; 10:1384
ultrasound machining (USM)
        10:1310
ultraviolet lamps 6:744; 18:2533–4
    for healing 18:2534
    sunlamps 5:658; 18:2533–4
ultraviolet radiation 6:744; 9:1237–8;
        18:2534
    from space 2:174–6
    uses
        fingerprinting 7:916
        food preservation 7:908;
            18:2533
        photolithography 10:1417
        stage lighting 16:2234
        to detect counterfeit banknotes
            5:584
        water sterilization 19:2666
    see also ultraviolet lamps
umbilical cord 6:777
uncertainty principle, Heisenberg
        6:770; 14:1883; 16:2249
undercarriage, retractable 18:2535–6
undersea habitats 18:2537–40
    see also aqualungs
underwater photography 3:369;
        18:2541–3
unified field theories 6:773; 14:1880,
        1954
Unified Thread series 15:2032–3
uniflow engines 16:2258
uniformitarianism 7:987
unit cells 5:598; 10:1359; 13:1744
UNIVAC machines 4:524

Universal coordinated time (UCT)
        17:2442
Universal Indicator 12:1692
universal joints 18:2544–5
universal serial bus (USB) sockets
        11:1474
Universe
    age 4:573
        clumping of material 4:576
        expanding 4:573; 5:672; 6:773
        fate 4:574
        history 4:575
            Big Bang 4:572, 573–4; 6:773
        missing mass in 4:575–6
        shape 4:574–5
        thermodynamics and 17:2416
uranium 14:1906–7; 18:2487,
        2546–8
    isotopes 6:764; 7:877; 8:1034;
        11:1539, 1544, 1551–2;
        14:1907; 18:2547
        decay series 14:1908, 1916
        separation (enrichment) 3:423;
            11:1537–8, 1544; 18:2548
    mining for 11:1457, 1462, 1537
        disposal of wastes 11:1547
    nuclear fission 2:248; 7:876, 877;
        11:1544, 1551–2; 14:1907;
        18:2548
    occurrence and extraction
        11:1457, 1462, 1537; 18:2546–7
    ore refining process 11:1537
    radioactivity 7:970; 14:1907;
        18:2546
    reprocessing 11:1538–9, 1549
    use in nuclear reactors 6:796;
        11:1537–9; 13:1831
    uses
        in aircraft 1:69
        in nuclear reactors 6:796;
            11:1537–9; 13:1831; 18:2548
        in nuclear weapons 11:1551–2
    waste disposal 11:1547, 1550
uranium carbide 3:426
uranium dioxide 11:1538
uranium hexafluoride 6:764; 8:1034;
        11:1537–8, 1539; 18:2546, 2548
uranium oxides 18:2546, 2547
uranium tetrafluoride 11:1538;
        18:2546
Uranus 13:1757, 1758, 1761;
        15:2118, 2122, 2123
    rings around 5:710; 15:2123
uranyl ions 18:2546
uranyl nitrate 18:2546, 2547
uranyl sulfate 11:1537
urea 4:453
    fertilizers 6:845
urea formaldehyde (UF) 19:2709
ureters 18:2549
urethra 18:2549
Urey, Harold 9:1234
urine, tests 5:684, 685; 12:1657;
        18:2457
URLs (uniform resource locators)
        9:1180, 1181
urograms 18:2549
urology 18:2549–50
    see also dialysis machines; kidneys
USB (universal serial bus) sockets
        11:1474
Uzi (submachine gun) 2:196

V

V1 (bomb) 2:286
V-2s (rocket missiles) 8:1144;
        14:1992
V/STOL (VTOL) aircraft 1:71, 77,
        78; 18:2551–3
    convertiplanes 8:1069; 18:2552
    see also helicopters

vaccines 8:1137; 10:1369, 1370;
        18:2554–7
    against biological weapons 4:440
    genetically-engineered 2:264–5,
        266; 7:978
    see also immunization
vacuoles, cell 3:412
vacuum 18:2558–60
    applications 18:2560
        in cans 3:381
        distillation 5:661, 663; 18:2560
        evaporation, of salt 14:2016
        measurement 18:2559–60
        partial 18:2558
        vacuum pumps 4:522; 18:2558
vacuum cleaners 18:2561–2
vacuum flasks (thermos bottles)
        17:2425
vacuum forming, thermoplastic
        (vacuum thermoforming)
        13:1773, 1775
vacuum tubes 1:124; 18:2480,
        2563–5
    in computers 2:169; 4:524; 6:754
    diodes 5:653; 6:750–1; 18:2480,
        2563–4
    pentodes 18:2565
    tetrodes 18:2564, 2565
    and thermionic emission 1:124;
        5:657; 18:2563
    triodes 1:124; 6:751; 18:2480,
        2564–5
    see also cathode-ray tubes
V agents 4:437
valency 4:442
Valium (diazepam) 12:1682; 13:1791
valves, heart 8:1045, 1046; 18:2568
    surgery 8:1049, 1051
valves, mechanical 18:2566–8
    on aerosol cans 1:40
    ball 18:2568
    bileaflet disk 18:2568
    brass instrument 3:319
    butterfly 18:2568
    cut-out 8:1103
    demand valves, in aqualungs 2:154,
        155
    disk 18:2568
    gate 18:2567, 2568
    globe 18:2568
    heart 18:2568
    internal combustion engine
        9:1173–4
        and cams 3:362
        exhaust valves 18:2568
        manufacture 1:101
    lift 18:2568
    nonreturn (check valves) 8:1103;
        18:2567–8
        for respirators 3:321
        for taps 13:1787
    piston 16:2256
    poppet 18:2568
    relief 8:1103
    rotary 16:2262
    selector 8:1103, 1104
    single-stage 2:154
    sleeve 1:74; 18:2568
    slide 18:2568
    spool 18:2566–7
        axial 16:2262
    stop 18:2568
    toilet 18:2457–8
valves, thermionic see vacuum tubes
vanadium pentoxide 1:24; 4:452;
        18:2488
Van Allen belts 14:1899–1900
van de Graaff generators 6:727
van der Waals forces 5:598; 15:2129
vapor density 5:617
vapor deposition
    chemical (CVD) 5:639; 10:1418

    using vacuums 18:2560
vaporization, latent heat of 4:463
vapor pressure 18:2569–70
vapors 10:1362
variance 16:2247
varnishes see lacquers and varnishes
vasectomy 13:1818
VASIs (visual approach slope indica-
        tors) 1:88
vasodilation 10:1376
vasopressin 8:1086
Vaucanson, Jacques de 9:1281
vault construction 18:2571–4
vaults (rooms) 14:2005
VDUs (visual display units) see
        computers, monitors
vector quantities 5:694–5; 16:2242
    and electromagnetism 6:749
veins, pulmonary 8:1045
Vela supernova remnant 14:1912
Velcro 6:835
velocity 3:422; 5:694, 695; 8:1144
    terminal 19:2611
vena cava, inferior and superior
        8:1045
vending machines 18:2575–7
    coin validation 4:509; 18:2575
    see also soft-drink dispensers
veneers 18:2578–9; 19:2710–11
Venera 15 and 16 (spacecraft) 12:1707
ventilation systems see heating and
        ventilation systems
ventilators, automatic 1:132
ventriculoscopes 6:785
vents, hydrothermal 10:1333;
        11:1567; 13:1780
venturi (choke) 3:396
Venturi effect 18:2580–1
    see also Bernoulli's effect
venturi meters 7:896
Venus (planet) 13:1757; 15:2118,
        2119–20, 2121
    mapping 12:1707; 17:2337
    traveling to 12:1600
Venus's flytrap 5:645
vermiculite (micafill) 8:1122; 9:1161
vernier scales (vernier gauges)
        18:2582
vertebrae, slipped disks, detection
        19:2723–4
vertebrates
    evolution 6:824
    smell used by 15:2105
Very Large Arrays (VLAS) 14:1909,
        1910–11
Very Large Crude Carriers (VLCCs)
        17:2351
very-large-scale integration (VLSI)
        see integrated circuits
Very Large Telescope (VLT) 17:2380
Very Long Baseline Array
        14:1910–11
very long baseline interferometry
        (VLBI) 14:1910–11
veterinary science and medicine
        18:2583–8
VHF omnidirectional ranging see
        VOR
video bugs 6:761
video cameras 18:2589–92
    charge-coupled devices 3:432;
        18:2590, 2591–2
    sound recording 15:2149
video conferencing 3:353; 17:2370
videomicrographics 10:1415
video-on-demand 3:354
videophones 3:415
Videoplace system 19:2604
video recorders 2:186, 188; 10:1311,
        1312; 19:2597–2602
    video cassettes 2:187–8; 10:1312;
        19:2600–2

video recorders (*cont.*)
 see also audio and video recording
video signals **17**:2393
video tape **10**:1312
vidicons **6**:742, 743; **17**:2384
Vietnam War
 chemical weapons **4**:438
  napalm **7**:883
 helicopters **8**:1068
villi **5**:*642, 643*, 644
vinegar **6**:842; **7**:911
vinyl acetate **7**:892–3; **13**:1771
 copolymers **12**:1696; **13**:1771
vinyl chloride *see* chloroethene
vinyl discs *see* phonography
vinyl floorings **7**:892–3
vinylidene chloride **7**:880; **13**:1771
 copolymers **13**:1771
violas **16**:2280
viol family **16**:2280
violincellos (cellos) **16**:2280
violin family **16**:2279–80
violins **16**:2280, 2281
 digital **17**:*2344*
ViOS (visual Internet operating
 system) browser **11**:1503
virtual reality (VR) **11**:1503;
 19:2603–8
 for surgery **17**:2332
 weather processes **4**:*534*
 see also flight simulators
viruses (computer) **4**:530, 531
viruses (microorganisms) **10**:1410
 bacteriophages **10**:1410
 and bioengineered vaccines **2**:264
 as biological weapons **4**:438
 and cancer **3**:378
 foot-and-mouth-disease (FMDV)
  2:261
 hepatitis B **12**:*1659*
 immune response to **8**:1136
 reproduction **14**:1957
 see also HIV (human immunodeficiency virus)
viscometers **19**:2611
viscose **3**:390; **6**:851; **7**:881; **13**:1769
viscosity **14**:1961; **19**:2609–11
 coefficient of **19**:2609, 2610, 2611
 SAE values **9**:1291
vision **6**:830–1; **9**:1240
 aids for impaired vision *see* accessibility aids
 persistence of **12**:1607
 quantifying **6**:832
 stereoscopic **6**:831; **16**:2263
 visual acuity **12**:1596
visual approach slope indicators
 (VASIs) **1**:88
visual display units (VDUs) *see* computers, monitors
visually coupled displays **19**:2604
visual purple **6**:831
vitamins **11**:1557–8; **19**:2612–14
 A **19**:2612, 2613, 2614
 antioxidant **11**:1558–9
 B complex **19**:2612, 2613, 2614,
  2727
 B₂ **5**:600; **6**:837; **19**:2613
 C **11**:1558–9; **19**:*2612*, 2613, 2614
 D **19**:2612, 2613
 deficiency **11**:1558; **19**:2612, 2613,
  2614
 E **7**:997; **11**:1558–9; **19**:2613
 as food additives **7**:914
 from fats **6**:837
 K **19**:2613
 supplements **19**:2614
vitreous humor **6**:830; **9**:1240
vitrification **4**:467
vitrification plants **11**:1550
VLSI *see* integrated circuits
vocal cords, growths **12**:1613

VOCs (volatile organic compounds,
 or components) **13**:1823;
 19:2641
vodka **5**:661; **16**:2217
voice *see* speech and language
voice-controlled wheelchairs **11**:1470
voice mail **17**:2367
voice recognition and synthesis
 2:169, 172; **19**:2615–17
 at automatic-teller machines **2**:192
 recognition **2**:172; **9**:1269;
  16:2202–3; **19**:2615–17
  for desktop publishing **5**:626
  and forensic science **7**:916
  and robotics **14**:1989; **19**:*2616,
   2617*
 synthesis **1**:22; **2**:172; **16**:*2200*,
  2202, 2203; **19**:2617
 see also natural-language processing
voice-stress analysis **13**:1808
volatile organic compounds, or components (VOCs) **13**:1823;
 19:2641
volcanoes **5**:*696*
 formation **5**:699
 and plate tectonics **13**:1778
Volta, Alessandro **2**:225; **6**:726, 737
voltage **4**:554; **6**:748
 measuring *see* potentiometers
 see also electromotive force
voltage dividers **13**:1821–2
voltage regulators **19**:2618–21
voltaic piles **6**:726
voltmeters **10**:1402, 1403
von Braun, Wernher **1**:42; **14**:1992
VOR (VHF omnidirectional
 ranging) **1**:67
 beacons **1**:88
vortex shedding **7**:897
Vostok, Lake **7**:998; **9**:1235
Voyager space probes **2**:217; **15**:2156
 Voyager 2 **15**:2118
  and Iapetus (moon) **3**:393
  and Neptune **5**:710; **15**:2118
Vulcan Air Defence System, Vulcan
 Gatling guns **1**:144; **2**:197
vulcanization **14**:1997, 2001; **18**:2454

W

walking frames **11**:1470–2
walkways *see* escalators and moving
 walkways
wall attachment effect (Coanda
 effect) **7**:898–9
wall paintings **13**:1743
Wall Street Journal (newspaper)
 11:1519
Wankel engines **9**:1170–1, *1173*,
 1175–6
WANs (wide area networks) **4**:537,
 539–40, 542
WAP (wireless access protocol)
 phones **8**:1147
warehousing **19**:2622–5
 see also forklifts
warfarin **12**:1677, 1678
warheads, torpedo **18**:2468
warships **19**:2626–33
washing machines **19**:2634–6
 and chaos theory **3**:431
 drums, polished **6**:736
 fuzzy logic **3**:431; **19**:2635–6
 used by the laundry industry
  9:1217–18
 see also dishwashers
washing pans, rotary **5**:638
Washington, D.C., mass transit and
 subways **10**:1348
wasps
 for biological control **1**:61
 gall **12**:1646

waste disposal **19**:2637–42
 burning in fluidized beds **7**:901;
  19:2639
 composting **6**:843; **10**:1411;
  19:2640
 exportation **6**:809
 incineration **19**:2638–9
 nuclear **6**:796; **11**:1539, **1547–50**;
  18:*2547*
 packaging waste **12**:1625
 refuse dumps **19**:*2637*
 removal **19**:2637–40
 special and hazardous waste
  19:2641, *2647*
 subsurface waste, detection **7**:994
 transfer stations **19**:2642
 using bacteria **10**:1411
 using reverse osmosis **12**:1610
 using yeast **19**:2727
 waste as a source of energy **6**:797;
  10:1411
 see also landfill; recycling; wastewater treatment
Waste Isolation Pilot Project (WIPP)
 11:1548
wastewater treatment (sewage treatment) **19**:2643–8
 ceramic diffusion plates **9**:*1199*
 fertilizers from **6**:844
 in fluidized beds **7**:901
 and septic tanks **5**:*674*; **19**:2648
 using algae **8**:1108; **13**:1803;
  19:2645
 using water hyacinths **13**:1803
 see also sewers
watches
 electronic **19**:2649–50
  LCD displays **5**:646; **19**:*2649*,
   2650
  LED displays **19**:2650
  radio-controlled **19**:2650
  tuning-fork watches **19**:2649–50
  TV watches **19**:2650
 mechanical **4**:483; **19**:2651–3
  automatic **19**:2653
  jewel bearings **2**:233; **19**:2653
 see also clocks
water **19**:2654–6
 in the atmosphere **10**:1396
 bonds in **4**:444; **19**:2654–5
 carbonated **15**:2109
 consumption **11**:1557
 cycle **19**:2665
 drinking **19**:2656, 2662–3
 on Earth, source **13**:1761
 from brackish or seawater *see*
  desalination
 hard **13**:1786–7; **19**:2656, 2666
 heavy *see* deuterium oxide
 in hot water systems, removal of
  salts **10**:1319
 jets, for cleaning **17**:2322–3
 phases **10**:1361
  phase diagrams **10**:*1360*
 physical properties **12**:1621;
  19:2654, 2655
 pure water polymer **12**:1620–1
 shortages **6**:809
 siphoning **15**:2083
 softening **12**:1699; **13**:1787;
  19:2656, 2666, 2730
 solvent power **19**:2655
 surface tension **10**:*1359*, 1361–2
 triple point **17**:2395
 and urban drainage **5**:674–5
 see also ice
water boatmen **10**:*1359*
water cannons
 law-enforcement **11**:*1533*, 1534;
  14:1972
 use in mining **11**:1461
water gas process **7**:959

water glass (sodium silicate) **1**:30
water hammer **8**:1111
water hyacinths **5**:608; **13**:1803
water hydrants **19**:*2667*
water-jet propulsion **10**:1365
watermarks **5**:583
water mills **19**:*2657*
water pumps **6**:801
water rams **19**:2658
water-repellent finishes **19**:2659–60
water skiing **2**:231
water supply **4**:476; **13**:1786–7;
 19:2661–7
 wells **19**:2683–4
 see also wastewater treatment
water tenders **6**:861
waterwheels **9**:1192; **13**:*1825*
 Lorenzian **3**:*431*
waterworks **19**:2662
Watson, James **7**:973
Watson-Watt, Sir Robert **14**:1893
Watt, James **11**:1458; **13**:1826;
 15:2055; **16**:2256
watt meters **10**:1403
watts **6**:729
wave functions, electron **6**:767–8
waveguides **19**:2668–71
wavelength **6**:739; **19**:2672
 of light **5**:641; **9**:1237
wave motion **19**:2672–4
 diffraction **5**:641; **19**:2672–3
  sound waves **15**:*2133*, 2134
 and the Doppler effect **5**:672
 and earthquakes **5**:707; **15**:*2047–8*
 electromagnetic waves **6**:739–40
 frequency **6**:739; **19**:2672
 light waves **5**:641; **9**:1236;
  14:1880; **19**:2673–4
 ocean waves **19**:2672, 2675
 superposition of waves **19**:2674
 velocity **19**:2672
 wavelength **6**:739; **19**:2672
 see also sound, waves
wave power **4**:549; **19**:2675–7
waves (oceanic) **19**:2672, 2674
 tidal (tsunamis) **18**:2509–11
wave-table cards **17**:2345
wax
 corrosion-prevention by **4**:*570*
 ear **8**:1041
 from oil refining **11**:1579
 sealing **1**:30
 uses
  food packaging **7**:908
  in water-repellent fabrics
   19:2660
weak nuclear force **6**:771, 773
weapons, nonlethal *see* nonlethal
 weapons
weather, study of *see* meteorology
weathering **7**:981
weaving **5**:2405–6
 cotton **5**:581, 582; **9**:*1283*
 rugs and carpets **7**:*893*, 894
 see also looms
webcams **18**:2592
Weber, Wilhelm **10**:1315
webers **10**:1313
Webley Tempest (air pistol) **8**:1025
web-offset printing **9**:1264;
 11:1517–18; **13**:1850
weed control **19**:2678–81
Wegener, Alfred **5**:707; **13**:1777
weigh stations **19**:2682
weight **12**:1725
weightlessness **6**:789
weirs, navigation **9**:1265
welding **10**:*1381*
 aluminum **1**:111; **11**:1529
 arc **1**:*111*; **3**:336; **8**:1119;
  10:1382–3; **11**:*1528*, 1529
 electron-beam **1**:111; **10**:1383

friction welding **7**:*934*; **10**:1384
  gas **10**:1382
  laser **10**:1383–4
  oxyacetylene **12**:1620
  plasma **10**:*1366*, 1383
  pressure **10**:1384
  ultrasonic **1**:111; **10**:1384
well logging **7**:991
wells
  oil exploration **11**:1571–3
  water **19**:2683–4
Westland Sea King helicopters
  8:1070
wet cleaning **5**:689
whales **19**:2733, 2734–5
  whaling and **19**:2685–8
whaling **19**:2685–8
wheat
  genetically-engineered **3**:303
Wheatstone, Charles **3**:353; **16**:2195,
  2263; **17**:2360
Wheelbarrow (robot) **3**:296; **14**:*1956*;
  18:*2471*
wheelchairs **11**:1469–70
wheel locks **8**:1024
wheels
  camber angles **16**:2261
  spoked, apparent backward motion
    in films **16**:2286
whey **5**:601, 603; **12**:1610
whiskey **1**:*97*; **5**:661; **16**:2215–17
white dwarves **14**:1954; **17**:2315,
  2316
white lead **12**:1628
Whitten Effect **12**:1691
Whittle, Frank **1**:75; **7**:965
wide area networks (WANs) **4**:537,
  539–40, 542
wide band code-division multiple
  access (WCDMA) **3**:416; **4**:540
Wide-Field Planetary Cameras
  2:176; **15**:*2154*, 2155; **17**:2381,
  2382
widescreen recording **5**:652
Wigner energy **11**:1535
WIMPS **4**:575
winches and windlasses **19**:**2689**
wind bracing **15**:2092, *2094*
windbreaks **6**:816–17
wind engines **19**:2695
windlasses *see* winches and windlasses
wind machines **15**:2136–7
windmills *see* wind power
Windows (operating system) **4**:525,
  539
windows
  double-glazed **15**:2140, 2141
  skyscraper, cleaning **15**:2095
  soundproofing **15**:2140
  see also stained glass
wind power **6**:793; **13**:1826;
  19:2690–5, **2690–5**
  and land reclamation **9**:1206, 1208;
  19:2695
winds
  Earth's surface **8**:*1097*
  see also hurricanes and tornadoes
  erosion by **6**:816–17, 819
  lunar **17**:2440
  trade **14**:1931, 2009
Windscale (Sellafield) **11**:1535
windshields
  automobile **1**:30; **7**:1001
wind speed, measurement **1**:63, 130
windsurfing **13**:*1840*; **14**:2013
wind tunnels **1**:*37, 38*; **19**:2696–9
  to test bridges **3**:327
  to test sails and rigging **14**:2012
winemaking **1**:98; **6**:840–1;
  19:2700–3
wings *see* aircraft, wings
wireframes **1**:*139*; **4**:536

wire guidance
  missile **11**:1466–7
  torpedo **18**:2468
wiretapping **6**:759
wiring systems **19**:2704–8
withdrawal symptoms, to drugs
  12:1685
wood
  fuel **2**:258
  laminated **19**:2711
  paper made from **12**:1637, 1638
  preservation **2**:159, *160*
  veneers **18**:2578–9; **19**:2710–11
wood alcohol *see* methanol
wood composites **19**:2709–11
  building with **19**:*2711*
woodwind instruments **14**:1965;
  19:2712–15
woodworking **19**:2716–18
  see also veneers
woofers **9**:*1284*, 1285
wool **6**:848–9, 850; **17**:2404, 2408
  glass **7**:1002, 1003
  spinning **16**:2214
Woolworth Building **3**:337; **15**:2092
word processors **19**:2719–20
  word-processing programs **5**:626;
    8:1150; **11**:1491
  see also desktop publishing;
    typewriters
work **5**:695; **12**:1726; **13**:1825
World Ocean Circulation
  Experiment **11**:1568
World Trade Center **15**:2092–3,
  2095
World War I
  aerial photography **1**:33
  aircraft **1**:41–2; **2**:212
    airships **1**:*92*
  bombsights **2**:287
  chemical weapons **4**:437, 438;
    8:1036
  flame throwers **7**:882
  gas masks **7**:953
  guns **8**:*1023*, 1026
  parachutes **12**:1641
  periscopes **12**:1674
  tanks **2**:162, 164, 168
World War II
  aerial photography **1**:34
  aircraft **1**:41; **2**:213; **15**:*2023*
    balloons **2**:218
    flight recorders **7**:884
    flying boats **15**:2036
    fuel-injection systems **7**:937
  ammunition **1**:118
    antitank guns **1**:119
    white phosphorus used in
      12:1700
  automatic rifles **8**:1025
  bombs **2**:284, 286; **3**:293
    atomic **11**:1551, 1552, 1553,
      1554
    disposal **3**:293
  bombsights **2**:287–8
  chemical weapons **4**:437, 438
  computers **4**:523
  cryptology **5**:593, 595–6
  flame throwers **7**:882, 883
  guns **8**:1027
    naval **8**:*1023*
  military bridges **3**:328
  motorcycles **11**:1489
  naval mines **11**:1454–5
  radio jamming **16**:2250
  radio receivers **14**:1904
  radio transmitters, power **17**:2420
  submarines, helicopters towed
    behind **8**:1070
  tanks **2**:164
  torpedoes **18**:2467
  V-2 missiles **8**:1144; **14**:1992

World Wide Web **8**:1147; **9**:1177,
  1178, 1179; **11**:1502–3
  multimedia applications **11**:1503
  see also search engines
worms
  muscles **11**:1504
  nematode **1**:61
    life span **7**:996
  on the seabed **11**:1567
WORM (write once read many)
  drives **5**:614
wow and flutter **8**:1076
wrapping
  packaging-wrap manufacture
    12:1626
  shrink **7**:908; **12**:1624
wrecks, destroying **15**:2023
wrenches
  manufacture **18**:2462
  pneumatic **13**:*1789*
Wright, Orville and Wilbur **1**:72, 77;
  2:211

X

X-43 (aircraft) **13**:1748; **17**:2320
xanthan gum **19**:2611
xenon **5**:*655*; **11**:1529
xenotransplants **13**:1734; **18**:2504
xerography **12**:1701–3
  body scans using **2**:281
xerophthalmia **11**:1558
X-ray fluorescence (XRF) **2**:158;
  4:447; **12**:1680; **16**:2196–7,
  2199; **19**:2724
X-ray imaging **19**:2721–4
  baggage **1**:*89*; **19**:2724
  of the body **12**:1657; **14**:1917;
    19:*2721*, 2722–3, *2724*
    of animals **18**:2584
    dental **5**:619
    fractures **3**:*300*
  of bombs **2**:295
  of fake statues and artwork **5**:584
  fluoroscopy **8**:1052; **19**:2723–4
  use in archaeology **2**:158
  xerography **2**:*281*
  X-ray astronomy **19**:2724
    and black holes **2**:268, *270*;
      19:*2724*
    and the Chandra telescope
      17:2381
    and stars **2**:174; **19**:2724
  X-ray crystallography, X-ray dif-
    fraction **2**:261, 262; **4**:462, 551;
    5:598–9, 641; **12**:1689; **19**:2724
  see also spectroscopy; X-ray fluores-
    cence
X rays **6**:744; **19**:2721
  anti-ballistic weapons **16**:2183
  detection **6**:744
  for etching silicon chips **9**:1168
  frequency **6**:739
  sources **19**:2721–2
  X-ray lasers **9**:1214
X-wing project **8**:1070
xylene (dimethylbenzene) **4**:498;
  8:1107-8
  from oil refining **11**:1578–9
  isomerization of **3**:406
xylophones **12**:1668, *1669*

Y

yachts **14**:*2008*, 2009
Yamato (ship) **5**:719–20; **10**:1319;
  17:2314; **19**:2626
yarn **17**:2405
  glass **7**:1003
  for stockings **8**:1090–1
  synthetic, preparation **6**:853
  see also spinning
yaw **1**:*70, 71*

years **5**:696; **17**:2441
yeast **6**:840; **10**:1409–10; **19**:2725–7
  enzymes in **6**:841–2
  and food spoilage **7**:905
  food yeast **19**:2726–7
  and protein production **6**:810;
    7:914; **13**:*1866*; **19**:2726–7
  industrial uses **19**:2727
  used in baking, brewing, and fer-
    mentation **2**:236, 237; **3**:*406*;
    19:2725–6
yellow cake **11**:1537
yellow fever **6**:811
  as a biological weapon **4**:438
  mosquitoes carrying **12**:*1644*
Yenisey-Angara River **8**:1115
yogurt **5**:603; **7**:904
Young, Thomas
  and energy **6**:786
  and light **9**:1236; **13**:1794
    double-slit experiment **14**:1880,
      1882; **19**:2673
Young's modulus (elastic modulus)
  5:713; **15**:2131; **16**:2229
yttrium **18**:2485, 2487
yttrium–aluminum garnet (YAG)
  9:1212; **18**:*2487*
Yucca Mountain **11**:*1547*

Z

zeolites **3**:406; **4**:471; **7**:953; **15**:2130;
  19:**2728–30**
  as catalysts **3**:406; **19**:2730
  synthesis **19**:2729
  ZSM-5 **19**:2729, 2730
zephyr **17**:2407–8
Zeppelin, Ferdinand von **1**:91
zeppelins **1**:91–2
  carrying bombs **2**:283
zero-level emission vehicles (ZLEVs)
  2:201
zidovudine (AZT) **12**:1688
Ziegler-Natta polymerization catalysts **4**:460; **13**:1770, 1810;
  14:2001
zinc **19**:2731–2
  alloys **19**:2731, 2732
    see also brass
  galvanizing with **4**:1571; **17**:2322,
    2323, 2325–6; **19**:2732
  production **19**:2731–2
  rolled **19**:2732
zinc blende (sphalerite) **9**:1219;
  19:2731
zinc carbonate **19**:2731
zinc oxide **10**:1352; **17**:2326;
  18:2529; **19**:2732
zinc phosphate **5**:619
zinc sulfide **19**:2731, 2732
zip codes **10**:1321–2, 1323, 1324–5
Zip drives and disks **4**:527; **5**:612
zippers **6**:835
  insertion of **4**:490
zircon **7**:988
zirconia **3**:426
zirconium dioxide **7**:936
zirconium oxide **12**:1609
zircons **16**:2271
ZLEVs (zero-level emission vehicles)
  2:201
zoetropes **1**:136
zone plates **9**:1230
zone refining **17**:2347
zoology **19**:2733–6
  see also entomology
zoonoses **18**:2586–7
zooplankton **10**:1332
zoptics **16**:*2186*
Zuider Zee **9**:1208
Zworykin, Vladimir **17**:2383
zymase **1**:98; **6**:841